THE
VAMPIRE
OMNIBUS

THE
VAMPIRE
OMNIBUS

EDITED BY PETER HAINING

First published in Great Britain in 1995 by Orion

This edition published in 2003 by Bounty Books,
a division of Octopus Publishing Group Ltd,
2-4 Heron Quays, London E14 4JP

Copyright © 1995 edited by Peter Haining

ISBN 0 7537 0850 7

A CIP catalogue record for this book is available from the
British Library

Printed and bound in Great Britain

In Memory of
PETER CUSHING
The Greatest Vampire Hunter of all

Contents

II: The Films

III: The Archetypes

Introduction

If one popular tale is to be believed then Bram Stoker had the idea for *Dracula* after eating a rather large helping of crab, while the book itself was the first great vampire novel. In fact, neither of these facts is true – although they are a clear indication as to why the famous vampire novel is still so popular almost a century after it was written and the whole topic of vampirism continues to exert such a fascination for readers all over the world.

The story of how Bram Stoker's creative juices were allegedly put into motion is worth the retelling. It was a tale that he himself liked to relate in the years following the publication of the book and reveals that the genial Irishman who spent many years of his life working in the theatre was as good at generating publicity for himself as for his employer, the great Victorian actor, Sir Henry Irving, whom he served as manager. Indeed, it all began with a quote that any modern publicist would probably love to pass on to gossip columnists about an author-client.

'The idea for the book came to me in a nightmare,' Stoker would rumble, stroking his large, red beard. 'One evening when I was dining with Irving I ate too much dressed crab and then spent all night long dreaming these weird dreams about a dead-alive man preying on the living!'

Although Stoker loved crab and did occasionally dream, the only part of the story which *is* true is that the idea for *Dracula* did begin to take shape in his mind after a evening meal at which Sir Henry Irving was present. The two men frequently dined together at the end of a performance, and one of their favourite eating spots was 'The

Beefsteak Room', located at the rear of the Lyceum Theatre where Irving was the star performer for almost twenty years. It was to this venue with its Gothic furnishings, candle-lit tables and sumptuous wine and food menu that the great actor also liked to invite his friends, business associates and the great and good of London society.

On an evening in April 1890, among his guests was a small, balding middle-European named Arminius Vambery, a professor from the University of Budapest who was then in London lecturing to invited audiences about Romanian folklore. He had earlier attended a performance of Irving's latest production – appropriately called 'The Dead Hand' – and afterwards been asked to join Irving's party for dinner. There he was sat between Sir Henry and Bram Stoker and for the rest of the night filled their heads with stories of the superstitions which abounded in his native land. Stories of witches, werewolves and the un-dead who were said to drink the blood of human beings . . .

Bram Stoker, who was already an author in his spare time and had written a number of short stories and two novels, *Under The Sunset* (1882) and *The Snake's Pass* which would be published later that year, could hardly fail to have been intrigued by Vambery's tales. It was the thought of those un-dead beings that specifically excited his interest, however, and in the months which followed he began to do some research into the topic in the British Museum. He also wrote to Vambery in Budapest about his idea and found the little Professor more than willing to elaborate on the story he had told over dinner . . .

The demands of running the eccentric and egotistical Henry Irving's life meant Stoker's opportunities for writing usually only occurred when he was on holiday at Whitby in Yorkshire and so it was to be almost six years before he completed the novel which was to be labelled among the greatest of all horror stories and make its central figure one of the immortals of literature. *Dracula* was finally published by Archibald Constable and Company of Westminster in June 1897 in a yellow binding with the title embossed in suitable blood red type. As was the common practice in those days, the volume was issued without a dust jacket.

Interestingly, the original title of the book – according to the contract Stoker signed with Constable – was *The Un-Dead*, and the title by which it is now so familiar was apparently not given to it until just before it was due to go to press. Two other important changes were also made to the manuscript, which was also unusual in being one of the earliest to have been type-written – a fact which was cleverly manifested in the book in the reference to Mina Harker's 'travelling typewriter'. (This is also a fact that the reader may care to bear in mind when he comes to the very last story in this collection . . .)

The first change appears to have taken place because one of the publisher's editors considered the text, as presented by Stoker, to be a little too long to be published economically at the firm's standard price of six shillings and so a whole chapter was excised. This episode has subsequently been much anthologised under the title of 'Dracula's Guest'. Secondly, a number of paragraphs were cut from the final entry in the book from Mina Harker's Journal. In these lines – which I have reprinted in this volume from a copy of the original manuscript kept in the Rosenbach Library in America – Dracula's Castle is destroyed.

Why these lines should have been cut is now purely a matter for conjecture. Was it that same editor's blue pencil again – though the logic seems less explicable? Or did Stoker perhaps feel he might one day write a sequel and so decided to leave the King of the Un-Dead's home still standing for such an eventuality? This is certainly a ruse that film-makers have used in one way or another over and over again in vampire pictures to facilitate the vampire's return.

The mystery will, however, have to remain unsolved – just as will two other unsubstantiated rumours which persist about the book. The first – a story repeated by H. P. Lovecraft, an admirer of Stoker and another master of horror fiction – that Bram's original text was so unpublishable that another author was approached to revise it; and, the second, a suggestion also floated in America that *Dracula* is actually a cryptic novelisation of the Jack the Ripper mystery based on certain secret information that was only known to Bram Stoker and a close circle of his friends!

What is beyond dispute, however, is that following the publication of *Dracula* in the form we now know it, the book began to make literary history. Though not an overnight best-seller – in fact the most fulsome praise for it came from Bram's own mother who wrote to him, 'No book since Mrs Shelley's *Frankenstein*, or indeed any other at all, has come near yours in originality or terror!' – the book began to sell steadily and finally crossed the Atlantic two years later, where it was published by Doubleday & McClure, priced $1.50. It was when the story was transferred to the stage, and in due course onto the cinema screen in 1931 by Universal with Bela Lugosi, that the legend of Dracula really took off.

A pillar of this legend was for some years the general public's misconception that Dracula was the first novel about vampires. It was not until the twentieth century was well underway, in fact, that researchers began to make the point that this claim was as false as Stoker's own that he owed his inspiration to an unsettled digestion. Today we know that vampires had been appearing in fiction for much of the nineteenth century; it was just that no other writer had enjoyed quite the same international success as Stoker.

The Vampire Omnibus is intended to set the record straight. For herein will be found representative examples of the stories of vampirism which precede Stoker's undeniable masterpiece, as well as the films which took the tradition into a new medium, and a cross-selection of just a few of the literally hundreds of short stories written in the past fifty years which have introduced new dimensions and ideas to the genre.

Just how far the popularity of the story of the living dead has come since Bram Stoker's day is evident by the attention given to each new vampire movie as well as the continuing stream of novels, all of which owe something to Stoker. Indeed, as recently as November 1992, Anne Billson the reviewer in that most distinguished of papers, *The Times*, felt moved to comment after wading through another batch of new titles, 'The vampire is shaping up to be bogeyman of the decade.'

In my contention, and I think it is supported by the sheer weight of material in this volume which is one of the most representative ever assembled, Dracula and his undead cohorts have been popular bogeymen for much of the last two hundred years, too.

It was Nietzsche, I think, who wrote, 'Talent is a vampire.' Herein the reader will find that the vampire in its turn has also attracted talent – the talent of outstanding writers and film-makers – and generated a legend that far exceeds anything Bram Stoker could have dreamed: dressed crab or not!

Requiescant in pace, Bram.

PETER HAINING,
October, 1994.

Preface

'THE DESTRUCTION OF CASTLE DRACULA!'

From Mina Harker's Journal, 6 November

The sun was almost down on the mountain tops, and our shadows fell long upon the snow. I saw the Count lying within the box upon the earth, some of which the rude falling from the cart had scattered over him. He was deathly pale, just like a waxen image, and the red eyes glared with the horrible vindictive look which I knew too well.

As I looked, the eyes saw the sinking sun, and the look of hate in them turned to triumph.

But on that instant, came the sweep and flash of Jonathan's great knife. I shrieked as I saw it shear through the throat; while at the same moment Mr Morris's bowie knife plunged into the heart.

It was like a miracle; but before our very eyes, and almost in the drawing of a breath, the whole body crumbled into dust and passed from our sight.

I shall be glad as long as I live that even in that moment of final dissolution, there was in the face a look of peace, such as I never could have imagined might have rested there.

The Castle of Dracula now stood out against the red sun and every stone of its broken battlements was articulated against the light. As we looked there came a terrible convulsion of the earth so that we seemed to rock to and fro and fell to our knees.

At the same moment, with a roar that seemed to shake the very heavens, the whole castle and the rock and even the hill on which it stood seemed to rise into the air and scatter in fragments while a mighty cloud of black and yellow smoke, volume on volume, in rolling grandeur, was shot upwards with inconceivable rapidity.

Then there was a stillness in nature as the echoes of that thunderous report seemed to come as with the hollow boom of a thunder-clap – the long reverberating roll which seems as though the floors of heaven shook. Then down in a mighty ruin falling whence they rose came the fragments that had been tossed skyward in the cataclysm.

From where we stood it seemed as though the once fierce volcano burst had satisfied the need of nature and that the castle and the structure of the hill had sunk again into the void. We were so appalled with the suddenness and the grandeur that we forgot to think of ourselves . . .

Bram Stoker,
From the original MS *of* DRACULA *(1897)*.

I
The Prototypes

The Skeleton Count
Or, The Vampire Mistress

ELIZABETH GREY

This extraordinary story which has lain forgotten in the pages of a weekly 'penny dreadful' for over 160 years is, without question, the earliest vampire serial story. Both it and its creator, a remarkably productive authoress who worked at the very heart of the London cheapjack publishing industry, have never before been acknowledged for their landmark contribution to the genre. The tale was published in The Casket, *'a weekly penny paper of the most sensational kind in which bloodthirsty Gothic short stories and serials predominated over a miscellany of brief articles, morbid poetry and news items', according to the late G. Ken Chapman, a leading antiquarian bookseller who first put me on the track of the story. Each weekly issue contained a gruesome woodcut on the front page illustrating the main piece of fiction inside – the titles of which speak for themselves: 'The Spectre Warning', 'The Witch of Marly', 'The Fiend of the Heath' and 'The Skeleton Count'. Although the word vampire only features in the sub-heading of this serial which* The Casket *began to run in the autumn of 1828, by the following year – and perhaps encouraged by the reception of the story? – the magazine was giving front page mention to epics such as 'The Vampires of London' and 'Der Vampyr!'*

Mrs Elizabeth Caroline Grey (1798–1869) who is credited with the authorship of this pioneer tale of the undead was a most interesting character about whom frustratingly little is known. What is on record is that she was born in London, and was the niece of a Miss Duncan, a favourite melodrama actress noted for playing charming heroines such as Alexina in Theodore Edward Hook's The Seige of Montgatz, *which ran for over a year at the Drury Lane Theatre from 1806–7. As a young woman, Elizabeth apparently ran a school for girls in the City Road, before marrying a journalist named Grey who worked on the* Morning Chronicle. *He introduced her to Edward Lloyd, then London's leading publisher of 'penny dreadfuls', and after a period as his secretary was made general editress of all his publications. Coping with the vagaries of the many hacks who supplied weekly copy for the magazines often meant she had to put pen to paper herself when an instalment failed to arrive on time. Eventually she began to write complete novels herself and in 1846 won a 100 Guinea prize for a melodrama called* The Ordeal By Touch, *which has been described by Montague Summers in his* Gothic Bibliography (1968) *as 'in many ways rather an absurd fiction, although by no means so absurd as the majority of self-dubbed "thrillers" of today'. Subsequently she wrote a number of similar books including* The Iron Mask (1847) *about an evil and mysterious astrologer,* The Horrors of Zindorf Castle (1850) *and* Murder Will Out (1860). *She lived a comfortable and active life and was still writing when she died, aged seventy-one.*

The story of 'The Skeleton Count' concerns Count Rodolph of Ravensburg who has made a pact with the Devil in return for eternal life. However, the condition of this agreement is that each night he is transformed into a fleshless skeleton – 'this horrible metamorphosis taking place precisely at sunset and continuing until sunrise the next day when the count resumes his natural shape', according to one of the early episodes. Quite where Mrs Grey got her inspiration for this grisly adventure is not known, although her aunt, Miss Duncan, did appear in the London production of The Bride of The Isles *(based on the vampire story by John Polidori which was staged in London in 1820 and to which I shall be returning in Part II), and Mrs Grey may well have attended this popular succès d'estime. Alternatively, the older woman might have suggested that the vampire tradition was ideal material for Elizabeth's kind of publication. In any event, Mrs Grey completed her story of the count and his vampire mistress and swiftly went on to other things – probably never giving it another thought and certainly unaware of its importance in the genre. Copies of* The Casket *have since become so impossibly rare that all traces of 'The Skeleton Count' might have disappeared had not the collector, David Phillips, unearthed a bound run of the magazine some years ago. It is from the yellowing and fragile pages of this that I have been able to extract the episode which is reprinted here. Apart from its own intrinsic importance, the story is fascinating because of its description of the*

reviving of a corpse in a manner not unlike that of Mary Shelley's
Frankenstein. *The element which is quite original, though, is the idea
of an animated skeleton! (For those readers interested in the fate of this
forerunner of* Dracula, *Count Rodolph finally returns to Ravensburg
200 years after the events described to find his castle in ruins. The
Devil, however, is cheated of his victim when the now less easily
frightened villagers corner the skeleton Rodolph one night and stake
him finally into a coffin.)*

*   *   *

Count Rodolph, after his impious compact with the prince of
darkness, ceased to study alchemy or to search after the elixir of
life, for not only was a long lease of life assured him by the demon, but
the same authority had declared such pursuits to be vain and delusive.
But he still dabbled in the occult sciences of magic and astrology, and
frequently passed day after day in fruitless speculation, concerning the
origin of matter, and the nature of the soul. He studied the writings
of Aristotle, Pliny, Lucretius, Josephus, Iamblicus, Sprenger, Cardan,
and the learned Michael Psellus; yet was he as far as ever from
attaining a correct knowledge of the things he sought to unveil from
the mystery which must ever envelope them. The reveries of the ancient
philosophers, of the Gnostics and the Pneaumatologists, only served
to plunge him into deeper doubt, and at length he determined to pass
from speculation to experiment, and put his half-formed theories to
the test of practice.

After keen study of the anatomy of the human frame, and many
operations and experiments on the corpse of a malefactor who had
been hanged for a robbery and murder, and which he stole from the
gibbet in the dead of night, and conveyed to Ravensburg Castle, with
the assistance of two wretches whom he had picked up at an obscure
hostelry in the town of Heidelberg, he resolved to exhume the corpse
of some one recently dead, and attempt its reanimation. The formula
of the necromancers for raising the dead did not suffice for their
restoration to life, but only for a temporary revivification; but in an
old Greek manuscript, which he found in the library of the castle, was
an account of how this restored animation might be sustained by
means of a miraculous liquid, for the distillation of which a recipe was
given.

Count Rodolph gathered the herbs at midnight, which the Greek
manuscript prescribed and distilled from them a clear gold-coloured

liquid of very little taste, but most fragrant odour, which he preserved in a phial. Having discovered that a peasant's daughter, a·girl of singular beauty, and about sixteen years of age, had died suddenly, and was to be buried on the day following that on which he had prepared his marvellous restorative, he set out on that day to Heidelberg to obtain the assistance of the fellows who had aided him in removing the corpse of the malefactor from the gibbet, and then returned to Ravensburg Castle, to prepare for his strange experiment.

At the solemn hour of midnight he departed secretly from the castle by a door in the eastern tower, of which he retained the key in his own possession, and bent his step to the church-yard of the neighbouring village. It was a fine moonlight night, but all the rustic inhabitants were in the arms of Morpheus, the leaden-eyed god of sleep, and the violator of the sanctity of the grave gained the churchyard unperceived. He found his hired associates waiting for him in the shadow of the wall, which was easily scaled, and being provided with shovels and a sack to contain the corpse, they set to work immediately. The fresh broken earth was soon thrown off from the lid of the coffin, which the resurrectionists removed with a screw-driver, and then the dead was disclosed to their view.

The corpse of the young maiden was lifted from its narrow resting place, and raised in the arms of the ungodly wretches whom Rodolph had hired, who deposited the inanimate clay on the margin of the grave, which they hastily filled up, and then proceeded to enclose in the sack the lifeless remains of the beautiful peasant girl. Having removed every trace of the sacrilegious theft which they had committed, one of them took the sack on his shoulders, and when he was tired his comrade relieved him, and in this manner they reached the castle. Count Rodolph led the way up the narrow stairs which led to his study chamber in the eastern turret, and having deposited the corpse upon the floor, and received their stipulated reward, the two resurrectionists were glad to make a speedy exit from a place which popular rumour began to associate with deeds of darkness and horror.

Having lighted a spirit lamp, which cast a livid and flickering light upon the many strange and mysterious objects which that chamber contained, and made the pale countenance of the corpse appear more ghastly and horrible, Count Rodolph proceeded to denude the body of its grave-clothes, which he carefully concealed, lest the sight of them, when the young maiden returned to life might strike her with a sudden horror which might prove fatal to the complete success of his daring experiment. He then placed the corpse in the centre of a magic circle which he had previously drawn upon the floor of the study, and covered it with a sheet. He had purchased some ready-made female apparel in the town of Heidelberg, and these he placed on the table in readiness for the use of the young girl, whom he felt sanguine of resuscitating.

Bertha had been, as was evidenced by her stark and cold remains, a maiden of surpassing symmetry of form and loveliness of countenance; no painter or sculptor could have desired a finer study, no poet a more inspiring theme. As she lay stretched out upon the floor of the study she looked like some beautiful carving in alabaster, or rather like a waxen figure of most artistical contrivance. Her long black hair was shaded with a purple gloss like the plumage of the raven, and her features were of most exquisite proportion and arrangement. But now her angelic contenance was livid with the pallid hue of death, the iron impress of whose icy hand was visible in every lineament.

Count Rodolph then took in his hand a magic wand, one end of which he placed on the breast of the corpse, and then proceeded to recite the cabalistic words by which necromancers call to life the slumbering tenants of the grave. When he had concluded the impious formula, an awful silence reigned in the turret, and he perceived the sheet gently agitated by the quivering of the limbs, which betokened returning animation. Then a shudder pervaded his frame in spite of himself, as he perceived the eyes of the corpse slowly open, and the dark dilated pupils fix their gaze on him with a strange and stolid glare.

Then the limbs moved, at first convulsively, but soon with a stronger and more natural motion, and then the young girl raised herself to a sitting posture on the floor of the study, and stared about her in a wild and strange manner, which made Rodolph fear that the object of his experiment would prove a wretched idiot or a raving lunatic.

But suddenly he bethought him of the restorative cordial, and snatching the phial from a shelf, he poured down the throat of the resuscitated maiden a considerable portion of the fragrant gold coloured fluid which it contained. Then a ray of that glorious intellect which allies man to the angels seemed to be infused into her mind, and beamed from her dark and lustrous eyes, which rested with a soft and tender expression on the handsome countenance of the young count. Her snowy bosom, from which the sheet had fallen when she rose from her recumbent position on the floor, heaved with the returning warmth of renewed life, and the Count of Ravensburg gazed upon her with mingled sensations of wonder and delight.

As the current of life was restored, and rushed along her veins with tingling warmth, the conscious blush of instinctive modesty mantled on her countenance, and drawing the sheet over her bosom, she rose to her feet, with her long black hair hanging about her shoulders, and her dark eyes cast upon the floor. Count Rodolph then directed her attention to the clothing which he had provided, so sanguine of complete success had the daring experimentalist been, and then he withdrew from the study while the lovely object of his scientific care attired herself.

When the Count of Ravensburg returned to his study, Bertha was sitting before the fire, attired in the garments he had provided for her, and he thought that he had never beheld a more lovely specimen of her sex. She rose when he entered, and kissed his hand, as though he were a superior being, and would have remained standing, with head bowed upon her bosom, as if in the presence of a being of another world, had he not gently forced her to resume the seat from which she had risen, and inquired tenderly the state of her feelings upon a return to life so strange and wonderful. But he found that she retained no remembrance of a previous existence, and all her feelings were new and strange, like those of Eve on bursting into conscious life and being from the hand of the Omnipotent. In her mysterious passage from life to death, and from death to new life, she had lost all her previous ideas and convictions, all her experience of the past, all that she had ever acquired of knowledge; and had become a child of nature, simple and unsophisticated as a denizen of the woods, with all the keen perceptions and untrained instincts of the untutored savage.

The young girl had braided up her flowing tresses of glossy blackness, and on her cheeks dwelt colour that might test a painter's skill, so rich yet delicate its hue, like the rosette tinge of some rare exotic shell, or that which a rose would cast upon an alabaster column. The young count felt himself irresistibly attracted towards the maiden, whom his science had endued with such a mysterious and preternatural existence, and she, on her part, regarded the handsome Rodolph with the wild, yet tender passion of frail humanity, mingled with the gratitude and devotion which she deemed due to one who stood to her in the position of her creator.

Thus the feelings which had so rapidly sprung up in her heart towards the only being of whom she had any conception, partook of a nature of a religious idolatry, but mingled with the grosser feelings of earth, like those which agitated in the bosom of the vestal whose sons founded Rome, or the virgin of Shen-si who was chosen from among all the women of the celestial empire to become the mother of the incarnate Foh.

'Thou art gloriously beautiful, my Bertha!' exclaimed the enamoured count, pressing her in his arms. 'Say that thou wilt be mine, and make me thy happy slave; thou should'st be loving as thou art loveable, beautiful child of mystery!'

'Love thee!' returned Bertha, a soft and tender expression dwelling in the clear depths of her dark eyes. 'I adore thee, my creator; my soul bows itself before thee, yet my heart leaps at thy glance, though I fear it is presumptuous for the work of thy hands to look on thee with eyes of love.'

'Sweet, ingenuous creature!' cried the Count of Ravensburg, kissing her coral lips and glowing cheeks. 'It is I who should worship thee! Thou art mine, Bertha, now and for ever. Henceforth I live only in thy smile!'

'For ever! Shall I remain with thee for ever? Oh, joy incomparable! My heart's idol, I adore thee!' and the beautiful Bertha wound her white arms about his neck, and pressed her lips to his, for in the new existence which she now enjoyed her feelings knew no restraint, and she yielded to every impulse of her ardent nature.

'Come, my Bertha,' said the enraptured Rodolph, 'this solitary turret must not be thy world; come with me, thy Rodolph, and be the mistress of Ravensburg Castle, as thou art already of its owner's heart.'

Passing his arm around the taper waist of the mysterious maiden, Rodolph took up the lamp, and quitting the eastern turret, they proceeded with noiseless steps to his chamber, where the first faint blush of day witnessed the consummation of their desires, nor did the torch of Hymen burn less brightly because no priest blessed their nuptial couch.

The presence in Ravensburg Castle of this young girl, which Rodolph, with that contempt for the opinion of the world which usually marked his actions, took no pains to conceal, became the engrossing topic of conversation in the servants' hall throughout the day, and as Rodolph had never before indulged in any intrigue, either with the peasant girls of the neighbouring village or the courtezans of Heidelburg, the circumstance seemed the more remarkable. But the beautiful Bertha seemed quite unconscious of the equivocal nature of her position in reference to the young count, and though her views of human nature became every moment more enlarged with the sphere of her existence, she still regarded Rodolph as a being of superior mould.

When night again drew his sable mantle over the sleeping earth, Rodolph and the mysterious Bertha sought their couch, and never had shone the inconstant moon on a pair so well matched as regarded physical beauty, or we may add as regarded their strange destiny – one gifted with almost superhuman powers of mind, yet in a few days to undergo so horrible a transformation, and far removed by that strange fate from ordinary mortals; the other endowed with such singular beauty yet doomed to the dreadful existence of one who had passed the boundaries of the grave, and returned to life!

With sonorous and solemn stroke the bell of the castle clock proclaimed the hour of midnight, and then Bertha slowly raised herself from her lover's body and slipping from the bed, attired herself in a half-unconscious state, and stole noiselessly from the room.

Her cheeks were pale, and her eyes had the wild and stolid glare which Rodolph had observed when she awakened from the slumber of the grave; she quitted the castle, and after gazing around her, as if uncertain which way to go, she proceeded towards the village.

She stopped opposite the nearest cottage, and then advanced to the window, and shook the shutters; the fastenings being insecure, they opened with little trouble, and a broken pane of glass enabled Bertha to introduce her hand, and remove the fastenings of the window. Then she cautiously opened the window, and entered the room – she ascended the stairs on tiptoe, and entered a chamber where a little girl was in bed and fast asleep. For a moment she shuddered violently, as if struggling to repress the horrible inclination which is the dread condition of a return to life after passing the portals of death, and then she bent her face down to the child's throat, her hot breath fanned its cheek, and the next moment her teeth punctured its tender skin, and she began to suck its blood to sustain her unnatural existence!

For such is the horrible destiny of the vampire race, of whom we have yet further mysteries and secrets to unfold; and such a being was she whom Count Rodolph had taken from the grave to his bed!

Presently the child awoke with a fearful scream, and its father, leaping from his bed in the next room, hurried to her succour, but Bertha rushed past him in the dark, and escaped from the house. The peasant found the little girl much frightened, and bleeding at the throat; but she had suffered no vital injury, and having ascertained this fact, he snatched up his match-lock, and hurried after the aggressor.

'A vampire!' exclaimed the peasant, turning pale with horror, as he distinctly saw, by the light of the moon, a young female hurrying from the village at a rapid pace.

The man gave chase to the flying Bertha, and gradually gaining ground, came within gun shot, just as she reached the shelving banks of the river, when he raised his weapon to his shoulder, and fired. The report echoed along the banks of the Rhine, and Bertha screamed as the ball penetrated her back, and tumbled headlong into the stream. The peasant hastened back to the village, satisfied that the horrible creature was no more, and the corpse of the vampire floated on the surface of the moonlit river.

The moon was that night at the full, and shed a flood of pearly light over the picturesque scenery of the Rhine, which, throughout its whole course, is a panorama of scenic beauty, every bend revealing some object interesting either for its historical reminiscences or legendary associations. There was the village, but now the scene of a horrible outrage – the castle, thrown into alternate light and shadow by the passing of the light fleecy clouds over the face of the moon – the town of Heidelberg, sloping from the Castle of the Palatine, and spanning the river with its noble bridge – and the Rhine, here shaded by the dark rocks which overhung the opposite bank, and there reflecting the silver light of the moon. The corpse of the vampire floated down the stream for some distance, and then it became arrested in its course by the bending of the river, and lay partly out of the water on the shelving bank.

And now commenced another scene of strange and startling interest – another phase in the fearful existence of the vampire bride! For as the beams of the full moon fell on the inanimate form of that being of mystery and fear, sensation seemed slowly to return, as when the magic spells of the Count of Ravensburg resuscitated her from the grave; her eyes opened, her bosom rose and fell with the warm pulsations of returning life; her limbs moved spasmodically, and then she rose from the bank, and shuddering at the recollection of what had occurred to her, she wrung the water from her saturated garments, and ran towards the castle at a pace accelerated by fear.

Having admitted herself into the castle, she sought the count's chamber with noiseless steps, and having taken off and concealed her wet clothes, she returned to his bed without his being aware that she had ever quitted it. The count was surprised to find that his mistress took no refreshment throughout the day, but he was led to consider it as one of the natural laws of her strange existence, and thought no more about it.

But in the village, the utmost excitement prevailed when it became known that the cottage of Herman Klans had been visited by a vampire during the night, and his little daughter bitten by the horrible creature. All day long the cottage of the mysterious visitation was beset by the wondering villagers, who crossed themselves piously, and wondered who the vampire could have been, and the services of the priest were called into requisition to prevent the little blue-eyed Minna becoming a vampire after death, as is supposed to be the case with those who have the misfortune to be bitten by one of those horrible creatures, just as a person becomes mad after the bite of a mad dog or cat.

According to the terms of the compact which had been entered into between Count Rodolph and the demon, its conditions did not come into operation until seven days after the signing of the dreadful bond, and as day after day flew on, Rodolph dreaded the necessity of acquainting Bertha with the terrible transformation which he must nightly undergo. But he knew how impossible it would be to keep his hideous and appalling metamorphosis a secret from his mistress, and he reflected that if he made her the confidant of his terrible fate it would be the more likely to remain unknown to the rest of the world. He accordingly nerved his mind to the appalling revelation which he had to make, and on the seventh day after his compact with Lucifer, he disclosed to her his awful secret.

'Bertha,' said he, in a sad and solemn tone, 'I am about to entrust thee with a terrible secret; swear to me that thou wilt never divulge it.'

'I swear,' she replied.

'Know, then,' continued the count, lowering his voice to a hoarse whisper, 'that, by virtue of a compact with the infernal powers of evil and of darkness, I am endowed with a term of life and youth amounting almost to the boon of immortality but to this inestimable gift, there is a condition attached which commences this night, and which I almost tremble to impart to thee.'

'Fear not, my Rodolph!' exclaimed his beautiful mistress, twining her round white arms about his neck, 'thy Bertha can never love thee less, and her soul the rather clings to thee more intensely for the preternatural gift which links thy destiny more closely to my own. For mine, too, is a strange and fearful existence, which I owe to thee, and therefore shall I cling to thee the more fondly for the kindred doom which allies us to each other while it lifts us far above ordinary mortals.'

'Then prepare thy ears for a dread revelation, Bertha,' returned the Count of Ravensburg. 'Each night of my future existence, at the hour of sunset, my doom divests me of my mortal shape, and I become a skeleton until sunrise on the morn ensuing. Now, thou knowest all, my Bertha, and be it thy care to prevent the dreadful secret from becoming known.'

'It shall, my brave Rodolph!' exclaimed Bertha, her eyes glittering with a strange expression, as she thought of the facility which her lover's strange doom would allow for her nocturnal absences from the castle. 'No eye but mine shall witness thy transformation, and I will watch over thee until thy return to thy natural shape.'

'Thanks, my Bertha!' returned Rodolph, embracing her. 'The hour draws nigh when I must relinquish for the night my mortal form; come, love, to our chamber, and see that no prying eye beholds the ghastly change.'

Bertha and her lover accordingly repaired to their chamber, and when the luminary of day sank below the horizon, leaving the traces of his splendour on the western sky, the Count Rodolph shrunk to a grisly skeleton, and fell upon the bed. Bertha shuddered as she witnessed the horrid transformation, and they lay down on the bed until midnight, the necessity of secrecy overcoming any repugnance she might otherwise have felt to the horrible contiguity of the skeleton, but when the castle clock proclaimed the hour of midnight with iron tongue, she rose from the bed, and locking the door of the chamber which contained so strange a guest, she stole from the castle to sate her unnatural appetite for human blood.

The moon rode high in the heavens on that night of unfathomable mystery and horror, and her silver beams shone through the chamber-window of Theresa Delmar, one of the loveliest maidens in the village of Ravensburg, revealing a snowy neck, and a white and dimpled shoulder, shaded by the bright golden locks which strayed over the pillow. The maiden's blue eyes were concealed by their thin lids and their long silken fringes, and her snowy bosom gently rose and fell beneath the white coverlet as the thoughts which agitated her by day, mingled in her dreams at night. Silence reigned in the thatched cottage, and throughout the village was only occasionally broken by the barking of some watchful house-dog.

But soon after midnight the silence was broken by a slight noise at the chamber window as if someone was endeavouring to obtain an entrance, and the flood of moonlight which streamed upon the maiden's bed was obscured by the form of a woman standing on the windowsill. Still Theresa slumbered on, nor dreamed of peril so near, for the woman had succeeded in opening the window, and in another moment she stood within the room.

With slow and cautious step she softly approached the bed whereon the maiden reposed so calmly, little dreaming how dread a visitant was near her couch, and then she shuddered involuntarily as she bent over the sleeping girl, and her long dark ringlets mingled with the masses of golden hair which shaded the white shoulder, and the partially exposed bosom of Theresa Delmar. Her lips touched the young girl's neck, her sharp teeth punctured the white skin, and then she began to suck greedily, quaffing the vital fluid which flowed warm and quick in the maiden's veins, and sapping her life to maintain her own!

Still Theresa awoke not, for the puncture made in her throat by the teeth of the horrible creature was little larger than that which would be made by a leech, and the vampire sucked long and greedily, for her long abstinence from blood had sharpened her unnatural appetite. Suddenly Theresa awoke with a start, doubtless caused by some unpleasant transition in her dreams, but she did not immediately cry out, for she felt no pain, and as yet she was scarcely conscious of her danger. But in a few seconds she was thoroughly awake, and her surprise and horror may be more easily imagined than described, when she found bending over her, and sucking her blood, the horrible creature that had but a few nights previously attacked Minna Klaus, and which the child's father thought he had destroyed.

Spell-bound by the glittering eyes of the vampire, she lay without the power to scream, until the appalling horror of her situation became too great for endurance, her quivering nerves were strung to their utmost power of extension, and a wild shriek burst from her lips. Even then the horrible creature did not leave its hold, but continued to suck from her palpitating veins the crimson current of her life, until footsteps were heard hastily approaching the chamber, and the lovely Theresa, whose screams seemed to have broken the fascination which had bound her in its thrall, struggled so violently that Bertha was compelled to relinquish her horrid banquet. Springing to the window, she effected her escape, just as heavy blows resounded on the door of the chamber, and her affrighted victim sank insensible on the bed.

'What is the matter, Theresa? Open the door!' exclaimed her terrified parents; but they received no answer.

Then Delmar broke open the door, and he and his wife rushed into the room and found their daughter lying insensible on the bed, with spots of blood on her throat and bosom, and the window wide open.

'The vampire has come to life again, and has attacked our Theresa!' exclaimed her mother. 'See the blood-marks on her dear neck! Raise the village, Delmar, to pursue the monster.'

'Oh, dear! where am I? Has it gone, mother?' inquired Theresa, as she recovered from her swoon, and gazed in an affrighted manner round the room.

'Yes, it has gone now, dear,' said her mother. 'What was it like?'

'Aye, what was it like?' added old Delmar. 'Perhaps it was not the same one that neighbour Klans shot at the other night.'

'Oh, yes! it was a young woman, and as much like Bertha Kurtel as ever one pea was like another,' replied the young girl, shuddering.

'Holy virgin!' exclaimed her mother, crossing herself with a shudder. 'Bertha Kurtel a vampire, and returned from the grave to prey upon our Theresea! Oh, horrible!'

Delmar hurriedly dressed himself, and catching up an axe, he hastened to call up Klans and others to pursue the vampire, and in a few minutes the whole village was in commotion. About twenty men armed themselves with whatever weapon came first to hand, and followed the direction which the vampire had taken when chased by Herman Klans on a former occasion. They searched every bush all round the village, to which they returned at sunrise without having found any trace of the object of their search. Delmar found his daughter somewhat faint from fright and loss of blood, but not otherwise injured by the vampire's attack. The greatest excitement prevailed in that usually quiet village, and all the morning, groups of men stood about the little street, or clustered round Delmar's cottage, conversing in low and mysterious whispers of the dreadful visitation which the village had a second time received.

'What a shocking thing it would be if a pretty girl like Theresa Delmar was to become a vampire when she dies,' observed one. 'And who knows what may happen now she has been bitten by one of those horrible creatures?'

'And poor little Minna Klaus,' said another.

'Ah, and we do not know how long the list may be if we do not put a stop to it,' added one of the rustic group. 'I have heard Father Ambrose say that they generally attack females and children.'

'Who can it be? that is what I want to know,' said old Klaus.

'Why, Theresa declares it was just like Bertha Kurtel,' returned another, shaking his voice to a whisper.

'Bertha Kurtel!' repeated a youth who had loved her who once bore that name. 'Bertha a vampire! impossible.'

'It is easily ascertained,' observed the gruff voice of the village blacksmith. 'We have only to take up the coffin and see if she is in it, as she ought to be. If we do not find her we shall know what's o'clock.'

'If it was not for her parents' feelings I really should like to be satisfied whether it is Bertha,' remarked old Delmar.

'Feelings!' repeated the smith, in a surly tone. 'Have we not all got our feelings? Are we to have our wives and children attacked in this manner, and all turned into vampires, and let other people's fine feelings prevent us from having satisfaction for it?'

'There is something in that,' observed Delmar, scratching his head with an air of perplexity.

'I would make one if anybody else would go,' said Herman Klaus, after a pause.

'And I will be another,' exclaimed the smith, looking around him. 'Now who will go and have a peep in the churchyard to see whose coffin is empty?'

Several expressed themselves ready, and others following their example the smith proceeded to the churchyard, backed by about twenty of the most resolute of the villagers, to reenact the scene which had taken place there but a few nights since. On arriving at the churchyard the smith and another immediately set to work to throw the earth out of the grave, which was soon accomplished, and amid the most breathless silence the smith proceeded to remove the lid of the coffin.

'Look here, neighbours,' said he, turning pale in spite of himself. 'The lid has been removed, and the coffin is empty!'

'So it is!' exclaimed Herman Klaus.

'Then is it not plain that Bertha is the vampire – the horrible creature that sucked the blood of Theresa Delmar and little Minna Klans?' said the smith, looking round upon the throng which had been swelled during the work of exhumation by idlers from the village.

'But where is she now? that is the question,' observed Herman Klans.

'This must be investigated,' said the smith. 'We must keep watch for the vampire, and catch it; then we must either burn it, or drive a stake through the creature's body, for they say those are the only methods that will effectually fix a vampire.'

The wondering group of peasants returned to the village, and great was the grief of the Kurtels at the horrible discovery that their daughter had become a vampire, and the youth who had so loved Bertha in her human state became delirious on hearing the confirmation of the suspicion which Theresa's assertion had first excited. The ordinary occupations of the villagers were entirely neglected throughout the day, and nothing was talked of but vampires and wehr-wolves, and other human transformations more terrific and appalling than any recorded in the metamorphoses of Ovid. Towards the evening the venerable seneschal of the Count of Ravensburg arrived in the village and had an interview with the Delmars, after which he visited the cottage of Herman Klans, and a vague rumour spread like wildfire from house to house, to the effect that the vampire was an inmate of Ravensburg Castle.

The communication made by the seneschal to Delmar and Klans was to the effect that, on the morning following the interment of Bertha Kurtel, a young female exactly resembling her in form, features, voice, and every individual peculiarity, had appeared in a mysterious manner at the castle, and had resided there ever since in the capacity of the count's mistress. No one knew who she was, where she came from, or how she obtained admission into the castle; and the occurrences in the village having reached the ears of the count's retainers and domestics, accompanied with the suspicion that the vampire was the revived Bertha Kurtel, the seneschal had hastened to the village to report his observations. The abstinence of the count's mistress from food was deemed corroborative of the suspicion that she was a vampire, and the seneschal's report caused the utmost excitement among the villagers. Symptoms of hostile intentions soon became visible, and in less than half an hour, more than a hundred men were proceeding in a disorderly manner towards the castle, armed with every imaginable weapon, and swearing to put an end to the vampire.

Count Rodolph and his beautiful mistress were sitting at a window which commanded a view of the road for some distance, the small white hand of Bertha locked in that of her lover, and whispering words of tenderness and love, when their attention was attracted by a disorderly mob approaching from the village.

'What can this mean?' said Rodolph, rising.

'Oh, this is what I have dreaded!' exclaimed Bertha, turning pale, and clasping her hands in a terrified manner: 'your studies have caused you to be suspected of necromancy, my Rodolph, they come to attack the castle.'

'I fear thou art right, dearest,' said the count: 'but we will give them a warm reception. Ho! a lawless mob menaces the castle with danger: make fast the gates; bar every door; bid my retainers man the battlements to repel the attack.'

'And sunset is approaching,' exclaimed Bertha, with a meaning glance at her lover.

'Do thou retire, sweet love, to thy chamber,' said Rodolph; 'fear not for me; I bear a charmed life, and neither sword nor shot will avail against it. If this lawless rabble be not dispersed when the dread moment comes all hope will be lost, and they shall behold the grisly change. Perhaps they may be struck with a sudden panic, and we may be enabled to fly into another country.'

Bertha retired after embracing the count, and shut herself up in her chamber. Preparations were immediately made to resist the attack of the insurgent villagers, who continued to advance upon the castle, yelling like savages, and breathing vengeance against the vampire mistress of Count Rodolph.

'Down with the vampire!' was the hoarse and sullen cry which rolled like distant thunder from a hundred throats, and then the mob drew up before the castle gates, and the smith struck them heavily with his ponderous hammer.

The count took an arquebuse and fired at the mob, very few of whom were provided with fire-arms; one of the peasants was wounded, and with a shout of rage and defiance a volley of shot, arrows, and stones was directed against the beleaguered castle. The smith continued to batter away at the gate, aided by several stalwart fellows with axes, and though several of the mob were killed by the fire of the men-at-arms, those who were endeavouring to force the gate were protected by the overhanging battlements, and continued to ply their implements with unwearied energy.

Could Rodolph turned pale, and shuddered as he listened to the wild cries of the assailants, not from fear, for apart from his invulnerability he was inaccessible to that feeling, but from the horrible ideas engendered from these shouts, having reference to the beautiful Bertha Kurtel. Had her resuscitation from the grave endowed her with the horrible nature of the vampire? Could that lovely creature sustain her renewed existence with the blood of her former companions? Horrible! yet, had she not hinted at something of the kind when he revealed to her the horrors of his own strange doom? It must be so, then; and he shuddered violently at the appalling idea.

'Down with the vampire!' was still the menacing cry which rose from the assailants, who at length succeeded in breaking down the gates, and rushed tumultuously into the court-yard, shouting and brandishing their weapons.

Undismayed by the fire from the battlements, they commenced an attack on the doors and windows of the castle, and now they were all crowded in the courtyard, Count Rodolph thought the moment favourable for a sally. Drawing his sword, and commanding a score of his armed retainers to follow him, he suddenly opened a door leading into the court-yard, and fell furiously on the flank of the assailants. For a moment they were thrown into confusion, but they quickly rallied, when Count Rodolph and his little party were surrounded and compelled to act on the defensive. The ruddy beams of the setting sun were already purpling the distant hills when the peasants marched upon the castle, and as his broad disk sank below the horizon, the aspect of the Count of Ravensburg suddenly underwent a marvellous change, and much as the insurgents had wondered to see arrows glance off from his body, and their swords rebound as if their stroke fell on a giant oak, how much greater was their astonishment when they beheld him suddenly transformed into a fleshless skeleton!

'It is some devise of Satan! – he is a sorcerer!' cried the stalwart smith, brandishing his huge hammer. 'Come on, mates – down with the vampire!'

'Down with the vampire!' echoed from the mob, and the count's retainers giving way on all sides, as much appalled as the peasants at this horrible metamorphosis, the assailants rushed into the castle by the open door, and marched from room to room, looking in every closet and under every bed, while the terrified Bertha flew from one apartment to another, until she at length sought refuge in the highest apartment of the eastern turret, that chamber which had witnessed her return from death to her renewed state of strange and horrible existence. She had locked and bolted the door of the study, but what availed these obstacles against a furious mob, animated by their success in gaining the castle, and bent upon destruction and revenge? The door cracked, yielded, was forced open, and several men rushed into the little chamber.

'Here she is! – here is the vampire!' cried the foremost, and despite her piercing shrieks and earnest supplications for mercy, the wretched Bertha was dragged out of the study, with her long black hair hanging in wild disorder about her shoulders, and her beautiful countenance pale with overpowering terror.

'Mercy, indeed! What mercy can we feel for a vampire?' cried the peasants, and the terrified creature was dragged down the turret stairs by one or two of the boldest, for few would venture to come in contact with the dreaded being.

As they reached the foot of the stairs a volume of smoke rolled along the passage, and the crackling of burning wood told them that some of their companions had set fire to the castle.

'Now what shall we do with the vampire?' said her remorseless captors.

'Throw her into the Rhine!' suggested one.

'Tie her up and shoot at her!' said another.

'What will be the use of that?' objected a third. 'Nothing but fire or a sharp stake will destroy a vampire. Let us shut her up in the castle, and burn her to ashes!'

'Yes, yes! burn the vampire!' shouted a score of voices.

'No, no! – I say, no!' cried the smith. 'Let us carry her to the churchyard, put her in her coffin again, and peg her down with a stake, so that she can never rise again.'

The suggestion of the smith was approved of, and the wretched Bertha was half-dragged and half-carried, more dead than alive, towards the village church. The flames were bursting forth from all parts of the castle when the lawless spoilers left it, and a red glow hung over its ancient towers; the work of destruction was rapid, and in a few hours nought but the bare and blackened walls were left standing.

On the destroyers of Ravensburg Castle reaching the churchyard, the almost lifeless form of Bertha Kurtel was dragged to the grave, which had been left open, and flung rudely into the coffin. Then a sharp pointed stake was produced, which had been prepared by the way, and the smith plunged it with all the force of his sinewy arms into the abdomen of the doomed vampire. A piercing shriek burst from her pale lips as the horrible thrust aroused her to consciousness, and as her clothes became dabbed with the crimson stream of life, and the smith lifted his heavy hammer and drove the stake through her quivering body, the transfixed wretch writhed convulsively, and the contortions of her countenance were fearful to behold. Thus impaled in her coffin, and while her limbs yet quivered with the last throes of dissolution, the earth was replaced and rammed down by the tread of many feet.

But those strange and terrible scenes were not yet ended. A young peasant of equal curiosity and boldness, and who had been engaged in the attack upon the castle and the horrible tragedy which followed it, was anxious to know more of the strange affair of the skeleton, which had been left in the courtyard where it fell, none of the villagers caring to interfere with so ghastly an object. He therefore stole away a little before midnight, and went towards the castle, where the fire was dying out, though a fiery glow was still reflected from the mouldering embers of beams and rafters. He advanced cautiously through the broken gates of the castle, and shuddered slightly as he perceived the skeleton of the Count of Ravensburg still lying on the pavement of the courtyard.

He determined to watch until daylight, and see what became of the grisly relics of mortality, which a few hours before had been the young and handsome Count of Ravensburg. The hours passed slowly on from midnight to the dawn of another day, and when the rising sun tinged the eastern sky with crimson and gold, a strange spectacle was witnessed by the solitary watcher in the court-yard of Ravensburg Castle.

The skeleton rose slowly from the pavement, and assumed the form of Count Rodolph, just as he appeared at the moment preceding his transformation on the evening before. A cold perspiration bedewed the brow of the peasant, and his hair stood erect with terror, on witnessing this sudden metamorphosis. The count looked up at the dilapidated walls and towers of his castle, and shuddered violently, and crossing the court-yard, passed through the broken gate.

The peasant then hastened to the village, and reported what he had seen, which was a source of much marvel to the rustic inhabitants. The story of the skeleton count, and his vampire mistress, quickly spread all over Germany, but the villagers were no more molested by vampires, for Bertha Kurtel was securely fixed in her coffin, and no ill effects ensued from her attacks upon Theresa Delmar and little Minna Klans.

The Vampyre's Story

JAMES MALCOLM RYMER

The discovery of 'The Skeleton Count' does, of course, cast doubts on the claim in many studies of horror fiction that another of Edward Lloyd's 'penny dreadfuls', Varney the Vampyre; or, The Feast of Blood, *which was published in 1847, was the first vampire novel in English. Certainly there can be no dispute that it was the first story to introduce those familiar leit motifs of undead creatures who rise from their graves at night and attack the living – in particular nubile young women – and who can only be stopped by a stake though their beating hearts. The saga was first issued in penny parts in the winter of 1847 and became so popular with readers that the author was compelled by Lloyd to keep it going for a total of 109 issues before Varney finally met his fate by leaping – of his own volition – into the lava pit at Mount Vesuvius.*

Montague Summers, the first great researcher into the history of Gothic literature and 'penny dreadfuls', attributes Varney to Thomas Peckett Prest, one of Lloyd's most prolific hack writers. But subsequent research has suggested that the real author was James Malcolm Rymer (1814–81) another writer of prodigious speed who began his working life as an engineer but apparently finding this occupation not fast enough for his taste turned himself into a very successful contributor to Edward Lloyd's presses. He would certainly have had dealings with Mrs Elizabeth Grey and the thought remains inescapable that she might just have suggested the idea for Varney the Vampyre *to him. That is certainly no more than speculation on my part, but it does seem likely that as the editress she would have encouraged such a project because of her earlier experience. Among*

Rymer's other contributions under a variety of pen-names such as Malcolm J. Merry and Malcolm J. Errym was a sensational novel of Victorian sexuality run riot, Ada the Betrayed *(1842), and* The Black Monk *(1844) about an evil and carnal old priest.*

The tale of Varney the Vampyre *begins during the time of Oliver Cromwell and in the ensuing years, the corpse-like man with his staring eyes and huge fangs, attacks dozens of victims, both men and women, until he finally takes his own life. It has been suggested that Rymer based his story on the weird events surrounding the life of a Sir Richard Verney, a blood-thirsty follower of King Charles and a rabid opponent of the Protector. Although there can be no argument that the story of Varney's life is often badly written and the events disjointed and even out of sequence — attributable, no doubt, to the demands placed upon Rymer to keep up the flow of blood and gore for his readers — it is also important as the first vampire story to contain an episode told in the first person. No writer previously had attempted to put himself into the mind of a member of the undead — which makes what follows another important landmark among the precursors of* Dracula . . .

*   *   *

In the reign of the First Charles, I resided in a narrow street, in the immediate neighbourhood of Whitehall. It was a straggling, tortuous thoroughfare, going down to the Thames; it matters little what were my means of livelihood, but I have no hesitation in saying that I was a well-paid agent in some of the political movements which graced and disgraced that period.

London was then a mass of mean-looking houses, with here and there one that looked like a palace, compared with its humbler neighbours. Almost every street appeared to be under the protection of some great house situated somewhere in its extent, but such of those houses as have survived the wreck of time rank now with their neighbours, and are so strangely altered, that I, who knew many of them well, could now scarcely point to the place where they used to stand.

I took no prominent part in the commotions of that period, but I saw the head of a king held up in its gore at Whitehall as a spectacle for the multitude.

There were thousands of persons in England who had aided to bring about that result, but who were the first to fall under the ban of the gigantic power they had themselves raised.

Among these were many of my employers; men, who had been quite willing to shake the stability of a throne so far as the individual occupying it was concerned; but who certainly never contemplated the destruction of monarchy; so the death of the First Charles, and the dictatorship of Cromwell, made royalists in abundance.

They had raised a spirit they could not quell again, and this was a fact which the stern, harsh man, Cromwell, with whom I had many interviews, was aware of.

My house was admirably adapted for the purposes of secrecy and seclusion, and I became a thriving man from the large sums I received for aiding the escape of distinguished loyalists, some of whom lay for a considerable time *perdu* at my house, before an eligible opportunity arrived of dropping down the river quietly to some vessel which would take them to Holland.

It was to offer me so much per head for these royalists that Cromwell sent for me, and there was one in particular who had been private secretary to the Duke of Cleveland, a young man merely, of neither family nor rank, but of great ability, whom Cromwell was exceedingly anxious to capture.

I think there likewise must have been some private reasons which induced the dictator of the Commonwealth to be so anxious concerning this Master Francis Latham, which was the name of the person alluded to.

It was late one evening when a stranger came to my house, and having desired to see me, was shown into a private apartment, when I immediately waited upon him.

'I am aware,' he said, 'that you have been confidentially employed by the Duke of Cleveland, and I am aware that you have been very useful to distressed loyalists, but in aiding Master Francis Latham, the duke's secretary, you will be permitted almost to name your own terms.'

I named a hundred pounds, which at that time was a much larger sum than now, taking into consideration the relative value. One half of it was paid to me at once, and the other promised within four-and-twenty hours after Latham had effected his escape.

I was told that at half-past twelve o'clock that night, a man dressed in common working apparel, and with a broom over his shoulder would knock at my door and ask if he could be recommended to a lodging, and that by those tokens I should know him to be Francis Latham. A Dutch lugger, I was further told, was lying near Gravesend, on board of which, to earn my money, I was expected to place the fugitive.

All this was duly agreed upon; I had a boat in readiness, with a couple of watermen upon whom I could depend, and I was far from anticipating any extraordinary difficulties in carrying out the enterprise.

I had a son about twelve years of age, who being a sharp acute lad, I found very useful upon several occasions, and I never scrupled to make him acquainted with any such affair as this that I am recounting.

Half past twelve o'clock came, and in a very few minutes after that period of time there came a knock at my door, which my son answered, and according to arrangement, there was the person with a broom, who asked to be recommended to a lodging, and who was immediately requested to walk in.

He seemed rather nervous, and asked me if I thought there was much risk.

'No,' said I, 'no more than ordinary risk in all these cases, but we must wait half an hour 'till the tide turns. For just now to struggle against it down the river would really be nothing else but courting observation.'

To this he perfectly agreed, and sat down by my fireside.

I was as anxious as he to get the affair over, for it was a ticklish job, and Oliver Cromwell, if he had brought anything of the kind exactly home to me, would as life order me to be shot as he would have taken his luncheon in the name of the Lord.

I accordingly went down to the water-side to speak to the men who were lying there with the boat, and had ascertained from them that in about twenty minutes the tide would begin to ebb in the centre of the stream, when two men confronted me.

Practised as I was in the habits and appearances of the times, I guessed at once who they were. In fact, a couple of Oliver Cromwell's dismounted dragoons were always well known.

'You are wanted,' said one of them to me.

'Yes, you are particularly wantèd,' said the other.

'But, gentlemen, I am rather busy,' said I. 'In an hour's time I will do myself the pleasure, if you please, of waiting upon you anywhere you wish to name.'

The only reply they made to this was the practical one, of getting on each side of me, and then hurrying me on, past my own door.

I was taken right away to St James's at a rapid pace, being hurried through one of the court yards; we paused at a small door, at which was a sentinel.

My two guides communicated something to him, and he allowed us to pass. There was a narrow passage without any light, and through another door, at which was likewise a sentinel, who turned the glare of a lantern upon me and my conductors. Some short explanation was given to him likewise during which I heard the words His Highness, which was the title which Cromwell had lately assumed.

They pushed me through this doorway, closed it behind me, and left me inside in the dark.

Being perfectly ignorant of where I was, I thought the most prudent plan was to stand stock still, for if I advanced it might be into danger, and my retreat was evidently cut off.

Moreover, those who brought me there must have some sort of intention, and it was better for me to leave them to develop it than to take any steps myself, which might be of a very hazardous nature.

That I was adopting the best policy I was soon convinced, for a flash of light suddenly came upon me, and I heard a gruff voice, say, –

'Who goes there? come this way.'

I walked on, and passed through an open door way into a small apartment, in the centre of which, standing by a common deal table on which his clenched hand was resting, I found Oliver Cromwell himself.

'So, sirrah,' he said, 'royalists and pestilent characters are to ravage the land, are they so? answer me.'

'I have no answer to make, your highness,' said I.

'God's mercy, no answer, when in your own house the Duke of Cleveland's proscribed secretary lies concealed.'

I felt rather staggered, but was certain I had been betrayed by some one, and Cromwell continued rapidly, without giving me time to speak.

'The Lord is merciful, and so are we, but the malignant must be taken by the beloved soldiers of the Commonwealth, and the gospel God-fearing men, who always turn to the Lord, with short carbines, will accompany you. The malignant shall be taken from your house, by you, and the true God-fearing dragoons shall linger in the shade behind. You will take him to the river side, where the Lord willing, there will be a boat with a small blue ensign, on board of which you will place him, wishing him good speed.'

He paused, and looked fixedly upon me by the aid of the miserable light that was in the apartment.

'What then, your highness?' I said.

'Then you will probably call upon us to-morrow for a considerable sum, which will be due to you for this good service to the Commonwealth; yea, it shall be profitable to fight the battles of the Lord.'

I must confess, I had expected a very different result from the interview, which I had been greatly in fear would have resulted, in greatly endangering my liberty. Cromwell was a man not to be tampered with; I knew my danger, and was not disposed to sacrifice myself for Master Latham.

'Your highness shall be obeyed,' I said.

'Ay, verily,' he replied, 'and if we be not obeyed, we must make ourselves felt with a strong arm of flesh. What ho! God-fearing Simpkins, art thon there?'

'Yes, the Lord willing,' said a dragoon, making his appearance at the door.

Cromwell merely made him a sign with his hand, and he laid hold of the upper part of my arm, as though it had been in a vice, and led me out into the passage again where the sentinels were posted.

In the course of a few moments, I was duly in custody of my two guards again, and we were proceeding at a very rapid pace towards my residence.

It was not a very agreeable affair, view it in whatever light I might; but as regarded Cromwell, I knew my jeopardy, and it would be perceived that I had not hesitated a moment in obeying him. Moreover, I considered, for I knew he was generous, I should have a good round sum by the transaction, which added to the fifty pounds I had received from the royalists, made the affair appear to me in a pleasant enough light. Indeed, I was revolving in my mind as I went along, whether it would not be worth while, almost entirely to attach myself to the protector.

'If,' I reasoned with myself, 'I should do that, and still preserve myself a character with the royalists, I should thrive.'

But it will be seen that an adverse circumstance put an end to all those dreams.

When we reached the door of my house, the first thing I saw was my son wiping his brow, as if he had undergone some fatigue; he ran up to me, and catching me by the arm, whispered to me.

I was so angered at the moment, that heedless of what I did, and passion getting the mastery over me, I with my clenched fist struck him to the earth. His head fell upon one of the hard round stones with which the street was paved, and he never spoke again. I had murdered him.

*

I don't know what happened immediately subsequent to this fearful deed; all I can recollect is, that there was a great confusion and a flashing of lights, and it appeared to me as if something had suddenly struck me down to the earth with great force.

When I did thoroughly awaken, I found myself lying upon a small couch, but in a very large apartment dimly lighted, and where, there were many such couches ranged against the walls. A miserable light just enabled me to see about me a little, and some dim dusky-looking figures were creeping about the place.

It was a hospital that the protector had lately instituted in the Strand.

I tried to speak, but could not; my tongue seemed glued to my mouth, and I could not, and then a change came upon my sense of sight, and I could scarcely see at all the dim dusky-looking figures about me.

Some one took hold of me by the wrist, and I heard one say, quite distinctly, –

'He's entirely going, now.'

Suddenly it seemed as if something had fallen with a crushing influence upon my chest, and then a consciousness that I was gasping for breath, and then I thought I was at the bottom of the sea. There was a moment, only a moment, of frightful agony, and then came a singing sound, like the rush of waters, after which, I distinctly felt some one raising me in their arms. I was dropped again, my limbs felt numbed and chill, an universal spasm shot through my whole system, I opened my eyes, and found myself lying in the open air, by a newly opened grave.

A full moon was sailing through the sky and the cold beams were upon my face; a voice sounded in my ears, a deep and solemn voice – and painfully distinct was every word it uttered.

'Mortimer,' it said, for that was my name, 'Mortimer, in life you did one deed which at once cast you out from all hope that anything in that life would be remembered in the world to come to your advantage. You poisoned the pure font of mercy, and not upon such as you can the downy freshness of Heaven's bounty fall. Murderer, murderer of that being sacredly presented to your care by the great Creator of all things, live henceforth a being accused. Be to yourself a desolation and a blight, shunned by all that is good and virtuous, armed against all men, and all men armed against thee, Varney the Vampyre.'

I staggered to my feet, the scene around me was a churchyard, I was gaunt and thin, my clothes hung about me in tattered remnants. The damp smell of the grave hung about them, I met an aged man, and asked him where I was. He looked at me with a shudder, as though I had escaped from some charnel house.

'Why, this is Isledon,' said he.

A peal of bells came merrily upon the night air.

'What means that?' said I.

'Why this is the anniversary of the Restoration.'

'The Restoration! What Restoration?'

'Why of the royal family to the throne, to be sure, returned this day last year. Have you been asleep so long that you don't know that?'

I shuddered and walked on, determined to make further inquiries, and to make them with so much caution, that the real extent of my ignorance should scarce be surmised, and the result was to me of the most astonishing character.

I found that I had been in the trance of death for nearly two years, and that during that period, great political changes had taken place. The exiled royal family had been restored to the throne, and the most remarkable revulsion of feeling that had ever taken place in a nation had taken place in England.

But personally I had not yet fully awakened to all the horror of what I was. I had heard the words addressed to me, but I had attached no very definite meaning to them.

I have already said that I was not yet fully alive to the horror of what I was, but I soon found what the words which had been spoken to me by the mysterious being who had exhumed me meant; I was a thing accursed, a something to be shunned by all men, a horror, a blight, and a desolation.

I felt myself growing sick and weak, as I traversed the streets of the city, and yet I loathed the sight of food, whenever I saw it.

I reached my own house, and saw that it had been burned down; there lay nothing but a heap of charred ruins where it once stood.

But I had an interest in those ruins, for from time to time I had buried considerable sums of money beneath the flooring of the lowest apartments, and I had every reason to believe, as such a secret treasure was only known to myself, that it remained untouched.

I waited until the moon became obscured by some passing clouds, and then having a most intimate knowledge of the locality, I commenced groping about the ruins, and removing a portion of them, until I made my way to the spot where my money was hidden.

The morning came, however, and surprised me at my occupation; so I hid myself among the ruins of what had once been my home for a whole day, and never once stirred from my concealment.

Oh, it was a long and weary day. I could hear the prattle of children at play, an inn or change-house was near at hand, and I could hear noisy drinkers bawling forth songs that had been proscribed in the Commonwealth.

I saw a poor wretch hunted nearly to death, close to where I lay concealed, because from the fashion of his garments, and the cut of his hair, he was supposed to belong to the deposed party.

But the long expected night came at last. It was a dark one, too, so that it answered my purpose well.

I had found an old rusty knife among the ruins, and with that I set to work to dig up my hidden treasure; I was successful, and found it all. Not a guinea had been removed, although in the immediate neighbourhood, there were those who would have sacrificed a human life for any piece of gold that I had hoarded.

I made no enquiries about any one that had belonged to me, I dreaded to receive some horrible and circumstantial answer, but I did get a slight piece of news, as I left the ruins, although I asked not for it.

'There's a poor devil,' said one; 'did you ever see such a wretch in all your life?'

'Why, yes,' said another, 'he's enough to turn one's canary sour, he seems to have come up from the ruins of Mortimer's house. By-the-by did you ever hear what became of him?'

'Yes, to be sure, he was shot by two of Cromwell's dragoons in some fracas or another.'

'Ah, I recollect now, I heard as much. He murdered his son, didn't he?'

I passed on. Those words seemed to send a bolt of fire through the brain, and I dreaded that the speaker might expatiate upon them.

A slow misty rain was falling, which caused the streets to be very much deserted, but being extremely well acquainted with the city, I passed on till I came to that quarter which was principally inhabited by money lenders who I knew would take my money without any troublesome questions being asked me, and also I could procure every accommodation required; and they did so, for before another hour had passed over my head, I emerged richly habited as a chevalier of the period, having really not paid to the conscientious man much more than four times the price of the clothing I walked away with.

And thus I was in the middle of London, with some hundreds of pounds in my pocket, and a horrible uncertainty as to what I was.

I was growing fainter and fainter still, and I feared that unless I succeeded in housing myself shortly, I should become a prey to someone who, seeing my exhausted condition, would, notwithstanding I had a formidable rapier by my side, rob me of all I possessed.

My career has been much too long and too chequered an one even to give the briefest sketch of. All I purpose here to relate is how I became convinced I was a vampyre, and that blood was my congenial nourishment and the only element of my new existence.

I passed on until I came to a street where I knew the houses were large but unfashionable, and that they were principally occupied by persons who made a trade by letting out apartments, and there I thought I might locate myself in safety.

As I made no difficulty about terms, there was no difficulty at all of any sort, and I found myself conducted into a tolerably handsome suite of rooms in the house of a decent-looking widow woman, who had two daughters, young and blooming girls, both of whom regarded me as the new lodger, with looks of anything but favour, considering my awful and cadaverous appearance most probably as promising nothing at all in the shape of pleasant companionship.

This I was quite prepared for – I had seen myself in a mirror – that was enough; and I could honestly have averred that a more ghastly and horrible looking skeleton, attired in silks and broad-cloth, never yet walked the streets of the city.

When I retired to my chamber, I was so faint and ill, that I could scarcely drag one foot after the other; and was ruminating what I should do, until a strange feeling crept over me that I should like – what? Blood! – raw blood, reeking and hot, bubbling and juicy, from the veins of some gasping victim.

A clock upon the stairs struck one. I arose and listened attentively; all was still in the house – still as the very grave.

It was a large old rambling building, and had belonged at one time, no doubt, to a man of some mark and likelihood in the world. My chamber was one of six that opened from a corridor of a considerable length, and which traversed the whole length of the house.

I crept out into this corridor, and listened again for full ten minutes, but not the slightest sound, save my own faint breathing, disturbed the stillness of the house; and that emboldened me so that, with my appetite for blood growing each moment stronger, I began to ask myself from whose veins I could seek strength and nourishment.

But how was I to proceed? How was I to know in that large house which of the sleepers I could attack with safety, for it had now come to that, that I was to attack somebody. I stood like an evil spirit, pondering over the best means of securing a victim.

And there came over me the horrible faintness again, that faintness which each moment grew worse, and which threatened completely to engulf me. I feared that some flush of it would overtake me, and then I should fall to rise no more; and strange as it may appear, I felt a disposition to cling to the new life that had been given to me. I seemed to be acquainted already with all its horrors, but not all its joys.

Suddenly the darkness of the corridor was cleared away, and soft and mellow light crept into it, and I said to myself, –

'The moon has risen.'

Yes, the bright and beautiful moon, which I had felt the soft influence of when I lay among the graves, had emerged from the bank of clouds along the eastern sky, its beams descending through a little window. They streamed right through the corridor, faintly but effectually illuminating it, and letting me see clearly all the different doors leading to the different chambers.

And thus it was that I had light for anything I wished to do, but not information.

The moonbeams playing upon my face seemed to give me a spurious sort of strength. I did not know until after experience what a marked and sensible effect they would always have upon me, but I felt it even then, although I did not attribute it wholly to the influence of the queenly planet.

I walked on through the corridor, and some sudden influence seemed to guide me to a particular door. I know not how it was, but I laid my hand upon the lock, and said to myself –

'I shall find my victim here.'

I paused yet a moment, for there came across me even then, after I had gone so far, a horrible dread of what I was about to do, and a feeling that there might be consequences arising from it that would jeopardise me greatly. Perhaps even then if a great accession of strength had come to my aid – mere bodily aid I mean – I should have hesitated and the victim would have escaped; but, as if to mock me, there came that frightful feeling of exhaustion which felt so like the prelude to another death.

I no longer hesitated; I turned the lock of the door, and I thought that I must be discovered. I left it open about an inch, and then flew back to my own chamber.

I listened attentively; there was no alarm, no movement in any of the rooms — the same death-like stillness pervaded the house, and I felt that I was still safe.

A soft gleam of yellow looking light had come through the crevice of the door when I had opened it. It mingled strangely with the moonlight, and I concluded correctly enough, as I found afterwards, that a light was burning in the chamber.

It was at least another ten minutes before I could sufficiently reassure myself to glide from my own room and approach that of the fated sleeper; but at length I told myself that I might safely do so, and the night was waning fast, and if anything was to be accomplished it must be done at once, before the first beams of early dawn should chase away the spirits of the night, and perhaps should leave me no power to act.

'What shall I be,' I asked myself; 'after another four-and-twenty hours of exhaustion? Shall I have power then to make the election of what I will do or what I will not? No, I may suffer the pangs of death again, and the scarcely less pangs of another revival.'

This reasoning — if it may be called reasoning — decided me; and with cautious and cat-like footsteps, I again approached the bed-room door which I had opened.

I no longer hesitated, but at once crossed the threshold, and looked around me. It was the chamber of the youngest of my landlady's daughters, who, as far as I could judge, seemed to be about sixteen years of age; but they had evidently been so struck with my horrible appearance, that they had placed themselves as little as possible in my way, so that I could not be said to be a very good judge of their ages or of their looks.

I only knew she was the youngest, because she wore her hair long, and wore it in ringlets, which were loose and streaming over the pillow on which she slept, while her sister, I remarked, wore her hair plaited up, and completely off her neck and shoulders.

I stood by the bed-side, and looked upon this beautiful girl in all the pride of her young beauty, so gently and quietly slumbering. Her lips were parted, as though some pleasant images were passing in her mind, and induced a slight smile even in her sleep. She murmured twice, too, a word, which I thought was the name of some one — perchance the idol of her young heart — but it was too indistinct for me to catch it, nor did I care to hear; that which was perhaps a very cherished secret, indeed, mattered not to me. I made no pretensions to her affections, however strongly in a short time I might stand in her abhorrence.

One of her arms, which was exquisitely rounded, lay upon the coverlit; a neck, too, as white as alabaster, was partially exposed to my gaze, but I had no passions – it was food I wanted.

I sprung upon her. There was a shriek, but not before I had secured a draught of life blood from her neck. It was enough. I felt it dart through my veins like fire, and I was restored. From that moment I found out what was to be my sustenance; it was blood – the blood of the young and the beautiful.

The house was thoroughly alarmed, but not before I had retired to my own chamber. I was but partially dressed, and those few clothes I threw off me, and getting into my bed, I feigned to be asleep; so that when a gentleman who slept likewise in the house, but of whose presence I knew nothing, knocked hardly at my door, I affected to awaken in a fright, and called out, –

'What is it? what is it? – for God's sake tell me if it is a fire.'

'No, no – but get up, sir, get up. There's some one in the place. An attempt at murder, I think, sir.'

I arose and opened the door; so by the light he carried he saw that I had to dress myself – he was but half attired himself, and he carried his sword beneath his arm.

'It is a strange thing,' he said; 'but I have heard a shriek of alarm.'

'And I likewise,' said I; 'but I thought it was a dream.'

'Help! help! help!' cried the widow, who had risen, but stood upon the threshold of her own chamber; 'thieves! thieves!'

By this time I had got on sufficient of my apparel that I could make an appearance, and, likewise with my sword in my hand, I sallied out into the corridor.

'Oh, gentlemen – gentlemen,' cried the landlady, 'did you hear anything?'

'A shriek, madam,' said my fellow-lodger; 'have you looked into your daughters' chambers?'

The room of the youngest daughter was the nearest, and into that she went at once. In another moment she appeared on the threshold again with a face as white as a sheet, then she wrung her hands, and said, –

'Murder! murder! – my child is murdered – my child is murdered, Master Harding,' – which I found was the name of my fellow-lodger.

'Fling open one of the windows, and call for the watch,' said he to me, 'and I will search the room, and woe be to any one that I may find within its walls unauthorised.'

I did as he desired, and called the watch, but the watch came not, and then, upon a second visit to her daughter, the landlady found she had only fainted, and that she had been deceived in thinking she was murdered by the sudden sight of the blood upon her neck, so the house was restored to something like quiet again, and the morning being now near at hand, Mr Harding retired to his chamber, and I to mine, leaving the landlady and her eldest daughter assiduous in their attentions to the younger.

How wonderfully revived I felt – I was quite a new creature when the sunlight came dancing into my apartment. I dressed and was about to leave the house, when Mr Harding came out of one of the lowest rooms, and intercepted me.

'Sir,' he said, 'I have not the pleasure of knowing you, but I have no doubt that an ordinary feeling of chivalry will prompt you to do all in your power to obviate the dread of such another night as the past.'

'Dread, sir,' said I, 'the dread of what?'

'A very proper question,' he said, 'but one I can hardly answer; the girl states, she was awakened by some one biting her neck, and in proof of the story she actually exhibits the marks of teeth, and so terrified is she, that she declared that she shall never be able to sleep again.'

'You astonish me.'

'No doubt – it is sufficiently astonishing to excuse even doubts; but if you and I, who are both inmates of the house, were to keep watch to-night in the corridor, it might have the effect of completely quieting the imagination of the young girl, and perhaps result in the discovery of this nocturnal disturber of the peace.'

'Certainly,' said I, 'command me in any way, I shall have great pleasure.'

'Shall it be understood, then, that we meet at eleven in your apartment or in mine.'

'Whichever you may please to consider the most convenient, sir.'

'I mention my own then, which is the furthest door in the corridor, and where I shall be happy to see you at eleven o'clock.'

There was a something about this young man's manner which I did not altogether like, and yet I could not come to any positive conclusion as to whether he suspected me, and therefore I thought it would be premature to fly, when perhaps there would be really no occasion for doing so; on the contrary, I made up my mind to wait the result of the evening, which might or might not be disastrous to me. At all events, I considered that I was fully equal to taking my own part, and if by the decrees of destiny I was really to be, as it were, repudiated from society, and made to endure a new, strange, and horrible existence, I did not see that I was called upon to be particular how I rescued myself from difficulties that might arise.

Relying, then, upon my own strength, and my own unscrupulous use of it, I awaited with tolerable composure the coming of night.

During the day I amused myself by walking about, and noting the remarkable changes which so short a period as two years had made in London. But these happened to be two years most abundantly prolific in change. The feelings and habits of people seemed to have undergone a thorough revolution, which I was the more surprised at when I learned by what thorough treachery the restoration of the exiled family was effected.

The day wore on; I felt no need of refreshment, and I began to feel my own proper position, and to feel that occasionally a draught of delicious life-blood, such as I had quaffed the night before was fresh marrow to my bones.

I could see, when I entered the house where I had made my temporary home, that notwithstanding that I considered my appearance wonderfully improved, that feeling was not shared in by others, for the whole family shrunk from me as though there had been a most frightful contamination in my touch, and as though the very air I had breathed was hateful and deleterious. I felt convinced that there had been some conversation concerning me, and that I was rather more than suspected. I certainly could then have left the place easily and quietly, but I had a feeling of defiance, which did not enable me to do so.

I felt as if I were an injured being, and ought to resist a something that looked like oppression.

'Why,' I said to myself, 'have I been rescued from the tomb to be made the sport of a malignant destiny? My crime was a great one, but surely I suffered enough, when I suffered death as an expiation of it, and I might have been left to repose in the grave.'

The feelings that have since come over me held no place in my imagination, but with a kind of defiant desperation I felt as if I should like to defeat the plan by which I was attempted to be punished, and even in the face of Providence itself, to show that it was a failure entailing far worse consequences upon others than upon me.

This was my impression, so I would not play the coward, and fly upon the first flash of danger.

I sat in my own room until the hour came for my appointment with Mr Harding, and then I walked along the corridor with a confident step, and let the hilt end of my scabbard clank along the floor. I knocked boldly at the door, and I thought there was a little hesitation in his voice as he bade me walk in, but this might have been only my imagination.

He was seated at a table, fully dressed, and in addition to his sword, there was lying upon the table before him a large holster pistol, nearly half the size of a carbine.

'You are well prepared,' said I, as I pointed to it.

'Yes,' he said, 'and I mean to use it.'

'What do they want now?' I said.

'What do who want?'

'I don't know,' I said, 'but I thought I heard some one call you by name from below.'

'Indeed, excuse me a moment, perhaps they have made some discovery.'

There was wine upon the table, and while he was gone, I poured a glass of good Rhenish down the barrel of the pistol. I wiped it carefully with the cuff of my coat, so there was no appearance upon the barrel of anything of the sort, and when he came back, he looked at me very suspiciously, as he said, –

'Nobody called me, how could you say I was called.'

'Because I thought I heard you called; I suppose it is allowable for human nature to be fallible now and then.'

'Yes, but then I am so surprised how you could make such a mistake.'

'So am I.'

It was rather a difficult thing to answer this, and looking at me very steadily, he took up the pistol and examined the priming. Of course, that was all right, and he appeared to be perfectly satisfied.

'There will be two chairs and a table,' he said, 'placed in the corridor, so that we can sit in perfect ease. I will not anticipate that anything will happen, but if it should, I can only say that I will not be backward in the use of my weapons.'

'I don't doubt it,' said I, 'and commend you accordingly. That pistol must be a most formidable weapon. Does it ever miss fire?'

'Not that I know of,' he said, 'I have loaded it with such extraordinary care that it amounts to almost an impossibility that it should. Will you take some wine?'

At this moment there came a loud knocking at the door of the house. I saw an expression of satisfaction come over his face, and he sprung to his feet, holding the pistol in his grasp.

'Do you know the meaning of that knocking,' said I, 'at such an hour?' and at the same time with a sweep of my arm I threw his sword off the table and beyond his reach.

'Yes,' he said, rather excitedly; 'you are my prisoner, it was you who caused the mischief and confusion last night. The girl is ready to swear to you, and if you attempt to escape, I'll blow your brains out.'

'Fire at me,' said I, 'and take the consequences – but the threat is sufficient, and you shall die for your temerity.'

I drew my sword, and he evidently thought his danger imminent, for he at once snapped the pistol in my face. Of course it only flashed in the pan, but in one moment my sword went through him like a flash of light. It was a good blade the money lender had sold me – the hilt struck against his breast bone, and he shrieked.

Bang! bang! bang! came again at the outer door of the house. I withdrew the reeking blade, dashed it into the scabbard just in time to prevent my landlady from opening the door, which she was almost in the act of doing. I seized her by the back of the neck, and hurled her to a considerable distance, and then opening the door myself, I stood behind it, and let three men rush into the house. After which I quietly left it, and was free to continue my existence as – VARNEY, THE VAMPYRE!

The Pale Lady

ALEXANDRE DUMAS & PAUL BOCAGE

The serialisation of Varney the Vampire *had hardly been brought to its shuddering conclusion than another landmark vampire story was published in France. 'The Pale Lady' was to prove important because it was the first such tale to be set in the Carpathian Mountains of Transylvania now universally accepted as the traditional home of the undead. (Despite the fact, of course, that history informs us that vampire myths can be traced back to the ancient cultures of the Greeks, Assyrians, Chinese and Indians.) Once again the author was a man of prodigious output, the journalist, novelist and dramatist, Alexandre Dumas (1802–70), known as the 'King of the Roman-Feuilleton', who has been credited with writing as many as 800 titles. The story appeared in a volume entitled* Les Mille et un Fantômes *(The Thousand and One Phantoms, 1849) a collection of weird tales each of which is narrated by a member of a group of people all of whom have had encounters with the supernatural. On the title page of the original French edition, a certain 'Paul Bocage' was credited as co-author, yet when the book was translated into English his name mysteriously disappeared, never to be reinstated. This is a regrettable error which I am happy to correct here for there is strong evidence that Bocage was something of an expert on European folklore, and wrote most, if not all of 'The Pale Lady' himself.*

As a journalist working in Paris, Bocage (1821–90) had already written about the supernatural for a number of publications before his association with Dumas began. In these he frequently cited as a source of reference a classic work, Histoire de Fantômes at de Demons, *and in this can be found several historical reports of vampires.*

Contemporary accounts of Bocage describe him as a 'favourite disciple of Dumas' who often called the older man, 'Maestro'. Dumas, for his part, was a writer always much more at home with stories of high adventure – such as The Count of Monte Cristo, The Three Musketeers *and* The Corsican Brothers – *than tales of horror. As A. Craig Bell has written in connection with* Les Mille at Une Fantômes *in his book,* Alexandre Dumas: A Biography and Study *(1950), 'Dumas was too absorbed in actual life, was too intensely human either to sense himself, or to make others sense, the ghoulish and the supernatural.' Two other biographers, A. Parran and P. Glinel share Bell's doubts about the extent of Dumas's involvement in the collection: 'Paul Bocage gave substantial assistance to Dumas,' they write, 'and in all probability wrote much of the collection himself.' As to the story of 'The Pale Lady', it is narrated by the woman of the title to the other members of the group explaining how she was attacked by a vampire in the dark recesses of the Carpathians. From the point of view of style it contrasts markedly with the two previous items because of the unhurried manner of its telling – and is, in fact, reminiscent of the Gothic Romances which had been so popular since the previous century. The fact remains, however, that tales such as this were now about to have to give way to the public's growing taste for the unashamed sensationalism of* Count Rodolph, Varney *and, shortly,* Dracula *himself.*

*   *   *

I

Among the Carpathians

I am a Pole by birth, a native of Sandomir, a land where legends become articles of faith, and where we believe in our family traditions as firmly as in the Gospel – perhaps more firmly. Not one of our castles but has its spectre, not one of our cottages but owns its familiar spirit. Among rich and poor alike, in castle and cot equally, the two principles of good and ill are acknowledged.

Sometimes the two are at variance and fight one against the other. Then are heard mysterious noises in passages, howls in old, half-ruined towers, shakings of walls – so terrible and appalling that cot and castle are both left desolate, while the inhabitants, whether peasants or nobles, fly to the nearest church to seek protection from holy cross or blessed relics, the only preservatives effectual against the demons that harass our homes.

Moreover in the same land two still more terrible principles, principles still more fierce and implacable, are face to face – to wit, tyranny and freedom.

In the year 1825 broke out between Russia and Poland one of those death struggles that seem bound to drain the life-blood of a people to its last drop, as the blood of a particular family is often exhausted.

My father and two brothers had risen in revolt against the new Czar, and had gone forth to range themselves beneath the flag of Polish independence, so often torn down, so often raised again.

One day I learnt that my younger brother had been killed; another day I was told that my elder brother was mortally wounded; lastly, after a long 24 hours during which I listened with terror to the booming of the cannon coming constantly nearer and nearer, I beheld my father ride in with a hundred horsemen – all that was left of three thousand men under his command. He came to shut himself up in our castle, resolved, if need be, to perish buried beneath its ruins.

Fearless for himself, my father trembled at the fate that threatened me. For him death was the only penalty, for he was firmly resolved never to fall alive into the hands of his enemies: but for me slavery, dishonour, shame might be in store.

From among the hundred men left him my father chose ten, summoned the Intendent of the Estate, handed him all the gold and jewels we possessed, and remembering how, at the date of the second partition of Poland, my mother, then scarcely a child, had found unassailable refuge in the Monastery of Sahastru, situated in the heart of the Carpathian Mountains, bade him conduct me thither. The cloister which had sheltered the mother would doubtless be no less hospitable to the daughter.

Our farewells were brief, notwithstanding the fond love my father bore me. By tomorrow in all likelihood the Russians would be within sight of the castle, so that there was not a moment to lose. Hurriedly I donned a riding-habit which I was in the habit of wearing when following the hounds with my brothers. The most trusty mount in the stables was saddled for me, my father slipped his own pistols, masterpieces of the Toula gunsmiths' art, into my holsters, kissed me and gave the order to start.

That night and next day we covered a score of leagues, riding up the banks of one of the nameless rivers that flow from the hills to join the Vistula. This forced march to begin with had carried us completely out of the reach of our Russian foes.

The last rays of the setting sun showed us the snowy summits of the

Carpathians gleaming through the dusk. Towards the close of next day we arrived at their base, and eventually during the forenoon of the third day we found ourselves winding along a mountain gorge.

Our Carpathian hills differ widely from Western ranges, which are civilised in comparison. All that nature has to show of strange and wild and grand is seen in its completest majesty. Their storm-beaten peaks are lost in the clouds and shrouded in eternal snow; their boundless fir-woods bend over the burnished mirror of lakes that are more like seas, crystal clear waters which no keel has ever furrowed, no fisherman's net ever disturbed.

The human voice is seldom heard in these regions, and then only to raise some rude Moldavian folksong to which the cries of wild animals reply, song and cries blending together to wake the lonely echoes that seem astounded to be roused at all.

Mile after mile you travel beneath the gloomy vaults of the forest interrupted only by the unexpected marvels which the waste reveals to the wayfarer at almost every step, moving his astonishment and admiration.

Danger lurks everywhere, danger compounded of a thousand varying perils; but there is no time to be afraid, the perils are too sublime to admit of common terror. Now it is the sudden formation of cataracts owing to the melting of the ice, which, dashing down from rock to rock, unexpectedly overwhelm the narrow path the traveller is following, a path traced by the sportsman and the game he pursues; now it is the fall of trees undermined by the lapse of time, which tear up their roots from the soil and come crashing down with a sound like that of an earthquake; now it is the onrush of a hurricane which enfolds the climber in storm-clouds riven by the darting zig-zags of the lightning, writhing and coiling like a serpent.

Then, after these Alpine peaks, after these primeval forests, as you have had giant mountains and boundless woods, you next have illimitable steppes, a veritable sea with its waves and tempests, barren, rugged wastes, where the eyes wander and lose themselves on the far-distant horizon. It is not terror now that seizes the spectator, it is irresistible melancholy, a profound sadness. The look of all the countryside, far as the eye can range, is everlastingly the same. You mount only to descend again slopes that are all alike; this you do twenty times over, searching in vain for a beaten track, till finding yourself thus lost in solitude, amid pathless deserts, you deem yourself alone with nature, and your melancholy turns into despair.

Movement seems a vain thing that will advance no whit; you will meet with neither village, nor castle, nor cottage, no smallest trace of human occupation. Only now and again, adding yet another note of sadness to the dreary landscape, a little lake, bare and treeless, without reeds or rushes or brushwood, lying asleep in the bottom of a ravine like another Dead Sea, bars your way with its greenish waters, from which rise at your approach a cloud of aquatic birds uttering long discordant screams. You make a detour; you climb the hill before you, you go down into another valley, you climb another hill, and this goes on and on till finally you come to the end of the range of foothills, which grow gradually lower and lower.

But now, if you make a bend to the south, the landscape recovers all its grandeur again and you catch sight of a new range, higher and more picturesque-looking and more inviting. It is all plumed with woods, and refreshed by countless watercourses. Shade and moisture give back life to the countryside; the tinkle of the hermit's bell is heard, a caravan is seen winding along the hillside. Finally, under the dying rays of the sinking sun, you sight, looking like a covey of white birds crouched side by side, the houses of a village grouped close together to guard against nocturnal attack.

For with life, danger is there again, and it is not now, as in the first range crossed, packs of wolves and bears that are to be feared, but hordes of Moldavian robbers.

However, we drew near our destination in spite of every difficulty. Ten days' constant travelling had sped without accident, and already we could make out the summit of Mount Pion, a giant a whole head taller than his fellow giants, on whose southern slopes lies the Monastery of Sahastru, to which I was bound. Another three days and we stood before the gates.

It was the end of August and the day had been one of blessing heat; the relief was intense when, towards four o'clock, we first began to inhale the fresh evening breeze. We had passed by the ruined towers of Niantzo, and were descending upon a plain just opening to view through a gap in the mountains. We could already, from the point we had reached, trace the course of the Bistriza, and note its banks besprinkled with red water-poppies and great white campanulas. We were making our way along the brink of a precipice at the foot of which rolled the river, as yet no more than a mountain torrent, our path being barely wide enough to allow our beasts to go two abreast.

The guide went first, perched sideways on his horse, singing a native stave to a monotonous air, the words of which I followed with no small interest and pleasure.

The singer was composer too. As for the tune, one must be a born mountaineer to appreciate to the full its wild melancholy and unsophisticated gloom. The words ran thus:

'In the marsh-lands of Stavila,
Where the fight has oft been sore,
    See yonder dead man lying!
'Tis no son of Illyria,
'Tis a brigand, fell and fierce,
Who beguiled a gentle maid,
    And robbed and burned and slew.

'A bullet sped like a hurricane
And struck the robber low,
    In his throat's a yatagan!
But for three long days, oh mystery,
Beneath the grim and lonely pine,
His warm blood wets the ground
    And strains red the Ovigan.

'His blue eyes shine no more;
Let us away, let none come nigh
    The swamp where the dead thief lies.
'Tis a vampire! The wild wolf
Runs howling from the horrid thing!
In terror o'er the bare hillside
    The vulture wings away.'

Suddenly a gun-shot rang out and a musket ball whistled through the air. The song stopped, and our guide rolled mortally wounded down the precipice, while his horse stood shivering on the brink, peering wonderingly into the depths of the abyss into which his master had disappeared.

Simultaneously a great shouting was raised, and we saw ourselves surrounded by a band of brigands, some thirty strong; we were entirely surrounded. All seized their weapons, and though caught unawares, my companions, being old soldiers inured to action, never lost their heads, but returned the fire vigorously. To give an example myself, I grasped a pistol, and seeing how disadvantageous our present position was, cried: 'Forward!' and spurred my horse in the direction of the level country.

But we had to do with mountaineers, who sprang lightly from rock to rock like very demons of the abyss, firing as they leapt, and never losing the menacing position they had taken up on our flank. Moreover, our attempt at escape had been foreseen. At a spot where the road widened and the mountain formed a small plain, a young chief awaited us at the head of ten or a dozen horsemen. On seeing us, they put their horses to a gallop, and dashed forward to charge us in front, while the rest who were pursuing us slipped down the mountain-sides and surrounded us on every side, so as to cut off our retreat completely.

The situation was very serious; yet, inured as I was from childhood to scenes of strife and bloodshed, I could examine my surroundings without a detail escaping me.

Our adversaries were one and all clad in sheepskins and wore enormous round hats garlanded with wild flowers, after the Hungarian fashion. Each carried a long Turkish firepiece; these they brandished in the air after discharging, uttering barbarous shouts the while. In their belts they had besides a curved sabre and a brace of pistols.

Their leader was a young man of barely twenty-two, with a pale face, long dark eyes and hair falling in ringlets about his shoulder. His costume consisted of the flowing Moldavian gown edged with fur and confined at the waist by a scarf of alternate gold and silken stripes. A curved sabre flashed in his hands, and four pistols glittered in his belt.

During the fight he kept up a string of hoarse, inarticulate cries, which scarcely seemed to belong to human speech; yet they sufficiently expressed his orders, for his men obeyed them implicitly, throwing themselves flat on the ground to avoid our fire, springing up anon to deliver their own, bringing down such as were still capable of defence, finishing off the wounded, and presently turning the fight into a mere butchery. Soon I had seen two-thirds of my defenders fall one after the other. Four only were left, who closed about me, never thinking of asking quarter, which they were certain not to receive, hoping one thing only, to sell their lives as dearly as possible.

Then the young chief gave a cry more expressive than ever, pointing his sabre at us. Doubtless the order was to envelop this final handful in a circle of fire, and shoot us down all together, for the long-barrelled Moldavian muskets covered us simultaneously. I felt our last hour was come; I raised my eyes and hands to heaven in a last supplication, and waited for death.

At this supreme moment I saw another young warrior descend – no, *descend* is not the word; I should say dash down, leaping from rock to rock. Then he halted, standing on a boulder, dominating the whole scene like a statue on its pedestal, and pointing to the field of carnage, pronounced the simple word:

'Enough!'

All eyes looked up at the voice. Each man appeared ready to obey this new leader. One bandit only raised his gun to his shoulder again, and fired.

One of our men gave a cry; the ball had broken his left arm. He turned instantly to rush at the man who had wounded him; but before his horse had taken four paces forward, a flash shone out above our heads, and the mutinous brigand rolled over, his skull shattered by a bullet.

Such a press of strong and varying emotions had brought me to the end of my strength, and I fell fainting to the ground.

When I recovered consciousness I was lying on the grass, my head supported against the knees of a man whose hand, very white and covered with rings, I could see about my waist. Standing in front of me, with arms crossed and his sabre under his arm, was the young Moldavian chieftain who had directed the attack against us.

'Kostaki,' my protector was saying in French and with a tone of authority, 'you must go this instant and draw off your men, and leave me to look after the girl.'

'Brother, brother,' replied the individual to whom these words were addressed, and who appeared to find extreme difficulty in containing himself; 'brother, beware of exhausting my patience. I leave you the Castle, leave the Forest to me. Within the Castle you are master, but here I am all-powerful. Here it would need but one word to compel you to obey me.'

'Kostaki, I am the elder – that is to say, I am master everywhere, in the Castle, no less than in the Forest, there as well as here. Oh yes! I am of the blood of the Brankovans as much a you. 'Tis Royal blood and is wont to be obeyed. I order, and I must be obeyed.'

'You order, you, Gregoriska; your lackeys, yes, but not my soldiers.'

'Your soldiers are brigands, Kostaki – brigands I will have hanged from the battlements of our towers, if they do not give me instant obedience.'

'Well, then, order them, and see if they obey!'

Then I felt my supporter draw away his knees and lay my head down softly against a stone. I followed him anxiously with my eyes, and I saw the same young chief who had tumbled, so to speak, from the skies into the middle of the fight, and whom hitherto I had only been able to catch a glimpse of, having swooned at the very instant he had first spoken.

He was a young man of twenty-four, of tall stature, with great blue eyes in which was legible a remarkable endowment of resolution and determination. His long flaxen hair, characteristic of the Slav race, fell about his shoulders like the Archangel Michael's, framing his young, fresh cheeks; his lips parted in a disdainful smile, showing a double row of pearls; his gaze was the eagle's confronting the lightning.

He was dressed in a kind of tunic of black velvet; a little cap, like that which the painter Raphael wears in his portraits, adorned with an eagle's feather, was on his head; he wore tight breeches and embroidered high boots. Round his waist was a sash containing a hunting-knife, while a shoulder-belt carried a short, double-barrelled carbine, the accuracy of which one of the bandits had just been given an opportunity of appreciating.

He extended his arm, and the gesture seemed to command the obedience even of his brother; he pronounced a few words in Moldavian, and these words appeared to produce a profound impression on the brigands.

Then, using the same language, the young chief spoke in his turn, and I could guess that his words were a mixture of threats and imprecations.

But to all his long and fierce harangue the elder of the two brothers vouchsafed not one word of reply.

The brigands bowed before his imperious glance, and, at a gesture from him, ranged themselves behind us.

'Well, so be it, Gregoriska,' said Kostaki, returning to the French tongue. 'The woman shall not be taken to the cavern, then; but she shall be mine none the less. She is to my taste, I have won her in fight, and I will have her.' And with the words, he darted towards me and lifted me in his arms.

'The woman shall be taken to the Castle, I repeat, and given into my mother's care; and I mean to see it is done,' replied my protector.

'My horse, bring me my horse!' cried Kostaki in Moldavian.

A dozen bandits sprang forward to obey, and led up the horse to their chief.

Gregoriska glanced around him, seized a masterless horse by the bridle, and leapt on its back without touching the stirrups.

Kostaki flung himself into the saddle almost as lightly as his brother, although he still held me in his arms, and dashed off at a gallop.

Gregoriska's steed seemed fired with the same spirit, and kept head and flank steadily on a level with the head and flank of Kostaki's mount.

It was a strange sight, the two horsemen speeding side by side, in gloomy silence, never losing one another for a single instant from view, though without seeming to look, giving the rein to their horses, which pursued a wild and desperate course through woods and amid rocks and precipices.

My head was thrown back so as to let me see Gregoriska's fine eyes fixed upon my own. Kostaki, observing this, raised my head, and I could henceforth see only his dark, sombre gaze, devouring my face. I dropped my lids, but in vain; through their shade I could still feel the same piercing glance penetrating to my inmost bosom and lacerating my heart. Then a strange hallucination took possession of me; I thought I was the lost Lenore of Bürger's famous ballad, in the act of being carried off by the spectral horse and horseman, and presently when I felt we were slackening speed, it was with a feeling of sheer terror I opened my eyes, firmly convinced I should see surrounding me only shattered graveyard crosses and open tombs.

What I did behold was hardly less gloomy, to wit, the inner courtyard of a Moldavian castle built in the fourteenth century.

2

The Castle of Brankovan

Then Kostaki let me slip out of his arms on to the ground, and in another moment got down beside me; but, quick as he had been, he had not been quick enough to anticipate Gregoriska. As the latter had said, within the Castle he was undisputed master.

Seeing the arrival of the two young chiefs and the strange woman they had brought along with them, the servants ran eagerly forward, but though their attentions were divided between Kostaki and Gregoriska, it was plain the greatest obsequiousness, the deepest respect, were reserved for the last named.

Two women approached; Gregoriska gave them an order in Moldavian, and signed me to follow them. The gesture was accompanied by a look expressive of so much respect that I did not hesitate to obey. Five minutes afterwards I was in a bedchamber, which, bare and uncomfortable as it must have appeared to the least exacting of mortals, was manifestly the best the Castle contained.

It was a vast, square apartment, provided with a sort of divan covered with green serge, serving as a seat by day and a bed by night.

Five or six great oak settles, an enormous cupboard or wardrobe, and in one corner of the room a canopied chair resembling a great, richly carved church stall, completed the furniture. As to window curtains or bed hangings, such things were out of the question. The way thither was by a staircase adorned with three statues, more than life-size, of dead and gone Brankovans, standing in niches.

In another few minutes the baggage was brought up, my trunks among the rest. The women offered to help me; but while repairing the disorder produced in my costume by the events of the day, I retained my long riding-habit, as better matching my hosts' personal appointments than any other costume I could have adopted.

Scarcely had I completed these little changes of dress when I heard someone knocking softly at the door.

'Come in,' I said, speaking naturally enough in French, French being, as you are aware, a second mother tongue to us Poles.

Gregoriska appeared, saying, 'Ah, madame, I am happy to know that you speak French!'

'And I too, sir,' I replied, 'I am happy to know that language, since, thanks to my doing so, I have been able to appreciate your generous conduct towards me. It was in that tongue you championed me against the evil designs of your brother, and in the same language I now offer you the expression of my heartfelt gratitude.'

'Thank you, madame. It was no more than natural I should take the side of a woman situated as you were. I was hunting in the mountain when I heard irregular but long-continued firing. I knew it must be a question of some attack by armed violence, and made for the scene of action. I arrived in the nick of time, thanks be to God. But may I ask you now, madame, by what strange chance a lady of distinction like yourself came to expose herself to the risks of our wild mountains?'

'I am a Pole, sir,' I replied. 'My two brothers have just been killed in the war against Russia; my father, whom I felt prepared to defend our Castle against the enemy, has doubtless rejoined them by this time. For myself, I was flying to escape from those scenes of massacre, and seeking, by my father's orders, an asylum in the cloister of Sahastru, where my mother in her youth and under similar circumstances, had found a secure refuge.'

'You are the foe of the Russians; so much the better!' cried the young man, 'this will be a strong point in your favour in our Castle here, and we shall require all our strength to sustain the struggle that is brewing. And now, as I know who you are, learn, madame, who we are; the name Brankovan is not unknown to you, is it, madame?'

I bowed assent.

'My mother is the last Princess of the name, the last descendant of that illustrious chief who was done to death by the Cantimirs, the caitiff courtiers of Peter I. My mother married as her first husband my father, Serban Waivady, a Prince as she was a Princess, but of less illustrious race.

'My father had been brought up at Vienna, where he had learnt to appreciate the advantages of civilisation. He resolved to make a European of me, and we started on travels embracing France, Italy, Spain and Germany.

'My mother — it is not a son's part, I know, to tell you what I am going to, but inasmuch as, for your own safety, it behoves you to know us intimately, you will understand the necessity for the revelation — my mother, who, during the earlier years of my father's absence, when I was still quite a child, had had guilty relations with a party chieftain (this,' added Gregoriska with a laugh, 'is what men who have wantonly attacked you are entitled in our country) — my mother, I saw, who had had guilty relations with a certain Count Giordaki Koproli, half Greek, half Moldavian, wrote to my father, confessing all and asking for divorce, declaring in support of her demand that she could not bear, Brankovan as she was, to continue the wife of man who deliberately day by day was making himself more and more of a stranger to his native land. Alas! my father was never called upon to agree to the request — one that may seem extraordinary to you, but which with us is looked upon as the simplest and most natural thing in the world; he had just died of an aneurism, from which he had long suffered, and it was I who received the letter.

'There was nothing for me to do, beyond expressing my heartfelt wishes for my mother's happiness. This I did in a letter, in which I announced to her the news of her widowhood. In the same letter I begged her permission to continue my travels, and this was readily granted.

'My fixed resolution had been to settle in France or Germany, so as to avoid meeting a man who hated me and for whom I could not possibly feel affection for, that is to say, my mother's second husband. But suddenly one day I received news that Count Giordaki Koproli had been assassinated, by all accounts at the hands of the old Cossack troopers of my father's.

'I hurried home; I loved my mother and understood her present isolation and her natural craving to have beside her at such a moment such persons as were bound to her by close ties of kinship. True she had never shown any very tender affection for me, but still she was my mother. One morning, without a word to announce my arrival, I entered the Castle of my ancestors.

'There I found a young man whom I took at first for a stranger, but whom I learnt later was my brother. This was Kostaki, the child of adultery, now legitimised by my mother's second marriage – Kostaki, the untamable being you have yourself seen, whose passions are his only law, who holds nothing sacred in all the world but his mother, who only obeys me as the tiger does the man that has mastered him by sheer force – and this with a never-ceasing growl of protest in vain hope of one day devouring me.

'Inside the Castle, within the home of the Brankovans and Waivadys, I am still master; but once outside its walls, once in the open country, he is again the savage child of the woods and mountains, resolved to make everything bend to his own iron will. How came he to yield today, what made his men obey another? I cannot say; perhaps force of habit, some relic of traditional respect. I should not care to put my authority to a second proof. Stay here, do not quit this room, this court, in a word the circuit of these walls – and I can guarantee your safety; take one step outside the Castle – and I can promise nothing, except to sacrifice my life in your defence.'

'Then cannot I continue my journey to the Monastery of Sahastru, as my father wished?'

'Try if you will; command, and I shall obey; but the end will be – I shall be left a dead man by the wayside, and you will never reach your destination.'

'What is to be done, then?'

'Best stay here and await events; have patience and profit by circumstances. Recognise that you are fallen into a bandit's den, and that your courage alone can save you, your presence of mind alone release you. My mother, despite her preference for Kostaki, the son of her love, is kind and generous. Moreover, she is a Brankovan, in other words a true princess. You shall be presented to her; she will defend you against the brute passions of Kostaki. Place yourself under her protection; you are fair to look upon and she will love you. Indeed,' he went on, looking at me with an indescribable expression on his face, 'who could see you and not love you? Come now to the hall where supper is prepared and where my mother waits you. Show neither embarrassment nor distrust, and speak Polish – no one understands that tongue here; I will translate your words to my mother, and rest assured I will only say what should be said. Above all, not a word of what I have just told you; not a breath of our mutual understanding. You do not know yet all the wiles and subterfuges of the most straightforward of my countrymen. Now come.'

I followed him down the staircase I have described, now lighted by pinewood torches burning in iron hands protruding from the walls. Evidently so unusual an illumination had been made in my honour.

Arrived at the great hall, Gregoriska threw open the door and pronounced a Moldavian word, which I learnt subsequently means 'the stranger'. Hereupon a tall, imposing woman came forward to meet us – the Princess Brankovan.

Her white hair was coiled in plaits about her head, on which rested a little cap of sable, surmounted by an aigrette, sign of her princely origin. She wore a sort of tunic of cloth of gold covered with pearls, falling over a long skirt of Turkish material, trimmed with the same fur as her headdress. In her hand she carried a rosary with amber beads, which she was turning rapidly between her fingers.

Beside her stood Kostaki, wearing the magnificent and imposing Magyar costume which lent him a still stranger and more exotic look than ever. It consisted of a gown of green velvet with ample sleeves, falling below the knee, breeches of red cashmere, and Turkish slippers of morocco leather embroidered in gold; his head was uncovered, and his long locks, so black as to be almost blue, tumbled about his bare neck, confined merely by the slender white line of the edging of a silken shirt.

He gave me an awkward bow, and said a few words in Moldavian which I could not understand.

'You can speak French, brother,' Gregoriska said to him. 'Madame is Polish, and understands the language.' Upon this, Kostaki made some remarks in French, which were all but as unintelligible to me as those he had uttered in Moldavian; but the Princess now extended her hand imperiously, and imposed silence on them both. I could plainly see she was telling her sons it was her place to receive me.

Then she began in Moldavian a speech of welcome, which the expression of her face made it easy to gather the drift of. She signed me to the table, offered me a seat by her side, embraced the whole house in a sweeping gesture, as if to tell me it was all at my disposal; then sitting down first with kindly dignity, she made the sign of the cross and began a prayer.

This ended, all took their places – places determined by etiquette, Gregoriska's being next below mine. I was a stranger, and consequently occupied a place of honour next to Kostaki, who sat beside his mother Smerande.

Gregoriska had likewise changed his dress. He now wore the Magyar tunic like his brother; only his was of garnet-red and his breeches of blue cashmere. A magnificent decoration hung at his neck – the Nisham of the Sultan Mahmoud.

The rest of the household supped at the same table, each in the due subordination given him by his position among the friends or dependents of the family.

The meal was a gloomy one; not once did Kostaki address me, though his brother took pains to converse with me and always in French. As for their mother, she offered me some of every dish herself, with the air of grave solemnity which never left her. Gregoriska had said truly, she was a veritable Princess.

After supper, Gregoriska came forward, and approaching his mother, explained to her in Moldavian the desire I must be feeling to be alone, and how needful rest was for me after the emotions of a day such as I had passed. Smerande bowed her head in assent, reached me her hand, kissed me on the brow, as she might have done to a daughter, and wished me a good night and sound repose in her Castle.

Gregoriska was right; I longed eagerly for a moment's solitude. So I thanked the Princess, who led me to the door of the hall, where I found waiting for me the two women who had previously attended me.

I made my bow to the mistress of the house, saluted her two sons, and retired to the same apartment, the room I had quitted an hour before to come down to supper. Meantime the divan had been converted into a bed, the only change that had been effected.

I thanked my tire-women, and informed them by signs that I would undress myself. On this they left the room at once, with marks of respect that showed they had received orders to obey me implicitly.

I was left alone in the vast apartment, which my light was insufficient even to illuminate from end to end; I could only make out bits at a time, as I moved my candle from place to place, never the whole room at once. The light was strangely blended, the moonbeams entering through the curtainless window, and struggling to diminish the glimmer of my taper.

Besides the door by which I had entered, and which opened on to the staircase, my room possessed two others, but massive bolts attached to these and fastening from inside, sufficed to reassure me on this score.

Next I examined the entrance door. Like the others, it was well provided with means of defence. Then I threw open my window, and found a sheer precipice beneath it.

I saw plainly enough that Gregoriska had made a deliberate choice of this particular chamber to ensure me against danger. Presently, coming back to my divan, I discerned a little note lying on a table by my bedside. I opened it and read in Polish:

'Sleep at ease; you will have nothing to fear, so long as you remain within the Castle walls. – *Gregoriska*.'

I followed the advice given me, and, weariness prevailing over all other feelings, I lay down and fell fast asleep.

3
The Two Brothers

Henceforward I was established at the Castle of Brankovan, and from that moment began the drama I am about to relate.

The two brothers both fell in love with me, each in his own peculiar way.

Kostaki did not wait a day before he told me he loved me, declared I should be his or no one's, swore he would kill me sooner than suffer me to belong to another, no matter who.

Gregoriska said nothing; but he lavished infinite care and solicitude upon me. All the resources of a brilliant education, all the recollections of a youth passed at the most famous Courts of Europe, were laid under contribution to please me. Alas! the task was only too easy; at the first sound of his voice, I had felt that he was the chosen one of my soul; at the first look of his eyes, I had felt my heart was his.

At the end of three months, Kostaki had repeated a hundred times over that he loved me. I detested him. At the end of the same period, Gregoriska had never spoken one word of love, and I knew that, ask me when he might, I should be his, heart and soul.

Kostaki had given up his out-of-door life altogether. He never left the Castle now, having for the time being abdicated his authority in favour of a sort of lieutenant, who came to him from time to time for orders, and disappeared to execute them.

Smerande likewise manifested a passionate affection for me, the intensity of which terrified me. She openly championed Kostaki, and seemed to be more jealous of me than he was himself. Only, as she understood neither Polish nor French, while I knew no Moldavian, she could not well make any pressing appeals to me in her boy's favour. Still she had learnt to say three words in French, which she would repeat to me every time her lips were laid upon my forehead:

'Kostaki aime Hedwig' – Kostaki loves Hedwig.

One day I learnt a terrible piece of news, which seemed to crown my misfortunes. The four men who had survived the fight with the brigands had been released, and had returned to Poland, under pledge that one of them should come back within three months to bring me news of my father's fate. One of the four did so come back, only to tell me our Castle had been taken, set fire to, and utterly destroyed, while my father had been killed in trying to defend it.

I was left all alone in the world. Kostaki redoubled his eager appeals and Smerande her tenderness; but I could now urge my mourning for my father as an obstacle. Kostaki only insisted the more, saying that the more lonely and forlorn I was, the more I needed a protector, while his mother was as importunate or perhaps more importunate than himself.

Gregoriska had spoken to me of the power the Moldavians possess over themselves in cases where they desire to keep their true feelings hid; and he was in himself a living example of this faculty. It was impossible to be more certain of the love of a man than I was of his; yet if I had been asked what proof I had to allege for my certainty, I could have given none. No one, in the Castle, had ever seen his hand touch mine, or his eyes seek mine. Jealousy alone could enlighten Kostaki as to his brother's rivalry, as my love alone could inform me of his love.

Nevertheless, I must admit, this excessive self-control of Gregoriska's troubled me. I believed, I felt he loved me, but how could I be sure? I wanted some tangible proof. I was still in this uncertainty, when one evening, just after I had retired to my room for the night, I heard a soft tapping at one of the two doors I have mentioned before as fastening on the inside. From the way the knocks were given, I guessed it was a friend. I went to the door and asked who was there.

'Gregoriska,' replied a voice whose accents there was little fear of my mistaking.

'What do you want with me?' I asked, trembling all over.

'If you trust me,' cried Gregoriska, 'if you believe me to be a man of honour, grant me what I ask.'

'And what is that?'

'Put out your light, as if you had gone to bed, and in half an hour's time open your door to let me in.'

'Come back in half an hour,' was my only and unhesitating answer. Then I put out my light and waited.

My heart beat violently, for I felt sure it was a question of some all-important eventuality. The half hour slipped by, and I heard the taps repeated more softly even than the first time.

Meanwhile I had withdrawn the bolts, so that I had merely to pull the door open.

Gregoriska came in, and, without his saying a word to that effect, I closed the door behind him and shot the bolts. He stood still a moment, mute and motionless, gesturing me to be silent. Then, assured that no immediate danger threatened us, he led me to the middle of the vast apartment, and, seeing from the way I trembled that I could hardly stand, brought me a chair. I sat down, or rather let myself sink helplessly into it.

'God in Heaven!' I exclaimed, 'what is the matter, and why these excessive precautions?'

'Because my life — though that is nothing — because your life, perhaps, depends upon the conversation we are going to have together.'

In great alarm, I seized his hand in mine, which he lifted to his lips, looking into my eyes the while to ask my pardon for such an act of presumption. I dropped my eyes before his — a confession of self-surrender.

'I love you,' he said in a voice as sweet and melodious as a song; 'do you love me?'

'Yes,' I told him.

'Are you ready to be my wife?'

'Yes.'

He drew his hand across his forehead with a deep-drawn sigh of happiness.

'Then you will not refuse to follow me?'

'I will follow you anywhere and everywhere!'

'You understand, of course,' he went on, 'that we can only win happiness by flight.'

'Oh, yes!' I cried, 'let us fly, let us fly!'

'Hush,' he said, shuddering, 'hush.'

'You are right,' and I went up to him trembling.

'This is what I have done,' he said; 'this is why I have been so long without confessing my love to you. It was because I desired, once secure of your affection, that nothing might have power to hinder our union. I am rich, Hedwig, enormously rich, but after the fashion of the Moldavian nobles — rich in lands, in flocks and herds, in serfs. Well, I have sold to the Monastery of Hango a million francs worth of land, cattle and villages. They have given me three hundred thousand francs of the purchase money in precious stones, a hundred thousand francs in gold, the rest in letters of credit upon Vienna. Will a million be enough for you?'

I pressed his hand. 'Your love would have been enough alone, Gregoriska, be sure of that.'

'Well, now, listen; tomorrow I am going to the Monastery of Hango to make my final arrangements with the Superior. He has horses ready for me; these horses will await us at nine o'clock, in hiding, a hundred paces from the Castle. After supper you are to go up to your room the same as today; the same as today you are to put out your light; the same as today you are to open the door and I will come in. But tomorrow, instead of my going out alone, you are to follow me; we will gain the gate opening on the country, we will find our horses, we will spring on their backs, and by next day's dawn we shall be thirty leagues away.'

'Ah! Why is it not next day's dawn already!'

'Hedwig, my darling!' – and Gregoriska pressed me to his heart; our lips met in a long kiss.

He had well said when I opened my chamber door to him that he was a man of honour; was well aware that without possessing my body, he possessed my heart.

The night passed without my having closed an eye. I pictured myself borne away in his arms as I had been by Kostaki. Only now, the ride which had been so fearful, so appalling, so grim, was a sweet, soft, entrancing motion, the very rapidity of which added a voluptuous charm, for speed has a charm and pleasure of its own. Daylight came at last, and I left my room. I seemed to detect something even more morose than usual in the greeting Kostaki vouchsafed me on my appearance. His smile was more than ironical, it was threatening, sinister. As for Smerande, her attitude seemed much as usual.

In the course of breakfast Gregoriska ordered his horses, without Kostaki paying any attention apparently to the circumstance. About eleven, he took leave of us, announcing that he would not be back before evening, and begged his mother not to delay dinner for him. Then, turning to me, he made his excuses for quitting me so suddenly.

He left the great hall, his brother staring after him until he crossed the threshold. As he did so, a lightning flash of hate and malignity shot from Kostaki's eyes that made me shudder.

The day passed amid such fears and anxieties as may be imagined. I had confided our projects to no living soul, hardly in my prayers had I dared to tell God of them; yet I felt as though these plans were known to all the world, that every look cast my way had power to penetrate my heart and read my inmost thoughts.

Dinner was a veritable torture; sombre and silent. Kostaki scarcely opened his mouth. When he did, it was only to address a curt phrase or two to his mother in Moldavian, and every time the tones of his voice made me shudder in spite of myself.

When I rose to go back to my room, Smerande kissed me as usual, and as she kissed me she spoke the sentence which for quite a week now I had not heard her utter:

'Kostaki loves Hedwig.'

The words pursued me like a threat; arrived in my chamber I seemed to hear a voice of fate still murmuring in my ear, 'Kostaki loves Hedwig,' – but Kostaki's love, Gregoriska had told me so, meant death.

About seven in the evening, as twilight was falling, I saw Kostaki cross the castle court; he wheeled round to look in my direction, but I started back to avoid his seeing me. I felt anxious, for as long as the situation of my window allowed me to follow his movements, I had observed that he was making his way towards the stables. I made bold to unbolt my door, and slipped into the next room, from the window of which I could see perfectly what he was about.

Yes, he was going to the stables. Presently he brought out his favourite horse, saddled the animal with his own hands, and this with a minute care that showed he attached the greatest importance to the smallest details. He wore the same costume as on the day I had first seen him, but on this occasion his only weapon was his sabre. His mount saddled, he cast his eyes once more to my window. Then, not seeing me, he leapt into the saddle, rode out by the same gate by which his brother had left the castle and would return, and away at a hard gallop in the direction of the Monastery of Hango.

Then my heart contracted in a spasm of dread; a fatal presentiment told me that Kostaki was going to meet and confront his brother.

I lingered at the window as long as I could make out the track, which a quarter of a league from the Castle made a bend, and disappeared among the first trees of the forest; but darkness was rapidly descending, and every trace of the road soon became invisible.

I lingered on and on. At last the very excess of my disquietude restored my energy, and as it was evidently in the great hall below that I was likely to receive the first tidings of one or other of the two brothers, I went down thither. My first look was for Smerande; but the calmness of her face told me she was under no special apprehension.

She was giving her orders for the customary supper, and places were laid as usual for the two brothers.

I dared not question anyone – indeed, who could I question? Nobody in the Castle, Kostaki and Gregoriska excepted, could speak either of the only two languages I knew myself.

The slightest sound set me trembling.

Nine o'clock was the ordinary hour for the meal. I had come down at half-past eight; I watched anxiously the minute hand, the movement of which was almost visible on the huge face of the Castle clock. Soon the quarter sounded, sad and solemn; then the hand went on its silent way again, and once more I watched the minutes marked off, slowly but surely.

A few minutes before nine I thought I heard a horse gallop into the courtyard. Smerande heard it too, and turned her head towards the window; but the night was too dark for her to see anything.

If she had but cast one glance at me, how easily she might have guessed what was passing in my heart. We heard but one horse only; indeed what else was to be expected? My heart told me only one horseman would return, but which?

Steps sounded in the ante-chamber – slow, heavy steps that seemed to oppress my soul. The door opened. I saw a shadow outlined in the gloom.

The shadow halted on the threshold. My heart trembled in suspense. The shadow came forward, and as it entered further and further into the lighted rooms I breathed again. Another second of such tension and my heart would have stopped beating.

Gregoriska stood before me, but pale as a dead man. To look at him was to see that something dreadful had happened.

'Is it you, my Kostaki?' asked Smerande.

'No, mother,' answered Gregoriska in a hoarse, toneless voice.

'Ah, it is you, is it?' she now said; 'and how long do you expect your mother to wait for you?'

'Why, mother,' protested Gregoriska, glancing at the time-piece, 'it is only nine o'clock.'

And indeed that moment the hour struck.

'Very true,' said Smerande. 'Where is your brother?'

In spite of myself, I could not help thinking it was the same question God had asked of Cain.

Gregoriska said nothing.

'Has no one seen Kostaki?' questioned Smerande.

The Vater (major-domo), after making inquiries of those around him, answered, 'about seven the Count went to the stable, saddled his horse himself, and set out on the road to Hango.'

At that moment my eyes met Gregoriska's. I cannot tell if it was reality or hallucination, but I seemed to see a drop of blood in the middle of his forehead.

I put my finger slowly to my own brow, indicating the spot where I thought I saw the stain. Gregoriska understood me; he took out his handkerchief and wiped his face.

'Yes, yes,' muttered Smerande.

'He must have fallen in with a bear or a wolf, and gone after it for his diversion.'

'Is that a reason for a son to keep his mother waiting? Where did you leave him, Gregoriska? tell me that.'

'Mother,' replied Gregoriska in a startled but firm voice, 'my brother and I did not set out together.'

'Well and good,' ended Smerande. 'Bring in supper, take your places at table, and shut the gates; those who are still outside must sleep outside.'

The first two orders were executed to the letter. Smerande took her place, while Gregoriska seated himself at her right, and myself at her left. Then the serving-men left the hall to carry out the third, that is, to shut the Castle gates.

At that moment a great noise rose from the courtyard and a terrified domestic dashed into the hall crying:

'Princess, Count Kostaki's horse has just galloped into the bailey riderless and dripping with blood.'

'Alas!' faltered Smerande, rising from her seat, pale and menacing, 'it was in like plight his father's horse came back one night.'

I looked at Gregoriska; he was not pale now, he was livid.

The fact is, Count Koproli's horse had dashed one evening into the Castle yard, dripping with blood, and an hour later the retainers had found his body covered with wounds, and brought it home.

Smerande now took a torch from the hands of one of the serving-men, walked to the door, threw it open, and went down the steps into the courtyard.

The horse, in a state of extreme terror, was being held in by main force by three or four grooms, who were doing all they could to soothe the animal. Smerande drew near, looked at the bloodstained saddle, and presently discovered the horse had received a wound in the face.

'Kostaki has been killed by a blow in front,' she said, 'in a duel, and by a single adversary. Search for the body, my lads; afterwards we will search till we find his murderer.'

As the horse had come back by the Hango gate of the Castle, all the men hurried out the same way, and soon we could see their torches flitting about the fields and diving into the forest, just as the fire-flies flash and gleam on a fine summer's evening in the plains about Nice or Pisa.

Smerande, as though convinced the search would soon be successful, stood waiting under the archway. Not a tear flowed from the eyes of the bereaved mother; yet it was plain that despair was tearing her entrails.

Gregoriska was behind her and I was next Gregoriska. On leaving the great hall he had made as if to offer me his arm, but had hesitated, and finally given up the intention, apparently afraid.

In about a quarter of an hour we saw a single torch reappear at the turning of the road, then two more, and finally the whole number. Only now, instead of being dispersed about the country, they were massed round a common centre — which it soon became manifest consisted of a litter and a man stretched upon it.

The funereal band advanced slowly but surely, and in another ten minutes was at the gateway. On observing the unhappy mother waiting for her dead son, the bearers uncovered instinctively, and marched sad and silent into the Castle yard.

Smerande joined the procession, and we came after her. In this order we all reached the great hall, where they laid down the body.

Then, with a gesture of supreme dignity, Smerande beckoned all to draw back, and, going up to the dead man, knelt down before him, parted the long hair which fell like a veil before his face, gazed long at his features, with dry eyes still, then, opening the Moldavian gown he wore, lifted the blood-stained shirt.

The wound was in the right side of the breast, and must have been made by a straight blade and a double-edged one. I remembered I had noticed that very day in Gregoriska's belt the long hunting-knife that served as a bayonet for his carbine.

I looked for the weapon now; but it had disappeared.

Smerande called for water, dipped her handkerchief in it and washed the wound. A gush of bright, fresh, scarlet blood welled up and reddened the lips of the gash.

The whole scene was at once odious and sublime. The vast gloomy hall, thick with the smoke of pine torches, the wild faces, the fiercely gleaming eyes, the strange dresses, the mother gazing at the still warm blood, and reckoning how long her son had been dead, the deep silence, only broken by the sobs of the bandits whose chief Kostaki had been, all was impressive and awe-inspiring to the last degree.

Lastly, Smerande put her lips to her son's brow; then, rising to her full height and tossing back the long coils of her white hair which had become unfastened, she cried, 'Gregoriska, Gregoriska!'

Gregoriska shuddered, shook his head, and coming out of his lethargy, answered, 'Yes, mother?'

'Come here, son, and hear me.'

Gregoriska obeyed with a shudder, but obey he did. The nearer he approached the corpse, the more abundantly did the red blood gush from the wound. Happily Smerande was not looking that way, for at sight of this accusing flood, she would have had no need to look further for the murderer.

'Gregoriska,' she went on, 'I know very well that you and Kostaki were enemies. I know quite well that you are a Waivady by your father, and he a Koproli by his; but through your mother you are both of you Brankovans. I know that you are a man of the Western cities, he a child of the Eastern hills; but still, by virtue of the womb that bore you both, you are brothers. Well! Gregoriska, I would know this, if you mean to lay your brother to rest beside his father without the oath of vengeance having been pronounced; if I may weep my dead in peace and confidence as a woman should, putting my trust in you to punish as a man's part is?'

'Tell me the name of my brother's murderer, madame, and command me; I swear that ere an hour is past, if you so order, he shall have ceased to live.'

'Nay! swear, Gregoriska, swear, under penalty of my curse, do you hear my son? swear the murderer shall die, that you will not leave one stone upon another of his house, that his mother, children, brothers, his wife or his betrothed, shall perish by your hand. Swear, invoking the anger of Heaven upon your head, if you fail to keep the sacred obligation. If you break the oath, be prepared for wretchedness, the execration of your friends, your mother's malediction.'

Gregoriska laid his hand upon the corpse. 'I swear the murderer shall die,' he said.

On this strange oath, of which I and the dead man alone perhaps could grasp the true sense, I saw, or I thought I saw, an appalling prodigy follow.

The dead man's eyes opened and fixed themselves on mine with a keener look than I had ever seen in them, and as though the double ray they shot had been a material thing, I felt a red-hot iron pierce to my very heart.

It was more than my strength could bear, and I swooned away.

4

The Cloister of Hango

When I came to myself, I was in my chamber, lying upon my bed, while one of my two tire-women was watching beside me.

I asked where Smerande was, and was told she was praying beside her son's body. Then I asked where Gregoriska was, and learned that he was at the Monastery of Hango.

Flight was needless, for was not Kostaki dead? Marriage was impossible; I could never wed a fratricide.

Three days and three nights dragged by, filled with strange and fantastic dreams. Awake or asleep, I could never lose sight of those two eyes glaring alive and eager in the dead face – a horrid vision!

On the third day Kostaki was to be buried, and early on that day they brought me a full suit of widow's weeds, saying Smerande sent them me. I dressed myself and came downstairs.

The rooms seemed utterly empty; every soul was in the Castle chapel. I made my way thither; and as I crossed the threshold, Smerande, whom I had not seen for three days, came forward to meet me in the doorway.

She looked like a carven image of Grief. Slow as a statue she laid her icy lips on my forehead, and in a voice that seemed to come from the tomb, she pronounced her customary phrase: 'Kostaki loves you.'

You can form no conception of the effect these words produced on me. This declaration of love, made in the present instead of in the past tense, this *loves you* instead of *loved you*, this passion from the world of the dead singling me out among the living, made a profound and terrible impression on my mind.

At the same time a strange, uncanny feeling crept over me that in very deed I was the wife of the dead man, and not the betrothed of the living brother. The coffin yonder drew me to him in spite of myself; I was attracted reluctantly and painfully, as they say a bird is fascinated by a serpent. I looked for Gregoriska, and saw him standing, pale and sad, beside a pillar. His eyes were raised to Heaven; I cannot say if he saw me.

The monks from Hango surrounded the bier, singing the funeral psalms of the Greek rite, sometimes melodious enough, more often harsh and monotonous. I longed to pray too, but the words died upon my lips; my mind was so confounded I seemed to be present at a consistory of demons rather than among a company of priests of God.

When they lifted the body to carry it to the grave, I tried to follow; but my strength failed me. I felt my limbs bend under me, and I leant against the doorway for support. Then Smerande approached me, signing to Gregoriska, who also came up in obedience to the gestures. Smerande addressed me in Moldavian.

'My mother bids me repeat to you word for word what she is going to say,' put in Gregoriska.

Smerande resumed, and when she had ended, he said:

'These are my mother's words,' and, translating into French:

'You weep my son, Hedwig; you loved him, did you not? I thank you for your tears and for your love; henceforward you are my daughter as truly as if Kostaki had been your husband – henceforth you have a country, a mother, a home. We will shed the guerdon of tears we owe the dead, then we will both remember our dignity and show ourselves worthy of him who is no more . . . I, his mother, you his wife! Farewell! return to your chamber; for myself, I will follow my son to his last resting-place. When I come back, I shall shut myself up with my grief, and when you see me again, I shall have conquered it. Rest assured I shall kill it, for I will not have it kill me.'

I could only reply by a groan to those affecting words. I returned to my room, and the funeral procession started and presently disappeared at the bend of the road. The Cloister of Hango was only half a league from the Castle as the crow flies; but irregularities of the ground forced the road to make wide detours, and to anyone following the highway, it was pretty nearly a two hours' journey.

We were in the month of November, and the days were short and chilly. At five in the afternoon it was quite dark. About seven I saw the torches reappear and the mourners returning. All was over; the dead man lay in the tomb of his fathers.

I have already described the strange fancy which had persistently possessed my mind ever since the fatal event which had put us all in mourning, and more particularly since I had seen those eyes, which death had closed, re-open and fix themselves on mine. Tonight, worn out by the emotions of the day, I felt more depressed than ever. I listened to the hours one after the other sounding on the Castle clock, and grew sadder and sadder the nearer the flight of time brought me to the minute when Kostaki must have died.

I heard a quarter to nine strike. Then an extraordinary sensation came over me, a sort of shuddering horror that ran over my whole body and froze it; then along with this an invincible drowsiness obscured my senses, weighed down my bosom and darkened my eyes. I stretched out my arms and stepped backwards to my bed, on which I fell in a half swoon.

Still my senses were not so completely deadened as to prevent my hearing a footstep approaching the door of my chamber. I seemed to notice the door opening, after which I neither saw nor heard anything more.

But I felt a sharp throb of pain at my neck, before I finally relapsed into complete unconsciousness.

At midnight I awoke, to find my lamp still burning. I tried to rise, but I was so weak I had to repeat the effort before I succeeded. However, I fought down this feebleness, and still feeling the same pricking sensation in my neck now that I was awake as I had felt in my sleep, I dragged myself along the walls as far as the mirror and looked at myself.

A pin-prick, or something like it, marked the carotid artery. I thought some insect had bitten me in my sleep, and as I was worn out with fatigue, I lay down and went to sleep again.

Next morning I awoke as usual; and as usual I made to spring out of bed the moment my eyes were open; but I experienced a feeling of extreme exhaustion such as I had felt only once before in my lfe, on the morning after I had been bled. I looked at my face in the glass, and I was struck with my own pallor.

The hours dragged by sad and sombre, and all day long I had an unaccustomed and unaccountable craving to stay where I was, every change of place or position being a weariness of the flesh.

Night came, and they brought me my lamp. My women, or so I understood from their signs, offered to stay with me; but I refused with thanks, and they left me to myself.

At the same time as before I began to feel the same sensations. I endeavoured this time to rise and summon help; but I could not get as far as the door. I heard vaguely the sound of the clock chiming a quarter to nine; then came footsteps, and the door opened. But I could neither hear nor see anything more; as on the first evening, I had fallen back fainting on my bed.

As before I felt a sharp pain at the side of my neck; as before, I roused at midnight, only now I awoke weaker and paler than ever.

Next day the same horrid fancy held undisputed possession of my mind. I had made up my mind to go down to Smerande, weak and feeble as I was, when one of my women came into my room, uttering the name of Gregoriska, who followed her across the threshold.

I tried to get up from my chair to receive him, but fell back again exhausted by the efforts. He gave a cry at the sight, and dashed forward to my assistance; but I had still strength enough left to wave him off.

'What are you come here for?' I asked him.

'Alas!' he said, 'I was coming to bid you farewell! I was coming to tell you that I am leaving a world that is intolerable to me without your love and your presence; I was coming to tell you I am retiring to a cell in the Monastery of Hango!'

'You must forego my presence, but my love is yours still, Gregoriska,' I returned. 'Alas! I love you still, and my great grief is, that henceforth such love is next door to a crime.'

'Then I may hope you will pray for me, Hedwig?'

'Yes; only I shall not have long to pray,' I added.

'What is wrong with you, tell me, and why are you so pale?'

'Wrong – wrong! Nay! doubtless God is taking pity on me, calling me to him.'

Gregoriska came near and took my hand, which I had not the strength to withdraw, and, looking me hard in the face, said:

'This pallor is not natural, Hedwig; what does it mean?'

'If I were to tell you what I think, Gregoriska, you would deem me mad.'

'No, no! tell me, Hedwig. I beseech you, tell me. We are here in a country that is like no other country, in a family that is like no other family. Tell me, tell me all, I beseech you.'

So I told him all – the strange hallucination which came over me at the hour when Kostaki must have died, the horror, the drowsiness, the icy chill, the prostration that laid me fainting on my bed, the sound of footsteps I seemed to hear, the opening door I seemed to see, and then the sharp pang of pain followed by a pallor and exhaustion growing greater day by day.

I had supposed my narrative would strike Gregoriska as merely the first stage of mania, and I concluded it with some natural timidity; but I saw, on the contrary, that he was profoundly impressed by what I had said.

He reflected a moment.

'So you fell asleep,' he asked, 'every evening at a quarter to nine?'

'Yes – in spite of all the efforts I make to resist the drowsiness.'

'Then, you seem to see the door open?'

'Yes – although I always bolt it.'

'Then, you feel a sharp pain in the neck?'

'Yes – though my neck shows scarcely any trace of a wound.'

'Will you let me see this trace?' he asked next.

In reply, I bent my head sideways so as to show the place, which he examined carefully.

'Hedwig,' he said, after a moment's silence, 'Hedwig, do you trust me?'

'Can you ask!' I cried indignantly.

'Do you believe my word?'

'As I believe in the Holy Gospels.'

'Very well, then, Hedwig; on my word, I swear you have not a week to live, unless you agree to do this very day what I am going to tell you . . .'

'And if I agree?'

'If you agree, you will be saved, perhaps.'

'Perhaps?'

But he would say no more.

'Come what may, Gregoriska,' I resumed, 'I will do whatever you bid me to do.'

'Then listen,' he said, 'and above all do not be too much alarmed. In your country, as in Hungary, there is a tradition.'

I shuddered, for I remembered the tradition in question.

'Ah!' he went on, 'then you know what I mean?'

'Yes!' I told him, 'yes, in Poland I have seen persons subject to this horrible fate.'

'You allude to vampires, do you not?'

'Yes, in my childhood I saw a dreadful sight in the cemetery of a village belonging to my father – the exhumation of forty peasants who had died one after the other, all in a fortnight, without an explanation of the cause of death. Seventeen exhibited all the marks of vampirism, that is to say, their bodies were found fresh, rosy, and looking as if still alive; the remainder were their victims.'

'And what was done to deliver the countryside from the scourge?'

'A stake was driven through their hearts, and this done, the bodies burned.'

'Yes, that is what is ordinarily done, but in your case it is not enough. To deliver you from the phantom, I must first know who it is, and, by God! I will know. Yes, if need be, I will fight hand to hand with him, be he who he may.'

'Oh, Gregoriska, you terrify me!' I cried in alarm.

'I said, "be he who he may", and I repeat it. But to bring this awful enterprise to a good end, you must agree to everything I am going to ask you to do.'

'Say on.'

'Be ready at seven this evening; come down to the chapel – and come alone. You must conquer your weakness, Hedwig, you *must*. There we will receive the nuptial benediction. Agree to this, beloved; to defend you efficiently, I must have the right, before God and men, to watch over your safety. We will return here when the rite is complete, and then – and then . . .'

'Oh! Gregoriska,' I ejaculated. 'If it is he, if it is Kostaki, he will kill you!'

'Have no fear, my beloved, my Hedwig; only agree.'

'You may rest assured I shall do whatever you ask.'

'Till tonight, then.'

'Yes, do you whatever is needful; I will second you to the best of my powers. Now go.'

He left me; and a quarter of an hour later, I saw a horseman bounding along the road to the Monastery, and knew it was Gregoriska.

No sooner had he vanished from my sight than I knelt down and prayed such prayers as are never uttered in your lukewarm irreligious Western land; thus occupied, I awaited seven o'clock, offering up to God and the Saints the holocaust of my meditations. I only rose from my knees as the clock struck the hour.

I was weak as a dying woman, pale as the sheeted dead. I threw a long, black veil over my head, and descended the stairs, supporting myself by the walls. I reached the chapel without having encountered a living soul.

Gregoriska was waiting for me there, along with Father Basil, Superior of the Cloister of Hango. My betrothed wore by his side a holy sword, heirloom of an old Crusader who had been at the taking of Constantinople with Villehardouin and Baldwin of Flanders.

'Hedwig,' he said, striking his hand upon his sword, 'with God's good help, here is a weapon will break the spell that threatens your life. Come boldly hither; this holy man is ready, after hearing my confession, to receive and sanctify our marriage vows.'

The ceremony began; never perhaps before had it been performed in simpler and at the same time more solemn guise. The Priest, or *Pope* according to the phraseology of the Greek Church, had neither acolyte nor assistant; with his own hands he placed the wedding crowns upon our heads. Both clad in mourning raiment, we marched about the altar, taper in hand; then Father Basil pronounced the ceremonial words, adding further:

'And now go, my children, and God give you force and courage to wrestle with the Enemy of Mankind. You are armed in your innocence and the justice of your cause; you will overcome the Demon. Go, and Heaven's blessing go with you.'

We kissed the holy books and left the chapel; then for the first time I rested on Gregoriska's arm, and at the touch of his valiant arm, at the contact of his noble heart, life seemed to flow back again into my veins. I felt confident of victory, now that Gregoriska was with me.

Half past eight struck. At the sound, Gregoriska spoke.

'Hedwig,' he said, 'we have no time to lose. Will you go to sleep as usual and slumber through it all? or will you remain up and dressed and see everything?'

'By your side I fear nothing; I will stay awake, I prefer to see it all.'

Gregoriska drew from his bosom a twig of box consecrated by the priest and still wet with holy water, and gave it me.

'Take this branch, ' said he, 'lie down on your bed, repeat thy prayers to the Virgin and wait. Fear nothing, God is with us. Above all, never quit hold of your talisman; with it you can command even the powers of hell. Do not cry nor call for help; pray, wait and hope.'

I lay down on the bed and crossed my hands over my bosom, on which I placed the branch the priest had blessed.

Meantime Gregoriska concealed himself behind the great canopied chair I have described before, which cut off a corner of the room.

I counted the minutes, one by one, and no doubt Gregoriska did the same. The clock struck the three quarters.

Instantly I felt the old drowsiness, the same sensations of horror and icy cold, creeping over me; but I put the holy branch to my lips, and found relief.

Then I heard distinctly the noise of slow and measured footsteps sounding on the stairs and coming nearer and nearer to the door. It opened slowly and noiselessly as if moved by a supernatural force, and then . . .

And then I beheld Kostaki, pale as I had seen him lying on the litter; his long dark hair falling about his shoulders dripped with blood; he wore his usual dress, only it was open at the breast, showing the bleeding wound.

He was dead, a corpse. Flesh, clothes, bearing, were those of a dead man; only the eyes, those awful eyes, were alive.

At the sight, strange to say, instead of an increase of terror, I felt fresh courage. Doubtless God gave me His courage that I might judge my position calmly, and defy the Powers of Evil. At the first step the spectre took towards my bed, I fixed my eyes boldly on his leaden orbs and held out the holy branch at him.

The phantom strove to advance, but a power stronger than his own held him rooted to the spot; he hesitated, muttering:

'Oh, she is not asleep, she knows all.'

He spoke in Moldavian, and yet I understood the sense of his words, as if they had been uttered in a tongue I was familiar with.

We stood face to face, and I could not withdraw my eyes from his. Presently, without needing to turn my head in his direction, I saw Gregoriska come out from behind the canopied stall, looking like the Angel of Destruction, and holding his sword in his right hand. With the left he made the sign of the cross and stepped slowly forwards, his sword's point threatening the spectre. On seeing his brother, Kostaki too drew his sabre with a screech of eldritch laughter; but scarcely had his sabre touched the consecrated steel ere the phantom arm fell back powerless and inert.

Kostaki heaved a sigh full of hatred and despair.

'What would you of me?' he asked his brother.

'In the name of the living God, I adjure you,' said Gregoriska, 'to answer my questions.'

'Speak,' replied the phantom, gnashing his teeth.

'Did I lay wait for you?'

'No.'

'Did I attack you?'

'No.'

'Did I strike you?'

'No.'

'You threw yourself upon my sword point and nothing else. Therefore in the eyes of God and men I am innocent of the crime of fratricide; therefore you have not received a divine mission, but an infernal behest; therefore you have left the tomb, not as a holy shade, but an accursed spectre. I command you, return to your tomb.'

'With her, yes!' cried Kostaki, making a supreme effort to reach and seize me.

'No! alone!' thundered Gregoriska in reply, 'this woman is mine.'

And as he pronounced the words, he touched with the point of his consecrated sword the raw wound in his brother's breast. Kostaki uttered a scream as if a falchion of fire had seared him, and, putting his left hand to his bosom, he took a step back.

Simultaneously, and keeping step by step with his ghostly adversary, Gregoriska advanced upon him; then, his eyes upon the dead man's eyes, his sword at his brother's breast, he began to drive the spectre before him slowly, sternly, solemnly. It was something like the passage of Don Juan and the Commendatore – the spectre recoiling before the consecrated blade and the irresistible will of God's Champion, the latter following him up pace for pace without a word. Both were breathless, both ghastly pale, the living man pushing the dead before him, forcing him to forsake the Castle that was his home in the past, for the tomb, his abiding place henceforth.

Oh, it was a horrid sight, a dreadful, dreadful sight!

And yet, urged by a superior force, a force mysterious, unknown, invisible, not knowing myself what I did, I rose from the bed and followed them. We descended the staircase, our only light Kostaki's blazing eye-balls. We traversed the gallery and the Castle yard; we passed the gate at the same measured pace – the phantom stepping backwards, Gregoriska with outstretched arm, myself behind them both.

The fantastic procession continued for a full hour. The dead man had to be led back to his tomb; only, instead of the beaten road, Kostaki and Gregoriska went straight to their end, paying scant heed to hindrances and obstacles. Indeed these had ceased to exist; beneath their feet rough places grew smooth, torrents dried up, trees fell back, rocks flew open. The same miracle worked for me as for them; but the heavens seemed to my eyes shrouded in a veil of darkness; moon and stars had disappeared and all I could see in the gloom was the flashing of the vampire's eyes of fire.

In this fashion we reached Hango, in this fashion we passed through the hedge of arbutus which fenced in the cemetery. The moment we were inside, I made out through the obscurity the tomb of Kostaki, side by side with his father's. Nothing was hid from me that night. At the edge of the open grave Gregoriska halted, saying,

'Kostaki, all is not yet over for you; a voice from Heaven tells me you will be pardoned if you repent. Promise to go back into your tomb, promise to leave it no more, promise to give God the devotion you have vowed to Hell.'

'Never,' replied Kostaki.

'Repent,' reiterated Gregoriska.

'Never.'

'For the last time, Kostaki, I appeal to you.'

'Never.'

'Well, then, call Satan to your help, as I call God to mine, and we shall see yet once again who will be victorious.'

Two cries rang out simultaneously and the swords crossed amid a myriad sparks; the fight lasted a minute, which seemed a century to me.

Kostaki fell; I saw the terrible sword whirl in the air, I saw it plunged into his body, nailing it to the freshly upturned earth. A last blood-curdling scream, which had nothing human about it, rent the air.

Gregoriska stood still over his adversary, but faintly and staggering. I ran up and caught him in my arms.

'Are you wounded?' I asked him anxiously.

'No,' he answered me, 'but in such a contest, dear Hedwig, 'tis not the wound that kills but the stress and struggle. I have striven with Death, and to Death I belong.'

'Beloved, beloved,' I cried, 'begone from here, and life will come back, perhaps.'

'No,' he said solemnly, 'here is my tomb, Hedwig. But waste no time, take a handful of this earth saturated with his blood and lay it on the bite he gave you; it is the only means to guard you in the future against his odious love.'

I shuddered, but obeyed. Stopping to gather up the blood-stained mould, I saw Kostaki's corpse pinned to the earth; the holy sword was through his heart, and an abundant jet of rich black blood gushed from the wound, as if he had died but an instant before. I kneaded a little mould with the blood, and applied the horrid talisman to my neck.

'Now, Hedwig, my adored Hedwig,' faltered Gregoriska in a thin, weak voice, 'listen heedfully to my last behests. Leave the country at the earliest opportunity; in distance lies your only safety. Father Basil had received my last instructions today, and he will carry them out. Hedwig, a kiss, the last, the only kiss, my Hedwig, before I die' – and with these words on his lips, Gregoriska fell dead beside his brother.

Under any other circumstances, in a graveyard, beside an open tomb, with two corpses lying side by side, I should have gone mad; but, I have already said so, God had given me a strength to match the terrible occurrences which He made me not only witness but play a part in.

I looked about me in search of help, and at that moment I saw the cloister door open, and the monks, Father Basil at their head, advancing towards me, two by two, carrying lighted torches and chanting the prayers of the dead.

Father Basil had just returned to the Monastery, and, foreseeing what had befallen, he had come straight to the cemetery, all his monks with him.

He found me, a living woman, standing over two dead men.

Kostaki's face was disfigured by a last hideous convulsion; but Gregoriska wore a calm and almost smiling aspect. As he had directed, the latter was buried by his sinful brother's side — God's servant keeping watch and ward over the Devil's.

Smerande, when she heard of this fresh calamity and the part I had played in it, desired to see me. She came to visit me at the Cloister of Hango, and learnt from my lips all that had happened that dreadful night.

I told her the fantastic history in all its dreadful details, but she heard me, as Gregoriska had, without a great surprise or horror.

'Hedwig,' she said to me, when I had finished, after a moment's silence, 'strange as the story is you have just told me, yet you have spoken only the plain truth. The race of the Brankovans is accursed to the third and fourth generation, because a Brankovan once killed a priest. But the curse is now run out; for though a wife, you are a virgin, and I am the last of my race. If my son has bequeathed you a million, take it. When I am gone, except for the few pious legacies I propose to leave, you shall have the remainder of my fortune. Now follow your bridegroom's advice, and return with all haste to the countries where God does not suffer the accomplishment of these appalling progidies. I need no one to help me mourn my sons. Farewell. Take no more heed of me; my lot to come concerns only myself and my God.'

And, kissing me on the brow as of old, she left me, to shut herself up in her bedchamber in the Castle of Brankovan.

A week later I started for France. As Gregoriska had hoped, my nights presently ceased to be haunted by the dreadful phantom. Health returned, and the only penalty remaining from my hideous adventure is this deathly pallor, which accompanies to the tomb every living creature that has once felt the embrace of a Vampire.

The Grave of Ethelind Fionguala

JULIAN HAWTHORNE

This is another landmark vampire story on two counts: first, it is the earliest on the theme to have been written by an American; and, secondly, because it might just have been read by Bram Stoker before he wrote Dracula. *'The Grave of Ethelind Fionguala' is the tale of an American artist travelling around Ireland who becomes fascinated by a sixteenth-century legend about a beautiful bride captured by a band of vampires and who is now said to haunt the scene of the crime. The tale was first published in the American publication,* Lippincott's Magazine, *in its May 1887 issue, where it appears to have passed without causing a single comment. A year later it was reprinted in Britain in another prestigious magazine,* Illustrated Sporting and Dramatic News *(now the* Illustrated London News) *where again it failed to attract any attention. Even when it was inexplicably retitled, 'Ken's Mystery' and collected with a selection of the author's other short stories under the title,* David Poindexter's Disappearance *in 1888, the silence was still resounding. It might be argued, therefore, that the chances of Bram Stoker having seen the item are slight: yet the facts are that he was also a contributor to* Illustrated Sporting and Dramatic News *(with 'The Judge's House' for the Christmas 1891 issue and 'The Squaw' for December 1893) and had been interested in the legends of his native Ireland since childhood (viz. his collection of fables,* Under The Sunset, *published in 1881). And here was an intriguing tale all about vampirism in County Cork! To my mind, the coincidences are certainly remarkable.*

The author of 'The Grave of Ethelind Fionguala', Julian Hawthorne

(1846–1934) was the son of the great nineteenth-century American realist writer, Nathaniel Hawthorne, and though Julian was talented in his own right as a journalist and creator of admittedly sensational fiction, lived forever in the shadow of his father. He even wrote a number of well-researched biographies – including one about his father – but was constantly subjected to comparisons with his parent which understandably embittered him. For a while he comforted himself in work and travel – and is believed to have based his vampire story on a legend he heard while visiting Dublin. But although Julian earned considerable sums of money from his prolific output of short stories for British and American magazines (not a few of which were horror and supernatural tales) he squandered the proceeds and in the early 1900s became involved in a series of fraudulent business ventures which ended with him being imprisoned. His work does, though, deserve a better fate than to be almost completely forgotten while virtually everything his father wrote is still in print. And if for no other reason than the fact that 'The Grave of Ethelind Fionguala' was the very first American vampire story and, even more importantly, may just have been another of the sparks that ignited Bram Stoker's imagination . . .

*　　　*　　　*

One cool October evening – it was the last day of the month, and unusually cool for the time of year – I made up my mind to go and spend an hour or two with my friend Keningale. Keningale was an artist (as well as a musical amateur and poet), and had a very delightful studio built onto his house, in which he was wont to sit of an evening. The studio had a cavernous fire-place, designed in imitation of the old-fashioned fire-places of Elizabethan manor-houses, and in it, when the temperature out-doors warranted, he would build up a cheerful fire of dry logs. It would suit me particularly well, I thought, to go and have a quiet pipe and chat in front of that fire with my friend.

I had not had such a chat for a very long time – not, in fact, since Keningale (or Ken, as his friends called him) had returned from his visit to Europe the year before. He went abroad, as he affirmed at the time, 'for purposes of study,' whereat we all smiled, for Ken, so far as we knew him, was more likely to do anything else than to study. He was a young fellow of buoyant temperament, lively and social in his habits, of a brilliant and versatile mind, and possessing an income of twelve or fifteen thousand dollars a year; he could sing, play, scribble, and paint very cleverly, and some of his heads and figure-pieces were really well done, considering that he never had any regular training in art; but he was not a worker. Personally he was fine-looking, of good height and figure, active, healthy, and with a remarkably fine brow, and clear, full-gazing eye. Nobody was surprised at his going to Europe, nobody expected him to do anything there except amuse himself, and few anticipated that he would be soon again seen in New York. He was one of the sort that find Europe agree with them. Off he went, therefore; and in the course of a few months the rumour reached us that he was engaged to a handsome and wealthy New York girl whom he had met in London. This was nearly all we did hear of him until, not very long afterward, he turned up again on Fifth Avenue, to every one's astonishment; made no satisfactory answer to those who wanted to know how he happened to tire so soon of the Old World; while, as to the reported engagement, he cut short all allusion to that in so peremptory a manner as to show that it was not a permissible topic of conversation with him. It was surmised that the lady had jilted him; but, on the other hand, she herself returned home not a great while after, and, though she had plenty of opportunities, she has never married to this day.

Be the rights of that matter what they may, it was soon remarked that Ken was no longer the careless and merry fellow he used to be; on the contrary, he appeared grave, moody, averse from general society, and habitually taciturn and undemonstrative even in the company of his most intimate friends. Evidently something had happened to him or he had done something. What? Had he committed a murder? or joined the Nihilists? or was his unsuccessful love affair at the bottom of it? Some declared that the cloud was only temporary, and would soon pass away. Nevertheless, up to the period of which I am writing, it had not passed away, but had rather gathered additional gloom, and threatened to become permanent.

Meanwhile I had met him twice or thrice at the club, at the opera, or in the street, but had as yet had no opportunity of regularly renewing my acquaintance with him. We had been on a footing of more than common intimacy in the old days, and I was not disposed to think that he would refuse to renew the former relations now. But what I had heard and myself seen of his changed condition imparted a stimulating tinge of suspense or curiosity to the pleasure with which I looked forward to the prospects of this evening. His house stood at a distance of two or three miles beyond the general range of habitations in New York at this time, and as I walked briskly along in the clear twilight air

I had leisure to go over in my mind all that I had known of Ken and had divined of his character. After all, had there not always been something in his nature – deep down, and held in abeyance by the activity of his animal spirits – but something strange and separate, and capable of developing under suitable conditions into – into what? As I asked myself this question I arrived at his door; and it was with a feeling of relief that I felt the next moment the cordial grasp of his hand, and his voice bidding me welcome in a tone that indicated unaffected gratification at my presence. He drew me at once into the studio, relieved me of my hat and cane, and then put his hand on my shoulder.

'I am glad to see you,' he repeated, with singular earnestness – 'glad to see you and to feel you; and to-night of all nights in the year.'

'Why to-night especially?'

'Oh, never mind. It's just as well, too, you didn't let me know beforehand you were coming; the unreadiness is all, to paraphrase the poet. Now, with you to help me, I can drink a glass of whisky and water and take a bit draw of the pipe. This would have been a grim night for me if I'd been left to myself.'

'In such a lap of luxury as this, too!' said I, looking round at the glowing fire-place, the low, luxurious chairs, and all the rich and sumptuous fittings of the room. 'I should have thought a condemned murderer might make himself comfortable here.'

'Perhaps; but that's not exactly my category at present. But have you forgotten what night this is? This is November-eve, when, as tradition asserts, the dead arise and walk about, and fairies, goblins, and spiritual beings of all kinds have more freedom and power than on any other day of the year. One can see you've never been in Ireland.'

'I wasn't aware till now that you had been there, either.'

'Yes, I have been in Ireland. Yes – ' He paused, sighed, and fell into a reverie, from which, however, he soon roused himself by an effort, and went to a cabinet in a corner of the room for the liquor and tobacco. While he was thus employed I sauntered about the studio, taking note of the various beauties, grotesquenesses, and curiosities that it contained. Many things were there to repay study and arouse admiration; for Ken was a good collector, having excellent taste as well as means to back it. But, upon the whole, nothing interested me more than some studies of a female head, roughly done in oils, and, judging from the sequestered positions in which I found them, not intended by the artist for exhibition or criticism. There were three or four of these studies, all of the same face, but in different poses and costumes. In one the head was enveloped in a dark hood, over-shadowing and partly concealing the features; in another she seemed to be peering duskily through a latticed casement, lit by a faint moonlight; a third showed her splendidly attired in evening costume, with jewels in her hair and ears, and sparkling on her snowy bosom. The expressions were as various as the poses; now it was demure penetration, now a subtle inviting glance, now burning passion, and again a look of elfish and elusive mockery. In whatever phase, the countenance possessed a singular and poignant fascination, not of beauty merely, though that was very striking, but of character and quality likewise.

'Did you find this model abroad?' I inquired at length. 'She has evidently inspired you, and I don't wonder at it.'

Ken, who had been mixing the punch, and had not noticed my movements, now looked up, and said: 'I didn't mean those to be seen. They don't satisfy me, and I am going to destroy them; but I couldn't rest till I'd made some attempts to reproduce – What was it you asked? Abroad? Yes – or no. They were all painted here within the last six weeks.'

'Whether they satisfy you or not, they are by far the best of yours I have ever seen.'

'Well, let them alone, and tell me what you think of this beverage. To my thinking, it goes to the right spot. It owes its existence to your coming here. I can't drink alone, and those portraits are not company, though, for aught I know, she might have come out of the canvas to-night and sat down in that chair.' Then, seeing my inquiring look, he added, with a hasty laugh, 'It's November-eve, you know, when anything might happen, provided it's strange enough. Well, here's to ourselves.'

We each swallowed a deep draught of the smoking and aromatic liquor, and set down our glasses with approval. The punch was excellent. Ken now opened a box of cigars, and we seated ourselves before the fire-place.

'All we need now,' I remarked, after a short silence, 'is a little music. By-the-by, Ken, have you still got the banjo I gave you before you went abroad?'

He paused so long before replying that I supposed he had not heard my question. 'I have got it,' he said, at length, 'but it will never make any more music.'

'Got broken, eh? Can't it be mended? It was a fine instrument.'

'It's not broken, but it's past mending. You shall see for yourself.'

He arose as he spoke, and going into another part of the studio, opened a black oak coffer, and took out of it a long object wrapped up in a piece of faded yellow silk. He handed it to me, and when I had unwrapped it, there appeared a thing that might once have been a banjo, but had little resemblance to one now. It bore every sign of extreme age. The wood of the handle was honey-combed with the gnawings of worms, and dusty with dry-rot. The parchment head was green with mould, and hung in shrivelled tatters. The hoop, which was of solid silver, was so blackened and tarnished that it looked like dilapidated iron. The strings were gone, and most of the tuning-screws had dropped out of the decayed sockets. Altogether it had the appearance of having been made before the Flood, and been forgotten in the forecastle of Noah's Ark ever since.

'It is a curious relic, certainly,' I said. 'Where did you come across it? I had no idea that the banjo was invented so long ago as this. It certainly can't be less than two hundred years old, and may be much older than that.'

Ken smiled gloomily. 'You are quite right,' he said; 'it is at least two hundred years old, and yet it is the very same banjo that you gave me a year ago.'

'Hardly,' I returned, smiling in my turn, 'since that was made to order with a view of presenting it to you.'

'I know that; but the two hundred years have passed since then. Yes; it is absurd and impossible, I know, but nothing is truer. That banjo, which was made last year, existed in the sixteenth century, and has been rotting ever since. Stay. Give it to me a moment, and I'll convince you. You recollect that your name and mine, with the date, were engraved on the silver hoop?'

'Yes; and there was a private mark of my own there, also.'

'Very well,' said Ken, who had been rubbing a place on the hoop with a corner of the yellow silk wrapper; 'look at that.'

I took the decrepit instrument from him, and examined the spot which he had rubbed. It was incredible, sure enough; but there were the names and the date precisely as I had caused them to be engraved; and there, moreover, was my own private mark, which I had idly made with an old etching point not more than eighteen months before. After convincing myself that there was no mistake, I laid the banjo across my knees, and stared at my friend in bewilderment. He sat smoking with a kind of grim composure, his eyes fixed upon the blazing logs.

'I'm mystified, I confess,' said I. 'Come; what is the joke? What method have you discovered of producing the decay of centuries on

this unfortunate banjo in a few months? And why did you do it? I have
heard of an elixir to counteract the effects of time, but your recipe
seems to work the other way – to make time rush forward at two
hundred times his usual rate, in one place, while he jogs on at his usual
gait elsewhere. Unfold your mystery, magician. Seriously, Ken, how
on earth did the thing happen?'

'I know no more about it than you do,' was his reply. 'Either you
and I and all the rest of the living world are insane, or else there has
been wrought a miracle as strange as any in tradition. How can I
explain it? It is a common saying – a common experience, if you will –
that we may, on certain trying or tremendous occasions, live years in
one moment. But that's a mental experience, not a physical one, and
one that applies, at all events, only to human beings, not to senseless
things of wood and metal. You imagine the thing is some trick or
jugglery. If it be, I don't know the secret of it. There's no chemical
appliance that I ever heard of that will get a piece of solid wood into
that condition in a few months, or a few years. And it wasn't done in a
few years, or a few months either. A year ago to-day at this very hour
that banjo was as sound as when it left the maker's hands, and
twenty-four hours afterward – I'm telling you the simple truth – it was
as you see it now.'

The gravity and earnestness with which Ken made this astounding
statement were evidently not assumed. He believed every word that he
uttered. I knew not what to think. Of course my friend might be
insane, though he betrayed none of the ordinary symptoms of mania;
but, however that might be, there was the banjo, a witness whose silent
testimony there was no gainsaying. The more I meditated on the
matter the more inconceivable did it appear. Two hundred years –
twenty-four hours; these were the terms of the proposed equation.
Ken and the banjo both affirmed that the equation had been made; all
worldly knowledge and experience affirmed it to be impossible. What
was the explanation? What is time? What is life? I felt myself
beginning to doubt the reality of all things. And so this was the mystery
which my friend had been brooding over since his return from abroad.
No wonder it had changed him. More to be wondered at was it that it
had not changed him more.

'Can you tell me the whole story?' I demanded at length.

Ken quaffed another draught from his glass of whisky and water
and rubbed his hand through his thick brown beard. 'I have never
spoken to any one of it heretofore,' he said, 'and I had never meant to
speak of it. But I'll try and give you some idea of what it was. You

know me better than any one else; you'll understand the thing as far as it can be understood, and perhaps I may be relieved of some of the oppression it has caused me. For it is rather a ghastly memory to grapple with alone, I can tell you.'

Hereupon, without further preface, Ken related the following tale. He was, I may observe in passing, a naturally fine narrator. There were deep, lingering tones in his voice, and he could strikingly enhance the comic or pathetic effect of a sentence by dwelling here and there upon some syllable. His features were equally susceptible of humorous and of solemn expressions, and his eyes were in form and hue wonderfully adapted to showing great varieties of emotion. Their mournful aspect was extremely earnest and affecting; and when Ken was giving utterance to some mysterious passage of the tale they had a doubtful, melancholy, exploring look which appealed irresistibly to the imagination. But the interest of his story was too pressing to allow of noticing these incidental embellishments at the time, though they doubtless had their influence upon me all the same.

'I left New York on an Inman Line steamer, you remember,' began Ken, 'and landed at Havre. I went the usual round of sight-seeing on the Continent, and got round to London in July, at the height of the season. I had good introductions, and met any number of agreeable and famous people. Among others was a young lady, a countrywoman of my own – you know whom I mean – who interested me very much, and before her family left London she and I were engaged. We parted there for the time, because she had a Continental trip still to make, while I wanted to take the opportunity to visit the north of England and Ireland. I landed at Dublin about the 1st of October, and, zigzagging about the country, I found myself in County Cork about two weeks later.

'There is in that region some of the most lovely scenery that human eyes ever rested on, and it seems to be less known to tourists than many places of infinitely less picturesque value. A lonely region too: during my rambles I met not a single stranger like myself, and few enough natives. It seems incredible that so beautiful a country should be so deserted. After walking a dozen Irish miles you come across a group of two or three one-roomed cottages, and, like as not, one or more of those will have the roof off and the walls in ruins. The few peasants whom one sees, however, are affable and hospitable, especially when they hear you are from that terrestrial heaven whither most of their friends and relatives have gone before them. They seem simple and primitive enough at first sight, and yet they are as strange and incomprehensible a race as any in the world. They are as superstitious, as credulous of marvels, fairies, magicians, and omens, as the men whom St Patrick preached to, and at the same time they are shrewd, sceptical, sensible, and bottomless liars. Upon the whole, I met with no nation on my travels whose company I enjoyed so much, or who inspired me with so much kindliness, curiosity and repugnance.

'At length I got to a place on the sea-coast, which I will not further specify than to say that it is not many miles from Ballymacheen, on the south shore. I have seen Venice and Naples, I have driven along the Cornice Road, I have spent a month at our own Mount Desert, and I say that all of them together are not so beautiful as this glowing, deep-hued, soft-gleaming, silvery-lighted, ancient harbour and town, with the tall hills crowding around it and the black cliffs and headlands planting their iron feet in the blue, transparent sea. It is a very old place, and has had a history which it has outlived ages since. It may once have had two or three thousand inhabitants; it has scarce five or six hundred to-day. Half the houses are in ruins or have disappeared; many of the remainder are standing empty. All the people are poor, most of them abjectly so; they saunter about with bare feet and uncovered heads, the women in quaint black or dark-blue cloaks, the men in such anomalous attire as only an Irishman knows how to get together, the children half naked. The only comfortable-looking people are the monks and the priests, and the soldiers in the fort. For there is a fort there, constructed on the huge ruins of one which may have done duty in the reign of Edward the Black Prince, or earlier, in whose mossy embrasures are mounted a couple of cannon, which occasionally sent a practice-shot or two at the cliff on the other side of the harbour. The garrison consists of a dozen men and three or four officers and non-commissioned officers. I suppose they are relieved occasionally, but those I saw seemed to have become component parts of their surroundings.

'I put up at a wonderful little old inn, the only one in the place, and took my meals in a dining-saloon fifteen feet by nine, with a portrait of George I (a print varnished to preserve it) hanging over the mantel-piece. On the second evening after dinner a young gentleman came in – the dining-saloon being public property of course – and ordered some bread and cheese and a bottle of Dublin stout. We presently fell into talk; he turned out to be an officer from the fort, Lieutenant O'Connor, and a fine young specimen of the Irish soldier he was. After telling me all he knew about the town, the surrounding country, his friends, and himself, he intimated a readiness to sympathise with whatever tale I might choose to pour into his ear; and I had pleasure in trying to rival his own outspokenness. We became excellent friends; we had up a half-pint of Kinahan's whisky, and the lieutenant expressed himself in terms of high praise of my countrymen, my country, and my own particular cigars. When it became time for him to depart I accompanied him – for there was a splendid moon abroad – and bade him farewell at the fort entrance, having promised to come over the next day and make the acquaintance of the other fellows. "And mind your eye, now, going back, my dear boy," he called out, as I turned my face homeward. "Faith, 'tis a spooky place, that graveyard, and you'll as likely meet the black woman there as anywhere else!"

'The graveyard was a forlorn and barren spot on the hill-side, just the hither side of the fort: thirty or forty rough head-stones few of which retained any semblance of the perpendicular, while many were so shattered and decayed as to seem nothing more than irregular natural projections from the ground. Who the black woman might be I knew not, and did not stay to inquire. I had never been subject to ghostly apprehensions, and as a matter of fact, though the path I had to follow was in places very bad going, not to mention a hap-hazard scramble over a ruined bridge that covered a deep-lying brook, I reached my inn without any adventure whatever.

'The next day I kept my appointment at the fort, and found no reason to regret it; and my friendly sentiments were abundantly reciprocated, thanks more especially, perhaps, to the success of my banjo, which I carried with me, and which was as novel as it was popular with those who listened to it. The chief personages in the social circle besides my friend the lieutenant were Major Molloy, who was in command, a racy and juicy old campaigner, with a face like a sunset, and the surgeon, Dr Dudeen, a long, dry, humorous genius, with a wealth of anecdotical and traditional lore at his command that I have never seen surpassed. We had a jolly time of it, and it was the precursor of many more like it. The remains of October slipped away rapidly, and I was obliged to remember that I was a traveller in Europe, and not a resident in Ireland. The major, the surgeon, and the lieutenant all protested cordially against my proposed departure, but, as there was no help for it, they arranged a farewell dinner to take place in the fort on All-halloween.

'I wish you could have been at that dinner with me! It was the essence of Irish good-fellowship. Dr Dudeen was in great force; the major was better than the best of Lever's novels; the lieutenant was overflowing with hearty good-humour, merry chaff, and sentimental rhapsodies anent this or the other pretty girl of the neighbourhood. For my part I made the banjo ring as it had never rung before, and the others joined in the chorus with a mellow strength of lungs such as you don't often hear outside of Ireland. Among the stories that Dr Dudeen regaled us with was one about the Kern of Querin and his wife, Ethelind Fionguala – which being interpreted signifies "the white-shouldered." The lady, it appears, was originally betrothed to one O'Connor (here the lieutenant smacked his lips), but was stolen away on the wedding night by a party of vampires, who, it would seem, were at that period a prominent feature among the troubles of Ireland. But as they were bearing her along – she being unconscious – to that supper where she was not to eat but to be eaten, the young Kern of Querin, who happened to be out duck-shooting, met the party, and emptied his gun at it. The vampires fled, and the Kern carried the fair lady, still in a state of insensibility, to his house. "And by the same token, Mr Keningale," observed the doctor, knocking the ashes out of his pipe, "ye're after passing that very house on your way here. The one with the dark archway underneath it, and the big mullioned window at the corner, ye recollect, hanging over the street as I might say – "

' "Go 'long wid the house, Dr Dudeen, dear," interrupted the lieutenant; "sure can't you see we're all dying to know what happened to sweet Miss Fionguala, God be good to her, when I was after getting her safe up-stairs – "

' "Faith, then, I can tell ye that myself, Mr O'Connor," exclaimed the major, imparting a rotary motion to the remnants of whiskey in his tumbler. " 'Tis a question to be solved on general principles, as Colonel O'Halloran said that time he was asked what he'd do if he'd been the Dook o' Wellington, and the Prussians hadn't come up in the nick o' time at Waterloo. "Faith," says the colonel, "I'll tell ye – "

' "Arrah, then, major, why would ye be interruptin' the doctor, and Mr Keningale there lettin' his glass stay empty till he hears – The Lord save us! the bottle's empty!"

'In the excitement consequent upon this discovery, the thread of the doctor's story was lost; and before it could be recovered the evening had advanced so far that I felt obliged to withdraw. It took some time to make my proposition heard and comprehended; and a still longer time to put it in execution; so that it was fully midnight before I found myself standing in the cool pure air outside the fort, with the farewells of my boon companions ringing in my ears.

'Considering that it had been rather a wet evening in-doors, I was in a remarkably good state of preservation, and I therefore ascribed it rather to the roughness of the road than to the smoothness of the liquor, when, after advancing a few rods, I stumbled and fell. As I picked myself up I fancied I had heard a laugh, and supposed that the lieutenant, who had accompanied me to the gate, was making merry over my mishap; but on looking round I saw that the gate was closed and no one was visible. The laugh, moreover, had seemed to be close at hand, and to be even pitched in a key that was rather feminine than masculine. Of course I must have been deceived; nobody was near me: my imagination had played me a trick, or else there was more truth than poetry in the tradition that Halloween is the carnival-time of disembodied spirits. It did not occur to me at the time that a stumble is held by the superstitious Irish to be an evil omen, and had I remembered it it would only have been to laugh at it. At all events, I was physically none the worse for my fall, and I resumed my way immediately.

'But the path was singularly difficult to find, or rather the path I was following did not seem to be the right one. I did not recognize it; I could have sworn (except I knew the contrary) that I had never seen it before. The moon had risen, though her light was as yet obscured by clouds, but neither my immediate surroundings nor the general aspect of the region appeared familiar. Dark, silent hill-sides mounted up on either hand, and the road, for the most part, plunged downward, as if to conduct me into the bowels of the earth. The place was alive with strange echoes, so that at times I seemed to be walking through the midst of muttering voices and mysterious whispers, and a wild, faint sound of laughter seemed ever and anon to reverberate among the passes of the hills. Currents of colder air sighing up through narrow defiles and dark crevices touched my face as with airy fingers. A certain feeling of anxiety and insecurity began to take possession of me, though there was no definable cause for it, unless that I might be belated in getting home. With the perverse instinct of those who are lost I hastened my steps, but was impelled now and then to glance back over my shoulder, with a sensation of being pursued. But no living creature was in sight. The moon, however, had now risen higher, and the clouds that were drifting slowly across the sky flung into the naked valley dusky shadows, which occasionally assumed shapes that looked like the vague semblance of gigantic human forms.

'How long I had been hurrying onward I know not, when, with a kind of suddenness, I found myself approaching a graveyard. It was situated on the spur of a hill, and there was no fence around it, nor anything to protect it from the incursions of passers-by. There was something in the general appearance of this spot that made me half fancy I had seen it before; and I should have taken it to be the same that I had often noticed on my way to the fort, but that the latter was only a few hundred yards distant therefrom, whereas I must have traversed several miles at least. As I drew near, moreover, I observed that the head-stones did not appear so ancient and decayed as those of the other. But what chiefly attracted my attention was the figure that was leaning or half sitting upon one of the largest of the upright slabs near the road. It was a female figure draped in black, and a closer inspection – for I was soon within a few yards of her – showed that she wore the calla, or long hooded cloak, the most common as well as the most ancient garment of Irish women, and doubtless of Spanish origin.

'I was a trifle startled by this apparition, so unexpected as it was, and so strange did it seem that any human creature should be at that hour of the night in so desolate and sinister a place. Involuntarily I paused as I came opposite her, and gazed at her intently. But the moonlight fell behind her, and the deep hood of her cloak so completely shadowed her face that I was unable to discern anything but the sparkle of a pair of eyes, which appeared to be returning my gaze with much vivacity.

' "You seem to be at home here," I said, at length. "Can you tell me where I am?"

'Hereupon the mysterious personage broke into a light laugh, which, though in itself musical and agreeable, was of a timbre and intonation that caused my heart to beat rather faster than my late pedestrian exertions warranted; for it was the identical laugh (or so my imagination persuaded me) that had echoed in my ears as I arose from my tumble an hour or two ago. For the rest, it was the laugh of a young woman, and presumably of a pretty one; and yet it had a wild, airy, mocking quality, that seemed hardly human at all, or not, at any rate, characteristic of a being of affections and limitations like unto ours. But this impression of mine was fostered, no doubt, by the unusual and uncanny circumstances of the occasion.

' "Sure, sir," she said, "you're at the grave of Ethelind Fionguala."

'As she spoke she rose to her feet, and pointed to the inscription on the stone. I bent forward, and was able, without much difficulty, to decipher the name, and a date which indicated that the occupant of the grave must have entered the disembodied state between two and three centuries ago.

' "And who are you?" was my next question.

' "I'm called Elsie," she replied. "But where would your honour be going on November-eve?"

'I mentioned my destination, and asked her whether she could direct me thither.

' "Indeed, then, 'tis there I'm going myself," Elsie replied; "and if your honour 'll follow me, and play me a tune on the pretty instrument, 'tisn't long we'll be on the road."

'She pointed to the banjo which I carried wrapped under my arm. How she knew it was a musical instrument I could not imagine; possibly, I thought, she may have seen me playing on it as I strolled about the environs of the town. Be that as it may, I offered no opposition to the bargain, and further intimated that I would reward her more substantially on our arrival. At that she laughed again, and made a peculiar gesture with her hand above her head. I uncovered my banjo, swept my fingers across the strings, and struck into a fantastic dance-measure, to the music of which we proceeded along the path, Elsie slightly in advance, her feet keeping time to the airy measure. In fact, she trod so lightly, with an elastic, undulating movement, that with a little more it seemed as if she might float onward like a spirit. The extreme whiteness of her feet attracted my eye, and I was surprised to find that instead of being bare, as I had supposed, these were incased in white satin slippers quaintly embroidered with gold thread.

' "Elsie," said I, lengthening my steps so as to come up with her, "where do you live, and what do you do for a living?"

' "Sure, I live by myself"; she answered; "and if you'd be after knowing how, you must come and see for yourself."

' "Are you in the habit of walking over the hills at night in shoes like that?"

' "And why would I not?" she asked, in her turn. "And where did your honour get the pretty gold ring on your finger?"

'The ring, which was of no great intrinsic value, had struck my eye in an old curiosity-shop in Cork. It was an antique of very old-fashioned design, and might have belonged (as the vender assured me was the case) to one of the early kings or queens of Ireland.

' "Do you like it?" said I.

' "Will your honour be after making a present of it to Elsie?" she returned, with an insinuating tone and turn of the head.

' "Maybe I will, Elsie, on one condition. I am an artist; I make pictures of people. If you will promise to come to my studio and let me paint your portrait, I'll give you the ring, and some money besides."

' "And will you give me the ring now?" said Elsie.

' "Yes, if you'll promise."

' "And will you play the music to me?" she continued.

' "As much as you like."

' "But maybe I'll not be handsome enough for ye," said she, with a glance of her eyes beneath the dark hood.

' "I'll take the risk of that," I answered, laughing, "though, all the same, I don't mind taking a peep beforehand to remember you by." So saying, I put forth a hand to draw back the concealing hood. But Elsie eluded me, I scarce know how, and laughed a third time, with the same, airy mocking cadence.

' "Give me the ring first, and then you shall see me," she said, coaxingly.

' "Stretch out your hand, then," returned I, removing the ring from my finger. "When we are better acquainted, Elsie, you won't be so suspicious."

'She held out a slender, delicate hand, on the forefinger of which I slipped the ring. As I did so, the folds of her cloak fell a little apart, affording me a glimpse of a white shoulder and of a dress that seemed in that deceptive semi-darkness to be wrought of rich and costly material; and I caught, too, or so I fancied, the frosty sparkle of precious stones.

' "Arrah, mind where ye tread!" said Elsie, in a sudden, sharp tone.

'I looked round, and became aware for the first time that we were standing near the middle of a ruined bridge which spanned a rapid stream that flowed at a considerable depth below. The parapet of the bridge on one side was broken down, and I must have been, in fact, in imminent danger of stepping over into empty air. I made my way cautiously across the decaying structure; but, when I turned to assist Elsie, she was nowhere to be seen.

'What had become of the girl? I called, but no answer came. I gazed about on every side, but no trace of her was visible. Unless she had plunged into the narrow abyss at my feet, there was no place where she could have concealed herself – none at least that I could discover. She had vanished, nevertheless; and since her disappearance must have been premeditated, I finally came to the conclusion that it was useless to attempt to find her. She would present herself again in her own good time, or not at all. She had given me the slip very cleverly, and I must make the best of it. The adventure was perhaps worth the ring.

'On resuming my way, I was not a little relieved to find that I once more knew where I was. The bridge that I had just crossed was none other than the one I mentioned some time back; I was within a mile of the town, and my way lay clear before me. The moon, moreover, had now quite dispersed the clouds, and shone down with exquisite brilliance. Whatever her other failings, Elsie had been a trustworthy guide; she had brought me out of the depth of elf-land into the material world again. It had been a singular adventure, certainly; and I mused over it with a sense of mysterious pleasure as I sauntered along, humming snatches of airs, and accompanying myself on the strings. Hark! what light step was that behind me? It sounded like Elsie's; but no, Elsie was not there. The same impression or hallucination, however, recurred several times before I reached the outskirts of the town – the tread of an airy foot behind or beside my own. The fancy did not make me nervous; on the contrary, I was pleased with the notion of being thus haunted, and gave myself up to a romantic and genial vein of reverie.

'After passing one or two roofless and moss-grown cottages, I entered the narrow and rambling street which leads through the town. This street a short distance down widens a little, as if to afford the wayfarer space to observe a remarkable old house that stands on the northern side. The house was built of stone, and in a noble style of architecture; it reminded me somewhat of certain palaces of the old Italian nobility that I had seen on the Continent, and it may very probably have been built by one of the Italian or Spanish immigrants of the sixteenth or seventeenth century. The moulding of the projecting windows and arched doorway was richly carved, and upon the front of the building was an escutcheon wrought in high relief, though I could not make out the purport of the device. The moonlight falling upon this picturesque pile enhanced all its beauties, and at the same time made it seem like a vision that might dissolve away when the light ceased to shine. I must often have seen the house before, and yet I retained no definite recollection of it; I had never until now examined it with my eyes open, so to speak. Leaning against the wall on the opposite side of the street, I contemplated it for a long while at my leisure. The window at the corner was really a very fine and massive affair. It projected over the pavement below, throwing a heavy shadow aslant; the frames of the diamond-paned lattices were heavily mullioned. How often in past ages had that lattice been pushed open by some fair hand, revealing to a lover waiting beneath in the moonlight the charming countenance of his high-born mistress! Those were brave days. They had passed away long since. The great house had stood empty for who could tell how many years; only bats and vermin were its inhabitants. Where now were those who had built it; and who were they? Probably the very name of them was forgotten.

'As I continued to stare upward, however, a conjecture presented itself to my mind which rapidly ripened into a conviction. Was not this the house that Dr Dudeen had described that very evening as having been formerly the abode of the Kern of Querin and his mysterious bride? There was the projecting window, the arched doorway. Yes, beyond a doubt this was the very house. I emitted a low exclamation of renewed interest and pleasure, and my speculations took a still more imaginative, but also a more definite turn.

'What had been the fate of that lovely lady after the Kern had brought her home insensible in his arms? Did she recover, and were they married and happy ever after; or had the sequel been a tragic one? I remembered to have read that the victims of vampires generally became vampires themselves. Then my thoughts went back to that grave on the hill-side. Surely that was unconsecrated ground. Why had they buried her there? Ethelind of the white shoulder! Ah! why had not I lived in those days; or why might not some magic cause them to live again for me? Then would I seek this street at midnight, and standing here beneath her window, I would lightly touch the strings of my bandore until the casement opened cautiously and she looked down. A sweet vision indeed! And what prevented my realizing it? Only a matter of a couple of centuries or so. And was time, then, at which poets and philosophers sneer, so rigid and real a matter that a little faith and imagination might not overcome it? At all events, I had my banjo, the bandore's legitimate and lineal descendant, and the memory of Fionguala should have the love-ditty.

'Hereupon, having retuned the instrument, I launched forth into an old Spanish love-song, which I had met with in some mouldy library during my travels, and had set to music of my own. I sang low, for the deserted street re-echoed the lightest sound, and what I sang must reach only my lady's ears. The words were warm with the fire of the ancient Spanish chivalry, and I threw into their expression all the passion of the lovers of romance. Surely Fionguala, the white-shouldered, would hear, and awaken from her sleep of centuries, and come to the latticed casement and look down! Hist! see yonder! What light – what shadow is that that seems to flit from room to room within the abandoned house, and now approaches the mullioned window? Are my eyes dazzled by the play of the moonlight, or does the casement move – does it open? Nay, this is no delusion; there is no error of the senses here. There is simply a woman, young, beautiful, and richly attired, bending forward from the window, and silently beckoning me to approach.

'Too much amazed to be conscious of amazement, I advanced until I stood directly beneath the casement, and the lady's face, as she stooped toward me, was not more than twice a man's height from my own. She smiled and kissed her finger-tips; something white fluttered in her hand, then fell through the air to the ground at my feet. The next moment she had withdrawn, and I heard the lattice close.

'I picked up what she had let fall; it was a delicate lace handkerchief, tied to the handle of an elaborately wrought bronze key. It was evidently the key of the house, and invited me to enter. I loosened it from the handkerchief, which bore a faint, delicious perfume, like the aroma of flowers in an ancient garden, and turned to the arched doorway. I felt no misgiving, and scarcely any sense of strangeness. All was as I had wished it to be, and as it should be; the mediæval age was alive once more, and as for myself, I almost felt the velvet cloak hanging from my shoulder and the long rapier dangling at my belt. Standing in front of the door I thrust the key into the lock, turned it, and felt the bolt yield. The next instant the door was opened, apparently from within; I stepped across the threshold, the door closed again, and I was alone in the house, and in darkness.

'Not alone, however! As I extended my hand to grope my way it was met by another hand, soft, slender, and cold, which insinuated itself gently into mine and drew me forward. Forward I went, nothing loath; the darkness was impenetrable, but I could hear the light rustle of a dress close to me, and the same delicious perfume that had emanated from the handkerchief enriched the air that I breathed, while the little hand that clasped and was clasped by my own alternately tightened and half relaxed the hold of its soft cold fingers. In this manner, and treading lightly, we traversed what I presumed to be a long, irregular passageway, and ascended a staircase. Then another corridor, until finally we paused, a door opened, emitting a flood of soft light, into which we entered, still hand in hand. The darkness and the doubt were at an end.

'The room was of imposing dimensions, and was furnished and decorated in a style of antique splendour. The walls were draped with mellow hues of tapestry; clusters of candles burned in polished silver sconces, and were reflected and multiplied in tall mirrors placed in the four corners of the room. The heavy beams of the dark oaken ceiling crossed each other in squares, and were laboriously carved; the curtains and the drapery of the chairs were of heavy-figured damask.

At one end of the room was a broad ottoman, and in front of it a table, on which was set forth, in massive silver dishes, a sumptuous repast, with wines in crystal beakers. At the side was a vast and deep fire-place, with space enough on the broad hearth to burn whole trunks of trees. No fire, however, was there, but only a great heap of dead embers; and the room, for all its magnificence, was cold – cold as a tomb, or as my lady's hand – and it sent a subtle chill creeping to my heart.

'But my lady! how fair she was! I gave but a passing glance at the room; my eyes and my thoughts were all for her. She was dressed in white, like a bride; diamonds sparkled in her dark hair and on her snowy bosom; her lovely face and slender lips were pale, and all the paler for the dusky glow of her eyes. She gazed at me with a strange, elusive smile; and yet there was, in her aspect and bearing, something familiar in the midst of strangeness, like the burden of a song heard long ago and recalled among other conditions and surroundings. It seemed to me that something in me recognized her and knew her, had known her always. She was the woman of whom I had dreamed, whom I had beheld in visions, whose voice and face had haunted me from boyhood up. Whether we had ever met before, as human beings meet, I knew not; perhaps I had been blindly seeking her all over the world, and she had been awaiting me in this splendid room, sitting by those dead embers until all the warmth had gone out of her blood, only to be restored by the heat with which my love might supply her.

' "I thought you had forgotten me," she said, nodding as if in answer to my thought. "The night was so late – our one night of the year! How my heart rejoiced when I heard your dear voice singing the song I know so well! Kiss me – my lips are cold!"

'Cold indeed they were – cold as the lips of death. But the warmth of my own seemed to revive them. They were now tinged with a faint colour, and in her cheeks also appeared a delicate shade of pink. She drew fuller breath, as one who recovers from a long lethargy. Was it my life that was feeding her? I was ready to give her all. She drew me to the table and pointed to the viands and the wine.

' "Eat and drink," she said. "You have travelled far, and you need food."

' "Will you eat and drink with me?" said I, pouring out the wine.

' "You are the only nourishment I want," was her answer. "This wine is thin and cold. Give me wine as red as your blood and as warm, and I will drain a goblet to the dregs."

'At these words, I know not why, a slight shiver passed through me.

She seemed to gain vitality and strength at every instant, but the chill of the great room struck into me more and more.

'She broke into a fantastic flow of spirits, clapping her hands, and dancing about me like a child. Who was she? And was I myself, or was she mocking me when she implied that we had belonged to each other of old? At length she stood before me, crossing her hands over her breast. I saw upon the forefinger of her right hand the gleam of an antique ring.

' "Where did you get that ring?" I demanded.

'She shook her head and laughed. "Have you been faithful?" she asked. "It is my ring; it is the ring that unites us; it is the ring you gave me when you loved me first. It is the ring of the Kern – the fairy ring, and I am your Ethelind – Ethelind Fionguala."

' "So be it," I said, casting aside all doubt and fear, and yielding myself wholly to the spell of her inscrutable eyes and wooing lips. "You are mine, and I am yours, and let us be happy while the hours last."

' "You are mine, and I am yours," she repeated, nodding her head with an elfish smile. "Come and sit beside me, and sing that sweet song again that you sang to me so long ago. Ah, now I shall live a hundred years."

'We seated ourselves on the ottoman, and while she nestled luxuriously among the cushions, I took my banjo and sang to her. The song and the music resounded through the lofty room, and came back in throbbing echoes. And before me as I sang I saw the face and form of Ethelind Fionguala, in her jewelled bridal dress, gazing at me with burning eyes. She was pale no longer, but ruddy and warm, and life was like a flame within her. It was I who had become cold and bloodless, yet with the last life that was in me I would have sung to her of love that can never die. But at length my eyes grew dim, the room seemed to darken, the form of Ethelind alternately brightened and waxed indistinct, like the last flickerings of a fire; I swayed toward her, and felt myself lapsing into unconsciousness, with my head resting on her white shoulder.'

Here Keningale paused a few moments in his story, flung a fresh log upon the fire, and then continued:

'I awoke, I know not how long afterward. I was in a vast, empty room in a ruined building. Rotten shreds of drapery depended from the walls, and heavy festoons of spiders' webs grey with dust covered the windows, which were destitute of glass or sash; they had been boarded up with rough planks which had themselves become rotten with age, and admitted through their holes and crevices pallid rays of light and chilly draughts of air. A bat, disturbed by these rays or by my own movement, detached himself from his hold on a remnant of mouldy tapestry near me, and after circling dizzily around my head, wheeled the flickering noiselessness of his flight into a darker corner. As I arose unsteadily from the heap of miscellaneous rubbish on which I had been lying, something which had been resting across my knees fell to the floor with a rattle. I picked it up, and found it to be my banjo – as you see it now.

'Well, that is all I have to tell. My health was seriously impaired; all the blood seemed to have been drawn out of my veins; I was pale and haggard, and the chill – Ah, that chill,' murmured Keningale, drawing nearer to the fire, and spreading out his hands to catch the warmth – 'I shall never get over it; I shall carry it to my grave.'

Let Loose

MARY CHOLMONDELEY

'Let Loose' represents yet another important step in the development of the vampire genre – being the earliest short story of 'Possession by the Dead', which Margaret L. Carter has defined in her study, The Vampire in Literature *(1989), as 'usually the draining of the victim's life-force or personality in order to be re-born in his or her body'. The theme was certainly a controversial one for a female author in the Victorian era, but Mary Cholmondeley (1859–1925) was no ordinary writer. Her life and work clearly label her as an early feminist, though at the time she was referred to (condescendingly or disparagingly, take your choice) as a 'New Woman' novelist. This reputation had been primarily established on the strength of her novel,* Red Pottage *(1899), which created a furor in the press because of its unstinted attack on the hypocrisy of the English middle classes. The outrage was seen to be all the greater because this was precisely the background from which Mary had come: she was the daughter of a rector, the Reverend Henry Cholmondeley of Hodnet in Stafford and a descendant of the great hymn writer, Bishop Heber. There was, however, no hint of this outspoken tone in her early writings for women's journals, but growing increasingly angry at the restrictions placed on the lives of the members of her sex, she began to plead for their emancipation in* Red Pottage *and her subsequent works such as* Prisoners *(1906),* The Lowest Rung *(1908) and* Under One Roof *(1918). Because of the frequent attacks on her in the press, Mary lived for the later part of her life in seclusion in a small cottage in the remote village of Ufford in Suffolk.*

The story of 'Let Loose' is set in a similar Yorkshire village not far from Pickering – a small, close-knit community much like Whitley Beaumont, also in Yorkshire, where her mother, Emily, had been born, and where Mary herself spent many happy holidays as a child. Evidence suggests that a local tradition inspired the story, but when it was first published in the April 1890 edition of Temple Bar, *Mary was promptly accused of plagiarism. Although she was quite used to attacks on her views, she could not accept this slur and promptly responded in the pages of* Temple Bar *with this statement: 'Since my story was written the author has been told that what was related as personal experience was partially derived from a written source. Every effort has been made, but in vain, to discover this written source.' Subsequent research has discovered that there was another vampire story written that same year entitled 'The Tomb of Sarah' by Frederick George Loring – which, though it can certainly be compared to 'Let Loose', was actually not published until the autumn of that year. Loring's story has since enjoyed something of a cult status and been endlessly reprinted in anthologies, though I prefer to agree with E. F. Bleiler's verdict in his* Guide to Supernatural Fiction (1983) *that it is 'a conventional vampire story, obviously derivative from Dracula'. (Though this hadn't been written yet!) Whatever the ramifications of the charge against Mary Cholmondeley, when the best of her short stories were collected together in 1902 under the title* Moth and Rust, *'Let Loose' was reprinted in the American edition but omitted from the British edition. I am, therefore, particularly pleased to reprint the original from the* Temple Bar *hereunder. (As a matter of interest, the* Temple Bar *magazine was responsible for publishing or reprinting several of the earliest vampire tales, and when, during the course of my researches, I came upon an anonymous story entitled 'Vautreau the Vampire' in the December 1879 issue I thought I had stumbled upon yet another landmark tale. How my hopes were dashed – for Vautreau turned out to be a rather engaging Parisian art dealer who far from 'vampirising' his artists actually put money and vitality into their careers!)*

*   *   *

A few years ago I took up architecture, and made a tour through Holland, studying the buildings of that interesting country. I had one companion on this expedition, who has since become one of the leading architects of the day. He was a tall grave man, slow of speech, absorbed in his work, and with a certain quiet power of overcoming obstacles which I have seldom seen equalled. A more careless man as to dress I have rarely met, and yet, in all the heat of July in Holland, I noticed that he never appeared without a high starched collar which had not even fashion to commend it at that time.

I often chaffed him about his splendid collars, and asked him why he wore them, but without eliciting any response. One evening as we were walking back to our lodgings in Middleberg I attacked him for about the thirtieth time on the subject.

'Why on earth do you wear them?' I said.

'You have, I believe, asked me that question many times,' he replied, in his slow, precise utterance; 'but always on occasions I was occupied. I am now at leisure, and I will tell you.'

And he did.

I have put down what he said, as nearly in his own words as I can remember them.

Ten years ago, I was asked to read a paper on English Frescoes at the Institute of British Architects. I was determined to make the paper as good as I possibly could, down to the slightest details; and I consulted many books on the subject, and studied every fresco I could find. My father, who had been an architect, had left me, at his death, all his papers and note-books on the subject of architecture. I searched them diligently, and found in one of them a slight unfinished sketch of nearly forty years ago, that specially interested me. Underneath was noted, in his clear small hand – *Frescoed east wall of crypt. Parish Church. Wet Waste-on-the-Wolds, Yorkshire (via Pickering).*'

The sketch had such a fascination for me that at last I decided to go there and see the fresco for myself. I had only a very vague idea as to where Wet Waste-on-the-Wolds was, but I was ambitious for the success of my paper; it was hot in London, and I set off on my long journey not without a certain degree of pleasure, with my dog Brian, a large nondescript brindled creature, as my only companion.

I reached Pickering, in Yorkshire, in the course of the afternoon, and then began a series of experiments on local lines which ended, after several hours, in my finding myself deposited at a little out-of-the-world station within nine or ten miles of Wet Waste. As no conveyance of any kind was to be had, I shouldered my little portmanteau, and set out on a long white road, that stretched away into the distance over the bare, treeless wold. I must have walked for several hours, over a waste of moorland patched with heather, when a doctor passed me, and gave me a lift to within a mile of my destination. The mile was a long one, and it was quite dark by the time I saw the feeble glimmer of lights in front of me, and found that I had reached Wet Waste. I had considerable difficulty in getting any one to take me in; but at last I persuaded the owner of the public-house to give me a bed, and quite tired out, I got into it as soon as possible, for fear he should change his mind, and fell asleep to the sound of a little stream below my window.

I was up early next morning, and inquired directly after breakfast for the way to the clergyman's house, which I found was close at hand. At Wet Waste everything was close at hand. The whole village seemed composed of a straggling row of one-storied grey stone houses, the same colour as the stone walls that separated the few fields enclosed from the surrounding waste, and as the little bridges over the beck that ran down one side of the grey wide street. Everything was grey. The church, the low tower of which I could see at a little distance, seemed to have been built of the same stone; so was the parsonage when I came up to it, accompanied on my way by a mob of rough, uncouth children, who eyed me and Brian, with half-defiant curiosity.

The clergyman was at home, and after a short delay I was admitted. Leaving Brian in charge of my drawing materials I followed the servant into a low panelled room in which at a latticed window a very old man was sitting. The morning light fell on his white head bent low over a litter of papers and books.

'Mr Er—?' He said looking up slowly, with one finger keeping his place in a book.

'Blake.'

'Blake,' he repeated after me, and was silent.

'I told him that I was an arhictect; that I had come to study a fresco in the crypt of his church; and asked for the keys.

'The crypt,' he said, pushing up his spectacles and peering hard at me. 'The crypt has been closed for thirty years. Ever since—' and he stopped short.

'I should be much obliged for the keys,' I said again.

He shook his head.

'No,' he said. 'No one goes in there now.'

'It is a pity,' I remarked, 'for I have come a long way with that one object,' and I told him about the paper I had been asked to read, and the trouble I was taking with it.

He became interested. 'Ah!' he said, laying down his pen, and removing his finger from the page before him, 'I can understand that. I also was young once, and fired with ambition. The lines have fallen to me in somewhat lonely places, and for forty years I have held the cure of souls in this place, where truly I have seen but little of the world, though I myself may be not unknown in the paths of literature. Possibly you may have read a pamphlet, written by myself, on the Syrian version of the Three Authentic Epistles of Ignatius?'

'Sir,' I said, 'I am ashamed to confess that I have not time to read even the most celebrated books. My one object in life is my art. *Ars longa, vita brevis*, you know.'

'You are right, my son,' said the old man, evidently disappointed, but looking at me kindly. 'There are diversities of gifts, and if the Lord has entrusted you with a talent, look to it. Lay it not up in a napkin.'

I said I would do so if he would lend me the keys of the crypt. He seemed startled by my recurrence to the subject and looked undecided.

'Why not?' he murmured to himself. 'The youth appears a good youth. And superstition! What is it but distrust in God!'

He got up slowly, and taking a large bunch of keys out of his pocket opened with one of them an oak cupboard in the corner of the room.

'They should be here,' he muttered, peering in; 'but the dust of many years deceives the eye. See, my son, if among these parchments there be two keys; one of iron and very large, and the other steel, and of a long and thin appearance.'

I went eagerly to help him, and presently found in a back drawer two keys tied together, which he recognised at once.

'Those are they,' he said. 'The long one opens the first door at the bottom of the steps which go down against the outside wall of the church hard by the sword graven in the wall. The second opens (but it is hard of opening and of shutting) the iron door within the passage leading to the crypt itself. My son, is it necessary to your treatise that you should enter this crypt?'

I replied that it was absolutely necessary.

'Then take them,' he said; 'and in the evening you will bring them to me again.'

I said I might want to go several days running, and asked if he would not allow me to keep them till I had finished my work, but on that point he was firm.

'Likewise,' he added, 'be careful that you lock the first door at the foot of the steps before you unlock the second, and lock the second also while you are within. Furthermore, when you come out lock the iron inner door as well as the wooden one.'

I promised I would do so, and, after thanking him, hurried away, delighted at my success in obtaining the keys. Finding Brian and my sketching materials waiting for me in the porch, I eluded the vigilance of my escort of children by taking the narrow private path between the parsonage and the church which was close at hand, standing in a quadrangle of ancient yews.

The church itself was interesting, and I noticed that it must have arisen out of the ruins of a previous edifice, judging from the number of fragments of stone caps and arches, bearing traces of very early carving, now built into the walls. There were incised crosses, too, in some places, and one especially caught my attention, being flanked by a large sword. It was in trying to get a nearer look at this that I stumbled, and looking down saw at my feet a flight of narrow stone steps, green with moss and mildew. Evidently this was the entrance to the crypt. I at once descended the steps, taking care of my footing, for they were damp and slippery in the extreme. Brian accompanied me, as nothing would induce him to remain behind. By the time I had reached the bottom of the stairs I found myself almost in darkness, and I had to strike a light before I could find the keyhole and the proper key to fit into it. The door, which was of wood, opened inwards fairly easily, although an accumulation of mould and rubbish on the ground outside showed it had not been used for many years. Having got through it, which was not altogether an easy matter, as nothing would induce it to open more than about eighteen inches, I carefully locked it behind me, although I should have preferred to leave it open, as there is to some minds an unpleasant feeling in being locked in anywhere, in case of a sudden exit seeming advisable.

I kept my candle alight with some difficulty, and after groping my way down a low and of course exceedingly dank passage, came to another door. I noticed that it was of iron, and had a long bolt, which, however, was broken. Without delay I fitted the second key into the lock, and pushing the door open after considerable difficulty, I felt the cold breath of the crypt upon my face. I must own I experienced a momentary regret at locking the second door again as soon as I was well inside, but I felt it my duty to do so. Then, leaving the key in the lock, I seized my candle and looked round. I was standing in a low vaulted chamber with a groined roof, cut out of the solid rock. It was difficult to see where the crypt ended, as further light thrown on any point only showed other rough archways or openings, cut in the rock, which had probably served at one time for family vaults. A peculiarity of the Wet Waste crypt, which I had not noticed in other places of that description, was the beautiful arrangement of skulls and bones which were packed about four feet high on either side. The skulls were symmetrically built up to within a few inches of the top of the low archways on my left, and the shin bones were arranged in the same manner on my right. *But the fresco!* I looked round for it in vain. Perceiving at the further end of the crypt a very low and very massive archway, the entrance to which was not filled up with bones, I passed under it, and found myself in a second much smaller chamber. Holding my candle above my head, the first object its light fell upon was – the fresco, and at a glance I saw that it was unique. Setting down some of my things with a trembling hand on a rough stone shelf hard by, which had evidently been a credence table, I examined the work more closely. It was a reredos over what had probably been the altar at the time the priests were proscribed. The fresco belonged to the earliest part of the fifteenth century, and was so perfectly preserved that I could almost trace the limits of each day's work in the plaster, as the artist had dashed it on, and smoothed it out with his trowel. The subject was the Ascension, gloriously treated. I can hardly describe my elation as I stood and looked at it, and reflected that this magnificent specimen of English fresco painting would be made known to the world by myself. Recollecting myself at last, I opened my sketching bag, and, lighting all the candles I had brought with me, set to work.

Brian walked about near me, and though I was not otherwise than glad of his company in my rather lonely position, I wished several times I had left him behind. He seemed restless, and even the sight of so many bones appeared to exercise no soothing effect upon him. At last, however, after repeated commands, he lay down watchful but motionless on the stone floor.

I must have worked for several hours, and I was pausing to rest my eyes and hands when I noticed for the first time the intense stillness that seemed to surround me. No sound from the outer world reached me. No sound from *me* could reach the outer world. The church clock which had clanged out so loud and ponderously as I went down the steps, had not since sent the faintest whisper of its iron tongue down to me below. All was silent as the grave. This *was* the grave. Those who had come here had indeed gone down into silence. I repeated the words to myself, or rather they repeated themselves to me.

Gone down into silence.

I was awakened from my reverie by a faint sound. I sat still and listened. Bats occasionally frequent vaults and underground places.

The sound continued, a faint, stealthy, rather unpleasant sound. I do not know what kinds of sounds bats make, whether pleasant or otherwise. Suddenly there was a noise as of something falling, a momentary pause – and then – an almost imperceptible but distinct jangle as of a key.

I had left the key in the lock after I had turned it, and I now regretted having done so. I got up, took one of the candles, and went back into the larger crypt, for though I hope I am not made nervous by hearing a noise for which I cannot instantly account, still, on occasions of this kind, I must honestly say I would rather they did not occur. As I came towards the iron door, there was another distinct (I had almost said hurried) sound. The impression on my mind was one of great haste. When I reached the door, and held the candle near the lock to take out the key, I perceived that the other one, which hung by a short string to its fellow, was vibrating slightly. I should have preferred not to find it vibrating, as there seemed no occasion for such a course; but I put them both into my pocket, and turned to go back to my work. As I turned I saw on the ground what had occasioned the louder noise I had heard, namely, a skull which had evidently just slipped from its place on the top of one of the walls of bones, and had rolled almost to my feet. There, disclosing a few more inches of the top of an archway behind, was the place from which it had been dislodged. I stooped to pick it up, but fearing to displace any more skulls by meddling with the pile, and not liking to gather up its scattered teeth, I let it lie, and went back to my work, in which I was soon so completely absorbed that I was only roused at last by my candles beginning to burn low and go out one after another.

Then, with a sigh of regret, for I had not nearly finished, I turned to go. Poor Brian, who had never quite reconciled himself to the place, was almost beside himself with delight. As I opened the iron door he pushed past me, and a moment later I heard him whining and scratching, and I had almost added beating, against the wooden one. I locked the iron door, and hurried down the passage as quickly as I could, and almost before I had got the other one ajar there seemed to be a rush past me into the open air, and Brian was bounding up the steps and out of sight. As I stopped to take out the key I felt quite deserted and left behind. When I came out once more into the sunlight there was a vague sensation all about me in the air of exultant freedom.

It was quite late in the afternoon, and, after I had sauntered back to the parsonage to give up the keys, I persuaded the people of the public house to let me join in the family meal which was spread out in the kitchen. The inhabitants of Wet Waste were primitive people, with the frank, unabashed manner that flourishes still in lonely places, especially in the wilds of Yorkshire; but I had no idea that, in these days of penny posts and cheap newspapers, such entire ignorance of the outer world could have existed in any corner, however remote, of Great Britain.

When I took one of the neighbour's children on my knee, a pretty little girl with the palest aureole of flaxen hair I had ever seen, and began to draw pictures for her of the birds and beasts of other countries, I was instantly surrounded by a crowd of children, and even grown-up people, whilst others came to their doorways and looked on from a distance, calling to each other in the strident unknown tongue which I have since discovered goes by the name of 'Broad Yorkshire.'

The following morning as I came out of my room, I perceived that something was amiss in the village. A buzz of voices reached me as I passed the bar, and in the next house I could hear through the open window a high-pitched wail of lamentation.

The woman who brought me in my breakfast was in tears, and in answer to my questions told me that the neighbour's child, the little girl whom I had taken on my knee the evening before, and plaything of the village, had died in the night.

I felt sorry for the general grief that the little thing's death seemed to cause, and the uncontrolled wailing of the poor mother took my appetite away.

I hurried off early to my work, calling on my way for the keys, and with Brian for my companion descended once more into the crypt, and drew and measured with an absorption that gave me no time that day to listen for sounds real or fancied. Brian, too, on this occasion seemed quite content, and slept peacefully beside me on the stone floor. When I had worked as long as I could, I put away my books with regret that even then I had not quite finished as I had hoped to do. It would be necessary to come again for a short time on the morrow. When I returned the keys late that afternoon, the old clergyman met me at the door, and asked me to come in and have tea with him.

'And has the work prospered?' he asked as we sat down in the long, low room, into which I had just been ushered, and where he seemed to live entirely.

I told him it had, and showed it to him.

'You have seen the original of course?' I said.

'Once,' he replied, gazing fixedly at it. He evidently did not care to be communicative, so I turned the conversation to the age of the church.

'All here is old,' he said. 'When I was young, forty years ago, and came here because I had no means of mine own, and was much moved to marry at that time, I felt oppressed that all was so old; and that this place was so far removed from the world, for which I had at times longings grievous to be borne; but I had chosen my lot, and with it I was forced to be content. My son, marry not in youth, for love, which truly in that season is a mighty power, turns away the heart from study, and young children break the back of ambition. Neither marry in middle life when the talk of a woman is become a weariness, so, you will not be burdened with a wife in your old age.'

I asked if the neighbouring villages were as antiquated as Wet Waste.

'Yes, all about here is old,' he repeated. 'The paved road leading to Dyke Fens is an ancient park road, made even in the time of the Romans. Dyke Fens which is very near here, a matter but of four or five miles, is likewise old, and forgotten by the world. The Reformation never reached it. It stopped here. And at Dyke Fens they still have a priest and a bell, and bow down before the saints. It is a damnable heresy, and weekly I expound it as such to the people, showing them true doctrine; and I have heard that this same priest has so far yielded himself to the Evil One that he has preached against me as withholding Gospel truths from my flock; but I take no heed of it, neither of his pamphlet touching the Clementine Homilies, in which he vainly contradicts that which I have plainly set forth and proven beyond doubt, concerning the word *Asaph*.'

The old man was fairly off on his favourite subject, and it was some time before I could get away. As it was he followed me to the door, and I only escaped because the old clerk hobbled up at that moment, and claimed his attention.

The following morning I went for the keys the third and last time. I had decided to leave early the next day. I was tired of Wet Waste, and a certain gloom seemed to my fancy to be gathering over the place. There was a sensation of trouble in the air, as if, although the day was bright and clear, a storm were coming.

This morning to my astonishment the keys were refused to me when I asked for them. I did not however take the refusal as final, and after a little delay I was shown into the room where as usual the clergyman was sitting, or rather on this occasion was walking up and down.

'My son,' he said with vehemence. 'I know wherefore you have come, but it is of no avail. I cannot lend the keys again.'

I replied that, on the contrary, I hoped he would give them to me at once.

'It is impossible,' he repeated. 'I did wrong, exceeding wrong. I will never part with them again.'

'Why not?'

He hesitated, and then said, slowly —

'The old clerk, Abraham Kelly, died last night.' He paused and then went on: 'The doctor has just been here to tell me of that which is a mystery to him. I do not wish the people of the place to know it, and only to me he has mentioned it, but he has discovered plainly on the throat of the old man, and also, but more faintly on the child's, marks as of strangulation. None but he has observed it, and he is at a loss how to account for it. I, alas! can account for it but in one way, but in one way.'

I did not see what all this had to do with the crypt, but to humour the old man, I asked what that way was.

'It is a long story, and haply to a stranger, it may appear but foolishness, but I will even tell it, for I perceive that unless I furnish a reason for withholding the keys you will not cease to entreat me for them.

'I told you at first when you inquired of me concerning the crypt, that it had been closed these thirty years, and so it was. Thirty years ago a certain Roger Despard, even the lord of the manor of Wet Waste and Dyke Fens, the last of his family, which is now, thank the Lord, extinct, died. He was an evil man of a vile life, neither fearing God nor regarding man, and the Lord appeared to have given him over to the tormentors even in this world, for he suffered many things of his vices, more especially from drunkenness, in which seasons, and they were many, he was as one possessed by seven devils, being an abomination to his household, and a root of bitterness to all, both high and low.

'And at last the cup of his iniquity being full to the brim he came to die, and I went to exhort him on his death-bed, for I heard that terror had come upon him, and that evil imaginations encompassed him so thick on every side, that few of them that were with him could abide his presence. But when I saw him I perceived that there was no place of repentance left for him, and he scoffed at me and my superstition, even as he lay dying, and swore there was no God and no angel, and all were damned even as he was. And the next day towards evening the pains of death came upon him, and he raved the more exceedingly, inasmuch as he said he was being strangled by the evil one. Now on his table was his hunting knife, and with his last strength he crept and laid hold upon it, no man withstanding him, and swore a great oath that if he went down to burn in hell, he would leave one of his hands behind on earth, and that it would never rest until it had drawn blood from the throat of another, and strangled him, even as he himself was being strangled. And he cut off his own right hand at the wrist, and no man dared go near him to stop him, and the blood went through the floor, even down to the ceiling of the room below, and thereupon he died.

'And they called me in the night, and told me of his oath, and I counselled that no man should speak of it, and I took the dead hand which none had ventured to touch, and I laid it beside him in his coffin; for I thought it better he should take it with him, so that he might have it, if haply some day after much tribulation he should perchance be moved to stretch forth his hands towards God. But the story got spread about, and the people were affrighted, so when he came to be buried in the place of his fathers, he being the last of his family, and the crypt likewise full, I had it closed, and kept the keys myself, and suffered no man to enter therein any more; for truly he was a man of an evil life, and the devil is not yet wholly overcome, not cast chained into the lake of fire. So in time the story died out, for in thirty years much is forgotten. And when you came and asked me for the keys I was at the first minded to withhold them, but I thought it was a vain superstition, and I perceived that you do but ask a second time for what is first refused; so I let you have them, seeing it was not an idle curiosity, but a desire to improve the talent committed to you, that led you to require them.'

The old man stopped, and I remained silent, wondering what would be the best way to get them just once more.

'Surely, sir,' I said at last, 'one so cultivated and deeply read as yourself cannot be biassed by an idle superstition.'

'I trust not,' he replied, 'and yet – it is a strange thing that since the crypt was opened two people have died, and the mark is plain upon the throat of the old man, and visible on the young child. No blood was drawn, but the second time the grip was stronger than the first. The third time, perchance – '

'Superstition such as that,' I said with authority, 'is an entire want of faith in God. You once said so yourself.'

I took a high moral tone which is often efficacious with conscientious humble-minded people.

He agreed, and accused himself of not having faith as a grain of mustard seed, but even when I had got him as far as that, I had a severe struggle for the keys. It was only when I finally explained to him that if any malign influence *had* been let loose the first day, at any rate, it was out now for good or evil, and no further going or coming of mine could make any different, that I finally gained my point. I was young, and he was old; and, being somewhat shaken by what had occurred, he gave in at last, and I wrested the keys from him.

I will not deny that I went down the steps that day with a vague, undefinable repugnance, which was only accentuated by the closing of the two doors behind me. I remembered then, for the first time, the faint jangling of the key, and other sounds which I had noticed the first day, and how one of the skulls had fallen. I went to the place where it still lay. I have already said these walls of skulls were built up so high as to be within a few inches of the top of the low archways that led into more distant portions of the vault. The displacement of the skull in question had left a small hole, just large enough for me to put my hand through. I noticed for the first time, over the archway above it, a carved coat of arms, and the name, now almost obliterated, of Despard. This, no doubt, was the Despard vault. I could not resist moving a few more skulls and looking in, holding my candle as near the aperture as I could. The vault was full. Piled high, one upon another, were old coffins, and remnants of coffins, and strewn bones. I think when I come to die, I would rather go home to the earth, than try to keep up appearances in a vault. The coffin nearest the archway alone was intact, save for a large crack across the lid. I could not get a ray from my candle to fall on the brass plates, but I felt no doubt this was the coffin of the wicked Sir Roger. I put back the skulls, including the one which had rolled down, and carefully finished my work. I was not there much more than an hour, but I was glad to get away.

If I could have left Wet Waste that day, I should have done so, for I had a totally unreasonable longing to leave the place; but I found that only one train stopped during the day at the station from which I had come, and that it would not be possible to be in time for it that day.

Accordingly I submitted to the inevitable, and wandered about with Brian for the remainder of the afternoon, and until late into the evening, sketching and smoking. The day was oppressively hot, and even after the sun had set across the burnt stretches of the wolds, it seemed to grow very little cooler. Not a breath stirred. In the evening, when I was tired of loitering in the lanes, I went up to my own room, and, after contemplating afresh my finished study of the fresco, I suddenly set to work to write the part of my paper bearing upon it. As a rule I write with difficulty, but that evening words came to me with winged speed, and with them a hovering impression that I must make haste, that I was much pressed for time. I wrote and wrote, until my candles guttered out, and left me trying to finish by the moonlight, which, until I endeavoured to write by it, seemed as clear as day.

I had to put away my MS., and feeling it was too early to go to bed, for the church clock was just counting out ten, I sat down by the open window and leaned out to try and catch a breath of air. It was a lovely night, and as I looked out my nervous haste and hurry of mind died down. The moon was sailing clear and tranquil over a fleckless sky; was touching the rugged village, the mist-dimmed trees, and ghostly wolds beyond, with a glory of her own.

The little stream below my window was not all that a stream should be. In the day time, fleets of unseaworthy refuse constantly hurried down it; it owned to dead kittens in the shallow places; but to-night it looked innocent and clear, under the loving eye of the moon that saw it, not as it was, but as it ought to be.

I sat a long time leaning against the window-sill. The heat was still intense. I am not, as a rule, easily elated or ready cast down, but as I sat that night in the lonely village on the moors, with Brian's head against my knee, how or why I know not, a great depression gradually came upon me.

My mind went back to the crypt and the countless dead who had been laid there. The sight of the goal to which all human life, and strength, and beauty, travel in the end, had not affected me at the time, but now, the very air about me seemed heavy with death.

What was the good, I asked myself, of working and toiling, and grinding down my heart and youth in the mill of long and strenuous effort; seeing that in the grave folly and talent, idleness and labour lie together, and are alike forgotten. Labour seemed to stretch before me till my heart ached to think of it, to stretch before me even to the end of life, and then came, as the recompense of my labour – the grave. Even if I succeeded, if after wearing my life threadbare with toil, I succeeded, what remained to me in the end? The grave. A little sooner, while the hands and eyes were still strong to labour, or a little later when all power and vision had been taken from them; sooner or later only – *the grave*.

I roused myself at last, when the moon came to look in upon me where I sat, and, leaving the window open, I pulled myself together, and went to bed.

I fell asleep almost immediately, but I do not fancy I could have been asleep very long when I was wakened by Brian. He was growling in a low muffled tone, as he sometimes did in his sleep, when his nose was buried in his rug. I called out to him to shut up, and as he did not do so, turned in bed to find my match box or something to throw at him. The moonlight was still in the room, and as I looked at him, I saw him raise his head and evidently wake up. I admonished him, and was just on the point of falling asleep when he began to growl again in a low savage manner that waked me most effectually. Presently he shook himself and got up, and began prowling about the room. I sat up in bed and called to him, but he paid no attention. Suddenly I saw him stop short in the moonlight; he showed his teeth, and crouched down, his eyes following something in the air. I looked at him in horror. Was he going mad? His eyes were glaring and his head moved slightly as if he were following the rapid movements of an enemy. Then with a furious snarl, he suddenly sprang from the ground, and rushed in great leaps across the room towards me, dashing himself against the furniture, his eyes rolling, snatching and tearing wildly in the air with his teeth. I saw he had gone mad. I leaped out of bed, and rushing at him caught him by the throat. The moon had gone behind a cloud, but in the darkness I felt him turn upon me, felt him rise up, and his teeth close in my throat. I was being strangled. With all the strength of despair I kept my grip of his neck, and dragging him across the room tried to crush in his head against the iron rail of my bedstead. It was my only chance. I felt the blood running down my neck. I was suffocating. After one moment of frightful struggle I beat his head against the bar, and heard his skull give way. I felt him give one strong shudder, a groan, and then I fainted away.

When I came to myself I was lying on the floor, surrounded by the people of the house, my reddened hands still clutching Brian's throat. Some one was holding a candle towards me, and the draught from the window made it flare and waver. I looked at Brian. He was stone dead. The blood from his great battered head was trickling slowly over my hands. His great jaw was fixed in something that – in the uncertain light – I could not see.

They turned the light a little.

'Oh God!' I shrieked. 'There! Look! look!'

'He's off his head,' said some one, and I fainted again.

I was ill for about a fortnight without regaining consciousness, a waste of time of which even now I cannot think without poignant regret. When I did recover consciousness I found I was being carefully nursed by the old clergyman and the people of the house. I have often heard the unkindness of the world in general inveighed against, but for my part I can honestly say that I have received many more kindnesses than I have time to repay. Country people especially are remarkably attentive to strangers in illness.

I could not rest until I had seen the doctor who attended me, and had received his assurance that I should be equal to reading my paper on the appointed day. This pressing anxiety removed, I told him of what I had seen before I fainted the second time. He listened attentively, and then assured me, in a manner than was intended to be soothing, that I was suffering from an hallucination, due, no doubt, to the shock of my dog's sudden madness.

'Did you see the dog after it was dead?' I asked.

He said he did. The whole jaw was covered with blood and foam; the teeth certainly seemed convulsively fixed, but the case being evidently one of extraordinary virulent hydrophobia, owing to the intense heat, he had had the body buried immediately.

My companion stopped speaking as we reached our lodgings, and went upstairs. Then, lighting a candle, he slowly turned down his collar.

'You see I have the marks still,' he said; 'but I have no fear of dying of hydrophobia. I am told such peculiar scars could not have been made by the teeth of a dog. If you look closely you see the pressure of the five fingers. That is the reason why I wear high collars.'

A True Story of a Vampire

COUNT ERIC STENBOCK

This curious story by an even more curious author was published just three years before Dracula *appeared and at the time when Bram Stoker was busy writing his tale of the vampire count. While Bram may not have read the story of a 'serpent vampire' – and as it only appeared in a limited edition of the author's short fictions entitled* Studies of Death *which was issued by David Nutt in December 1894, the chances are slight – Count Stenbock himself was at the time one of the most talked-about and controversial figures in London and Stoker would undoubtedly have known about him. Stenbock has been described as a person whose life was more fantasy than reality; a man with a waxen complexion and lank, flowing hair, who dressed almost exclusively in evening dress with a flowing cloak. He was said to receive guests in his London flat while sitting in a coffin (shades of Bela Lugosi in his declining years!) and had an obsession with weird creatures – keeping a toad as a 'familiar' which sat on his shoulder as he ate and an enormous snake which coiled around his feet. There were even dark rumours that he practised black magic.*

Eric Magnus Andreas Harry Stenbock (1859–95) was born in Estonia of an ancient but decaying noble family. He was sent to Oxford to study, but was expelled for the kind of exhibitionism and disgraceful behaviour with other boys which became the pattern for his life when he later settled in London thanks to a lavish grant from his family. Almost at once he cultivated the strangest of lifestyles, enjoying anything to do with death and decay. On one occasion he exclaimed to a friend: 'Death is a dirty doorway to a wonderful region where there will be no London fogs and none of the evils that trouble the poets and artists here.' Stenbock rarely went out by day and lit his home only with black candles. He could indeed have been an almost perfect model for Dracula, though he is best remembered in literary histories for his decadent eccentricities which were out of the ordinary in even the perverse and fin-de-siècle London of the 1890s. The count was a drug user and heavy drinker which contributed to his early end, though not before he had founded the 'Idiots Club' which he claimed had branches in London and Estonia where some of the members, he said, were 'more dead than alive'. His own death from cirrhosis of the liver coincided with the first day of Oscar Wilde's trial which may well explain why his notoriety was soon overshadowed. But even then Stenbock's eccentric legend was not quite finished: because before his funeral in Brighton his heart was extracted from his body and sent back to Estonia to be preserved in a jar of fluid among other family remains! The count's undoubted interest in vampirism is evident in several of his now very rare collections of poetry – notably 'The Lunatic Lover' in which a vampire arrives in a dream – as well as in stories like 'A Dream' and the item reprinted here. There are probably very few stranger vampire tales – and certainly not one by a writer who, if not a model for a vampire, might almost have been one himself!

*   *   *

Vampire stories are generally located in Styria; mine is also. Styria is by no means the romantic kind of place described by those who have certainly never been there. It is a flat, uninteresting country, only celebrated for its turkeys, its capons, and the stupidity of its inhabitants. Vampires generally arrive at night, in carriages drawn by two black horses.

Our Vampire arrived by the commonplace means of the railway train, and in the afternoon. You must think I am joking, or perhaps that by the word 'Vampire' I mean a financial vampire. No, I am quite serious. The Vampire of whom I am speaking, who laid waste to our hearth and home, was a *real* vampire.

Vampires are generally described as dark, sinister-looking, and singularly handsome. Our Vampire was, on the contrary, rather fair, and certainly was not at first sight sinister-looking, and though decidedly attractive in appearance, not what one would call singularly handsome.

Yes, he desolated our home, killed my brother – the one object of my adoration – also my dear father. Yet, at the same time, I must say that I myself came under the spell of his fascination, and, in spite of all, have no ill-will towards him now.

Doubtless you have read in the papers *passim* of 'the Baroness and her beasts'. It is to tell how I came to spend most of my useless wealth on an asylum for stray animals that I am writing this.

I am old now; what happened then was when I was a little girl of about thirteen. I will begin by describing our household. We were Poles; our name was Wronski: we lived in Styria, where we had a castle. Our household was very limited. It consisted, with the exclusion of domestics, of only my father, our governess – a worthy Belgian named Mademoiselle Vonnaert – my brother, and myself. Let me begin with my father: he was old and both my brother and I were children of his old age. Of my mother I remember nothing: she died in giving birth to my brother, who was only one year, or not as much, younger than myself. Our father was studious, continually occupied in reading books, chiefly on recondite subjects and in all kinds of unknown languages. He had a long white beard, and wore habitually a black velvet skull-cap.

How kind he was to us! It was more than I could tell. Still it was not I who was the favourite. His whole heart went out to Gabriel – Gabryel as we spelt it in Polish. He was always called by the Russian abbreviation – Gavril – I mean, of course, my brother, who had a resemblance to the only portrait of my mother, a slight chalk sketch which hung in my father's study. But I was by no means jealous: my brother was and has been the only love of my life. It is for his sake that I am now keeping in Westbourne Park a home for stray cats and dogs.

I was at that time, as I said before, a little girl; my name was Carmela. My long tangled hair was always all over the place, and never would be combed straight. I was not pretty – at least, looking at a photograph of me at that time, I do not think I could describe myself as such. Yet at the same time, when I look at the photograph, I think my expression may have been pleasing to some people: irregular features, large mouth, and large wild eyes.

I was by way of being naughty – not so naughty as Gabriel in the opinion of Mlle Vonnaert. Mlle Vonnaert, I may intercalate, was a wholly excellent person, middle-aged, who really did speak good French, although she was a Belgian, and could also make herself understood in German, which, as you may or may not know, is the current language of Styria.

I find it difficult to describe my brother Gabriel; there was something about him strange and superhuman, or perhaps I should rather say praeterhuman, something between the animal and the divine. Perhaps the Greek idea of the Faun might illustrate what I mean; but that will not do either. He had large, wild, gazelle-like eyes: his hair, like mine, was in a perpetual tangle — that point he had in common with me, and indeed, as I afterwards heard, our mother having been of gipsy race, it will account for much of the innate wildness there was in our natures. I was wild enough, but Gabriel was much wilder. Nothing would induce him to put on shoes and stockings, except on Sundays — when he also allowed his hair to be combed, but only by me. How shall I describe the grace of that lovely mouth, shaped verily 'en arc d'amour'. I always think of the text in the Psalm, 'Grace is shed forth on thy lips, therefore has God blessed thee eternally' — lips that seemed to exhale the very breath of life. Then that beautiful, lithe, living, elastic form!

He could run faster than any deer: spring like a squirrel to the topmost branch of a tree: he might have stood for the sign and symbol of vitality itself. But seldom could he be induced by Mlle Vonnaert to learn lessons; but when he did so, he learnt with extraordinary quickness. He would play upon every conceivable instrument, holding a violin here, there, and everywhere except the right place: manufacturing instruments for himself out of reeds — even sticks. Mlle Vonnaert made futile efforts to induce him to learn to play the piano. I suppose he was what was called spoilt, though merely in the superficial sense of the word. Our father allowed him to indulge in every caprice.

One of his peculiarities, when quite a little child, was horror at the sight of meat. Nothing on earth would induce him to taste it. Another thing which was particularly remarkable about him was his extraordinary power over animals. Everything seemed to come tame to his hand. Birds would sit on his shoulder. Then sometimes Mlle Vonnaert and I would lose him in the woods — he would suddenly dart away. Then we would find him singing softly or whistling to himself, with all manner of woodland creatures around him — hedgehogs, little foxes, wild rabbits, marmots, squirrels, and such like. He would frequently bring these things home with him and insist on keeping them. This strange menagerie was the terror of poor Mlle Vonnaert's heart. He chose to live in a little room at the top of a turret; but which, instead of going upstairs, he chose to reach by means of a very tall chestnut-tree, through the window. But in contradiction of all this, it was his custom to serve every Sunday Mass in the parish church, with hair nicely combed and with white surplice and red cassock. He looked as demure and tamed as possible. Then came the element of the divine. What an expression of ecstasy there was in those glorious eyes!

Thus far I have not been speaking about the Vampire. However, let me begin with my narrative at last. One day my father had to go to the neighbouring town – as he frequently had. This time he returned accompanied by a guest. The gentleman, he said, had missed his train, through the late arrival of another at our station, which was a junction, and he would therefore, as trains were not frequent in our parts, have had to wait there all night. He had joined in conversation with my father in the too-late-arriving train from the town: and had consequently accepted my father's invitation to stay the night at our house. But of course, you know, in those out-of-the-way parts we are almost partriarchal in our hospitality.

He was announced under the name of Count Vardalek – the name being Hungarian. But he spoke German well enough: not with the monotonous accentuation of Hungarians, but rather, if anything, with a slight Slavonic intonation. His voice was peculiarly soft and insinuating. We soon afterwards found out he could talk Polish, and Mlle Vonnaert vouched for his good French. Indeed he seemed to know all languages. But let me give my first impressions. He was rather tall with fair wavy hair, rather long, which accentuated a certain effeminacy about his smooth face. His figure had something – I cannot say what – serpentine about it. The features were refined; and he had long, slender, subtle, magnetic-looking hands, a somewhat long sinuous nose, a graceful mouth, and an attractive smile, which belied the intense sadness of the expression of the eyes. When he arrived his eyes were half closed – indeed they were habitually so – so that I could not decide their colour. He looked worn and wearied. I could not possibly guess his age.

Suddenly Gabriel burst into the room: a yellow butterfly was clinging to his hair. He was carrying in his arms a little squirrel. Of course he was bare-legged as usual. The stranger looked up at his approach; then I noticed his eyes. They were green: they seemed to dilate and grow larger. Gabriel stood stock-still, with a startled look, like that of a bird fascinated by a serpent. But nevertheless he held out his hand to the newcomer. Vardalek, taking his hand – I don't know why I noticed this trivial thing – pressed the pulse with his forefinger. Suddenly Gabriel darted from the room and rushed upstairs, going to his turret-room this time by the staircase instead of the tree. I was in terror what the Count might think of him. Great was my relief when he came down in his velvet Sunday suit, and shoes and stockings. I combed his hair, and set him generally right.

When the stranger came down to dinner his appearance had somewhat altered; he looked much younger. There was an elasticity of the skin, combined with a delicate complexion, rarely to be found in a man. Before, he had struck me as being very pale.

Well, at dinner we were all charmed with him, especially my father. He seemed to be thoroughly acquainted with all my father's particular hobbies. Once, when my father was relating some of his military experiences, he said something about a drummer-boy who was wounded in battle. His eyes opened completely again and dilated: this time with a particularly disagreeable expression, dull and dead, yet at the same time animated by some horrible excitement. But this was only momentary.

The chief subject of his conversation with my father was about certain curious mystical books which my father had just lately picked up, and which he could not make out, but Vardalek seemed completely to understand. At dessert-time my father asked him if he were in a great hurry to reach his destination: if not, would he not stay with us a little while: though our place was out of the way, he would find much that would interest him in his library.

He answered, 'I am in no hurry. I have no particular reason for going to that place at all, and if I can be of service to you in deciphering these books, I shall be only too glad.' He added with a smile which was bitter, very very bitter: 'You see I am a cosmopolitan, a wanderer on the face of the earth.'

After dinner my father asked him if he played the piano. He said, 'Yes, I can a little,' and he sat down at the piano. Then he played a Hungarian csardas – wild, rhapsodic, wonderful.

That is the music which makes men mad. He went on in the same strain.

Gabriel stood stock-still by the piano, his eyes dilated and fixed, his form quivering. At last he said very slowly, at one particular motive – for want of a better word you may call it the relâche of a csardas, by which I mean that point where the original quasi-slow movement begins again – 'Yes, I think I could play that.'

Then he quickly fetched his fiddle and self-made xylophone, and did, actually alternating the instruments, render the same very well indeed.

Vardalek looked at him, and said in a very sad voice, 'Poor child! you have the soul of music within you.'

I could not understand why he should seem to commiserate instead of congratulate Gabriel on what certainly showed an extraordinary talent.

Gabriel was shy even as the wild animals who were tame to him. Never before had he taken to a stranger. Indeed, as a rule, if any stranger came to the house by any chance, he would hide himself, and I had to bring him up his food to the turret chamber. You may imagine what was my surprise when I saw him walking about hand in hand with Vardalek the next morning, in the garden, talking livelily with him, and showing his collection of pet animals, which he had gathered from the woods, and for which we had had to fit up a regular zoological gardens. He seemed utterly under the domination of Vardalek. What surprised us was (for otherwise we liked the stranger, especially for being kind to him) that he seemed, though not noticeably at first – except perhaps to me, who noticed everything with regard to him – to be gradually losing his general health and vitality. He did not become pale as yet; but there was a certain languor about his movements which certainly there was by no means before.

My father got more and more devoted to Count Vardalek. He helped him in his studies: and my father would hardly allow him to go away, which he did sometimes – to Trieste, he said: he always came back, bringing us presents of strange Oriental jewellery or textures.

I knew all kinds of people came to Trieste, Orientals included. Still, there was a strangeness and magnificence about these things which I was sure even then could not possibly have come from such a place as Trieste, memorable to me chiefly for its necktie shops.

When Vardalek was away, Gabriel was continually asking for him and talking about him. Then at the same time he seemed to regain his old vitality and spirits. Vardalek always returned looking much older, wan, and weary. Gabriel would rush to meet him, and kiss him on the mouth. Then he gave a slight shiver: and after a while began to look quite young again.

Things continued like this for some time. My father would not hear of Vardalek's going away permanently. He came to be an inmate of our house. I indeed, and Mlle Vonnaert also, could not help noticing what a difference there was altogether about Gabriel. But my father seemed totally blind to it.

One night I had gone downstairs to fetch something which I had left in the drawing-room. As I was going up again I passed Vardalek's room. He was playing on a piano, which had been specially put there for him, one of Chopin's nocturnes, very beautifully: I stopped, leaning on the banisters to listen.

Something white appeared on the dark staircase. We believed in ghosts in our part. I was transfixed with terror, and clung to the banisters. What was my astonishment to see Gabriel walking slowly down the staircase, his eyes fixed as though in a trance! This terrified me even more than a ghost would. Could I believe my senses? Could that be Gabriel?

I simply could not move. Gabriel, clad in his long white night-shirt, came downstairs and opened the door. He left it open. Vardalek still continued playing, but talked as he played.

He said – this time speaking in Polish – *Nie umiem wyrazic jak ciechi kocham* – 'My darling, I fain would spare thee; but thy life is my life, and I must live, I who would rather die. Will God not have any mercy on me? Oh! Oh! life; oh, the torture of life!' Here he struck one agonized and strange chord, then continued playing softly, 'O Gabriel, my beloved! my life, yes *life* – oh, why life? I am sure this is but a little that I demand of thee. Surely thy superabundance of life can spare a little to one who is already dead. No, stay,' he said now almost harshly, 'what must be, must be!'

Gabriel stood there quite still, with the same fixed vacant expression, in the room. He was evidently walking in his sleep. Vardalek played on: then said, 'Ah!' with a sign of terrible agony. Then very gently, 'Go now, Gabriel; it is enough.' And Gabriel went out of the room and ascended the staircase at the same slow pace, with the same unconscious stare. Vardalek struck the piano, and although he did not play loudly, it seemed as though the strings would break. You never heard music so strange and so heart-rending!

I only know I was found by Mlle Vonnaert in the morning, in an unconscious state, at the foot of the stairs. Was it a dream after all? I am sure now that it was not. I thought then it might be, and said nothing to anyone about it. Indeed, what could I say?

Well, to let me cut a long story short, Gabriel, who had never known a moment's sickness in his life, grew ill: and we had to send to Gratz for a doctor, who could give no explanation of Gabriel's strange illness. Gradual wasting away, he said: absolutely no organic complaint. What could this mean?

My father at last became conscious of the fact that Gabriel was ill. His anxiety was fearful. The last trace of grey faded from his hair, and it became quite white. We sent to Vienna for doctors. But all with the same result.

Gabriel was generally unconscious, and when conscious, only seemed to recognize Vardalek, who sat continually by his bedside, nursing him with the utmost tenderness.

One day I was alone in the room: and Vardalek cried suddenly, almost fiercely, 'Send for a priest at once, at once,' he repeated. 'It is now almost too late!'

Gabriel stretched out his arms spasmodically, and put them round Vardalek's neck. This was the only movement he had made for some time. Vardalek bent down and kissed him on the lips. I rushed downstairs: and the priest was sent for. When I came back Vardalek was not there. The priest administered extreme unction. I think Gabriel was already dead, although we did not think so at the time.

Vardalek had utterly disappeared; and when we looked for him he was nowhere to be found; nor have I seen or heard of him since.

My father died very soon afterwards: suddenly aged, and bent down with grief. And so the whole of the Wronski property came into my sole possession. And here I am, an old woman, generally laughed at for keeping, in memory of Gabriel, an asylum for stray animals – and – people do not, as a rule, believe in Vampires!

Grettir at Thorhall-Stead

FRANK NORRIS

Frank Norris is widely regarded as one of America's nineteenth-century literary giants, as well as being the country's first important writer of naturalistic novels. Less well known is the fact that he was also the man who introduced to vampire fiction the concept of the 'Animated Dead' – the undead revived by another will – with his tale of 'Grettir of Thorhall-Stead' published in Everybody's Magazine in April 1903. The story is set in the ice-bound, hostile wastes of Iceland and there is something very reminiscent about the horrible, shambling entity that comes out of the snows to the one that appears in the final confrontation between Frankenstein and his creature in the Arctic. The major inspiration for Norris' story is, though, undoubtedly the legend of the terrible battle between Grettir and the fearsome Glamr recorded in the ancient Norse fable of the Grettirsaga. The American expert on horror and fantasy fiction, Sam Moskowitz, who was responsible for tracking down the story in its original printing, believes it to be, 'a neglected masterpiece of the art of the supernatural'.

It comes as something of a surprise to those people who only think of Norris as the man who pioneered the trend towards naturalism in America in the same way that Emile Zola had done in France, to discover that he was at all interested in the supernatural let alone that he made several important contributions to the genre. Yet such are the facts about Benjamin Franklin Norris (1870–1902) – to give him his full name which he understandably shortened. He was a journalist, war correspondent (in South Africa and Cuba), publisher's editor and writer, and from these experiences created such enduring classics as *his novel of alcoholism and murder,* McTeague *(1899) and the story of the opening up of the American West by the railways in* The Octopus *(1901). Yet among his other works can be found a novel such as* Vandover and the Brute *(1894), which Dorothy Scarborough described in her study,* The Supernatural in Modern English Fiction *(1917) as, 'The most revolting story of lycanthropy – a study in soul degeneration akin to the moral decay that George Eliot has shown in the character of Tito Melema, but grosser and utterly lacking in artistic restraint'; and powerful short stories like 'The Ship That Saw A Ghost' and 'The Ghost in the Crosstrees'. All of these together with 'Grettir at Thorhall-Stead' surely entitle Norris to also be counted among the leading writers of horror fiction of his time . . .*

✷   ✷   ✷

I

Glamr

Thornhall the bonder had been to the great Thingvalla, or annual fair of Iceland, to engage a shepherd, and was now returning. It had been a good two-days' journey home, for his shaggy little pony, though sure-footed, was slow. For the better part of three hours on the evening of the second day he had been picking his way cautiously among the great boulders of black basalt that encumbered the path. At length, on the summit of a low hill, he brought the little animal to a standstill and paused a moment, looking off to the northward, a smile of satisfaction spreading over his broad, sober face. For he had just passed the white stone that marked the boundary of his own land. Below him opened the little valley named the Vale of Shadows, and in its midst, overshadowed by a single Norway pine, black, wind-distorted, was the stone farmhouse, the byre, Thorhall's home.

Only an Icelander could have found pleasure in that prospect. It was dreary beyond expression. Save only for the deformed pine, tortured and warped by its unending battle with the wintry gales, no other tree relieved the monotony of the landscape. To the west, mountains barred the horizon – volcanic mountains, gashed, cragged, basaltic, and still blackened with primeval fires. Bare of vegetation they were – sombre, solitary, empty of life. To the eastward, low, rolling sand dunes, sprinkled thinly with gorse, bore down to the sea. They shut off a view of the shore, but farther on the horizon showed itself, a bitter, inhospitable waste of grey water, blotted by fogs and murk and sudden squalls. Though the shore was invisible, it nonetheless asserted itself. With the rushing of the wind was mingled the prolonged, everlasting thunder of the surf, while the taint of salt, of decaying kelp, of fish, of seaweed, of all the pungent aromas of the sea, pervaded the air on every hand.

Black gulls, sharply defined against the grey sky, slanted in long tacking flights hither and thither over sea and land. The raucous bark of the seal hunting mackerel off the shore made itself occasionally heard. Otherwise there was no sign of life. Veils of fine rain, half fog, drove across the scene between ocean and mountain. The wind blew incessantly from off the sea with a steady and uninterrupted murmur.

Thorhall rode on, inclining his head against the gusts and driving wind. Soon he had come to the farmhouse. The servants led the pony to the stables and in the doorway Thorhall found his wife waiting for him. They embraced one another and – for they were pious folk – thanked God for the bonder's safe journey and speedy return. Before the roaring fire of drift that evening Thorhall told his wife of all that had passed at the Thingvalla, of the wrestling, and of the stallion fights.

'And did you find a shepherd to your liking?' asked his wife.

'Yes, a great fellow with white teeth and black hair. Rather surly, I believe, but strong as a troll. He promised to be with me by the beginning of the winter night. His name is Glamr.'

But the summer passed, the sun dipped below the horizon not to reappear for six months, the winter night drew on, snow buried all the landscape, hurricanes sharp as boarspears descended upon the Vale of Shadows; in their beds the dwellers in the byre heard the grind and growl of the great bergs careering onward through the ocean, and many a night the howl of hunger-driven wolves startled Thorhall from his sleep; yet Glamr did not come.

Then at length and of a sudden he appeared; and Thorhall on a certain evening, called hastily by a frightened servant, beheld the great figure of him in the midst of the kitchen floor, his eyebrows frosted yet scowling, his white teeth snapping with cold, while in a great hoarse voice, like the grumble of a bear, he called for meat and drink.

From thenceforward Glamr became a member of Thorhall's household. Yet seldom was he found in the byre. By day he was away with the sheep; by night he slept in the stables. The servants were afraid of him, though he rarely addressed them a word. He was not only feared, but disliked. This aversion was partly explained by Glamr's own peculiar disposition – gloomy, solitary, uncanny, and partly by a fact that came to light within the first month of his coming to the Vale of Shadows.

He was an unbeliever. Never did his broad bulk darken the lich-gate of the kirk; the knolling of the matin and the vesper-bell put him in a season of even deeper gloom than usual. It was noticed that he could not bear to look upon a cross; the priest he abhorred as a pestilence. On holy days he kept far from home, absenting himself upon one pretext or another, withdrawing up into the chasms and gorges of the hills.

So passed the first months of the winter.

Christmas day came, and Christmas night. It was bitter, bitter cold. Snow had fallen since second cockcrow the day before, and as night closed in such a gale as had not been known for years gathered from off the Northern Ocean and whirled shrieking over the Vale of Shadows. All day long Glamr was in the hills with the sheep, and even above the roaring of the wind his bell-toned voice had occasionally been heard as he called and shouted to his charges. At the candle-lighting time he had not returned. The bonder and his family busked themselves to attend the Christmas mass.

Some two hours later they were returning. The wind was going down, but even yet shreds of torn seaweed and scud of foam, swept up by the breath of the gale, drove landward across the valley. The clouds overhead were breaking up, and between their galloping courses one saw the sky, the stars glittering like hoar frost.

The bonder's party drew near the farmhouse, and the servants, going before with lanthorns and pine torches, undid the fastenings of the gate. The wind lapsed suddenly, and in the stillness between two gusts the plunge of the surf made itself heard.

Then all at once Thorhall and his wife stopped and her hand clutched quickly at his wrist.

'Hark! what was that?'

What, indeed? Was it an echo of the storm sounding hollow and faint from some thunder-split crag far off there in those hills toward which all eyes were suddenly turned; was it the cry of a wolf, the clamour of a falcon, or was it the horrid scream of human agony and fury, vibrating to a hoarse and bell-like note that sounded familiar in their ears?

'Glamr! Where is Glamr?' shouted Thorhall, as he entered the byre. But those few servants who had been left in charge of the house reported he had not yet returned.

Night passed and no Glamr; and in the morning the search-party set out toward the hills. Half way up the slope, the sheep – a few of them – were found, scattered, half buried in drifts; then a dog, dead and frozen hard as wood. From it led a track up into the higher mountains, a strange track indeed, not human certainly, yet whether of wolf or bear no one could determine. Some had started to follow when a lad who had looked behind the shoulder of a great rock raised a cry.

There was the body of Glamr. The shepherd was stretched upon his back, dead, rigid. The open eyes were glazed, the face livid; the tongue protruding from the mouth had been bitten through in the last agony. All about the snow was trampled down, and the bare bushes crushed and flattened out. Even the massive boulder near which the body had been found was moved a little from its place. A fearful struggle had been wrought out here, yet upon the body of Glamr was no trace of a wound, no mark of claw or hand. Only among his footprints was mingled that strange track that had been noticed before, and as before it led straight up toward the high part of the mountains.

The young men raised the body of the shepherd and the party moved off toward the kirk and the graveyard. Even though Glamr had shunned the mass, the priest might be prevailed upon to bury him in consecrated ground. But soon the young men had to pause to rest. The body was unexpectedly heavy. Once again, after stopping to breathe, they raised the bier upon their shoulders. Soon another helper was summoned, then another; even Thorhall aided. Ten strong men though they were, they staggered and trembled under that earthly weight. Even in that icy air the perspiration streamed from them. Heavier and still heavier grew the burden; it bore them to the earth. Their knees bowed out from under them, their backs bent. They were obliged to give over.

Later in the day they returned with oxen and a sledge. They repaired to the spot where the body had been left; then stared at each other with paling faces. In the snow at their feet there was the impression made by the great frame of the shepherd. But that was all; the body was gone, nor was there any footprint in the snow other than they themselves had made.

A cairn was erected over the spot, and for many a long day the strange death of the shepherd of the Vale of Shadows was the talk of the countryside. But about a month or so after the death of Glamr a strange sense of uneasiness seemed to invade the household of the byre. By degrees it took possession of first one and then another of the servants and family. No one spoke about this. It was not a thing that could be reduced to words, and for the matter of that, each one believed that he or she was the only one affected. This one thought himself sick; that one believed himself merely nervous. But nevertheless a certain perplexity, a certain disturbance of spirit was in the air.

One evening Thorhall and his wife met accidentally in the passage between the main body of the house and the dairy. They paused and looked at each other for no reason that they could imagine. Thus they stood for several seconds.

'Well,' said Thorhall at length, 'what is it?'

'Ay,' responded his wife, 'Ay, what *is* it?'

'Nothing,' he replied; and she, echoing his words, also answered 'Nothing.'

Then they laughed nervously, yet still looking fixedly into each other's eyes for all that.

'I believe,' said Thorhall the next day, 'that I am to be sick. I cannot tell – I feel no pain – no fever – and yet – '

'And I, too,' declared his wife. 'I am – no, not sick – but distressed. I – I am troubled. I cannot tell what it is. I sometimes think I am *afraid*.'

A week later, on a certain evening just after curfew, the whole family was aroused by a wild shriek as of someone in mortal terror. Thorhall and his wife rushed into the dairy whence the cry came and found one of the maids in a fit upon the floor.

When she recovered she cried out that she had seen at one of the windows the face of Glamr.

II

Grettir

The cold, bright Icelandic summer shone over Thorhall's byre and the Vale of Shadows. There was no cloud in the sky. The void and lonely ocean was indigo blue. But still the prospect was barren, inhospitable. Only a few pallid flowers, hardy bluebells and buttercups, appeared here and there on the sand dunes in the hollows beneath the gorse and bracken. In the lower hills, on the far side of the valley, a tenuous skim of verdure appeared. At times a ptarmigan fluttered in and out of the crevices of these hills searching for blueberries; at times on the surfaces of the waste of dunes a sandpiper uttered its shrill and feeble piping. Always, as ever, the wind blew from off the ocean; always, as ever, the solitary pine by the farmhouse writhed and tossed its gaunt arms; always the gorse and bracken billowed and weltered under it. The sand drifted like snow, encroaching forever upon the cultivated patches around the house. Always the surf – surge on surge – boomed and thundered on the shore, casting up broken kelp and jetsam of wreck. Always, always forever and forever, the monotony remained. The bleakness, the wild, solitary stretches of sea and sky and land turned to the eye their staring emptiness. At long intervals the figure of a servant, a herdsman or at times Thorhall himself moved – a speck of black on the illimitable grey of nature – across the landscape. Ponies, shagged, half wild, their eyes hidden under tangled forelocks, sometimes wandered down upon the shore – their thick hair roughing in the wind – to snuff at the salty seaweeds. The males sometimes fought on the shore, their hoofs thudding on the resounding beach, their screams mingling with the incessant roar of the breakers.

Once even, at Eastertide, during a gale, an empty galley drove ashore, a *snekr* with dragon prow, the broken oars dangling from the thole-pins; and in the waist of her a Viking chieftain, dead, the salt rime rusting on his helmet.

With the advent of summer the mysterious trouble at the farmhouse in the Vale of Shadows disappeared. But the fall equinox drew on, the nights became longer; soon the daylight lasted but a few hours and the sun set before it could be said to have actually risen.

As the winter darkness descended upon the farmhouse the trouble recommenced. During the night the tread of footsteps could be heard making the rounds of the byre. The fumbling of unseen fingers could be distinguished at the locks. The low eaves of the house were seized in the grip of strong hands and wrenched and pulled till the rafters creaked. Outhouses were plucked apart and destroyed, fences up-rooted. After nightfall no one dared venture abroad.

Thorhall had engaged a new shepherd, one Thorgaut, a young man, who professed himself fearless of the haunted sheep-walks and farmyard. He was as popular where Glamr had been disliked. He made love to the housemaids, helped in the butter-making, and rode the children on his back. As to the Vampire, he snapped his fingers and asked only to meet him in the open.

The snow came in August, and was followed by sleet and icy rains and blotting sea-fogs. As the time went on the nightly manifestations increased. Windows were broken in; iron bars shaken and wrenched; sheep and even horses killed.

At length one night a terrible commotion broke out in the stables – the shrill squealing of the horses and the tramping and bellowing of cows, mingled with deep tones of a dreadful voice. Thorhall and his people rushed out. They found that the stable door had been riven and splintered, and they entered the stable itself across the wreckage. The cattle were goring each other, and across the stone partition between the stalls was the body of Thorgaut, the shepherd, his head upon one side, his feet on the other, and his spine snapped in twain.

It chanced that about this time Grettir, well known and well beloved throughout all Iceland, came into that part of the country and one eventide drew rein at Thorhall's farmhouse. This was before Grettir had been hunted from the island by the implacable Thorbjorn, called The Hook, and driven to an asylum and practical captivity upon the rock of Drangey.

He was at this time in the prime of his youth and of a noble appearance. His shoulders were broad, his arms long, his eye a bright blue, and his flaxen hair braided like a Viking's. For cloak he wore a bearskin, while as for weapons he carried nothing but a short sword.

Thorhall, as may be easily understood, welcomed the famous outlaw, but warned him of Glamr.

Grettir, however, was not to be dissuaded from remaining overnight at the byre.

'Vampire or troll, troll or vampire, here bide I till daybreak,' he declared.

Yet despite the bonder's fears the night passed quietly. No sound broke the stillness but the murmur of the distant surf, no footfall sounded around the house, no fingers came groping at the doors.

'I have never slept easier,' announced Grettir in the morning.

'Good; and Heaven be praised,' declared the bonder fervently.

They walked together toward the stables, Thorhall instructing Grettir as to the road he should follow that day. As they drew near, Grettir whistled for his horse, but no answering whicker responded.

'How is this?' he muttered, frowning.

Thorhall and the outlaw hurried into the building, and Grettir, who was in the advance, stopped stock-still in the midst of the floor and swore a great oath.

His horse lay prone in the straw of his stall, his eyeballs protruding, the foam stiff upon his lips. He was dead. Grettir approached and examined him. Between shoulder and withers, the back – as if it had been a wheat-straw – was broken.

'Never mind,' cried the bonder eagerly, 'I have another animal for you, a piebald stallion of Norway stock, just the beast for your weight. Here is your saddle. On with it. Up you go and a speedy journey to you.'

'Never!' exclaimed Grettir, his blue eyes flashing. 'Here will I stay till I meet Glamr face to face. No man did me an injury that he did not rue it. I sleep at the byre another night.'

Dark as a wolf's mouth, silent as his footfalls, the night closed down. There was no moon as yet, but the heavens were bright. Steadily as the blast of some great huntsman's horn, the wind held from the northeast. The sand skimming over the dunes and low hills near the coast was caught up and carried landward and drifted in at crevice and door-chink of the farmhouse. A young seal, lost, no doubt, from the herd that had all day been feeding in the offing – barked and barked incessantly from a rock in the breakers. In the pine tree by the house a huge night-bird, owl or hawk, stirred occasionally with a prolonged note. By and by the weather grew colder, the ground began to freeze and crack. Inside in the main hall of the house, covered by his bearskin cloak, Grettir lay wakeful and watching. He reclined in such a manner – his head pillowed on his arm – that he could see the door. At the other end of the hall the fire of drift was dying down upon the flags. On the other side of the partition, in the next room, lay the bonder, alternately dozing and waking.

The time passed heavily, slowly. From far off toward the shore could be heard the lost seal raising from time to time his hoarse, sobbing bark.

Then at length a dog howled, and an instant after the bonder spoke aloud. He had risen from his bed and stood in the door of his room.

'Hark! Did you not hear something?'

'I hear the barking of the seal,' said Grettir, 'the baying of the hound, the cry of the night-bird, and the break of the surges; nothing else.'

'No. This was a footstep. There. Listen!'

A heavy footfall sounded crunching in the snow from without and close by. It passed around and in front of the house; and the wooden shutter of a window of the hall was plucked at and shaken. Then an outhouse was attacked – a shed where in summertime the calves were fed. Grettir could hear the snap and rasp of splintering boards.

'It has a strong arm,' he muttered.

Once more the tread encircled the house. In a very short time it sounded again in front of the byre.

'It has a long stride,' said Grettir.

The tread ceased. For a long moment there was silence, while the scurrying sand rattled delicately against the house like minute hailstones. Suddenly a corner eave was seized. Something tugged at it, wrenching, and the thatch gave with the long swish of rent linen.

'It has a tall figure,' said Grettir.

For nearly a quarter of an hour these different sounds continued, now distinct, now confused, now distant, now near at hand. Suddenly from overhead there came a jar and a crash, and Grettir felt the dust from the rafters descend upon his face; the Vampire was on the roof. But soon he leaped down and now the footsteps came straight to the door of the hall. The door itself was gripped with colossal strength. In the crescent-shaped openings of the upper panels a hand appeared, black against the faint outside light, groping, picking. It seized upon the edge of the board in the lower bend of the crescent and pulled. The board gave way, ripped to the very door-sill; then an arm followed the hand, reaching for one of the two iron bars with which the door was fenced. Evidently it could not find these, for the effort was soon abandoned and another panel was split and torn away. The cross-panel followed, the nails shrieking as they were drawn out from the wood. Then at last the door, shattered to its very hinges, gave way, leaving only the bars set in the stone sockets of the jamb, and against the square of grey light of the entrance stood, silhouetted, the figure of a monster. Stood but for a moment, for almost at once the bars were pulled out.

The Vampire was within the house, the light from the smouldering logs illuminating the face.

Glamr's face was livid. The pupils of the eyes were white, the hair matted and thick. The whole figure was monstrously enlarged, bulked like a *jotun*, and the vast hands, white as those of the drowned, swung heavily at his sides.

Once in the hall, he stood for a long moment looking from side to side, then moved slowly forward, reaching his great arms overhead, feeling and fumbling with the roofbeams with his fingers, and guiding himself thus from beam to beam.

Grettir, watching, alert, never moved, but lay in his place, his eyes fixed upon the monster.

But at length Glamr made out the form stretched upon the couch and came up and laid hold of a flap of the bearskin under Grettir's shoulders and tugged at it. But Grettir, bracing his feet against the footboard of the couch, held back with all his strength. Glamr seized the flap in both hands and set his might to pull, till the tough hide fetched away, and he staggered back, the corner of skin still in his grip. He looked at it stupidly, wondering, bewildered.

Then suddenly the bonder, listening from within his bolded door, heard the muffled crashing shock of the onset. The rafters cracked, the byre shook, the shutters rocked in their grooves, and Grittir, eyes alight, hair flying like a torch, thews rigid as iron, leaped to the attack.

Down upon the hero's arms came the numbing, crushing grip of the dead man's might. One instant of that inhuman embrace and Grettir knew that now peril of his life was toward. Never in all his days of battle and strength had such colossal might risen to match his own. Back bore the wrestlers, back, back toward the sides of the hall. Benches ironed to the wall were overturned, wrenched like paper from their fastenings. The great table crashed and splintered beneath their weight. The floor split with their tramping, and the fire was scattered upon the hearth. Now forward, now back, from side to side and from end to end of the wrecked hall drove the fight. Great of build though the fighters were, huge of bone, big of muscle, they yet leaped and writhed with the agility, the rapidity of young lambs.

But fear was not in Grettir. Never in his life had he been afraid. Only anger shook him, and fine, above-board fury, and the iron will to beat his enemy.

All at once Grettir, his arms gripped about the Vampire's middle, his head beneath the armpit, realized that the creature was dragging him toward the door. He fought back from this till the effort sent the blood surging in his ears, for he knew well that ill as the fight had fared within the house it must go worse without. But it was all one that he braced his feet against the broken benches, the wreck of the table, the every unevenness of the floor. The Vampire had gripped him close and dragged and clutched and heaved at his body, so that the white nails drove into his flesh, and the embrace of those arms of steel shut in the ribs till the breath gushed from the nostrils in long gasps of agony.

And now they swayed and grappled in the doorway. Grettir's back was bent like a bow and Grettir's arms at fullest stretch strained to their sockets, till it seemed as though the very tendons must tear from off the bones. And ever the foul thing above him drew him farther and yet farther from out the entrance-way of the house.

'God save you, Grettir!' cried the bonder, 'God save you, brave man and true. Never was such a fight as this in all Iceland. Are you spent, Grettir?'

Muffled under the arms of his foe, the voice of Grettir shouted: 'Stand from us. I am much spent, but I fear not.'

Then with the words, feeling the half-sunk stone of the threshold beneath his feet, he bowed his knees, and with his shoulder against the Vampire's breast drove, not, as hitherto, back, but forward, and that with all the power of limb and loin.

The Vampire reeled from the attack. His shoulder crashed against the outer doorcase, and with that gigantic shock the roof burst asunder. Down crushed and roared the frozen thatch, and then in that hideous ruin of splintering rafters, grinding stones, and wreck of panel and beam the Vampire fell backward and prone to the ground, while Grettir toppled down upon him till his face was against the dead man's face, his eye to his dead eye, his forehead to his front, and the grey bristle of his beard between his teeth.

The moon was bright outside, and all at once, lighted by her rays, Grettir for the first time saw the Vampire's face.

Then the soul of him shrank and sank, and the fear that all his days he had not known leaped to life in his heart. Terror of that glare of the dead man's gaze caught him by the throat, till his grip relaxed, and his strength dwindled away and he crouched there motionless but for his trembling, looking, looking into those blind, white, dead eyes.

And the Vampire began to speak:

'Eagerly has thou striven to match thyself with me, and ill hast thou done this night. Now thou art weak with the fear and the rigor of this fight, yet never henceforth shalt thou be stronger than at this moment. Till now thou hast won much fame by great deeds, yet henceforth ill-luck shall follow thee and woe and man-slayings and untoward fortune. Outlawed shalt thou be, and thy lot shall be cast in lands far from thine home. Alone shalt thou dwell and in that loneliness, this weird I lay upon thee: Ever to see these eyes with thine eyes, till the terror of the Dark shall come upon thee and the fear of night, and the twain shall drag thee to thy death and thy undoing.'

As the voice ceased, Grettir's wits and strength returned, and suddenly seizing the hair of the creature in one hand and his short sword in the other, he hewed off the head.

But within the heart of him he knew that the Vampire had said true words, and as he stood looking down upon the great body of his enemy and saw the glazed and fish-like eyes beneath the lids, he could for one instant look ahead to the days of his life yet to be, to the ill-fortune that should dog him from henceforth, and knew that at the gathering of each night's dusk the eyes of Glamr would look into his.

Thorhall came out when the fight was done, praising God for the issue, and he and Grettir together burned the body and, wrapping the ashes in a skin, buried them in a corner of the sheep-walks.

In the morning Thorhall gave Grettir the piebald horse and new clothes and set him a mile on his road. They rode through the Vale of

Shadows and kissed each other farewell on the shore where the road led away toward Waterdale.

The clouds had gathered again during the dawn and the rain was falling, driven landward by the incessant wind. The seals again barked and hunted in the offing, and the rough-haired ponies once more wandered about on the beach snuffing at the kelp and seaweed.

Long time Thorhall stood on the ridge watching the figure of Grettir grow small and indistinct in the waste of north country and under the blur of the rain. Then at last he turned back to the byre.

But Grettir after these things rode on to Biarg, to his mother's house, and sat at home through the winter.

The Blood Fetish

MORLEY ROBERTS

In the years preceding the First World War, vampire stories set in even more remote parts of the world saw the genre develop still further. The great explorer, Sir Richard Burton, for instance, offered an entire collection of stories from India entitled, Vikram the Vampire *(1893); while George Soulie's translation of 'The Corpse The Blood Drinker' from a Chinese book,* Strange Stories From The Lodge of Leisures *(1913) indicated that the vampire had been a part of that great nation's history for centuries. The fact the tradition also existed in that other vast continent, Africa, was demonstrated by this next story, 'The Blood Fetish' by Morley Roberts which is not only highly unusual, but has also never been anthologised before. If I indicate no more than it is the grisly tale of a severed hand that resorts to vampirism in order to sustain itself, I think the reader will be in no doubt that the word unusual is an understatement if anything! I have a feeling, too, that the story must have had quite an impact on the readers of the* Strand Magazine *when it appeared in October 1908. Sadly, though, this famous magazine which gave the world Sherlock Holmes and made Sir Arthur Conan Doyle a household name, did little for Morley Roberts who contributed just as frequently and sometimes every bit as ingeniously as the creator of the Great Detective. He is today virtually forgotten, except among those collectors who treasure the rare volumes of his novels and short stories.*

Morley Roberts (1857–1942) was born in London, the son of an Income Tax inspector, but spent much of his early life travelling around the world which accounts for the variety of settings of his stories. In 1876, for instance, he was helping to rebuild railways in

Australia. This was followed by cattle ranching in America, projects in India, Africa, the South Seas and Central America, not to mention a period at sea, before he finally returned home and devoted the rest of his life to fiction writing. His first success as a novelist was with The Adventures of the Broad Arrow *(1897) a 'lost race' story set in Australia which contains a vivid picture of the Australian outback that is obviously drawn from personal experience. This was followed by similar tales of fantasy and the macabre including* The Colossus *(1899),* The Degradation of Geoffrey Alwith *(1908),* The Serpent's Fang *(1930) and* The White Mamaloi *(1931), plus a string of weird stories for the* Strand *and* Pearson's Magazine *like 'A Thing of Wax', 'Out of the Great Silence', 'The Man With The Nose', 'The Fog' (a notable tale about London being threatened with a terrible doom) and 'The Blood Fetish' which he indicated was inspired by a curious incident that happened to him while he was living in Africa. It is, I think, one of his very best short fictions and certainly unique among all the vampire stories I have read . . .*

* * *

Outside the tent the forest was alive and busy, as it is for ever in the tropics of Africa. Birds called with harsh strange notes from dark trees, for, though the forest was even more full of creeping shadows, the sun had not yet sunk beyond the western flats through which the Kigi ran to the sea. Monkeys chattered and howled: and beneath this chorus was the hum of a million insects, that voice of the bush which never ceases. The sick man in the tent moved uneasily and looked at his companion.

'Give me something to drink, doctor,' he said.

The doctor supported his head while he drank.

'Were there any of your drugs in it?' asked the patient.

'No, Smith,' said the doctor.

'My taste is morbid,' said Smith. 'I shan't last long, old chap.'

Dr Winslow looked out into the forest, into the night, for now it was night very suddenly.

'Nonsense,' said Winslow. 'You'll live to take your collection home and be more famous than you are now.'

'Am I famous?' asked Simcox Smith. 'I suppose I am in my way. I'm thought to know more than most about this country and the devilish ways of it. Every one acknowledges that, or everyone but Hayling.'

He frowned as he mentioned the name.

'He's no better than an ignorant fool,' he remarked. 'But we see strange things here, doctor.'

The doctor sighed.

'I suppose so,' he said, 'but what fools we are to be here at all.'

The dying man shook his head.

'No, no, I've learnt a lot, old chap. I wish I could teach Hayling. I meant to, and now I can't. He'll spend all his time trying to discredit my – my discoveries.'

'Lie quiet,' said the doctor, and for long minutes Simcox Smith and the anthropologist said nothing. He lay thinking. But he spoke at last.

'I've not bought that thing from Suja,' he said.

'Don't,' said Winslow.

'You think it's a fraud?'

'I'm sure of it,' said Winslow.

Simcox Smith laughed.

'You are as bad as Hayling.'

He put out his hand and drew Winslow closer to him.

'Suja showed me what it did,' he said. 'I saw it myself.'

'On what?' asked Winslow quickly.

'On a prisoner, one who was killed when you were away.'

'And it did – '

'Did something! My God, yes,' said the anthropologist, shivering.

'What?' asked the doctor curiously, but with drawn brows.

'He grew pale and it got red. I thought I saw the wrist,' said Simcox Smith. 'I thought I saw it. I *did* see it.'

Winslow would have said it was all a delusion if Smith had been well. He knew how men's minds went in the rotten bush of the West Coast. He had had seen intellects rot, and feared for his own.

'Oh,' said Winslow.

The sick man lay back in his bed.

'I'll buy it and send it to Hayling.'

'Nonsense,' said Winslow; 'don't.'

'You don't believe it, so why shouldn't I send it? I will. I'll show Hayling! He's a blind fool, and believes there are no devilish things in this world. What is this world, old chap, and what are we? It's all horrible and ghastly. Fetch Suja, old chap.'

'Nonsense, lie down and be quiet,' said Winslow.

'I want Suja, the old rascal, I want him,' said Smith urgently. 'I must have it for Hayling. I'd like Hayling or some of his house to grow pale. They'll see more than the wrist. Oh God! what's the head like?'

He shivered.

'I want Suja,' he said moaning, and presently Winslow went out and sent a boy for Suja, who came crawling on his hands and knees, for he was monstrously old and withered and weak. But his eyes were alive. They looked like lamps in a gnarled piece of wood. He kneeled on the floor beside Smith's bed. Smith talked to him in his own tongue that Winslow could not understand, and the two men, the two dying men, talked long and eagerly while Winslow smoked. Suja was dying, had been dying for twenty, for fifty years. His people said they knew not how old he was. But Smith would die next day, said Winslow. Suja and Smith talked, and at last they came to an agreement. And then Suja crawled out of the tent.

'Get me a hundred dollars out of my chest,' said Smith. 'And when I am dead you will give him my clothes and blankets; all of them.'

'All right if you say so,' said Winslow. He got the hundred dollars out, and presently the old sorcerer came back. With him he brought a parcel done up in fibre and a big leaf, and over that some brown paper on which was a label in red letters, 'With great care.' It was a precious piece of paper, and not a soul thereabouts but Suja would have touched it. The red letters were some dreadful charm, so Suja had told the others.

'This is it,' said Suja.

'Give him the money,' said Smith eagerly.

He turned to Suja and spoke quietly to him in his own tongue.

'It's not mine, Suja, but John Hayling's. Say it.'

Winslow heard Suja say something, and then he heard the words, 'Shon 'Aylin'.'

Simcox Smith looked up at Winslow.

'He gives it to Hayling, Winslow,' he said triumphantly.

'Is that part of the mumbo jumbo?' asked Winslow, half contemptuously. But somehow he was not wholly contemptuous. The darkness of the night and the glimmer of the lamp in the darkness, and the strange and horrible aspect of the sorcerer affected him.

'Shon 'Aylin',' mumbled Suja, as he counted his dollars.

'Yes, it's part of it,' said Smith. 'It won't work except on the one who owns it and on his people. It must be transferred. We gave it to the slave who died.'

'It's a beastly idea,' said Winslow.

'You'll send it for me,' said Smith. 'You must.'

'Oh, all right,' said Winslow.

With trembling hands Smith put the packet into a biscuit tin.

Old Suja crept out into the darkness.

'I believe anything with that old devil in the tent,' said Winslow. Smith giggled.

'It's true, and it's Hayling's. I always meant to send it to him, the unbelieving beast,' he said. 'I wish I was going to live to see it. You'll send it, Winslow?'

'Yes.'

'You promise on your word of honour?' insisted Smith.

Reluctantly enough, Winslow gave his word of honour, and Smith was satisfied. And at ten o'clock that night he died in his sleep.

Winslow packed up all his papers and collections, and sent him down to the coast by carriers and canoe. The packet containing the fetish which Smith had bought from the ancient sorcerer he sent by post to England. He addressed it to A. J. Hayling, 201 Lansdown Road, St John's Wood. By this time Winslow had recovered his tone. He believed nothing which he could not see. He was angry with himself for having been affected by what Smith and old Suja had said and done.

'It's absurd, of course,' said Winslow, with bent brows. He added, 'but it's a beastly idea.'

When he sent the fetish away he wrote a letter to go with it, saying that Simcox Smith had often spoken to him of his rival in England. He described briefly what had occurred at the time of Smith's death, and gave some brief details of old Suja. He was obviously very old, and all the natives for miles round were frightened of him. Nevertheless, there was, of course, nothing in the thing. Latterly the climate and overwork had obviously affected Smith's mind. 'I should not send it if he had not made me promise to do so on my word of honour,' wrote Winslow.

He dismissed the matter from his mind, and the parcel and letter went home by the next Elder Dempster boat.

Mr Hayling was rather pleased than otherwise to hear of Simcox Smith's decease, although he said 'poor fellow,' as one must when a scientific enemy and rival dies. They had quarrelled for years when they met at the Society's rooms, and had fought in the scientific journals. Hayling was an anthropological Mr Gradgrind. He wanted facts, and nothing but facts. He believed he was a Baconian, as he knew nothing of Bacon. It had never occurred to him that there was any mystery in anything. There was nothing but ignorance, and most men were very ignorant. The existence of men, of things, of the universe, of matter itself, were all taken for granted by him, in the same way they are taken for granted by the average man. What made Simcox Smith (who had a *penchant* for metaphysics) once jokingly called the

Me-ness of the Ego was an absurdity. It was idiocy. When a man begins to think what made himself an Ego and what constitutes his 'Me,' he is the on the verge of insanity unless he is a great philosopher.

'Simcox Smith is an ass,' said Hayling, quite oblivious to the fact that Smith had done good work in many directions and offered some conjectural hypotheses to the world which had much merit and might some day rank as theories. 'Simcox Smith is an ass. He believed in occultism. He believed, I am prepared to swear, in witchcraft. He mistook the horrible ideas of a savage race for realities. Would you believe it, he even said that everything believed in utter and simple faith had a kind of reality? He said this was a law of nature!'

Obviously Simcox Smith had been mad. But some easily affected and imaginative people said it was a dreadful idea, just as Winslow had said the notion of Suja's blood fetish was a beastly one. Imagine for an instant that the idea was true! It meant that the frightful imaginations of madmen had a quasi existence at least! It meant that there was a dreadful element of truth (for who knew what truth was?) in any conceived folly. A man had but to imagine something to create it. One of Smith's friends really believed this. He was an atheist, he said, but he believed (in a way, he added, as he laughed) that mankind had really created a kind of anthropomorphic deity, with the passions and feelings attributed to him by belief and tradition. No wonder, said this friend of Smith's, that the world was a horrible place to any one who could grasp its misery and had ears for its groans.

It must be acknowledged that this idea of Simcox Smith's was a horrible one. It really affected some men. One tried it on a child (he was very scientific, and believed in experiments he could more or less control) and the child saw things which threw it into a fit and injured it for life. Nevertheless, it was a very interesting experiment, for something happened to the child (there were odd marks on it) which looked like something more than suggestion, unless it is all true that we hear of stigmata. Perhaps it is, but personally I have an idea (I knew Smith) that there is something in his damnable creating theory.

But to return to Hayling. He got the parcel from the Coast, and he read Winslow's letter.

'Poor fellow,' said Hayling; 'so he's dead at last. Well, well! And what is this that he sends? A blood fetish? Ah, he thinks he can convert me at the last, the poor mad devil.'

He opened the parcel, and inside the matting and the leaves, which smelt of the West Coast of Africa (the smell being muddy and very distinctive to those who have smelt it), he found a dried black hand, severed at the wrist joint. There was nothing else, only this hand.

'Humph,' said Hayling, who had nerves which had never been shaken by the bush and the fevers of the bush, and had never heard black men whispering dreadfully of the lost souls of the dead. 'Humph.'

He picked it up and looked at it. It was an ordinary hand, a right hand, and there was nothing remarkable about it at first. On a further look the nails seemed remarkably long, and that gave the hand a rather cruel look. Hayling said 'humph,' again. He examined it carefully and saw that it was very deeply marked on the palm.

'Very interesting,' said Hayling. Curiously enough (or rather it would have been curious if we didn't know that the strongest of us have our weak spots), he had a belief or some belief in palmistry. He had never acknowledged it to a soul but a well-known palmist in the west of London. 'Very interesting. I wonder what Sacconi would say of these lines?'

Sacconi was the palmist. He was an Irishman.

'I'll show it to Sacconi,' said Hayling. He packed it up in its box again and put it in a cupboard, which he locked up. He dismissed the matter, for he had a good deal to do. He had to write something about Simcox Smith, for instance, and he was working on totemism. He hardly thought of the dried hand for some days.

Hayling was a bachelor, and lived with a niece and a housekeeper. He was a nice man to live with unless one knew anything about anthropology and totems and such like, and Mary Hayling knew nothing about them whatever. She said 'Yes, uncle dear,' and 'No, uncle dear,' just as she ought to do, and when he abused Simcox Smith, or Robins-Gunter, or Williams, who were rivals of his, she was always sympathetic and said it was a shame.

'What's a shame?' asked Hayling.

'I don't know, dear uncle,' said Mary Hayling.

And Hayling laughed.

Then there was the housekeeper. She was fair, stout and ruddy, and very cheerful in spite of the fact that skulls and bones and specimen things in bottles made her flesh creep. She knew nothing whatever about them, and wondered what they mattered. Why Mr Hayling raged and rumbled about other men's opinions on such horrid subjects she didn't know. However, she took everything easily, and only remonstrated when the fullness of the house necessitated skulls being exposed to public view. The passage even had some of them and the maids objected to dusting them, as was only natural. Hayling said he didn't want 'em dusted, but what would any housekeeper who was properly constituted think of that? She made the girls dust them, though she herself shivered. She even saw that they wiped glass bottles with awful things inside them. She and the housemaid cleaned up Mr Hayling's own room and opened the cupboard where the hand was. The girl gave a horrid squeak as she put her hand in and touched it.

'Oh, law, ma'am, what is it?' asked Kate.

'Don't be a fool, girl,' said Mrs Farwell, with a shiver. 'It's only a hand.'

'Only – oh Lord! I won't touch it,' said the girl. 'There's a dead mouse by it.'

'Then take out the dead mouse,' said the housekeeper. The girl did so, and slammed the cupboard door to and locked it. The mouse was a poor shrivelled little thing, but how interesting it would have been to dead Simcox Smith neither Kate nor the housekeeper knew. It went into the dustbin as if it did not bear witness to a horror.

That afternoon Mrs Farwell spoke to Hayling.

'If you please, sir, there's a hand in that cupboard, and I couldn't get Kate to clean it out.'

'A hand! Oh yes, I remember,' said Hayling. 'The girl's a fool. Does she think it will hurt her? How did she know it was there? I wrapped it up. Some one's been meddling.'

'I don't think so, sir,' said Mrs Farwell, with dignity. 'She is much too frightened to meddle, and so am I.'

'Mrs Farwell, you are a fool,' said Hayling.

'Thank you, sir,' said Mrs Farwell.   When Mrs Farwell had sailed out of the room Hayling opened the cupboard and found the hand out of its package.

'Some one *has* been meddling,' growled Hayling. 'They pretend that they are frightened and come hunting here to get a sensation. I know 'em. They're all savages, and so are all of us. Civilization!'

He gave a snort when he thought of what civilization was. That is an anthropological way of looking at it. It's not a theological way at all.

He looked at the hand. It was a curious hand.

'It's contracted a little,' said Hayling. 'The fist has closed, I think. Drying unequally. But it's interesting; I'll show it to Sacconi.'

He put the hand into its coverings, and took it that very afternoon to Sacconi.

Personally Hayling believed in chiromancy. As I have said, it really was his only weakness. I never used to believe it when he argued with me, but now I have my doubts. When Sacconi took the thing into his own white and beautiful hands and turned it over to look at the palm, his eyebrows went up in a very odd way. Hayling said so.

'This, oh, ah,' said Sacconi. His real name was Flynn. He came from Limerick. 'This is very odd – very – '

'Very what?' asked Hayling.

'Horrible, quite horrible,' said Sacconi.

'Can you read it, man?'

Sacconi grunted.

'Can I read the *Times*? I can, but I don't. I've half a mind not to read this. It's very horrible, Hayling.'

'The devil,' said Hayling; 'what d'ye mean?'

'This is a negro's hand.'

'Any fool can see that,' said Hayling rudely.

'A murderer's hand.'

'That's likely enough,' said Hayling.

'A cannibal's hand.'

'You don't say so!' said Hayling.

'Oh, worse than that.'

'What's worse?'

Sacconi said a lot that Hayling denounced as fudge. Probably it was fudge. And yet –

'I'd burn it,' said Sacconi, with a shiver, as he handed it back to Hayling, and went to wash his hands. 'I'd burn it.'

'There's a damn weak spot in you, Sacconi,' said the anthropologist.

'Perhaps,' said Sacconi, 'but I'd burn it.'

'Damn nonsense,' said Hayling. 'Why should I?'

'I believe a lot of things you don't,' said Sacconi.

'I disbelieve a lot that you don't,' retorted Hayling.

'You see, I'm a bit of a clairvoyant,' said Sacconi.

'I've heard you say that before,' said Hayling, as he went away.

When he got home again he put the hand in the cupboard. He forgot to lock it up. And he locked the cat up in his room when he went to bed.

There was an awful crying of cats, or a cat, in the middle of the night. But cats fight about that time.

And when Kate opened the door of Hayling's working-room in the morning she saw the hand upon the hearthrug, and gave a horrid scream. It brought Mrs Farwell out of the drawing-room, and Hayling out of the bathroom in a big towel.

'What the devil — ' said Hayling.

'What is it, Kate?' cried Mrs Farwell.

'The hand! the hand!' said Kate. 'It's on the floor.'

Mrs Farwell saw it. Hayling put on his dressing-gown, and came down and saw it, too.

'Give that fool a month's notice,' said Hayling. 'She's been meddling again.'

'I haven't,' said Kate, sobbing. And then Mrs Farwell saw the cat lying stretched out under Hayling's desk.

'It was the cat. There she is,' said Mrs Farwell.

'Damn the cat,' said Hayling. He took Kate's broom and gave the cat a push with it.

The cat was dead.

'I don't want a month's notice,' said Kate, quavering, 'I'll go now.'

'Send the fool off,' said Hayling angrily. He took up the cat, of which he had been very fond, and put it outside, and shut the door on the crying girl and Mrs Farwell. He picked up the hand and looked at it.

'Very odd,' said Hayling.

He looked again.

'Very beastly,' said Hayling. 'I suppose it's my imagination.'

He looked once more.

'Looks fresher,' said Hayling. 'These fools of women have infected me.'

He put the hand down on his desk by the side of a very curious Maori skull, and went up-stairs again to finish dressing.

That morning the scentific monthlies were out, and there was so much of interest in them that Hayling forgot all about the hand. He had an article in one of them abusing Robins-Gunter, whose views on anthropology were coloured by his fanaticism in religion. 'Imagine a man like that thinking he is an authority on anything scientific,' said Hayling. It was a pleasure to slaughter him on his own altar, and indeed this time Hayling felt he had offered Robins-Gunter up to the outraged deity of Truth.

'It's a massacre,' said Hayling; 'it's not a criticism — it's a massacre.'

He said 'Ha-ha!' and went to town to hear what others had to say about it. They had so much to say that he remained at the club till very late, and got rather too much wine to drink. Or perhaps it was the whisky-and-soda. He left his working-room door open and unlocked.

Kate had gone, sacrificing a fortnight's wages. Mrs Farwell said she was a fool. Kate said she would rather be a fool outside that house. She also said a lot of foolish things about the hand, which had a very silly effect upon the housekeeper. For how else can we account for what happened that night? Kate said that the beastly hand was alive, and that it had killed the cat. Uneducated superstitious girls from the country often say things as silly. But Mrs Farwell was a woman of nerves. She only went to sleep when she heard her master come in.

She woke screaming at three o'clock, and Hayling was still so much under the influence of Robins-Gunter's scientific blood and the club whisky that he didn't wake. But Mary Hayling woke and so did the cook, and they came running to Mrs Farwell's room. They found her door open.

'What's the matter? what's the matter?' screamed Mary Hayling. She brought a candle and found Mrs Farwell sitting up in bed.

She was as white as a ghost, bloodlessly white. 'There's been a horrible thing in my room,' she whispered.

The cook collapsed on a chair; Mary Hayling sat on the bed and put her arms round the housekeeper.

'What?'

'I saw it,' whispered Mrs Farwell. 'A black man, reddish black, very horrible – '

She fainted, and Mary laid her down.

'Stay with her,' said Mary. 'I'll go and wake my uncle.'

The cook whimpered, but she lighted the gas and stayed, while Mary hammered on Hayling's door. He thought it was thunderous applause at a dinner given him by the Royal Society. Then he woke.

'What is it?'

Mary opened the door and told him to get up.

'Oh, these women,' he said.

His head ached. He went up-stairs cursing and found Mrs Farwell barely conscious. The cook was shaking like a jelly, and Hayling thrust her aside. He had some medical training before he turned to anthropology, and he took hold of the housekeeper's wrist, and found her pulse a mere running thread.

'Go and bring brandy,' said Hayling, 'and fetch Dr Sutton from next door.'

He was very white himself. So far as he could guess she looked as if she were dying of loss of blood. But she didn't die. Sutton, when he came in, said the same.

'She's not white only from fainting, she's blanched,' he declared.

He turned back her nightgown, and found a very strange red patch on her shoulder. It was redder than the white skin, and moist. He touched it with a handkerchief, and the linen was faintly reddened. He turned and stared at Hayling.

'This is very extraordinary,' he said, and Hayling nodded.

He tried to speak and could not. At last he got his voice. It was dry and thick.

'Don't you think the patch is the shape of a hand?' asked Hayling.

'Yes, rather,' replied Sutton; 'somewhat like it, I should say.'

They were all in the room then: Mary Hayling and the cook. There was no other person in the house. They could have sworn that was a fact. They heard a noise below.

'What's that?' asked Hayling.

'Some one gone out of the front door, sir,' said the trembling cook.

'Nonsense,' said Hayling.

But the door slammed. When he ran down he found no one about. He went up-stairs again shaking. For he had looked for something in his own room and had not found it.

The next day there was a curious paragraph in all the evening papers.

'The freshly severed hand of a negro was picked up early this morning in Lansdown Road, St John's Wood, just outside the residence of the well-known anthropologist, Mr A. J. Hayling. The police are investigating the mystery.'

But Hayling destroyed the article in which he proposed to massacre poor credulous Simcox Smith.

The Land of the Time-Leeches

GUSTAV MEYRINK

A number of German writers were also among the early contributors to the development of the vampire short story. Two much reprinted examples are 'Wake Not The Dead' by Johann Ludwig Tieck, written about 1820, and the anonymous 'The Mysterious Stranger' which was published in 1860. The first is a fairly traditional tale of a woman raised from her grave by a sorcerer to ravage the countryside as a vampire; while the second concerns Azzo van Klatka, a vampire of amazing strength who can summon wolves to his aid. A highlight of this story is the battle for supremacy between Klatka and a man with an artificial spring-arm which gets him mistaken as a vampire, too! Both stories, however, lack the originality of 'The Land of the Time-Leeches' by Gustav Meyrink, arguably Germany's most famous horror-meister. This extraordinary tale of creatures who – to quote the author – 'like blood-suckers drain from our hearts, Time, the very sap of life', was written in 1920 and has only once previously appeared in English in a now forgotten magazine called The Quest, *in its issue of July 1920.*

Gustav Meyrink (1868–1932) led a life almost as bizarre and troubled as the stories he wrote. Born the illegitimate son of a German aristocrat and his actress-mistress, Meyrink had an unhappy childhood and as a young writer was soon in trouble with the law for shocking and annoying the bourgeoisie. As a dedicated pacifist, his early books also incensed the authorities and though only banned during World War I, were actually burned by the Nazis in the second. Throughout all this persecution, however, Meyrink never stopped working – developing his gifts as a satirist, proving himself to be one of the earliest 'Expressionist' writers, and 'certainly the foremost twentieth-century novelist of the supernatural', according to E. F. Bleiler. Meyrink had apparently formed an interest in the occult in his twenties and developed a theory that the spiritual world was opposing civilization, so that when he wrote The German Philistine's Horn *(1909) he immediately found himself the centre of a controversy which would never leave him. Other works with strong elements of the supernatural followed including* The Waxworks *(1907),* The Green Face *(1916) and* At The Threshold of the Beyond *(1923). In 1915 he published the book which made him internationally famous,* The Golem, *about a huge, artificial clay man brought to life by a rabbi in Prague in order to protect his ghetto from a pogrom. The story, based on an old Jewish folk-tale, has subsequently been filmed several times, most notably with Paul Wegener who has become as identified with the role as Karloff with Frankenstein's creature and Lugosi with Dracula.*

*　*　　*　*　　*　*

In the churchyard of the secluded and out-of-the-world little town of Runkel my grandfather's body is laid 'to eternal rest.' His gravestone is thickly overgrown with moss and the date well-nigh obliterated; but below it, standing out in gilt[1] and as fresh as though they were cut yesterday, are four letters ranged round a cross, thus:

$$\begin{array}{c|c} V & I \\ \hline V & O \end{array}$$

'VIVO' – 'I live.' Such was the meaning I was told, when as a boy I read the inscription for the first time. The word at once impressed itself as deeply on my soul as if the dead had uttered it from underneath the sod.

'VIVO' – 'I live,' a strange watch-word for a tombstone! Even to-day it re-echoes in my heart; whenever I think of it, I feel as I felt long since when first I stood before that grave. In my imagination I see my grandfather – though I had never known him in the flesh – lying there, untouched by decay, with folded hands, eyes open clear as crystal, motionless; like one who has escaped corruption in the midst of the realm of mould, with silent patience awaiting resurrection.

---

[1] Cp. the Golden Gate of the Osiric Garden, end of *Der Golem*.

I have since visited many a churchyard of many a town; ever have my steps been directed there by a vague desire, for which I could not account, to read once more that word on some chance stone. Twice only have I found it – that cross-encircling 'VIVO' – once in Danzig, once in Nuremburg. In both cases Time's finger has rubbed out the name; in both the 'VIVO' shines out fresh and untouched as if instinct with life.

I had been told in my youth, and had always believed, that my grandfather had not left behind a single line in his own writing. All the more excited was I then when one day I discovered in a secret drawer of an old writing-desk – an ancient family heirloom – a packet of notes which had evidently been written by him. They were enclosed in a book-cover, on which I read the strange sentence:

'How shall man escape death if not by ceasing to wait and hope?'

At once I felt light up within me that mysterious 'VIVO,' which had ever throughout my life accompanied me with a faint shimmer, dying away a thousand times only to revive without any apparent outer cause in dreams or waking moments. If I had at times believed some chance had put that 'VIVO' on his tombstone – a parson's choice perhaps – now, with this sentence on the book-cover before me, I knew for sure and certain the 'VIVO' must have had a deeper meaning for him; must doubtless hint at something that filled the whole life of my father's father. And indeed, as I read on, page after page of his bequest to me confirmed my first intuition.

Most of the notes are of too private a nature to have their contents revealed to other eyes. It must suffice if I touch lightly on those details which led to my acquaintance with Johann Hermann Obereit.

It appeared from these memoirs that my grandfather was a member of a society called the 'Philadelphians,' an order claiming that its roots go back to ancient Egypt and hailing as its founder the legendary Hermes Trismegistus. Even the secret grips and signs of recognition were given. The name of Johann Hermann Obereit frequently occurred. He was a chemist and apparently an intimate friend of my grandfather's; indeed he seemed to have lived in the same house with him at Runkel. I wished naturally to learn more about the life of my extraordinary ancestor and about that hidden world-renouncing philosophy the spirit of which spoke out of every line he had written. I accordingly decided to go to Runkel to find out whether by chance any descendants of Obereit were still there and if they had any family records.

One can scarcely imagine anything more dream-like than this tiny little town of Runkel, slumbering away in spite of the screams and cries of Time, like some forgotten relic of the Middle Ages, with its crooked streets and passages, silent as the dead, and grass-grown, rugged cobble-stones, beneath the shadow of the ancient rock-built castle of Runkelstein, the ancestral seat of the Princes of Wied.

The very first morning after my arrival I felt myself irresistibly drawn to the little churchyard. There the days of my youth woke again to memory, as I stepped from one flower-carpeted mound to another in the sweet sunshine and read mechanically from the stones the names of those who slumbered beneath. Already from afar I recognized my grandfather's with its glittering mystic inscription. But on drawing near I found I was no longer alone.

An old white-haired, clean-shaven man of sharp-cut features was sitting there, with his chin resting on the ivory handle of his walking-stick. As I approached he glanced at me with strangely vivid eyes, as of one in whom the likeness to a well-remembered face had awakened a host of memories. He was dressed in old-fashioned clothes, high collar and stock – one might almost have said like a family portrait in Louis Philippe or early Victorian style.

I was so astonished at a sight so out of keeping with present-day surroundings, moreover my brooding thoughts were so deeply sunk in what I had gathered from my grandfather's writings, that scarcely knowing what I did I uttered half-aloud the name 'Obereit.'

'Yes, my name is Johann Hermann Obereit,' said the old gentleman without showing the least surprise. I nearly stopped breathing. And what I learned from the conversation that followed was even less calculated to diminish my astonishment.

It is indeed not an every-day experience to find oneself face to face with a man to all appearances not much older than oneself yet who had lived so long – some century and a half, he said! I felt like a youth in spite of my already white hair, as we paced side by side, while he spoke of Napoleon and historic persons he had known long years ago, as one would speak of people who had died the other day.

'In Runkel,' he said with a smile, 'I am believed to be my own grandson.' He pointed to a tomb we were passing and which bore the date 1798. 'By right I should be lying there,' he continued. 'I had the date put on to avoid the curiosity of the crowd for a modern Methuselah. The "VIVO",' he added, as if divining my thought, 'will be put on only when I am dead for good.'

Almost at once we became intimate friends; and he soon insisted on my staying with him. A month thus passed; and we sat up many a night engaged in deep discourse. But always when I would have asked the purport of the sentence on the book-cover that contained my grandsire's papers, he deftly turned the conversation. 'How shall a man escape death if not by ceasing to wait and hope?' What could it mean?

One evening – indeed the last we passed together – our talk had turned on the old witch-trials. I was contending that they must all have been highly hysterical women, when suddenly he said: 'So you do not believe a man may leave his body and travel, say, to Blocksberg?' 'Shall I show you now?' he asked, looking sharply at me.

I shook my head. 'I admit only this much,' I said, laughing. 'The so-called witches got into a kind of trance by taking narcotic drugs, and were then firmly persuaded they rode through the air on broomsticks!'

He remained sunk in thought. 'You will perhaps say that I too travelled only in imagination,' he murmured half aloud, and relapsed again into meditation.

After a while he rose slowly, went to his desk and returned with a small book.

'Perhaps you may be interested in what I wrote down here when first I made the experiment many long years ago. I must tell you I was still very young and full of hopes.'

I saw from his indrawn look that his memory was going back to far-off days.

'I believed in what men call life, till blow after blow fell on me. I lost whatever one may value most on earth – my wife, my children – all. Then fate brought about my meeting with your grandfather. It was he who taught me to understand what our desires are, what waiting is, what expectation, what hope is; how they are interlocked with one another; how one may tear the mask off the faces of those ghostly vampires. We called them the Time-leeches; for like blood-suckers they drain from our hearts Time, the very sap of life. It was here in this room that he taught me the first step on the way towards the conquest of death and how to strangle the vipers of hope. And then . . .' – he hesitated for a moment. 'And then I became like a block of wood that does not feel whether it be touched gently or split asunder, plunged into water or thrown into fire. Since then there has been, as it were, a certain void within me. No more have I looked for consolation; no more have I needed it. Wherefore should I seek it? I know I *am*. Since then only is it that *I live*. There is a fundamental difference between "I live" and "*I live*." '

'You say that so simply; and yet it is terrible,' I interrupted, deeply moved.

'It only seems to be so,' he assured me smilingly. 'Out of this heart-stableness there streams a sense of beatitude of which you can scarcely dream. It is like a sweet melody that never ceases – this "I am." Once born it cannot die – neither in sleep, nor when the outer world wakes our senses for us again, nor even in death.

'Shall I tell you why men now die so early and no longer live for a thousand years as it is written of the patriarchs in the scriptures? They are like the green watery shoots of a tree. They have forgotten that they belong to the trunk, and so they wither away the first autumn. But I wanted to tell you how I first left my body.

'There is an old, old doctrine, as ancient as mankind itself. It has been handed on from mouth to ear until this day; but few know it. It teaches how to step over the threshold of death without losing consciousness He who can rightly do so is henceforth master of himself. He has gained a new self, and what till then seemed his self becomes henceforth a tool just as now our hands and feet are organs for us.

'Heart-beat and breath are stilled as in a corpse when the newly rediscovered spirit goes forth – when we go forth as once did Israel from the fleshpots of Egypt, and the waters of the Red Sea stood as walls on either side.

'Long and oft had I to practise, nameless and excruciating were the tortures I had to undergo, before I succeeded finally in freeing myself consciously from the body. At first I felt myself, as it were, hovering – just as we think ourselves able to fly in dreams – with knees drawn up yet moving quite easily.

'Suddenly I began gliding down. I found myself in a black stream running as it were from the south to the north. In our language we call it the flowing backwards of the Jordan. There was a roaring of waters, a buzzing of blood in the ears. In great excitement many voices – though I could not see their owners – cried out on me to turn back. A trembling seized upon me, and in dumb fear I swam towards a cliff that rose from the waters before me. Standing there in the moonlight was a naked child. But the signs of sex were absent, and in its forehead it had a third eye, like Polyphemus of old. It stood stock still, pointing with its hand to the interior of the island.

'I advanced through a wood on a smooth white road, but without feeling the ground beneath my feet. When I tried to touch the trees and shrubs around me I could not feel them. It was as though there were a thin layer of air between them and me which I could not penetrate. A phosphorescence as from decaying wood covered every object and made seeing possible. But their outlines seemed vague and and loose and soft like molluscs, and all seemed strangely over-sized. Featherless birds, with round staring eyes, swollen like fattened geese and huddled together in a huge nest, hissed down at me. A fawn, scarce able to walk yet as big as a full-grown deer, lay in the moss and lazily turned its fat pug-dog-like head towards me.

'There was a toad-like sluggishness in every creature I happened to see.

'By and by the knowledge of where I was dawned on me – in a land as real as our own world and yet but a reflection of it, in the realm of those unseen doubles that thrive upon the marrow of their terrestrial counterparts, that exploit their originals and grow into ever huger shapes, the more the latter eat themselves up in vain hoping and waiting for happiness and joy. If the mothers of young animals are shot off and their little ones waste and waste away longing in faith for their food until they die in the tortures of starvation, spectral doubles grow up in this accursed spirit-land, and like spiders suck up the life that trickles from the creatures of our world. The life-powers of all that thus wane away in vain hopes, become gross shapes and luxurious weeds in this Leech-land, the very soil of which is impregnated by the fattening breath of time spent in vain waiting and wasting.

'As I wandered on I came to a town full of people. Many of them I knew on earth. I reminded myself of their countless vain and abortive hopes; how they walked more and more bowed down year after year, yet could not drive out of their hearts the vampires – their own demonic selves that devoured their Life and their Time. Here I saw them staggering about swollen into spongy monsters with huge bellies, bulging eyes and cheeks puffed with fat.

'First I noticed a bank which displayed in its windows the announcement:

> FORTUNA
> LOTTERY OFFICE
> EVERY TICKET
> WINS
> THE FIRST PRIZE

Out of it came thronging a grinning crowd carrying sacks of gold, smacking their puffed lips in greasy contentment – phantoms in fat and jelly of all who waste their lives on earth in the insatiable hunger for a gambler's gains.

'I entered a vast hall; it seemed like a colossal temple whose columns reached the sky. There, on a throne of coagulated blood, sat a monstrous four-armed figure. Its body was human but its head a brute's – hyæna-like, with foam-flecked jaws and snout. It was the war-god of the still savage superstitious nations who offer it their prayers for victory over their foes.

'Filled with horror and loathing I fled out of the atmosphere of decay and corruption which filled the place, back into the streets, but only to be dumbfounded again at the sight of a palace which surpassed in splendour any I had ever seen. And yet every stone, every gable, mullion, ornament, seemed strangely familiar; it was as if I had once built it all up in fancy for myself. I mounted the broad white marble steps. On the door-plate before me I read . . . my own name – JOHANN H. OBEREIT! I entered. Inside I saw myself clad in purple sitting at a table groaning with luxuries and waited on by thousands of fair women slaves. Immediately I recognized them as the women who had pleased my senses in life, though most of them but as a passing moment's whim.

'A feeling of indescribable hatred filled me when I realized that this foul double of mine had wallowed and revelled here in lust and luxury my whole life; that it was I myself who had called him into being and lavished riches on him by the outflow of the magic power of my own self, drained from me by the vain hopes and lusts and expectations of my soul.

'With terror I saw that my whole life had been spent in waiting and in waiting only – as it were an unstaunchable bleeding to death; that the time left me for feeling the *present* amounted to only a few hours.

'Like a bubble burst before me whatever I had hitherto thought to be the content of my life. I tell you that whatever we seem to finish on earth ever generates new waiting and hoping. The whole world is pervaded by the pestiferous breath of the decay of a scarcely-born present. Who has not felt the enervating weakness that seizes on one when sitting in the waiting-room of a doctor or lawyer or official? What we call life is the waiting-room of death!

'Suddenly I realized then and there what Time is. We ourselves are forms made out of Time – bodies that seem to be matter, but are no more than coagulated Time. And our daily withering away towards the grave – what is it but our returning unto Time again, waiting and hoping being but the symptoms of this process, even as ice on a stove hisses away as it changes back to water again?

'I now saw that, as this knowledge woke in my mind, trembling seized upon my double, and that his face was contorted with terror. Then I knew what I had to do; to fight unto the death with every weapon against those phantoms that suck our life away like vampires.

'Oh! they know full well why they remain invisible for man, why they hide themselves from our eyes – those parasites of our life! – even as it is the devil's most foul device to act as if he did not exist. Since then I have for ever rooted out of my life the two ideas of hoping and waiting.'

'I am sure,' I said, when the old gentleman fell to silence, 'I should break down at the first step, if I tried to tread the terrible way along which you have walked. I can well believe that by incessant labour a man may benumb the feeling of waiting and hoping in his soul; but . . .'

'Yes, but only *benumb* it,' he interrupted. 'Within you the waiting still remains alive. You must put the axe to the root. Become as an automaton in this world, as one dead though seemingly alive. Never reach out after a tempting fruit, if there is to be the shortest waiting for it. Do not stir a hand; and all will fall ripe into your lap. At the beginning, and for long perchance, it may be like a wandering through desert plains void of all consolation; but suddenly there will be a brightness round you and you will see all things – beautiful and ugly – in a new and unexpected splendour. Then will there be no more "importance" and "unimportance" for you; every event will be equally "important" and "unimportant." You will become "horned" by drinking the dragon's blood, and be able to say of yourself: I fare forth into the shoreless sea of an unending life with snow-white sails.'

These were the last words Johann Hermann Obereit spoke to me. I have not seen him again.

Many years have passed since then and I have tried as well as I could to follow his doctrine; but waiting and hoping will not wane from my heart.

I am too weak, alas! to root out these weeds; and so I no longer wonder that on the countless gravestones so very seldom does one find the legend:

$$\begin{array}{c|c} \text{V} & \text{I} \\ \hline \text{V} & \text{O} \end{array}$$

The Elder Brother

CHARLES CALDWELL DOBIE

'The Elder Brother' represents another landmark because the mesmerising Elena with her 'bright red lips and hair as sleek and shining as
the wing of a blackbird' who appears in this story is the first native
American vampire. As I have shown, earlier writers like Julian
Hawthorne and Frank Norris had already explored the vampire
theme, but had located the events abroad. Charles Caldwell Dobie's
atmospheric tale is set among the Greek emigrants of San Francisco
where the fears and superstitions of the old world have not been
completely swept aside in the new. The story was published in the
prestigious monthly, Harper's Magazine, which had earlier run Frank
Stockton's 'psychic vampire' story, 'A Borrowed Month', set in
Switzerland in which a man crippled with rheumatism discovers that
by force of will he can extract energy and vitality from his friends; and
would later publish Helen R. Hull's thriller about the animated dead
in New York, 'Clay-Shuttered Doors' (May 1926). Both of these, like
Charles Dobie's story, have remained unjustly neglected.

The author of 'The Elder Brother', Charles Caldwell Dobie (1881–
1943) was a writer of realistic novels and short stories in the same style
as Frank Norris, according to Stanley Kunitz and Howard Haycraft in
Twentieth Century Authors (1950), who refer to him as 'an essentially
romantic storyteller who thinks of himself as a realist in style'. Dobie
was born in San Francisco and lived there all his life, becoming very
much identified with the city and surviving its devastating Earthquake
and Great Fire. The early death of his father meant that Charles had to
start work at fourteen as an office boy in an insurance company, but he
had been writing stories ever since his childhood and finally managed to

sell some of these to the Smart Set *magazine around the years of the
First World War. He rose rapidly to fame after the publication of his
first novel,* The Blood Red Dawn *(1920) which enabled him to devote
all of his energies to writing and his reputation was ensured with
further works such as* The Arrested Moment *(1927) and* San Francisco
Tales *(1935). He had a particularly intimate knowledge of the city, its
history and people and this was often evident in his stories. A report
that his mother was an amateur fortune teller of Greek origin who
enthralled him with tales about the superstitions that were still current
in her native country may or may not be apochryphal. It does, though,
add a nice element of* frisson *to the events which unfold in the next few
pages . . .*

*   *   *

Last week my landlady said in the midst of the evening meal, 'You
must see to it that you are early to your dinner to-morrow night,
Josef Vitek, for I have a great treat in store for you.'

Now hearing my landlady talk thus I felt sure that she was planning
some brave dish, and so to plague her I answered:

'I am not sure that I shall be here at all. My Greek friend is to
celebrate his name-day and he has said something to me about a feast.'

'His name-day!' cried my landlady in scorn, for she cares little for
my Greek friend. 'And what unmannerly thing is that, I should like to
know? In Alsace we have no such foolishness.'

'Nor in my country, either . . . But it seems it stands in place of a
birthday. And it falls upon the day called after the saint a man is named
for.'

'Do not tell me,' my landlady cried out, 'that such a stupid lout is
named for a saint!'

'Well,' I retorted gravely, 'since he is a Christian what else is left? . . .
You would not have him named for the devil?'

At this my landlady put two hands upon her hips and wagged her
old head from one side to another. 'Christian, indeed! Then why does
he not have a birthday like decent folks?'

'Perhaps he does,' I answered. 'That I do not know. But is there
anything to prevent one having a name-day, too? . . . And think how
many, being named for the same saint, feast upon the same day? It is
almost as good as Easter or Christmas . . . No, I do not agree with you:
for my part I think it is a good arrangement. And what is more, I
should say that any excuse for feasting serves a good turn.'

'To hear you talk, Josef Vitek, one would fancy that you were worn down to a shadow with lean living . . . I do not know what sort of outlandish fare your Greek friend can provide you, but if you are willing to risk it I suppose there is no more to be said.'

I looked at my landlady out of the corner of my eye. Her face was very red and in a moment I thought she might have wept from her disappointment and anger. Yet the longer her vexation, the more happily I knew she would smile in the end, so I said:

'I know some of the things he will serve me: broth of chicken with a taste of lemon and little bitter-sweet olives in the Greek fashion. And like as not, lamb baked with eggplant. And rice fried in butter. And in the end a curd of goat's milk.'

'And you call that a feast? Lamb and bitter olives and goat's-milk curd? . . . Shall I tell you what you would have at my table? Well then, a roast duck with noodles for one thing. And a batter pudding with all manner of preserves in the centre for another. To say nothing of nuts and raisins and little red apples with your coffee. If you can match that anywhere in San Francisco, well and good. But for my part I would not trade so much as the little red apples for anything you have named me.'

Now my landlady had named everything that she knew was my delight and there was so much sorrow bound up in her anger that I put up my finger as if an idea suddenly had come to me, and I replied:

'Now that I think on it, my Greek friend's name-day is a week from to-morrow! So I shall have both feasts!' And I threw back my head, laughing.

With that my landlady gave me a merry box on the ears and cried out gayly:

'Josef Vitek, you are a trial and no mistake! Fancy what a scare you gave me! Here was I, with a duck all dressed and ready for tomorrow's roasting, and noodles freshly rolled and cut into thin strips, and a guest all invited! Well, that which ends happily ends best.'

'A guest!' cried I. 'Now that is as it should be. And pray what is his name?'

'*His* name! Do you not think that one man at my table is worry enough? Besides I have only a single duck. Nay, this guest which I have invited is a woman. Not just any woman, mind you, but one who has a rare gift. For if everything is as it should be with her, at the end of the meal she can look into your teacup and tell you whatever the future has in store for you.'

'What!' I exclaimed. 'Can it be that you are asking a gipsy to sup with you?'

At this my landlady's face grew red again. 'Do you think I am quite a fool, Josef Vitek? I have not lived a decent life these many years to end by sitting at the same table with a thieving witch.'

'Well,' I answered, 'I am glad of that. But in Bohemia we have gipsies for such traffic. Although there was once an old woman in Polna, where I was born, who could tell marvelous things with a strand cut from your hair . . . In a teacup, did you say? Yes, come to think of it, gipsies look at your palm or they spread out cards before them.'

'As my guest can do also if she has the mind for it. Indeed, there are no end to the pleasant things she can tell you, any way she chooses.'

'If they be only pleasant things then it is well,' said I. 'But I remember that once my mother sent the strand from a lock of my sister's hair to the woman I told you of. And she sent back word: In less than a twelvemonth the child will die. And so it was.'

'Well, what better can one expect from one who tells a fortune from a strand of human hair?' demanded my landlady. 'For my part I should say that such a creature was in league with the devil. Doubtless she bewitched this sister of yours. And you must know, Josef Vitek, that there are such things as vampires.'

'Vampires!' I repeated. 'And what are they, pray?'

And with that my landlady told me so many stories concerning them that I forgot to eat the apple tart which she had set before me and I had to run all the way to my evening baking.

I was so late to my task that all my comrades were at their places when I entered, short of breath from my running, and my Greek friend who worked beside me looked up and said:

'What is the matter, Josef Vitek? One would think that you had seen your grandfather's ghost.'

'Well,' I answered, laughing, 'and if I had, I should certainly not run from it. For, as I remember, my grandfather was a kindly old man and his ghost would be a very gentle ghost, I am sure. But,' I went on, recalling my landlady's tales, 'I could not have run faster if I had met a vampire.'

At this my Greek friend turned pale. 'Hush, Josef Vitek!' he cried. 'It is not good for a Christian to so much as mention such creatures. For you must have heard the dreadful things they do.'

'Ah, then you have them in Greece, too! And are they the same sort that my landlady talks of: lost souls who rise up from their graves at midnight to drain the heart's blood from a man?'

'Yes,' whispered my Greek friend, 'they are the same in every country. And the worst of it is, you could not guess it if you saw one. At midnight, did you say? . . . Josef Vitek, they may *rise* from their graves at that hour but when they return is another matter. They are abroad at all seasons and they are always very beautiful, so that a man loses his heart to them . . .'

'Can you mean,' asked I, 'that there are no ugly ones, nor any men among them?'

'If there are I have yet to hear of it. I have a friend who has great knowledge of them. He is a seventh son and has the gift of discerning things that others cannot see. If one can trust his report, their lips are always red and their eyes two burning coals. And when all other wiles fail they let down great strands of blue-black hair to lure a man with its perfume. And they have little sharp white teeth.'

'Barring the little sharp white teeth,' said I, 'they have a pleasant sound.'

'They have, indeed!' replied my Greek friend, turning away with a shudder.

And with that I whipped off my coat and began to toss from the mixing pails enough dough for my first kneading.

All night as I plied my trade I thought about fortune tellers, and seventh sons, and vampires with little sharp white teeth, until these things were all mixed up in my mind like the very dough which finally I pushed into the oven. I wondered what this friend of my landlady would be like: an old gnarled witchlike creature or something dark and flashing in the manner of a young gipsy? And I watched my Greek friend going about his tasks with the bitter smile that is usually on his red lips turned to grave silence.

All this made me solemn also, but in the end I said to myself:

'Josef Vitek, do not be a fool! There are no such things as vampires abroad. This landlady of yours is full of such old-wives' tales. And as for your Greek friend, he is a sly dog and has stooped to many a trick to give himself a laugh at the expense of another. Even now he is probably thinking, "What sport to watch this simpleton from Polna swallow however large a dish of lies I set before him!" '

And I went home in the early morning light, misty as it usually is in San Francisco, whistling gaily; so that my landlady, meeting me at the threshold, said:

'That is right, my son. Be happy while there is time for it. For no one knows what is in the future.'

To which I replied, laughing:

'But to-night, at your table, I shall learn everything.'

'So much the more reason,' she answered, 'that you sing now at daybreak.'

'But I thought this friend of yours told only pleasant things.'

My landlady looked at me and shook her head. 'When you are as old as I am, Josef Vitek, you will learn that bitterness lies at the bottom of every sweet cup.'

'If there is only sweetness at the beginning,' I said, 'I shall be content.'

To which she made answer:

'So think we all until the draught is drained.'

Now this friend of my landlady who told only pleasant fortunes was neither a gnarled old witch nor a brown gipsy. She was very beautiful, with flashing eyes and bright red lips and hair as sleek and shining as the wing of a blackbird.

Her name was Elena and when she looked into my teacup she said:

'Josef Vitek, there is much sweetness in store for you . . . And a tear or two!' And she smiled in a curious way that hid her teeth.

But teacup fortunes were not to her taste, so she called to my landlady for a deck of cards.

'Now, Josef Vitek,' she commanded, 'shuffle these cards and cut them three times and make a wish, and then we shall see what we shall see.'

To shuffle the cards and to cut them was no great matter, but when it came to wishing there was much time wasted; for at once a flood of wishes crowded in upon me and, try as I would, I could not tell which to decide upon.

'Come, now,' said my landlady impatiently, 'you are holding everything back! There must be a thousand things a youth like you can wish for!'

'That is just it!' I cried. 'A thousand things to wish for and only one wish!'

But in the end I said to myself, 'Josef Vitek, if you wish just to be happy you will do well. For to be happy is to get every wish no matter how many.' And I laughed to myself, thinking how clever I was, and straight-way I cut the cards three times.

Then Elena spread out the cards before her and from the beginning she began to see marvellous things: journeys by land and water, pieces of money, an envious friend, and much feasting. I kept my counsel until she named this last circumstance and at once I cried out to my landlady.

'See, this is the name-day of my Greek friend which has turned up in the cards. Now if that is not wonderful I should like to know what is!'

To which the landlady replied:

'Not a bit more wonderful than the envious friend. If he is not that heathenish Greek, then I have never heard a fortune told in my life.'

As for Elena, she kept on sorting and discarding and turning up cards, and all the while finding astonishing things. But when it came to the matter of my wish she shook her head, saying:

'Sometimes your wish seems in your hand and then it vanishes . . . No, I have never seen quite the like of it before – to come and go in this fashion!'

'Well,' thought I, 'nobody can be always happy!' And I remembered Miriam whom I had loved. And I sighed as I had done that first evening when she had let me buy her a sweet-meat in the Greek coffee-house where she had danced.

As I sighed, the woman before me threw away the cards and looked straight into my eyes so that I felt a pleasant chill run over me. And she said again, smiling her discreet smile that concealed her teeth:

'Josef Vitek, give me your hands palms upwards. For your real fortune is withheld from the cards as it was from the teacup.'

So I gave her my hands palms upward, and she bent them back with her cool touch, and again that pleasant chill ran over me, and again she turned two burning eyes upon me as she said:

'You have a cold heart, Josef Vitek. And there are many women who will weep because of you. But there is one woman that stands out from all the rest: she shall sit at table with you one night as I do here. And she shall hold your hand thus and her heart will beat fast, as mine does!'

With that she brought my hands up to her breast and I felt the beating of her heart, and at once the pleasant chill which had swept me changed to fire and I felt my cheeks burn as I heard my landlay saying in a cold voice:

'Come, drink your coffee, Josef Vitek! . . . We have had enough of fortune telling for one evening.'

Now as soon as my landlady had spoken thus I remembered that it was time to go to work and I rose from the table. And at once Elena rose also, saying:

'If you are going in my direction, Josef Vitek, I shall walk with you.'

At these words my landlady frowned, motioning me with her head against the invitation. But I thought to myself, 'What concern can it be of hers whom I walk with to my work? I am no goose to be herded hither and thither!'

So I answered without looking at my landlady:

'Whatever is your direction is mine!'

And I waited while she covered herself in a cloak coloured like a flame.

We went out into the night, but my landlady did not so much as follow us to the door. I felt ashamed to see her treat a guest so, and at the foot of the stairs I said to my companion:

'My landlady never follows anyone to the door at night. The chill air is not good for her.'

'Night is for youth, Josef Vitek!' she replied. And I felt her hand touch mine.

I felt her hand touch mine and it was as if Miriam had touched me, only with a difference: this touch set me shivering. Yet I did not feel cold. And while I was still pondering this strange circumstance, she said:

'Josef Vitek, which way shall we walk?'

'Wherever you will!' I answered, scarcely knowing what I said.

We turned our steps in the opposite direction from what should have been my course. But somehow my night's task at the bakery where I work seemed very far away, like a tale that had been told. And presently we stood upon the top of a hill in a little public square with a plume of cypress trees upon its crest. And San Francisco lay before us, twinkling its thousand eyes.

Then Elena said to me softly, 'Josef Vitek, you are a cold youth and no mistake . . . Come closer.'

But instead of obeying her, I drew back as if a cold wind had touched me. And with that she gave a toss of her head as one does who is displeased and her blue-black hair fell in a dark shower over her shoulders. Her blue-black hair fell in a dark shower over her shoulders and a strange perfume filled the air and I heard her say again:

'Come closer, Josef Vitek, there is nothing to fear!'

And at that moment I felt two burning lips against my throat.

I came home at my appointed hour, in the chill of morning, and as usual my landlady was waiting for me at the head of the stairs. Her face had a stern look and she said coldly:

'Josef Vitek, already your Greek friend has been here asking for you. He came almost at daybreak and there was nothing to do but lie concerning you. So I said, "He is sleeping now after a night of pain."

And he went away with an unsatisfied look upon his face as if he knew that I had deceived him. If he comes again I shall bring him to you.'

And having said her say, she went into her room, closing the door. All the time I have lived with my landlady she had never spoken so coldly to me. Yet in my room everything was as it always was – a plate of fruit on the table before my bed, and a little mound of spice cakes near it such as are my delight, and the coverlet turned down. And I thought:

'She must love you still, Josef Vitek, or she would not put apples and spice cakes upon your table. She must love you still, Josef Vitek, or she would not tell a lie for you.'

And I remembered my mother, almost as I had last seen her on that day I fled my country – standing in the door with an Austrian officer opposite her, saying, 'No, my son Josef Vitek is not here . . . Only this morning he went out into the fields with his father' – while all the time I was peering at her from a huge chest in which she had once stored her linen.

And thinking it all over, I said aloud to myself, 'My landlady is not my mother and my Greek friend is not an Austrian officer. And the lie that was told this morning was not to save me from fighting for an enemy. But it was told to spare me unpleasantness, and in that they were both alike . . . Yes, Josef Vitek, there are beautiful lies just as there are beautiful women.' And as I said this I shut my eyes and the vision of that public square, plumed with cypress trees, rose before me and I smelled the strange perfume of unbound hair.

As I stood there a knock came on my door, and before I could answer my Greek friend pushed his way into my room.

Yes, before I could answer, my Greek friend pushed his way into my room and his little glinting eyes travelled from the cap upon my head to the untouched bed, and he said bitingly:

'Ah, Josef Vitek, and have you been in such pain that you could not rest except upon your two feet?'

I drew myself up proudly. 'I have not been in pain at all, my friend . . . In fact, everything has been as it should with me. You see, my landlady was mistaken.'

At that my Greek friend smiled a knowing smile. 'Josef Vitek,' he said, 'there are three things that keep a man from his daily task: being sick, or drunk with wine, or under the spell of a woman . . . Now your own testimony sets at naught the first circumstance, and the testimony of my eyes sets at naught the second. There remains only the third excuse . . . Well, we are all human, Josef Vitek, and you are young in the bargain. I was once so myself.'

And for a moment a shadow crossed his face and I knew that he too was thinking of Miriam, for had he not loved her also? . . . As for me, I felt the hot blood rising to my cheeks and the laughter of my Greek friend filled the room.

When my Greek friend had departed I threw myself on my bed, but my sleep was filled with strange dreams; so I awoke at my appointed time feeling as tired as when I had first lain down. And instead of going into my landlady's kitchen for the evening meal, I tiptoed out into the night, thinking:

'To-morrow she will be better humoured . . . Besides, I must be beforehand to my task, to make up for my absence. I shall not even take time to eat.' For, if the truth were known, I did not feel hungry.

But it seemed that I was not to go to my task that night, for as I turned the first corner whom should I see but Elena, standing with her flame-coloured cloak blowing in the wind. And suddenly I felt cold all over and my teeth chattered and I said to myself, 'I must go roundabout before she sees me!' But ere I could retrace my steps I felt her eyes upon me and I heard her voice say:

'Ah, Josef Vitek, so there you are! And whither do you go at such an early hour?'

'To my task,' I answered as coldly as I could in spite of my beating temples.

'To your task, Josef Vitek? . . . *To your task?* . . . On such a night as this, with the moon just rising and the stars waiting to be fanned into a flame? . . . Come, this is not a night for *work*, Josef Vitek!' And as she spoke my night's task seemed very far away, and yet a voice within me made me answer:

'What are a rising moon and flaming stars to me, who must labour and sweat? . . . A man must eat, and unless he be a rich man or a king, he must earn it.'

'Be a king, then, for to-night, Josef Vitek!' she cried, touching me with a finger that burned in spite of its chill. And at that moment all my strength went out of me and I felt my resolution fall as a ripe field before a shining sickle.

On that night we did not climb upward to the public square with its crest of plumed cypresses, but instead we rode out to the sea; for the air was clear and there was no mist to chill us. And we sat in the yellow sand with the perfume of lupines mingling with the wet smell of the ocean, while far off in the west, hanging above the water, the evening star burned so brightly that even the moon could not shame it. And again Elena's teeth flashed in the dusk, and again she let down her blue-black hair, and again her two lips burned my throat. And again I forgot everything that was or ever had been. For it was as if the sea crept in and covered us.

When morning came Elena rose, shaking the sand from her tangled hair, and she left me without a word. And with her going it was as if the sea fell back also, uncovering me, and I remembered everything that was or ever had been. I thought of my native village and my landlady and my nightly task. But the thing that I thought of more than any of these was the monastery near Polna where once I plied my trade as baker. And I recalled the rose garden in which the pious men walked in the noon sunlight and where the bees grew heavy with sweetness, and the hush and peace that fell on the old grey walls at evening, and the tinkling of bells. Yes, I once had plied my trade in such a place even before I knew that trade perfectly, for my good mother had said, 'My son Josef is but a lad – and where better can a lad be than in the shelter of a holy place? Perhaps, who knows, he may end it by being a holy man.' And remembering her hopes for me, I wept, burying my face in the sand.

Thus I lay until noon, and then I rose and went back to the crowded town and to my lodgings. But my landlady was not at the door to greet me, neither were there apples nor spice cakes upon my table; and the coverlet had not been turned down.

Again I rose from sleep at the appointed time, thinking to be beforehand to my task, and again I went out softly so that I might escape the ill-humour of my landlady, and again Elena stood upon the corner waiting. And again when she spoke to me and touched me with her cool fingers I felt my resolution fall as a ripe field before a shining sickle.

And thus the days passed, with my nightly task at the bakery where I work growing farther and farther away, like a tale that had been told. And in all this time I saw nothing of my landlady: for in the morning she was not on hand to greet me and at night I stole out without breaking bread at her table. Only my Greek friend came with news from my comrades, and yet I cared for no word he uttered. It was as if nothing in life mattered except the coming of night and Elena in her flame-coloured cloak. Not even when he said to me, 'Josef Vitek, you cannot go on thus forever . . . presently you will return to find your place taken at the bakery,' did I feel the least uneasiness. If the truth were known, I but laughed at him, and the next day he said:

'If you do not work, Josef Vitek, how shall you live? . . . Who will pay your landlady if you earn no money, and where will you find lodgings?'

'Once I thought of these things,' I returned, 'but what are food and lodgings to me now?'

And looking at me sharply, he said:

'Josef Vitek, you are talking like one already dead. It must be that a woman has bewitched you . . . Come, is she more beautiful than Miriam?'

'She is different,' I answered. 'When Miriam was near I felt a *sweet* pain in my heart.'

He turned away with a hard laugh and presently he said:

'To-morrow is my name-day, Josef Vitek. Have you forgotten that you are pledged to my feast?'

'I cannot come without Elena,' I answered.

'As you will,' returned my Greek friend. 'At a name-day feast there is always room for whatever guests come at the eleventh hour.'

So he departed with my promise. But once he was gone, I thought: 'What will Elena say to a feast? Perhaps she will not like the idea.' And I was disturbed. But that night when I told her of it, she said: 'A feast, did you say? And will there be men there?'

'Yes,' I answered, remembering my Greek friend's last name-day, 'scores of them.'

A strange ravenous look came into her eyes and her lips smiled a discreet smile, concealing her teeth.

'Come let us make haste, Josef Vitek!' she breathed softly. 'For if there is one thing I like above anything in the world, it is a feast.'

And with that her lips grew fuller and more red.

Truly, in spite of many faults, my Greek friend is a brave giver of feasts. Even if my landlady had been minded to provide fare for threescore guests she could not have done better. For the most part it was all as I had prophesied: broth of chicken with a dash of lemon, little bitter-sweet olives, lamb baked with eggplant, and at the end a curd of goat's milk. Only there was chicken as well, fried in sweet butter, and sea bass for those who wished it. And with every course strange and warming drinks: mastica, and mavro-daphne, and retzina, and cognac. And between the courses melancholy music to which the men danced, holding one another's hands in a long line, with the women sitting at the snow-white tables looking on. Yes, between the courses the men danced together, and Elena at my side said:

'What a strange custom! Do you do thus in Bohemia?'

'Nay,' I answered, 'in my country we dance to gay music with the skirts of our partners flying in the breeze.'

'Then let us dance together, Josef Vitek,' she cried, 'when all this sad gliding is finished.'

'As you will,' I replied. And as soon as they had finished I threw a coin to the musicians and I called to them:

'Can you not play us a gay tune? Come, play us a gay tune and *we* shall dance for you!'

With that the feasters broke into a laugh and clapped their hands and the head musician, striking his bow against the strings, began a wild tune that set my pulses leaping. I looked down into Elena's eyes and I said:

'Are you ready? Are you ready to dance with me, knowing nothing of a single measure which I shall tread?'

For answer she rose, pressing her body against mine, and I heard her say between closed teeth:

'Dance, Josef Vitek! Dance and leave such things as measures to Greeks and fools!'

So we danced, and to this day I cannot say what steps were traced by us. For we were like two leaves blown in the wind and I could not even say who led or who followed. But at once I thought:

'It is thus that witches upon broomsticks dance!'

And I felt the hot breath of Elena in my face and I said to myself:

'Josef Vitek, this is not a gay dance! This is not a gay dance for there is something terrible in it!'

And thus we whirled and leaped and swayed and presently the music stopped and I heard the company crying out their pleasure. And with that we stood still . . . We stood still, with the company crying out their pleasure, and presently a press of men swept us toward our table and I felt the hand of my Greek friend upon my shoulder, and I heard his voice saying:

'Come with me, Josef Vitek, for I have something to say to you.'

And though I was loth to leave Elena even for a moment, I went with him and stood apart.

'Josef Vitek,' he said, 'such dancing and such a woman are not for you.'

I felt the blood warm in my face. 'You are right!' I answered in my pride. 'But for that matter there is not a man among us who can measure up to her.'

He looked at me sharply and this time he laughed. 'Josef Vitek, you are a child and no mistake . . . At your age all men are fools!'

I was about to speak when a laugh like silver broke in upon me. Elena stood at my elbow.

'At his age, did you say? . . . Tell me, pray, at what age then are they wise?' And she threw a glance of fire at my Greek friend and I felt my heart grow cold.

She threw a glance of fire at my Greek friend and his little eyes became two points of flame, and he reached over to a near-by table and poured amber wine into an empty glass and gave it to her. She held the glass almost to her lips, then dashed it to the floor. 'Give me red wine or nothing!' she cried.

An ugly look came over the face of my Greek friend and I saw him set his teeth together. Yet he did as she commanded, and presently she stood before us, sipping at red wine in a strange manner which left me shuddering. And as she stained her red lips further with the last drop, she said to my Greek friend:

'Let *us* dance together!'

To which he replied:

'I dance only in the fashion of my country.'

'And I,' she answered, 'in the fashion of any who will pay the piper!'

With that my Greek friend tossed a coin upon the platform where the players sat gossiping and at once they caught up their instruments and began a slow melancholy tune. Then Elena and my Greek friend stepped out upon the floor and she danced in *his* fashion with little snakelike glidings, until she seemed herself just such a creature intent on charming whom she would. And as the music quickened my Greek friend leaped before her like some spellbound thing, and her black hair tumbled in a dark shower about her shoulders, and her smile became wider and wider until I saw her teeth unguarded for the first time.

I saw her teeth unguarded for the first time and I turned away shuddering: *for they were small and sharp and pointed!*

They sat all night, Elena and my Greek friend, at a table which had no third seat; while I stood in a far corner of the room – sick with dread and envy and I know not what. And all night long Elena sipped red wine, and my Greek friend, wine the colour of amber. And neither turned eyes in my direction.

And at dawn Elena rose, slipping on her cloak of flame, and my Greek friend followed after her. They halted for a moment before the door and I thought:

'Shall I warn him against her? Shall I tell him what manner of woman she is to drain the heart's blood from a man?'

But almost at once I grew bitter and I said to myself: 'Has he no eyes of his own?'

And so I let them go together out into the dawn.

For myself, I turned my steps in the direction of my lodgings. The morning air was dank and misty and I felt sick and weary and full of strange confusion. At one moment I longed again for Elena and in the next I hated her. And in the moments that I hated her I thought of my Greek friend, wondering what was to become of him and whether I had done right to let him go thus without protest. But always, in the end, bitterness had its way and I would mutter:

'Does a man who is despoiled warn the thief?'

Thus I came to my lodgings, still at odds with myself. And no landlady stood upon the threshold to greet me. And my room was clean and cold and unadorned, so that I thought of my cell back in that monastery near Polna where I had once plied my trade. Yes, in the grey morning light it seemed as if it might well be that very place, except that here there was no peace. And shivering, I lay down to wait the appointed hour for me to go to my task.

I rose at evening, still sick at heart, and I went softly out into the dusk lest my landlady should hear me. And as I turned in the direction of the bakery where I work – whose shadow should cross my path but the shadow of my Greek friend! For a moment I drew back, but he said quickly:

'Ah, Josef Vitek, I have been waiting for you! . . . Come, let us go to our task together.'

I felt my heart beat fast, but there was nothing to do but go with him and thus we walked in silence, and I thought:

'Is he laughing, Josef Vitek? Or does he repent the wrong he did you?'

And looking at his face, as dark as a shuttered house, I could not answer.

But when we reached the bakery, entering the narrow wash-room where the men gather, I felt his hand upon my shoulder. I felt his hand upon my shoulder in the fashion of an elder brother, and at that moment every one pressed forward full of questions concerning my absence, and I heard my Greek friend say:

'Do not bother him! Cannot you see how pale and spent he is? For a week or more he has been in the hands of the devil. Yes, for a week he has been in the hands of the devil and it is only by a miracle that you have him with you to-night.'

And suddenly, looking at my Greek friend, I understood everything, and I said to as many as could hear me:

'Comrades, he is only half right . . . For a week or more I *have* been in the hands of the devil. But it was not a miracle that saved me. Instead, I was saved by nothing so truly as by this friend of mine, himself.'

And with that my Greek friend broke out into his old laugh, half bitterness and half scorn, but his fingers gripped my shoulder in a way which told me that my words had pleased him.

When morning came my Greek friend walked back with me to my lodgings, and I thought:

'Yes, he has become like an elder brother, indeed. Even now he will not trust me to danger. I might be a child in my first week at school.'

And the thought pleased me because I had always fancied this Greek friend of mine a man without affection. And walking home in the cool grey dawn, I said to him:

'Did you not mark her red lips last night when you danced with her?'

'Yes,' he answered.

'And her eyes like two burning coals?'

'Yes.'

'And her blue-black hair with its perfume?'

'Yes.'

'And at the end, her little sharp white teeth?'

'Yes.'

'Then, did you not fear that she would drain your heart's blood?'

My Greek friend shook his head. 'There is little wine in a cracked jug, Josef Vitek.'

At that moment we both looked up and I felt my Greek friend's hand in mine: a cloak of flame was billowing in the morning air and Elena stood waiting on the corner near my lodgings.

For a moment my heart beat fast. And I heard my Greek friend say between his teeth:

'Courage, brother!'

And we passed her swiftly and her taunting laugh floated after us.

My Greek friend halted at the foot of the stairs to my lodgings and I said farewell to him. But he did not go at once. Instead I saw him standing, as I mounted upward, like the keeper to some forbidden gate.

I entered the house and at the door to my landlady's room I stopped and beat upon it.

'Who is there?' I heard her cracked voice call out.

'It is Josef Vitek,' I cried back.

'Well?'

'I have come home again,' I said, and I went swiftly to my room.

I went swiftly to my room and laid myself down, closing my eyes. And presently I heard the door open gently. I lay quite still, pretending I was fast asleep; and between my half-opened lids I saw my landlady creep gently in and place spice cakes and red apples and grapes upon my table.

As she left again, closing the door softly, a single tear dropped upon my pillow. And I gave a happy sigh and fell into a deep sleep.

I, The Vampire

HENRY KUTTNER

Of all the dozens of American 'pulp' magazines that appeared during the Twenties and Thirties none published more vampire stories than the legendary Weird Tales *and this may, indeed, have helped generate the interest in the subject which prompted Hollywood into making the major series of horror movies in the decade prior to the Second World War. During the thirty years of its existence (from 1923 to 1954)* Weird Tales *published literally hundreds of stories in which a vampire was either the central figure or the final revelation. Seabury Quinn, the magazine's hugely popular undertaker-turned-writer, featured the undead perhaps more than anyone else in his cases about a psychic detective, Jules de Grandin; while among those who followed his example were Robert Bloch, August Derleth, Robert E. Howard, Manly Wade Wellman and Ray Bradbury – men who owed the start of their writing careers to* Weird Tales *and later became household names. Henry Kuttner, the author of this next story, also made his debut in the magazine with an outstandingly gruesome story, 'The Graveyard Rats' (1936) about a greedy cemetery watchman who battles with a horde of rats in the burrows of a graveyard for the spoils from a rich man's grave. Mike Ashley in his* Who's Who in Horror and Fantasy Fiction *(1977) says of this story that it is 'regarded by some as one of the most horrifying stories ever written'. In the years which followed Kuttner proved himself not only an exceptional writer of pure horror but also a versatile author of fantasy and science fiction.*

  Henry Kuttner (1914–58) was born in Los Angeles of German, Jewish, English, Irish and Polish extraction. His childhood was somewhat harsh when his father, a bookshop owner, died when he was five, and his mother was forced to run a boarding house to support him and his two older brothers. It was while he was at High School that Kuttner began to write when he discovered fantasy fiction in the pages of Amazing Stories *– and following the publication of 'The Graveyard Rats' he never looked back. After his marriage to another writer, Catherine Moore, the couple were recruited by Hollywood for film and TV work and consequently Kuttner's fictional output dropped considerably. He did, though, always find time to encourage other writers and was a major influence on Ray Bradbury and several of the other younger generation of American fantasy and horror writers who feature later in this book. He was tragically only forty-two when he died suddenly from an acute coronary. 'I, The Vampire', written for* Weird Tales *in February, 1937, is another landmark variation on our theme, being one of the first stories in which the vampire is portrayed sympathetically as a tragic victim of circumstance, capable of self-sacrifice. It also offers an insider's view of the making of horror movies – thus neatly leading up to the second section of this collection . . .*

* * *

I

The Chevalier Futaine

The party was dull. I had come too early. There was a preview that night at Grauman's Chinese, and few of the important guests would arrive until it was over. Indeed, Jack Hardy, ace director at Summit Pictures, where I worked as assistant director, hadn't arrived – yet – and he was the host. But Hardy had never been noted for punctuality.

I went out on the porch and leaned against a pillar, sipping a cocktail and looking down at the lights of Hollywood. Hardy's place was on the summit of a hill overlooking the film capital, near Falcon Lair, Valentino's famous turreted castle. I shivered a little. Fog was sweeping in from Santa Monica, blotting out the lights to the west.

Jean Hubbard, who was an ingenue at Summit, came up beside me and took the glass out of my hand.

'Hello, Mart,' she said, sipping the liquor. 'Where've you been?'

'Down with the *Murder Desert* troupe, on location in the Mojave,' I said. 'Miss me, honey?'

I drew her close. She smiled up at me, her tilted eyebrows lending a touch of diablerie to the tanned, lovely face. I was going to marry Jean, but I wasn't sure just when.

'Missed you lots,' she said, and held up her lips. I responded.

After a moment I said, 'What's this about the vampire man?'

She chuckled. 'Oh, the Chevalier Futaine. Didn't you read Lolly Parsons' write-up in *Script*? Jack Hardy picked him up last month in Europe. Silly rot. But it's good publicity.'

'Three cheers for publicity,' I said. 'Look what it did for *Birth of a Nation*. But where does the vampire angle come in?'

'Mystery man. Nobody can take a picture of him, scarcely anybody can see him. Weird tales are told about his former life in Paris. Going to play in Jack's *Red Thirst*. The kind of build-up Universal gave Karloff for *Frankenstein*. The Chevalier Futaine' — she rolled out the words with amused relish — 'is probably a singing waiter from a Paris café. I haven't seen him — but the deuce with him, anyway. Mart, I want you to do something for me. For Deming.'

'Hess Deming?' I raised my eyebrows in astonishment. Hess Deming, Summit's biggest box-office star, whose wife, Sandra Colter, had died two days before. She, too, had been an actress, although never the great star her husband was. Hess loved her, I knew — and now I guessed what the trouble was. I said, 'I noticed he was a bit wobbly.'

'He'll kill himself,' Jean said, looking worried. 'I — I feel responsible for him somehow, Mart. After all, he gave me my start at Summit. And he's due for the D.Ts any time now.'

'Well, I'll do what I can,' I told her. 'But that isn't a great deal. After all, getting tight is probably the best thing he could do. I know if I lost you, Jean — '

I stopped. I didn't like to think of it.

Jean nodded. 'See what you can do for him, anyway. Losing Sandra that way was — pretty terrible.'

'What way?' I asked. 'I've been away, remember. I read something about it, but — '

'She just died,' Jean said. 'Pernicious anemia, they said. But Hess told me the doctor really didn't know what it was. She just seemed to grow weaker and weaker until — she passed away.'

I nodded, gave Jean a hasty kiss, and went back into the house. I had just seen Hess Deming walk past, a glass in his hand.

He turned as I tapped his shoulder. 'Oh, Mart,' he said, his voice just a bit fuzzy. He could hold his liquor, but I could tell by his bloodshot eyes that he was almost at the end of his rope. He was a handsome devil, all right, well-built, strong-featured, with level grey eyes and a broad mouth that was usually smiling. It wasn't smiling now. It was slack, and his face was bedewed with perspiration.

'You know about Sandra?' he asked.

'Yeah,' I said. 'I'm sorry, Hess.'

He drank deeply from the glass, wiped his mouth with a grimace of distaste.

'I'm drunk, Mart,' he confided. 'I had to get drunk. It was awful – those last few days. I've got to burn her up.'

I didn't say anything.

'Burn her up. Oh, my God, Mart – that beautiful body of hers, crumbling to dust – and I've got to watch it! She made me promise I'd watch to make sure they burned her.'

I said, 'Cremation's a clean ending, Hess. And Sandra was a clean girl, and a damned good actress.'

He put his flushed face close to mine. 'Yeah – but I've got to burn her up. It'll kill me, Mart. Oh, God!' He put the empty glass down on a table and looked around dazedly.

I was wondering why Sandra had insisted on cremation. She'd given an interview once in which she stressed her dread of fire. Most write-ups of stars are applesauce, but I happened to know that Sandra did dread fire. Once, on the set, I'd seen her go into hysterics when her leading man lit his pipe too near her face.

'Excuse me, Mart,' Hess said. 'I've got to get another drink.'

'Wait a minute,' I said, holding him. 'You want to watch yourself, Hess. You've had too much already.'

'It still hurts,' he said. 'Just a little more and maybe it won't hurt so much.' But he didn't pull away. Instead he stared at me with the dullness of intoxication in his eyes. 'Clean,' he said presently. 'She said that too, Mart. She said burning was a clean death. But, God, that beautiful white body of hers – I can't stand it, Mart! I'm going crazy, I think. Get me a drink, like a good fellow.'

I said, 'Wait here, Hess. I'll get you one.' I didn't add that it would be watered – considerably.

He sank down in a chair, mumbling thanks. As I went off I felt sick. I'd seen too many actors going on the rocks to mistake Hess's symptoms. I knew that his box-office days were over. There would be longer waits between pictures, and then personal appearances, and finally Poverty Row and serials. And in the end maybe a man found dead in a cheap hall bedroom on Main Street, with the gas on.

*

There was a crowd around the bar. Somebody said, 'Here's Mart. Hey, come over and meet the vampire.'

Then I got a shock. I saw Jack Hardy, my host, the director with whom I'd worked on many a hit. He looked like a corpse. And I'd seen him looking plenty bad before. A man with a hangover, or a marijuana jag, isn't a pretty sight, but I'd never seen Hardy like this. He looked as though he was keeping going on his nerve alone. There was no blood in the man.

I'd last seen him as a stocky, ruddy blond, who looked like nothing so much as a wrestler, with his huge biceps, his ugly, good-natured face, and his bristling crop of yellow hair. Now he looked like a skeleton, with skin hanging loosely on the big frame. His face was a network of sagging wrinkles. Pouches bagged beneath his eyes, and those eyes were dull and glazed. About his neck a black silk scarf was knotted tightly.

'Good God, Jack!' I exclaimed. 'What have you been doing to yourself?'

He looked away quickly. 'Nothing,' he said brusquely. 'I'm all right. I want you to meet the Chevalier Futaine – this is Mart Prescott.'

'Pierre,' a voice said. 'Hollywood is no place for titles. Mart Prescott – the pleasure is mine.'

I faced the Chevalier Pierre Futaine.

We shook hands. My first impression was of icy cold, and a slick kind of dryness – and I let go of his hand too quickly to be polite. He smiled at me.

A charming man, the Chevalier. Or so he seemed. Slender, below medium height, his bland, round face seemed incongruously youthful. Blond hair was plastered close to his scalp. I saw that his cheeks were rouged – very deftly, but I know something about make-up. And under the rouge I read a curious, deathly pallor that would have made him a marked man had he not disguised it. Some disease, perhaps, had blanched his skin – but his lips were not artificially reddened. And they were as crimson as blood.

He was clean-shaved, wore impeccable evening clothes, and his eyes were black pools of ink.

'Glad to know you,' I said. 'You're the vampire, eh?'

He smiled. 'So they tell me. But we all serve the dark god of publicity, eh, Mr Prescott? Or – is it Mart?'

'It's Mart,' I said, still staring at him. I saw his eyes go past me, and an extraordinary expression appeared on his face – an expression of amazement, disbelief. Swiftly it was gone.

I turned. Jean was approaching, was at my side as I moved. She said, 'Is this the Chevalier?'

Pierre Futaine was staring at her, his lips parted a little. Almost inaudibly he murmured, 'Sonya.' And then, on a note of interrogation, 'Sonya?'

I introduced the two. Jean said, 'You see, my name isn't Sonya.'

The Chevalier shook his head, an odd look in his black eyes.

'I once knew a girl like you,' he said softly. 'Very much like you. It is strange.'

'Will you excuse me?' I broke in. Jack Hardy was leaving the bar. Quickly I followed him.

I touched his shoulder as he went out the French windows. He jerked out a startled oath, turned a white death-mask of a face to me.

'Damn you, Mart!' he snarled. 'Keep your hands to yourself.'

I put my hands on his shoulders and swung him around.

'What the devil has happened to you?' I asked. 'Listen, Jack, you can't bluff me or lie to me. You know that. I've straightened you out enough times in the past, and I can do it again. Let me in on it.'

His ruined face softened. He reached up and took away my hands. His own were ice-cold, like the hands of the Chevalier Futaine.

'No,' he said. 'No use, Mart. There's nothing you can do. I'm all right, really. Just – overstrain. I had too good a time in Paris.'

I was up against a blank wall. Suddenly, without volition, a thought popped into my mind and out of my mouth before I knew it.

'What's the matter with your neck?' I asked abruptly.

He didn't answer. He just frowned and shook his head.

'I've a throat infection,' he told me. 'Caught it on the steamer.'

His hand went up and touched the black scarf.

There was a croaking, harsh sound from behind us – a sound that didn't seem quite human. I turned. It was Hess Deming. He was swaying in the portal, his eyes glaring and bloodshot, a little trickle of saliva running down his chin.

He said in a dead, expressionless voice that was somehow dreadful, 'Sandra died of a throat infection, Hardy.'

Jack didn't answer. He stumbled back a step. Hess went on dully.

'She got all white and died. And the doctor didn't know what it was, although the death certificate said anaemia. Did you bring back some filthy disease with you, Hardy? Because if you did I'm going to kill you.'

'Wait a minute,' I said. 'A throat infection? I didn't know – '

'There was a wound in her throat – two little marks, close together. That couldn't have killed her, unless some loathsome disease – '

'You're crazy, Hess,' I said. 'You know you're drunk. Listen to me: Jack couldn't have had anything to do with – that.'

Hess didn't look at me. He watched Jack Hardy out of his bloodshot eyes. He went on in that low, deadly monotone:

'Will you swear Mart's right, Hardy? Will you?'

Jack's lips were twisted by some inner agony. I said, 'Go on, Jack. Tell him he's wrong.'

Hardy burst out, 'I haven't been near your wife! I haven't seen her since I got back. There's – '

'That's not the answer I want,' Hess whispered. And he sprang for the other man – reeled forward, rather.

Hess was too drunk, and Jack too weak, for them to do each other any harm, but there was a nasty scuffle for a moment before I separated them. As I pulled them apart, Hess's hand clutched the scarf about Jack's neck, ripped it away.

And I saw the marks on Jack Hardy's throat. Two red, angry little pits, white-rimmed, just over the left jugular.

2

The Cremation of Sandra

It was the next day that Jean telephoned me.

'Mart,' she said, 'we're going to run over a scene for *Red Thirst* tonight at the studio – Stage 6. You've been assigned as assistant director on the pic, so you should be there. And – I had an idea Jack might not tell you. He's been – so odd lately.'

'Thanks, honey,' I said. 'I'll be there. But I didn't know you were in the flicker.'

'Neither did I, but there's been some wire-pulling. Somebody wanted me in it – the Chevalier, I think – and the big boss phoned me this morning and let me in on the secret. I don't feel up to it, though. Had a bad night.'

'Sorry,' I sympathized. 'You were okay when I left you.'

'I had a – nightmare,' she said slowly. 'It was rather frightful, Mart. It's funny, though, I can't remember what it was about. Well – you'll be there to-night?'

I said I would, but as it happened I was unable to keep my promise. Hess Deming telephoned me, asking if I'd come out to his Malibu place and drive him into town. He was too shaky to handle a car himself, he said, and Sandra's cremation was to take place that afternoon. I got out my roadster and sent it spinning west on Sunset. In twenty minutes I was at Deming's beach house.

The house-boy let me in, shaking his head gravely as he recognized me.

'Mist' Deming pretty bad,' he told me. 'All morning drinking gin – straight – '

From upstairs Hess shouted, 'That you, Mart? Okay – I'll be down right away. Come up here, Jim!'

The Japanese, with a meaning glance at me, pattered upstairs.

I wandered over to a table, examining the magazines upon it. A little breath of wind came through the half-open window, fluttering a scrap of paper. A word on it caught my eye, and I picked up the note. For that's what it was. It was addressed to Hess, and after one glance I had no compunction about scanning it.

'Hess dear,' the message read. 'I feel I'm going to die very soon. And I want you to do something for me. I've been out of my head, I know, saying things I didn't mean. Don't cremate me, Hess. Even though I were dead I'd feel the fire – I know it. Bury me in a vault in Forest Lawn – and don't embalm me. I shall be dead when you find this, but I know you'll do as I wish, dear. And, alive or dead, I'll always love you.'

The note was signed by Sandra Colter, Hess's wife. This was odd. I wondered whether Hess had seen it yet.

There was a little hiss of indrawn breath from behind me. It was Jim, the house-boy. He said, 'Mist' Prescott – I find that note last night. Mist' Hess not seen it. It Mis' Colter's writing.'

He hesitated, and I read fear in his eyes – sheer, unashamed fear. He put a brown forefinger on the note.

'See that, Mist' Prescott?'

He was pointing to a smudge of ink that half obscured the signature. I said, 'Well?'

'I do that, Mist' Prescott. When I pick up that note. The ink – not dry.'

I stared at him. He turned hastily at the sound of footsteps on the stairs. Hess Deming was coming down, rather shakily.

I think it was then that I first realized the horrible truth. I didn't believe it, though – not then. It was too fantastic, too incredible; yet something of the truth must have crept into my mind, for there was no other explanation for what I did then.

Hess said, 'What have you got there, Mart?'

'Nothing,' I said quietly. I crumpled the note and thrust it into my pocket. 'Nothing important, anyway. Ready to go?'

He nodded, and we went to the door. I caught a glimpse of Jim staring after us, an expression of – was it relief? – in his dark, wizened face.

The crematory was in Pasadena, and I left Hess there. I would have stayed with him, but he wouldn't have it. I knew he didn't want anyone to be watching him when Sandra's body was being incinerated. And I knew it would be easier for him that way. I took a short cut through the Hollywood hills, and that's where the trouble started.

I broke an axle. Recent rains had gullied the road, and I barely saved the car from turning over. After that I had to hike miles to the nearest telephone, and then I wasted more time waiting for a taxi to pick me up. It was nearly eight o'clock when I arrived at the studio.

The gateman let me in, and I hurried to Stage 6. It was dark. Cursing under my breath, I turned away, and almost collided with a small figure. It was Forrest, one of the cameramen. He let out a curious squeal, and clutched my arm.

'That you, Mart? Listen, will you do me a favour? I want you to watch a print – '

'Haven't time,' I said. 'Seen Jean around here? I was to – '

'It's about that,' Forest said. He was a shrivelled, monkey-faced little chap, but a mighty good cameraman. 'They've gone – Jean and Hardy and the Chevalier. There's something funny about that guy.'

'Think so? Well, I'll phone Jean. I'll look at your rushes tomorrow.'

'She won't be home,' he told me. 'The Chevalier took her over to the Grove. Listen, Mart, you've *got* to watch this. Either I don't know how to handle a grinder any more, or that Frenchman is the damnedest thing I've ever shot. Come over to the theatre, Mart – I've got the reel ready to run. Just developed the rough print myself.'

'Oh, all right,' I assented, and followed Forrest to the theatre.

I found a seat in the dark little auditorium, and listened to Forrest moving about in the projection booth. He clicked on the amplifier and said, 'Hardy didn't want any pictures taken – insisted on it, you know. But the boss told me to leave one of the automatic cameras going– not to bother with the sound – just to get an idea how the French guy would screen. Lucky it wasn't one of the old rattler cameras, or Hardy would have caught on. Here it comes, Mart!'

I heard a click as the amplifier was switched off. White light flared on the screen. It faded, gave place to a picture – the interior of Stage 6.

The set was incongruous – a mid-Victorian parlour, with overstuffed plush chairs, gilt-edged paintings, even a particularly hideous what-not. Jack Hardy moved into the range of the camera. On the screen his face seemed to leap out at me like a death's-head, covered with sagging, wrinkled skin. Following him came Jean, wearing a tailored suit – no one dresses for rehearsals – and behind her –

I blinked, thinking that my eyes were tricking me. Something like a glowing fog – oval, tall as a man – was moving across the screen. You've seen the nimbus of light on the screen when a flash-light is turned directly on the camera? Well – it was like that, except that its source was not traceable. And, horribly, it moved forward at about the pace a man would walk.

The amplifier clicked again. Forrest said, 'When I saw it on the negative I thought I was screwy, Mart. I saw the take – there wasn't any funny light there. Look – ' The oval, glowing haze was motionless beside Jean, and she was looking directly at it, a smile on her lips. 'Mart, when that was taken, Jean was looking right at the French guy!'

I said, somewhat hoarsely, 'Hold it, Forrest. Right there.'

The images slowed down, became motionless. Jean's left profile was toward the camera. I leaned forward, staring at something I had glimpsed on the girl's neck. It was scarcely visible save as a tiny, discoloured mark on Jean's throat, above the jugular – but unmistakably the same wound I had seen on the throat of Jack Hardy the night before!

I heard the amplifier click off. Suddenly the screen showed blindingly white, and then went black.

I waited a moment, but there was no sound from the booth.

'Forrest,' I called. 'You okay?'

There was no sound. The faint whirring of the projector had died. I got up quickly and went to the back of the theatre. There were two entrances to the booth, a door which opened on stairs leading down to the alley outside, and a hole in the floor reached by means of a metal ladder. I went up this swiftly, an ominous apprehension mounting within me.

Forrest was still there. But he was no longer alive. He lay sprawled on his back, his wizened face staring up blindly, his head twisted at an impossible angle. It was quite apparent that his neck had been broken almost instantly.

I sent a hasty glance at the projector. The can of film was gone! And the door opening on the stairway was ajar a few inches.

I stepped out on the stairs, although I knew I would see no one. The white-lit, broad alley between Stages 6 and 4 was silent and empty.

The sound of running feet came to me, steadily growing louder. A man came racing into view. I recognized him as one of the publicity gang. I hailed him.

'Can't wait,' he gasped, but slowed down nevertheless.

I said, 'Have you seen anyone around here just now? The – Chevalier Futaine?'

He shook his head. 'No, but – ' His face was white as he looked up at me. 'Hess Deming's gone crazy. I've got to contact the papers.'

Ice gripped me. I raced down the stairs, clutched his arm.

'What do you mean?' I snapped. 'Hess was all right when I left him. A bit tight, that's all.'

His face was glistening with sweat. 'It's awful – I'm not sure yet what happened. His wife – Sandra Colter – came to life while they were cremating her. They saw her through the window, you know – screaming and pounding at the glass while she was being burned alive. Hess got her out too late. He went stark, raving mad. Suspended animation, they say – I've got to get to a phone, Mr Prescott!'

He tore himself away, sprinted in the direction of the administration buildings.

I put my hand in my pocket and pulled out a scrap of paper. It was the note I had found in Hess Deming's house. The words danced and wavered before my eyes. Over and over I was telling myself, 'It can't be true! Such things can't happen!'

I didn't mean Sandra Colter's terrible resurrection during the cremation. That, alone, might be plausibly explained – catalepsy, perhaps. But taken in conjunction with certain other occurrences, it led to one definite conclusion – and it was a conclusion I dared not face.

What had poor Forrest said? That the Chevalier was taking Jean to the Cocoanut Grove? Well –

The taxi was still waiting. I got in.

'The Ambassador,' I told the driver grimly. 'Twenty bucks if you hit the green lights all the way.'

3
The Black Coffin

All night I had been combing Hollywood – without success. Neither the Chevalier Futaine nor Jean had been to the Grove, I discovered. And no one knew the Chevalier's address. A telephone call to the studio, now ablaze with excitement over the Hess Deming disaster and the Forrest killing, netted me exactly nothing. I went the rounds of Hollywood night life vainly. The Trocadero, Sardi's, all three of the Brown Derbies, the smart, notorious clubs of the Sunset eighties – nowhere could I find my quarry. I telephoned Jack Hardy a dozen times, but got no answer. Finally, in a 'private club' in Culver City, I met with my first stroke of good luck.

'Mr Hardy's upstairs,' the proprietor told me, looking anxious. 'Nothing wrong, I hope, Mr Prescott? I heard about Deming.'

'Nothing,' I said. 'Take me up to him.'

'He's sleeping it off,' the man admitted. 'Tried to drink the place dry, and I put him upstairs where he'd be safe.'

'Not the first time, eh?' I said, with an assumption of lightness. 'Well, bring up some coffee, will you? Black. I've got to – talk to him.'

But it was half an hour before Hardy was in any shape to understand what I was saying. At last he sat up on the couch, blinking, and a gleam of realization came into his sunken eyes.

'Prescott,' he said, 'can't you leave me alone?'

I leaned close to him, articulating carefully so he would be sure to understand me. 'I know what the Chevalier Futaine is,' I said.

And I waited for the dreadful, impossible confirmation, or for the words which would convince me that I was an insane fool.

Hardy looked at me dully. 'How did you find out?' he whispered.

An icy shock went through me. Up to that moment I had not really believed, in spite of all the evidence. But now Hardy was confirming the suspicions which I had not let myself believe.

I didn't answer his question. Instead, I said, 'Do you know about Hess?'

He nodded, and at sight of the agony in his face I almost pitied him. Then the thought of Jean steadied me.

'Do you know where he is now?' I asked.

'No. What are you talking about?' he flared suddenly. 'Are you mad, Mart? Do you – '

'I'm not mad. But Hess Deming is.'

He looked at me like a cowering, whipped dog.

I went on grimly: 'Are you going to tell me the truth? How you got those marks on your throat? How you met this – creature? And where he's taken Jean?'

'Jean!' He looked genuinely startled. 'Has he got – I didn't know that, Mart – I swear I didn't. You – you've been a good friend to me, and – and I'll tell you the truth – for your sake and Jean's – although now it may be too late – '

My involuntary movement made him glance at me quickly. Then he went on.

'I met him in Paris. I was out after new sensations – but I didn't expect anything like that. A Satanist club – devil-worshippers, they were. The ordinary stuff – cheap, furtive blasphemy. But it was there that I met – him.

'He can be a fascinating chap when he tries. He drew me out, made me tell him about Hollywood – about the women we have here. I bragged a little. He asked me about the stars, whether they were really as beautiful as they seemed. His eyes were hungry as he listened to me, Mart.

'Then one night I had a fearful nightmare. A monstrous, black horror crept in through my window and attacked me – bit me in the throat, I dreamed, or thought I did. After that –

'I was in his power. He told me the truth. He made me his slave, and I could do nothing. His powers – are not human.'

I licked dry lips. Hardy continued:

'He made me bring him here, introducing him as a new discovery to be starred in *Red Thirst* – I'd mentioned the picture to him, before I – knew. How he must have laughed at me! He made me serve him, keeping away photographers, making sure that there were no cameras, no mirrors near him. And for a reward – he let me live.'

I knew I should feel contempt for Hardy, panderer to such a loathsome evil. But somehow I couldn't.

I said quietly, 'What about Jean? Where does the Chevalier live?'

He told me. 'But you can't do anything, Mart. There's a vault under the house, where he stays during the day. It can't be opened, except with a key he always keeps with him – a silver key. He had a door specially made, and then did something to it so that nothing can open it but that key. Even dynamite wouldn't do it, he told me.'

I said, 'Such things – can be killed.'

'Not easily. Sandra Colter was a victim of his. After death she, too, became a vampire, sleeping by day and living only at night. The fire destroyed her, but there's no way to get into the vault under Futaine's house.'

'I wasn't thinking of fire,' I said. 'A knife – '

'Through the heart,' Hardy interrupted almost eagerly. 'Yes – and decapitation. I've thought of it myself, but I can do nothing. I – am his slave, Mart.'

I said nothing, but pressed the bell. Presently the proprietor appeared.

'Can you get me a butcher-knife?' I measured with my hands. 'About so long? A sharp one?'

Accustomed to strange requests, he nodded. 'Right away, Mr Prescott.'

As I followed him out, Hardy said weakly, 'Mart.'

I turned.

'Good luck,' he said. The look on his wrecked face robbed the words of their pathos.

'Thanks,' I forced myself to say. 'I don't blame you, Jack, for what's happened. I – I'd have done the same.'

I left him there, slumped on the couch, staring after me with eyes that had looked into hell.

It was past daylight when I drove out of Culver City, a long, razor-edged knife hidden securely inside my coat. And the day went past all too quickly. A telephone call told me that Jean had not yet returned home. It took me more than an hour to locate a certain man I wanted – a man who had worked for the studio before on certain delicate jobs. There was little about locks he did not know, as the police had sometimes ruefully admitted.

His name was Axel Ferguson, a bulky, good-natured Swede, whose thick fingers seemed more adapted to handling a shovel than the mechanisms of locks. Yet he was as expert as Houdini – indeed, he had at one time been a professional magician.

The front door of Futaine's isolated canyon home proved no bar to Ferguson's fingers and the tiny sliver of steel he used. The house, a modern two-story place, seemed deserted. But Hardy had said *below* the house.

We went down the cellar stairs and found ourselves in a concrete-lined passage that ran down at a slight angle for perhaps thirty feet. There the corridor ended in what seemed to be a blank wall of bluish steel. The glossy surface of the door was unbroken, save for a single keyhole.

Ferguson set to work. At first he hummed under his breath, but after a time he worked in silence. Sweat began to glisten on his face. Trepidation assailed me as I watched.

The flashlight he had placed beside him grew dim. He inserted another battery, got out unfamiliar-looking apparatus. He buckled on dark goggles, and handed me a pair. A blue, intensely brilliant flame began to play on the door.

It was useless. The torch was discarded after a time, and Ferguson returned to his tools. He was using a stethoscope, taking infinite pains in the delicate movements of his hands.

It was fascinating to watch him. But all the time I realized that the night was coming, that presently the sun would go down, and that the life of the vampire lasts from sunset to sunrise.

At last Ferguson gave up. 'I can't do it,' he told me, panting as though from a hard race. 'And if I can't, nobody can. Even Houdini couldn't have broken this lock. The only thing that'll open it is the key.'

'All right, Axel,' I said dully. 'Here's your money.'

He hesitated, watching me. 'You going to stay here, Mr Prescott?'

'Yeah,' I said. 'You can find your way out. I'll – wait awhile.'

'Well, I'll leave the light with you,' he said. 'You can let me have it sometime, eh?'

He waited, and, as I made no answer, he departed, shaking his head.

Then utter silence closed around me. I took the knife out of my coat, tested its edge against my thumb, and settled back to wait.

Less than half an hour later the steel door began to swing open. I stood up. Through the widening crack I saw a bare, steel-lined chamber, empty save for a long, black object that rested on the floor. It was a coffin.

The door was wide. Into view moved a white, slender figure – Jean, clad in a diaphanous, silken robe. Her eyes were wide, fixed and staring. She looked like a sleep-walker.

A man followed her – a man wearing impeccable evening clothes. Not a hair was out of place on his sleek blond head, and he was touching his lips delicately with a handkerchief as he came out of the vault.

There was a little crimson stain on the white linen where his lips had brushed.

4
I, The Vampire

Jean walked past me as though I didn't exist. But the Chevalier Futaine paused, his eyebrows lifted. His black eyes pierced through me.

The handle of the knife was hot in my hand. I moved aside to block Futaine's way. Behind me came a rustle of silk, and from the corner of my eye I saw Jean pause hesitatingly.

The Chevalier eyed me, toying negligently with his handkerchief. 'Mart,' he said slowly. 'Mart Prescott.' His eyes flickered toward the knife, and a little smile touched his lips.

I said, 'You know why I'm here, don't you?'

'Yes,' he said. 'I – heard you. I was not disturbed. Only one thing can open this door.'

From his pocket he drew a key, shining with a dull silver sheen.

'Only this,' he finished, replacing it. 'Your knife is useless, Mart Prescott.'

'Maybe,' I said, edging forward very slightly. 'What have you done to Jean?'

A curious expression, almost of pain, flashed into his eyes. 'She is mine,' he shot out half angrily. 'You can do nothing, for – '

I sprang then, or, at least, I tried to. The blade of the knife sheared down, straight for Futaine's white shirtfront. It was arrested in midair. Yet he had not moved. His eyes had bored into mine, suddenly, terribly, and it seemed as though a wave of fearful energy had blasted out at me – paralyzing me, rendering me helpless. I stood rigid. Veins throbbed in my temples as I tried to move – to bring down the knife. It was useless. I stood as immovable as a statue.

The Chevalier brushed past me.

'Follow, he said almost casually, and like an automaton I swung about, began to move along the passage. What hellish hypnotic power was this that held me helpless?

Futaine led the way upstairs. It was not yet dark, although the sun had gone down. I followed him into a room, and at his gesture dropped into a chair. At my side was a small table. The Chevalier touched my arm gently, and something like a mild electric shock went through me. The knife dropped from my fingers, clattering to the table.

Jean was standing rigidly near by, her eyes dull and expressionless. Futaine moved to her side, put an arm about her waist. My mouth felt as though it were filled with mud, but somehow I managed to croak out articulate words.

'Damn you, Futaine! Leave her alone!'

He released her, and came toward me, his face dark with anger.

'You fool, I could kill you now, very easily. I could make you go down to the busiest corner of Hollywood and slit your throat with that knife. I have the power. You have found out much, apparently. Then you know – my power.'

'Yes,' I muttered thickly. 'I know that. You devil – Jean is mine!'

The face of a beast looked into mine. He snarled, 'She is not yours. Nor is she – *Jean*. She is Sonya!'

I remembered what Futaine had murmured when he had first seen Jean. He read the question in my eyes.

'I knew a girl like that once, very long ago. That was Sonya. They killed her – put a stake through her heart, long ago in Thurn. Now that I've found this girl, who might be a reincarnation of Sonya – they are so alike – I shall not give her up. Nor can anyone force me.'

'You've made her a devil like yourself,' I said through half-paralyzed lips. 'I'd rather kill her – '

Futaine turned to watch Jean. 'Not yet,' he said softly. 'She is mine – yes. She bears the stigmata. But she is still – alive. She will not become – *wampyr* – until she has died, or until she has tasted the red milk. She shall do that tonight.'

I cursed him bitterly, foully. He touched my lips, and I could utter no sound. Then they left me – Jean and her master. I heard a door close quietly.

The night dragged on. Futile struggles had convinced me that it was useless to attempt escape – I could not even force a whisper through my lips. More than once I felt myself on the verge of madness – thinking of Jean, and remembering Futaine's ominous words. Eventually agony brought its own surcease, and I fell into a kind of coma, lasting for how long I could not guess. Many hours had passed, I knew, before I heard footsteps coming toward my prison.

Jean moved into my range of vision. I searched her face with my eyes, seeking for some mark of a dreadful metamorphosis. I could find none. Her beauty was unmarred, save for the terrible little wounds on her throat. She went to a couch and quietly lay down. Her eyes closed.

The Chevalier came past me and went to Jean's side. He stood looking down at her. I have mentioned before the incongruous youthfulness of his face. That was gone now. He looked old – old beyond imagination.

At last he shrugged and turned to me. His fingers brushed my lips again, and I found that I could speak. Life flooded back into my veins, bringing lancing twinges of pain. I moved an arm experimentally. The paralysis was leaving me.

The Chevalier said, 'She is still – clean. I could not do it.'

Amazement flooded me. My eyes widened in disbelief.

Futaine smiled wryly. 'It is quite true. I could have made her as myself – undead. But at the last moment I forbade her.' He looked toward the windows. 'It will be dawn soon.'

I glanced at the knife on the table beside me. The Chevalier put out a hand and drew it away.

'Wait,' he said. 'There is something I must tell you, Mart Prescott. You say that you know who and what I am.'

I nodded.

'Yet you cannot know,' he went on. 'Something you have learned, and something you have guessed, but you can never know me. You are human, and I am – the undead.

'Through the ages I have come, since first I fell victim to another vampire – for thus is the evil spread. Deathless and not alive, bringing fear and sorrow always, knowing the bitter agony of Tantalus, I have gone down through the weary centuries. I have known Richard and Henry and Elizabeth of England, and ever have I brought terror and destruction in the night, for I am an alien thing. I am the undead.'

The quiet voice went on, holding me motionless in its weird spell.

'I, the vampire, I, the accursed, the shining evil, *negotium perambulans in tenebris* . . . but I was not always thus. Long ago in Thurn, before the shadow fell upon me, I loved a girl – Sonya. But the vampire visited me, and I sickened and died – and awoke. Then I arose.

'It is the curse of the undead to prey upon those they love. I visited Sonya. I made her my own. She, too, died, and for a brief while we walked the earth together, neither alive nor dead. But that was not Sonya. It was her body, yes, but I had not loved her body alone. I realized too late that I had destroyed her utterly.

'One day they opened her grave, and the priest drove a stake through her heart, and gave her rest. Me they could not find, for my coffin was hidden too well. I put love behind me then, knowing that there was none for such as I.

'Hope came to me when I found – Jean. Hundreds of years have passed since Sonya crumbled to dust, but I thought I had found her again. And – I took her. Nothing human could prevent me.'

The Chevalier's eyelids sagged. He looked infinitely old.

'Nothing human. Yet in the end I found that I could not condemn her to the hell that is mine. I thought I had forgotten love. But, long and long ago, I loved Sonya. And, because of her, and because I know that I would only destroy, as I did once before, I shall not work my will on this girl.'

I turned to watch the still figure on the couch. The Chevalier followed my gaze and nodded slowly.

'Yes, she bears the stigmata. She will die, unless' – he met my gaze unflinchingly – 'unless I die. If you had broken into the vault yesterday, if you had sunk that knife into my heart, she would be free now.' He glanced at the windows again. 'The sun will rise soon.'

Then he went quickly to Jean's side. He looked down at her for a moment.

'She is very beautiful,' he murmured. 'Too beautiful for hell.'

The Chevalier swung about, went toward the door. As he passed me he threw something carelessly on the table, something that tinkled as it fell. In the portal he paused, and a little smile twisted the scarlet lips. I remembered him thus, framed against the black background of the doorway, his sleek blond head erect and unafraid. He lifted his arm in a gesture that should have been theatrical, but, somehow, wasn't.

'And so farewell. I who am about to die – '

He did not finish. In the faint greyness of dawn I saw him striding away, heard his footsteps on the stairs, receding and faint – heard a muffled clang as of a great door closing. The paralysis had left me. I was trembling a little, for I realized what I must do soon. But I knew I would not fail.

I glanced down at the table. Even before I saw what lay beside the knife, I knew what would be there. A silver key . . .

II
The Films

The Bride of the Isles

'LORD BYRON'
(James Robinson Planche)

The famous gathering of literati in June 1816 at the Villa Diodati beside Lake Geneva in Switzerland which included the poets, Lord Byron and Percy Shelley, Byron's physician, John William Polidori, and Shelley's young mistress, Mary Godwin, not only inspired the classic horror novel, Frankenstein, *but also a novella,* The Vampyre, *and a third, incomplete, work,* A Fragment of a Novel. *Curiously, in the case of* Frankenstein *and* The Vampyre *both were wrongly attributed in their first editions:* Frankenstein *to Percy Shelley (who had merely written a Foreword to his mistress's book) and* The Vampyre *as 'a Tale by Lord Byron' in the April 1, 1819 issue of* The New Monthly Magazine. *(Does the date of this publication have any relevance, I wonder!) The mistake over* Frankenstein *was quickly remedied, however, but the belief that Byron had written* The Vampyre *persisted for some years, even when a stage version was launched in 1820, first in London at the Theatre Royal and then at the Theatre Royal, Dublin. At both venues a sixpenny souvenir 'novelisation' was on sale to theatregoers (undoubtedly one of the earliest examples of a 'tie-in' publication) and this carried on its title page the words: 'The Bride of the Isles, A Tale Founded on the Popular Legend of the Vampire by Lord Byron.' A copy of the rare Irish issue ('Printed and sold by J. Charles, 57, Mary-Street, Dublin') now in my possession also reprints on the first page ten lines of verse stated to be, 'Lord Byron's description of a Vampire'. The intention of the publisher to convince his customers that Byron is the author is abundantly clear. Nor is his oportunism finished there: for below the title is the admonition: 'From which is taken*

*the much-admired piece of that name now performing with un-
bounded applause.'*

*Who wrote this novelisation is, therefore, a complete mystery:
though we do know that the stage adaptation of Polidori's tale was
created by a certain James Robinson Planche (1796–1880), reputedly
one of the most prolific dramatists of his time. Planche had begun
writing for the theatre in 1818 and was responsible for introducing a
number of innovations into the theatre including historical accuracy in
stage costumes and settings. For The Vampyre he also introduced a
new form of stage trap-door – a 'Vampire Trap' – which enabled the
central character to make a spectacular entrance. Interestingly, in the
light of the Byron controversy, Planche devoted a lot of his later
energies to getting proper copyright protection for theatrical scripts:
though whether the publication of 'The Bride of the Isles' by 'Lord
Byron' played any part in his campaign can now only be a matter for
speculation! The man to appear as Lord Ruthven, the first stage
vampire, was Thomas Potter Cooke (1786–1864), a former merchant
seaman who had lead an adventurous life at sea after running away to
join the navy at the tender age of ten. After being shipwrecked off
Cuxhaven, Cooke returned to dry land and joined the Royal Theatre
company in 1804 where he immediately displayed a talent for acting.
Not surprisingly, he was very good at playing sea-faring roles –making
almost 800 appearances in the famous nautical melodrama,* Black-
eyed Susan *– but was also a considerable success in* The Bride of the
Isles *which, after lengthy spells in London and Dublin, transferred to
the Porte St. Martin in Paris for almost a year. He is said to have played
the vampire with 'great gusto', glaring malevolently at his victims and
the audience in turn. The most bizarre element to a modern
theatregoer would probably be the fact that the story is set in Scotland
and Ruthven the Vampire wears a kilt! Today Cooke's contribution in
introducing the vampire to its first new medium outside print is
scarcely known and little acknowledged. The republication of* The
Bride of the Isles *for the first time at last allows me to record his
contribution.*

*   *   *

There is a popular superstition *still extant* in the southern isles of
Scotland, but not with the force as it was a century since, that the
souls of persons, whose actions in the mortal state were so wickedly
attrocious as to deny all possibility of happiness in that of the next;

were doomed to everlasting perdition, but had the power given them by infernal spirits to be for awhile the scourge of the living.

This was done by allowing the wicked spirit to enter the body of another person at the moment their own soul had winged its flight from earth; the corpse was thus reanimated – the same look, the same voice, the same expression of countenance, with physical powers to eat and drink, and partake of human enjoyments, but with the most wicked propensities, and in this state they were called Vampires. This second existence, as it may not improperly be termed, is held on a tenure of the most horrid and diobolical nature. Every *All-Hallow E'en*, he must wed a lovely virgin, and slay her, which done, he is to catch her warm blood and drink it, and from this draught he is renovated for *another* year, and free to take *another* shape, and pursue his Satannic course; but if he failed in procuring a wife at the appointed time, or had not opportunity to make the sacrifice before the moon set, the Vampire *was no more* – he did not turn into a skeleton, but literally vanished into air and nothingness.

One of these demoniac sprites, Oscar Montcalm, of infamous notoriety in the Scotch annals of crime and murder, (who was decapitated by the hands of the common executioner), was a most successful Vampire, and many were the poor unfortunate maidens who had been sacrificed to support his supernatural career, roving from place to place, and every year changing his shape as opportunity presented itself, but always choosing to enter the corpse of some man of rank and power, as by that means his voracious appetite for luxury was gratified.

Oscar Montcalm had seen, and distantly adored in his mortal state, the superior beauty of the Lady Margaret, daughter of the Baron of the Isles, the good Lord Ronald; but, such was his situation, he had not dared to address her; however, he did not forget her in his Vampire state, but marked her out for one of his victims, in revenge for the scorn with which he had been treated by her father.

Lady Margaret, though lovely and well proportioned, entered her twentieth year unmarried, nor had she ever been addressed by a suitor whom she could regard with the least partiality, and with much anxiety she sought to know whether she should ever enter into wedlock, and what sort of person her future lord would be. With credulity pardonable to the times in which she lived, and the narrow education then given to females, even of rank, she consulted Sage Seer and Witch, as to this important event; but it is not to be wondered at that she met with many contradictions, every one telling a different tale. At length urged on by the irresistible desire to pry into futurity, she repaired with her two maidens, Effie and Constance, to the CAVE of FINGAL, where, cutting off a lock of her hair, and joining it to a ring from her finger, she cast it into the well, according to the directions she had received from Merna, the Hag of the mountains, who had instructed the fair one as to this expedition.

No sooner was the ring flung into well than a dreadful storm arose; the torches, which the attendant maidens had borne, were extinguished, and the immense cave was in utter darkness: loud and dreadful was the thunder, accompanied by a horrid confusion of sounds, which beggars description.

Margaret and her companions sunk on their knees; but they were too stupified with horror: to pray, or to endeavour to retrace their way out of this den of horrors. Of a sudden, the cave was brilliantly illuminated. But with no visible means of light, for there were neither torch, lamp, or candle. Solemn music was heard, slow and awfully grand, and in a few minutes two figures appeared, one heavy morose in countenance, and clad in dark robes, who announced herself as Uno, the spirit of the storm, and touching a sable curtain, discovered to the view of Margaret the figure of a noble young warrior, Ruthven, earl of Marsden, who had accompanied her father to the wars. Again the storm resounded, the curtain closed, and the cave resumed its darkness; but this was only transient – the brilliant light returned – Una was gone, and the light figure, dressed in transparent robes, sprinkled over with spangles remained. With her wand she pulled aside the curtain, and a young man of interesting appearance was visible, but his person was a stranger to the fair one. Ariel, the spirit of the Air, then waved her hand to the entrance of the cave, as a signal for them to depart, and bowing low, they withdrew, amid strains of heart thrilling harmony, rejoiced to find themselves once more in an open space, and they happily returned in safety to the baron's castle. The Lady Margaret was well pleased with what she had seen, as promising her two husbands, though she was somewhat puzzled by calling to mind a couplet that Ariel had repeated three or four times, while the curtain remained undrawn.

> 'But once, fair maid, will you be wed,
> 'You'll know no second bridal bed.'

What could this mean? Surely she would never stoop to illicit desires or intrigue? She thought she knew her own heart too well.

The Vampire had seen into the designs of Margaret to visit the Cave of Fingal, and he sought out Ariel and Uno, to whom, by virtue of his supernatural rights, he had easy access. The spirit of the air would not befriend him, but the spirit of the storm assisted him to pry into futurity; and to suit his views, she presented the figure of Ruthven, earl of Marsden. In the mean time, Marsden had the good fortune to save Lord Ronald's life in the battle, and the wars being ended, or at least suspended for a time, he invited the gallant youth home with him to his castle, to pass a few months amid the social rites of hospitality and the pleasures of the chase.

The Lady Margaret received her father with dutiful affection, and gratitude to providence for his safe return, and she beheld young Marsden with secret delight; but when informed that he had preserved the baron from overpowering enemies, her gratitude knew no bounds, and she looked so beautiful and engaging, while returning her thankful effusions for the service he had rendered her father, that the earl could not resist the impulse, and from that hour became deeply enamoured of the lovely fair one.

Marsden's rank and birth were unexceptionable but his fortune was very inadequate to support a title, which made him (added to the love of military glory) enter into the profession of arms, of which he was an ornament.

Margaret was an only child, and her father abounding in wealth and honours; it might therefore be presumed that an ambition might lead him to form very exalted views for the aggrandizement of his heiress; and so he had, but perceiving how high his preserver stood in the good graces of his darling child, and that the passion was becoming mutual, he resolved not to give any interruption to their happiness, but if Marsden could win Margaret to let him have her, as a rich reward for the service he had performed amid the clang of arms.

Parties were daily formed by the baron for the chace, hawking, or fishing, while the evening was given to the festive dance, or the minstrels tuned their harps in the great hall, and sang the deeds of scottish chiefs, long since departed, amongst whom the heroic Wallace was not forgot.

The loves of Ruthven and Lady Margaret were now generally known throughout the islands and congratulations poured in from every quarter.

A day was fixed for the nuptials, and magnificent preparations were made at the castle for the celebration of the ceremony, when the sudden and severe illness of the baron caused a delay. He wished them not to defer their marriage on his account; but the young people, in this instance, would not obey him, declaring their joys would be incomplete without his revered presence.

The baron blessed them for this instance of love and filial duty, but he still felt a strong desire to have the marriage concluded.

The baron was scarce recovered, when he and Ruthven were summoned to the field of battle, a war having broke out in Flanders, and the marriage was deferred till their return; and taking a most affectionate leave of the Lady Margaret, the father and lover left the castle, and the fair one in the charge of old Alexander, the faithful steward, with many commands and cautions respecting the edifice and the Lady, whom they both regarded as a gem of inestimable value, with whom they were loath to part, but imperious duty and the calls of honour allowed no alternative.

Robert, the old Steward's son, attended the baron abroad; and Marsden took his own servant the faithful Gilbert. They were successful in several skirmishes with the enemy, but in the final engagement Ruthven lost his life, dying in the arms of the Lord of the Isles, who mourned over him as for a beloved son, and he ordered Robert and Gilbert, who were on the spot, to convey the body to a place beyond the carnage, that when the battle was over he might see it, (if he himself survived,) and have the valued remains interred in a manner that became an earl and a soldier, dying in defending his country's cause.

The battle ended, for the glory and success of Great Britain, and the good Baron of the Isles was unhurt, so was Robert, but Gilbert was amongst the slain.

Lord Ronald, fatigued with the sharp action of the day, in which he had borne his part with a vigour surprising to his time of life, for his head was now silvered over with the honourable badge of age, repaired to his tent to take some refreshment and an hour's rest on his couch, to invigorate his frame. The couch eased his weary limbs, but his eyes closed not, and all his thoughts were on Ruthven, and the distress the sad news would give to his dear child. He arose, and with trembling fingers penned a letter to her, describing the melancholy event, and exhorting her, for the sake of her father, to support this trial with resignation and patience, and bow to the dispensations of Providence, who orders all things eventually for the best, however severe and distressing they seem at the time. He ended his letter by observing that he should return to the castle of the Isles without delay, being anxious to fold her in his arms, and that he should bring the corpse of the brave Marsden to his native land.

The letter being sent off expressly by one of his retainers, the baron ordered some soldiers to attend with a bier, and taking Robert for their guide they went to fetch the body of Ruthven, and in the mean time he had a small tent erected for its reception, surmounted by a sable flag.

But this posthumous attention of the good baron was all in vain, for after a long absence, Robert and the soldiers returned, with the unwelcome news that the body of the gallant Scot was not to be found, but the spot where it had been deposited by the servants was still marked with the blood that had flowed from his gaping wounds and it was presumed that the enemy had found the corpse, and had conveyed it away to some obscure hole out of revenge for the slaughter he had dealt among their leaders before his fall. This event added materially to Ronald's regret and sorrow, for the natives of the Isles of Escotia held a traditional superstition, that while the body lay unburied the spirit wandered denied of rest. He offered rewards for the body without success, and was at length obliged, though with much reluctance, to drop the affair.

The baron was obliged to pay his duty in England to his sovereign before he repaired to the Isles. Unexpected events detained him two months at the British court, but he at last effected his departure to his long wished for home.

A courier made known his approach, and Lady Margaret, attended by the whole household, dressed in their best array, came forth to meet him, headed by the aged minstrel, and they received their lord with joyous shouts and lively strains, about half a mile from the gates of the castle.

Lord Ronald, as the carriage descended a steep hill that led into the valley, had a full view of the party approaching to meet him, and his heart felt elate at the compliment. He could discern his daughter; but how came it she was not in sables? Surely Ruthven, her betrothed lover, deserved that mark of respect to his memory! But he could observe that she was gaily dressed, and her high plume of feathers waving in the light breeze that adulated the air. The baron cast a look on his own deep mourning, and sighed; he was not pleased – but worse and worse. As he gained a nearer view, he perceived that his daughter was handed along, most familiarly by a knight. I had hoped, said he to himself, that Margaret would have rose superior to the inconstancy and caprice attributed to her sex. Can it be possible, that she has so soon forgot the valiant accomplished Ruthven! Oh, woman! woman! are ye all alike? As the vehicle entered the valley, Ronald quitted it, to receive the welcome of his child and retainers.

Powers of astonishment! was it, or was it not, illusion? By what miracle did he behold Ruthven, earl of Marsden, standing before him, and Lady Margaret hanging with chaste expressions of delight on his arm; there was a scar on his forehead, and he was much paler than before the battle, but no other alteration was visible. As for Robert, he stood aghast, his hair bristled up and his joints trembled, and altogether would have served as a good model of horror to a painter or statuary.

Ruthven stretched forth his hand – 'You seem astonished, my good lord,' said he, 'to find me here before you, or, indeed to find me here at all. I was discovered by some peasants returning from their daily labour, nearly covered with fern and leaves, ['Yes' said Robert, 'that was Gilbert's work and mine.'] by means of a little dog, who had scented out my body from its purposed concealment. They were very poor, and my clothes and decorations were a strong temptation, to which they yielded, they agreed to strip me, sell the clothes, and divide the spoil. While they were thus occupied, they perceived signs of life, and their humanity prevailed over every other consideration, I was conveyed to one of their cottages, and well attended. The man had a wonderful skill in herbs and simples, therefore my cure was rapid, but previous to my leaving them, I well rewarded every one who had been instrumental in my preservation and freely forgave the intended plunder they had confessed to me, as it was the means directed by fate to prolong my existence, and restore me to my angelic Margaret.

'When I recovered, I found the British forces had quitted Flanders, but I could not learn which direction my friend the baron (you my dear lord) had taken; so I hastened to Scotland with all the speed my situation would admit of, and we were retarded at sea by adverse winds. I found my dear betrothed, and her fair damsels, in deep mourning for my supposed loss; but I soon changed her tears for smiles, and her sables for gayer vestments: but at first her surprise, like yours, Lord Ronald, was too great to admit of utterance, but in time we became composed and grateful, and we agreed not to inform you of my existence, but astonish you on your arrival.'

The baron greeted his young friend most warmly and testified his hope that no more ill-omened events would disappoint the nuptials of the brave earl and Margaret, whom he tenderly clasped to his bosom, and kissing each cheek, remarked that she was the living image of his dear departed wife. He then turned to the old harper, and bidding him strike up a lively strain, proceeded to the castle, where all was joy and festivity; again resounded the song, and again the damsels, with their swains shewed off their best reels *a-la Caledonia*.

In the old steward's room a plenteous board was spread, for the upper servants and retainers of the hospitable Lord of the isles, who ordered flowing bowls and well replenished horns to the health of Ruthven and Margaret.

Some of the party were remarking on the wonderful preservation of Marsden's earl by the Flemish peasants, instead of plundering and leaving him to perish, as many would have done to an almost expiring enemy.

'*Almost expiring!*' said Robert, whose cheeks had not yet recovered their usual hue since the meeting in the valley with Ruthven.

'*Almost Expiring!*' he repeated; 'I am certain the body of the earl was dead – aye, as dead as my great grandsire – when I and Gilbert carried him from the field of battle; and when we left him under the fern he was as cold as ice, and the blood from his wounds coagulated – No, no, he never came to life again; this Ruthven you have here must be a Vampire.'

'*A Vampire! a Vampire!*' resounded from all the company, with loud shouts of laughter at poor Robert's simplicity. 'Perhaps you are a *Vampire*,' said his sweetheart, Effie, joining in the mirth, 'so I shall take care how I trust myself in your power.'

Robert did not reply, and all the rest of the night he had to stand the bantering jests of his companions.

But Robert was right; Marsden's earl died on the field of battle, and the moment the servants quitted the corpse, the Vampire, wicked Montcalm, whose relics lay smouldering beneath a stone in Fingal's cave, watching the moment, took possession, and reanimated the body; the wounds instantly healed, but the face wore a pallid hue, the invariable case with the Vampires, their blood not flowing, in that free circulation which belong to real mortals.

The story told by the Vampire was a fabrication, respecting the peasants, to impose on Lord Ronald and the Lady Margaret as to the appearance of the supposed Ruthven, and he well succeeded.

On previously consulting the Spirit of the Storm, the Vampire had discovered that Margaret would be courted by Ruthven, earl of Marsden; he also discovered, in his peep into futurity, that the young hero would be slain in battle, and this seemed to him a glorious opportunity to obtain possession of the lovely Margaret, and make her his victim, renovate his Vampireship, and go on in the most diabolical career, hurling destruction on the human race, and drawing them into crime after crime, till they sunk into the gulph of eternal infamy.

It now wanted a month to All Hallow E'en and it so chanced, that in that year the next coming moon would set on that very eve from its full orbit. The Vampire repaired to the cave of Fingal, and by magic means, which he well knew how to put in execution, he raised up some infernal spirits, whom he asked for orders. They told him they would consult their ruler Beelzebub, and he was to come on the third eve from thence for an answer.

This, then, was the decree – he must wed a virgin, destroy her, and drink her blood, before the setting of the moon on All Hallow E'en, or terminate into mere non-entity; and if the maid was unchaste, the charm was dissolved. If he succeeded he was to quit the form of earl Marsden and get egress into some other corpse to give it animation.

The supposed death of Ruthven had caused Margaret to imbibe the idea that the two figures she had seen in Fingal's cave, and Ariel's couplet prophetic but of one marriage, now made out by his fall, he being only a betrothed lover, and the stranger knight she regarded as her future spouse; but the return of the earl again puzzled her, and she knew not what to think, but at length resolved on another visit to the mystic cavern. Possibly ashamed of confessing this weakness to her maidens, or, what is more probable, conscious that from the terrors they had experienced in attending her there, she could not persuade them to go a second time, she went alone, and soon after midnight, when all the castle was hushed in sound repose, save the Vampire, who beheld from the lofty casement, the temporary flight of the enterprising Margaret. How did he thirst for her blood – how willingly would he have immolated the lovely maid that moment, and paid the infernal tribute, but for one clause that interposed and saved her from his fangs. This was the necessity of his being first legally married, in all due form, to the intended victim. He regarded her with a diabolical and malicious scowl, while, by as bright a star light as ever illumined the heavens, he saw her tripping through the park's wide avenues of stately firs. He wondered where she was going, and felt apprehensive that some event was in agitation that might deprive him of his bride. The Vampire had just concluded to follow her, when a heaviness, he could neither resist or shake off, overpowered him and sealed his eyes in a deep sleep.

Margaret, in much perturbation and a beating heart, gained the way to the cave; but the interior was so dark that she was obliged to grope on her hands and knees to the magic well, and cast in the accustomed charm. The thunder rolled, and the storm commenced, but with not one quarter of the violence as on her preceding visit. The music followed in an harmonious strain, and the spirits of the storm and air soon stood before her. The beauty, the innocence, of the noble maid, her virtues and her benevolence, had interested these mystical beings in her behalf – yes, even the stern and oft obdurate Una felt for Margaret, and wished to save her. They could not alter the decree of fate, nor had they power over the Vampires; the only thing that remained was to warn the inquirer, if possible, of her danger. For this purpose, they unfolded the curtain, and presented to her view, the real Ruthven on the field of battle, bleeding and a corpse. She heard his last sigh, saw his last convulsive motion; – *a grizzly fleshless skeleton stood by his side, and at that moment entered his corpse, which sprung up reanimated.* Margaret knew well the traditional tales of the Vampires, and shudderd as she beheld one before her; for what could be more plain? No further vision was shewn her – she was warned from the cave, and the fair one returned to the castle, dejected and spiritless. What did this mean? Ruthven, her adored Ruthven, could be no Vampire – impossible – so accomplished, so clever, superior in most things to others of his rank. – She past the intervening hours in a very restless state, till they met at their morning repast in the small saloon. The Vampire handed her to a chair; she remembered the scene in the cave, and shrank back with a feeling of disgust; but this was not lasting; the labours of the spirit of the storm and the air had not their intended effect; like advice given to young maidens that accords not with the inclination, it sank before the fascination of the object beloved, and she regarded what had been shewn her as wayward spite in Una and Ariel; so ready are we to twist circumstances to act in conformity with our own inclination.

The dews of night, the chilling breeze, the damp of the magic cave of Fingal, joined to the fatigue and agitation of the noble maiden, caused a fever which confined her to her chamber several days, and again delayed the marriage. The Vampire grew impatient, and before the Lady Margaret was scarce convalescent, he began to press for the nuptial ceremony, with what the good baron thought indecorous haste, though he made all possible allowance for repeated disappointments and youthful passions.

Robert, much better read than the warrior, his master, in the traditional tales of his country, and its popular superstitions, had not yet got the better of his shock at the re-appearance of Ruthven in his native valley, when he felt convinced that marsden's earl died of his wounds on the field of battle at Flanders. 'Aye, by the holy rood, he did,' would the youth often mutter to himself – 'May I never live to be married to my gentle Effie, and it wants but three days and three nights to that happy morn, if I did not see Ruthven's eye-strings crack, and heart's veins burst asunder: this is a Vampire, and this is the moon when those foul fiends pay their tribute, and now he is all impatience to wed my young mistress, forsooth — Yes, yes, 'tis plain enough: but what is the use of saying any thing about it, my father and all the servants laugh at me; even my intended turns into ridicule, any thing I advance on that subject, and calls me Robert, the Vampire hunter: but I will not be deterred from doing my duty like an honest servant, let them jeer as they will. I am resolved to tell the baron all that I know, that is, all I think of his guest, and then he may please himself, and come what will, my conscience will be clear.'

Robert had courage to face a cannon, and never turned his back on the bravest foe, but he felt daunted at the disclosure he meant to make to Lord Ronald; the subject was awkward, and the Vampire (if Vampire he was) might take a summary revenge on him for his interference. Yet his resolution was not shaken, and seeking the cellar-man he procured a glass of cordial and a horn of ale to revive his spirits, and then, finding himself what he called his own man again, he sought the baron, whom he happened to find a one and taking his evening walk in the grounds, while Margaret and her lover were sitting at their music.

Robert told his tale with much hesitation and faultering, but the baron heard him with more patience than he expected, and made him recount every particular of his suspicions. ' 'Tis strange! 'Tis marvellous strange!' replied the good Lord Ronald; 'for I have seen many persons from Flanders, and yet they never heard of the earl of Marsden being saved by the peasants: one would have thought such news would have spread like wildfire.'

'Neither does he go to mass or prayer,' observed Robert, 'as a christian warrior ought to do; nor does he take salt on his trencher.* And All-Hallow-E'en is fast approaching,' continued Robert: 'this is the fatal moon, and my young mistress —'

'Shall never be his,' exclaimed the baron 'till the moon sets, and the night, so tragic and pregnant of evil to many a spotless maid, is gone by; then if Ruthven is Marsden's true earl, he may have my Margaret. She shall then be his, and I will turn all my fish-ponds into bowls for whiskey punch, and the great fountain in the fore court shall flow with ale till not a Scot around can stand upon his legs, or he is no well-wisher to me or mine; but if he is an infernal Vampire, his reign will be

---

* This remark of Robert's was another popular Superstition of the Isles.

over. Faith, by St. Andrew, I know not what to think, but I have had fearful dreams, portentous of evil to my ancient house.'

The baron dismissed Robert with a present, and many encomiums on his fidelity and zeal for him and the Lady Margaret. 'My father,' said the honest fellow, 'has lived with you from youth to age: I was born within these walls, and my deceased mother suckled your amiable heiress; treachery in me would be double guilt: No, I would die to serve the house of Ronald!'

When the baron entered his daughter's appartment, a groupe met his eyes, very ill calculated to give him pleasure in his present frame of mind full of supernatural ideas, and teeming with dread suspicions; Margaret had changed her robes of plaid silk for virgin white, her neck chain, bracelets, and other ornaments of filagree silver, most exquisitely wrought. Ruthven was also dressed with elegance. The fair one's attendants were also in their best. The steward and the physician of the household were present, and the chaplain stood with the sacred book in his hand.

'We were waiting for you, my dear Lord Baron,' said the Vampire, Ruthven; 'I have persuaded my lovely betrothed to be mine this very evening. We have been so very unfortunate, that I dread further delay, and think every hour teeming with evil till she is mine irrevocably.'

'You have no rival,' answered the baron, much alarmed and piqued: 'you are secure in Margaret's love and my consent. My friends and tenants will ill brook such privacy; they have been accustomed to see the daughters of the Lord of the Isles wedded in public pomp and magnificence, and to share in the festive and abundant hospitalities. – No, by the shades of my ancestors, I will have no such doings.'

Ruthven pleaded hard, but the baron heeded not his arguments or eloquence, for the more he seemed bent on espousing Margaret then, the old lord thought more on Robert's report and his own suspicions. Margaret, infatuated by the spell that cast an illusion over her senses, seemed to forget her proper dignity and the delicate decorum of her sex, and joined in the solicitations of her lover. 'My dear father,' said the beauteous maiden, 'Ruthven and myself are in unison with each other's sentiments: we seek not in pomp and glare for happiness; we place our prospects of future bliss in elegant retirement and domestic pleasures. Allow us to be now united, I entreat you, and you can afterwards treat your neighbours, retainers, and servants, as plenteously as you like, but I shrink from the idea of a public marriage.'

Ruthven took the hand of his betrothed, which she presented to him with the most endearing smiles, while her eyes were modestly bent down and her cheeks covered with roseate blushes, and never did Lady Margaret look so irresistibly captivating as at that moment.

The baron, while she was speaking, trembled with emotion – Not for a single hour, said he, mentally, would I defer their happiness on account of bridal pomp, if I thought all was right; but I will not risk the sacrificing so much loveliness, and that my only child, the image of my lost Cassandra, to a Vampire; but he did not like to disclose the suspicions he had imbibed, for if they were founded in error, how grossly ridiculous would he appear, and he resolved to delay the nuptials, and stay the test of the moon. He therefore said, 'It is my pleasure to give a full month to splendid preparation, 'tis but a short delay, and let me have the satisfaction to have the nuptials as I would wish them to be, in honour of Marsden's earl and Ronald's daughter.'

The baron observed the lover give a start at the words 'a full month,' and his eyes shot forth a most malicious glance. He still held Margaret's hand. 'Nonsense! my good friend,' said he, – 'this is not fair, from one warrior to another – Chaplain, begin the ceremony.'

The enraged baron flung off his guard, snatched the book from the hands of the priest, and bade Margaret retire with her maidens to another room, accusing Ruthven of being a Vampire.

This was strongly resented by the accused, and, indeed, every one took his part, and laughed at the suggestion. This raised his passion so high that he was declared by the physician to be insane, and they coercively conveyed him to his chamber, and barred him in, where he was on the point of becoming frantic indeed, from the thoughts that the marriage might now take place in spite of his injunctions, for he was more convinced than ever of Ruthven being a supernatural imposter, or he would never have acted so uncourteous to a knight in his own castle.

Robert having heard from his father, the old steward, of the interruption of the marriage, through the baron's mania, in thinking the Earl of Marsden a Vampire, and his lord's confinement in the western turret, observed that he supposed the nuptials then were all off – His parent answered no, that the young people were not forced to obey such whims; that Lady Margaret was retired for an hour to regain her composure, and the chaplain would then perform the ceremony. 'And who is to be the bride's father?' said Robert. 'I am to have that honour,' replied the steward. – 'And much good may it do you,' said the son; 'but if I was you, I'd cater better for the noble lady Margaret than to give her to an evil spirit' – 'Go to, for an ungracious bird,' exclaimed Alexander; 'you are as mad as your master; poor Effie will have but a crazy husband at the best of it.' 'Better a crazy one, than a blood thirsty Vampire, father,' observed Robert, who quitted the room, vexed at the loud peal of laughter, which was now set up against him.

Robert went out into the park, but returned privately into the castle by a bye path and a private door, of which he had a key, having procured it some time before he went to the wars, for he was then a rakish youth, and loved to steal out to the village dance or festival, after he was supposed to retire to rest for the night; but now, he was contracted to the languishing blue-eyed Effie he was reformed, and voluntarily relinquished all such stolen delights. The key was now regarded by him as a treasure. 'It helped me,' said he to himself, to sow my wild oats; 'it shall now aid me to perform a more laudable purpose. Little did I think to see the good Baron of the Isles a captive in his own castle; and for what, but that he is in too much possession of his senses to sacrifice his lovely virgin daughter to a Vampire, for such, by the holy rood, is this fine Earl of Marsden. Why his face is the image of death itself, and his eyes glare; yet my Lady Margaret forsooth! thinks him very handsome, now she is under the influence of the wicked spell; the real Ruthven looked not so when he came to woo the noble fair one; but he says 'tis through his wounds in battle: I think by St. Cuthbert, he has had time enough to get his complexion again, and he eats and drinks voraciously, it makes me sick to see him as I stand in waiting, and no salt – faugh!'

This long soliloquy brought the faithful youth to the door of the baron's prison; he drew the bolts and entered; his Lord was pacing the chamber with unmeasured strides, and beating his forehead, while heavy sighs burst from his aged bosom. He started and stood still on Robert's entrance.

'Friend or foe,' said he. 'Friend,' replied Robert, 'and when I prove otherwise to my most noble master and commander, may I be siezed by the foul fiend and made food for vulture.'

'I am not mad,' said the good old veteran, 'but I think I may say, I am distracted with grief;' 'You are no more mad than I my lord; I do not join in that absurd tale; but hasten and arm yourself? The marriage is to take place almost immediately – let us hasten and prevent it, ere it is too late.'

Lord Ronald was doubly shocked – his suspicions of the Vampire was increased by this obstinate persisting in the nuptials against his command, and the want of tenderness and filial love testified by his daughter. How changed was Margaret! did she choose for her bridal hours those of confinement to her sire – had she not supposed him insane, it is not to be thought she would have suffered him to be thus treated; this then was her season for connubial joys – the sudden insanity of her only surviving parent, he who had so ardently strove not only to fulfil his own duties, but to supply the place as far as possible of the late lady Cassandra, his amiable wife, and he felt there was no sting so keen as a child's ingratitude. The barbed arrow seemed to touch his very vitals, and for the first time in his life the brave Ronald shed tears.

'Take courage, my lord,' said Robert, 'if they dare still to oppose your authority, this trusty falchion, this well tried steel, shall prove if Ruthven is common flesh and blood or no.'

'Moderation! moderation! Robert,' replied the Baron, as he led the way to Lady Margaret's apartment, where he did not arrive one minute too soon – the ceremony was on the point of commencing, and 'tis possible a few of the first words had been pronounced by the priest.

The Baron's entrance caused a universal consternation – the maidens shrieked, and the Vampire began to bluster, but Lord Ronald took prompt measures. He solemnly protested that he was in the full use and exercise of his senses, and charged his daughter, on the penalty of incurring his curse, not to enter into wedlock with Marsden's Earl till he sanctioned it. She did not choose to disobey on such an awful threat, but casting a look of anguish and tenderness on her lover, she burst into tears, and leaning on the arms of her sympathizing maidens, withdrew to her chamber, where throwing herself on a couch, gave way to a full tide of sorrow. 'Cruel father,' she exclaimed! 'ridiculous superstition! I feel I never shall be the bride of my truly adored and adoring Ruthven, so many fatal interruptions seem as if the fates forbid our union – spirits of the storm and air, are ye not too in league against me?'

The Vampire now besought the baron's forgiveness and friendship, attributing his recent behaviour to excess of love, that did not brook delay; he also interceded for the chaplain, whom Lord Ronald was about to dismiss for his presumption, and peace was again restored in the Castle of the Isles.

Wine was called for, and a repast was spread and the Vampire so artfully strove against the suspicions of the Baron, that the prejudices of the latter were nearly done away; and Robert blamed for his credulous folly; yet the false Earl could not obtain from the old nobleman a promise to allow him to wed before the setting of the moon, for Ronald still adhered to that test, nor would abridge, aught of a term that now waxed very short.

The Vampire concealed his chagrin and feigned content; he thought it best to keep a firm footing in the castle, as some chance might still operate in his favour, founding his hopes on the spell he had obtained over Lady Margaret, and the strong affection with which she beheld him, and he scarcely admitted a doubt of success, if he could get the Baron and Robert out of the way; for no one else in the castle had the least doubt of his being the real Earl of Marsden.

The Baron, however, watched with great vigilance, and Robert never stirred from a station he had taken that commanded a view of the door of Lady Margaret's chamber. Time seemed to ride on swift pinions with the Vampire – his fears were stronger than his hopes – he had never been so foiled before in his attempts, and he thought it best to provide against the coming danger, and leave the mistress alone for her allegiance to Robert, persuade her to wed himself, and then sacrifice her to pay his annual demoniac tribute. This would serve two purposes, renew his Vampire-ship, and be a deadly revenge on the interfering Robert, on whom he longed to wreak his diabolical rage.

It seemed rather a difficult achievement to gain the affections of a young and certainly most virtuous maiden, (who was to be married in a few hours to the object of her first choice) from that object, but the Vampire's case grew desperate, and he resolved to try if the charm would operate.

While Robert was watching the lady the Vampire resolved to seize on the more ignoble prize, and he assailed Effie with every alluring temptation. He told the poor girl that he was tired of pursuing the match with Lady Margaret, and abhorred the thoughts of allying himself to such a piece of dotage as the credulous Baron, who was grown superannuated, and only fit to sit amongst the old wives a-spinning, and tell legendary tales of hobgoblins, and water sprites. He said Effie's beauty and innocence had charmed him – that she wanted nothing but dress and rank to be level with her mistress, and that would be hers by marrying Marsden's Earl.

'But I am ignorant, and can neither play music, sing, dance, or do the honours of a table, like Lady Margaret.' This reply pleased the Vampire; it seemed one of a very yielding nature, if she had no scruples but what arose from a fear of her own demerits.

'All these can soon be taught,' said the deceiver. 'I must seek some lady of fallen fortune, but elegant accomplishments, to polish your native gracefulness; she shall be your companion in my absence, and your tutoress, and I will join in the delightful task; therefore that can be no objection.' Effie raised several other difficulties, but all were successfully combated, and the Vampire Earl promised to make the forsaken Robert amends for the loss of his bride by a noble sum and a pretty damsel from off his own estate.

Effie yielded; and though by this act she justly incurred censure and reproach, yet we must do her the justice to remember, that the Vampire had a tongue to charm his victims, and eyes that are described like the fascination of a basilisk; and to have a powerful Earl sighing for her love, might have tempted a higher maid than the simple Effie, the mere child of nature.

Having gained her consent, he hastened to secure his prize; he persuaded her that they must instantly flee, lest the lynx-eyed Robert should grow jealous, and interrupt their promised happiness; he therefore told her, to meet him in an hour, at the end of the long avenue in the castle park, and he would be prepared with a horse to convey her to the next convent, (about five miles distant,) where the priest could join their hands.

That he intended to wed Effie was too true; in that promise lurked no deceit, but the ceremony over, he meant to take her into an adjacent wood, offer up his sacrifice by immolating her with his own hands, and drinking her heart's blood; then seek out some noble form just departed – enter it – and woo Lady Margaret in a new character, and finally triumph over the Baron, for he hated all who opposed him in his designs.

Poor unsuspecting Effie, thy head ran on nothing but the glare of thy expected coronet, and thou felt no pity for thy so lately loved Robert, or thy kind and generous mistress, though both were to be betrayed by this clandestine step.

She was true to her appointment and crossed the park with light steps – the Vampire was in waiting – he assisted her to mount the horse, and then sprung up behind her – The steed bounded off like lightning. In an instant Robert rushed from a copse and cried out for the fugitives to stop, but instead of obeying him the Vampire spurred his horse to quicken him on. The Baron had taken Robert's post to watch the Lady Margaret while the latter made an excursion for air; his gun was loaded, and vengeance nerved the young soldier's arm with so sure an aim that the corporeal part of the Vampire fell mortally wounded to the ground, dragging Effie after it loudly shrieking, and all her new raised love extinguished – for the illusion had vanished, and the image of Robert again filled her virgin heart. Most happily for her future peace the secret of her consenting to the supposed Earl's passion was known to her alone – there had been no witness of that degrading incident so fatal to her integrity; and Robert, believing she was carried off against her will all ended well – she was espoused to her faithful suitor at the appointed time, and made an excellent wife; for her direliction had made her watchful over herself – she often thought of the precipice on which she had stood and trembled. Her beauty long after her marriage gained her admirers, but they were soon dismissed with spirit, and taught to keep at a proper distance, for Effie was now proof against seduction.

But to return to the Vampire. He lay bleeding on the ground, while Robert conveyed Effie to the castle, cautioning her to secrecy as she valued his life, for he knew not what might be the result of this act, if it was indeed Marsden's Earl he had slain. He sought the Baron who was much vexed at the recital, though he acknowledged that Robert had much provocation, and Ruthven's elopement with Effie was an insult on the Lady Margaret not to be borne. The Lord of the Isles and his faithful follower repaired to the spot where the latter had left the treacherous Earl.

'I wonder,' said Robert, as they proceeded hither, and calling to mind the scene in Flanders, 'whether we shall find his lordship there, or whether Beelzebub has given him a second lift.' The Vampire, however, was there, bleeding copiously, but in full possession of his senses. He declared life to be ebbing fast, and that he forgave Robert his death wound; also, he ascribed his carrying off Effie as a mere frolic to alarm her and that he had intended to convey her back in safety to the castle. 'I do not like such jests,' said the indignant Robert, 'and you have paid for an act you had better have left alone.'

The false earl then proceeded to state, on the oath of a dying man, that he was no Vampire. This gave a sad pang both to the baron and Robert, and the former testified his regret at the conduct such suspicions had given rise to. He then demanded of Ruthven if he had any commission to charge him with, and it should be punctually executed.

'Swear it,' exclaimed the Vampire, eagerly.

The baron drew forth his sword and swore on it.

'Give me that topaz ring from off your finger,' said the Vampire; 'let me die with it on, in token of your renewed amity, and allow it to be buried with me.' To this the Lord Ronald most readily consented.

'Next' said the Vampire, drawing it forth from his bosom, where it hung extended by an hair chain, 'take this ring of twisted gold, and cast it into a well that stands on the north side of Fingal's Cave — 'tis a charm given by the mighty Stuffa. I shall thus have a vow performed that will give peace to my soul, and save it from wandering after it has quitted its mortal clay-built tenement. In a few minutes I shall be no more — draw my body aside into the copse, and to-morrow at your return you can seek it, and give me burial; but for the present conceal my death from all you meet: name it not until the ring is in the cave.'

In a few minutes the Vampire seemed to die with a heavy groan, and the afflicted baron and his attendant proceeded to obey the last injunction thus-received, both conscience-stricken at having thus treated Marsden's Earl, and feeling assured, from the manner of his death, that he was a mortal man. They returned to the castle to prepare for their journey to the cave; but mentioned not the decease of Ruthven; and even Effie was imposed on to believe that the wounds, though they had bled much, were but trifling. This gave much comfort to the damsel, as it cleared her Robert of a deed of blood.

The Baron and Robert set out as soon as it dawned, for the cave of Fingal, to perform what they thought an imperious duty, for as such they considered a posthumous request made under such distressing circumstances.

Little did the credulous pair suspect that they were now made the agents of the wicked Vampire, for this is the true story of the magic ring.

The outer part of the Vampire was not subject to disease, and it was invincible to the sword. If they could contrive to have Stuffa's ring flung into the well of the cave of Fingal within twenty-four hours after the death wound it was restored to its vile career for the appointed time, and for that season the malignant spirit hovered round the body.

The good Lord of the Isles and Robert arrived safe there, and with little difficulty found the well, for report had spread its situation far and wide owing to its magic qualities. Lord Ronald cast in the ring — instantaneously a hissing, as if of snakes, followed, but soon all was silent as the grave.

They left the cavern and found themselves in the midst of a pelting storm, and their horses, which they had left tied to a tree, were unloosened and they sought in vain for them. As they continued their search a sweet musical voice was heard by the wanderers.

'Tis Ariel bids you haste away,
'Tis Ariel warns you not to stay;
Hie and stop a horrid scene,

> 'Tis the fatal *Hallow E'en*,
> Haste and save the destined fair
> From the treacherous Vampire's snare!'

'Robert,' said the Baron, 'did you hear ought or do my ears deceive me? – again was the verse repeated with this additional stanza –

> 'Lose not time but quickly see
> Whose the triumph is to be,
> Margaret must be no more,
> Or the Vampire's reign is o'er'

'Tis plane enough, my lord; Ariel, who is always reckoned a benign spirit, warns us – We are deceived – Oh this cursed Vampire! I see it now, he made us tools for his own purpose.'

'Nonsense, my good fellow,' said the Baron, 'it must be some new plot against my peace – a real Vampire, for we left Marsden's Earl quite dead.'

'Oh, he was dead enough in Flanders,' observed Robert, 'but he seems to have as many lives as the Witch of Endor's tabby cat. My mind forbodes horrid things – No harm, however, in getting home quick.'

But they were involved in the intricacies of the forest, and it required both patience and perseverence to find the right track; at length they succeeded, and walked on with rapid strides, for the evening wore away. At this juncture some horsemen overtook them – It was quite dusk and objects scarce discernible.

'Hoy, Holla, my good foresters! can you put us in the way for Baron Ronald's castle; the Lord of the Isles we mean, said the foremost of the caveliers?'

'What want you there?' replied the Baron, (himself) 'let us know ere we guide you, for we are going thither.'

'I am Hildebrand, Lord Gowen's sister's son, sent by my mother to pay my respects and duty to him as becomes a nephew and a godson, nor has he seen me since my infancy.'

'Welcome! Welcome!' exclaimed the Baron, 'son of my beloved Ellen, I am thy uncle, but by some strange accidents, here on foot with one single follower.'

' 'Tis lucky, replied the youth, springing from his steed and embracing the Baron, that we have some led horses in our train.' Lord Ronald and Robert were glad to hear of this seasonable supply, and mounting the noble beasts, set off at full speed.

Hildebrand; as they rode along, was made acquainted with recent events by his worthy uncle – he was struck with terror, and felt much interested for the Lady Margaret; for young Gowen had imbibed from the Countess, (his mother) a strong belief of the existence of Vampires, and he intimated, though respectfully, to his venerable uncle, that he had done wrong by throwing the ring into the well, as by that means it was most probable, the wicked sprite had acquired reanimation.

Again the storm arose and served to retard their progress, for the steeds affrighted at the vivid and incessant lighting, could with difficulty be got forward. At length they arrived at the copse, and Robert with two of Earl Gowen's serving men dismounted to seek for the body, but it was not there. 'Just as I thought to find it,' said the former, 'beshrew me it is an industrious sprite; but the moon will soon set,' and as the benign Ariel sang –

> 'Let's haste and save the destin'd fair
> From the treacherous Vampire's snare.'

They spurred their horses, and the storm having made a temporary stop they were soon across the park. Music was sounding – they could distinguish the harper's strain – the great hall was lighted up most brilliantly – a sumptuous altar had been erected at one end – and for the third time, the marriage ceremony was about to begin, when the Baron, Lord Gowen and Robert rushed in and secured the intended bride, who fainted immediately, for in the person of her noble cousin she beheld the form shewn her by Una and Ariel in the cave of Fingal, and the Vampire's charm vanished away like snow before the meridian sun.

The Vampire seemed armed with supernatural strength – he resisted all their efforts to subdue him – and their swords made no impression – he struggled hard to bear away the Lady Margaret from the midst of her protectors, and the amazing efforts of the Vampire spread horror and alarm, for that he was an evil sprite no one now doubted. He had returned to the castle that evening, and said he came with the Baron's consent, (who had undertaken a sudden journey) to wed the Lady Margaret, and had brought her father's ring as a token. All was now bustle, preparation and joy, till the unexpected entrance of the Lord of the Isles and his companions, and had it not been for the providence of Gowen seeking the castle that night, the fiend would have triumphed, for they could not have got home on foot time enough to save her.

But the fiend was not to be overpowered – he jumped on the temporary altar sword in hand (after having wounded and bit with his teeth several of the domestics) insisting he would yet have his bride. In an instant the scene changed – the moon set – the thunder rolled over the castle, and the bolt fell on the Vampire – he rolled lifeless upon the floor, and after a terrific yell, melted into air, incorporeal and invisible to every eye. Thus ended the wicked sprite.

Some months after this event Margaret was happily united to Earl Gowen, with whom she led a happy life till they both sunk into the grave, venerable with age, making good the prediction of the spirits of the cave of Fingal –

'Ne'er but once was she to wed,
Or have a second bridal bed.'

Les Vampires

EUGENE SUE

The vampire theme was first introduced into the cinema as early as 1915 in a serial, Les Vampires, *made by the great French film maker Louis Feuillade (1873–1925), which cinema historian David Robinson had called, 'a huge masterpiece of crime and horror . . . which audiences took time out of the First World War to be thrilled and chilled by'. At the time Feuillade began to make the silent picture he was already the undisputed master of the crime serial and brought enormous energy and creativity to all his films. He had made his name with his very first serial,* Fantomas *(1912–13), about a man of mystery operating on both sides of the law, which was then the most successful film ever seen in Paris. Feuillade decided to produce* Les Vampires *as direct competition for another series,* Mysteries of New York, *then being shown by a rival company, Pathé. He took for his inspiration the huge French novel,* The Mysteries of Paris *by Eugene Sue, and cast one of his favourite actresses Musidora (Jeanne Roques, 1889–1957), who had starred in several of his earlier productions. With her voluptuous figure daringly displayed in a black leotard and with bat-like wings affixed to her arms, she was to prove the most piquant sex icon of the age. Already known as the French cinema's original femme fatale, by staring in* Les Vampires *she became the first film 'vamp', too. Indeed, so strikingly sexual did she appear in the early episodes that the Paris police contemplated banning the picture on moral grounds – but a visit to the prefecture by the irresistible Musidora flashing her lustrous eyes soon put a stop to any such threat. Once Feuillade had started shooting, he frequently changed the storyline: occasionally when some of the actors, working while on leave from the services, were*

suddenly required back at the Front which necessitated their 'deaths',
or else from audience reactions he had received from his distributors.
Such elements notwithstanding, he injected great pace and excitement
into the serial about a young investigator's campaign to bring to
justice a group of satanic criminals, Les Vampires, lead by the
mysterious Dr Nox – the Grand Vampire in disguise – and his equally
fiendish assistant, Irma Vep (the anagram was obvious to everyone in
the cinema audience). A problem which arose from the unpunctuality
of Jean Ayme, playing the Grand Vampire, and which seriously began
to threaten the serial meeting its weekly deadlines, was ingeniously
resolved by Feuillade. He had Musidora shoot and kill Dr Nox and
become the undisputed star herself. The story of crimes, robberies,
kidnappings and poisonings at which Irma Vep was invariably at the
centre then continued unabated for twenty-four episodes. Despite its
importance in the French cinema, Les Vampires *was feared lost for*
many years until 1987 when a pile of cans containing the episodes
were located in a vault and the whole picture was painstakingly
restored to its original length of over seven hours and reshown at a
number of cinema festivals in France and London.

Eugene Sue (1804–57) is remembered as the prime innovator of
the sensational roman-feullton serials which so delighted French
readers in the middle years of the nineteenth century and which were
later to inspire the Grand Guignol *plays and early silent movies like*
Les Vampires. *The Mysteries of Paris (1843–44), his most famous*
serial, with its unrelentingly grim portrait of the Parisian underworld,
its crime, criminals, sex and sinners, proved hugely popular with
readers and inspired many other writers to abandon the more
traditional Gothic forms of romance in favour of tales of social
realism. Two authors in particular, the Englishman, George
Reynolds, and the American, George Lippard, unashamedly cashed in
on his popularity with their own Mysteries of London *(1844–48)*
and Mysteries of Philadelphia *(1844–5) respectively. In the follow-*
ing extract from The Mysteries of Paris, *the investigator Rudolph is*
looking for a room to rent where he hopes to be able to infiltrate Les
Vampires. It also describes his first encounter with a mysterious
woman (Irma Vep) who drops a handkerchief marked with the initials
'D.N.' (those of her associate, Dr Nox). In the light of the previous
story, it is interesting to note that Sue chose the name Polidori for
another of the central characters in his tale . . .

* * *

The dark and damp staircase seemed doubly dingy on this gloomy winter's day. The entrance to each of the apartments of this house had, to the observant eye, a physiognomy peculiar to itself. Thus, the door which led to the commander's abode was freshly painted of a brown colour, grained in imitation of wainscot; a copper-gilt handle shone on the lock, and a handsome bell-rope, with a red silk tassel, was in striking contrast with the mouldy antiquity of the walls.

The door of the second story, inhabited by the fortune-teller and pawnbroker, presented a singular aspect. A stuffed owl, a bird signally cabalistic and symbolical, was nailed over the room-door by the feet and wings; and a little wicket, latticed with iron wire, enabled those within to examine their visitors previous to admitting them.

The dwelling of the Italian quack doctor, who was suspected of pursuing a frightful avocation, was also distinguished by the strangeness of the entrance. His name was done in horses' teeth, inlaid on a tablet of black wood, screwed on the panels; and the bell-rope, instead of the classic termination of a hare's or a deer's foot, was appended to the wire by the dried fore-arm of an ape; this withered limb, with its five articulated fingers and its perfect nails, had something of the horrible in its appearance. One might have taken it for the hand of a child!

As Rudolph passed by this ominous-looking door, he fancied that he heard the sound of smothered sobs; then, all at once, an agonized, convulsive, horrible cry, which seemed as if wrung from the inmost soul of some wretched sufferer, awakened the echoes of that silent house. Rudolph shuddered: then, quick as thought, he rushed to the door, and pulled the bell violently.

'What ails you, sir?' asked the astonished porter.

'That cry!' said Rudolph; 'did you not hear it?'

'Yes sir, I heard it; no doubt it is one of M. Cæsar's patients having a tooth drawn — or perhaps two.'

This explanation seemed plausible, but it did not satisfy Rudolph. He had rung the bell violently; yet no one came to answer him. He could hear several doors shut in succession; and through a glass bull's-eye which was above the door, Rudolph indistinctly saw a haggard, cadaverous, and pallid countenance. A perfect forest of wild, red hair crowned that hideous visage, which was fringed below by a long beard of the same colour. This hideous face disappeared in a moment. Rudolph felt completely petrified.

Brief as had been the vision, he believed that he recognized those features. Those green eyes, that shone bright as aqua-marine beneath

those staring and yellow eyebrows – that livid paleness – that slender
and prominent aquiline nose, the nostrils of which, strangely dilated
and arched outward, exposed the nasal septum – reminded him in a
fearful manner of a certain Polidori, whose name had been so
execrated by Murphy in his conversation with Baron de Graun.
Although Rudolph had not seen Polidori for sixteen or seventeen
years, he had a thousand reasons for not forgetting him: the only thing
that contradicted his remembrance was, that the man, whom he
fancied he saw in the person of this fair-skinned and red-haired quack,
was extremely dark. If Rudolph (supposing his conjectures to be
correct) felt no surprise at finding a man whose learning, great talent,
and intelligence, he knew, fallen to such a state of degradation,
perhaps of infamy – it was because he also knew that these rare and
noble gifts were allied to so much perversity, such wild, unbridled
passions, desires so foul, and, beyond all, to such an affected scorn and
contempt of the world, as might induce this man, when overtaken by
want, to prefer degraded and dishonourable modes of subsistence;
nay, even to enjoy a fiendish satisfaction that he was hiding beneath his
ignoble pursuits the precious treasures of a highly-gifted mind. But, we
must repeat that, although he had last seen Polidori in the prime of life,
and although he must be about the same age as the charlatan, there
were still between the two persons certain differences so remarkable,
that Rudolph remained in great doubt as to whether they were one and
the same person. At length turning to Pipelet, he inquired – 'Has M.
Bradamanti long resided in this house?'

'About a year, sir; now I recollect, he came in January quarter. He is
a very punctual lodger; he cured my dreadful rheumatism – '

'Mrs Pipelet tells me that there are certain horrible reports about
him.'

'She has told you of them?'

'Make yourself quite easy; I am very discreet.'

'Well, sir, I don't believe there's the least truth in these reports – and
I never will believe it – I trust I have too much modesty to do anything
of the kind,' rejoined Pipelet, blushing, and preceding his new lodger
to the next landing-place.

More than ever resolved to clear up his doubts – feeling that
Polidori's presence in the same house might greatly interfere with his
projects, and experiencing a growing inclination to put the worst
interpretation on the horrible cry he had heard, Rudolph resolved to
assure himself of this man's identity, and followed the porter to the
upper story, where was situated the apartment he wished to rent.

Miss Dimpleton's lodging, next-door neighbour to the chamber for which Rudolph was in treaty, was easily recognized, thanks to a charming gallantry of the painter who has been described as the mortal foe of Pipelet. Half-a-dozen chubby little Cupids, very freely and spiritedly painted in the style of Watteau, were grouped about a shield. One held a thimble, another a pair of scissors, another a flat-iron, and another a hand-glass; and in the midst of them, in pink letters on a sky-blue ground, was 'Miss Dimpleton, dressmaker;' the whole being surrounded by a garland of flowers, which stood out in admirable relief from the sea-green colour of the door. This beautiful little panel had all the better effect from its strong contrast with the filthiness of the staircase.

At the risk of opening afresh Alfred's wounds, Rudolph said, pointing to the door: 'That, I suppose, is the work of M. Cabrion?'

'Yes, sir; he took the liberty of spoiling the painting of the door, by daubing it over with those fat, indecent brats, stark naked, which he called 'Coopids.' If it hadn't been for the entreaties of Miss Dimpleton, and M. Red Arms' weakness, I would have scratched all that out, as I also would this palette, filled with horrid-looking monsters, amongst whom you may detect their equally abominable creator – you may know him by his sugar-loaf hat.'

And, there, sure enough, on the door of the room Rudolph was about to engage, might be seen a palette surrounded by all sorts of odd, strange-looking figures, the witty conceit of which might have done honour to Callot. Rudolph followed the porter into a good-sized room, which communicated with a small bed-room, and was lighted by two windows which opened upon the Rue du Temple. Some wild fancies, which had been painted on the same door, had been scrupulously respected by M. Germain. Rudolph had many reasons for wishing to occupy this apartment; therefore, modestly placing in the porter's hand forty *sous*, he said to him: –

'This apartment exactly suits me; here is the deposit. I will send my furniture in to-morrow. But let me beg of you not to efface that palette. It is so very funny. Don't you think so?'

'Funny! Oh, sir! I have seen every one of those monsters in my nightmares; hunting me, sir, in my dreams, with Cabrion at the head of them, till I have awoke in a cold sweat: oh, there was a horrid chase!'

'I can imagine that they were not pleasant visitors. But tell me, have I any need to see your M. Red Arm about the hiring of this apartment?'

'No, sir; he seldom comes here, except now and then on business with Mother Burette. I always treat directly with the lodgers. I will only further trouble you for your name?'

'Rudolph.'

'Rudolph what?'

'Plain Rudolph, M. Pipelet.'

'I am satisfied, sir; I did not ask from idle curiosity – names and inclinations are free.'

'Tell me, M. Pipelet, cannot I call to-morrow upon poor Morel, as a next neighbour, to ask if I can be of any use to him, since my predecessor, M. Germain, was so good to him?'

'Oh, yes, sir, that can be done; it is true that will not be of much use to him, as they are to be turned out; but still it will ease his mind.' Then, as if struck with a sudden thought, Pipelet, looking slyly at his new lodger, said: 'I understand, I understand: it is a beginning, so that you can also call by-and-by, with a good grace, upon the little neighbour next door!'

'Oh! I reckon upon that as certain.'

'There is no harm in that, sir – it is the custom – understand, I mean honourably; and I am sure Miss Dimpleton has heard us in the room, and is in a fever to see us go down again. I will make a noise on purpose with the key, and if you look behind, you will see her watching us.' And, sure enough, Rudolph perceived that the door, which was so handsomely decorated with the Cupids à la Watteau, was ajar, and, through the narrow opening, he could see the turn-up tip of a little rosy nose, and a large inquisitive black eye; but, as he slackened his step, the door suddenly slammed to. 'Did I not tell you, sir, that she was watching us?' said the porter; then he added: 'Pray excuse me, one moment, while I step into my warehouse.'

'Where is that?'

'At the top of that ladder is the landing upon which opens the door of Morel's garret, and behind a panel of the wainscot is a little dark hole, where I keep my leather; the partition is so warped and full of cracks, that I can see and hear there as if I was in their room. It is not, God, knows, that I wish to act the spy upon them – on the contrary. But pray excuse me for a minute or two, sir, while I get my bit of leather. If you will be good enough to step down stairs, I will rejoin you.'

And so saying, Pipelet began to mount the crazy ladder, an ascent which seemed perilous at his years.

Rudolph threw a last glance at Miss Dimpleton's door, as he reflected that that young girl, the companion of poor Goualeuse, was doubtless acquainted with the retreat of the Schoolmaster's son, when he heard some one in the lower story come out of the apartment of the charlatan; he distinguished the light step of a female, and the rustle of a silk dress. Rudolph stopped for an instant, lest he should intrude. Hearing no more, he went down. Arrived at the second landing-place, he saw and picked up a handkerchief that lay upon the lower stair – doubtless it belonged to the female who had just left the lodging of Polidori. He took it to one of the narrow-stair-case windows, and examined it. It was magnificently trimmed with costly lace, and embroidered in one of the corners were the initials D. N., surmounted by a ducal coronet. The handkerchief was literally soaked with tears. Rudolph's first impulse was to follow the person from whose hand this mute evidence of grief had fallen, with the intention of restoring it; but reflecting that such a step might be taken for impertinent curiosity, he determined to keep it as the first link in the chain of a mysterious adventure, in which he had found himself suddenly and unintentionally involved. On arriving at the porter's lodge, he said to Mrs Pipelet: 'Did not a female come down stairs just now?'

'No, sir – but a very fine *lady*, tall and slender, in a large black veil did. She came from the apartment of M. Bradamanti. Little Hoppy went for a coach, in which the lady has just gone away. But what astonished me was to see that little blackguard get up behind the coach. I dare say, though, it was to see where the lady goes to; for he is as mischievous as a magpie, and active as a ferret, spite of his club-foot.'

'So, then,' thought Rudolph, 'the charlatan will most likely discover this lady's name and address, since doubtless it is he who has ordered Hoppy to follow her.'

'Well, sir, does your room suit you?' asked the portress. 'It suits me excellently! I have hired it: to-morrow I will send in my furniture.'

'May heaven bless you for coming by our door, sir; we shall have one good lodger the more.'

'I hope so, Mrs Pipelet. It is understood that you will see to my little domestic affairs. To-morrow my goods will be brought. I will see them arranged myself.' And Rudolph left the lodge.

The results of the visit to the house of the Rue du Temple were sufficiently important, alike to the solution of the mystery he hoped to penetrate, and to the noble curiosity with which he found out every occasion of doing good, and of preventing evil. On reflection, he thought he had achieved the following results: That Miss Dimpleton *must* be acquainted with the residence of François Germain, the

Schoolmaster's son. A young woman, who, according to some appearances, might unfortunately be the Marchioness d'Harville, had made, for the morrow, an appointment with the Commander, which might ruin her for ever; and, for a thousand reasons, Rudolph took a most lively interest in his friend D'Harville, whose peace and honour seemed so cruelly compromised.

An honest and laborious artizan, crushed by the most frightful misery, was about to be turned into the street with his family by Red Arm.

Further, Rudolph had involuntarily come upon some traces of an adventure in which the charlatan, Cæsar Bradamanti (perhaps Polidori), and a lady, who appeared to be of rank and fashion, were the chief actors.

And lastly, the Owl, recently emerged from the hospital, to which she had been taken after the scene in the Allée des Veuves, had some very suspicious communications with Mother Burette, fortune-teller and money-lender, who occupied the second floor of this house.

Having carefully noted these points of information, Rudolph returned to his house in the Rue Plumet, there to contemplate his next move in the mystery . . .

Nosferatu

PAUL MONETTE

*The archive records of early films give the impression that there were
quite a number of silent vampire movies made around the time of
Louis Feuillade's serial,* Les Vampires. *Although no trace of the actual
prints of these elusive shorts still exist, their titles are recorded in
several major British, European and American filmographies:*
Vampires of the Coast *(1909),* The Vampire's Tower *(1913),* The
Vampire's Clutch *(1914),* Vampires of the Night *(1914),* Tracked By
A Vampire *(1914) and* A Village Vampire *(1916). All without
exception, however, used the word vampire as another – presumably
crowd-drawing – alternative to vamp or femme fatale. What was
undoubtedly the first genuine vampire movie was* Nosferatu *made in
Germany by the young German expressionist director, Friedrich
Murnau in 1922. It, too, could have suffered the same fate as those
early 'vamp' pictures: because the film was actually an unauthorised
version of Bram Stoker's* Dracula *which his widow successfully
prosecuted and won an order that all copies should be destroyed! Two
years prior to making* Nosferatu, *Murnau had made a successful foray
into horror literature with* Der Januskopf, *an adaptation of Robert
Louis Stevenson's* Dr Jekyll and Mr Hyde. *Searching round for similar
material he came across Stoker's novel and swiftly adapted it for the
screen with only the most cosmetic changes. The location was
switched from Transylvania to Germany; the vampire's name was
altered to Count Orlock; and the word Nosferatu – a Romanian
term for a vampire that causes its male victims to become impotent –
was substituted for the title as being more sinister. (The word had
actually appeared in the original novel in one of Dr Van Helsing's*

dialogues). Murnau cast the appropriately named Max Schreck (Schreck means Fear in German) as the skeletal-looking Orlock, complete with bald head, pointed ears and rat-like features. His performance has been described as probably the most hideous vampire ever to appear on the screen. The picture was certainly a sensation when it was released in Germany in March 1922, but within two months Florence Stoker had heard all about it and begun legal proceedings. Although the distributors, the Prana Company of Berlin, attempted to deny infringement, this was summarily dismissed. After a succession of unsuccessful appeals, the final decision that all copies of Nosferatu *were to be destroyed was handed down in July 1925. Fortunately for subsequent generations of film-lovers a few prints had already been sureptitiously made for distributors outside Europe, and though Mrs Stoker was able to prevent any of these from being shown in London, the picture reached America and opened there in December 1929, thereby beginning the legend of* Nosferatu . . .*

In 1979 another leading German film director-producer-screenwriter, Werner Herzog, already famous for* The Mystery of Kasper Hauser *(1974) and* Heart of Glass *(1976), decided to remake the Murnau classic in colour, and now that the story had long been in the public domain to restore the original names of the characters – even including Count Dracula – though retaining the German setting. The charismatic actor Klaus Kinski brought Schreck's animated corpse-like vampire back to the screen, with the beautiful Isbella Adjani playing Lucy Harker again facing the awful challenge that only by sacrificing herself to Dracula can she free her husband, Jonathan, from his clutches. Paul Monette (1959–), the versatile young American novelist and scriptwriter, who is himself a great admirer of the Murnau classic, here relates the climactic episode which made both the original version of* Nosferatu *and Werner Herzog's superlative remake such unforgettable cinema experiences . . .*

*   *   *

The fever struck during the night. A morning fog had settled on the town, and several people gathered on the hospital steps to clamour for medicine that didn't exist. Doctor van Helsing came out to try to comfort them, but they preferred to be enraged. They accused him and all the authorities of Wismar of hiding the truth about the contamination till it was too late to flee to high country. They accused him of having a cure he was saving for the rich. They were half of them fevered themselves. They would have thrown eggs and overripe fruit, but they didn't dare waste a morsel of food.

The doctor stumbled back in and sadly gave the word to his guards to disperse the crowd. He fled to his office, covering his ears against the cries of people beaten and defeated, sent home empty-handed. The situation was grave and would be graver still with every hour that passed. Five hundred, perhaps, had been stricken already, and they were well into the first stage – chills and high fever, hallucinations, loss of appetite. The town was still on its ghastly holiday. The whole municipal apparatus had been disbanded. Doctor van Helsing still had a staff about him at the hospital, but only because the nurses and guards felt safer there, as if on sanctified ground. It was all an illusion, of course. There was no safe place in Wismar.

The doctor knew he could do nothing now but wait. In two or three days, thousands would have passed the crisis of the third stage. Then they would have enough dead to heap in a charnel house, but there would also be some few survivors – a quarter of the town if they were lucky. And it was for those few that the hospital was being kept ready, to nurse them back to health from their weakened state. But van Helsing couldn't help but wonder, as he sat in his office without any skill to help the suffering in Wismar, if the crowd wasn't right. If he'd listened to Lucy from the very beginning, couldn't he have ensured the evacuation of the children, at least? He looked out of his window, across the square to the empty schoolhouse, and wept for the fate of his fellow man.

Lucy came in unannounced, her manner grave and purposeful. She waited in the doorway till he'd finished crying. When he looked up, weary and defeated, she went to his desk and spread out her plans for the neighbourhood hospitals. Her knowledge of the course of the plague was impressive, and her scheme for the recuperative period was more sophisticated than van Helsing's own. He began to feel hope again as he listened to the calm in Lucy's voice.

'I blame myself,' he said when she had finished.

'No,' she replied. 'We are all to blame. But I think it may still be possible to stop this horror at the source.'

'What do you mean?' he asked. She was scanning among his shelves, looking through his books for something she had only cast a glance at when she was here before. After a moment, she pulled out a heavy volume. She laid it down on the desk, and he read the word that burned across the cover: *Nosferatu*.

'Jonathan chants this word whenever the fever is high,' she

explained. 'I have listened to all his delirious memories. He has had dealings with a vampire.'

'No such thing,' the doctor replied with a firm shake of his head. 'If you read every book on these shelves, Lucy, you would see that the superstitions of the past have begun to yield to the enlightment of science. There is a long way yet to go, but the terrors of the darkness have at last been engaged. Your husband suffers from the plague. Do not get caught up in delusions.'

'I am absolutely certain,' she said. 'I have seen the vampire with my own eyes.'

'Your husband's illness has worn you out. You must go home and rest.' He would not listen. He knew the hysterical theories would be starting up around the town. But he expected more control from Lucy, who'd had the courage to see the plague coming from the moment the first rumours had reached Wismar. Now that he'd seen the plans she drew up for the care of survivors, he wanted to appoint her as his assistant in the coming struggle. He couldn't afford to have her playing with will-o'-the-wisps.

'I beg you, doctor. Help me to crush this monster.' If she had to do it alone, she knew she would surely die. Doctor van Helsing was her last chance. 'Jonathan says he has brought coffins filled with polluted earth, by sea from Varna. I think he had hidden them all over Wismar, to hide himself from the light of the day. If you will only help me find them, we can kill him in his lair. But we must search them out *now*, while he still sleeps. Tonight, it will be too late. Tonight, he comes to take me.'

While she spoke, she trembled with dread. The doctor concluded there was nothing he could do. She had the fever now herself. He came around his desk and held her in his arms, silently cursing the darkness that had swept her up. He could only humor her now.

'Of course, my dear, of course. You go on home. I will come to you as soon as I have finished getting ready here.' In a couple of hours, he knew, she would be too weak to leave her bed. This hallucination would pass, and another would take its place. 'I will bring a stake to drive into the vampire's heart,' he lied, 'and together we will track him down.'

He led her out to the hallway and instructed his most trusted guard to see her home. Her eyes were dull as she walked away. She knew he had not believed her. She carried the book of vampires under one arm and cast an agonized look at the town she would have to save on her own. Every hour, the situation grew more extreme. The rats would overrun a house without any warning, crushing against the doors in such vast numbers that they broke inside. They ate up all the food and mangled anyone trapped within. Reports were abroad in the town that a hundred women had died in the night, from fear alone.

When they crossed the canal and came along the chestnut alley in front of Lucy's house, she dismissed the guard quite curtly. She was turning to go inside when she heard a shriek from the garden. She thought the rats had taken the house next door, and she fumbled with the key in the lock, though she knew she had nothing to fear for herself. There was an invisible zone of protection around her. It was Jonathan she had to keep safe.

But before she could hasten inside, Schrader appeared from the side of the house, staggering out of the garden. He was holding his dead wife in his arms, and he wailed with pain, though he didn't seem to see Lucy at all. He wandered the dangerous night all alone. The rats had nipped at his feet wherever he walked, and he kicked them away and strangled them in his bare hands. Twice he was seized with a sense of overwhelming danger, so he hid behind trees while the vampire passed in shadow. Nothing stopped his searching. Though Mina had taken a darker lover, he bore all the love he had like a beacon and tried to find her in time to save her. Just after dawn, he fainted from exhaustion in a deserted street. The rats were around him in a ring, the moment he hit the ground, but the raging love inside him held them back. They let him alone and went for choicer prey.

But what good did it do him now? He swore revenge against the indifferent sky and buried his anguished face in Mina's neck. That is when Lucy, helpless to give him comfort, noticed the two ripe puncture wounds on the side of Mina's throat, the last of the blood crusted around them. It was not fever, then. Nor madness, either. She clutched her book more tightly as she recalled the two white scars on Jonathan's throat.

Her brother walked away beneath his burden, heartbroken and alone, without so much as a word of recognition. She tried to banish the image from her mind as she came in and called to her husband. But the hope that he might not have heard the commotion fled when she saw his sombre face.

'He came to tell us what he saw in his travels through the town,' said Jonathan grimly, raising his head from the pillow. 'All is lost. The plague has reached as far as Riga. The fever there is one day advanced ahead of ours. They roast their pets in the street. A baby has been born with the head of a rat.' He looked at her with the strangest glare of accusation, as if to demand what words of relief she dared speak now. 'He said he believed that Mina had fled to the countryside, that the country air would calm her nerves. When the world ends, Lucy, does a man only lie to himself? He told me all these terrors, all the while convincing himself they wouldn't come to him. And then he glanced out the parlour window, and he *saw* her!'

Jonathan pointed a bony finger toward the garden, then fell back and closed his eyes, weary from so much talking. Lucy didn't know what to say. She could not assure him that every pair of lovers in Wismar wouldn't end just as tragically, just as far apart. What she hadn't expected was this distance in him. She'd prepared for a thousand agonies, her death included – but not for losing Jonathan. Late the night before, she'd defied the vampire. She said she could love enough for two if Jonathan couldn't return it. But could she? And could she go off to the weird, unspeakable meeting with the darkness if she weren't secure in Jonathan's love?

She sat by the fire, very near him, and turned the pages of the vampire book. In a moment, she knew he would sink into sleep, and then he would start to murmur the tale of his journey once again. It came in no particular order, and gypsies and nuns were mixed in together with innkeepers, coachmen, and wolves. But she'd heard out all the scenes with the Count, and she saw the lonely castle very clearly. She knew he had snatched up her pendant. Knew that he slept in a tomb beneath a dome. Things that Jonathan didn't even know he knew, he babbled out of his haunted dream.

But as the dream had not yet started, she found herself drawn to the language of dread that filled the book in her lap. '*Nosferatu*,' she whispered when she saw the name. God of the Undead. He is as a shadow, and he makes no mark on a mirror. Abandon hope, all whom he approaches.' She turned the page. She felt she had read these things before, a long time past. Softly, to herself, she read aloud the antidote. 'Though the vampire be an unnatural being, he must obey some natural laws. The sign of the cross bans him. A consecrated host will bar his retreat. If a woman pure of heart should make him forget the cry of the cock, the first light of day will destroy him forever.'

She looked out the parlour window, down the sun-shot garden to the summer house at the far end. She didn't see any way out. She would have to court him all night long, and trick him into staying past his time. Curious, how it made her calm. Now that she knew the specific task, she saw she would simply *have* to survive it. There was

so much despair and madness in Wismar now, the people might not
know the horror was over unless she came back to tell them.

'Why?' cried Jonathan out of his sleep, fighting to get away from a
thing he couldn't name. 'Why?'

'Because,' she said, looking out on the fallen leaves and speaking
half to herself, 'we've forgotten the dark side of nature. That is why. It
has not forgotten us.'

The day passed all too quickly. Most of the time, she sat by
Jonathan's side in the parlour, stroking his fevered brow. He had
ceased to rave in his sleep, as if he had told all the story that could fit
into words. Whenever he stirred and broke through to consciousness,
she fed him milk and toast, though he'd developed the plague
victim's revulsion for food. He was painfully thin and pale, and he
surfaced with a wounded look on his face, as if he felt betrayed by his
own body.

But there were moments, two or three that day, when he looked
upon Lucy's tender countenance and came all the way back to the life
they shared. Hardly a word would pass between them then, yet they
gazed in each other's eyes and renewed the indestructible bond they'd
made the day they married. She remembered it all so clearly. They
stood outside the chapel, the blossoms of a cherry tree raining down
upon them, and Jonathan turned and said: 'I promise you, Lucy, our
life will be as happy as a dream.' And so it had been.

Toward the middle of the afternoon, he struggled to speak. She
gave him a sip of water, and then he whispered: 'If only we'd known
how much we had. It has all fled away from us, Lucy. I should have
kissed you more.'

'Don't grieve, my darling,' she said. 'We had it then, and we know
it now. More we cannot ask. I love you better in the present hour,
dark though the world around us grows, than ever I have before.
Now is all we have, and now is more to me than a thousand kisses.'

'I will love you forever,' he swore to her, tears in his eyes, 'no
matter if time itself should stop.' And he took her hand in both of his
and slipped back into a peaceful sleep.

It must have been after three – the sun was shining sidelong
through the naked branches of the trees – when she heard a
commotion in the street outside. She went to the door and opened it
wide, fearful of nothing the daylight had to offer. At the house
opposite, two well-dressed gentlemen were carrying a sofa down the
steps of a house whose door was marked with a white cross. They

were stealing from the dead. They already had a pushcart piled high with booty. In spite of herself, Lucy hurried across the street to berate them.

'What are you doing, you fools? Why are you stealing *now*?' They stopped dead in their tracks and stared at her. She could see they were wild with fever. 'Don't you understand,' she begged them, 'the plague is your redemption. You are free at last of all possessions. Let the rats *have* your houses! Let them sit in your armchairs and sleep in your beds. Tomorrow you must begin to live without these props. The world will be utterly naked again.'

But they looked at her quite as if *she* were the one all crazed with fever. They shouldered her aside and heaved their sofa up on the pile. They went away arguing what was whose, pushing their cart to the next house chalked with death. Lucy hurried back across the street and shut herself in. She saw it did no good to act the prophet. They would wake to the new world and see for themselves, or they would die with the old world in the night. Yet she wept for an hour, all alone at the window above the canal, for all those men who clung to the past like a dying animal. She could not hate them. No more than she could hate the vampire, who struggled with an agony all his own. Hate had made no headway in her heart. She'd banished it long since.

It was coming close on dusk when she went and fetched her jewel case. She walked to the sofa where Jonathan slept in the parlour. She lifted the lid and took up a handful of consecrated wafers. She crumbled them up and dropped them like a trail, in a narrow circle around the place where he would sleep the night. He groaned and struggled as if it were a cage, but she did not stop till she was done. She bent over and examined her work with meticulous care, making sure there was no break in the circle. When he was all protected, she sat by his side a final time, smoothing his forehead with the cool of her hand till he quieted down again.

'Good night, dear Jonathan,' she said, her voice breaking. 'Be happy, won't you? I do not know when I will see you again, but I go with your face imprinted on my heart. I will not forget you, no matter where the darkness leads me.'

He did not hear a word of it, nor did he feel the tear that fell upon his cheek. She wiped it away as if it were some final sorrow she could bear alone. She rose and went away without a backward look, lest she falter in her resolve. She climbed the stairs in the gathering twilight. She came into her bedroom and lit the candles in the sconces, though the glow did not serve to warm her as it used to. She clapped her hands to shoo the cat out of the room, but it left at its own pace, slow as a creature spellbound.

Passionlessly, she stood at the mirror and took off her clothes. She folded each thing neatly and put it in the proper drawer, as if there was something safe in keeping all the order that she could. When she was naked, she cast an indifferent glance at her frail and fully human body. There was no vanity in her. She wore this body as a weapon now, and nothing more. She could scarcely recall the girl who used to study her skin for blemishes and fret about a tooth she thought looked crooked, who wept with rage if she couldn't comb a stray curl from her marvellous hair. The mirror had nothing to show her, least of all herself.

She went to the window and looked out into the dark. There were bats wheeling in the air above her garden. The rats moved by in procession along the edge of the canal. Though there were no wolves within a hundred miles of Wismar, she could hear a howling close as the neighbour's house. The denizens of the night made ready to adore her. They gathered in endless audience, as if the word had spread that they would have a queen at last. There seemed to be a babble of voices rising on the air. They chanted her damnation, and she did not flinch to hear it. the clock on the church tower chimed, with long resounding echoes.

It's time, she thought as the chimes mounted to midnight, *finally it's time*. She was possessed by the strangest feeling of impatience, like someone condemned at the gallows who wants the ceremony finished, who waves away the priest so as to get it all over with now. The twelfth bell rang, and she felt a wave of power course through her with a murderous desire. She turned to the ground of her sacrifice.

Dracula was already there, waiting inside the door. They had no need to take each other's measure anymore. She did not have to speak her answer. She walked across the room to her bed, and she drew back the linen counterpane as she had a thousand nights before. She lay back among the pillows, her dark hair spread out wantonly. For a moment of awesome stillness, the world seemed to hold its breath. The vampire didn't move. Could it be the dread and modesty had fallen to him? She looked more ready than he was. Seemed to know more how the night would go.

He came to her soundlessly and knelt beside the bed. He put out his hands to touch her, then let them fall to his sides, as if they were not worthy of the whiteness of her flesh. His lip curled up, and his fangs shone dully in the candlelight. She turned her face slightly away as he moved forward, so as to give him the full expanse of her throat. For hundreds of years he'd approached a victim swiftly, puncturing at the neck with an expert speed, without preliminary exploration. but this he came to lingeringly. The razor teeth touched flesh and held a long moment before he made the incision. An unbearable tension of forces gathered to act.

And when the flesh first tore, the cut was so small that only a single drop of blood came beading out. It was weighted like a teardrop, and he drank it like a rare elixir. His body shuddered with glory. He took it drop by drop for what must have been an hour. He hunched like a man praying. Lucy stared off into the light of a single candle, conscious still, and thought it did not hurt at all. She felt a kind of numbness in her throat, twin to the numbness that gripped her heart and would not let him enter. She could almost pretend it wasn't happening. She could see Jonathan's face as clearly as she hoped she would. It covered her mind like the summer sky.

Later – neither could say how long – he let the fangs sink into the vein and began to drink, but ever so slowly still. She felt it like a burning at first, and she groped the air with her hand as if to plead with him to stop. He caught up her hand in his and gathered it to his cloak to comfort her. She could feel the beating of his heart like a bell tolling. Then she ceased to struggle. The numbness spread out from her neck, all the way down her arm to the hand he held. She felt herself falling, but not into sleep. She was sure she would never sleep again.

It was more a state of suspension that she entered – as if this moment would go on forever, no matter what else should ever come to follow it. She began to wave in and out of visions, but through all of it, she never lost control. She had so little fear that she decided to explore this part like a cave. The more she could bear to see firsthand, the more likely it was she would beat him in the end. So she entered the incalculable night.

Black bats beat their wings in the darkness, rising out of the nightmare like herons off a marsh. Their mouths were opened wide, but all their cries were soundless. They lived in a great cathedral, far away on a moor, and the god who blessed it once was long forgotten. They kept a vigil in a night without end, waiting for their queen. She was walking down the aisle in a white dress, toward a broken altar. The cross was gone. The chalice was gone. Only the Bible remained, but when she turned the page, the word that blazed like a tongue of fire was *Nosferatu*.

She was on a dark ship that sailed the canals of Wismar. But as it

passed under a bridge, it went underground. On either side, gigantic
spiders tested the air with their feelers, then reared back and groped
with two front legs. A creature like a crab filled the tunnel in front of
the ship, and as they went beneath his twitching legs, his dead eyes
rolled, and she felt the shell slide over her skin. The tunnel went on and
on, till she became aware of men lined up in a row on the stone bank.
They were still as mummies, and their mouths gaped open.

Everything in the night was hungry, and yet the further she travelled
into it, the more she saw they could not prey on her. The corpses
leaned against the walls, exhausted and alone. Their clothes were
tattered, and their flesh fell off them like wax along a candle. They
stood frozen in unfinished gestures, not living and not quite dead. She
sailed by them like a ghost, and she knew that if they reached to touch
her, their hands would catch hold of nothing but the air. She saw, as
never before, how precarious was the vampire's grip on life. Dracula
had crawled somehow to the lip of the cave, where he hung by a single
thread, and all the hellish world beneath him tried to pull him back.

When was it, deep in the night, that she felt him crying as he drank?
She put her arms around his neck and drew him ever closer. She
opened her lips and made a hushing sound. She wondered how he'd
ever thought he had the power to bring her down with him. She knew
the life was going out of her, but she had no fear of death, and now
there was no chance that he could detain her, here among the Undead.
It required a cast of mind she simply didn't possess – a sense of secrecy
and guilt, of longing without a name, of terror to live in time.

The candles had guttered and gone out by the time the church clock
struck four. The vampire barely breathed. The fangs held on in the
vein, but for the longest time he took nothing in. It was too exquisite to
dream of all that was left, like a pool as deep as the world, just his
alone. He did not hear the panic of his children, thronging out in the
night. They groaned and howled and pleaded for him to make an end
of it and bring her to the kingdom. His hands had begun to roam her
body as it cooled and hovered on the brink of death. He had the whole
of eternity to keep her by his side, but he knew there would never again
be a night like this. For once he was more alive than not. He savoured
the stroke of time like an open window letting in the moon.

And though she was far gone now, and deeply under his spell, she
was crouched in the corner of her mind where the air was free of
phantoms, and she counted every minute like a nun at her rosary. A
half hour more. She heard the rage of the powers of darkness, moaning
at the windows and calling warnings. She was not sure the house could

stand up, with the furies bearing down like a hurricane. But she held his head and stroked the pulses in his skull and met him trance for trance. They were so entwined, so locked to a single fate, that there ceased to be any difference between her pain and his. They seemed to lie here like mirrors set face to face, excluding all the world besides. She had half a mind to go with him, flee this sorrowful trap of mortal life forever. And it only made her count the minutes harder.

The vampire heaved a sigh that broke a thousand hearts. He lifted away from her neck, and the look in his eyes was full of dreams. He saw the first light of day as if he didn't understand the significance of it. The rising sun had caught the tip of the tallest steeple in Wismar, and the high gables of the houses at the eastern end of town were bathed in a reddish light. An ominous silence had fallen on the landscape as the creatures of the night withdrew to their lairs. Their final warning didn't even reach him. He had forgotten himself – he who endured five hundred years of knowing nothing else, night after night.

A cock crowed out in the morning air. Another, and then another. The sun lit up the topmost branches of the blighted trees. He made as if to rise, by instinct only. He couldn't see why he should not stay here, where he thought he had come to life again. Her hands around his neck restrained him, so he moved to disengage them. But she moaned so pitifully then, as he tugged to pull away, that he made his fatal error. He looked into her eyes.

There was hardly a breath left in her, and she was whiter than the pillows where she lay, but she gathered all the force still grappling after life and whispered this command: 'Take me with you, Master. Do not leave me here alone!'

And he knew he could not go without her. But he had to finish every drop of blood that beat inside her before he could carry her to his bed. He bent again to her neck, bit in, and sucked with a deep abandon. Her eyes were mad with pain as she stared at the brightening window. Please, she begged the dawning day. She could not last another second.

A ray of the sun streaked in. It touched the tip of his shoulder and glanced away to a patch of wall. He fell from her, writhing as if a spear had lodged in the bone. He turned in rage, his mouth widened to a rictus and wet with gore, his eyes glazed with vengeance. But it wasn't an enemy he could take and ravage. It was only the sun, and it grew and grew till it flooded the room, because it could not help itself. He caught at his own throat as the breath froze in his lungs. He stood, and it seemed he was going to throw himself through the window, to stop the torture blistering his skin like white-hot bars of iron.

But he was only drawing the drapes. It did no good, of course. The light was all over the room by now. Yet he was frantic to dim the room, even as he choked and plummeted to death. He backed against the foot of the bed and spread his cape to shield his queen. For that is what he was trying to do – save *her*, though he had to die himself. He gave her one last agonized look over his shoulder. He did not seem to have the least idea that she had tricked him to his fate. His eyes were great with sorrow, as if he thought he'd failed her.

She saw it was over at last. She was all but dead as she stared at him, but she was too good, or she understood him now too well, to let him die in such despair. She smiled as if to say the night was magic. His own face lit with triumph, and though he fell, his last thought as he slipped away to his final sleep was this: he had tasted love like any other man.

He lay in a heap on the floor, released from his ancient prison. Lucy looked into the sun. The sky outside her window was bright with the constant image of the man she loved. She had kept it like a faith. She moved her lips to speak his name. *I love you always*, she whispered, a smile of perfect mildness breaking on her face. And the light went out.

The Bat

BELA LUGOSI

It was by the merest chance that a young actor named Bela Lugosi (1882–1956) did not appear in Friedrich Murnau's Nosferatu. *Lugosi was then living and working in Berlin and had already made an appearance in the Jekyll and Hyde story,* Der Januskopf, *which starred Conrad Veidt. The young, Hungarian born actor was eager for work, and once again presented himself when Murnau was casting for his vampire movie. Legend has it that Lugosi wanted to play Waldemar Hutter (the re-named Jonathan Harker), but was considered too youthful-looking. His disappointment was, of course, to be completely overturned eleven years later in Hollywood when he became the first — and authorised — screen Dracula. Lugosi had emigrated to America in 1921, hoping for a more rewarding career, and for the first few years appeared on the stage in New York. Because of his mid-European background he was a natural choice for the leading role in a stage version of* Dracula, *written by the English actor, Hamilton Deane, which reached Broadway in 1927 after two successful years in Britain. Lugosi duly made the part very much his own, playing the Count for a year in New York and then two more years around the nation's big cities. In 1931, legend has it, the popularity of the play reached the ears of Universal Pictures who bought the rights and assigned director Tod Browning to make a screen version. Three leading actors were initially considered for the central role: Lon Chaney, the famous 'Man of a Thousand Faces'; Paul Muni, the star of* Scarface; *and Conrad Veidt who, like Lugosi, had come to Hollywood seeking international fame. There is little doubt that Chaney was the favourite for the role, but he died while the film was in post production, and, short of time, Browning opted for Lugosi who was, of course, already familiar with the part. Aided by Browning's sense of the weird, a number of atmospheric sets and Lugosi's heavy, deliberate and inimitable accent growling, 'I-am-Dracu-la', the resulting movie proved a cinema landmark. It also gave the screen a personification of dark evil that has never been surpassed. Co-starring with Lugosi were Edward Van Sloane as Professor Van Helsing, a role he, too, had played on the stage; with David Manners as Jonathan Harker, Helen Chandler as Mina and Dwight Frye as the madman, Renfield. Reviewers on both sides of the Atlantic did not, however, share the enthusiasm for* Dracula *which it has enjoyed in the past sixty years. The* New York Times *found it, 'an inadequate reproduction of Bram Stoker's famous novel', while Leonard Wallace in the* British Film Weekly *complained, 'Personally, this reviewer finds the subject revolting.'*

Revolting or not, the film at a stroke made Bela Lugosi one of the immortals of the cinema, while the picture itself was the instigation of a host of vampire movies which have continued unabated to this day. Sadly, Lugosi did not make the most of his fame – instead of concentrating on the kind of quality horror films for which he was so obviously suited, he accepted roles in a number of abysmal productions and ruined his reputation. His private life also became a mess of marital problems and, later, drug addiction. Writing of this element of Lugosi's life, Ephraim Katz says in his International Film Encyclopedia *(1979), 'He allowed the vampire image to become part of his real life – he began giving interviews while lying in a coffin and in his later films played parodies of himself as Dracula. He was even buried in his Dracula cape.' Nothing, though, can diminish the importance of Lugosi's performancce as the first Count on the screen. With his vocal gifts, he was also something of a storyteller, too, and in 1955, the year before he died, read the following story on NBC Radio claiming that it was actually based on fact. True or not, just imagine as you read it Lugosi's voice speaking and I am sure the effect will be as chilling as anything else you find in these pages . . .*

❋   ❋   ❋

Your fancy may crawl away from the tale I am about to tell you – in fact you may not believe it. But in order to tell you about the haunted house and what occurred there I must go back a little way in time. You know that I am married a fourth time. Yes, you know that.

You have heard about my – my other wives. You know that I come from the black mountains of Hungary where, in the arms of my old nurse, I heard the tales of vampires and saw their victims. Ah, yes, as I grew older and could take notice of things about me I saw many a young man and young woman pale and sicken and seem to die with no cause given. I had a sceptical mind. I read widely. I made a brave attempt to laugh off such nonsense. Folklore gone mad, I told myself. I would shake off the charnel-house odours of such foul superstitions . . .

And then, I met the woman. Her age was indeterminable. She was an actress. She was not outstandingly beautiful. Her hair was a pale brown. Her skin was deathly pale at times; at other times it was a blood, blood red – that was when she had been fed. Her mouth was thin and ravenous. Her teeth were tiny, and pointed. She had been married many times. There had been many lovers. One never asked what had become of them. Men feared her – and went to her at her command. Husbands left their wives because of her.

I had a wife, too, and two sons. Yes, I have two sons of whom I have never spoken. They are grown boys now. I have never seen them since I – I left. I have never, from that day to this, sent so much as a picture postcard home. Nor have I had one. How should I? I burned all my bridges behind me when I left more than fifteen years ago. It was safer to have no communication of any earthly kind. I wish I could say that I did not care, that the thought of those two young men of mine did not matter to me. But I do care, it does matter. However, to get back . . . At that time I was living the normal life of a young man of the town. I had played Romeo, with some success. I was said to be of outstanding appearance. I had a genial disposition and a happy outlook on life.

Then I met – her. The very first time I was introduced to her I broke out into a deathly cold sweat. My heart and pulse raced and then seemed to stop, dead. I lost control of my limbs and faltered in my speech. I was never happy in her presence. I felt always sick and dizzy and depleted. Yet I could not remain away from her. She never bade me come to her, not in words. There was never any of the conventional trapping of assignations. I simply went to her, at odd hours of the day and night, impelled by an agency I neither saw nor heard.

I lost weight. I hardly slept. I had seen other young men fade and wither before my eyes and had heard the village folk whisper the dread cause. But when it came to me, I did not know it for what it was.

It was my mother who forced me to flee the country and never to return to it again until that woman and every trace of her vanished from the sight of men . . .

This that I am telling you is the truth. It can be verified if you are curious or incredulous.

I came to America. After a time, my health returned to me. I tried, on two other occasions, to find human love, to marry and have a home as other men have. You have heard the results. One marriage lasted twenty-four hours . . . The other . . . I can only say she, the faithful one, was there and gave me to understand that if ever I felt love again, attempted marriage, she would stand between me and fulfillment.

For many months, for years I dared not think of love or of marriage. I was determined to stay alone.

And then I met my present wife. She was my secretary. She, too, is of Hungarian descent. She was born here. She, too, was raised on the folklore of the countryside, the tales of vampires and ghouls and unspeakable things.

She loved me, she has told me, at first sight. Something in her ached for me. I did not love her – not at first. I had put love from me. Then, day after day, as she worked for me and with me, did little things for me I had not thought to ask her, a craving for companionship, for a woman in my heart and in my home once more took hold of my very vitals.

But I wanted to put her to the test. For weeks before I dared to tell her that I loved her, wanted to marry her I – I tortured her. They were not nice things, the things I did to her. I cannot speak of them. Perhaps it was to test her . . . perhaps it was an attempt to placate that – that other one. Whatever it was, and however shamed my heart, I caused her such suffering as made the tears stream down her face for hours and hours at a time . . . but she never faltered, never turned away from me.

And so, nearly two years ago we were married and found this house. We thought, 'We will make it safe against invasion of any kind.' And so we have locks on all the doors, locks that cannot be unlocked by any hands but mine. And no one is admitted to this house unless that person is well known to us. No appointments are made over the phone. We have five hounds and one of them is white and his name is Bodri. He *knows*. The windows, as you can see, are screened and barred and locked. On the landing of each stairway is a large cushion upon which one of the hounds sleeps at night . . . no footstep, human or otherwise, can mount or descend these stairs without their knowing it.

And there are times when they howl in the night . . . howl fearfully though no eye, not even mine, can see what they are howling at. And so, in spite of all these precautions *the house is haunted!*

I knew it, first, when the dogs began to howl. I knew it when I first saw the white fur rise on Bodri's body, saw his ears flatten and his red eyes dilate.

I knew it when, in the dead of night, there came the sound of something dragging around the house.

And then, that first night in this house and every night thereafter the bat has come. The first night I saw that bat, monstrously big and with but one eye, flattened against the window.

'It began to be a monomania with both of us – to kill that bat. We had the feeling that if we ridded ourselves of that thing we would be free. We told Bodri to get it. We even hired exterminators to come up and watch for the creature and kill it. We had all kinds of men here lying in wait for it. They finally told us we were imagining it – there was no bat visible. We knew that they thought we were mad.

Months went by and then, one night, Bodri got it. We heard him howling in the darkness. He came into the house and he had it in his mouth, limp, dead, hideous beyond words. With a sick heart and shuddering flesh I went into the garden and there, in the dead of night, I dug a grave for it. I dug a hole deep enough to bury the Giant of Tarsus. I went back to the house, and to bed.

The next night came. We had a little festive dinner, my wife and I. We drank wine and were very gay. We even talked of the time when we might go back to Hungary, back to Lugos. In the midst of our happy talk, it happened.

My wife heard it first. I could tell that she had heard it by the look on her face. I went to the window. The bat was back again. Not the same one you say? But yes, it was.

I went into the garden with Bodri beside me. I dug up that deep pit again. The bat was gone. The ground was undisturbed but the bat – was – *gone!*

That is my story. In Lugos it would not be thought so strange, nor disbelieved. So often and so frightful is this sort of thing over there, even today, that the townspeople of Lugos often keep their dead for days and sometimes weeks to be sure they have died a Christian death and not the hideous, half-death of the vampires. But I do hope that I have not *frightened* you . . .

Son of Dracula

PETER TREMAYNE

Universal Pictures followed their success with Dracula *and its sequel* Dracula's Daughter *(based on Stoker's much anthologised tale, 'Dracula's Guest') by inventing a son for the Count and casting in the lead role the offspring of the man who should have been the original Dracula, Lon Chaney jnr. Though never as versatile or charismatic a star as his father, Lon did give a few memorable screen performances – in particular as Lennie in the film of John Steinbeck's* Of Mice and Men *(1940) – but is perhaps best remembered for his 'monster' roles in the Forties as Frankenstein's creature, the Mummy, the Wolfman and Dracula. The idea for his third picture in the Universal triology had come from Curt Siodmak, the German-born scriptwriter and novelist, probably best remembered for his much-filmed novel,* Donovan's Brain *(1942), about a criminal's brain which is kept alive and controls the minds of others. In Hollywood, Curt had already written* The Invisible Man Returns *(1940),* Frankenstein Meets The Wolf Man *(1941) and* I Walked With A Zombie *(1942) and was thoroughly familiar with the sequel syndrome. His basic idea for* Son of Dracula *was turned into a screenplay by Eric Taylor, though it was Curt's older brother, Robert, who directed the picture. Co-starring with Lon Chaney jnr, were Louise Allbritton as Katherine Caldwell; Robert Paige (Frank Stanley), Frank Craven (Dr Harry Brewster), George Irving (Colonel Caldwell), J. Edwards Bromberg (Professor Lazlo) and Adeline Reynolds as Zimba. The* Son of Dracula *is also a landmark because it introduced several 'firsts' into cinematic vampire lore. It was the first picture to show a vampire transforming into a bat, thanks to the special effects wizardry of John P. Fulton; the first film in which a vampire was seen to have no reflection in a mirror; and the first (of many) in which the central character thinly disguised his real identity as Count Alucard – Dracula spelt backwards. Audiences at the time loved the picture and the* Los Angeles Times *of 19 November 1943 declared it was 'really eerie' and added that Lon Chaney jnr, 'is fast catching up with his father in the ability to project a horrid atmosphere'. Some later writers, however, have seen this movie as the forerunner of the series of dreadful, low-budget vampire pictures which appeared in the next decade – but not Donald Glut. 'This film is not generally accepted as a classic Dracula film,' he has written in* The Dracula Book, *'and many snobbish film aficionados dismiss it as ludicrous. I contend, though, that* Son of Dracula *is the slickest and most entertaining of the trilogy.'*

This view is shared by Peter Tremayne (1943–) who has always had a nostalgic regard for the Universal horror movies and first saw Son of Dracula *as a teenager. Now a full-time writer of horror and fantasy fiction, those films – plus Bram Stoker's original novel – have inspired his own Dracula trilogy,* Dracula Unborn *(1977),* The Revenge of Dracula *(1978) and* Dracula, My Love *(1980), which have been published on both sides of the Atlantic, with* Dracula, My Love *being optioned for filming. In 1993, the three titles were reissued in a single volume as* Dracula Lives! *Peter's adaptation of the screenplay is here published for the first time – and forms a tribute to the original picture as well as re-emphasising the undoubted pleasure that it has given to millions of viewers during the past half century.*

*   *   *

The trees clustered over the narrow pathway making it gloomy and forbidding. The young woman, dark haired and attractive, pushed her way along the track with a determined set to her mouth and chin. Now and again the dank verdure of the forest gave way to a swampy clearing. Such areas were more dangerous than the narrow confines of the forest path for they were simply areas of foetid mire from which malodorous fumes assailed her nostrils.

She shivered slightly as she saw the muddy, weed-veined waters ripple and undulate now and then as an alligator, with its broad snout, pushed its log like way across the blackness of the swamp, between the sinister looking clumps of sawgrass.

Katherine Caldwell had lived near these swamps most of the twenty-three years of life. Indeed, these same swamps formed part of her father's vast plantation. While she was not fearful, nevertheless, she had a deep respect for the area. There were a hundred ways to meet an untimely death in this humid wilderness, from 'gators to water snakes, not to mention the feline predators who roamed around the dark wastes during the nocturnal hours.

Pushing through overhanging branches, she spied her destination. A rotting wood shack nestling almost hidden in the undergrowth. From its advanced state of dilapidation, it appeared that the hut had been deserted as a human habitation for many years. Kay knew that this was not so. She stopped before the ramshackle cabin and called softly.

'Queen Zimba?'

There was no reply.

She moved forward cautiously to the stoop and called again.

A throaty chuckle answered this time from the darkness of the open door beyond the stoop.

A figure stirred in the darkness.

For many years Kay had known the old Hungarian refugee who had come to dwell in isolation in the swamps. No one knew her real name. Many said that 'Queen' Zimba, as everyone had come to call her, was the genuine article; a queen of the Manush gypsies who once dwelt in the brooding Carpathian Mountains of Eastern Europe. Others dismissed her a charlatan. Kay did not. Several times she had consulted the crone to see what fortune was outlined on the palms of her hands. Kay was a great believer in the fates and the old woman's powers of divination.

'Queen Zimba,' she began respectfully, 'tonight is my engagement party. I am marrying Frank Stanley in a fortnight. Can you tell me what my palms say?'

She did not move from the foot of the stoop but thrust out her hands, palms upward. A silver dollar piece was resting on one palm.

The crone moved forward into the light, a caricature of an aged gypsy fortune teller. Her bent figure moved slowly, utilising the heavy stick, as she came forward to stand before Kay. The silver dollar swiftly vanished.

'Ah, I see you now, Kay Caldwell,' she breathed, her eyes like gimlets. 'Let me look at your hands.'

She took them and peered down. Suddenly a stream of unintelligible sounds broke from her thin, dried lips as she broke into her native dialect. Zimba's eyes rolled and her skin, even though tanned brown by years of constant exposure to the elements, seemed to blanch.

Kay started back, fearfully.

'What is it? What do you see, Queen Zimba?'

'I cannot tell,' wheezed the old woman, dropping Kay's hands as if they were red hot.

'You must!' insisted Kay. 'Is my marriage to be an unhappy one?'

The bright eyes of the woman were upon her.

'Flee from this place, child. Seek the sanctuary of a Church. After tonight, it will be too late.'

'Why? I don't understand. I am to be married.'

'Then you will marry a corpse and live in a grave! Be gone!'

With the hag's hideous shriek of laughter ringing in her ears, Kay turned and fear caused her to run headlong back along the pathway to where she had left her car at the edge of the forest.

Behind her, the sounds of the swamp and forest suddenly ceased. Queen Zimba put her head to one side listening in puzzlement. Then she heard a curious flapping sound behind her. Slowly the old woman turned. On the stoop, or rather hovering above it, level with her head was a large black bat, its great wings beating at the air. Tiny red malignant eyes bore into the now wide, horrified eyes of the old woman.

She shrieked loudly as the terrifying creature dived straight for her eyes, its talons outstretched.

Queen Zimba's heart had stopped in fear even before her blood spattered the stoop and her frail, twisted body sank to the ground.

'That's odd,' Frank Stanley frowned, looking down the length of the depot platform as the train pulled out. 'Kay said her guest would be arriving on the train. Did you see anyone who fitted her description get off, Harry?'

Dr Harry Brewster shook his head in reply. Brewster was an elderly man, in his mid-60s. Slow, thoughtful and always with a briar-pipe clenched between his teeth. He had stood *in loco parentis* to Frank, who was half his age, for many years, ever since, as a boy, Frank's parents had been killed in an automobile accident. He smiled now at his handsome, eager companion. In two weeks, young Frank would be marrying Kay Caldwell and Brewster justly felt that he was losing a son.

Dark Oaks Siding was not really a railroad depot. It was just a long wooden platform beside the railroad tracks with a couple of store houses, one of which served as a ticket and telegraph office. Over the years, several houses had grown up in the vicinity, so there was a small community at Dark Oaks, though not big enough to call the place a

town. But the depot had really been built to serve the Caldwell's Dark
Oaks plantation back in the 1870s when the country was cotton-
hungry and the great southern plantations, like Dark Oaks, were
attempting to recover from the deprivations of the bitter war with the
north. Trains originally stopped at Dark Oaks merely to load cotton.
Now the cotton trade was gone and the community had sunk into
genteel squalor, although the local folks still respected the Caldwells,
especially old Colonel Caldwell who had done his best to keep their
small community in existence.

Brewster pointed to where Caleb Brown, the station master, was
overseeing some boys stacking curious looking oblong boxes which
had been unloaded from the train.

'Let's ask Caleb, just in case Kay's friend missed the train. You
know what foreigners are. Did she say that he could speak English?'

Frank nodded agreement.

'I know for certain Kay can't speak Hungarian or Rumanian or
whatever the language is where this queer bird comes from, so he must
speak English.'

Brewster sighed.

'Did she tell you much about him? Curious, her inviting him to her
engagement party out of the blue like this?'

'She met him during her recent trip to Europe, Harry. He's from
Transylvania or some such place. Owns a castle, or so he told her, and
says that he is a count. Told her he wanted to visit America. Well, you
know what Katherine is like. She immediately asked him to come
down here as a house guest when he came to the States. We only knew
he was arriving this morning when he sent a telegram from
Montgomery.'

'Well, she should have come to meet him herself instead of roping us
in to pick up this elusive count,' complained Brewster, pausing to
relight his briar and casting another look around. 'Where is he?'

They had reached the spot where Caleb Brown was organising the
lifting of the boxes which had been off-loaded from the train.

He nodded sourly to them both.

'Any sign of a foreign guy coming off the train?' Frank asked.
'We've come down here to meet him.'

Caleb rubbed his chin.

'Foreign guy, you say? Well, no passengers came off the train at all,
Mister Stanley.'

'Did anyone leave a message for us, then? Did you get a wire saying
that they'd miss the train? The message would be for Miss Caldwell.'

Caleb shook his head again.

'No message. But if one does come through, I can get it sent on to the mansion.' Locals always called the great Caldwell plantation house 'the mansion'. 'What's the name of this party you be lookin' fer?'

Frank Stanley thrust his hand into his pocket and drew out the piece of paper on which Kay had written the name.

'It's a guy called Alucard. Count Alucard.'

Caleb Brown whistled softly.

'Well, see here . . .' He caught Frank by the sleeve and pointed to one of the boxes. It was an oblong trunk of polished ebony. It reminded Frank uncomfortably of a coffin. On the top of the trunk was the name 'Alucard'.

'Well, at least his luggage has arrived safely,' muttered Brewster. 'If not himself. Do the other boxes belong to him as well?'

Caleb spat sourly.

'They surely do. All addressed to Dark Oaks Depot, to be collected. And lookee here . . .' he pointed to where one of the accompanying boxes had tumbled and been knocked open when it had been off-loaded from the train. Frank and Harry could see that it was filled with nothing but earth. 'Is this Alucard guy some sort of joker, Mister Stanley? Now what's a body want to travel around with boxes of earth fer?'

The celebration party was over at the Dark Oaks mansion. The guests had departed and the servants were beginning to tidy up. Old Colonel Caldwell had given his final blessing to Kay and Frank before announcing that he was retiring for the night. He was not as youthful and strong as he once had been and he felt tired. It had been a long evening, but he didn't begrudge Kay. She had never looked more beautiful nor happier in young Frank's arms. The colonel felt a regret that Kay's mother was not alive to see this day. Now the colonel felt able to make his excuses and leave the bright summer's night to the young lovers.

He entered his bedroom and crossed to the window. It was a beautiful moonlit night and so he decided to leave the curtains open. But as the air was slightly chill he moved to the glowing embers of the fire and reached for the poker to stir the coals into a warming display of sparks and flames.

It was at that moment that he heard the curious sound of flapping wings and, frowning, turned back to the window. Hovering outside was a gigantic bat which seemed to be staring at him through the glass with small, bead-like, malignant red eyes. Then the creature suddenly seemed to evaporate into a mist, a white ethereal mist that seeped through the window-frame and reformed; reformed into the figure of a tall, powerfully built man whose face was contorted with evil, his lips pulled back from sharp white teeth.

Old Colonel Caldwell came out of his shocked stupor and lurched fearfully for the bellrope but the dark figure swept forward and seized him by the throat with one powerful hand, lifting him bodily from the floor. Colonel Caldwell tried to lash out with the poker still gripped in his hand, but to no avail. He was thrown to the floor. The tall man followed him down. As the colonel continued to thresh wildly, trying to fight off the powerful figure, his foot dislodged some burning coals from the fire, spilling them onto the carpet where they began to smoulder and catch light.

Dr Harry Brewster came down the ornate stairway of the mansion and gazed at the tear-stained face of Kay, seated on a couch in the hall. Her hands gripped those of Frank who was vainly trying to comfort her.

'Well?' demanded Frank as Brewster paused awkwardly before them.

'I don't know. The fire was started accidentally. It's out now. The servants have it under control. But what started it, I can't say for sure. We'll have to speak with the sheriff tomorrow and he can see if I've missed something.'

'But what caused daddy's death?' interrupted Kay. She was not concerned with the minor fire in the colonel's room which had alerted the servants to go to his aid. The colonel had been found stretched dead on the floor, a look of terror on his contorted features such as she never wanted to see on a human face again.

It had been Frank who had telephoned for Dr Brewster to come back to the house immediately.

'A massive heart attack,' replied Brewster after a moment or so. It was the only logical explanation. The colonel must have threshed and contorted in pain and caused the fire to start. But there were several other things which mystified Brewster. There were the strange puncture marks on the colonel's neck; marks like animal bites. There was also a bruising as if he had been held by the throat by some powerful force. And there was the odd, pallid texture of the skin as if the colonel was anaemic, though all his life he had been a rugged, florid-faced man. And then there was the room's disarray almost as if the colonel had been engaged in a struggle. These were questions which Brewster could not answer. Above all, Brewster had known Caldwell all his life and if there was a man he would say was certain not to have a cardiac arrest it was the colonel.

'Anyway, Kay,' he went on, 'I am prescribing a mild sedative for you tonight. Don't worry. I will stay here the rest of the night and we can sort things out with the sheriff tomorrow.'

'I am staying as well,' insisted Frank.

There came the sound of a ringing on the front door bell.

Brewster said: 'I'll see to it. You take Kay to her room, Frank. I'll come up to administer the sedative shortly.'

As Frank obeyed, his arm around the girl, leading her up the staircase, Brewster opened the door. A tall, powerful man, dressed curiously for the hour in a tuxedo and a long, black cloak, lined in red satin, stood at the door. His face was pale, strong boned, with almost unnaturally thin red lips. His eyes were dark, seeming to be without pupils which gave them an abnormal quality. They appeared to be flecked with red specks, evil and malignant, but Brewster put it down to a trick of the porch lighting. A small thin moustache adorned the man's upper lip.

'I am Count Alucard,' the man announced almost sepulchrally. His voice was strong but heavily accented.

Brewster frowned. So this was the strange Hungarian guest whom Kay had been expecting earlier in the day.

'I am the family doctor, Doctor Brewster,' he replied. 'I am afraid it is a bad time to call, count.'

The nobleman raised an eyebrow in silent query.

'Colonel Caldwell has just died.'

'So? This death was expected?' The lisping foreign intonation was nonetheless firm.

'No. It was a sudden heart attack.'

'So? May I convey my condolences to Miss Katherine in person?'

Why did Brewster feel his hackles rise at the count's familiar form of address to Kay?

'I'm afraid not,' he replied shortly. 'Miss Caldwell has just gone to bed with a sedative. You'll appreciate that she has received a terrible shock. Tonight was her engagement party . . .'

'Engagement?' the question was a short staccato breath.

'She is to marry in a fortnight. She is engaged to my ward, Frank Stanley.'

Did a look of anger cross the previously bland expression of the man? Brewster could not be sure.

'Then I shall leave my card,' the count replied, suiting the action to the word. The card was an ornate pasteboard with Gothic lettering announcing 'Count Alucard, Castle Alucard, Borgo Pass, Transylvania'. 'I will call on Miss Katherine in the next day or so when she has rested. I shall be taking accommodations within the area. Goodnight.'

Brewster watched the man stride away, pausing for a moment or two before closing the door. This European nobleman whom Kay had picked up was surely a curious bird, he thought a little uneasily.

Something caused Kay to come awake. It was night and the moon was shining brightly through her bedroom window. She felt peaceful and languid. She sat up, head to one side, listening. She was sure someone was calling her. It was not Frank. It was someone she felt she needed to go to; to go to at once. She did not question why. Obedient to the urging of her mind, she swung out of bed and put a robe around her nightgown before making her way onto the darkened landing.

The servants were all in bed and she met no one as she descended the ornate staircase and across the gloomy hall to the door.

Outside, the night was bright and silent.

Again she thought she heard her name being called.

She moved off, not even realising that she was barefoot. Some instinct made her feel eager to reach the owner of the voice which was calling. She began to hurry, almost running in her desire to reach her destination.

She found that her footsteps were guiding her towards the old swamp area of the plantation. Yet she had no thoughts for the wild cats, those feline nocturnal predators, nor even the snakes or swamp creatures of the night. She ran eagerly on along the paths, not minding the stones and twigs under her bare feet. The path now darkened as the trees closed in on her shutting out the moonlight.

It was some time before she came to the old swamp and stood in front of the hut that was the home of the hermit fortune teller 'Queen' Zimba.

She did not go to the hut but paused on the edge of the swamp and stared out across its dark, dank surface. She felt a sense of anticipation, almost of sexual exaltation, thrill her body.

The surface of the swamp began to bubble, it heaved and swirled as if guided by a strange force. Suddenly, a great oblong trunk emerged in the centre of the swamp, like a cork popping up after being immersed in water. As she watched, a mist began twisting from the sides of the trunk as if alive; twisting and whirling and reforming into the solid figure of Count Alucard, standing with his pallid face in the silver moonlight; powerful arms folded across his chest, a grim smile on his thin red lips.

Even as Kay watched the trunk, with Alucard standing on it as firmly as if on dry ground, it seemed to be guided mysteriously to the shore, gliding across the foetid pool to where Kay stood waiting, her head thrown back, her arms held outwards in a wanton gesture of surrender. Standing above her, as she strained eagerly towards him, Alucard smiled confidently down.

'And you shall be flesh of my flesh; blood of my blood; kin of my kin; my bountiful wine press for a while. You shall be my companion and my helper. This is a young country, with young, fresh blood, and here I will take my vengeance on those puny mortals who dare to think they can thwart my will and purpose.'

'I am yours, my love!' cried Kay with abandon. 'Take me! I am yours forever!'

Frank Stanley was half out of his mind with rage as he drove his automobile up to the darkened portals of the Dark Oaks mansion. The news that Katherine had married Alucard had left him with a mixture of shock and disbelief. It had been Harry Brewster who had given him the news. He had heard it from old Clem Butler, the local justice of the peace, who was given to gossiping. That morning, Clem told Brewster that he had been awakened before dawn with Kay and a foreign man, whom he later discovered was Alucard, standing outside and demanding that he marry them immediately. What could he do? It was odd, especially when Clem knew Kay was engaged to young Frank. But there was no reason to refuse to perform the marriage.

Harry had called round to Frank's apartment to break the news to him as gently as he could. It was not the sort of news that could be broken gently. As soon as Brewster had left, Frank had telephoned Kay to seek an explanation. She had confirmed her marriage to Alucard, as if Frank had been a perfect stranger. He could not believe it when she simply put the 'phone down on him after he demanded to know why he had been jilted.

The rage did not abate as he drove. Instead it grew to such proportions that he soon found himself with his old service revolver in his pocket as he rang on the bell of Dark Oaks where, only two, or was it three?, nights before, he had been celebrating his engagement party – his engagement to Kay. Kay who had laughed and danced that night in his arms . . .

The door swung open. The tall, grim figure of Alucard stood there and regarded him with a mocking smile.

'Where's Kay?' Frank demanded bluntly.

'My wife, the Countess, does not wish to see you,' replied Alucard, enunciating slowly and emphasising Kay's new status as if using it as a weapon.

Frank ground his teeth for the words struck him like knife wounds. 'I will see her!'

'Why?' demanded Kay's cold voice. She emerged from the dining room and came to stand by Alucard, her hand upon his arm. The gesture was not lost on Frank. It infuriated him the more.

'Kay . . . what has happened?' demanded Frank. 'What does this mean? You loved me . . . a few days ago you were going to marry me.'

'I owe you no explanation, Frank. Please go now.'

A red rage burned in Frank's mind. He drew out the revolver.

'I think you owe me that much, Kay. This man has turned your mind and I will not allow it!'

The barrel came up to Alucard's chest. The Count's mocking smile simply broadened.

'Don't be a total fool, Frank,' Kay said coldly.

'I don't know what your game is, mister,' snarled Frank to Alucard, 'but you're not getting away with it.'

Kay breathed out with a long hiss of a breath and, as if seeking protection, moved behind Alucard's tall figure.

'You are a stupid fool, young man,' drawled the count. 'She is mine and will be mine for all eternity.'

Something snapped in Frank's mind then. He pressed the trigger, scarcely knowing what he was doing. The explosion seemed deafening. It was followed by a scream.

Frank blinked and stared aghast, not believing what he saw.

Kay, who had been standing behind Alucard, had fallen to the floor with a red stain spreading over her bosom. Alucard was untouched, yet he did not appear to have moved from the spot.

'Kay!' cried Frank in anguish. But from the blood stain and the way the body had fallen it was obvious that she was dead. Was he losing his mind? How could this be?

'You fool!' snarled the count. 'You pale, puerile mortal.'

Frank gazed in helpless bewilderment.

'But how . . . how . . . ? You were standing in front of her and yet . . .'

Suddenly the tall figure seemed to dissolve, dissolve and reform. A giant bat hung in the air before Frank, flapping its relentless black wings.

With a scream of terror, Frank fired another shot wildly. He was sure that he had hit the creature – he could not have missed from this range, but the bullet seemed to pass through it. With that realisation, Frank turned and fled moaning in terror from the house. The creature, its wings flapping, rose and followed him leisurely.

Frank ignored his automobile and fled on foot down the long drive through the old Caldwell cemetery, dodging and twisting through the headstones and grave markers, while all the time just behind and above him, the great black bat followed, its wings pulsating in the air.

Frank twisted and dodged among the tombstones. He was mumbling now, his mind unhinged by the inexplicable horror he had witnessed.

The bat was gaining on him, swooping closer, ever closer, and poised ready to strike.

Exhausted, Frank found himself stumbling and then falling behind a great stone carved cross at the edge of the graveyard. At that moment the clouds passed from the face of the moon and the bright rays of moonlight caught that cross and sent its shadow across Frank's heaving body.

The bat seemed to jerk backwards and its shape began to dissolve and change until the tall figure of Alucard was standing only a few yards away, one hand raised as if shielding his eyes. There were no other clouds in the night sky and the bright light continued to shine down creating the image of the cross on the exhausted back of Frank Stanley.

With a growl of anger, Alucard turned and strode out of the ancient cemetery, back in the direction of the house.

'So you see, Lazlo,' Harry Brewster said to his elderly companion, seated on the other side of the hearth, warming himself before the fire, 'when young Frank confessed to me that he had killed Kay, I immediately went up to Dark Oaks mansion.'

Professor Lazlo had been a psychiatrist at the hospital in Tuscaloosa where Brewster had interned many years before. They were old friends and he had arrived only an hour before in Dark Oaks, coming immediately in response to Brewster's frenzied telephone call. He had settled into a fireside chair and demanded that Brewster go carefully over the events of the last few days.

'Go on, Harry,' Lazlo lisped slightly, his Eastern European accent giving a dramatic quality to his voice. 'You went to see if you could assist in what you thought was a shooting? The death or, at least, the wounding of Miss Katherine Caldwell?'

Brewster raised his arms helplessly.

'Well, I was astonished when this count, Alucard, invited me in with a smile and called for Kay. There she was, sound in mind and limb. No sign of a gunshot wound or even a scratch. When I told them that Frank was convinced that he had killed her ... well, they both laughed. Alucard took me by the arm – by God, professor, he has a powerful grip – and guided me to the door. Frank was just a silly boy, whose mind was easily turned to fantasy, he said. Then I realised there were no longer any servants in the house. Alucard said that he and Kay had decided not to receive any more visitors at the house and to get rid of all the servants.'

Lazlo leant forward with interest.

'So? Did he say why?'

'Just that his work would force them to sleep during the daylight hours and thus make them unsociable people, even for servants to attend.'

'Did you ask him what this work was?'

'Experiments. That's all he said. Scientific experiments.'

'Then what happened?'

'Well, Frank was clearly out of his mind. Whatever had happened had unhinged him. I thought that Kay was unusually cold blooded about the whole business when I had mentioned his condition to her. She used to be so loving and caring towards Frank. Now she seems totally besotted by this Count Alucard. He seems to dominate her entirely. I gave Frank a sedative and found him a bed in our local hospital.'

'But something else happened?' pressed Lazlo.

'The next thing was that Frank absconded. I called Sheriff Japhet. The sheriff had a report that he had been seen up near the old Caldwell family cemetery. Japhet went there with a deputy and found Frank. I am afraid he was insane. When the sheriff arrested him, he noticed that the crypt contained a new coffin, the lid was askew, and there was Kay's body lying in it – dead. Yet I had seen her alive only an hour before! Frank kept mumbling that he had killed her and so the sheriff charged him with her homicide and incarcerated him in the local jailhouse until a psychiatrist could be sent for.'

Brewster paused and shuddered.

'What worries me, makes me really afraid, is the fact that I saw Kay alive and well after Frank had said he had shot her.'

'And that was when you telephoned me to come here, eh, my old friend? You need my advice, *hein*?'

Brewster nodded.

The old professor gave a deep sigh.

'You know, my friend, that I have practised not only as a psychiatrist but that I have a knowledge of the occult? As you know, I came to this country from Hungary, from the Carpathian Mountains. In my part of the world most people accept certain things which are dismissed as mere superstitions by this new country of ours.'

'What are you saying, professor? Are you saying that Frank is *not* insane? That all this talk about killing Kay, of her being alive again, of being chased by Alucard in the form of a bat, is true? Do you believe Frank, professor?'

The old professor inclined his grey head.

'I am afraid I do, my friend,' he said softly. 'The signs are all there. We are dealing with the great Undead himself.'

Brewster frowned, perplexed.

'I don't follow you.'

With a sigh, Lazlo pulled out a piece of paper and, taking a pen, wrote on it. Then handed it to Brewster.

'There, what is that name, please?'

'Why, Alucard. Count Alucard,' he read, still wondering.

'Read the name backwards,' instructed Lazlo.

Slowly Brewster re-spelt his name and then whistled.

'It spells Dracula. *Count Dracula*? But surely those stories of vampires are just myths and legends?'

'No myth, my good friend. Ask anyone who lives in Transylvania if Dracula is a myth. No, I am convinced that this Alucard is either a victim, or a direct descendant, of the original Dracula.'

'A man who was supposed to have lived six centuries, a vampire living on the blood of human beings . . . ?' gasped Brewster.

'Who in their turn became Undead ones, troubled, cursed souls, who are doomed to wander the earth for all eternity.'

'I can't believe it . . .'

Lazlo had suddenly risen to his feet, his face had paled, and he was pointing to the door.

Brewster turned round and stared. A white opaque mist was seeping under the door, swirling and taking shape until the tall, powerful figure of Count Alucard suddenly materialised before their eyes.

Brewster swallowed hard.

'I don't believe it . . .' he gasped.

The red, malignant eyes of Alucard turned on him. The thin red lips drew back from his sharp white teeth in a sneer.

'You do not believe the evidence of your own senses?'

'Well I believe that you are what you appear to be,' snapped Lazlo.

Alucard turned and regarded him with hatred.

'Of course. You are from the old country, Professor Lazlo. I have heard of you. An enemy to all my kin. You have knowledge of my kind. But he . . .' he gestured to Brewster, 'there are many such as he. They cannot believe for they are foolish. They believe only what they can touch, taste or measure. That is for the good. I have had to leave my dry, inhospitable homeland, with its old and tired people, to seek the rich blood of the New World. Here I shall thrive for another millennium! Here is a new beginning! Here I will continue my vengeance and spread it over the ages for time is now on my side.'

He took a step towards Brewster.

'Look at me! You will join me. Yes, and you, too, Lazlo. We will begin to spread . . .'

Lazlo's hand dived into the pocket and brought out an ornate silver crucifix.

Alucard took a step back and threw up a hand to cover his terrified face.

As Lazlo advanced, Alucard took another step back and began to evaporate into a mist which seemed to fall and twist and drain out under the door.

Brewster stood still, his face covered with beads of sweat, his hands trembling.

'The Undead thing is gone now,' Lazlo said confidently.

'Professor,' whispered Brewster in horrified disbelief, 'did I really see what I thought I saw?'

Inside the solitary jailhouse cell, Frank Stanley lay on his cot, head in hands, his crumpled body a sign of his despair. The noise came faintly at first, the soft flapping as of wings. Outside the tiny barred window of the cell, as if attracted by the dim interior light bulb which shone on the prisoners in the town jail both day and night, a giant black bat hovered, flapping its wings.

The bat seemed to insinuate itself through the bars and hover a moment or two in the cell before transforming itself into human shape.

The tall, attractive figure of Katherine Caldwell stood looking down at Frank Stanley's sleeping form. She stood smiling, her lips unnaturally red against her pallid features. The smile made her teeth seem sharp and unnaturally white.

'Frank,' she whispered, reaching forward and shaking his shoulder.

Frank came awake suddenly, his eyes staring up at her in shock.

'You're dead!' he blurted, the blood draining from his features.

Kay smiled, almost mischievously.

'Not dead but Undead, Frank. I will exist forever, for all eternity and now I wait for you to join me.'

Frank started upwards on his bed, unable to believe his eyes.

'Listen to me, Frank, for the dawn will come soon. We do not have long. There is much you want to know but there is no time as yet to explain. Believe only this, Frank. Before I met Alucard in Europe, I had discovered all about vampire lore. I realized that he's Count Dracula. To attain eternal life I was willing to become a vampire. But that does not mean to say that I do not love you, Frank.'

'I do not understand what you mean,' Frank said, her words beyond him.

'I mean, I married Alucard solely for the gift of immortality. Now I want you to destroy him, Frank. I will tell you where he rests. You must come there just before dawn and burn his coffin. It will destroy him if he cannot find a resting place. Then we can be together; together forever; forever, Frank!'

Frank Stanley gazed into her earnest, beautiful face wanting with his whole being to believe her. This was surely the Kay he knew, the Kay he loved.

'How can I get out of here?' he muttered.

'In this new form, I have powers. I can send forth an elemental mist that will mesmerise the sheriff and his deputy and open the locks of all the doors in this place. All you have to do is follow my directions . . . will you join me, Frank? Join me for all eternity?'

It was still dark when Frank Stanley reached the edge of the swamp area and began to push through the heavy undergrowth. His passage was made difficult by the fact that he was carrying a large can of gasoline which he had stolen from the sheriff's garage, along with a box of matches. Behind him he could hear the wailing of the siren of Sheriff Japhet's prowl-car as it took up the chase now that his escape had been discovered.

Frank scrambled and staggered along the slushy stream towards one of the old drainage tunnels which had once carried sewerage from the workers' houses on the Caldwell plantation into the main river. It was a dark cavern of a place, secured by rusting iron gates.

He paused. Should he trust the shadow which took the shape of the girl he once loved? Was Kay really still alive? He shivered and glanced anxiously at the sky. It would soon be dawn. The birds had begun to stir and twitter expectantly and there was a soft light on the eastern horizon.

Determinedly he pushed open the creaking iron gate and entered the drainage tunnel. It was ten feet in width and the same in height with a sludge-filled stream pushing down its centre. He had not gone far along it before he saw the oblong wooden box. Alucard's coffin. The lid was askew and he saw that it was empty. A little further on was another coffin. He moved cautiously to it. Katherine Caldwell lay in a shallow coma, her eyes half open, the voluptuous red lips drawn back from her sharp white teeth. Frank shuddered.

He turned, knowing what he had to do. He could hardly believe the grim determination with which he set his hands to action. He emptied half of the can of gasoline over Alucard's box, paused a moment to light a match. The box flared up brightly.

Almost at once he heard a terrible shriek. At the gate to the tunnel stood the tall, powerful figure of Alucard. He was staring aghast at the inferno of his sanctuary.

'Put it out! Put out that fire, I say!' he cried, racing forward as if he would throw himself into the flames. The intense heat beat him back.

Then, realising that his resting place was no more, he turned, teeth grinding in rage, blood flecks on his lips, and seized Frank by the throat with one powerful hand.

'You have destroyed me, you puny, pale mortal, but I will destroy your life as you have destroyed my eternity!'

Frank felt himself edging into unconsciousness as the strength of those superhuman fingers closed on his windpipe. Then, miraculously, the pressure was suddenly gone. He staggered back, retching, hand trying to massage his throat, gasping for air.

In front of him, Alucard had turned to face the entrance to the tunnel. Frank saw the look of utter horror and fear on the great Undead's features. The tunnel was aglow with the ominous light of dawn. Alucard raised a hand, as if to shield his eyes from its increasing light, and took an involuntary step backward – straight into the flowing, muddy waters.

He screamed terribly as he suddenly fell backwards into the running water. Frank stared aghast as Alucard raised an imploring hand, the hand which had been immersed in the water. It seemed to be dissolving as if in a vat of acid. The flesh withered away and for a moment Frank saw only the skeleton of the hand and then the brittle bones were also dissolving.

Before Frank's sickened gaze, the body of Alucard disintegrated and dissolved, its elemental components being washed, like so much sludge, in the rushing waters of the sewerage stream.

It took Frank several long moments before he could recover himself. By then the sun was well above the horizon and light was flooding through the entrance of the passage. He knew full well what he must do as the final act to this terrible, insane nightmare. Taking the can with the remaining gasoline, he went to Kay's coffin and stared down a moment. Did she know that he was there? He bent forward and allowed himself to kiss her pale, cold forehead. Did she stir? Then, pressing his lips together with determination, he splattered the remaining gasoline over her and her coffin.

He stepped back and struck a match, not hesitating but throwing it into the coffin.

He was unprepared for the terrible shriek of anguish that issued from the writhing form as the flames took hold. The coffin and its grisly contents erupted in a great conflagration which no mere fire could have created.

After it had died down, after there was nothing else but charred matter to be seen, he knew that he had done the right thing. He had saved Kay's soul, at least, from the evil of the vampire. Now he turned into the bright dawn light with some inner peace and strength. He could face what was to come because, whatever she had become, Kay had loved him to the end and he had saved her from eternal damnation. He would return and give himself up to the sheriff — but of what had taken place he vowed never to speak.

Cat People

VAL LEWTON

Amidst the dross of vampire films made in the decade between the end of the Second World War and the late Fifties when Britain's Hammer Films began a new era for the genre – for example The Vampire's Ghost *(1945),* Abbott and Costello Meet Frankenstein *(with Bela Lugosi, 1948) and* Mother Riley Meets The Vampire *(ditto Lugosi, 1952) – there was one small collection of minor classics produced in America. These were the cheaply-made but uniquely stylish films created for RKO by the producer-director Val Lewton (1904–51). Beginning with* Cat People *in 1942, and followed by* I Walked With A Zombie *(1942),* Isle of the Dead *(1945) and* Bedlam *(1946), Lewton created stark, black-and-white movies of mounting terror in which what was inferred and unseen rather than any actual horror on the screen was what gripped audiences. Carlos Clarens in his* History of the Horror Films *(1967) maintains that* Cat People *and* Isle of the Dead *were 'the spiritual children of Carl Dreyer's* Vampyre', *but equally they were also the intensely personal creations of a brilliant imagination.*

Born Vladimir Ivan Leventon in Russia, Lewton emigrated to America as a young man and for a time worked as a journalist, poet, author and occasional pornographer – one of his books, Yasmine, *was considered such strong meat that it was only sold under the counter in US bookstores! Thereafter he entered the world of films as an editorial assistant to David O. Selznick in the early Thirties. He wrote a number of screenplays before being hired by RKO in 1942 to head a special unit set up to make cheap horror pictures. 'This was so penny-pinching,' film historian Alan Stanbrook has written, 'that it would not stretch to proper sets, so Lewton had to cannibalise the left-overs from Orson Welles' The Magnificent Ambersons which had been shot in the same studio.' To make his budget go still further, Lewton even drew on one of his own stories for his first picture, Cat People, the tale of a Serbian woman living in America who believes she is descended from a race of cat women who can turn into panthers when aroused. The inspiration for this was 'The Bagheeta' which Lewton had written for the legendary pulp magazine, Weird Tales, in July 1930. It was, he said, based on an actual legend he had heard as a child in the Caucasus mountain ranges of Russia where there are supposed to be were-beasts who could change their shape into those of humans. But the fear of the supernatural that the characters in his story experienced were just the same as those people like himself who had emigrated and brought with them to the New World felt, and he had no difficulty in transposing the locale from Ghizikhan to New York. With ingenious use of clever camera angles, shadows produced by lighting effects, and the occasional off-screen sounds, Lewton let his audience create their own terrors – and by this method succeeded beyond anyone's expectations. In the next few hectic years he created a body of work that has proved hugely influential on many later horror film directors. Tragically, the overwork killed Lewton, and he died of a heart attack aged just forty-six. Here, though, as a memorial to the man and his little dynasty of film terrors, is the story that began the legend . . .*

*   *   *

The church bells of Ghizikhan pealed out slow, lazy music to mark the end of the morning prayer. Kolya turned his head idly to look at the village. From his vantage-point in the open porch of the armourer's shop where he was engaged in polishing the swords and other weapons which his uncle had chosen to place on display that day, Kolya could see the entire length of Ghizikhan's single street. It was early and the long shadows of the Caucasian peaks fell like dark, irregular bars across the valley. Only through the gap between Mount Elbruz and the volcanic peak of Silibal came sunlight, falling squarely upon the village. In this pleasant light the folk of Ghizikhan went about their early morning tasks. At the well the maidens jostled one another, giggling as they drew up water. Kolya's eyes, although he had just grown to manhood, avoided this group, but turned with interest upon the shepherds who were having a last, long draught at the inn door before going on to relieve the men who had guarded the flocks through the night hours.

It was a sight that Kolya could see any time, and, yawning, he turned back to the task in hand, the scouring of a new sword blade with water and white sand. Diligently he worked the scouring-cloth back and forth, his long, fair hair falling down over his forehead as he bent to the task. Of a sudden a cry went up at the other end of the village, and Kolya's head was upflung as if by magic.

Two men were running towards the inn. Between them they carried a shapeless bundle. Kolya could only catch the colours of the object – red and white. As they ran they cried out: 'A Bagheeta! A Bagheeta! We have seen her!'

Kolya identified the burden which they carried between them. It was a sheep, torn to death by a panther. Dropping the scouring-cloth, Kolya ran to where a knot of men had gathered about the two shepherds. He forced his way towards the centre of the crowd until he could hear the words of one of the men: '– black as wood from a fire, bigger than any natural leopard – a monster, I tell you! Varla and I came upon her at her meal. With my own eyes I saw her – you can measure for yourselves – from here to here,' the shepherd indicated a huge, bloody rent in the flank of the slain sheep, 'she took one mouthful. A real Bagheeta – I swear it!'

The men around him crowded closer to see the evidence. It was true; an enormous mouth had made those long gashes in the carcass.

The *hetman* of Ghizikhan, pulling at his virgin white beard, questioned the shepherd: 'Fool, what did you do? Did you let the beast escape so that it may enjoy such a feast as this from our table whenever he wills it?'

The shepherd protested: 'It was a real Bagheeta, I tell you, *Hetman!* What could we do? Varla shot at her, but you know that no bullet can harm a Bagheeta – not even a silver bullet. She just snarled at us and walked away.'

'Walked away?' the *hetman*'s tones were dubious.

'Yes, *Hetman*, I have said it so: walked away, just turned and walked away. She knew we couldn't hurt her. Both Varla and I are married men, you know!'

'Aye, *Hetman*, I believe them.' It was Davil who spoke, Davil the old minstrel, who in his youth had killed a Bagheeta. 'This Bagheeta must be the same leopard we hunted all these last three days. If it had been a real leopard its skin would have been drying on the walls of your house by now, *Hetman*, but only a pure youth who can resist her blandishments can kill a Bagheeta. You must select a pure youth to hunt down this were-beast – a real St Vladimir, pure of heart as a virgin.'

'Nonsense! These are old wives' tales, falser than your rhymes, Davil,' Rifkhas the huntsman, whose very garments smelled always of the forest, spoke out heatedly. 'What is this beast, you say – a black leopard? To the east, beyond Elbruz, they are as common as black crows are in our land! It was the hard winter and the heavy snows which have driven them here. One good shot from my old rifle and your Bagheeta will be deader than the sheep he's killed. Do not forget, Davil, that I too have killed one of these black kittens, and with a rifle and a lead ball – I saw no signs of magic or sorcery.

'I have grown sick of these old lies which send our young men frightened into the forest. Believe me, it is safer in the forest than before the coffee-pots in the *khan*. King God has made man lord above the beasts and they all fear him.'

But by now the women of Ghizikhan had swarmed to the scene of the excitement, and their loud outcries drowned out the old huntsman's logic. Shrill voices explained the myth to those too young to know the significance of a black leopard among the spotted ones.

It is a were-beast, they said, half leopard and half woman, the reincarnation of a virgin who has died from wrongs inflicted upon her by sinful men, and who comes again to the world so that she may prey upon the flocks of the sinful. Only a pure youth, one who has lain clean and alone, can hope to slay the mystic beast. He must ride out against the Bagheeta with only a sword at his side and a prayer to King God upon his lips. The Bagheeta, so the women said, will change at his coming into a beautiful woman and attempt to coerce him into an embrace. If she is successful, if the youth kisses her, his life is forfeited. Changing again into a black leopard, the Bagheeta will tear him limb from limb. But, if he remain steadfast in his purity, then surely will he slay the beast.

Kolya listened eagerly. It was not the first time he had heard the legend. When they had done talking he looked again at the dead sheep. The bloody, mangled flesh, bearing clear marks of the enormous fangs which had rent it so hideously, sent little shivers up his spine. He had often heard Davil sing his song of the slaying of the Bagheeta, and standing in the warm sunlight, Kolya grew cold thinking on the dark forest and the dark beast, only its golden eyes visible in the night. He could see vividly the heavy, crushing paws, the curving claws, the red and rending mouth.

Suddenly the *hetman*'s voice rang clearly above the chatter of the women: 'Who among the *Jighitti* – the good, brave horsemen of our village – is pure of heart and free of sin? Let him stand forward, sword in his right hand!'

A silence fell upon the villagers, and all eyes were turned, first to the face of one youth and then to the face of another. All upon whom the eyes of the villagers fell turned blood-red and averted their faces.

The *hetman* grew impatient. He began to call the young men by name: 'Rustumsal? What! And you but sixteen! Fie upon the women of Ghizikhan! Valodja? Shame! Badyr? Shamyl? Vanar?'

All shook their heads.

Then Kolya, his heart pounding with excitement, stepped forward. In his right hand he held his sword, silent declaration of his intention. Behind him he could hear his mother shrilling: '*Hetman*, he is too young! It is but yesterday that he rode in the *Jigitovka*. Only two days has he worked as a man among men.'

The *hetman* paid no attention to her.

Bending forward so that he might look into Kolya's eyes, he asked: 'How old are you?'

Kolya answered sturdily: 'Sixteen.'

'And you have never laid yourself beside a woman, nor lusted after her with your eyes?'

'No,' said Kolya.

The *hetman* doffed his karakul *chapka* and with it still clasped in his hand, pointed to Kolya. A shout went up. Kolya the orphan, nephew of the armourer, had been chosen to hunt down the Bagheeta.

An hour later the men of the village, accoutred as if for war or holiday, rode out from Ghizikhan in a long cavalcade. Kolya, dressed in his best *kaftan* of Burgundy-coloured silk, a sleek black *chapka* set jauntily on his head, and wreaths of flowers about his horse's neck, rode at their head. At his side hung the best sword from his uncle's shop. The Silver Maid, his uncle called it, and for no price would he sell it, neither to prince nor commoner, saying always: 'Only by the grace of King God was I able to forge such a sword. One cannot sell God's gifts for gold.'

Beside Kolya rode the *hetman*, and behind them the two old enemies, David the minstrel and Rifkhas the huntsman, wrangling as they rode.

'I have lived in the woods my whole life,' the huntsman was saying, 'and not one, but many of these Bagheetas have I seen killed with bullets. The Russians pay well for their black skins.'

Davil silenced his arguments with a burst of song:

'I ride beneath the silver stars,
　　All in my war array;
I ride beneath the silver stars
　　To break Bagheeta's sway.

'The stars are bright and bright am I
　　Clad in my war array.
The land about does gloomy lie,
　　And Bagheeta's sway.

'I ride with flowers in my hair
　　And grim sword at my side,
Among the youths I am most fair
　　And in war foremost ride.

'To me unknown a maiden's wiles:
　　For see, my heart is pure.
God looks upon my head and smiles:
　　For see, my heart is pure.'

'Blah!' said Rifkhas, spurring his horse a bit so as to catch up with Kolya and leave Davil to ride by himself, singing the song which he had composed many years ago in celebration of his own victory over a Bagheeta.

Kolya heard the song behind him go on and on as they rode forward to where the shepherds had seen the leopard.

'Unfeared by me the Deva's call,
　　The war's grim chance of death,
But here soft footsteps thud and fall,
　　And quickly comes my breath.'

The lad shuddered. He could well imagine the sinuous body of the beast, black as the night it walked through, creeping through the tree trunks in the forest. How dark the forest would be after the moon had gone down! Kolya's horse quivered. It was as if his master's agitation had been conveyed to her too, and that she also knew of the trial ahead of them. Davil's song went on:

'Of death alone I have no fear,
　　Nor yet of sword hurt deep,
But now a silent move I hear,
　　From darkness gold eyes peep.

'My brave horse trembles in his fear,
    And tighter grows my rein.
Somewhere from night two gold eyes peer
    And mark his frightened pain.'

A restive horse in the darkness of the midnight forest; a silent and unseen foe, waiting to leap from ambush, to strike one down with huge paws, to rend one with enormous teeth; Kolya could almost smell the foetid, hot breath which was to issue from the gaping jaws. Yet all this must be true; had not the minstrel killed just such a beast in his youth? Was not this the very song inspired by the feat? Kolya gazed nervously into the green depths of the forest, crowding in upon the trail. Somewhere in its fastnesses was the Bagheeta, crouched, waiting, confident in its supernatural powers.

Rifkhas' voice was speaking to his ear: 'I'm sorry that they're not letting you carry a gun, lad. You could wait for the Bagheeta by the water hole. He must drink after his kill. Didst ever note how the cats go to the water but when they have eaten a rat in the granary? These leopards, black or spotted, are but big cats; they too must drink after they eat. You could shoot the beast easily if the light were good. But these fools, full of old wives' tales, they make it difficult for you. When the good King God has given us gunpowder, what sense is there to send you into the forest with but a sword in your hand? Likewise, when God gives mankind a full moon to hunt by, why in the name of the seven Peris must they make you wait until the moon has set before you go a-hunting? Why? Because old women like Davil are frightened of the dark, and they would have you be frightened also. Have no fear! There is no beast nor were-beast that will not run from a man. Have no fear, Kolya. I, who have been a huntsman for thirty years, tell you that.'

From behind them came the voice of the other old man. He had changed his tune. It was no longer slow, measured and fearsome, the words filled with dread. It came forth exultantly, as if he had just conquered fear. He sang:

'But now I tremble once again,
    For here a fair maid comes.
I tremble with no thought of pain
    For here a fair maid comes.

'Her lips are scarlet pomegranates,
    Her cheeks like Kavkas' snows,
Her eyes are tense as one who waits
    For sounds of ringing blows.

'Her speech is all of lovely things
    That are in other climes,
Of butterflies with silver wings
    And bells with silken chimes.

'She lifteth up her laughing mouth
    And I bend down my own.'

Davil's voice fell. Deep and fearsome it pounded against Kolya's ears:

'What is this chill wind from the south?
    This noise of bone on bone?'

Kolya's heart skipped a beat. What if he were to have no warning? What if he were to be so entranced by the Bagheeta's charms that he were to kiss her?

Davil's chant answered the question for him:

'I fear, I fear and gaze at her
    Who looks with such a mien;
I fear, I fear and strain from her
    Whose yellow eyes are keen.

'Out sword! Out sword! Bagheeta's eyes
    Look now into your own.
Out sword! Out sword! He only dies
    Who must the kiss atone.

'With tooth and claw Bagheeta flies
    Straight at my armoured throat,
And now so close his yellow eyes
    That I have falsely smote —'

Kolya's imagination conjured up the gleaming eyes, the hot breath of the beast, its claws sinking into his shoulder. He could feel the sense of helplessness as he was torn from the saddle — the weight of the giant cat upon his body.

Rifkhas' cranky voice, speaking in the calming tones of prose, allayed his fears.

'I'd like to have your chance at this beastie, Kolya,' Rifkhas was saying. 'One black pelt like that would supply me with wine and caresses for an entire year — aye, even an old fellow like myself could buy the soft arms of women with the price of such a pelt. It's a rare chance you have. If only these fools would let you go on foot. You

can't hunt leopards on horseback. Why, the sound of your horse's
hoofs will echo for miles about. Get off your horse and creep to the
water hole, being careful to see that he doesn't get the wind of you;
that's the only way you'll get close enough to Master Bagheeta to kill
him with a sword.

'Mind what I tell you, Kolya, and forget all these old women who'd
tell you that a leopard can change into a woman just because it
happens to be black instead of spotted. Mind what I tell you, Kolya,
and with the money you get for the pelt you can set up an armourer's
shop of your own.'

Behind him, Kolya could hear Davil still singing, describing his own
encounter with the dread and mystic beast long, long ago. The fierce
half-joy of the conflict and the anguish of those long-healed wounds
were in the voice of the old minstrel as he sang:

> 'Deep, deep I strike, again, again;
>   Deep do his talons rend.
> I am oblivious of my pain
>   And fast my blows descend.
>
> 'With horrid shriek he falls aback,
>   And now my sword is free.
> Again he leapeth to attack,
>   But now my sword is free.
>
> 'Half-way in air the leaping beast,
>   The cleaving sword, have met;
> Now may the herdsmen joyful feast,
>   For sword and beast have met!'

'*Stoi!*' The *hetman*'s command cut short both Davil's song and the
movement of the cavalcade. The men grouped themselves about the
leader as he explained to them how they could best aid Kolya in his
adventure. They had arrived at the copse where the Bagheeta had been
seen, he told them, and they would now surround the place in such a
way as to turn back the Bagheeta if he, sensing Kolya's innocence,
were to attempt an escape. None of the men, he warned them, must
dare to engage the creature. This was safe only for Kolya, who was
pure of heart.

With the point of his spear the *hetman* drew a rough map in the sand
showing the copse and the hollow between two steep cliffs in which it
was situated. To each man he designated a certain post at which to
watch. He told them that if the Bagheeta approached their positions

they must raise up their sword with the cross-like hilts uppermost and loudly sing the hymn of Saint Ivan. Thus, and thus only, could they turn the were-beast back.

At a word from their leader the men galloped off, shouting, to their positions. Only Davil and Rifkhas remained with Kolya and the *hetman* to wait for the coming of night and the dark of the moon.

It was still late afternoon and, although a pale slice of luminous white moon already rode high in the heavens – sure indication that it would set early – Kolya and the men with him still had a long while to wait before he could ride forth in search of the Bagheeta. Davil was all for passing the time in prayer and the singing of songs, but Rifkhas brought forth an earthen jug of wine and a pack of greasy playing-cards. Soon the three grown men were hard at it, playing one game of cards after another.

Kolya was left to his own devices. He fussed with his horse, watering it at the brook and removing the bridle so that it could graze at will. This took only a short time, and then Kolya was again left with nothing to occupy him but his own fears of the night's trial.

He turned his attention to the copse before him. It was dark with the shadows of the larch and fir trees growing on either side of the brook. This stream had, in the course of the centuries, cut itself a hard bed through the solid rock. Its either bank was precipitous. No animal, Kolya thought to himself, could drink from the stream unless somewhere there was a cleft in the rocky banks. If he were to follow Rifkhas' advice he would have to find such a spot where the leopard could come to drink and there await the Bagheeta's coming.

'But, there will be little need to find the Bagheeta,' he reasoned. 'She will come creeping upon me and, when she divines that I am pure of heart and have no knowledge of women, then she will turn herself into a maiden, and so lure me to my death.'

On whispering feet, darkness came stealing into the little glen in which they had halted. The beech leaves, quivering in the evening wind, lisped a plaintive song of nervous fear to Kolya's heart. The same breeze, straying through the pine boughs, struck deep soughing chords. Then, as the sun finally set, plunging the land into intense darkness, the evening noises quieted. Robbed of light by which to continue their card game, the three older men sat quietly. Even the horses ceased their trampling and champing in the place where they had been tethered. A cloud was over the slim, silver moon, shaped ominously, Kolya imagined, like a Persian dagger.

Some current of the upper air swept the cloud from before the moon's face. The *hetman*, looking up, remarked that the moon would set in another hour.

Kolya walked to where he had tied his horse. He saddled the animal carefully, glad to crowd fear out of his mind with activity. Putting his knee sharply against his mount's belly, Kolya jerked the girth tight. Then he bridled the horse, feeling with anxious fingers in the darkness to see that the check strap was properly set. When he had done all this he led the beast to where the *hetman*, Davil and Rifkhas sat about a tiny fire that they had kindled, more for light than for warmth.

The *hetman* lectured him: 'Pray earnestly, Kolya. Ask forgiveness for your sins. This is a creature of deep sin that you go to fight. Only through sin may it vanquish you. It will tempt you in many ways, but you must resist evil. The sign of the cross and the prayers of our people are most potent against magic. Keep your lips clean from its lips, and your heart clean from the evil it will try to teach you. Only in this way may you hope for victory.'

Davil spoke to him: 'Have no fear, Kolya. If your heart is pure, and you resist the blandishments of the Bagheeta – beautiful as she may become – then surely King God will send strength to your sword. I can see you now, riding back to us in the morning with the slain were-beast over your saddle bow –'

Rifkhas cut him short: 'I can see you too, Kolya! But I can see what a fool you will look if you follow the advice of this impotent old rhymester. There is but one way to hunt – whether you hunt leopards or were-leopards, it makes no difference – and that way is to go stealthily – and not on horseback with a clanking sword at your side. Do what I have told you to do and you will not fail to find the Bagheeta: go to the water hole and wait – else you will not see hair nor hide of the creature all the long night through.'

The crescent moon edged down below the horizon.

'It is time, Kolya,' said the *hetman*. 'May King God bless you, pure of heart.'

Kolya mounted, and wheeling his horse, rode toward the forest at a foot pace.

'Mind what I have told you,' Rifkhas shouted after him.

As the first slender saplings of the wood brushed against him, Kolya could hear Davil singing:

'I ride beneath the silver stars,
  All in my war array.

I ride beneath the silver stars
To break Bagheeta's sway.'

His sword swung reassuringly at Kolya's side. From behind him the
second verse of Davil's song came floating to his ears.

'The land about does gloomy lie,
And black Bagheeta's way.'

The distance muffled the other words of Davil's ballad. But Kolya
could remember them. They sang through his mind as the wood grew
denser and denser about him. He had often heard them before. Some
verses brought him courage. He recalled:

'I ride with flowers in my hair,
And grim sword at my side,
Among the youths I am most fair,
And in war foremost ride.

'To me unknown a maiden's wiles:
For see; my heart is pure.
God looks upon my head and smiles:
For see; my heart is pure.'

Other verses brought him dread:

'King God, look on my woeful plight:
Pity and give me aid.
Hang out the moon to give me light
And guide my palsied blade.'

The trees rustled in the light night currents. Each falling leaf, each
snapping twig, brought sharp ice to the skin of Kolya's back. Clumps
of deeper darkness – some fallen tree or jagged stump – denser than the
overflowing night, caused Kolya to tighten his reins and grip fast the
hilt of his sword. Out of earshot of the *hetman* and the others, Kolya
drew his sword slowly from its sheath. The weight of the weapon, its
fine balance, brought no comfort to his disturbed mind. The empty
sheath banged now and again against his leg, making him wince at
each contact. It would be just so softly, and with just such lack of
warning, that the Bagheeta would spring upon him from the dark
thickets at either side of the path.

Slowly, drawing rein again and again so that he might strain his ears
for some sound of his mystic foe, Kolya traversed the wood. Now so

frightened was he by the menacing stillness of the forest that he would have preferred to return to the men; but fear of the taunts which he knew to be the lot of a coward forced him on.

Again he rode through the wood. Again he peered right and left for some sign of the beast, fearful always of seeing golden eyes glow at him from the pitch blackness of the night. Every rustle of the wind, every mouse that scampered on its way, flooded his heart with fear, and filled his eyes with the lithe, black bulk of the Bagheeta, stalking toward him on noiseless paws. With all his heart he wished that the beast would materialize, stand before him, allow him opportunities to slash and thrust and ward. Anything, even deep wounds, would be better than this dreadful uncertainty, this darkness haunted by the dark form of the were-beast.

Near to the place where he had entered the forest, Kolya turned his horse about and rode through again. This time a greater fear had crept into his heart. What if the were-cat were to take advantage of its magical powers? It had done so with Davil. He remembered how he had gone, while still a student at the riding-school, to the village well to wash the blood from his face after a spill, and of how Mailka, the daughter of Davil, had placed her arm about his shoulder, so that with the corner of her apron she might wipe the blood from his forehead. He remembered now with a sense of horrible fear how he had longed to crush her to him, how some strange well-spring in his blood had forced him, against his own will, closer to her. It was only the passing of Brotam, the shepherd, which had prevented him from folding Mailka to his heart. And Mailka was not beautiful, nor willing for embraces. How then would he resist the Bagheeta, beautiful and inviting? He was sick with fear. His stomach was like a pit of empty blackness, as black as the night, as black as the Bagheeta.

It was with relief that he reached the opposite end of the woods and remembered that so far he had not come upon the Bagheeta. Somehow this thought gave food and drink to his fainting heart. If the Bagheeta were so strong, if these tales of supernatural power were true, why then did it not appear and make away with him? It must be, he thought to himself, an ordinary, spotted leopard which had frightened the shepherds in the morning. With this in mind, Kolya began to make plans to find and kill the beast.

'Thrice have I ridden through the wood on this side of the stream,' he deliberated; 'then it is reasonable that the Bagheeta, if it is such a creature, is on the other side of the stream. I will go there.'

Where the stream narrowed a bit, Kolya jumped his horse across, landing with a thud on the firm bank of the opposite side.

Twice he rode through the woods on this side of the stream, making, at intervals, little sorties through the forest as far as the cliffs which bound the copse on either side. He could find no trace of the Bagheeta.

Intent upon the hunt now Kolya had lost all fear. 'It must be,' he reasoned, 'just as Rifkhas told me, that I must hunt the beast on foot, waiting for him at the water hole.'

With this plan in mind, Kolya rode directly along the bank of the creek. The high walls of the creek bed, Kolya clearly saw, would prevent even a creature as agile as a leopard from going to the water's edge for a drink. Then, of a sudden, his horse shied back. Before him, Kolya could see where a slide on each side of the creek had made a sloping pathway to the water. Dismounting, he inspected the place. Hoof marks and paw prints were indubitable proof that the place was in use by all the animals of the vicinity. Kolya led his horse a little way from the bank and tethered it stoutly to an oak sapling.

He divested himself of his *kaftan* and sword belt, pulled his dagger from its sheath and stuck it through the waistband of his breeches. Then, sword in hand, he returned quietly to the water hole. Carefully he stole down half-way to the water and then, flattening his back against the wall of the cut, prepared to wait.

Even as he settled himself in a comfortable position, the falling of a pebble attracted his attention to the other bank of the stream. He could distinguish nothing. The water was as dark as the night. But from the water came a lapping sound. Something was drinking there at the edge of the creek. Kolya strained his eyes. He could see nothing. But as he continued to stare into the darkness he caught a gleam of eyes, yellow, round and burning as the burnished brass of the altar rail. Again Kolya heard the sound of water being lapped up by the rough tongue of the animal. The round, golden eyes were hidden as the creature drank.

Lifting his left hand to his mouth, Kolya ran his tongue across the palm and across the back of his fingers. Lifting it cautiously above his head he held it, palm forward, toward the Bagheeta. The palm of his hand felt colder than the back; the wind was blowing toward him. There was no danger of the Bagheeta taking his scent. But there was the danger that the Bagheeta might go back by the way he had come, without passing Kolya's ambush.

Slowly, ever so slowly, Kolya bent and picked up a large stone. With all his strength he threw it into the bushes on the other bank of the stream, then braced himself to cleave down his sword with all his might. The stone landed on the farther bank with a crash. Gold eyes turned up and, with the shriek, the Bagheeta flung herself across the stream and began to climb past Kolya.

With bated breath he waited until the powerful haunches had lifted the creature until its eyes were on a level with his own. For one moment the beast stared straight into his eyes; then Kolya's sword plunged down slashing the black leopard's shoulder. The Bagheeta shrieked piercingly and fell back a few feet. Again Kolya struck at it, but the beast, snarling, rolled free. Kolya gathered himself and lunged forward with the point as if toward a human opponent. A great feeling of satisfaction flooded his heart as he felt the blade sink deep into the thick neck of the Bagheeta. There was a choking sound, the quick pant and insuck of painful breathing, and then silence. The Bagheeta was dead.

'It was so easy. It was so easy!' Kolya repeated the phrase again and again in wonderment.

Dawn was breaking. Thin, grey light began to filter into the wood. Mists and vapours like grey wraiths whirled without rhyme or reason between the tree trunks. Stiff-legged, body and tail relaxed, with blood flowing over the sandstone on which it lay, Kolya could see the Bagheeta. The heavy jaws gaped wide open, and the boy could see clearly the long, thick fangs of the beast. Its paws were thrust out stiffly, the claws, cruel as Tartar simitars, still unsheathed.

Kolya laughed a bit hysterically. It had been so easy, it had been so easy to kill this fearsome thing of dreadful aspect and terrible strength. Two cuts and a single thrust of his sharp sword had killed the Bagheeta. Tough sinews, tearing fangs and rending jaws had been subdued by the steel of his sword. There had been no magic trial of virtue and morals. Davil was a liar, and Rifkhas a true man.

Kolya sat down upon a stone to rest himself, his eyes still drawn to the inert body of the leopard.

'How they will laugh at Davil when I tell them what a liar he is!' Kolya thought to himself. 'How fat and respected he has grown on that one lie these many years! That song of his — with its beautiful maiden and terrible struggle — why, every child in Ghizikhan knows it by heart, and even the *hetman* believes it. What a lie!'

But then doubts began to steal into Kolya's mind. He thought deeply: 'If this is untrue, if a Bagheeta is but a black leopard, no more dangerous than a spotted one, why then even the story about Lake

Erivan having been created by the tears of God as he wept for the crucifixion of his only Son might be untrue. And the story of Saint Ilya the Archer and his arrows of fire, giving courage to the pure of heart in perilous places, might also be a lie. Even God might be a lie!'

But the grey dawn was ghostly. The trees moved mysteriously in the light winds and the half-light of the morning, and the mountain towered dimly towards the sky. Who knew what dread creatures stalked abroad in the mist? The trees might fall in upon him, the mountains topple to crush him! Kolya put the unreality of God quickly from his mind. A ray of light touched the peak of Silibal and it shone, rose-coloured and white, against the blue of the morning.

Birds began to twitter in the bushes. A deer came to the water hole to drink, but, upthrusting her muzzle at the scent of the slain leopard, trotted off otherwheres.

'How they will laugh when I tell them what a liar Davil has been these many years!'

Stretching himself, Kolya rose, smiling, and prepared to return to where he knew the *hetman* and the *jigits* of the village awaited him.

He donned his *kaftan* and sword belt, replaced his dagger in its sheath, and started to cleanse his bloody sword with a wisp of grass. As he started on this task, a thought struck him. No, he must let the sword remain bloody – proof of the conflict. He laid it down in the grass carefully. Then, wondering at the weight and size of the animal, Kolya dragged the Bagheeta to where he had tethered his horse. The mare plunged and curvetted at the sight of the dead animal and at the smell of its coagulating blood. When he had secured the body to the high cantle with thongs, Kolya picked up his bloody sword, untethered the horse and mounted into the saddle deliberately.

As the horse nervously threaded its way under the double burden of victor and vanquished, Kolya rode slowly out of the wood with the reins held tight in his left hand. His mind was busy. A thought had come to him. For years Rifkhas had said that a Bagheeta was but a black leopard among the spotted ones. The people of the village had only laughed at him. Davil, the liar, they loved and respected. Rifkhas, they thought a strange man, a little mad from having lived so long alone in the woods.

'Even if they believed me,' Kolya was thinking, 'they would laugh at Davil only for a day, and then what? Then, no one would fear the Bagheeta any more. And so, no longer,' Kolya reasoned, 'would I be honoured as a man who had slain a Bagheeta.'

He said to himself: 'Surely there must be some reason for this lie.

Others have invented it so that they might appear brave and good in the eyes of the village.'

And Mailka, Mailka would certainly never give herself to one who had betrayed her father's secret. How warm and softly firm her arm had felt against his shoulder that day she had washed his wounds by the well.

'I will do as Davil has done.' Kolya spoke decisively. 'I shall tell them that I first saw the Bagheeta as a beautiful maiden, bathing at the water hole, her body surrounded by a white light. That she called me by name and spoke to me courteously – and that, enchanted by her beauty, I had forgotten all warning and bent to kiss her. Then, I shall say that an arrow of fire sprang through the sky. Knowing it for the sign of Ilya the Archer, I will say that I took warning from this and, springing away from the maiden, drew my sword. So fast that I could not even see the change, the Bagheeta transformed herself again into a leopard and sprang at me. I shall tell them that we fought for an hour and then, just as I was ready to drop my sword from weariness, a great strength surged through me and I killed the beast. Even as Davil has done, so will I do.'

At a sharp trot Kolya rode through the outskirts of the wood. Before him, cooking their breakfasts around little fires, were the men of Ghizikhan. With a great shout of triumph, Kolya struck heels to his horse and charged toward them. The men raised their voices in a hail of welcome which sounded thin and shrill among the mountains.

Kolya began to shout the words of Davil's song as he rode toward them:

'Half-way in air the leaping beast,
  The cleaving sword, have met.
Now may the herdsmen joyful feast,
  For sword and beast have met.

'I rode beneath the silver stars
  And broke Bagheeta's sway –'

Kolya lifted his bloody sword high in the air, the cross of the hilt extended toward heaven, as if giving the victory to God. The men doffed their sheepskin caps and knelt in prayer at this proof of King God's all-powerful goodness.

'Blah!' said Rifkhas the huntsmen, as he knelt with the rest.

Dracula – Prince of Darkness

JIMMY SANGSTER

The year 1958 was to provide another landmark in the history of the vampire film when Hammer Films in England launched what ultimately became as successful a series as the original Universal movies – not to mention making a household name of the star, Christopher Lee. A year earlier, Hammer had released a very popular new version of Frankenstein, *and understandably commissioned the same scriptwriter, the versatile Jimmy Sangster (1927–), to adapt Stoker's novel. Sangster's storyline remained remarkably faithful to the original, but the picture itself was to have the advantage over its predecessors of being filmed in technicolour. The tall, mesmerising Lee (who had appeared in the earlier* Frankenstein *swathed under yards of bandages) made his Dracula an unforgettable figure, complete with grey-streaked hair, wild red eyes and glistening fangs. Clothed all in black, he brought tremendous vitality and sense of power to the role, in complete contrast to Lugosi's more measured performance. The film, and its sequels, were bathed in blood and gore, not to mention featuring a constant stream of well-endowed young actresses into whose throats Dracula was forever sinking his fangs. In the Hammer series, Christopher Lee created a quite new interpretation of the anti-hero and his was soon to become the performance against which all others would be judged – while in Peter Cushing (who had also starred in* Frankenstein) *as Van Helsing, director Terence Fisher found a perfect foil for Lee. Fisher also produced one of the most dramatic climaxes seen in any vampire film when Van Helsing ripped open some curtains to let in the dawn sunlight and Dracula literally crumbled to dust in front of the audience's eyes: a special*

284 THE VAMPIRE OMNIBUS

effects triumph that had been beyond the capabilities of earlier film makers. (Parts of this grisly sequence were even cut from the film by the British censor and have only been seen in the Far East.) Dracula was a big success at the box office and was soon followed by a flood of sequels: Brides of Dracula *(1960),* Dracula – Prince of Darkness *(1966),* Dracula Has Risen From The Grave *(1968) & etc. However, while Peter Cushing continued happily reprising his role, Lee grew increasingly dissatisfied with the quality of the scripts and how far the plots had departed from the original concept. Finally, in 1973, after making* The Satanic Rites of Dracula, *Christopher refused to appear in any more, and though he has since starred in a great many other pictures still remains forever associated with his role as the vampire Count.*

While the first Dracula *was undoubtedly the most faithful of all the Hammer series,* Dracula – Prince of Darkness *was perhaps the most inventive. For this time Jimmy Sangster had the ingenious idea of starting the film where the first had ended – Lee turning to dust – and reintroduced him in what Donald Glut has described as 'one of the most majestic bloodbaths the screen has ever seen' with a bleeding corpse being suspended over Dracula's ashes to revitalise him. The movie was one more triumph for Sangster who had begun his working life at Hammer as a clapper boy and risen dramatically to become the company's leading scriptwriter and latterly a director. Now living and working in Hollywood, Jimmy has rightly been described as one of the most influential figures in the legend of Hammer Films. In his script for* Dracula – Prince of Darkness, *a group of English travellers, Charles Kent (Francis Matthews), his wife, Diana (Suzan Farmer) and sister-in-law, Helen (Barbara Shelley) unwisely visit the Count's Castle in the Carpathian Mountains despite the warnings of Father Shandor (Andrew Keir) and there the voluptuous Helen becomes Dracula's first victim. The vampire next turns his attentions to Diana who is only rescued just in time by her husband and taken to the apparent safety of Father Shandor's monastery. The following episode continues their experiences and includes the scene of a vampire being staked which was the first time such a thing had ever been shown on the screen, and a finale that introduced another method of killing a member of the undead – but again one that had never been previously used in the movies . . .*

*   *   *

That night, as she slept, Diana felt herself once again back in Castle Dracula, penned in a corner as a faceless shape raised its wings and came at her. Faceless because she did not let herself remember those cruel features. She raised her arms against his talons and tried to beat him off.

But there was only the coarse edge of the blanket on her bed, rasping against her cheek and tangling in her arms as she flailed out.

Diana opened her eyes and stared at the ceiling for a minute. She fought to calm herself. Her heart was beating wildly. It was ridiculous: she was safe in the monastery, well guarded, out of the clutches of that obscene creature.

There was a faint tapping sound. She could not tell whether it was real or part of her drowsy imaginings. It came again. Branches tapping the wall . . . a gust of rain pattering on the low roof of the monastery . . .

There were three louder taps, quite distinct this time and quite real. Diana sat bolt upright in bed and stared at the window.

It was slightly misted over inside, and a clinging fog brushed it outside. But the face at the window was clear enough – the tormented, mouthing, imploring face of Helen.

Diana shivered. She sat where she was, not daring to move. She wanted to cry out but could not.

Helen's lips moved. 'Please,' she was saying inaudibly; 'please . . .'

Diana got out of bed. When her feet touched the cold stone floor she felt the impulse to turn and go in search of Charles. But Helen raised her hands and clawed at the window, and her mouthings grew frantic. Diana was drawn irresistibly towards the misted panes.

Helen's face was bleached and agonized. Close to the window, it was possible to hear her.

'Please . . . let me in, Diana. It's cold out here. So cold.'

Diana hesitated. She glanced back at the door. If only Charles would come in. If only Father Shandor were close at hand, ready to make the decisions.

'Diana, I beg you . . .' Helen was pressed to the glass in utter, desperate self-abasement. 'It's all right now. Everything is all right. I've escaped from him. Please . . . it's freezing out here.'

Diana unlatched the window. As the catch grated free, she started to pull the window open.

The night air was harsh, and the fog seethed in like a wild, leaping thing. And Helen snarled. It was a bestial snarl of triumph. Through the tendrils of fog her hand struck down and grasped Diana's wrist.

The grip was cruel. Diana tried to throw herself back, away from the window and into the safety of her cell. But Helen pulled, and now her hand struck down and she sank her teeth in Diana's wrist.

Diana screamed. Helen let go and disappeared. But the frame of the window was filled suddenly and hideously with the gloating face of Dracula, his arms raising his cloak as though to catch Diana up in his suffocating embrace.

Behind her there was a crash as the door was flung open. Dracula retreated swiftly into the night like a bird of prey scared off by a sudden noise.

Diana fell. She felt herself going backwards, and then Charles was holding her and helping her towards the bed.

'What happened?'

It was Father Shandor's voice. She was vaguely aware of him striding towards the window. He closed it and fastened it securely, then swung round and pounced on her. Charles snapped a protest, but Shandor took her by the shoulders and shook her furiously.

'Tell me – what happened?'

Diana reached out for Charles. He took a step towards her and then froze, staring at her wrist as she held it out. Shandor's head turned and he, too, looked. Then he growled: 'Hold her.'

She was free. He let go, and Charles came to put his arm round her. Shandor took up the oil lamp that was burning on the small corner table.

'Hold out her hand.'

Charles seized Diana's arm and twisted it towards Shandor so that two tiny puncture marks and the faint globules of blood oozing from them were exposed. Shandor's left hand gripped her fingers so that they could not move. With his right hand he brought the lamp forward and pressed the scorching glass against the marks.

Agony raced up Diana's arm and consumed her. She screamed and tried to fight away. Charles held fast, and there was no shaking Father Shandor off.

The burning pain had to stop . . . had to be made to stop . . . she couldn't endure any more, couldn't let herself be engulfed . . . had to stop, stop, stop . . .

'For pity's sake,' Charles was crying, 'enough!'

Shandor pulled the lamp away from her wrist. The pain abated; but the cool air on the seared flesh redoubled it, and Diana whimpered once and collapsed. She was conscious of being picked up and laid on the bed. In the far distance, Shandor was shouting: 'Brother Mark . . .

salve and bandages . . .' And Charles was close to her, murmuring to her. She wanted to reach up and put her arms round him but was too exhausted and too frightened that the slightest movement might bring on a new refinement of torture.

'We were just in time,' said Shandor.

There was a shuffle of feet. She heard the men muttering together, and then something very cold was smeared on her wrist. It burned with an icy fire, intolerable for a few seconds and then numbing the pain. The ice fought with the flame. She tried to think of something else, to be conscious only of the rest of her body; but the throbbing in her arm pounded everything else into insensibility.

'Are there strangers in the monastery?' Shandor was asking.

'None, Father.' It was Brother Mark, allowing himself to sound gently offended. 'Your orders were that we should admit no one. But there is the wagoner, you will recall, spending the night outside the main gates. We sent food out to him.'

'A wagoner. Yes. Perhaps we would have been better advised . . .' Shandor broke off and said abruptly: 'Mr Kent, come with me. No, do not worry: your wife will be all right. Brother Mark will bandage her wrist and stay with her.'

Again Diana wanted to reach out and hold Charles in her arms. She wanted him to stay with her. But they were going. They went out of the room and their footsteps hurried away along the resonant corridor.

She opened her eyes and met Brother Mark's solicitous gaze. When she made a feeble indication that she wanted to sit up, he put his arm behind her and lifted her. It made it easier for him to complete the bandaging. When he had finished, she sat on the edge of the bed. She did not want to succumb again. She did not want to rest, to sleep, to lay herself open to nightmares.

Brother Mark understood without their needing to exchange a word. He sat on the hard chair against the wall, folded his hands in his lap, and sank into a reverie. She knew that if she wished to talk he would respond at once. But their shared silence was what she needed most at this moment. She was grateful to him for his gentle intuition.

A rap at the door broke the spell. Brother Mark was on his feet at once. He went to the door and opened it.

A man with a striking but ravaged face stood in the opening. He half crouched as though waiting for a blow – or as though, thought Diana obscurely, waiting to spring.

'Ludwig.' Brother Mark sounded surprised. 'What are you doing out of your room?'

'My room is being used for highly important matters.' The man called Ludwig looked round the door at Diana with an odd mixture of deference and slyness. 'Father Shandor sends his compliments, madam. Would you do him the honour of joining him in his study?'

Brother Mark began to protest. 'But I have instructions . . .'

Ludwig raised a lordly hand. Diana knew nothing of his position in the monastery, but she could see that his manner baffled Brother Mark. There was no denying the authority in it, however. She reached instinctively for a robe from behind the door and drew it over her shoulders.

'Everything is under complete control, Brother,' Ludwig said loftily to Mark. 'There is no cause for concern.'

Before there could be any further argument, he was ushering Diana out into the chilly corridor. He walked quickly as though eager that they should both keep an urgent appointment. She wondered what new developments there had been, and what Shandor and her husband had discovered.

Ludwig darted ahead of her to open a door. He tapped sharply on it and opened it without waiting for a reply. Then he stood aside and waved Diana in.

She advanced into a room which must undoubtedly be Father Shandor's study. The bookshelves mellowed the harshness of the floor and walls, and the finely polished old desk was, in these surroundings, a luxury in itself.

But there was no sign of Father Shandor.

Behind her she heard the faint click of the lock. She swung round.

Ludwig had gone. He had not followed her into the room. But standing with his back to the door, staring at her with leisurely appreciation, was Count Dracula.

Terror bubbled up in her throat. Before she could unleash it in a cry for help, Dracula raised his right arm and pointed one savage claw at her. His eyes blazed as though the fires of hell had been rekindled behind them.

Diana could make no sound. She stared into those demoniacal eyes and felt that she would soon fall down, down into those pits of flame. His hypnotic gaze drew her on. Without moving an inch she was somehow being wrapped in his embrace. They stood apart yet she was getting closer and closer to him.

Dracula took a step forward. She sweated with fear yet yearned for him.

His hand gestured at her throat.

Half seeing the movement of command, she was still a captive of his eyes. Again he had to wave his hand before her eyes; and then she understood. Her hand went of its own accord to the crucifix at her throat, and slowly she undid the clasp at the back of her neck and threw it aside.

Dracula smiled. Without releasing Diana from the spell of his gaze, he tore open the front of his white shirt, with its fastidiously bunched lace at the throat. The sharply pointed nail of his little finger sketched a line down his bare chest; then it drove in, pressed home . . . and there was a puncture from which the blood began to flow.

With his free hand he reached out for Diana. She did not resist. He caught her arm and drew her close, guiding her head towards the slow, steady flow of blood.

She saw the darkness of it against his chest, and felt an anguished greed for the taste of it. But now the spell had been broken. His eyes no longer dominated hers. Freed from that burning trance, she struggled against the remorseless clutch of his hand. Dracula growled like a beast which would not give up its prey. He let go of her arm quickly and seized her by the hair, pressing her head against his chest.

Diana struck out again and again. She was able to draw her head back long enough to scream. At last it came – a reverberating scream that was answered by another snarl from Dracula.

'Diana . . . !'

It was Charles. But far away down a corridor: too far away.

Diana fought to free herself. If she could only run to the door . . . if she could hold him off for only a few seconds . . .

There was a sudden crash of glass. Dracula did not slacken his grip, but twisted Diana and himself round to face the window.

The face of Ludwig grimaced at them. He beckoned, and then jabbed forward again with his elbow to send more glass showering to the floor.

Dracula's fist came round brutally against Diana's head. She reeled, and felt him gathering her up in his arms. The room spun past them, Dracula leapt at the window, and the remains of the glass splintered and sprayed around them.

The nightmare had claimed her again. Charles had left her, gone away from her, and now he would never find her. Charles . . . never again.

They were racing into the night, into the waiting hell of the undead.

*

Father Shandor had taken Charles with him from Diana's room straight to the main gate. He had seemed to guess exactly what he was going to find. After a cautious study of the wagon under the trees, to make sure that there was nobody lurking in its shadow, he went to it and clambered up, dragging Charles bodily up after him with one heave of his muscular arm.

There were two long boxes on the wagon. Boxes . . . or coffins. Shandor raised the lid of one, and in the faint glow of light from the monastery windows Charles saw a thin layer of earth at the bottom of the coffin.

'Yes,' said Shandor bitterly. 'Unpardonable of me not to have anticipated such a move.'

From beneath his robe he drew two crucifixes. One he placed in the centre of the earth in the coffin. He nodded to Charles, indicating that he should lift the lid of the other box, and then laid the second crucifix in the faint dusting which lay there also.

'The wagoner,' he said, 'was probably the faithful Klove. Faithful . . . if one may dignify his slavish subservience to his evil master with such a word. He brought the creatures of darkness here in daylight while they were still asleep – ready to awaken when night fell upon the land. But now' – he nodded at the coffins – 'that will prevent them from returning to their resting-place at daylight. If we haven't caught them by that time, they will be exposed to the sun and will be destroyed.'

'So we have no time to waste,' said Charles.

'I should have listened to you earlier. When evil is abroad, one must never delay, never rest.'

There was a babble of voices from the courtyard within the monastery. Shandor swung round, appalled. The uproar sounded quite out of keeping with the holy traditions of the place.

They both jumped from the wagon and hurried back through the gates. A monk let out a gasp of relief and moved towards Shandor.

'Brother Peter, this commotion – '

'We have caught the woman, Father. She was hiding in the stables.'

'Ah. And Dracula?'

Brother Peter shook his head.

Shandor thought for a moment, then said? 'Take her to . . . to Ludwig's cell.'

Brother Peter ran off. Shandor took Charles's arm and led him back into the monastery.

'If you wish to see the destruction of the horror spawned by Count Dracula, come with me. But I warn you it is not a sight for the squeamish.'

Charles said nothing but continued to walk beside Shandor. The two men made their way to the cell in which Ludwig worked. He was there, but not the Ludwig who had been so proud of his handiwork. Now he cowered in a corner as though sensing that something terrible was about to happen. Cowering . . . and yet, thought Charles uneasily, somehow sure of himself. He could not define the change in Ludwig, but felt that he was in possession of his faculties again: he was frightened yet covertly gleeful.

He turned to whisper something to Shandor, to draw attention to this almost imperceptible difference; but Shandor was already issuing orders.

'Brother Peter, take Ludwig out.' He raised his voice. 'Let the woman be brought in.'

Ludwig scuttled towards the door – and again Charles was disturbed by something sly and exultant in the last glance he cast back into the cell.

When he had gone, two brawny monks came in, with Helen struggling wildly between them.

Charles forgot Ludwig. He forgot everything. He saw and heard only Helen. The room was filled with the evil of her. Beneath the mask of hatred he tried to recognize the lineaments of the dry but well-meaning woman who had been his sister-in-law; but there was nothing left of her. Her teeth gleamed, her mouth slavered. When Shandor took a step towards her she fought like a demon to be free and hurl herself at him. When Charles came to stand beside Shandor, to give help when that help was needed, she screamed with awful laughter. If she could bite either of them, they would be hers . . . or Dracula's. Charles tried not to look at those vicious, venomous teeth.

Shandor said, without turning his head: 'Bear in mind, Mr Kent, that this is not the woman you knew. This is not your brother's wife. She is dead. What remains – what you see before you – is a shell . . . and what it contains is unadulterated evil. When we destroy it, we destroy only the evil.'

The monks began to drag Helen towards the table on which Ludwig had so recently worked so assiduously at the creation of beauty. Shandor swept up a few brushes and fragments of paper which still lay there.

Helen struggled and howled. Her body was taut and limp by turns, thrashing and turning and contorting with inhuman energy. But the monks held firm.

As they threw Helen by main force on to the table, another monk came in with a sharpened wooden stake about a foot long. The wood gleamed in the light, and there was a faint piny smell about it: it had been newly shaven and sharpened within the last few minutes. The newcomer handed it to Shandor, and then produced a heavy club mallet.

Shandor turned towards the table.

Helen was spreadeagled so that only her head could move. It twisted incessantly from side to side, and she spat and cursed until the room seethed with her fury.

Shandor raised his eyes, remote from her for a moment. He prayed silently.

Then he placed the sharpened stake over Helen's left breast, and raised the hammer.

Charles felt his stomach contract. He wanted to bend double, to hug his pain and sickness. He ought not to have come, ought never to have seen this. No man ought ever to look on this.

But he could not take his eyes away.

Shandor's arm swung down.

The scream that rang through the room was nothing human. It was the last terrible howl of a soul in torment. The stake thrummed for a second like a taut wire and then was still.

Charles looked away.

'Mr Kent,' said Shandor gently, 'it's over now.'

He took Charles by the arm and led him to the table. Reluctantly Charles looked down.

The face of the old Helen had been restored. It was as prim as ever, but more peaceful than he had ever seen it; a thousand times more peaceful than that of the hideous creature who had been here only a few minutes ago.

The monks began to intone a prayer. Shandor and Charles stood with bowed heads. Then Shandor said:

'Come . . . you need a drink.'

As they went to the door, Shandor's foot jarred against something metallic. It clanked a few inches along the floor. Shandor stooped and picked up a metal bar. Charles did not understand why he should have gone so rigid. He swung round towards the window. It was open a few inches. There had been four bars on the inside. Now, Charles saw, there were only two. The fragment which Shandor held in his hand had been carefully sawed off.

'Ludwig!' murmured Shandor. 'Was he trying to get away from us, after all this . . . ?' He stared at the window as though to pierce the secrets of the night. 'Could it be . . . his old master calling him . . . Ludwig striving to reach him?' He sprang into life and whirled back towards the door. 'We can't let him roam about loose if there is any such yearning in his mind.'

Charles had to hurry to keep up with Shandor, whose long legs strode resolutely down the corridor. At the corner, in shadow, the two of them almost stumbled over the huddled form of Brother Peter. He moaned as Father Shandor touched him, and brought his hands up to explore the back of his head tenderly.

'Ludwig,' he mumbled. 'Where . . . ?'

There was a scream. Charles recognized Diana's voice at once. He shouted, and ran madly towards her door. Shandor came after him.

Together they charged into the door and blundered across the threshold – in time to see Dracula gather up Diana in his arms and take a great leap that carried him through the splintering glass of the window.

'The wagon!' snapped Shandor.

They raced to the main door and out into the darkness. As they reached the gates they saw that the wagon was still there, but two horses were in the shafts and a dark figure was waiting on the driver's seat. Dracula hurled himself at the wagon and threw Diana up between the coffins. Then he sprang to the seat beside the driver, and the horses jolted forward under the flick of the whip. The driver leaned forward, and as his hood fell back from his face it was clear that he was Klove.

A dark figure scuttled across the path of the horses.

'Take me with you, master. Take me with you . . .'

Shandor had the gates open and ran forward as the horses slowed, with Charles at his heels. Dracula saw them coming and let out a feral howl. Ludwig was swept mercilessly aside and hurled to the ground. The horses tugged forward again and went at a fiendish pace down the bumpy track towards the road.

'Horses!' cried Charles. 'Horses – quickly!'

'We will go after them,' said Shandor, 'but not in panic.'

He turned back towards the monastery. Ludwig was grovelling on the earth. Shandor stared down at him in a dark anger which turned slowly to compassion. As they reached the main door, where Brother Mark was waiting with three or four of the brothers, Shandor said:

'Take Ludwig back to his cell. Be gentle with him – but be very careful of him.'

Charles was impatient to be out of the building. To be on horseback in pursuit of Dracula was all that counted. Every second lost was a second nearer to the pit for Diana.

But Shandor insisted on their going to his study. There he produced a rifle from behind one of the bookshelves. It was a surprising thing to find in this setting.

'They will head for the castle,' he said, as though this were some leisurely academic discussion. 'Once there he will be safe – and your wife will be lost forever. We must stop him before he gets there.'

'Then let's start *now*,' Charles implored. 'In an hour or so – '

'An hour or so?' Shandor shook his head. 'You were in no state to judge time or distance when we brought you here. The castle is a full day's ride from the monastery.'

'But that makes it worse.'

'It is to our advantage. It will soon be light, and already he will be thinking of returning to his coffin. Klove will have to make it ready for him – and will have to guard your wife during the hours of daylight. She will be safe until sunset. Here . . .'

He loaded the rifle and handed it to Charles, then began to search through the drawers of his desk.

'It would be better if you kept it,' said Charles. 'It's your rifle. You're used to it . . .'

'For hunting game. I am not used to shooting human beings. Klove is a human being and you may need to use it against him. I may bend the laws of my office at times, but there is a limit to what I can do.' Shandor tugged at his lower lip. 'We shall need some newly sharpened stakes. Come . . . you and Brother Mark can saddle the horses while I make my preparations.'

They rode through the last hour of darkness and into the flush of dawn. As it grew lighter they could see the tracks of wheels in the dusty road ahead of them. The skid marks and swirls of dust at corners showed what a rate Klove must be maintaining. Dracula would be asleep in his coffin now, but his loyal servant would not slacken the pace. And Diana . . . ? Charles urged his horse on. Bound or unconscious, stunned or awake and alive to terror, his wife was in the power of the vampire. When sunset came she could be eternally in his power.

The day drew on. Shandor insisted that they stopped for a while to rest the lathered horses, though Charles was in a mood to flog them till they dropped. Afternoon settled on the mountain peaks, and gradually the light began to wane once more.

'We'll never make it,' sobbed Charles.

Soon they would be at the crossroads and still the wagon was ahead of them. It was incredible that Klove should have kept up such a speed, yet no more incredible than the other devil-inspired things which had already happened.

Shandor reined in his horse. He stared up at the slopes of the jagged, interlocked hills:

'We must cut across country. It's rough going, but we may just have a chance of intercepting them below the castle.'

They turned their horses towards the wild slopes. It was a grim scramble up through scrubland, skirting the outcrop of dark forest and then picking a stumbling way over a wilderness of small stones.

Darkness raced them, flowing greedily down the slopes like a tide rippling in to cut them off.

When Charles had given up hope and was urging his mount on simply because it was as meaningless to stop as to go on, the castle rose suddenly above them, to their left. Immediately ahead was the road. And there were no recent tracks in the dust: the wagon had not yet passed this way.

Shandor slid from his horse and tethered it to a tree. Charles followed suit. They were getting their breath back when they heard the unmistakable rumble of wheels. Cautiously they picked their way through a clump of trees to a bend in the road.

The wagon was moving slowly now. The horses strained up the slope. Klove was alone on the seat. Behind him the coffins bumped and jarred as one wheel went into a rut.

Shandor glanced at Charles and raised an eyebrow. The two of them stepped out into the road. Charles raised the rifle and drew a bead on Klove.

Klove stared straight at them for a moment without taking in what their presence meant. Then, his mouth dropping slackly open, he pulled in the horses. The rifle was aimed unwaveringly at him.

Shandor said: 'This is far enough. Get down from there.'

Klove sat quite still as though debating this order. Then he edged to one end of the seat and let his right hand fall to his side. There was the swift flash of a blade, a knife was in his hand, he was thrusting himself forward to hurl it at Shandor . . . and Charles squeezed the trigger.

Klove seemed to have been punched in the chest. He jolted back, hung suspected on the edge of the box, and then toppled off to the ground. His knife fell a long way away. Klove did not stir.

Shandor took a step towards the wagon. Before he could reach it, the horses reared up with whinnies of fright, and bolted. Charles had to leap away as they thundered towards him. Foam smeared their distended nostrils as they went like mad things at the last stretch of the hill. They were racing for home – the dark castle looming over them, no more than a quarter of a mile away now.

Charles and Shandor freed their mounts and set off in pursuit.

They were within yards of the careering, swaying wagon as it headed for the bridge over the moat. The rear wheels spun and screeched, not gripping the road. As the horses pounded on to the bridge, the offside rear wheel jammed in a strut whose far end was secured in the castle wall. There was a shriek of wood and iron, and a splintering as the wheel collapsed. The horses were chokingly brought to a halt. One went down to its knees, bellowing.

The wagon began to tilt slowly over to one side. One of the coffins slid towards the edge. It was checked for a moment, then there was another jolt and it went over the edge of the bridge.

Shandor and Charles reined in. They watched the coffin hit the ice and slither across it, fetching up against the green-stained stonework of the castle.

There was another long, grim box still on the wagon. Charles flung himself down from his horse and ran towards the precariously balanced wagon. Shandor was close behind him. The wagon shifted ominously beneath them as they got a grip on the lid of the coffin and raised it.

In the bottom of the box, tied hand and foot, was Diana. Her eyes were wide open. At first Charles was sure that she did not see him – that she was already possessed, already one of Dracula's minions. Then a tear trickled down her cheek and she tried to smile.

Charles reached down towards her, but Shandor grabbed his arm. 'I'll look after her. You take care of . . . of *him*.'

Charles looked over the edge of the drop and saw the light fading in the ice of the moat. The other coffin was a dark hulk against the wall.

'You must hurry,' Shandor urged. 'The light's going.'

Charles lowered himself from the wagon to the bridge, and then slithered down the steep bank to the ice. The moat was a dark chasm between the bank and the lowering castle.

He tested the ice. It creaked beneath his weight but seemed solid enough – and it had certainly borne the weight of the box containing Dracula.

Charles walked towards the coffin.

The last red finger of sunset was withdrawn from the highest turret of the castle. He could hardly see the fastenings of the lid, which were much more complex than those on the box in which Diana lay. He fumbled to free the catches.

'Too late!' The voice came from the bridge. He paused and looked up. Shandor, with Diana beside him, resting on his arm, was shaking violently. 'It's too late, Kent. Get away from there at once. It's too late.'

Charles half turned back towards the coffin, undecided. As he did so, the lid flew back with a crash, and a long, bony hand stabbed out at him. The talons closed on his wrist, as cold and as unbreakable as iron.

Diana screamed.

Charles tried to brace his feet so that he could grapple with the creature rising from the coffin, but on the ice there was no foothold.

'Shoot him!' Diana was crying. 'Why don't you shoot?'

'It would do no good, my dear.'

Charles saw Diana snatch the rifle from Shandor; and then Dracula was triumphantly out of the box. The two of them lurched towards the wall. Charles struck the Count across the face, but the effort overbalanced him, and Dracula resettled his grip and began to drag him contemptuously along.

There was the crack of a gun. A long chip of ice was blasted from the surface a few feet away. A small fountain of water bubbled up. Charles felt Dracula sway to one side.

The water rippled across the ice and then ebbed away again.

'Yes!' cried Shandor. 'Running water . . . !'

There was another shot. And another. Dracula drew in a hissing breath like a curse, and thrust the two of them against the wall. Yet another bullet struck into the ice nearby, and this time a long, dangerous crack zigzagged across the surface.

With a snarl of rage Dracula let go. Charles was free. He half skidded, half ran away. The ice bent perilously beneath his feet, and cold water clutched at one ankle. He threw himself forward, let himself go, and went prone on the ice, sliding at last to safety against the bank.

As he scrambled up on to the grass, he heard a score of grinding, screeching cracks behind him. Shandor re-loaded and fired again, and the smack of the bullet was followed by a torment of breaking ice. Fissures joined up and water bubbled over the raw edges.

Dracula was trying to edge along the wall to a buttress by which he might hoist himself up to safety.

Breathless, Charles made an effort to reach the top of the bank and rejoin Diana. But he was nearly exhausted. And the frenzied movements of that dark figure on the ice were as hypnotic as the deadly creature had always been.

Shandor aimed again; and fired.

It was as though he had taken one end of the breaking ice in his hand and torn a massive strip from it. The surface on which Dracula stood was ripped away from the rest, and began to tilt. The vampire let out a vengeful howl and raised his claws towards the two on the bridge. Then he fell, groped for support that wasn't there, and plunged into the water. Up to his armpits, he managed for a few seconds to cling to the ice. Then another fragment came away and slowly, remorselessly, he was sucked down.

The wicked face was thrown back for an instant, the mouth making a last wild appeal to a thousand guardian demons. Then the water closed over it. The dark cloak swirled on the surface like a sombre lily before it, too, was drowned.

Charles groped his way to the top of the bank, and Diana hurried to meet him. Shandor followed at a tactfully slow pace. He kept his eyes on the moat as though afraid that this might still not be the end, that the scourge of Carpathia might still have escaped utter destruction.

But on the surface of the dark water were fragments of ice and nothing more. Count Dracula had gone and would never return.

Incense For The Damned

SIMON RAVEN

Although some earlier vampire films, especially those from Hammer, had contained elements of sex and sensuality as part of their storylines, Incense For The Damned, *made in 1969, was the forerunner of what are now known as 'Sex-Vampire' pictures. As David Pirie has explained in his book,* The Vampire Cinema (1977), *'The idea of vampirism as a straight sexual perversion minus any supernatural connations at all was first properly mooted in mainstream fiction by Simon Raven in his novel,* Doctors Wear Scarlet . . . Incense For The Damned *based on that book inaugurated the British sex-vampire in 1969.' It was a film that did not reach the screen without its fair share of problems, however. Initially, Terence Fisher the Hammer director was keen to make the picture, but instead the rights went to Titan Films. Their director Robert Hartford-Davis had trouble of one kind or another throughout the entire shooting and editing process and then took legal action – demanding that his name be removed from the credits. There were difficulties with the casting, too, Patrick Mower and Imogen Hassell finally being cast as the lovers who develop a taste for vampirism. The picture did, though, closely follow the plot of Simon Raven's novel about a young professor who uses the sucking of blood as a substitute for proper sexual intercourse. His condition, apparently, has been brought about as a result of his clashes with the 'bloodsuckers of the academic world'. Once made, however,* Incense For The Damned, *then became bogged down in a further legal dispute which delayed its release until 1972. Nevertheless, it can still be viewed in hindsight as the instigator of a whole school of such movies, including* The Vampire Lovers *(an explicit version of Joseph Sheridan*

Le Fanu's Carmilla *with heavy emphasis on the lesbian undertones),*
Lust For A Vampire *(vampirism at a girl's finishing school) and* Twins
of Evil *(about a battle between puritans and vampires).*

Simon Raven *(1927–) the much-admired novelist, dramatist, critic
and essayist, has made a reputation for tackling controversial subjects
in his works of fiction. Apart from* Doctors Wear Scarlet, *which he
wrote in 1960, he has poked fun at the establishment in* The Rich Pay
Late *(1964), the morals of society in* Friends in Low Places *(1965) and
the Army in* Sound The Retreat *(1971). The first chapter of* Doctors
Wear Scarlet *is virtually a self-contained short story and is reprinted
hereunder as a reminder of the ground-breaking movie that it inspired
and which deserves a greater appreciation – not to mention rescreen-
ing again at some time other than on very late night television!*

                    ∗   ∗   ∗

'The place must have been a Venetian stronghold,' said Piers.
        We were outside looking at the low, square tower, with its
narrow pointed windows and crenellated walls, which the light of
morning revealed. The wind was still strong; but it had stopped
raining now, and there was promise that the blanket of white cloud
above us might later yield to the sun.

'They must have had a troop of soldiers here,' Piers went on,
'keeping watch over the mountains.'

'I hope,' I said, 'that they were frequently relieved. One night in the
place is enough.'

'We shan't be able to move Richard for a day or two,' said Roddy,
who on account of some slight experience in the field was acknowledged by us as a kind of crude medical expert.

'Just how bad is he?' I asked.

'Very weak,' said Roddy with a puzzled look. 'As far as I can tell he
just needs rest and food. Building up. But it will be some time before he
can take much of anything solid.'

'So long as we can keep that woman away from him,' Piers said, 'he
will be all right.'

Roddy looked at him thoughtfully.

'Will she come back?'

'Oh yes.'

'She bolted fast enough when we appeared last night.'

'She was taken unawares. But soon she will pull herself together, and she will wait for her opportunity, and then she will . . .' His voice trailed away.

'Will what?' said Roddy.

'. . . will return, for Richard.'

'The three of us should be able to manage her.'

'She will have . . . resources,' Piers said.

For a time we were silent. The towering peaks crowded about us, but there was a gap between two of the mountains through which I glimpsed a green plain far below. Familiarity, I thought, security: home.

'We'd best go in and look to Richard.'

When we returned into the fort, Richard, for the first time, was awake. He was still as white as marble and he looked desperately weak; but he smiled softly at us and said, without apparent surprise –

'So you got here all right. Piers . . . Anthony . . . and you, Roddy. It was good of you to come.'

'We came as soon as we could.'

'Where did you sleep?'

'Here. With you.'

'No blankets,' said Richard, turning his head with effort and looking round the inside of the fort. 'You must have been cold.'

'Never mind that,' said Roddy; 'don't worry about us. Sleep.'

'Yes,' said Piers, 'you must sleep.'

But Richard was still gazing, restless and anxious, round the bare stone walls.

'Where is . . . Chriseis?' he said at length.

'She went away last night when we came.'

'We will take care of you now.'

'You must watch for her,' said Richard. 'She will come back. She . . . is . . . clever.'

Then his eyes closed and he fell asleep.

But later that day, early in the afternoon, he awoke once more. We gave him some yoghurt, which he swallowed with difficulty, and a little wine. And then he seemed disposed to talk.

'You must watch for Chriseis. If she comes back, I shall not be able to fight her. Neither, perhaps, will you. Even when I was well and strong . . . when I first met her months ago in Corinth . . . I could not fight her. But then, of course, I thought she was something different . . . liberation, escape.

'A dreary town, Corinth. Modern and hard. How should such a creature come from those everyday streets, the bright shops, the neat houses? But she was there, and she found me, and I thought she loved me. And indeed I loved her. For herself and the escape I thought she offered. But even then I couldn't . . . I couldn't . . .'

He broke off and looked despairingly at Piers, who put out a hand and began to stroke the tumbled hair back from his forehead.

'Never mind, my dear, never mind. We understand. Don't force yourself to tell us.'

'But I want to tell you. You must all know.'

His voice was becoming urgent and he raised his head from the pillow.

'I couldn't . . . make love . . . like a man.'

His head sank back and he seemed much relieved.

'But Chriseis, she said it didn't matter, there were other things. And so there were – fearful, ugly things. But I went with her, dazed, not really knowing what I did, but helping her all the same, because, you see, I felt I had betrayed her by my lack of manhood, and now she meant so much I couldn't leave her. And so together we did these things.'

He gave a soft moan and looked at Piers once more.

'And then,' he went on, 'I had to leave Corinth for a time, to go to Athens and then to Delphi, where I had work. Some of the way she came with me, but after a time she had to return to Corinth. For a while I missed her desperately, but then it got better, and I began to realize that what I really needed was to forget her, was to have my own proper friends once more. That was when I wrote to Piers to ask him to come in the summer.'

He stretched out a hand to Piers, who took it lightly and rubbed it between his own to warm it.

'But later,' said Richard, 'when I had done my work and returned to Corinth, she came to me again. I had hoped she wouldn't . . . that she would have forgotten me and found someone else. But within a week of my return to Corinth – I had more work there, you see, and had to go back – within a week, she came to me. And it was then that something different began between us. We no longer went out and did . . . the things we used to. She turned herself entirely on to me, and thenceforth all the suffering was mine. You know what I mean, Piers. I can see it in your eye. But you, Anthony? And Roddy?'

A frustrated look appeared on Roddy's face. He opened his mouth as if to ask a question, but thought better of it when he saw Piers shake his head.

'You will find out, Roddy, as time goes on,' said Richard, who had apparently noticed this exchange. 'You will find out. For the present you must just understand that she made me suffer and began to make me ill. I tried to get away. Although I wanted her to go on making me suffer, at that time I was still strong enough to want to escape from her also, and in the end I decided to leave for Crete several weeks before I had planned. I found the strength to leave without telling her; but she followed me to Athens and found me. Do you know, I was *glad* to be found. But I was also desperate, because I now knew that she was going to kill me. Sooner or later she would have taken everything she could, and then I would be dead. So from Athens I wrote to Anthony, begging him to bring you and follow me to Crete; because I was still strong enough and clear enough to know that I must have help, and that you, who were my friends, would help me. And now you have come . . .

'Now you have come, but there is still danger. For I know she is not far from here, and soon she will come back. . . .'

He broke off, and then returned to the story of his love.

'So when we got to Crete, I became less and less clear, but all the time I knew that you would come. But somehow Chriseis knew too, and persuaded me to come with her to Hydra, thinking to elude you. The police were interested in us, she said, and we must go where we were not known. And then the monks in Hydra would make me strong. They would make me so strong that she would be able to love me, in her vile way, for ever, and yet I would never again get weak. So I listened to her lies and believed them; but although she tried to prevent me I left a clue for you, so that you could follow. I managed to speak to the old man, Arnold, though even then her influence was so strong that I found myself speaking in riddles, and whether I was trying to cheat her or trying to cheat you I shall never know. Still, it was a simple riddle, so I suppose you understood. . . .

'By the time we had gone to Mount Ida and then on to Hydra, I was very ill. So ill that I cannot remember how I was brought there. But the monks made me well. In a few days they made me so strong that I could stand up to her; and then I insisted that we went back to Crete. Because I was terrified that you would not find Arnold, or would not understand my riddle, and in any case all this was still in June: so that at this time you had yet to come to Crete; and by going there straight away I might hope to find you. And in the end Chriseis gave way. She let me charter a caique owned by a German, and we came round to the coast near Sphakion. I wanted to go to Heraclion and wait there for you; but she didn't want this, because she hated you and was also afraid, or so she said, that there might be trouble with the police. And since I was already beginning to get weaker again, I gave in to her and let her bring me to Sphakion. From there she took me to several villages, while I was growing weaker all the time; but always the villagers seemed to understand what she was doing, and they would drive us out after a day or two, until at last we ended up here on the mountain. We have been here for days now. And all the time I have been growing weaker and weaker . . . Why did they have no charity, those villagers? Why did they not try to save me, instead of turning me away with her? I suppose they were afraid of what she might do. For all the time they could see what she was doing to me. How I was growing weaker. . . .

'But now you have come and I shall get well. All I need is rest and food. The monks in Hydra have a special wine, and they did some other things, so that I became well very quickly. But even without their wine and their care, I shall get well in time, if I can only rest. And if that fiend will stay away from me,' he said, his voice quivering with anger and disgust, 'so that the life within me can grow. Watch for her, Anthony, and you, Piers. Watch for her, Roddy. She is not far away, I know, and she will come again. . . .'

And suddenly, as had happened that morning, his eyes closed and he fell asleep.

By now it was early evening and we must make some sort of plan.

'The mayor must be told,' said Roddy.

'He said he would wait.'

'He has already waited a night and a day. We must tell him that we shall be here at least another night, and warn him how difficult it will be to carry Richard down. . . . It may be possible to bind him to one of the mules — but then it could be days before he is strong enough to stand it. . . . But in any case we must speak with the mayor. Courtesy requires it.'

Piers and I nodded.

'But it is important,' Piers said, 'that *two* of us stay here with Richard. In case that woman comes.'

Roddy looked at him with a question in his eye, but seeing how intent was Piers' face, he just nodded in agreement.

'And whoever goes,' said Piers, 'must take care. He must go fast and not linger . . . for anything.'

'It is not far,' said Roddy, 'and there is nothing on this mountain to frighten me. So I had better go.'

'That will be good,' said Piers. 'But remember: *go fast*.'

Roddy gave him another questioning look, but again simply nodded. He rose and made ready to go.

'It is only early evening,' he said. 'I shall be back before dark.'

Richard, disturbed by Roddy's movements, awoke once more.

'Where are you going, Roddy?' he said.

'To speak with friends who have helped us. They are not far.'

'You are going alone?'

'Yes.'

'Take care, Roddy.'

Roddy smiled.

'You needn't worry about me,' he said.

A shadow came into Richard's eyes.

'Lift me to the door,' he said. 'I want to look outside. And to speed Roddy on his way.'

Roddy looked startled, then embarrassed, then deprecating. But Piers signed to me, and together we helped Richard from his bed and supported him to the door. It was the first time we had seen him uncovered by blankets; his clothes were tattered and he smelt abominably. Roddy lifted one of the blankets from the litter on the floor and placed it, like a shawl, round Richard's shoulders and over his chest. Then, having made a vague salute, he started down the steps.

'Wait,' called Richard.

Roddy turned to face us.

'Some say,' said Richard strangely, 'that Zeus was reared on this island. Over in the other mountains to the East. Others say that his tomb is in those same mountains. The tomb of Zeus . . . But either way, he is strong in this island, and we should pray to him: I for my strength, you for safe passage, and all of us for deliverance.'

Roddy shifted uneasily on the steps.

'It is already evening,' he said. 'I must not wait – '

Richard interrupted him with a movement of his hands. Piers flashed a look at him over Richard's shoulder, a look which said 'pity him and do as he asks.'

'I shall not be long,' Richard said.

So Roddy stood quiet, waiting politely, impatience still stirring in the muscles under his eyes.

Then Richard, leaning on Piers and myself but lifting his voice in a curiously powerful fashion when one considered the low tones in which he had spoken hitherto, called out his prayer to the mountains opposite. He invoked the deity, he asked for the strength to be put back into his limbs, he solicited a safe passage for Roddy, and he requested a good deliverance for us all. The prayer, as he had promised, was brief; and he concluded by asking for a sign.

'Father,' he called out over the mountains, 'send us a sign.'

For a moment no one moved. Then Roddy, saluting once more, began to descend the steps.

'Wait,' called Richard again. And again Roddy turned and stood waiting.

As he turned, a huge black eagle appeared in the sky above us. For a moment it seemed to hover like a hawk, then it swooped down over our heads, so near that the rush of its wings was almost deafening, and soared up again, turning at the same time, till it was once more hovering high above. Again it descended, flying almost into our faces, and again soared up and turned to hover above us. Then it swooped a third time, to ascend, as before, into the sky above our stronghold. And now it hovered, and made as if to swoop yet once more; but before it had come down more than a few yards, it made a wide and beautiful turn and flew away from the declining sun towards the mountains in the East.

'I wouldn't have wanted to miss that,' called Roddy cheerfully. 'Thank you for making me stay.'

He waved gaily. All of us answered his wave, though Richard, who was leaning very hard on the arm I had round him, waved very weakly. Then Roddy turned away; whistling a bar or two of our own regimental march he walked quickly down the graceful steps, turned the corner at the bottom, waved once more as he turned, and was then lost to view. Piers and I made to help Richard inside.

'What did you notice about that eagle?' asked Richard.

'It was a noble bird,' Piers said.

'It was,' said Richard. 'But there are four of us, and the eagle only swooped three times.'

As the evening deepened, Richard slept. Piers and I lit the storm-lantern and sat over it on two large rocks we had carried in from outside.

'Why are you so anxious for Roddy?' I said. 'What danger could there be for him?'

'The same as there could be for us. If that woman came here.'

'And that is . . . ?'

'. . . best not thought about unless it has to be faced.'

I roused myself to press Piers further.

'Piers . . . It is all very well, this fashion of sparing our feelings. But we are adult men, Roddy and I, and we have a right to know what is going on. When you were still in doubt, then you were probably justified in not committing yourself. But there has clearly been no real doubt in your mind for a long while now. And so now, since Roddy and I are sharing in the dangers, we must be allowed to share in your knowledge.'

'I cannot help feeling you have both been slightly obtuse.'

'Myself, possibly. But there is excuse for Roddy. His education has been of an uncomplicated nature.'

Piers looked over at Richard and stirred moodily above the lantern.

'Very well, Anthony,' he said. 'But it is not the sort of thing I can bring myself to explain twice. I will tell you both together when Roddy gets back.'

He rose to look through one of the windows.

'It is nearly dark now,' he said; 'I wonder what is keeping him.'

'The way may be longer than he remembered.'

'Shorter if anything. The storm made it stretch for a hundred miles.'

'He may be having a difficult time with the mayor and his men. They can hardly be anxious to stay another night.'

'You underrate them. They need never have come in the first place. And I suspect – I know – that it is not only for Richard's sake they have helped us.'

'For what other?'

'For their own. That woman is a danger to all men. To all men and all women too.'

'Then why did they not deal with her themselves?'

'They are afraid of her in a fashion in which they think we cannot be afraid. They believe in her power.'

'But so do you.'

'Yes – and that is one reason why I am not anxious to explain it. But I only believe in part. I share their fear all right. But another side of me, the Western, educated, *Lancaster* side forbids me to be afraid. So I can just make shift to face her.'

The night was down outside, and still Roddy did not come.

'Perhaps the dark overtook him while he was still with the mayor. In which case he might choose to spend the night with him.'

'He would know that we worried for him,' said Piers; 'he would come back.'

'And there can be no question of fear . . .'

'He was brave when you knew him in the Army?'

'Yes. And you can see that he is still brave.'

'But perhaps . . . on the mountain . . . in the night . . .'

'He showed no fear last night,' I said.

'Last night he was fighting a storm, the kind of enemy to which he is accustomed. But now . . .'

'It is the only kind of enemy he acknowledges. If there is another, he does not know of it.'

'He may begin to . . . feel that it is there. So long as he does not realize too late. . . .'

But for some time now Piers' eyelids had been drooping. Each time they nearly closed he had forced them back. But plainly the need for sleep was making him desperate.

'I must sleep for a while,' he now said, 'Can you keep watch, Anthony? Wake me in two hours, and then I will watch for you. It . . . should be all right like that . . . I think . . . unless . . . But wake me on the instant if you hear any noise at all.'

Without another word he settled himself in a corner and fell asleep.

I took a book from the valise we had brought and began to read in the light of the storm-lantern. The book was heavy to my hands, however, the words drifted in front of my eyes, there was not a flicker of response in my brain. I thought of Tyrrel on the night on which everything had started; of Cambridge and of Walter and of Marc Honeydew; of Piers – 'I've seen him three times, Anthony, and each time he was dead'; of how I went to Ludlow to persuade Roddy – 'All that is needed is a little common sense, Anthony, and a lack of superfluous scruple.' I thought of the dinner with Tyrrel before we left, of Penelope's telephone call that night, and of our lighthearted journey across France and Italy; of Venice; of Heraclion with its blind sea-front; of Cnossos and Ratty Arnold . . . 'He likes islands. He likes Crete, but he likes other islands as well, because water is best . . . $αοιστου$ $μεν$ $υδωρ$ . . . ariston men hydor . . . ariston men hydor . . . hydor . . . hydor . . .' until I awoke with a start, and this is what I saw.

I saw that the door was half open, and that just inside it was standing a woman, dressed in black trousers and a kind of black tunic above them. She also had on a medium length black cape, which was held together in front by a short gold chain. It was the same woman as we had surprised the night before; but on that occasion she had fled so swiftly, and I had been so numbed by the storm and so dazzled by the white light of the lantern, that I had taken in no detail about her. But now, though newly awoken, I saw with great clarity every detail of her dress and her appearance. That beneath the trousers was a pair of what looked very like Mess Wellingtons, the upper portions of which were concealed under the trouser legs; that on her throat, just above the gold chain which secured her cloak, was a small silver brooch; that her black hair was long and very glossy in appearance for a woman who had just spent a night in the open and many days living in extreme discomfort; that her complexion was white yet healthy, her nose well proportioned, her forehead narrow; that her chin was delicate; and that her eyes were very bright.

It was these bright eyes that were fixed on me now. They were not looking into my own eyes, but just played generally, though seemingly without moving, over my face and the upper part of my body. Sometimes the light caught her brooch and it would flash; sometimes it caught her eyes, which then became brighter than ever. So she stood, while her eyes explored me; and then I realized, not with horror but with a comfortable feeling of resignation, that I could not move. I could shift my gaze, turn my head, even raise a hand; but I could not move my body; and I could not speak. I was not afraid, I was simply numb. I had realized, dimly and without urgency, that I must wake Piers, so I had made to get to my feet and go to him; but my body would not stir. Then I had opened my mouth to call out to him; but no words, not even the faintest sound, would come. I was paralysed; I had made my effort and in a distant, theoretical way regretted my failure: but now I knew, with a kind of grim satisfaction, that I could do nothing more, and I settled with interest and almost with pleasure to watch what happened next.

First of all the woman closed the door. She did not turn; she just moved one arm behind her and pushed it gently home. Then, still letting her eyes play over me, she unfastened her cloak and dropped it on the floor. After this, she walked slowly towards me, smiled with considerable charm, and muttered something in Greek which I did not understand. Taking her eyes off me, she passed on to where Piers was slumped in the corner. I was still fixed to my seat, but as before I could still turn my eyes to follow her. I saw her stand over Piers and regard him with attention. For a while she stood there, playing her eyes over him in the same way as she had done to myself, but all the time muttering in a low, soft voice, a neutral voice, neither of hatred nor desire, but perhaps of incantation. After which she stooped down over him, opened one of his eyes with finger and thumb, looked closely into it, and then let the eyelid drop. I was conscious of faint curiosity: why had she paid so much more attention to Piers, who was safely asleep, than to myself who was at least partially conscious? But the thought, vague and untroubling in any case, soon passed from me. Meanwhile the woman was standing up again, and now, after a last low mutter over Piers, she began to move towards Richard.

When she reached the pathetic shape of clammy blankets, she knelt down on the floor beside them and started to moan softly. She passed her hand over the feet and legs, up over the stomach, stroking and fondling, then on to the chest and throat. At this stage, her moaning struck a higher and more intense key; her caresses were slower and more loving; while her face, of which I could see the right profile, became at once fierce with longing and tender with an effort of love. She stroked Richard's forehead and his cheeks. She passed her fingers lightly over his closed eyes. She smoothed his hair and touched him behind the ears. And then she arched her body and brought her face down over his, being about, as I thought, to kiss him on the lips: but just as her face was almost touching his, she seemed to wrench it to one side; she bared her teeth, until her whole face seemed one hideous grin, and then, with a movement as quick as a snake's, she struck into Richard's naked throat.

And still I could not move or speak; still I felt neither fear nor horror, only interest and the very faintest misgiving. Richard was awake now. I was near enough to see his eyes: into them came a look of utter loneliness and despair; a look which, as he saw my eyes on his, turned to one of pleading and of prayer, and thence, as I continued to regard him without moving, to one of sorrowful reproach. 'Save me,' his eyes had said, 'before the life is drained out of me'; and then, 'You have yielded to her and betrayed your friend.' But still I could do nothing, still I watched with interest and was untouched in my heart, by the terrible message in those eyes.

Then Richard, seeing that there would be no help from me and knowing that his life was fast leaving him, must have steeled himself to make one final call for help. For the muscles of his face knotted in the desperate summoning of his strength; his eyes bulged and his forehead narrowed and stretched in his agony; and out of his mouth came a great groan of despair and desolation, a call for pity, a call for salvation, a call for love.

The woman, sunk into his throat with lust, did not heed his cry for pity. Myself, lost and paralysed, could interpret but remained indifferent to his plea for salvation. But Piers, whatever the depths to which his sleeping soul had been willed by the woman, awakened to Richard's cry for love. He stirred, sat up, rubbed his eyes and then looked straight at Richard and the woman. His eyes became bright with hatred, brighter than the eyes of the woman had been. He crossed the room in four quick steps; he seized the woman by her shoulders; and with all his strength he wrenched her away from Richard, whose eyes closed, whose head lolled, whose whole body seemed to shrink and sag.

Piers hurled the woman down on the floor. He put one knee on her chest. He placed both hands round her throat and he began to squeeze. He squeezed until the veins and sinews stood out in his neck; until the sweat was running in streams down his face, until his whole body was jerking in spasms, half of rage and half of effort, which struck at him as the multiple lash might strike at a trussed man under the cat. All the time his eyes grew brighter and harder; until at last, after one final and tremendous spasm, which seemed like some supreme and brutish orgasm, he slowly loosened his hands, stood up and back so that I might see what he had done.

'Now are you answered?' he shouted into my face.

On the floor I could see the body of the woman. All of it was limp and easy now. Except for the face: for her mouth was still caught in the hideous grin which she had worn as she struck her face at her victim; and spread over her cheeks and lips, dribbling from the bared white teeth, was the blood wet and shining red, which she had drunk from Richard Fountain's throat.

For a long time I remained without moving. I have a vague recollection of watching Piers drag the body of a woman into a corner and of seeing him busy himself with Richard; but I related none of this to myself or to any kind of reality, for I was still debarred from reality. Gradually, however, I began to come out of my daze, to think and feel as Anthony Seymour, the friend of Piers Clarence and Richard Fountain, and to comprehend the enormity of what I had seen. I put my head between my knees; then rose slowly from the seat of rock, my limbs cramped and bitterly cold, my stomach heaving and contracting with horror and guilt.

'Richard . . . will he be all right?'

'I think so,' said Piers; 'but I only got her in the nick of time.'

'What can I . . . ? Oh, Piers. So sorry . . . I . . .'

Piers got up from beside Richard and smiled at me.

'It wasn't your fault, Anthony. Why do you think I felt desperately sleepy so very suddenly? I can usually go for days . . . No. You couldn't help it, and Richard of all people will understand why.'

'How did you awake?'

'I don't know. I heard Richard . . . with my soul, I think. His call was too strong for her. But even then she nearly . . . got the better of me. You saw how hard I was . . . trying?'

'Yes.'

'It wasn't anger, Anthony. All that effort, effort of body *and* mind, was really needed. She was a strong woman in more ways than one.'

'And Richard will really be all right?'

'I think so,' he said. 'He's very weak indeed. But when he knows the danger is gone for good . . .'

He paused for a moment.

'Is it gone for good?' he said.

He looked at me very oddly.

'We have gone through too much,' he murmured at last, 'to take any more chances now.'

He went to one corner where Roddy had left a walking stick which he had been shaping, earlier in the day, from a branch he had found.

'Lucky Roddy forgot this,' said Piers softly.

And then, 'You realize, Anthony, that if I am *right* in doing . . . what I am now going to do — and we shall have no way at all of knowing — then there may be . . . consequences for Richard. Even afterwards. Nobody knows really.'

'We must deal with them as and when they arise,' I said, not really understanding.

Piers rummaged in the valise and took out a large clasp knife.

'Take her outside, Anthony.'

I went to the body of the woman and took it by the shoulders. With some difficulty I dragged it to the door, which Piers opened for me, and then on to the topmost of the wide and graceful steps outside. There was a light cold wind and a trace of dawn.

Piers joined me. He was carrying the storm-lantern and Roddy's stick, which he had sharpened down to a point. He put the lantern down and with great care sawed the stick in two with the knife about nine inches above the sharp end. Then he looked about in the light of the lamp and selected a large, flat-bottomed stone.

'Hold up the lantern, Anthony.'

He knelt down on one knee and placed the point of the stake he had made over the heart of the thing which had been Chriseis.

'Now keep this upright with your other hand.'

I clasped the stake some six inches above the point; and Piers, drawing a deep breath, raised the stone high above his head with both hands, so that he might be able to strike down again with all the strength of his two arms.

Dark Shadows

MARILYN ROSS

Television has, of course, shown (and sometimes shown time and time again) all the most popular vampire movies. Yet it has only once transmitted an entire vampire series, Dark Shadows, *which actually became so popular in the late Sixties that it ran as a daily soap opera all over America and earned ratings figures that would be the envy of* Dallas *and* Hawaii Five-O. *Vampire short stories have certainly occasionally been used as episodes in some of the popular anthology series such as Rod Serling's* Night Gallery *in America and ITV's* Mystery and Imagination *in Britain; while adaptations of Stoker's novel have also been produced by TV channels on both sides of the Atlantic starring such familiar names as John Carradine, Denholm Elliott and Jack Palance.* Dark Shadows *was rather different from all of these, however. Producer Dan Curtis and his scriptwriter Sam Hall took the Gothic trappings of Dracula and grafted them onto a centuries-old New England house, Collinwood, inhabited by one Barnabas Collins, a mysterious and rather sinister figure in whom the residents of nearby Collinsport went in fear and trembling. When Barnabas – who was played by the fine Shakesperean actor, Jonathan Frid – first arrived in the series he was supposedly from England and planned to reoccupy his old family home. He was a man with a sallow skin and gaunt features, thought not unattractive, and wore a caped coat and carried a fancy cane with a silver top in the shape of a wolf's head. Like the Dracula of the movies, he was believed to make nocturnal attacks on young girls and roamed the local graveyard at night and dabbled in black magic. As the show grew in popularity, however, Barnabas became less villainous and eventually mellowed into a rather tragic and romantic figure of the kind beloved by watchers of soaps, and then proceeded to carry out a one-vampire campaign against other supernatural foes who materialised in the area with alarming frequency to threaten his neighbours. Barnabas Collins was not called the good vampire for nothing! The success of the series generated all manner of merchandising from t-shirts to games and in 1970 a full-length cinema movie,* House of Dark Shadows, *was produced by Dan Curtis starring the regular actors from the TV series including Jonathan Frid, Joan Bennett and Grayson Hall. When* Dark Shadows *finally came off the air in 1971 after completing over one thousand hours of broadcasting it had created a little piece of television – and vampire – history.*

A number of Barnabas Collins' confrontations with witches, mummies, ghosts, werewolves and demons were recounted by 'Marilyn Ross' in a series of books published at the time and eagerly collected by fans of the series. The author's name was actually a pseudonym of the prolific American mystery and adventure writer, Michael Avallone jnr (1924–) whose many credits have included ghosting stories for Boris Karloff. In 'The Secret of Collinwood', he tells the story of how Barnabas was saved from the life of a vampire and begin his battle against the forces of evil. And, incidentally, become probably the most unlikely TV soap hero of all!

*   *   *

Dusk was falling as Dr Julia Hoffman made her way to the old house of Collinwood where Barnabas Collins and his servant, Willie Loomis, lived. She halted a few feet from the entrance and watched the sun moving close to the horizon. Then with a look of determination on her attractive face she went to the door and knocked.

In the depths of the cellar Willie heard the knock. He was baffled and annoyed, but set off to answer the door. When he opened it, Julia took him by surprise and barged in before he could say a word. He stood there gaping at her and looking more flustered than usual.

He gasped, 'Dr Hoffman, I'm afraid you can't come in right now!'

Julia was all assurance. 'I'm in, Willie. Would you tell Mr Collins I'd like to see him?'

Willie looked uneasy. 'He ain't here. He's away. He's in Portland on business.'

She let him see she didn't believe him and in a sharp tone demanded, 'When will he be back?'

'I don't know,' Willie stammered, 'I don't. He didn't say!'

Julia smiled sourly. 'Shouldn't be too long now, should it, Willie?'

He gaped again. 'What do ya mean?'

'The sun just went down.'

'That don't make sense,' Willie protested.

'I think it does.'

'You'd better go,' Willie warned her. 'He won't like it if he comes and finds you here.'

'He might like it less if I went without seeing him,' Julia said.

'I don't understand you,' Willie said worriedly.

She gave him another of her sour smiles. 'I don't expect you to.'

'Come back when Mr Barnabas is here,' the servant pleaded.

'Strange,' she said. 'I have the feeling he is here now.'

'Do you really?' The question came to her from the door at the rear of the house. She glanced quickly and saw that it was Barnabas, a thin smile on his lips. 'How astute of you, Doctor.'

Willie looked at them nervously. 'He just came back.'

'Yes,' Barnabas said in his clipped British accent, 'that is so. I have just returned. And you may go, Willie. That will be all.'

Willie hesitated, then with a gulp said, 'Yes, sir.'

When they were alone Barnabas said, 'You wanted to see me, Doctor?'

'Yes.'

He continued to smile at her. 'I'm delighted. It's not often I have such a charming visitor. You must pardon the condition of this house. The restoration is coming slowly.'

She said, 'You've taken on a huge and expensive task.'

He shrugged. 'Money isn't important to me. And I like the challenge of the project. Besides, I love this house.'

'I'm sure you must,' she said, pointedly. 'And you must expect to remain here a long time to get all the renovations completed.'

'That depends,' he said. 'You must come into the drawing room and have a sherry.'

'Thank you,' she said.

The elegantly appointed and paneled drawing room had been the first room to be completely restored. He indicated the cut-glass chandelier with its array of flickering candles throwing a soft yet satisfying light over the room.

'Can you imagine anything more romantic than candlelight?' he asked her.

'It is lovely.'

Barnabas indicated a high-backed chair. 'Make yourself comfortable, dear lady, while I get the wine.' He moved to the sideboard as she sat down. 'I'm surprised you dare venture out so close to dark by yourself. After the tragedy of Carolyn's death, not to mention that of Nancy Hodiak, I'd think you'd be terrified.'

'My training has taught me not to give way to fear,' Julia said.

Barnabas had poured sherry from a dusty bottle into two exquisite tiny wine glasses. Now he handed one to her with an amused expression on his gaunt, attractive face. 'I forgot about your being a doctor.'

She took the glass and looked up at him pleasantly. 'But you mustn't,' she protested. 'It is one of the most important things about me. My character has been moulded by my training.'

'Try the wine,' Barnabas said. 'I think you will approve.'

She took a sip of it. 'Dry! Lovely!'

'An ancient vintage,' he said. 'I found some in the cellars here. This old place is a treasure house.'

Taking another sip of the wine, she said, 'I hope you don't resent my intruding this way.'

'You came at an opportune time,' he said.

She looked up into his deep-set eyes. 'I felt it wouldn't do any good to arrive earlier.'

He showed no reaction to her words. He was the epitome of an urbane, civilized man. Moving to a spot before the fireplace he stood with his wine glass in hand studying her.

'No,' he said. 'You would not have found me earlier.' And then he added, 'I have an idea you are a rather complex person, Dr Hoffman.'

She smiled. 'You may call me Julia. All my friends do.'

'And I should like to be regarded as a friend. So let me be Barnabas to you.'

'Agreed,' she said. 'It's strange you should describe me as complex. I have been having exactly the same thoughts about you.'

He raised his eyebrows. 'Few of us are as simple as we appear on the surface. Life shapes us, moulding the good and evil.'

'We do have our good and our evil sides, don't we?' Julia agreed, looking at him earnestly from her chair.

'All of us.'

She said, 'The tragedy is when we allow the evil in us to dominate our actions.'

Barnabas looked bleak. 'There are times when one has no choice.'

'I disagree,' Julia said. 'There must always be a choice.'

'Your experience is somewhat limited,' he said with irony. 'Forgive my disagreeing. But I have lived much longer than you. I know many things which you cannot have encountered.'

'Still, you shouldn't allow yourself to become cynical or despairing,' the woman doctor warned him. 'You mustn't be like the man Ambrose Bierce wrote of, who 'damned his fellows for his own unworth, And, bad himself, thought nothing good on earth.' Remember that?'

Barnabas smiled grimly. 'I don't think I've ever heard it before. But I can tell you that there are persons condemned to a life of evil who would fight against it if they knew of a way. Those who claim it is easy to be evil are entirely wrong. It is much easier to be good.'

'Your philosophical views amaze me, Barnabas,' Julia Hoffman said. 'I have looked on you as a cynical sophisticate from London.'

'As you suggested, none of us are as one-dimensional as we may seem,' he told her.

She put aside her empty wine glass. 'I feel I understand you a lot better for this short conversation.'

'And I, you,' he said. 'Would you care for more wine?'

'Thank you, no,' she said.

He studied her with those deep-set eyes. 'What can I do for you, Doctor?'

She met his gaze with an earnest one of her own. 'The question is, what can *I* do for *you*.'

He frowned. 'I don't understand.'

Julia stood up. 'Perhaps this will help you to understand.' And she reached into her purse and removed a cross. She held it up before him in a dramatic fashion. His face suddenly took on a tortured expression and he at once turned his back on the cross, and on her.

In a strained voice, he said, 'So you know.'

'Yes.'

'How long?'

'Since the evening you came to pay your condolences.'

He sighed. 'You were very brave to come here, Doctor. Please put that cross away.'

'I will if you will promise me my safety. I must talk to you.'

'You need have no fear of me,' he said.

'I'd like to be your friend,' she said, putting the cross back in her purse.

Barnabas turned to her with a sad look on his gaunt, sallow face. 'Now I understand all your talk about good and evil.'

'I said those things because I believe you want to be a good man, Barnabas,' she told him gravely.

'Thank you,' he said with irony. 'It's not often I'm given the benefit of the doubt.'

'In your present state you might live forever,' she said. 'You might transform yourself into the form of a bat and even somehow escape the stake and mallet treatment Dr Stokes gave poor Carolyn. But no matter how you elude justice, you will always remain a tormented soul.'

He spread his hands. 'I would be the last to deny that.'

'What would you say if I told you I could change you? Transform you into a normal human being?'

He stared at her. 'I'd say you were crazy. A crazy dreamer!'

Julia spoke earnestly, 'Listen to me. I've done a great amount of research in the past month on blood samples of your victims. I've learned that you carry in your bloodstream a very destructive cell.'

'You are serious?' he asked tensely.

'Quite serious,' she assured him.

'Go on.'

'I'm convinced that the existence of this cell keeps you the way you are. If the cell could be eliminated, I believe you'd be able to live a perfectly normal life.'

Barnabas was staring at her. 'This is amazing! Tell me more!'

Julia smiled. 'I've conducted experiments on isolated samples of the cell and the results were successful.'

His deep-set eyes were fixed on her. 'You give me hope.'

'I want to.'

'But you should despise me! Hate me! Run from me in fear,' he protested.

'I don't feel that way about you at all.'

He gave a deep sigh, seeming stunned. 'I don't know whether you're sincere or mad.'

'If I weren't sincere, if I had no belief in you, I never would have come here.'

'No?'

'No. Why would I deliberately place my own life in danger?'

'You took that risk when you knocked on my door.'

'Because I think you deserve another chance,' she said quietly.

'I have lost hope that such a chance is possible.'

'You aren't resigned to being one of the living dead, are you? You would like to live a normal life, wouldn't you?'

'Do you think anyone could enjoy an existence like this? To roam the world by night, shut off from all you love? To be a thing of evil, hated by everyone caught in your shadow?'

'Then you do want to escape your curse,' she said.

'I do!'

'Then give me a chance to conduct this experiment on you.'

He turned away from her. 'I don't deserve your help.'

'Let me be the judge of that.'

'I sacrificed Carolyn. My own flesh and blood. Elizabeth's daughter.'

Julia said, 'Because you couldn't help yourself.'

'Her death is still on my head,' he said, his fists clenched as he was tormented by the thought.

'That is past. We mustn't think about it.'

He looked at her again. 'You're a very generous woman.'

'Not really. But I am a doctor.'

'And?'

'I've sworn an oath to dedicate myself to the healing art and make no exceptions.'

Barnabas, smiling bitterly, quoted the Hippocratic oath: 'I will use treatment to help the sick according to my ability and judgment. But never with a view to injury or wrongdoing. And whatsoever I shall see or hear in the course of my profession, if it be what should not be published abroad, I will never divulge, holding such things to be holy secrets.'

'You have an excellent memory,' she complimented him quietly.

'And so many things to remember,' he said in a sad voice.

'You are a challenge to me. One I cannot resist. I'm confident I will succeed.'

'What if you fail?'

She shrugged. 'You should be no worse off than you are now.'

'You misunderstood me,' he said. 'I'm thinking of what such a failure might do to you, not what its effect would be on me.'

'How interesting,' she said.

'Well?' He waited for her reply.

'I would go on seeking a cure for your condition. I wouldn't be discouraged.'

'I like that,' he said thoughtfully.

'What is your answer?'

He smiled in his melancholy fashion. 'I have not seen the light of day for almost two hundred years! I'm willing to try, Doctor. When do you want to begin?'

It was Julia's wish to begin as soon as she could set up a makeshift lab in the old house, and Barnabas was ready to give her every cooperation. So within a few days they started the experiment. Barnabas became more enthusiastic and hopeful with every passing day. And Julia managed to keep the experiments a secret from all the others at Collinwood.

She came to admire Barnabas more as the treatments went on. She had always felt he was worthy of being saved and now she had become obsessed with this desire. They talked of many things during the successive nights of his treatments. She considered him perhaps the most interesting male she'd ever met.

One night as he sat with his coat off and his sleeve rolled up while Julia prepared a hypodermic needle, he asked her, 'How do you think the experiment is working out?'

She smiled his way. 'There have been a few hopeful results.'

'Can't we rush things?' he pleaded. 'It means so much to me.'

She came and gave him the injection. 'You must be patient. I'll be increasing the dosage as time goes on.'

'How many injections will there be altogether?'

Julia put the hypodermic aside. 'I can't say just yet.'

'You must have some idea?' he insisted.

She considered. 'It may be a matter of months. Perhaps a hundred or more injections.'

'Do you think you can manage to keep your coming here at night from the others that long?' he worried.

'It doesn't matter if they think we're seeing each other, as long as they don't guess why,' she said with a thin smile.

He rolled down his sleeve and put on his jacket. 'Won't Professor Stokes be jealous?' he asked with a twinkle in those deep-set eyes.

She blushed, forgetting for a moment she was a doctor and Barnabas her patient, and she said, 'There is no romance between Professor Stokes and myself.'

'Oh?' he said. 'I was under the impression there was.'

'He is a typical bachelor.'

'You never can be sure,' Barnabas said.

She turned away to work at the improvised arborite counter and in a tight voice told him, 'And many people see me as a typical old maid.'

'Then they are surely wrong,' Barnabas said in a gentle voice. 'You are a dear person whom any man would be glad to marry. I personally dislike the "typical old maid" idea as much as the "typical old bachelor" one. There are no such people. To enter into marriage merely requires meeting the right person. Those who remain single simply haven't met that person.'

Julia turned to him with an amused expression. 'Are you speaking from experience, Barnabas?'

He nodded. 'A long one. More than two hundred years. Don't forget that.'

She laughed. It was a private joke between them. It was good to be able to laugh again. For the time being there were no more nightmare episodes taking place at Collinwood or in the area. The sheriff had not let up in his determination to locate the monster, but most of the ugliness had been relegated to the past. They were all trying to blot out the horror and live with some degree of enjoyment in the present. Julia felt the probable success of her experiment with Barnabas justified this attitude on their parts.

She said, 'You've told me so little about your life and all the adventures you've encountered.'

'Plenty of time for that.'

'Perhaps you will lose your memory of those things as the experiment progresses,' she warned him.

'Much of it would be best forgotten,' he said, his handsome face briefly shadowed.

'I'm sorry,' she said, 'I shouldn't have gone into that.'

'No. It doesn't matter,' Barnabas said. 'What does matter is the possibility that I may be able to go on living here for a normal lifetime and end my days here with a normal death.'

She studied his melancholy yet attractive face. 'That really is terribly important to you, isn't it?'

'After being one of the living dead for two hundred years there is nothing I want more,' Barnabas said. 'I love this place and I'd like to remain here.'

'Let's hope you'll be able to,' Julia said quietly.

'If the experiment fails,' Barnabas said with a furrowed brow, 'I can only hope to go the same way as Carolyn. Better to have it ended with a stake through my heart than to continue as a creature of evil.'

'Will you still think that if I have to break the news that I haven't succeeded?'

He gave her an unhappy look. 'I can't predict my attitude. It is possible I may revert to the vampire state I was in when you first began the treatments. If this should happen, please try to understand. And for my sake do all you can to see that I'm destroyed.'

Touched by his sad desperation, she said, 'I'll do more than that, Barnabas. I'll make sure the others know that you told me this. That they come to understand the sort of man you really are.'

His smile was tinged with bitterness. 'So few of us can be sure of what we are. I don't attempt to say that I know.'

Her eyes were tender as she said, 'I know. And I will tell them if I fail. But I don't want to even think of failure yet. I've never been so confident about an experiment before.'

And Julia meant what she said. In the month that followed she pursued Barnabas' treatment with a fanatical devotion. And it was inevitable that they would come to know each other better and become fonder of each other as time passed. Often, when she'd given him the required injection and made the routine tests afterwards, they would wander out into the night. On certain nights they walked and talked until dawn showed in the sky and it was time for Barnabas to retire to his coffin for the daylight hours.

Julia learned more about the countryside and its history than she had ever known. And Barnabas was becoming increasingly optimistic about his chances of recovering from his vampire state. So preoccupied was he about this that it was doubtful if he was aware of something else that was happening. Julia Hoffman was falling in love with him.

It was one of the beautiful moonlit nights and Barnabas and Julia were strolling back from Widows' Hill. He gave her a warm smile and said, 'This has been one of the most perfect nights of my life.'

She looked up at him with tenderness mirrored on her attractive face. 'I've never felt more content.'

'You've changed,' he told her. 'In your manner you're much more a woman and less a doctor. I approve of that.'

'Thanks to you,' she joked. 'You've passed on some of your old world charm to me.'

'I wish there were more I could do for you,' he said, suddenly serious. 'And I will, if I ever recover. I wish there were some way of expediting the experiment.'

Julia warned him, 'We're proceeding at a very safe pace. Aren't you satisfied with the progress?'

He halted, erect and handsome in the moonlight. 'How can you ask me that? Don't you know how happy you've made me?'

'Have I, Barnabas?' Her tone was soft.

'I feel as though the life I was living is years behind me instead of only a month. It's such a gratifying thing to me not to feel the need for blood.' And as he finished saying this he touched his cold lips gently to her forehead. It was the kiss of a grateful friend, though Julia might have assumed it meant more.

A few nights later after Barnabas received his injection he left Julia to finish up in the lab and went into the drawing room of the old house. There he removed a cleverly designed little music box from a chest and studied it with a sad smile. He touched the lid of the box so that it tinkled out its tune with crystal clarity. And the thin music of the old box took him back many years in thought.

Julia entered from the hallway with her medical bag in hand. 'Isn't it delightful!'

Barnabas beamed at her. 'A family heirloom.'

She smiled. 'I'm glad you're in such a happy mood. I spoke to Professor Stokes today. The fact that there have been no attacks recently has almost convinced him that the vampire has disappeared. And the police have lifted the curfew.'

Barnabas was pleased. 'Julia, I owe it all to you! I don't know how I shall ever be able to thank you.'

She said, 'It would be pointless now, anyway. We must wait until we achieve total success. Where did you get the music box?'

'It was hidden away here,' he said. 'It belonged to someone I knew many years ago.'

Julia listened, enthralled. 'It's very beautiful.'

Barnabas gave her a meaningful smile. 'I intend to give it to someone soon. Someone I love very much.'

Julia felt the rush of warm blood to her cheeks. Speechless and full of hope, she lowered her gaze to the music box quickly.

Return to 'Salem's Lot

STEPHEN KING

The credit for having inspired TV's first straightforward vampire miniseries belongs to Stephen King (1946–), the American writer tagged 'the world's master of horror' whose second novel, 'Salem's Lot (1975), was adapted for the small screen by CBS in 1979. This macabre, imaginative story of a small town in Maine where all the residents begin to disappear after the arrival of a sinister, bald stranger, was directed by Tobe Hooper and starred David Soul as the writer who returns to the scene of his childhood only to find it has become a living hell since the appearance of the mysterious Richard Straker (James Mason). Although by no means the best film adaptation of King's work, 'Salem's Lot did demonstrate that his stories could make good TV, and several of his subsequent vampire stories have also been adapted for filming. The original novel remains one of Stephen's personal favourites and he has also revealed that it was actually based on a real incident. 'In the early 1800's,' he explained a few years back, 'a whole sect of Shakers, a rather strange, religious persuasion at best, disappeared from their village (Jeremiah's Lot) in Vermont: the town remains uninhabited to this day.' The success of the miniseries prompted a sequel, though not for television, but the cinema instead. This was Return to 'Salem's Lot (1987) directed by Larry Cohen for Warner Brothers and starring James Dixon. According to producer Paul Kurta the movie was 'based on characters created by Stephen King' and was inspired by the author's short story, 'One For The Road', also set in 'Salem's Lot. It had been written ten years earlier for the March/April 1977 issue of a small rural publication, the Maine Magazine. The film, it has to be said, was hugely disappointing, one critic even stating that the best it deserved was to have 'a stake driven through it'. Apart from 'One For The Road' King has also written a novella featuring the town entitled 'Jerusalem's Lot' (1976) which although it has not been filmed, has been adapted for audiocassette read by Colin Fox.

Stephen King's interest in the vampire theme was, he says, prompted by reading Dracula – although as a writer he was always determined if he tackled the theme to move the setting from the darker reaches of Europe to the New England countryside where he had grown up and which he knew best. The success of this relocation in 'Salem's Lot – which critic Douglas E. Winter has called, 'the single most influential of King's books upon other writers of horror fiction' – inspired him to use the concept again in a number of his later novels, including Christine (1983), Pet Cemetery (1983) IT (1986) and The Tommy-knockers (1987), as well as in a clutch of short stories, 'The Oracle and the Mountains' (1981), 'Popsy' (1987) and 'The Night Flier' (1988). What most of Stephen's admirers would really like, however, is a book-length sequel to 'Salem's Lot – but at the time of writing he shows no sign of setting about it just yet. In the interim, then, the story below will serve as a reminder of that benchmark novel and the movies it inspired. Not to mention providing a chance to return once again – albeit briefly – to that haunted small town in Maine which is now deep under a snow blizzard but far from inactive . . .

*   *   *

It was a quarter past ten and Herb Tooklander was thinking of closing for the night when the man in the fancy overcoat and the white, staring face burst into Tookey's Bar, which lies in the northern part of Falmouth. It was the tenth of January, just about the time most folks are learning to live comfortably with all the New Year's resolutions they broke, and there was one hell of a northeaster blowing outside. Six inches had come down before dark and it had been going hard and heavy since then. Twice we had seen Billy Larribee go by high in the cab of the town plough, and the second time Tookey ran him out a beer – an act of pure charity my mother would have called it, and my God knows she put down enough of Tookey's beer in her time. Billy told him they were keeping ahead of it on the main road, but the side ones were closed and apt to stay that way until next morning. The radio in Portland was forecasting another foot and a forty-mile-an-hour wind to pile up the drifts.

There was just Tookey and me in the bar, listening to the wind howl around the eaves and watching it dance the fire around on the hearth. 'Have one for the road, Booth,' Tookey says, 'I'm gonna shut her down.'

He poured me one and himself one and that's when the door cracked open and this stranger staggered in, snow up to his shoulders and in his hair, like he had rolled around in confectioner's sugar. The wind billowed a sand-fine sheet of snow in after him.

'Close the door!' Tookey roars at him. 'Was you born in a barn?'

I've never seen a man who looked that scared. He was like a horse that's spent an afternoon eating fire nettles. His eyes rolled toward Tookey and he said, 'My wife – my daughter –' and he collapsed on the floor in a dead faint.

'Holy Joe,' Tookey says. 'Close the door, Booth, would you?'

I went and shut it, and pushing it against the wind was something of a chore. Tookey was down on one knee holding the fellow's head up and patting his cheeks. I got over to him and saw right off that it was nasty. His face was fiery red, but there were grey blotches here and there, and when you've lived through winters in Maine since the time Woodrow Wilson was President, as I have, you know those grey blotches mean frostbite.

'Fainted,' Tookey said. 'Get the brandy off the backbar, will you?'

I got it and came back. Tookey had opened the fellow's coat. He had come around a little; his eyes were half open and he was muttering something too low to catch.

'Pour a capful,' Tookey says.

'Just a cap?' I asks him.

'That stuff's dynamite,' Tookey says. 'No sense overloading his carb.'

I poured out a capful and looked at Tookey. He nodded. 'Straight down the hatch.'

I poured it down. It was a remarkable thing to watch. The man trembled all over and began to cough. His face got redder. His eyelids, which had been at half-mast, flew up like window shades. I was a bit alarmed, but Tookey only sat him up like a big baby and clapped him on the back.

The man started to retch, and Tookey clapped him again.

'Hold onto it,' he says, 'that brandy comes dear.'

The man coughed some more, but it was diminishing now. I got my first good look at him. City fellow, all right, and from somewhere south of Boston, at a guess. He was wearing kid gloves, expensive but thin. There were probably some more of those greyish-white patches on his hands, and he would be lucky not to lose a finger or two. His coat was fancy, all right; a three-hundred-dollar job if ever I'd seen one. He was wearing tiny little boots that hardly came up over his ankles, and I began to wonder about his toes.

'Better,' he said.

'All right,' Tookey said. 'Can you come over to the fire?'

'My wife and my daughter,' he said. 'They're out there . . . in the storm.'

'From the way you came in, I didn't figure they were at home watching the TV,' Tookey said. 'You can tell us by the fire as easy as here on the floor. Hook on, Booth.'

He got to his feet, but a little groan came out of him and his mouth twisted down in pain. I wondered about his toes again, and I wondered why God felt he had to make fools from New York City who would try driving around in southern Maine at the height of a northeast blizzard. And I wondered if his wife and his girl were dressed any warmer than him.

We hiked him across to the fireplace and got him sat down in a rocker that used to be Missus Tookey's favourite until she passed on in '74. It was Missus Tookey that was responsible for most of the place, which had been written up in *Down East* and the *Sunday Telegram* and even once in the Sunday supplement of the Boston *Globe*. It's really more of a public house than a bar, with its big wooden floor, pegged together rather than nailed, the maple bar, the old barn-raftered ceiling, and the monstrous big fieldstone hearth. Missus Tookey started to get some ideas in her head after the *Down East* article came out, wanted to start calling the place Tookey's Inn or Tookey's Rest, and I admit it has sort of a Colonial ring to it, but I prefer plain old Tookey's Bar. It's one thing to get uppish in the summer, when the state's full of tourists, another thing altogether in the winter, when you and your neighbours have to trade together. And there had been plenty of winter nights, like this one, that Tookey and I had spent all alone together, drinking scotch and water or just a few beers. My own Victoria passed on in '73, and Tookey's was a place to go where there were enough voices to mute the steady ticking of the death-watch beetle – even if there was just Tookey and me, it was enough. I wouldn't have felt the same about it if the place had been Tookey's Rest. It's crazy but it's true.

We got this fellow in front of the fire and he got the shakes harder than ever. He hugged onto his knees and his teeth clattered together and a few drops of clear mucus spilled off the end of his nose. I think he was starting to realize that another fifteen minutes out there might have been enough to kill him. It's not the snow, it's the wind-chill factor. It steals your heat.

'Where did you go off the road?' Tookey asked him.

'S-six miles s-s-south of h-here,' he said.

Tookey and I stared at each other, and all of a sudden I felt cold. Cold all over.

'You sure?' Tookey demanded. 'You came six miles through the snow?'

He nodded. 'I checked the odometer when we came through t-town. I was following directions . . . going to see my wife's s-sister . . . in Cumberland . . . never been there before . . . we're from New Jersey . . .'

New Jersey. If there's anyone more purely foolish than a New Yorker it's a fellow from New Jersey.

'Six miles, you're sure?' Tookey demanded.

'Pretty sure, yeah. I found the turnoff but it was drifted in . . . it was . . .'

Tookey grabbed him. In the shifting glow of the fire his face looked pale and stained, older than his sixty-six years by ten. 'You made a right turn?'

'Right turn, yeah. My wife —'

'Did you see a sign?'

'Sign?' He looked up at Tookey blankly and wiped the end of his nose. 'Of course I did. It was on my instructions. Take Jointner Avenue through Jerusalem's Lot to the 295 entrance ramp.' He looked from Tookey to me and back to Tookey again. Outside, the wind whistled and howled and moaned through the eaves. 'Wasn't that right, mister?'

'The Lot,' Tookey said, almost too soft to hear. 'Oh my God.'

'What's wrong?' the man said. His voice was rising. 'Wasn't that right? I mean, the road looked drifted in, but I thought . . . if there's a town there, the ploughs will be out and . . . and then I . . .'

He just sort of tailed off.

'Booth,' Tookey said to me, low. 'Get on the 'phone. Call the sheriff.'

'Sure,' this fool from New Jersey says, 'that's right. What's wrong with you guys, anyway? You look like you saw a ghost.'

Tookey said, 'No ghosts in the Lot, mister. Did you tell them to stay in the car?'

'Sure I did,' he said, sounding injured. 'I'm not crazy.'

Well, you couldn't have proved it by me.

'What's your name?' I asked him. 'For the sheriff.'

'Lumley,' he says. 'Gerald Lumley.'

He started in with Tookey again, and I went across to the telephone. I picked it up and heard nothing but dead silence. I hit the cutoff buttons a couple of times. Still nothing.

I came back. Tookey had poured Gerard Lumley another tot of brandy, and this one was going down him a lot smoother.

'Was he out?' Tookey asked.

'Phone's dead.'

'Hot damn,' Tookey says, and we look at each other. Outside the wind gusted up, throwing snow against the windows.

Lumley looked from Tookey to me and back again.

'Well, haven't either of you got a car?' he asked. The anxiety was back in his voice. 'They've got to run the engine to run the heater. I only had about a quarter of a tank of gas, and it took me an hour and a half to . . . Look, will you *answer* me?' He stood up and grabbed Tookey's shirt.

'Mister,' Tookey says, 'I think your hand just ran away from your brains, there.'

Lumley looked at his hand, at Tookey, then dropped it. 'Maine,' he hissed. He made it sound like a dirty word about somebody's mother. 'All right,' he said. Where's the nearest gas station? They must have a tow truck – '

'Nearest gas station is in Falmouth Centre,' I said. 'That's three miles down the road from here.'

'Thanks,' he said, a bit sarcastic, and headed for the door, buttoning his coat.

'Won't be open, though,' I added.

He turned back slowly and looked at us.

'What are you talking about, old man?'

'He's trying to tell you that the station in the Centre belongs to Billy Larribee and Billy's out driving the plough, you damn fool,' Tookey says patiently. 'Now why don't you come back here and sit down, before you bust a gut?'

He came back, looking dazed and frightened. 'Are you telling me you can't . . . that there isn't . . . ?'

'I ain't telling you nothing,' Tookey says. 'You're doing all the telling, and if you stopped for a minute, we could think this over.'

'What's this town, Jerusalem's Lot?' he asked. 'Why was the road drifted in? And no lights on anywhere?'

I said, 'Jerusalem's Lot burned out two years back.'

'And they never rebuilt?' He looked like he didn't believe it.

'It appears that way,' I said, and looked at Tookey. 'What are we going to do about this?'

'Can't leave them out there,' he said.

I got closer to him. Lumley had wandered away to look out the window into the snowy night.

'What if they've been got at?' I asked.

'That may be,' he said. 'But we don't know it for sure. I've got my Bible on the shelf. You still wear your Pope's medal?'

I pulled the crucifix out of my shirt and showed him. I was born and raised Congregational, but most folks who live around the Lot wear something – crucifix, St Christopher's medal, rosary, something. Because two years ago, in the span of one dark October month, the Lot went bad. Sometimes, late at night, when there were just a few regulars drawn up around Tookey's fire, people would talk it over. Talk around it is more like the truth. You see, people in the Lot started to disappear. First a few, then a few more, then a whole slew. The schools closed. The town stood empty for most of a year. Oh, a few people moved in – mostly damn fools from out of state like this fine specimen here – drawn by the low property values, I suppose. But they didn't last. A lot of them moved out a month or two after they'd moved in. The others . . . well, they disappeared. Then the town burned flat. It was at the end of a long dry fall. They figure it started up by the Marsten House on the hill that overlooked Jointner Avenue, but no one knows how it started, not to this day. It burned out of control for three days. After that, for a time, things were better. And then they started again.

I only heard the word 'vampires' mentioned once. A crazy pulp truck driver named Richie Messina from over Freeport way was in Tookey's that night, pretty well liquored up. 'Jesus Christ,' this stampeder roars, standing up about nine feet tall in his wool pants and his plaid shirt and his leather-topped boots. 'Are you all so damn afraid to say it out? Vampires! That's what you're all thinking, ain't it? Jesus-jumped-up-Christ in a chariot-driven sidecar! Just like a bunch of kids scared of the movies! You know what there is down there in 'Salem's Lot? Want me to tell you? Want me to tell you?'

'Do tell, Richie,' Tookey says. It had got real quiet in the bar. You could hear the fire popping, and outside the soft drift of November rain coming down in the dark. 'You got the floor.'

'What you got over there is your basic wild dog pack,' Richie

Messina tells us. 'That's what you got. That and a lot of old women who love a good spook story. Why, for eighty bucks I'd go up there and spend the night in what's left of that haunted house you're all so worried about. Well, what about it? Anyone want to put it up?'

But nobody would. Richie was a loudmouth and a mean drunk and no one was going to shed any tears at his wake, but none of us were willing to see him go into 'Salem's Lot after dark.

'Be screwed to the bunch of you,' Richie says. 'I got my four-ten in the truck of my Chevy, and that'll stop anything in Falmouth, Cumberland, *or* Jerusalem's Lot. And that's where I'm goin'.'

He slammed out of the bar and no one said a word for a while. Then Lamont Henry says, real quiet, 'That's the last time anyone's gonna see Richie Messina. Holy God.' And Lamont, raised to be a Methodist from his mother's knee, crossed himself.

'He'll sober off and change his mind,' Tookey said, but he sounded uneasy. 'He'll be back by closin' time, makin' out it was all a joke.'

But Lamont had the right of that one, because no one ever saw Richie again. His wife told the state cops she thought he'd gone to Florida to beat a collection agency, but you could see the truth of the thing in her eyes – sick, scared eyes. Not long after, she moved away to Rhode Island. Maybe she thought Richie was going to come after her some dark night. And I'm not the man to say he might not have done.

Now Tookey was looking at me and I was looking at Tookey as I stuffed my crucifix back into my shirt. I never felt so old or so scared in my life.

Tookey said again, 'We can't just leave them out there, Booth.'

'Yeah. I know.'

We looked at each at each other for a moment longer, and then he reached out and gripped my shoulder. 'You're a good man, Booth.' That was enough to buck me up some. It seems like when you pass seventy, people start forgetting that you are a man, or that you ever were.

Tookey walked over to Lumley and said, 'I've got a four-wheel-drive Scout. I'll get it out.'

'For God's sake, man, why didn't you say so before?' He had whirled around from the window and was staring angrily at Tookey. 'Why'd you have to spend ten minutes beating around the bush?'

Tookey said, very softly, 'Mister, you shut your jaw. And if you get urge to open it, you remember who made that turn onto an unploughed road in the middle of a goddamned blizzard.'

He started to say something, and then shut his mouth. Thick colour

had risen up in his cheeks. Tookey went out to get his Scout out of
the garage. I felt around under the bar for his chrome flask and filled
it full of brandy. Figured we might need it before this night was over.

Maine blizzard – ever been out in one?

The snow comes flying so thick and fine that it looks like sand and
sounds like that, beating on the sides of your car or pickup. You
don't want to use your high beams because they reflect off the snow
and you can't see ten feet in front of you. With the low beams on, you
can see maybe fifteen feet. But I can live with the snow. It's the wind I
don't like, when it picks up and begins to howl, driving the snow into
a hundred weird flying shapes and sounding like all the hate and pain
and fear in the world. There's death in the throat of a snowstorm
wind, white death – and maybe something beyond death. That's no
sound to hear when you're tucked up all cosy in your own bed with
the shutters bolted and the doors locked. It's that much worse if
you're driving. And we were driving smack into 'Salem's Lot.

'Hurry up a little, can't you?' Lumley asked.

I said, 'For a man who came in half frozen, you're in one hell of a
hurry to end up walking again.'

He gave me a resentful, baffled look and didn't say anything else.
We were moving up the highway at a steady twenty-five miles an
hour. It was hard to believe that Billy Larribee had just ploughed this
stretch an hour ago; another two inches had covered it, and it was
drifting in. The strongest gusts of wind rocked the Scout on her
springs. The headlights showed a swirling white nothing up ahead of
us. We hadn't met a single car.

About ten minutes later Lumley gasps: 'Hey! What's that?'

He was pointing out my side of the car; I'd been looking dead
ahead. I turned, but was a shade too late. I thought I could see some
sort of slumped form fading back from the car, back into the snow,
but that could have been imagination.

'What was it? A deer?' I asked.

'I guess so,' he says, sounding shaky. 'But its eyes – they looked
red.' He looked at me. 'Is that how a deer's eyes look at night?' He
sounded almost as if he were pleading.

'They can look like anything,' I says, thinking that might be true,
but I've seen a lot of deer at night from a lot of cars, and never saw
any set of eyes reflect back red.

Tookey didn't say anything.

About fifteen minutes later, we came to a place where the
snowbank on the right of the road wasn't so high because the

ploughs are supposed to raise their blades a little when they go through an intersection.

'This looks like where we turned,' Lumley said, not sounding too sure about it. 'I don't see the sign – '

'This is it,' Tookey answered. He didn't sound like himself at all. 'You can just see the top of the signpost.'

'Oh. Sure.' Lumley sounded relieved. 'Listen, Mr Tooklander, I'm sorry about being so short back there. I was cold and worried and calling myself two hundred kinds of fool. And I want to thank you both – '

'Don't thank Booth and me until we've got them in this car,' Tookey said. He put the Scout in four-wheel drive and slammed his way through the snowbank and onto Jointner Avenue, which goes through the Lot and out to 295. Snow flew up from the mudguards. The rear end tried to break a little bit, but Tookey's been driving through snow since Hector was a pup. He jockeyed it a bit, talked to it, and on we went. The headlights picked out the bare indication of other tyre tracks from time to time, the ones made by Lumley's car, and then they would disappear again. Lumley was leaning forward, looking for his car. And all at once Tookey said, 'Mr Lumley.'

'What?' He looked around at Tookey.

'People around these parts are kind of superstitious about 'Salem's Lot,' Tookey says, sounding easy enough – but I could see the deep lines of strain around his mouth, and the way his eyes kept moving from side to side. 'If your people are in the car, why, that's fine. We'll pack them up, go back to my place, and tomorrow, when the storm's over, Billy will be glad to yank your car out of the snowbank. But if they're not in the car – '

'Not in the car?' Lumley broke in sharply. 'Why wouldn't they be in the car?'

'If they're not in the car,' Tookey goes on, not answering, 'we're going to turn around and drive back to Falmouth Centre and whistle for the sheriff. Makes no sense to go wallowing around at night in a snowstorm anyway, does it?'

'They'll be in the car. Where else would they be?'

I said, 'One other thing, Mr Lumley. If we should see anybody, we're not going to talk to them. Not even if they talk to us. You understand that?'

Very slow, Lumley says, 'Just what are these superstitions?'

Before I could say anything – God alone knows what I would have said – Tookey broke in. 'We're there.'

We were coming up on the back end of a big Mercedes. The whole hood of the thing was buried in a snowdrift, and another drift had socked in the whole left side of the car. But the taillights were on and we could see exhaust drifting out of the tail-pipe.

'They didn't run out of gas, anyway,' Lumley said.

Tookey pulled up and pulled on the Scout's emergency brake. 'You remember what Booth told you, Lumley.'

'Sure, sure.' But he wasn't thinking of anything but his wife and daughter. I don't see how anybody could blame him, either.

'Ready, Booth?' Tookey asked me. His eyes held on mine, grim and grey in the dashboard lights.

'I guess I am,' I said.

We all got out and the wind grabbed us, throwing snow in our faces. Lumley was first, bending into the wind, his fancy topcoat billowing out behind him like a sail. He cast two shadows, one from Tookey's headlights, the other from his own taillights. I was behind him, and Tookey was a step behind me. When I got to the trunk of the Mercedes, Tookey grabbed me.

'Let him go,' he said.

'Janey! Francie!' Lumley yelled. 'Everything okay?' He pulled open the driver's-side and leaned in. 'Everything – '

He froze to a dead stop. The wind ripped the heavy door right out of his hand and pushed it all the way open.

'Holy God, Booth,' Tookey said, just below the scream of the wind. 'I think it's happened again.'

Lumley turned back toward us. His face was scared and bewildered, his eyes wide. All of a sudden he lunged towards us through the snow, slipping and almost falling. He brushed me away like I was nothing and grabbed Tookey.

'How did you know?' he roared. 'Where are they? What the hell is going on here?'

Tookey broke his grip and shoved past him. He and I looked into the Mercedes together. Warm as toast it was, but it wasn't going to be for much longer. The little amber low-fuel light was glowing. The big car was empty. There was a child's Barbie doll on the passenger's floormat. And a child's ski parka was crumpled over the seatback.

Tookey put his hands over his face . . . and then he was gone. Lumley had grabbed him and shoved him right back into the snowbank. His face was pale and wild. His mouth was working as if he had chewed down on some bitter stuff he couldn't yet unpucker enough to spit out. He reached in and grabbed the parka.

'Francie's coat?' he kind of whispered. And then loud, bellowing: '*Francie's coat!*' He turned around, holding it in front of him by the little fur-trimmed hood. He looked at me, blank and unbelieving. 'She can't be out without her coat on, Mr Booth. Why . . . why . . . she'll freeze to death.'

'Mr Lumley – '

He blundered past me, still holding the parka, shouting: '*Francie! Janey! Where are you? Where are youuu?*'

I gave Tookey my hand and pulled him onto his feet. 'Are you all – '

'Never mind me,' he says. 'We've got to get hold of him, Booth.'

We went after him as fast as we could, which wasn't very fast with the snow hip-deep in some places. But then he stopped and we caught up to him.

'Mr Lumley – ' Tookey started, laying a hand on his shoulder.

'This way,' Lumley said. 'This is the way they went. Look!'

We looked down. We were in a kind of dip here, and most of the wind went right over our heads. And you could see two sets of tracks, one large and one small, just filling up with snow. If we had been five minutes later, they would have been gone.

He started to walk away, his head down, and Tookey grabbed him back. 'No! No, Lumley!'

Lumley turned his wild face up to Tookey's and made a fist. He drew it back . . . but something in Tookey's face made him falter. He looked from Tookey to me and then back again.

'She'll freeze,' he said, as if we were a couple of stupid kids. 'Don't you get it? She doesn't have her jacket on and she's only seven years old – '

'They could be anywhere,' Tookey said. 'You can't follow those tracks. They'll be gone in the next drift.'

'What do you suggest?' Lumley yells, his voice high and hysterical. 'If we go back to get the police, she'll freeze to death! Francie *and* my wife!'

'They may be frozen already,' Tookey said. His eyes caught Lumley's. 'Frozen, or something worse.'

'What do you mean?' Lumley whispered. 'Get it straight, goddamn it! Tell me!'

'Mr Lumley,' Tookey says, 'there's something in the Lot – '

But I was the one who came out with it finally, said the word I never expected to say. 'Vampires, Mr Lumley. Jerusalem's Lot is full of vampires. I expect that's hard for you to swallow – '

He was staring at me as if I'd gone green. 'Loonies,' he whispers.

'You're a couple of loonies.' Then he turned away, cupped his hands around his mouth, and bellowed, '*FRANCIE! JANEY!*' He started floundering off again. The snow was up to the hem of his fancy coat.

I looked at Tookey. 'What do we do now?'

'Follow him,' Tookey says. His hair was plastered with snow, and he *did* look a little bit loony. 'I can't just leave him out here, Booth. Can you?'

'No,' I says. 'Guess not.'

So we started to wade through the snow after Lumley as best we could. But he kept getting further and further ahead. He had his youth to spend, you see. He was breaking the trail, going through that snow like a bull. My arthritis began to bother me something terrible, and I started to look down at my legs, telling myself: A little further, just a little further, keep goin', damn it, keep goin' . . .

I piled right into Tookey, who was standing spread-legged in a drift. His head was hanging and both of his hands were pressed to his chest.

'Tookey,' I says, 'you okay?'

'I'm all right,' he said, taking his hands away. 'We'll stick with him, Booth, and when he fags out he'll see reason.'

We topped a rise and there was Lumley at the bottom, looking desperately for more tracks. Poor man, there wasn't a chance he was going to find them. The wind blew straight across down there where he was, and any tracks would have been rubbed out three minutes after they was made, let alone a couple of hours.

He raised his head and screamed into the night: '*FRANCIE! JANEY! FOR GOD'S SAKE!*' And you could hear the desperation in his voice, the terror, and pity him for it. The only answer he got was the freight-train wail of the wind. It almost seemed to be laughin' at him, saying: *I took them Mister New Jersey with your fancy car and camel's-hair topcoat. I took them and I rubbed out their tracks and by morning I'll have them just as neat and frozen as two strawberries in a deepfreeze* . . .

'Lumley!' Tookey bawled over the wind. 'Listen, you never mind vampires or boogies or nothing like that, but you mind this! You're just making it worse for them! We got to get the –'

And then there *was* an answer, a voice coming out of the dark like little tinkling silver bells, and my heart turned cold as ice in a cistern.

'*Jerry . . . Jerry, is that you?*'

Lumley wheeled at the sound. And then *she* came, drifting out of the dark shadows of a little copse of trees like a ghost. She was a city woman, all right, and right then she seemed like the most beautiful woman I had ever seen. I felt like I wanted to go to her and tell her how glad I was she was safe after all. She was wearing a heavy green pullover sort of thing, a poncho, I believe they're called. It floated all around her, and her dark hair streamed out in the wild wind like water in a December creek, just before the winter freeze stills it and locks it in.

Maybe I did take a step toward her, because I felt Tookey's hand on my shoulder, rough and warm. And still – how can I say it? – I *yearned* after her, so dark and beautiful with that green poncho floating around her neck and shoulders, as exotic and strange as to make you think of some beautiful woman from a Walter de la Mare poem.

'Janey!' Lumley cried. '*Janey!*' He began to struggle through the snow toward her, his arms outstretched.

'No!' Tookey cried. '*No, Lumley!*'

He never even looked . . . but she did. She looked up at us and grinned. And when she did, I felt my longing, my yearning turn to horror as cold as the grave, as white and silent as bones in a shroud. Even from the rise we could see the sullen red glare in those eyes. They were less human than a wolf's eyes. And when she grinned you could see how long her teeth had become. She wasn't human anymore. She was a dead thing somehow come back to life in this black howling storm.

Tookey made the sign of the cross at her. She flinched back . . . and then grinned at us again. We were too far away, and maybe too scared.

'Stop it!' I whispered. 'Can't we stop it?'

'Too late, Booth!' Tookey says grimly.

Lumley had reached her. He looked like a ghost himself, coated in snow like he was. He reached for her . . . and then he began to scream. I'll hear that sound in my dreams, that man screaming like a child in a nightmare. He tried to back away from her, but her arms, long and bare and as white as the snow, snaked out and pulled him to her. I could see her cock her head and then thrust it forward –

'Booth!' Tookey said hoarsely. 'We've got to get out of here!'

And so we ran. Ran like rats, I suppose some would say, but those who would weren't there at night. We fled back down along our own backtrail, falling down, getting up again, slipping and sliding. I kept looking back over my shoulder to see if that woman was coming after us, grinning that grin and watching us with those red eyes.

We got back to the Scout and Tookey doubled over, holding his chest. 'Tookey!' I said, badly scared. 'What – '

'Ticker,' he said. 'Been bad for five years or more. Get me around in the shotgun seat, Booth, and then get us the hell out of here.'

I hooked an arm under his coat and dragged him around and somehow boosted him up and in. He leaned his head back and shut his eyes. His skin was waxy-looking and yellow.

I went back around the hood of the truck at a trot, and I damned near ran into the little girl. She was just standing there beside the driver's-side door, her hair in pigtails, wearing nothing but a little bit of a yellow dress.

'Mister,' she said in a high, clear voice, as sweet as morning mist, 'won't you help me find my mother? She's gone and I'm so cold – '

'Honey,' I said, 'honey, you better get in the truck. Your mother's – '

I broke off, and if there was ever a time in my life I was close to swooning, that was the moment. She was standing there, you see, but she was standing *on top* of the snow and there were no tracks, not in any direction.

She looked up at me then, Lumley's daughter Francie. She was no more than seven years old, and she was going to be seven for an eternity of nights. Her little face was a ghastly corpse white, her eyes a red and silver that you could fall into. And below her jaw I could see two small punctures like pinpricks, their edges horribly mangled.

She held out her arms at me and smiled. 'Pick me up, mister,' she said softly. 'I want to give you a kiss. Then you can take me to my mommy.'

I didn't want to, but there was nothing I could do. I was leaning forward, my arms outstretched. I could see her mouth opening, I could see the little fangs inside the pink ring of her lips. Something slipped down her chin, bright and silvery, and with a dim, distant, faraway horror, I realized she was drooling.

Her small hands clasped themselves around my neck and I was thinking: Well, maybe it won't be so bad, not so bad, maybe it won't be so awful after a while – when something black flew out of the Scout and struck her on the chest. There was a puff of strange-smelling smoke, a flashing glow that was gone an instant later, and then she was backing away, hissing. Her face was twisted into a vulpine mask of rage, hate, and pain. She turned sideways and then . . . and then she was gone. One moment she was there, and the next there was a twisting knot of snow that looked a little bit like a human shape. Then the wind tattered it away across the fields.

'Booth!' Tookey whispered. 'Be quick, now!'

And I was. But not so quick that I didn't have time to pick up what he had thrown at that little girl from hell. His mother's Douay Bible.

*

That was some time ago. I'm a sight older now, and I was no chicken then. Herb Tooklander passed on two years ago. He went peaceful, in the night. The bar is still there, some man and his wife from Waterville bought it, nice people, and they've kept it pretty much the same. But I don't go by much. It's different somehow with Tookey gone.

Things in the Lot go on pretty much as they always have. The sheriff found that fellow Lumley's car the next day, out of gas, the battery dead. Neither Tookey nor I said anything about it. What would have been the point? And every now and then a hitchhiker or a camper will disappear around there someplace, up on Schoolyard Hill or out near the Harmony Hill cemetery. They'll turn up the fellow's packsack or a paperback book all swollen and bleached out by the rain or snow, or some such. But never the people.

I still have bad dreams about that stormy night we went out there. Not about the woman so much as the little girl, and the way she smiled when she held her arms up so I could pick her up. So she could give me a kiss. But I'm an old man and the time comes soon when dreams are done.

You may have an occasion to be travelling in southern Maine yourself one of these days. Pretty part of the countryside. You may even stop by Tookey's Bar for a drink. Nice place. They kept the name just the same. So have your drink, and then my advice to you is to keep right on moving north. Whatever you do, don't go up that road to Jerusalem's Lot.

Especially not after dark.

There's a little girl somewhere out there. And I think she's still waiting for her good-night kiss.

Interview With The Vampire

ANNE RICE

The international success of Francis Ford Coppola's version of Bram Stoker's Dracula *(1993) starring Gary Oldman as the Count, Winona Ryder as Mina and Anthony Hopkins as the indefatigable Van Helsing, shows every sign of launching a whole new cycle of vampire pictures. Indeed, Coppola had already announced a sequel to his box office triumph entitled* The Van Helsing Chronicles *which will see Anthony Hopkins reprising his role in an original story told from the vampire hunter's point of view; while Neil Jordan, the director of* The Company of Wolves *(1984) and* The Crying Game *(1993), has scored as big a hit with* Interview With The Vampire *starring Tom Cruise and Brad Pitt. This is based on the best-selling novel of the same name by Anne Rice which has itself been the inspiration for several more novels about its central character, a charismatic vampire called Lestat, played by Tom Cruise in the film. (A co-star in the movie was to have been River Phoenix the highly acclaimed young American actor who died of a drug overdose in October 1993 just before filming was due to begin in New Orleans.)*

Lestat is unlike any other vampire to be found in fiction: a merciless, sadistic eighteenth-century member of the undead who, 200 years later, has found life in modern America much more conducive to his taste in victims. He has, however, spared one man, Louis, whom he has turned into a vampire and now shares his secrets. It is this Louis who relates their story to a young chronicler in the novel. The exploits of this pair and their associates are being continued in a series of novels entitled The Vampire Chronicles *which began with* Interview With The Vampire *(1976) and have continued in* The Vampire Lestat

(1985), The Tale of the Body Thief *(1992) and* Queen of the Damned *(1988). The enormous popularity of the saga already promises to ensure Lestat a reputation as international as that of Dracula himself. The originality of the books is a tribute to the ingenuity of their creator, Anne Rice (1941–), who was born and brought up in New Orleans and has used the scenes of the American South as the background to the stories, as well as drawing on her Roman Catholic upbringing to explore the religious and moral elements of vampirism. As one of her admirers, Patricia Skarda, the author of* The Evil Image: Two Centuries of Gothic Short Fiction and Poetry *(1986) has pointed out, 'The sadism of Rice's novels places her in the decadent tradition of horror fiction, where mutilation and death take on a mystical glory. Their historical settings, however, demonstrate her careful research and her protagonists' psychological torments usually overpower the violence inflicted and received.' What Anne Rice has done is to give the vampire legend a whole new dimension by exploring the psyche of the undead, and in the following extract from* Interview *dispels some of the longest-held beliefs about those who must have the blood of life to ensure their undead existence. Her vision promises much for the future of the vampire in both fiction and on the cinema screen . . .*

*   *   *

'You want to know how it happened, how I became a vampire.'
'Yes,' said the boy. 'How did you change, exactly?'
'I can't tell you exactly,' said the vampire. 'I can tell you about it, enclose it with words that will make the value of it to me evident to you. But I can't tell you exactly, any more than I could tell you exactly what is the experience of sex if you have never had it.'

The young man seemed struck suddenly with still another question, but before he could speak the vampire went on. 'As I told you, this vampire Lestat, wanted the plantation. A mundane reason, surely, for granting me a life which will last until the end of the world; but he was not a very discriminating person. He didn't consider the world's small population of vampires as being a select club, I should say. He had human problems, a blind father who did not know his son was a vampire and must not find out. Living in New Orleans had become too difficult for him, considering his needs and the necessity to care for his father, and he wanted Pointe du Lac.

'We went at once to the plantation the next evening, ensconced the blind father in the master bedroom, and I proceeded to make the change. I cannot say that it consisted if any one step really – though one, of course, was the step beyond which I could make no return. But there were several acts involved, and the first was the death of the overseer. Lestat took him in his sleep. I was to watch and to approve; that is, to witness the taking of a human life as proof of my commitment and part of my change. This proved without doubt the most difficult part for me. I've told you I had no fear regarding my own death, only a squeamishness about taking my life myself. But I had a most high regard for the life of others, and a horror of death most recently developed because of my brother. I had to watch the overseer awake with a start, try to throw off Lestat with both hands, fail, then lie there struggling under Lestat's grasp, and finally go limp, drained of blood. And die. He did not die at once. We stood in his narrow bedroom for the better part of an hour watching him die. Part of my change, as I said. Lestat would never have stayed otherwise. Then it was necessary to get rid of the overseer's body. I was almost sick from this. Weak and feverish already, I had little reserve; and handling the dead body with such a purpose caused me nausea. Lestat was laughing, telling me callously that I would feel so different once I was a vampire that I would laugh, too. He was wrong about that. I never laugh at death, no matter how often and regularly I am the cause of it.

'But let me take things in order. We had to drive up the river road until we came to open fields and leave the overseer there. We tore his coat, stole his money, and saw to it his lips were stained with liquor. I knew his wife, who lived in New Orleans, and knew the state of desperation she would suffer when the body was discovered. But more than sorrow for her, I felt pain that she would never know what had happened, that her husband had not been found drunk on the road by robbers. As we beat the body, bruising the face and the shoulders, I became more and more aroused. Of course, you must realize that all this time the vampire Lestat was extraordinary. He was no more human to me than a biblical angel. But under this pressure, my enchantment with him was strained. I had seen my becoming a vampire in two lights: The first light was simply enchantment; Lestat had overwhelmed me on my deathbed. But the other light was my wish for self-destruction. My desire to be thoroughly damned. This was the open door through which Lestat had come on both the first and second occasion. Now I was not destroying myself but someone else. The overseer, his wife, his family. I recoiled and might have fled from Lestat, my sanity thoroughly shattered, had not he sensed with an infallible instinct what was happening. Infallible instinct . . .' The vampire mused. 'Let me say the powerful instinct of a vampire to whom even the slightest change in a human's facial expression is as apparent as a gesture. Lestat had preternatural timing. He rushed me into the carriage and whipped the horses home. "I want to die," I began to murmur. "This is unbearable. I want to die. You have it in your power to kill me. Let me die." I refused to look at him, to be spellbound by the sheer beauty of his appearance. He spoke my name to me softly, laughing. As I said, he was determined to have the plantation.'

'But would he have let you go?' asked the boy. 'Under any circumstances?'

'I don't know. Knowing Lestat as I do now, I would say he would have killed me rather than let me go. But this was what I wanted, you see. It didn't matter. No, this was what I thought I wanted. As soon as we reached the house, I jumped down out of the carriage and walked, a zombie, to the brick stairs where my brother had fallen. The house had been unoccupied for months now, the overseer having his own cottage, and the Louisiana heat and damp were already picking apart the steps. Every crevice was sprouting grass and even small wild-flowers. I remember feeling the moisture which in the night was cool as I sat down on the lower steps and even rested my head against the brick and felt the little wax-stemmed wildflowers with my hands. I pulled a clump of them out of the easy dirt in one hand. "I want to die; kill me. Kill me," I said to the vampire. "Now I am guilty of murder. I can't live." He sneered with the impatience of people listening to the obvious lies of others. And then in a flash he fastened on me just as he had on my man. I thrashed against him wildly. I dug my boot into his chest and kicked him as fiercely as I could, his teeth stinging my throat, the fever pounding in my temples. And with a movement of his entire body, much too fast for me to see, he was suddenly standing disdainfully at the foot of the steps. "I thought you wanted to die, Louis," he said.'

The boy made a soft, abrupt sound when the vampire said his name which the vampire acknowledged with the quick statement, 'Yes, that is my name,' and went on.

'Well, I lay there helpless in the face of my own cowardice and fatuousness again,' he said. 'Perhaps so directly confronted with it, I might in time have gained the courage to truly take my life, not to whine and beg for others to take it. I saw myself turning on a knife then, languishing in a day-to-day suffering which I found as necessary as penance from the confessional, truly hoping death would find me unawares and render me fit for eternal pardon. And also I saw myself as if in a vision standing at the head of the stairs, just where my brother had stood, and then hurtling my body down on the bricks.

'But there was no time for courage. Or shall I say, there was no time in Lestat's plan for anything but his plan. "Now listen to me, Louis," he said, and he lay down beside me now on the steps, his movement so graceful and so personal that at once it made me think of a lover. I recoiled. But he put his right arm around me and pulled me close to his chest. Never had I been this close to him before, and in the dim light I could see the magnificent radiance of his eye and the unnatural mask of his skin. As I tried to move, he pressed his right fingers against my lips and said, "Be still. I am going to drain you now to the very threshold of death, and I want you to be quiet, so quiet that you can almost hear the flow of blood through your veins, so quiet that you can hear the flow of that same blood through mine. It is your conscious-ness, your will, which must keep you alive." I wanted to struggle, but he pressed so hard with his fingers that he held my entire prone body in check; and as soon as I stopped my abortive attempt at rebellion, he sank his teeth into my neck.'

The boy's eyes grew huge. He had drawn farther and farther back in his chair as the vampire spoke, and now his face was tense, his eyes narrow, as if he were preparing to weather a blow.

'Have you ever lost a great amount of blood?' asked the vampire. 'Do you know the feeling?'

The boy's lips shaped the word *no*, but no sound came out. He cleared his throat. 'No,' he said.

'Candles burned in the upstairs parlour, where we had planned the death of the overseer. An oil lantern swayed in the breeze on the gallery. All of this light coalesced and began to shimmer, as though a golden presence hovered above me, suspended in the stairwell, softly entangled with the railings, curling and contracting like smoke. "Listen, keep your eyes wide," Lestat whispered to me, his lips moving against my neck. I remember that the movement of his lips raised the hair all over my body, sent a shock of sensation through my body that was not unlike the pleasure of passion. . . .'

He mused, his right fingers slightly curled beneath his chin, the first finger appearing to lightly stroke it. 'The result was that within minutes I was weak to paralysis. Panic-stricken, I discovered I could not even will myself to speak. Lestat still held me, of course, and his arm was like the weight of an iron bar. I felt his teeth withdraw with such a keenness that the two puncture wounds seemed enormous, lined with pain. And now he bent over my helpless head and, taking his right hand off me, bit his own wrist. The blood flowed down upon my shirt and coat, and he watched it with a narrow, gleaming eye. It seemed an eternity that he watched it, and that shimmer of light now hung behind his head like the backdrop of an apparition. I think that I knew what he meant to do even before he did it, and I was waiting in my helplessness as if I'd been waiting for years. He pressed his bleeding wrist to my mouth, said firmly, a little impatiently, "Louis, drink." And I did. "Steady, Louis," and "Hurry," he whispered to me a number times. I drank, sucking the blood out of the holes, experiencing for the first time since infancy the special pleasure of sucking nourishment, the body focused with the mind upon one vital source. Then something happened.' The vampire sat back, a slight frown on his face.

'How pathetic it is to describe these things which can't truly be described,' he said, his voice low almost to a whisper. The boy sat as if frozen.

'I saw nothing but that light then as I drew blood And then this next thing, this next thing was . . . sound. A dull roar at first and then a pounding like the pounding of a drum, growing louder and louder, as if some enormous creature were coming up on one slowly through a dark and alien forest, pounding as he came, a huge drum. And then there came the pounding of another drum, as if another giant were coming yards behind him, and each giant, intent on his own drum, gave no notice to the rhythm of the other. The sound grew louder and louder until it seemed to fill not just my hearing but all my senses, to be throbbing in my lips and fingers, in the flesh of my temples, in my veins. Above all, in my veins, drum and then the other drum; and then Lestat pulled his wrist free suddenly, and I opened my eyes and checked myself in a moment of reaching for his wrist, grabbing it, forcing it back to my mouth at all costs; I checked myself because I realized that the drum was my heart, and the second drum had been his.' The vampire sighed. 'Do you understand?'

The boy began to speak, and then he shook his head. 'No . . . I mean, I do,' he said. 'I mean, I . . .'

'Of course,' said the vampire, looking away.

'Wait, wait!' said the boy in a welter of excitement. 'The tape is almost gone. I have to turn it over.' The vampire watched patiently as he changed it.

'What happened then?' the boy asked. His face was moist, and he wiped it hurriedly with his handkerchief.

'I saw as a vampire,' said the vampire, his voice now slightly detached. It seemed almost distracted. Then he drew himself up. 'Lestat was standing again at the foot of the stairs, and I saw him as I could not possibly have seen him before. He had seemed white to me before, starkly white, so that in the night he was almost luminous, and now I saw him filled with his own life and own blood: he was radiant, not luminous. And then I saw that not only Lestat had changed, but all things had changed.

'It was as if I had only just been able to see colours and shapes for the first time. I was so enthralled with the buttons on Lestat's black coat that I looked at nothing else for a long time. Then Lestat began to laugh, and I heard his laughter as I had never heard anything before. His heart I still heard like the beating of a drum, and now came this metallic laughter. It was confusing, each sound running into the next sound, like the mingling reverberations of bells, until I learned to separate the sounds, and then they overlapped, each soft but distinct, increasing but discrete, peals of laughter.' The vampire smiled with delight. 'Peals of bells.

' "Stop looking at my buttons," Lestat said. "Go out there into the trees. Rid yourself of all the human waste in your body, and don't fall so madly in love with the night that you lose your way!"

'That, of course, was a wise command. When I saw the moon on the flagstones, I became so enamoured with it that I must have spent an hour there. I passed my brother's oratory without so much as a thought of him, and standing among the cottonwood and oaks, I heard the night as if it were a chorus of whispering women, all beckoning me to their breasts. As for my body, it was not yet totally converted, and as soon as I became the least accustomed to the sounds and sights, it began to ache. All my human fluids were being forced out of me. I was dying as a human, yet completely alive as a vampire; and with my awakened senses, I had to preside over the death of my body with a certain discomfort and then, finally, fear. I ran back up the steps to the parlour, where Lestat was already at work on the plantation papers, going over the expenses and profits for the last year. "You're a rich man," he said to me when I came in. "Something's happening to me," I shouted.

' "You're dying, that's all; don't be a fool. Don't you have any oil lamps? All this money and you can't afford whale oil except for that lantern. Bring me that lantern."

' "Dying!" I shouted. "Dying!"

' "It happens to everyone," he persisted, refusing to help me. As I look back on this, I still despise him for it. Not because I was afraid, but because he might have drawn my attention to these changes with reverence. He might have calmed me and told me I might watch my death with the same fascination with which I had watched and felt the night. But he didn't. Lestat was never the vampire I am. Not at all.' The vampire did not say this boastfully. He said it as if he would truly have had it otherwise.

'*Alors*,' he sighed. 'I was dying fast, which meant that my capacity for fear was diminishing as rapidly. I simply regret I was not more attentive to the process. Lestat was being a perfect idiot. "Oh, for the love of hell!" he began shouting. "Do you realize I've made no provision for you? What a fool I am." I was tempted to say, "Yes, you are," but I didn't. "You'll have to bed down with me this morning. I haven't prepared you a coffin." '

The vampire laughed. 'The coffin struck such a chord of terror in me I think it absorbed all the capacity for terror I had left. Then came only my mild alarm at having to share a coffin with Lestat. He was in his father's bedroom meantime, telling the old man good-bye, that he would return in the morning. "But where do you go, why must you live by such a schedule!" the old man demanded, and Lestat became impatient. Before this, he'd been gracious to the old man, almost to the point of sickening one, but now he became a bully. "I take care of you, don't I? I've put a better roof over your head than you ever put over mine! If I want to sleep all day and drink all night, I'll do it, damn you!" The old man started to whine. Only my peculiar state of emotions and most unusual feeling of exhaustion kept me from disapproving. I was watching the scene through the open door, enthralled with the colours of the counterpane and the positive riot of colour in the old man's face. His blue veins pulsed beneath his pink and greyish flesh. I found even the yellow of his teeth appealing to me, and I became almost hypnotized by the quivering of his lip. "Such a son, such a son," he said, never suspecting, of course, the true nature of his son. "All right, then, go. I know you keep a woman somewhere; you go to see her as soon as her husband leaves in the morning. Give me my rosary. What's happened to my rosary?" Lestat said something blasphemous and gave him the rosary. . . .'

'But . . .' the boy started.

'Yes?' said the vampire. 'I'm afraid I don't allow you to ask enough questions.'

'I was going to ask, rosaries have crosses on them, don't they?'

'Oh, the rumour about crosses!' the vampire laughed. 'You refer to our being afraid of crosses?'

'Unable to look on them, I thought,' said the boy.

'Nonsense, my friend, sheer nonsense. I can look on anything I like. And I rather like looking on crucifixes in particular.'

'And what about the rumour about keyholes? That you can . . . become steam and go through them.'

'I wish I could,' laughed the vampire. 'How positively delightful. I should like to pass through all manner of different keyholes and feel the tickle of their peculiar shapes. No.' He shook his head. 'That is, how would you say today . . . bullshit?'

The boy laughed despite himself. Then his face grew serious.

'You mustn't be so shy with me,' the vampire said. 'What is it?'

'The story about stakes through the heart,' said the boy, his cheeks colouring slightly.

'The same,' said the vampire. 'Bull-shit,' he said, carefully articulating both syllables, so that the boy smiled. 'No magical power whatsoever.'

III
The Archetypes

Uncle Vlad

CLIVE SINCLAIR

When, almost a century ago, Bram Stoker began to research information in the British Museum for his projected novel about vampires, one of the first entries he came across under Romanian folklore concerned a historical figure with the intriguing name of Vlad the Impaler, better known as 'Dracul'. And in the subsequent books and documents which he consulted about this fifteenth-century warlord, Stoker undoubtedly found a model for his King of Vampires, Count Dracula. Vlad was in truth, though, a man whose cruelty and blood-lust far surpassed anything that Bram Stoker subsequently used in his novel. He was born Vlad Tepes Dracula about 1431, the second son of Vlad II – better known as 'Dracul' – and ruled the unsettled nation of Wallachia from 1448 to the time of his assassination in 1476. From an early age his motto was 'It is better to be feared than loved' and he set about subjugating both his own people and his enemies with the same utmost ruthlessness. According to some accounts it is said that Vlad killed between 40,000 and 100,000 people during his short lifetime, the majority of them Turks. He apparently earned his infamous nickname from his practice of impaling prisoners onto huge stakes which were then displayed to public view; and sometimes he even used smaller stakes to nail the hats of those who displeased him on their heads! On another infamous occasion, after having treated a host of his impoverished peasants to a lavish feast in his castle because he 'did not like the sight of poor people', he ordered them all to be boarded up in the dining room and set the place on fire. 'I did this,' he explained later to his horror-struck courtiers, 'so that no one will be poor in my realm!' Legend also has it that Vlad occasionally ate his meals *surrounded by the corpses of his victims, and took an unholy delight in torturing naked women – a factor which has led to suggestions that he was sexually abnormal and may well have been impotent, too. Although there is no evidence that this monster of cruelty actually drank blood, his grisly reputation certainly provided Bram Stoker with some of the background details for his book – not least being the location of the story and the central character's name. In a curious twist of fate, however, Vlad is nowadays better known as the man who inspired Dracula rather than as one of the most gruesome psychopaths in history and almost certainly the role model for Ivan the Terrible who based a number of his tortures on those practised by the Wallachian warlord.*

Although the fame of Dracula has also brought Vlad the Impaler to public notice, he has rarely featured in vampire fiction. One of the few examples is the following tale by Clive Sinclair (1948–) who is a PhD and has written a number of stories with strong historical and sexual elements including his collection, For Good or Evil *(1991) and the novels* Bibliosexuality *(1973) and* Blood Libels *(1985). Clive was born in London and educated at the University of East Anglia and the University of California at Santa Cruz before working for a while as a copywriter and then as the Literary Editor of the* Jewish Chronicle. *In 1981 he won the Somerset Maugham award for his book,* Hearts of Gold, *and in 1983 was voted 'one of the 20 Best Young British Novelists'. His story 'Uncle Vlad' is important not only for introducing Vlad to the short story game, but as an outstanding tale in its own right which combines Gothic terror and contemporary horror in a unique blend of fact and fiction. It also happens to centre around a sumptuous feast – and a visit to Vlad's infamous Castle . . .*

*   *   *

A small puff of powder cleared and I saw my aunt touch my uncle on his white cheek with such exquisite precision that she left lip marks like the wings of a ruby butterfly. I watched her for nine times nine swings of the golden pendulum as she walked from guest to guest leaving behind trails of silver dust that sparkled in the lamplight. It was as though the entire effort of her toilet was not so much designed to establish a character as to create an impression that would leave a colourful insignia on the memory. Her voice floated on her breath, a soft wind that bent and bared the necks of her listeners before her; I heard her whisper imaginary family secrets to an English aesthete who made notes behind her back:

'I believe that Lupus thinks that Vlad married me on purely scientific principles as the best specimen he could find of a modern butterfly.'

The asthete laughed. 'Well, Countess,' he said. 'I hope he won't stick pins into you.'

Then they both swirled away in a creamy whirl of silk out into the milky way of moonlight and left behind the delicate blooms and rouged cheeks. Uncle Vlad smiled at my aunt's joke and followed her silhouette as it flitted among the lace curtains, but he remained where he was, still standing beneath the candelabra, wax dripping on to his white hair, holding several glass jars, some containing ether, others containing frantic beating moths, one containing champagne.

Our family is old and distinguished, descended from the ancient mountain lords down into a lowland mansion. Uncle Vlad, tall and grand, the head of the house, is himself called after our most famous ancestor Vled the Impaler, who finally drove the Turks from Europe, so named because of his sanguine habit of tossing Turkish captives into the air and catching them on the point of a spear. We have a portrait in the Great Hall of Vled standing in a full field of flowers amid the dying Turks who, pierced through the middle, and waving their arms and legs, look like a multitude of ecstatic butterflies. Beneath this scene in now smoked grey this legend is painted in Roman print – *Vled I called The Impaler.* 'Vlad' is the modern corruption of the venerable Vled, the result of an obscure etymological whim. However, there is no disguising the physical similarities; it is all but impossible to detect a difference between the painting of Vled and the face of Uncle Vlad. Uncle Vlad is an honoured lepidopterist, but, as a rule, does not sail about honey fields in short trousers; instead he goes out at night and gathers moths by candlelight. He exchanges these easily, because of his skill and their unique paleness, for the more brightly coloured varieties, which he mounts, simply, by driving a needle through their bodies. Uncle Vlad's pursuit is looked upon with much interest by the distant Viennese branch of our family which maintains, to a doctor, that it is a genuine genetic manifestation of his more barbaric prototype; while another more émigré branch claims that Uncle Vlad is a veritable paragon of the pattern of behaviourism in that, having seen the painting of Vlad at an early age, he has ever since sought to realize the contents within the limitations of his own civilized environment. Uncle Vlad believes greatly in tradition.

Every year, on a fixed day, the entire family gathers at our home to celebrate the generations with a gorgeous extravagance. My uncle and aunt occupy weeks in anticipation of the fantastic evening, working

and reworking menus, always seeking a sublime gastronomic equilib-
rium, so that the discards look like nothing more than the drafts of
meticulous lyric poems. And what poets they are! Garbure Béarnaise,
Truites au Bleu, Grives au Genievre, Canard au Sang, Crêpes Flambés
aux Papillons. They strive to astonish the most sophisticated taste, the
only applause they seek is the thick sound of the satisfied tongue
clapping the palatine papillae. Once Uncle Vlad said to my aunt, at the
supreme moment before the food is collected, 'Should we not share the
secrets of our art with the swine that starve?' And she replied, 'Let
them eat words.'

Our family is proud and jealous of its dark arboreal rebus.
     This year, being the first congregation since my coming of age, I was
permitted to help in the preparations. On the eve, I went out alone into
the nocturnal wood, carrying my rods and nets, and followed the
overgrown path to the gilt river. And there I sat in silence for many
hours until my nets were full, very content, for there are few sights
more beautiful than that of the silver fish struggling in the moonlight. I
left the fish where they were, because it was vital to keep them alive,
and commenced the journey back, proud that I had completed my task
so well. But I had gone no more than a kilometre towards the residence
when I heard a rustling of dead leaves and the final cry of a bird in pain.
I pushed my way through the bushes in the direction of the sound and
came into the perfect circle of a moonbright glade. The air was full of
the melodious song of a score or more of thrushes. The birds were all
on the ground, trapped in Uncle Vlad's subtle snares, and they did not
look real but seemed to be some eccentric ornament of the night.
     Uncle Vlad himself, dressed by the shadows as a harlequin, was
stepping among the thrushes and killing them one by one by gently
pressing their soft necks between his thumb and forefinger. Each
death, save for the single scream and the frightened flap of the wings,
was conducted in complete silence: until the survivors sang again.
Uncle Vlad saw me and allowed me to help.
     'My boy,' he whispered to me as we worked, 'how was the fishing?'
     'It was good, Uncle,' I replied. 'I caught twenty trout.'
     When we had finished Uncle Vlad collected all the tight bodies into a
little bundle and opened a sack of the finest silk. But before he dropped
the birds into it he bit off their heads. Fine tributaries of blood ran
from his swelling lips.
     'The thrushes always come to this spot,' he said, 'they cannot resist
my special snails.'

The kitchen was already full with the shadowy figures of our servants when we returned, and my aunt was throwing resinous logs into the dancing flames. One of the anonymous cooks was apparent through a vaporous curtain of steam, stirring a dull copper soup-pot bubbling with boiling water and vegetables.

'There must be no garlic in the Garbure Béarnaise!' Uncle Vlad called out as we entered.

'Of course not, my dear,' replied my aunt. 'Did you do well?'

Uncle Vlad emptied his bag out on to the ancient wooden table, and at once long fingers fluttered out of the obscurity and plucked the feathers from the bodies. Then the birds were split open with sharp knives and stuffed till they were full with peppercorn and juniper. When this was done to the satisfaction of my uncle the breasts were sewn up, and the birds wrapped in slices of pork lard, and bound, ready to be cooked.

'We shall eat well tomorrow,' said my aunt to me.

Exactly one hour before we were due to dine, when all our guests were safely arrived, we killed the ducks. We took seven regal mallards from the lake and suffocated them by wringing their necks and pressing their breasts. The carcasses were given to the cooks, under the supervision of my aunt, to dress and draw, while Uncle Vlad and I went out with a large tank to collect the patient trout. And when we carried it back into the kitchen the oval tank seemed to have a shining lid, so full was it with fish. The remains of the ducks were ready in the great meat press waiting only for my uncle to add his libation of red wine. Then the press was turned and the blood and wine was caught as it ran, by Uncle Vlad, in goblets of gold and poured into a silver bowl. Pure vinegar was heated in large pans, over the oven, until it boiled.

'Throw in the fish while they still live,' ordered my aunt, 'and let them cook until they shrivel and turn steel blue.'

Thus everything was made complete, and we went into the incandescent dining-room to join our guests.

The English aesthete, protégé of my blonde cousin Adorian, and Madeleine, adored but adopted daughter of the childless union of the Count Adolphus and the Countess Ada, were the only visitors I did not recognize from an earlier year.

'My dear, you look absolutely *ravissant*,' said myopic Countess Ada, 'you simply must meet Madeleine.'

However, before that happened the implacable gong gave out with sonorous tidings of the approaching pabulum and, at the sound, we all took our places, according to the established decorum, at the ebony table. I sat in velvet, as always, between my aunt and the ageing mistress, so old as to have been long accepted as a second or rather parallel wife, of General X. The Garbure Béarnaise was served in ochre bowls of rough clay, the Truites au Bleu came on dishes of silver garlanded with circle of lemon and round potatoes, and the Grives au Genièvre were carried high on plates of the finest porcelain. The bones crunched deliciously beneath white teeth, knives and forks flashed like smiles as they moved, faces shone, and the wind glowed like a living thing in the crystal glasses. Then amid a fanfare of the oohs and aahs of aroused and admiring appetites the Canard au Sang was brought on and, as Uncle Vlad flamed the pieces of meat with the sauce of blood and wine and a bottle of cognac, I looked toward Madeleine for the first time.

Her face was the shape of a slightly more serious moon than our own, and her nocturnal hair was as black as the ravens that fly in the hills beyond our lands. She seemed to be searching some distant horizon, for her crescent eyebrows hovered like the wings of a gliding bird, and her mouth was slightly open as if she were holding the most delicate bird's egg between her lips. When she noticed that I was regarding her so curiously she smiled a little and she blushed.

As was the custom, after the main course, our smooth glasses were filled with champagne, and we left the decadent table, before the dessert was served. The wonders of our cuisine were praised, by a familiar chorus, to the heights of our moulded ceilings; but my aunt went outside with the English asthete to discuss synaesthesia, and Uncle Vlad took the opportunity to catch some moths. I looked for Madeleine, but I could not find her.

'I say, young fellow,' mumbled ancient Count Adolphus through his moustaches, 'have you seen Madeleine yet?'

But I did not see Madeleine again until the butterflies burst into ardent applause when we all sat down for the Crêpes aux Papillons. There was something indescribably wonderful, that night, in watching those blazing palettes puff away in smoke; it was very much as if the colours evaporated into the air and were absorbed by our breath. The crêpes too seemed suffused with this vibrant energy; it must be said, Uncle Vlad had created the most brilliant dessert of his life. I wondered afterwards if the extraordinary vitality had communicated itself to Madeleine, if her cheeks had grown roses, but when I looked I saw that she was already walking away from the table.

'I do believe that that young lady has dropped her handkerchief,' observed the mistress of General X. 'If I were you, young man, I should return it to her.'

I nodded. I could hear the violins beginning to play discordant themes in the ballroom.

The dance opened with a grand flourish of wind instruments and took off around the room on the resonant wings of the flutes and strings, and joined, in counterpoint, the butterflies released simultaneously by Uncle Vlad. My uncle and aunt, as much concerned with the macula lutea as with the more alimentary organs, had carefully planned to fill in the musical space with the most unusual sights. A pellucid cube of the purest crystal was suspended from the centre of the ceiling and rotated on a fixed cycle by means of a concealed clockwork motor, creating an optical illusion, for in each of the faces a single eye was carved, and in each of the eyes a prism had been planted; so that, as it revolved above the dancing floor, it caught the occasional beam of light and projected visionary rainbows. Benevolent Uncle Vlad, having led the dancers with my aunt in an energetic pas de deux, stood resting against an ormulu commode, pouring out tall glasses of punch from a commodious bowl, happily recording the performance of his decorated insects.

'Ah, Nephew,' he remarked as I emerged from among a crowd of dancers, 'have you noticed that spinal quiver in the little beasts when a certain note is sounded, high C, I believe?'

'As a matter of fact I have not,' I replied. 'I am trying to find Madeleine to return a handkerchief.'

Countess Ada and Count Adolphus came capering by and called out. 'She is beside the flowers in the garden.'

Madeleine was standing all alone beneath the moon, in the centre of a crazy path, skirted by a row of yellow gaslights and ghostly trees. As I approached nearer to her, along that long lane, I fancied that she was looking, as if fascinated, at the illuminated cupolas, each of which was nightly adorned with the tingling jewellery of bats. And I was reminded what a newcomer Madeleine really was, for this singular display was almost a family phenomenon; indeed, by coincidence, all true members of our family have a small but distinctive brown birth mark on the cheek that is said to resemble two open wings. Poor General X, as a result of this, was forced to grow a bushy beard, not because of his military manner, nor because of his virile dignity, but because he developed an unfortunate twitch.

'Hello,' I spoke into the night, 'hello.' I do not think that I have seen anyone look so beautiful as Madeleine looked at that moment with the full curve of her throat outlined against the blackness as if by the inspired stroke of an artist's brush.

She jumped a little, like a sleeper awakened, and turned towards me. Her brown eyes were excited and shining like an indian summer. 'The night is so wonderful,' she said, 'I feel enchanted.'

'Let us walk together,' I replied, 'and I will show you the garden.'

Madeleine took my arm and in the instant that I felt the warm flesh of her own bare arm brush carelessly against my cold hand I experienced a sensation I can only call an emotional tickle; as if some hitherto secret nerve end had been suddenly revealed and stimulated. That arm of hers was a marvellous thing, it was no single colour but a multitude of hues and tints, and covered with the finest down, except inside the elbow, where the smooth skin was pale and shy and utterly desirable. The flowers were everywhere but the famous roses were all spaced out before the french windows, so that they encircled the building like some blossoming necklace. Madeleine reached out to pick one of the blossoms but managed only to prick her finger. She gave a little cry, and stared at the finger which was rapidly dropping beads of blood.

'Let me see,' I said, 'I know how to make it better.' And I took the wounded finger between my thumb and forefinger and squeezed it, very carefully, until the last few drops of blood came like red flowers, then I carried it to my lips and sucked away any hurt. I bandaged the flushed tip with Madeleine's own handkerchief.

She smiled.

'Will you dance?' I asked.

The slight dizzyness I had felt when I tended Madeleine's hurt was heightened by our mazy movement around the dance floor to the sound of a jazzy waltz; though it was not, in fact, at all an unpleasant feeling, rather like being drunk on champagne bubbles.

'Look!' shouted Countess Ada to my aunt. 'Look who Madeleine is dancing with.'

Madeleine coloured slightly, which only made her the more radiant, then as she raised her face to me the spectrum burst all over her, and all else retreated into spectral shades. In the magic of that moment I completely forgot that the entire illusion was due to the clever artifice of my uncle and aunt and quite unconsciously pulled Madeleine closer to me, she responded with a shiver along her back, as if she were waving invisible wings, and I drifted over a dream-like sea holding on to Madeleine's warm body. I have no idea how long that moment lasted, but in those seconds or minutes I experienced an extraordinary sensation: my senses were literally magnified, I saw her skin as mixtures of pure colour, I felt her every movement; the beat of her heart, the air in her lungs, the blood in her veins. But Madeleine suddenly broke the spell.

'Oh, no!' she cried. 'We have danced over a butterfly.'

When, at last, a sliver of sun shone through the leadlight windows and exploded over the trumpet section, the dancers all leaned against one another and walked from the floor into the corridors and dimness of the receding night. I led Madeleine by the hand to her chamber.

'I must sleep now,' she said, 'but we will meet again in the afternoon?'

'Yes, you must sleep,' I replied as I touched her tired eyelids with my fingertips, 'but I will plan a picnic for when you awaken, and I will show you the ruined castle of Vled.' I returned to the ballroom to find my uncle and aunt, to congratulate them upon their success, and found them both upon their knees collecting up the bruised bodies of the fallen butterflies. I joined them, to complete the family group, crawling about as if we were posing for a portrait of a surreal autumn in a sparkling land of leaves without trees.

'Your designs were wonderful, the execution was superb,' I said to them both, 'even I ignored the methods for the sake of the effect.'

'Everything worked perfectly,' agreed my aunt, 'and what is more you and Madeleine liked each other.'

'Yes, I wanted to speak to you about that,' I began. 'I have asked Madeleine to come with me beyond the woods, and I would like to take some food and wine with us,' I paused, 'so will you be kind enough to show me the cellars?'

Uncle Vlad looked very pleased with himself and beamed at my aunt as if all credit for my request was owed to him. 'Of course, with pleasure,' he replied, with that smile of his, and added: 'Tell me, Nephew, do you intend to kiss her?'

No light at all came into the cellars except, that is, from the illumined rectangle at the head of the stairs, where the old oaken door was left open. I had never been into the cellars before, so it was all strange to me, but Uncle Vlad walked among the rows upon rows of green bottles as if this weird underwater world were his natural habitat.

'We are standing directly beneath our small lake,' he informed me. 'The cellars were designed that way deliberately so as to control the air temperature in here.'

Soon I was moving about freely on my own, and the longer I remained in the cellars the more I felt that I too belonged to this profound environment, that I was in truth the nephew of my uncle.

The air was rich with the smells of the earth, the cellars were like a distillation of night and the world, the essence of the veil, the antithesis of those bright tedious rooms where everything is visible at once, where you forget that you are breathing. There should be an art to capturing beauty; it becomes merely banal when it is not hunted. Uncle Vlad emerged from the depths of a particularly dusty rack of vintage carrying two bottles of red wine by their swans' necks, one in each hand.

'These should be just the thing,' he said as he rubbed a label, 'Château Margaux.'

Then we went much deeper, beyond where the wine was stored, until we came to a dank natural cave which smelt very strongly of pelardon. Uncle Vlad picked up a few small rounds of the aged goats' cheese, carefully wrapped and tied in dusky vine leaves, and weighed them in his hands. 'Perfect,' he adjudged, 'just ripe. Now all you require is some pâté de foie gras.'

'You must beware of the sun,' said Madeleine, regarding my pale complexion with some concern. 'I do not want you to burn because of showing me the castle.'

She gave me her straw bonnet to wear, and the blue ribbons flew in the breeze on the slope of the hill. Lupus, the great dog, ran on through the waving corn and the poppies and waited for us, barking, at the start of the woods. Several birds flew out in a straight line squawking with alarm. The woods were much cooler and greener than the sandy daylight, a delightful diurnal anachronism, an eden free from gardeners; what is more, I knew all the paths. Lupus darted ahead and chased rabbits through the undergrowth; usually he caught them. I carried the picnic on my back in a creamy satchel made from a pelt of the softest goatskin, and led Madeleine by the hand, watching all the tonal variations that the light and the shade of the sun and the different leaves made over her body. It seemed that the life in her had come to the surface and was showing itself in his ebb and flow of moving colours. I chose the spot very carefully and spread a chequered cloth over the ground, and I put out all the food on it in the crafty design of a rather ingenious check mate. We sat beneath the tall trees in the long grass. The picnic was excellent; the pâté provided the expected largesse, the cheese had just the right temperament, and I continually filled the glasses with the flowing wine. Madeleine ate a yellow pear for her dessert, and the juice dripped from her fingers; her black hair was just touching emerald leaves, also pear-shaped, and the attracted flies flew round her head like a halo.

'That was a lovely picnic,' she said, smiling. 'What shall we do now?'

'I must tell you something, Madeleine,' I confessed, by way of a reply, after some assumed consideration. 'I dabble in paronomasia.'

Madeleine put down the core of the pear. 'I thought that the game would be chess,' she gave me a sly smile, 'but now I suppose that it will be a crossword puzzle, am I right?'

She was right, of course. Nevertheless, I took a black crayon from the satchel and wrote on the white squares of the cloth – *many alive devils enliven living even in novel evils.*

'Oh, well,' laughed Madeleine, 'we all have our acrostics to bear.'

I don't know why, it certainly was not because Madeleine had beaten me at my own game, but her response made me shiver. Madeleine must have noticed because she touched my cheek with her lips.

'You are cold,' she said.

'There,' I said after we pushed through the last of the overgrown bushes, 'is Vled's castle.'

The ruined keep stood erect and solitary on the motte in melancholy grandeur. Ravens flew about the grey merlons in great circles. As we watched, the setting sun shone red through holes in the broken walls giving the whole, for a brief while, the appearance of a cavernous skull with bloodshot sockets. Although I had seen the same sight many times it still exerted over me an irresistible and hypnotic fascination; as if there really were some powerful force behind those empty carmine eyes. Then the sun deepened to purple and streaks of fiery clouds opened labial wounds in the sky. The castle looked even blacker, and all the more compelling. Madeleine did not blink, she stood transfixed, staring into the approaching gloom; her eyes reflected what she saw. I felt her hand tighten in mine and grow colder all the time; her entire being seemed frozen on the threshold of an irreversible event like a reluctant swimmer poised on the edge of a diving board. I touched her left breast with my right hand, just enough to feel the flesh.

'Will you go in, Madeleine?' I asked. She came without a word.

The graves of my ancestors were all covered with historic weeds, and the moat was dry, but a wooden table and twelve wooden chairs remained within the hollow keep. We walked through the grounds with all the care and respect due to fallen stones and came into the dining hall. It was evening. I lit many candles and covered the table with the chequered cloth and spread out upon it the remains of the picnic; there were a few cheeses, a little pâté, much fruit, and most of a bottle of wine, so that I was able to compose a creditable still life. It glowed in the glimmering light. On the walls beside where Madeleine sat there was the famed mural which represented, in picturesque detail, the narrative of Vled's many military victories, also, by way of interludes, either for himself or the spectator, the artist had included the faded delights of Vled's more carnal conquests. Even as I looked a single moonbeam suddenly shot as swift as an arrow through a crack in the annals and flashed directly on to Madeleine's face and neck.

'This is the most extraordinary supper,' she murmured, very coyly, 'that I have ever eaten.' She smiled across at me and I saw at once, in the luminous night, that her upper lip was shaped exactly like the famous long-bow old Vled had used to lick the Turks. It quivered a little beneath my gaze, and the more I studied that priceless object the more I was filled with an increasing need to make it mine. I wanted to taste that secret egg. Then the light changed, or she moved. I followed the graceful arch of her neck to where her ear disappeared among her rich hair and I felt again, though I knew not why, that I had to possess that mysterious lobe that hung so full like a liquid jewel. Madeleine became in that chance instant of illumination a collection of individual treasures and temptations; I had never done it before, but I knew then that I had to kiss her. My desire was inevitable, as inevitable as the flame that burned above the candle.

In the courtyard beyond the keep, in the centre of a thirsty fountain, a small statue of Cupid was slowly falling to pieces.

There is an old belief in our family to the effect that any passion, if held strongly enough, can so influence the prevailing atmosphere as to establish conditions favourable for the realization of that same passion. It happened in the gathering night that Madeleine got up from her place at a table of crumbling foods and walked towards me, slowly, languorously, through the undulant waves and splashes of candlelight and wax. I couldn't take my eyes from her mouth; the tongue was just visible through the open lips; the teeth looked sharp and white. I rose too, unawares, in a state of hard anticipation. We met, quickly, flesh against flesh; and I knew, by a kind of ecstatic instinct, exactly what I had to do.

I put my hands on Madeleine's hot cheeks, making a prize cup of my hands and her cervix, and tilted her head to one side. She looked at me with a sleepy look, and half closed her eyes. Her lips started to move. I placed my face on Madeleine's offered neck and began to kiss her, moving my tongue over her smooth skin, seeking, seeking, pressing, until I could feel the blood pumping through her jugular vein. Then I took a roll of the powdered flesh between my lips so that it was pressed against my teeth. I had to hold Madeleine tight, for her whole body was swept again and again with a series of short but violent tremors. I could feel her breathing right into my ear, her warm breath came in gasps and clung to me for a few seconds before vanishing. I sank my teeth into the skin and pushed, harder, harder – suddenly a great wave seized me and with a convulsive spasm of my cervical spine I bit deeper into Madeleine's vein. Then my mouth was filled with her blood and I think I heard her shriek of pleasure through my own blaze of delight.

It was a perfect kiss! I kissed Madeleine until I had to stop for breath; by then she was quite relaxed, and the arms which had clutched me so firmly hung limp by her sides. I carried her gently to the table and rolled her over the chequered cloth so that she finished on her back. Her arms got in a bit of a tangle, so I straightened them out for her. And I leaned back in a chair, well satisfied. As I did so a rather large *acherontia atropos* flew into a candle flame and fell burning on to Madeleine's cheek. She was too weak to brush it off; her hands fluttered as vainly as the moth's wings.

'Madeleine,' I whispered in her ear as I blew off the ashes, 'now you are really one of the family.'

Sanguinarius

RAY RUSSELL

While there is no evidence that Vlad the Impaler actually drank human blood, the same cannot be said of Countess Elizabeth Bathory of Castle Csejthe in north-western Hungary, whose legend as the 'Vampire of Csejthe' also came to Bram Stoker's attention during the writing of Dracula. The Countess is reputed to have murdered as many as 700 young women in the belief that their blood would rejuvenate her, and her lust for it was such that apart from taking drafts from bodies as soon as they had been killed and were hanging like sides of beef from the ceilings in her castle dungeon, she even bathed in the liquid tapped from her victims. So unbelievably awful were Elizabeth's activities that despite the procession of young girls who went to her castle ostensibly to be servants and were never seen again – not to mention the rumours which began to circulate – it was only when the number of blood-drained corpses proved to be too numerous to bury within the castle walls and some were carelessly dumped in a nearby forest, that the authorities were forced to take action against a woman who held the life of inferiors to be worthless and believed herself to be above the law. Born in 1560 to a family whose seal depicted three wolf's teeth, Elizabeth was undoubtedly promiscuous from her early teens but gave no indication of her penchant for blood until after the death of her soldier husband, Count Ferenc Nadasdy in 1604. It was her desire to attract new, younger lovers as her beauty faded that made her search for a remedy to stop her ageing. An old superstition related by one of her servants that blood was supposed to contain special preservatives turned her, almost overnight, into a human vampire. At once she began to use her

*authority to lure young girls to the castle and then order her terrified
servants to kill them. Some reports claim that she even had werewolf
tendencies – using her teeth to tear strips of flesh from the bodies of
some of her victims and then sucking these dry of blood. When
Elizabeth was finally seized in 1611 she maintained a haughty disdain
towards the charges laid against her: perhaps aware that as a member
of the nobility there was no law on the Hungarian statute books which
could be used to execute her. Instead, the trial judge who was clearly
appalled at the litany of blood-letting which was recited to him by the
Countess's servants and the few victims still awaiting their fate in the
dungeons, ordered that she should be walled-up alive in one of the
castle's remotest rooms with an access only big enough to allow food
to be passed inside. There she was condemned to spend the rest of her
days. Elizabeth died in this 'tomb' just three years later in August 1614
– and with her passing the legend of the 'Bloody Countess' was born.*

*The story of Countess Elizabeth Bathory has subsequently been told
in several scholarly works of non-fiction; a novel,* The Lady of
Cachtice *by Jozo Niznansky; and in a Hammer movie made in 1972
which starred Ingrid Pitt. Like the legend of Vlad, it is another theme
that few short story writers have chosen to tackle, with perhaps Ray
Russell (1924–) the only notable success. Russell was for some years
an executive editor at* Playboy *magazine and published a number of
stories which combined sex and horror, as well as writing several
himself including* The Case Against Satan *(1962) about a struggle
between the Devil and a young girl, and* Incubus *(1976) which dealt
with demonic possession. In the following pages he sets out to recreate
the world of Countess Bathory in an evocative style that might just
have been translated from her native Hungarian into English by an
Elizabethan writer such as Jonson, Marlowe or even Shakespeare – all
of whom were her contemporaries. And in her we have the woman
who, with Vlad the Impaler, was Dracula's other parent . . .*

I

A Key to Secret Places

O LORD,
High on its jutting promontory, gaunt and austere, Castle Csejthe still
stands, dark and muted now, its tenants none but rats and spiders,
nesting birds, and one lone wretch, Elisabeth, Thy servant. In my

sleepless desolation, I think upon those great rooms I am constrain'd to see no more, and roam in fancy through them, gliding like an insubstantial phantom through those high, broad, livid veils of dust that, when they catch the moonlight and a vagrant breeze, shimmer and ponderously sway, thus doubtless spawning village talk of ghosts – vast, shapeless, silent, silver minions now that once were solid men and women. Sometimes a bird, flapping and cawing, will start a shrill reverberation drifting through those bleak, abandon'd halls, filling their enormous emptiness with memories of screaming, and of pitiless laughter, and of the sharp cries of fleshly lust.

I do not starve for food, but pine for faces, and for the cherish'd sound of speech. The serfs whose task it is to hand my fare in through the narrow chink risk death by the whispers they afford me in their pity, yet they are good of heart, and when I plead with them and beg them but to speak, to utter any words, be they ever so plain and paltry, these lowly folk cannot gainsay me.

From them, I glean that in the village, in every inn and cottage, the church itself not excepted, all but one colour may be seen in draperies and raiment and every manner of trapping: no soul will dare display a thing of crimson. The sun itself is shunn'd when, at the close of day, it sinks into its scarlet bath; and should a wayfarer, ignorant of this strange conceit, enter the village, and he attir'd in red, be in no more than a kerchief of the offending hue, that garment is stripp'd from him, and burnt, and he is told, 'We of Nyitra are sore surfeited with that colour; by firm decree we do not name it, we think not of it, we have forbade our eyes to look upon it evermore.'

Soon I will die, O Lord, and the fetters of mortality will be stricken from my limbs, and I will straightway fly into Thy Presence, into the waiting embrace of Thine Arms. The thought of that liberation is the sole thing that sustains me in my harsh imprisonment, and allows me to endure these final solitary days, seal'd off by stone and mortar from this world, from the blue of the very sky, denied all human congress, speaking naught, seeing no one, inaccessible to all save Thee.

The others are already dead – some dispatch'd mercifully, some torn and broken by protracted torture, then burnt while yet they liv'd. I alone (and how alone!) remain, passing the cheerless days with this my screed, a captive in a single room of this which was my castle.

Fifteen I was, and lovely, when first I came to Castle Csejthe as the bride of Ferencz Nadasdy. My flesh was as pearl, lit from within, the faint blue tracery of the veins lightly visible; my hair, a tumble of raven's plumage that fell to below my waist: mine eyes, large and lustrous; my mouth, full-lipp'd and carmine. (Do women of the village now, I wonder, blanch the proscrib'd colour of their lips?)

We had met not many months before, in my father's house, where Nadasdy had been an honour'd guest. He was handsome and masterful, a scant six years older than mine own few years. His sweet demeanour, the lightning flashes of his eyes, his melodious laugh, his arms, hard with latent puissance: these things commended him to me, and quicken'd my blood. No man had yet enjoy'd me, but I knew full well that Ferencz yearn'd to do so. He paid me compliments, bestow'd flowers and other gifts upon me, seldom left my side.

I took my refuge in coyness, and reciprocated by presenting him with a dainty wooden box made of interlocking panels, a product of Cathayan cunning, impossible to open lest one knew the secret sequence of its intricate design. It had belong'd to my mother.

'There is a sweetmeat within,' I told him. 'It is thine to savour, if thou canst extract it.'

At first, he tried without success to gain entry, his fingers vainly prodding and prying. 'Canst find no way into that little toy, Count Ferencz?' I said, amus'd at his efforts. 'How wilt thou find thy way into my heart?'

He laugh'd, and solv'd the problem simply – by crushing the box between his two strong hands and victoriously chewing the sweetmeat, his eyes aglint with mischief.

I feign'd vexation. 'Brute strength,' I coldly said. 'It is a thing to please foolish girls . . .'

'But it does not please Elisabeth Bathory,' he rejoin'd, 'kin to bishops, cardinals, princes, kings. So be it. Pose me other problems, little Bathory, and Ferencz of Nyitra will solve them all!'

'Sayest thou? Then look upon these . . .' I shew'd him three eggs, which artisans had stain'd with divers patterns, each delightful, yet each different.

'Painted eggs,' said Ferencz, with a shrug. 'Dost think I cannot open them, as thou thought I could not open that little box?'

He reach'd for the eggs, but I stay'd his hand. 'This is a problem for thy *mind*, Count Ferencz, not thy sinews,' I explain'd. 'Each of these eggs is pleasing to the eye, and yet each is different from its sisters. It is hard to choose among them, they are so beautiful. It is not so?'

'It is so – if that be thy wish.'

'But once the pretty shells are peel'd away, one egg will taste much like another.'

'Doubtless. Does thy discourse have a theme?'

'Only this,' I said: 'It is even so with women. Outwardly, one of us may seem more fair than others; but when our shells are crack'd . . .'

He smil'd; his white teeth gleam'd. 'The riddling wisdom of the Bathorys is well-renown'd,' he admitted, 'but Nadasdy wit can match it. Look thou here . . .' He gestur'd toward three carafes which stood on my father's table. 'Outwardly, all these are quite the same,' he said, 'but do not be deceiv'd. One contains strong Bathory wine . . .' He drank deeply from the wine carafe. 'One contains water . . .' He drank of the water. 'And one is full of emptiness.' He flung the empty carafe to the floor's stone flagging, where it was sunder'd into shards. He walk'd closer to me and look'd long into mine eyes before he spoke. 'It is even so with women,' he said, echoing my words. 'Elisabeth, God willing, I would quench my thirst with strong Bathory wine — not tasteless water.'

'And if . . .' I found it difficult to speak. 'And if I fain prove full of emptiness, Count Ferencz?'

'My love should fill thee,' he swore.

That same night, when my old nurse, Ilona Joo, was undressing me, I ask'd of her, 'What think thee of the young Nadasdy?'

'A noble gentleman,' she replied, 'and all report him gracious, brave, and godly.'

'But of his person, what of that, Ilona? Is he not comely and well-favour'd?'

Ilona laugh'd at this, and said, 'The time is past, my lady, when such things caught my fancy; and yet I deem Count Ferencz most agreeable to the eye.'

'Ilona,' I said as I climb'd into my bed, 'would marriage to him suit me, dost think?'

'Thou art young,' she answer'd, 'but it may be that thou art ready for reaping. The Bathorys are people of high blood. Thy brother, since the time his cheek first sprouted pallid down, has never yet been sated, and neither green-bud maids nor matrons far past ripe have been enough to glut him. Thine aunts and uncles, all, crave without end; thy noble cousin Zsigmond . . . tut, tut, thou mak'st me talk of things not meet.'

'Is marriage, then, not meet? For it is *that* I bade thee speak of, dear old goose.'

'Marriage, my child,' she said, after smoothing my coverlet, 'is a key to a lock'd casket, full of many things.'

'What kind of things?' I ask'd her.

'Things unknown,' she said. 'Bright things, most oft, but . . .'

'But *what*, Ilona?'

'But naught. It is time thou wert asleep.' She blew out the candles. 'Good night, my little bud, and dream of pleasing things.'

I did. I dream'd of Ferencz. That same week, he ask'd for and receiv'd my hand, for he was look'd upon with favour by my father.

The wedding feast was prodigal, and spoken of throughout the land. Hundreds of guests attended, pounds of viands and gallons of drink were consum'd. The king himself was present, and his Prime Minister, my cousin. Another kinsman of mine, a great prince of Transylvania, sent gifts and lordly greetings across the miles. There was dancing, and there were songs of minstrels; and some of the men, my brother among them, giddy with the fumes of wine, quarrel'd and brawl'd and laugh'd and, I doubt not, had their way of serving maids in the priviest recesses of my father's house.

Through all of this, my glance would catch the eye of Ilona; but she said naught, proffer'd me scant regard, and I was sore distress'd at this and could, at length, endure her silence no whit more; hence went to her, and took her two old hands in mine.

'Dear friend,' I chided, 'whence come these glances? Have I done ought to vex thee?'

'No, my lady,' she said.

'Why, then, rejoice with me,' I begg'd her. 'This is a merry time. Put off thy glumness and thy frowns, or I will think thou dost not wish to see me happy.' I then perceiv'd that both her cheeks were wet. 'Dear nanny, weepest thou? Pray do not, lest mine own tears flow.'

'I weep to think of time's too hurried passage,' she replied. 'For fifteen years thou hast been my tender charge, and now . . .'

'Ilona,' I said, 'dost think I am a heartless ingrate who would leave thee behind? Thou'lt come with us, and be with me alway.'

'Oh, lady,' she said in a rush of warmth, 'those words are a benison to mine ears!'

And so, on that same day, I, my husband, and my nurse departed for Nyitra; and soon I was to behold Castle Csejthe for the first time.

Vasty, it stood upon high ground, o'erlooking all the countryside, and was, in truth, a bastion'd citadel, for the rich and noble of that region, in times past, being much given to feuds and bloodshed, had need of suchlike strongholds to subdue their equals and oppress their lessers. Such castles, too, gave protection 'gainst the invading Turk, rampant in our land. In the months to come, Ferencz was to shew me every inch of this his home, but this detailing was to wait upon his ardour: we had not been within the walls of Csejthe ten minutes ere he lifted me aloft in his strong arms, and with a lusty laugh, carried me up a winding, wide, stone staircase to our chambers.

'Now, Elisabeth; pale, trembling little Bathory,' he whisper'd when we were quite alone, 'I will do that I swore to do; fill thy maiden emptiness with my love.'

In later days, I was to recollect the words of old Ilona Joo, and her likening of marriage to a key that opened seal'd and secret places, denizen'd by things unknown. For such it prov'd.

II

A Courier in the Night

It was at first, a key to joy.

As in the old tale of the slumbering princess, Nadasdy's kiss awaken'd me, open'd mine eyes to piercing colours I had not hitherto beheld. I flourish'd, ripen'd, thriv'd, like some lush tropic bloom. Each sense was made more keen, the air itself more sharp and clear, lung-lancing, as is air upon a mountain top, for indeed to peaks of pleasure Ferencz led me, slowly to start with, step by timorous step, then setting out with more audacity, striving together, each succouring the other, climbing first to one ledge, then to a higher, and then to yet a higher and more dizzying ridge, finally to soar as if on wings and to attain, both in the same heart-bursting moment, that cloud-capp'd ultimate point.

This arduous and ardent mountain scaling was not the work of any single night; rather, it was a task spread over many weeks and months. Not ever had I known such blinding gladness; its very existence this side of Heaven's gates I had not once suspected. And thus I fell to worshipping my Ferencz as I would a god. His lithe young body was a shrine at which I knelt, bowing happily before his might, paying him tender homage, grateful, humble, awed by the majesty and marvel of his transfiguring power.

He, too, was close to Heaven in such moments, for he would cry aloud: 'God! O, God! My God!' as if the Deity had appear'd, in a supernal flash, before his eyes.

Once, in the dark, I, in my foolish innocence, ask'd him: 'Why dost thou call upon God when thou art with me thus?' He seemed bemus'd by my question, and I was oblig'd to mimic him as best I could, calling out as was his wont: ' "Oh God! My God!" ' until he laugh'd. 'Why sayest that?' I ask'd again.

'In faith, I do not know,' he said, and I could feel him smiling in the darkness, for with my fingertips I trac'd his lips. 'It is a thing men say; no more.' We lay not speaking for a time, and I knew that he was thinking on my question. At length, he spoke again: 'Perchance 'tis this . . .' He held me closer, and his voice was quiet. 'This joy that we twain make together is but a gift; a gift from Him; the brightest thing of all that He has given us. It gilds the drabness of our world, makes music out of silence. When I say that, when any man or woman says it, we are thanking Him for the gift.'

This I could well understand, for in his wise I thank'd my private god, my Ferencz, for his bounty.

Our life together was an idyll. Having no need for other folk, we saw but few, content within our universe of love. Troubadours, from time to time, would pass our way and sing some lay or other and pass on; the reverend father from the village church would come to say a simple mass and hear confession; messengers would bring dispatches to Ferencz, which he would read, and frown upon, and give grumbling reply; purported wizards of the woods and flame-hair'd gypsies would wander near the castle, gathering weeds and herbs, and would smile up at us and we would nod from out our window; villagers would bring provender to the castle kitchens; but these were all.

When love did not demand our urgent services, Ferencz and I would roam the whole of Csejthe, within and without. Mighty it was, and arrogant, its arrogance proclaim'd by it's high, unbroken, battle-mented walls; its overhanging bartizans and galleries from which attackers could be shower'd with missiles and archers' shafts; its projecting turrets, palisades, and towers. Ferencz would extol the main wall's strength and the loftiness of its parapet, pointing with family pride to every bulwark and rampart, praising the crenels and merlons, explaining patiently the purposes of glacis, escarp, counter-scarp, and machicolation, until my brain would spin and I would yawn, and he would make a show of anger, causing us both to laugh.

The castle's depths we plumb'd, descending into dungeons where, in former times, dread punishments were suffer'd by unhappy captives. There stood the infernal rack, and branding irons and thumbscrews, and that grim table called in French *peine forte et dure*, whereon helpless wretches were constrain'd to lie under intolerable iron weights until the breath of life was press'd from them. 'Tokens of bygone tyranny,' my husband call'd these fell objects. 'God grant no human soul again scream out his final hours here.'

'Amen to that,' I said.

It was my husband's custom, when we address'd ourselves to the sweet rites of Venus, to allow no mortal thing to interrupt us. Minstrels were silenc'd at such times, no messengers admitted to the castle, no thing or person given leave to sully the unmingled rapture of our love.

It yet befell, one rain-thick night, when the lightning and the thunder fill'd the eyes and ears, and we oblivious to it all, so deep immur'd within our love were we, that a wayfarer approach'd the castle. He came on foot, his pummel'd body bent forward into the driving slant of the rain, his clinging raiment heavy and dark with wet. More than once, he slipp'd in the slick brown mud and fell, sliming himself from head to foot, but each time he rose and clamber'd on, desperate to reach the castle, his eyes intent upon the great portcullis that barr'd his entry. At length, his vigour spent, his bosom heaving, he fell against the outer wall and tried to regain his breath. This done, he commenc'd to pound and shout, raising his voice high above the shriek of the wind, demanding word with Count Nadasdy. A wracking cough shook him more than once, and nearby twists of lightning balefully blanch'd his face, but when the spasms were subsided, he resum'd. All this, I learn'd of later.

From one of the castle bartizans, a helmeted guard at last looked down. 'Away with thee!' he cried to the forlorn figure below.

The wayfarer persisted: 'Grant me entrance! Raise the portcullis, I beseech thee!'

'Have done with that!' the guard call'd down. 'Count Ferencz will see no one! Be off!' And he fix'd an arrow to his crossbow.

'Scullion!' the wayfarer cried. 'Is this the welcome thou affordest a courier of the king?'

'A courier?' the guard rejoin'd. 'Unmounted, like a churl?'

'My steed lies dead a league from here. Open, I say!'

'King's courier?' the guard call'd down again. 'What sign proclaims thee this?'

'Sign enough!' the fellow roared: 'Thy caitiff head upon a pike, when the king hears how thou useth me!'

By this time, the tumult had reach'd my husband's ears, and disengaging himself from mine arms, he gave orders to admit the man. With a sour creaking of chains and winches, the portcullis was rais'd, and at length the courier enter'd the great hall. A stoup of hot wine was put into his hands, and this he drank off at a draught. 'My lord,' he then said to Ferencz, 'these from His Majesty.' And handed certain papers to my husband.

When he had read them, frowning more deeply even than his wont, he pass'd them to me, but I could make small substance of them, darken'd as they were by bristling words such as 'defence' and 'border,' 'the marauding Turk' and 'loyal Magyar lords.' Looking up, I ask'd, 'What mean these papers, Ferencz?'

'They may be digested and distill'd to one hard word.' He turn'd to me, and I could see his gentle nature reinforc'd with manly steel as he, with sorrow, spoke that one word: 'War.'

The happenings of that night were swift and melancholy. I found myself helping Ferencz into his battle garb and gear, asking him tearful questions touching upon his return, but answers had he none, and I could see his thinking was already far from Nyitra and from me. Then, at the open portal, clad though I was but in my nightdress, my bare feet wet and cold upon the drench'd flagging, the raging elements all wild and out of tune around us, he bade me kiss him.

This I did, in a frenzy, throwing my arms about him, crying, 'Live, Ferencz! Live for me!'

He smiled down upon my upturn'd face. 'Little Bathory,' he said, 'player with painted eggs and Cathay boxes. God's my guardian, thou my guerdon: how else, then, can it be but I will triumph over Death and foe alike?'

And, on these words, he rode into the whirling storm.

I stood, I know not how long, in the portal, nearly naked, the icy rain pasting my nightdress to my body as 'twere a shining skin; until Ilona, rous'd from her sleep, clucking words of comfort, led me back to my bed, peel'd the dripping garment from me, warm'd me with blankets, and sat with me until I wept myself at last to troubled sleep.

III

An Angry Burning Ember

Now stretch'd a span of time bereft of bliss, like to an arid desert waste which one traverses without hope, on bleeding feet, one's skin aflame, the flesh and humours parch'd beyond endurance, the very soul a festering cicatrix. Such was my lot, with Ferencz gone.

By dint of tender arts, Nadasdy had, as 'twere, spread out for my delight a table heap'd with dishes exquisite and rare, delicious Afric fruits, pungent saucers, succulent meats, all hitherto untasted by my palate – cruelly to sweep away that feast with harsh abruptness, consigning me again to the flat gruel that had been my erstwhile fare.

Cozen'd by heartless war, I pin'd, I mourn'd; the hours of my husband's absence were like the heavy weights of the *peine forte et dure*, each more insupportable than the last, pil'd upon my bosom without pity by a tormenting fiend, until my heart was crush'd within my breast and I cried out in bitter anguish. Daytime was passing desolate; but in the night, my bed transmogrified into an hideous rack on which my aching flesh was torn, I writh'd and thrash'd upon the sheets, despairing and distrait, my teeth worrying the coverlet as might a bitch, my briny tears making the pillow sodden.

From such nights would I wake dull, unrestor'd, and pale, with swollen eyes, my spirit bleak. In such sorry case was I that I would rage at the servants who brought my morning morsel, even at my faithful old Ilona; and at one such time she said, 'What pains my lady?'

'Love,' I sigh'd, 'no other thing than love for my departed consort.'

She took my hand. 'It is as I have fear'd would come to pass,' she said, nodding her grey head. 'Thou wast dry tinder till Count Ferencz struck his flint and spark'd thee; now, lacking his cool quenching, thou art an angry ember, my poor child; thou burnest.'

'Oh, my old friend, indeed I burn!' I moan'd tears brimming in mine eyes. 'Red glowing irons sear me to the bone, impale me deep, plunge hot into my vitals. I am in dire distraction!'

As if alone and speaking to herself, Ilona murmur'd, 'Abandon'd thus to such a scorching fever, what fearsome, all-consuming blaze might not this child become?' Then, looking down at me, she said, 'No other thing within this mortal sphere do I desire but thy happiness. There, there, my child, there, there . . .' And she strok'd my dry, hot hand.

'Thou art so wise, Ilona,' I said, my head in her ample lap, 'are there not medicines to avail against such sore distress?'

'None, none, my lady,' she replied. 'Fasting and prayer excepted, I know none.'

'These have I tried, at the priest's urging, but they are unavailing. Dost know of some diversions, then? Puzzles and games to tease the mind away from the throbbing wound?'

'None, child; none that are wholesome.'

'Are there unwholesome pastimes, then?' I marvell'd. 'My fancy cannot picture pleasures that are vile. To be vile, yet pleasing? This surely is a paradox, Ilona.'

'I chatter'd idly; think not of this,' she said. Patting my hand more heartily, she further spake: 'Thou passeth thy days too much alone here, now that thy good Count is gone. None but serfs and servants, and cold priests, hold discourse with thee. This must not be, for thou art young, and have sore need of merriment. In attendance should be those whose arts would fain relume thy heart, as pipers, poets, minstrels.'

'Sweet nanny, they are with their warlike masters, striking tabours, and bawling songs of brave exploits. All men of mettle or mirth are far away.'

'Then what of ladies?' ask'd Ilona.

I pouted and pac'd. 'The ladies hereabout are lack-wits,' I rejoin'd, 'who prate of naught but gowns and silly gossip.'

Thus did it go, and thus I languish'd for full many a day, and word of my distemper spread slowly through all Nyitra. From time to time, but all too seldom, letters would be brought from Ferencz, swearing his love anew, importuning me to free my mind of worry. These messages would I press to my bosom, and to my thirsting lips, and place beneath my pillow when I slept.

One morn, when I was lolling in my bath, Ilona, as she fetch'd my towel, disclos'd that there awaited in the adjacent chamber a lady, who, hearing of my drear existence, had forthwith come to cheer me.

'Name her,' I said, with some alacrity.

'Alas, I cannot,' said Ilona, drying my glistening limbs as I stepp'd from the tub, 'and, indeed, I know naught of her station, or if it is meet that you have concourse with her. She is not, I think, a gentlewoman, and yet, in sooth, her aspect is most gracious and commends her . . .'

'Ilona, leave off prattling! Go to the lady, use her with courtesy, ask what her name be, and – '

'My name,' now spake a purring voice, 'is Dorottya.'

I looked up, undrap'd as I was, to see my visitant standing in the archway, tall, full-bodied, beautiful, attir'd all in black, her skin paler than mine, her tresses red as fire. It was one of the persons I had glimps'd, now and again, from out my window, quietly gathering barks and grasses. 'Have I leave to enter, Countess?' she ask'd, most deferentially.

I nodded, and she mov'd soundlessly into the chamber, her eyes not once leaving mine. Then, her glance flickering quickly down the length of my dewy frame, she enquir'd, 'Is it my lady's pleasure, after bathing, to be rubb'd with scented oil?'

Once more I nodded, and Ilona held out for her to see the phial of oil with which she customarily anointed me. 'With my lady's permission,' said Dorottya, 'may I proffer a balm of mine own concoction, distill'd of aromatic woodland herbs?' She pull'd the stopper from a tiny urn, and instantly the air was all infus'd with heady fragrance. 'To soft skins such as thine, Countess, it is as sweet as lover's lips,' she said.

I smiled my approval, and Ilona reach'd for the urn, but Dorottya did not surrender it. 'Let not rough hands perform this subtle office,' she urg'd. 'Rather, if it please my lady, let myself be thine anointer.'

Again I smil'd, words frozen on my lips by the unswerving eyes of my new friend, and discarding my towel, I reclin'd upon my bench to await the soothing unction.

Dorottya knelt beside the bench, and pour'd the olent oil into her palm. 'Leave us,' she bade Ilona.

IV

The Village Girl

How shall I say what comfort Dorottya afforded me; what panacea flow'd from her, in the days that follow'd, to ease my loneliness? Her voice, as rich and dark as sable, was in itself a healing balsam; her gentle, stroking hands unparallel'd in smoothing cares away. To her, I felt that I could speak of all things: trifles, fears, delights, puzzles that piqued my curiosity, small vexing shames too delicate to confess even to Ilona. Dorottya was a vessel that receiv'd and understood them all. She assuag'd my fears, confirm'd my joys, bestow'd upon me peace and absolution beyond the gifts of any priest.

Of herself, she spoke little. 'Dorottya,' I asked her straight one day, 'whence comest thou; what are thy people?'

'I am a woman of the wood, Countess,' she said. 'Some call us gypsies, others deem us fairies. Those who fear our wisdom and our crafts say we are witches.'

'That is no answer at all,' I told her, laughing, 'but let is pass.'

She said, 'I would not leave my lady unsatisfied.'

'It is no matter,' I assur'd her, 'but tell me this: are there others of thine ilk or kin hereabout?'

'More than my lady might suppose,' she said.

'Why do thy people keep their own counsel, and eschew the company of others?'

'Our ways are oft misrender'd, and false readings put on what we do: out of such ill perceivings rise discord and strife.'

'Do I misrender or misread thee, Dorottya? Doth discord come of these fair hours together?'

'No, my lady. But thine affections complement mine own.'

At first, Dorottya paid visits to the castle of an hour or more; these visits I persuaded her to lengthen; finally I gave instructions to Ilona that the woman of the wood was to be granted domicile in chambers next to mine.

It must not be suppos'd that Dorottya's ministrations dislodg'd all thought of Ferencz from my mind, or that my love for him had lessen'd with the lessening of my loneliness. Indeed, some of my new friend's arts seem'd meant by fate to cleave Ferencz more close to me, and fan our love, and sanctify it with issue. For Dorottya's discourse of herbs and vegetals and suchlike held me blandish'd: how ragwort and colewort do enliven virile humours, whereas chaste-tree and water lily quench the generative powers of the man; how mugwort, pennyroyal, fetherfew, and savine are most beneficent to the womb; how saffron is so priz'd for its medicinable effects that, in Nuremberg, if pharmacists adulterate or otherwise dilute it, they are some burnt and some interr'd alive. By this and other learned talk did Dorottya amuse me, likewise by suave anointings and by little games most easing to my nature.

From all of this, Ilona drew away, her aspect clouded by disapprobation. Anger'd by this, I call'd her to task. 'Fie, Ilona,' I said. 'It speaks most ill of thee to mope thus.'

'I beg my lady's pardon,' she said coldly.

'Was it not thee, Ilona,' I pursu'd, 'who said that she desir'd, above all else, my happiness? Why, then, these frowns?'

'My lady,' she said haltingly, 'this gypsy woman is not of thy station . . .'

'No more are thee.'

'. . . And yet, ye twain are lock'd for hours together; I hear the plashing of thy bath, and laughter, and low talking, and strange long silences, and sudden cries . . .'

'Dost decree, then, that I weep and groan, which heretofore has been my portion?'

Ilona gabbl'd on, as if I had not spoken: 'Such silences, such laughter, and such cries, as I was wont to hear more happily, when thou wert closeted with thy lord the Count . . .'

'Enough of this!' I shouted in displeasure. 'Thy brain is addl'd with thine age, and poison'd with ignoble jealousy! What, shall a married lady, the mistress of a mighty castle, be censur'd and diminish'd by her ancient nurse? Hath the fair structure and proportion of mankind been now inverted, dangled by its heels? Do lackeys reign, and servants sit in judgment? Oh, then is Chaos surely come!'

So generous and open was Dorottya that, learning of old Ilona's foolish opposition, she ventur'd to suggest a remedy. 'Among my people, there are cordials, broths, and simples to charm away these cholers, and to lull and pacify such peevish minds . . .'

'I would not drug the good old woman,' I said.

'She will no more be drugg'd than is the fever'd, raving patient, when physick'd into calm by healthful draughts. I prithee, Countess, place thy trust in me and in my arts.'

And so, with sprinkling of some powdery dust into Ilona's nightly cup of mead, that source of sad annoy was purg'd. My nurse, quite cur'd of retrograde and waspish thought, was coax'd into a smiling mollitude, her eye no longer darken'd by unseemly doubts, but well-content and fix'd as on some distant blissful scene.

'She is the happier now,' I was assur'd by Dorottya.

'Yes, it is good,' I quite agreed. 'I would not have the dear dame vex'd and sorrow'd.'

With fresh zeal, then, did I address myself to all those revels which Dorottya had devis'd to fill my heart, made empty by my warrior husband's fealty to the king.

'What would my lady say,' croon'd Dorottya one eve, 'if I were to bid welcome to such others as would cheer thee?'

'Bid welcome *here*, dear Dorottya? What sort of others?'

'Some, as myself, the gypsy breed,' she said. 'Others, maybe, of different stamp – young village maids of jolly temper, whose rustic songs and dances would regale thee.'

I thought upon this before answering, 'I know not if such company would find favour with the Count.'

'The Count?' laughed Dorottya. 'I see no Count. Say, rather, if such company would find favour with the Countess.'

I knew not what to answer: fill my husband's home with wild gypsies and ungentle village girls, suffer rude songs and peasant gambols to taint these ancestral halls? I waver'd, said not yes or no; and Dorottya did not persist. 'If thou art hesitant, I will not press,' she said, 'for it is only thine own merriment, and my sworn duty to preserve it, that brought the notion to my thoughts. Let us say no more of this. At any rate, it is past time for my lady's bath . . .'

Never had I enjoy'd such frequency of bathing and oiling, save since the day Dorottya had come to me. Surrendering to her services, I let my imagination dwell upon the sport she had suggested, the singing and the dancing of the simple village folk, the carefree ways of gypsies. As Dorottya rubb'd me from head to foot with scented ointment (I sipping all the while from a chalice of wine she had mull'd for me), my presentments fell away, and in a drowsy voice I let her know that it would not be untoward if, at some time soon, she invited certain gay companions to the castle.

'I would not do a thing the Countess thinks unseemly,' she replied.

'Nay,' I said, with clos'd eyes, 'do it, sweet Dorottya, I pray. I give you leave . . .' And, with this, I was asleep, warm'd by the wine, naked and bath'd and oil'd upon my bench.

Whether an hour I doz'd, or more, I never knew, but when I awaken'd, I was irk'd to see a stranger in my chambers, a young girl, scarcely out of childhood, rudely garbed but comely. I reach'd out, startl'd, for my towel, and with it covered most of my nakedness, crying out, 'Who art thou? What dost thou here?'

'Please m'lady,' the girl stammer'd, afrighted and distrait. ''Twas Mistress Dorottya commanded me to appear before thee . . .' And she look'd, with some trepidation I bethought me, over my shoulder, where, I now discover'd, Dorottya stood.

' "*Commanded*"?' I said to Dorottya sharply. 'Dost now command here, gypsy woman?'

'The girl is mewling,' smiled Dorottya. 'She is but a village simpleton I had brought hither for thy diversion, Countess. For, sure, thou gavest leave to do so.'

'I may have done,' I said, my brain still wrapp'd in foggy sleep, 'I do not now recall. But whilst I am all ungirt, can it be meet?'

'Faith, lady,' chided Dorottya, 'are we not all women here, whatever our condition? No harm can come of such an audience, surely.'

Dorottya's words calm'd my first misgivings. 'Thou art welcome,' I said, extending my hand for the girl to kiss. But she instead fell forward on her knees and kiss'd mine unshod foot.

This much surpris'd me, and I giggl'd, drawing my foot away and saying, 'Nay, foolish girl, I am no pope that thou must pay me homage thus.'

'But Mistress Dorottya —' the girl began to say.

'Silly wench,' said Dorottya, 'dost thou so soon offend the Countess?'

I interven'd: 'But there is no offence. Arise, girl, do not kneel thus, as if at thy prayers.'

'Truly,' said Dorottya, with a merry laugh, 'we hope to be more jocund than folk are wont to be at vespers!'

With this I did concur with all my heart, and ask'd of Dorottya, 'What frolic, then, shall we try with our new friend?'

'None at all,' said Dorottya, 'whilst she is thus begrim'd with village dirt.' (And true it was, the girl was most uncleanly.)

'What then?' I ask'd, still clutching at my towel.

'Why,' said Dorottya, 'would it not prove saucy sport for us to play at being handmaidens to the girl? To let this lowly person once enjoy the ministrations highborn ladies do?'

'It is thy thought, then . . . ?'

'But a passing thought, a vagrant fancy,' Dorottya answer'd with a shrug. 'If thou likest it not . . .'

'It suits me well,' I rejoin'd. 'To bathe the girl, and then anoint her?'

'For a beginning,' Dorottya made reply, adding: 'Surely it is innocent, and Christian?'

'So it is!' I laughed.

And thus, with many a smile and slap and sportive cry, Dorottya and I stripp'd bare the girl of her mean attire, and lifted her into my tub. She squeal'd to feel the water, and howl'd as we scrubb'd her with the brush. Such squirming did she do that I was drench'd from head to foot, but this was no great matter for I was still unclad, and Dorottya, in concord with the occasion, had divested herself of her garments, as well.

It was at this time that Ilona enter'd the chamber, was gaily told to be about her business and leave us young ladies to our play, but persisted, and through the girl's pretty shrieks, at length made her message understood; it was none other than the news that, from the highest parapet of Csejthe, a vigil guard had seen and made known the approach of mounted men.

'What men?' I laugh'd, still in the spirit of our romp. 'We have no need of men!'

'Count Ferencz and his retinue,' my nurse replied.

V

Sins Without Faces

Ferencz! The mention of that cherish'd name at once restor'd me to my former self. 'Dorottya,' I quickly said, 'this girl must not be found here; secrete her where my lord will not come upon her . . .'

'It will be done,' Dorottya replied, urging the girl out of the tub.

'Ilona, dear,' I said, 'fetch here my nightdress, remove the tub and blot away this water.'

These things were swiftly done, and it was not long ere Dorottya, now dress'd, appear'd again within my chamber and assur'd me that the girl was safely hid away. 'Is it my lady's wish,' she ask'd, 'that I, as well, hide from the Count?'

'No, good Dorottya!' I said. 'Thou art my trusted friend. Stand here at my side, for the Count will wish to meet thee, I am certain. Later, thou wilt be given leave to retire to thine own chamber, for the Count will wish to be alone with me.'

'Oh, that is sure,' said Dorottya, with a tinct of slyness that made my cheeks all roseate with blushing.

And, while my face was yet thus flush'd, my dear Ferenz, he gone from me these many weeks, enter'd my chamber. His face was made gaunt by weariness, and he walk'd with a halting step that spoke, with mute eloquence, of grievous wounds. I rush'd into his arms, and felt him crush me hungrily to his bosom; I wept with joy; and neither of us spoke for many moments.

Then what a torrent of sweet words cascaded from us twain! What sighs, what vows, what bright renewals of our love! Until, at length, his eye first catching sight of Dorottya, Ferenz ask'd, 'And this lady: who is she?'

'A dear and valu'd friend, by name Dorottya,' I replied. 'She hath done much to make my days less bleak.'

'Why, then,' he said to her, 'I am beholden to thee, mistress.'

'Such duty is but pleasure, good m'lord,' said Dorottya. 'But now I see thou'rt tired, and I beg leave to retire.'

Ferencz nodded graciously, and Dorottya repair'd to her own rooms. This caus'd my husband to lift his eyebrows: 'She dwelleth here?' he ask'd.

'Sweet Ferencz, do not scold,' I said. 'She is a kind and most devoted lady; without her, I fear I would have gone quite mad with sorrow. Pray let her stay.'

'It matters not,' he answer'd, with a wan smile. 'For a while, at least, she may stay.'

Then did I help remove my husband's battle gear, and rubb'd his wounds, and coo'd soft words into his ear as we lay upon our bed; and soon had brought him to a pitch of glowing love, and we did cleave as we were wont to do before his leaving.

How happy was I then! how luminous! how tingling and alive!

After a time, Ferencz turn'd to me and said, 'Elisabeth, a secret hides behind thine eyes, a darkness. Tell me of it.'

'I have no secrets from thee, Ferencz,' I replied, 'and if a darkness thou divinest in me, it is the shadow of the loneliness I felt when thou wert far away.'

'Is not that shadow now dispell'd by my return?'

'It is, beloved husband, oh it is!'

But still did Ferencz stubbornly persist.

'This Dorottya,' he said. 'What traffic does she have with thee?'

'Friendship, gentle Ferencz, nothing more. Solace for my lonely hours. Am I to pine without companions? May no one cheer my heart when thou art gone from me?'

He then did stroke my hair, and spoke more low, and call'd me his little raven. 'Elisabeth, there are abroad in this world things thou know'st not of, such things that it were better thou shouldst be struck blind than look upon, struck deaf than bend thine ear to.'

'What breed of things, Ferencz?' I ask'd, masking my fearfulness, for his voice had taken on a thickness much disquieting to me.

'Things of black night,' he said, in hollow tones.

'Thy words afright me, though I glean them not,' I said.

'My little one, my pearl: in elder time, before Christ shed his blood for us, unholy joys were known . . .'

'Why dost thou tell me of them, Ferencz, and in a voice so full of haunt that I am chill'd unto my marrow?'

'I do *not* tell thee of them,' he said, 'I do *not*. For these sweet ears, such stuff would not be meet. And yet, I do most earnestly abjure thee: pray to God, read deeply of thy Scripture.'

'I do, I have; both prayer and Book have always fill'd my days.'

'Let them fill thy nights as well, Elisabeth,' he said, 'for there are sins without faces; sins that, in their shame, shun the glare of honest day and creep unseen into the soul. Such guileless souls as thine are lodestones to them. Therefore, pray; steep thyself in Holy Writ. Be mindful of that blessed Paul of Tarsus, and those of whom he wrote.'

'Wrote what, Ferencz?'

'Of those who "changed the glory of the uncorruptible God into an image made like to corruptible man," ' he answered, ' "and wor-shipp'd and serv'd the creature more than the Creator . . ." '

'Ferencz, these words are naught but fumes to make me giddy! Desist, I do beseech thee, and let us talk of blither things!'

Fatigue of battle took its toll, however, and soon Ferencz was in a deep sleep. I, rested by my earlier nap, and made still more awake by my returning warrior's kisses, lay for a time, with open eyes, beside him. Then, sleep evading me, I arose and crept quietly into Dorottya's rooms, thinking to talk with her if she be still awake.

Her bed was empty. This was most curious, and I went in search of her. I walk'd through halls and antechambers, peeped within alcoves and nooks, and still I found her not. Then, from far off, I thought I heard a cry.

So faint it was, that I at first deem'd it a figment or, at most, a passing bird. Then, as I turn'd into another corridor, I heard the sound again, more clearly and much closer, and knew with certainty it was a human cry; or more precisely, scream.

Again it rang out: high and sharp and piercing, the scream of one so sore excruciated that all mark of sex or age was lost – man, woman, child, crone, any of these could have utter'd it in dire extremity.

Downward I delv'd into the castle's bowels, into dominions dark and rank with damp effluvium of must, on stone steps slick with parlous grume – and, of a sudden, very near to me, that scream reach'd shrilly out once more, and I was much afraid, for, turning, I perceiv'd that it had issued from no other place than that horrendous dungeon wherein, long since, despairing victims had been tortur'd unto death!

Chill'd by fear, my flesh acrawl and prickl'd, I yet did muster courage and approach'd, on timorous feet, that evil room.

VI

The Smell of Pain

The torture chamber's heavy iron door was but an inch ajar, and yellow torchlight flicker'd out through this discrepancy. The screams had stopp'd, but now I heard another sound: the voice of Dorottya.

'I will return to thee at dawn,' she said, 'at which hour wilt thou be more acquiescent to my wishes. Indeed, by that time thou wilt beg, if need be, on thy knees for the privilege of serving me.'

The door, with shriek of hinges, open'd wider, and I back'd into the shadows. Dorottya appear'd, her dark eyes smouldering, her face agleam with sweat. She turn'd to close and lock the iron door, but ere she did so, I stepp'd forth and challeng'd her by name. She spun around, astonish'd, then, making out my face in the half-dark, spake: 'My lady here, and at such an hour?'

'That question should be mine,' I said.

'A matter of mere discipline,' she smil'd. 'Nothing of such high import that it should trouble thee.' And, so saying, she began to lock the dungeon door.

'No happening in this castle is too low of import for mine ears,' I said. 'What dost thou here, Dorottya?'

She sigh'd. 'Why, then, I see thou art distrustful. It is no more than this: when, earlier, thou bad'st me hide the village girl in some recess where Count Nadasdy would not find her, I, in my haste, could think of no place better than these dungeons, where no one treads. I lock'd the girl herein, and charg'd her to be silent. Later, as I lay alone abed, I heard the silence of this night disturb'd by the foolish wench's cries. Fearing the Count would hear them, I arose, descended hither, and abjur'd her to be quiet. She would not; she demanded I release her; I told her to be patient and she would gain thereby, with fair rewards and bounty; but the stubborn creature still persisted until, at last, I was oblig'd to chastise her. That, my lady, is the simple sum.'

'How chastise her?' I ask'd.

'Such trifling things must not concern my lady.'

'*How* chastise her, Dorottya?' I repeated sternly.

She stood unspeaking for a moment, her eyes as hard as flint. Then, smiling thinly, she replied: 'By means most honour'd with long use and old tradition the world over, even in far-off heathen lands, and most particularly in the noble canons of thy Christian law.' She push'd open the dungeon door. 'Will it please my lady pass approval on my handiwork?'

I fear'd to step inside that place of ancient horror, but the steady eyes of Dorottya, narrow with mockery, goaded me, and with a shuddering breath, I took heart and pass'd through the iron door. In the erratic, twitching torchlight, I saw again the rack, the brazier of old irons and ashes, the cages, chains, the instruments of crushing and of tearing, the ghastly slab of the *peine forte et dure*. And then my breath caught suddenly in my lungs, as I saw the village girl.

Naked from head to toe, she hung motionless and silent in this place that smell'd of pain. Her feet dangled inches off the dungeon floor. Her arms stretch'd straight above her head, and the weight of her small body, slight though it was, dragg'd upon her thumbs, purpled and swollen in the leathern thongs that bound them. Her back and nates were cover'd by a tangle of glistering welts. Briny blood ooz'd thickly from the freshest of these, making its sluggish way down the serpentine length of her body in thin rivulets, thence to gather into heavy droplets at her toe-tips and drip evenly into a pool of ruby slime under her feet. The metrical slow dripping of her lifeblood was the only sound in the dungeon, and the foetid air hung still as Death.

I whisper'd in revulsion, 'Oh, God in Heaven, Dorottya – hast slain this unoffending child?'

'Nay,' Dorottya said, grinning, 'she is but senseless from the blows. A little salt rubb'd briskly on her rawest weals, and she will shew thee life enough! Wouldst have me demonstrate?'

'Pile one abomination on another?' I cried.

'Tut, lady, 'twould be healthful to the wretch,' Dorottya rejoin'd.

'This is a monstrous thing,' I said. 'How dar'd thou trespass thus, and so abuse my confidence?'

'My lady likes it not?'

'Thou knowest well I like it not!'

'My lady finds some flaw?' she said with a sneering lilt. 'Some thing not done or poorly wrought? My lady would *improve* my efforts?' She thrust into my hand a coil'd black whip, still thick with blood: my fingers jump'd from it as they would jump from a venomous reptile, and the ugly length of hide fell to the floor.

Dorottya pick'd up the whip. 'Wilt add thy signature to this piece of work?' she taunted.

I dash'd it from her hand. 'Art mad?'

She cluck'd her tongue in mocking admonition. 'So squeamish art thou, Countess?' And ere I could reply, she added: 'So squeamish – *and a Bathory?*'

'Thy words lack all concord and sense,' I told her. 'In what wise does my name have aught to do with this?'

'Oh, lady, 'tis a large and lustrous name, known far and wide, familiar to the ears of great and humble . . .'

'Thou speakest wildly, Dorottya!' I said, and stepp'd forward to cut down the hapless girl.

'Sayest thou so?' snapp'd Dorottya, seizing my shoulder and staying me. 'Here is a marvel, then, indeed! What? Thou, a Bathory, unknowing of the fame that shineth from thy family's escutcheon? This is surpassing modesty, my lady; innocence so pure, unspoilt, and rare that Reason's own sweet self is ravag'd!'

'Let loose mine arm,' I said, 'and help me dress this poor girl's sorry gashes, or *thou* wilt hang thus in her stead, I swear!'

'Ah!' crow'd Dorottya in triumph. 'Now speaks the true Bathory voice!'

'What meanest thou, by this vain harping on my name?'

Dorottya shook her head in wonderment. 'Dost, thou, in truth, not know?'

My blank looks gave reply; and Dorottya, with a bestial snarl, look'd past me, toward the dungeon door, and said, *'Enlighten her.'*

I swiftly turn'd, and gave a cry of sharp surprise. There in the open door of that vile chamber – not livid in disgust and loathing, not mouth agape and wide of eye with unbelieving awe, but, rather, with lips curving in a calm and curious smile – stood my husband.

VII

The Enlightenment

Ferencz stood in the doorway for an unending moment, not speaking, his eye darting from me, to Dorottya, to the tormented victim hanging from the ceiling; then he advanc'd into the chamber, easefully, unhurried, his smile broadening the while. 'Enlighten my little spouse?' he said at last. 'Cast her out naked from that Eden of sweet ignorance she hath so happily inhabited? Crease that unlin'd brow? Darken those starry eyes? Bow those alabaster shoulders with the heavy, horrid burthen of knowledge? What saith Elisabeth: shall I indeed enlighten thee?'

Terror and fearful portent rose like a freezing mist, enveloping my body, choking the words in my throat. My Ferencz, who was my world, my god, to look and speak thus cold, ironical, and strange? To be so alter'd and unlike his own fair self in every aspect? If this could be, then nothing in this sphere or in the vast eternal firmament was constant, staunch, and love itself a lie.

Yet, though fear transfix'd me, my first words were of the unlucky village girl, for I said: 'Enlighten me if't please, thee, Ferencz, but not until that blameless maid is loos'd from out her crippling bonds.'

He look'd up at the hanging girl, and at her blackening thumbs, and said to Dorottya: 'The purpose hath been serv'd, methinks, the lesson learn'd. Cut down the little drab.'

With one of sundry cruel blades that lay about the cell, Dorottya server'd the thongs from the wall-hook whereat they were affix'd; the ceiling pulley squeak'd; and the girl slump'd to the damp stone floor, a silent, naked, bleeding heap of flesh.

'Enlightenment hath been ask'd for,' Ferencz said when this was done, 'and indeed it seems most timely. Enlightenment by dint of words; but first by dint of action . . .'

What follow'd then was so abhorrent, that to think upon it even now, after the lapse of years, makes my gorge to seethe and rise within me.

'Sit thee down,' said Ferencz, and push'd me into a chair affix'd with manacles, and these he lock'd upon my hands and feet. 'Thou'lt not be much discomfited,' he said, 'for I do not mean to light the pan of coals that lieth under the iron seat. This is but to assure thy fixity.' A kind of vise he tighten'd, not ungently, at my temples, saying: 'And this to keep thy head from motion.' He then display'd two small iron rings, about the same circumference as florins. 'And these?' he chuckl'd. 'Why, these will make it certain thou'lt not miss the smallest trifle of my enlightenment.' He, quickly and with deftness, forc'd the iron rings around my very eyeballs, in such wise as to keep my lids from lowering, obliging me to stare, unblinking, at whatever lay before me.

Ferencz then, to my mounting anguish, gather'd the gloating Dorottya into his arms, and kiss'd her with excess of zeal; and did not stop with kissing, that perfidious pair, but, unmindful of all decency, like ruttish beasts that lack the benefit of soul to guide them, did foully slake their lusts in that rank cell, amongst the cunning tools of agony, within an arm's length of the insensate village girl, whilst I, unable to turn my head from the infernal scene, beheld, with stinging, bulging eyes, each moment of that union, unto its final hideous gasp.

Arising then from his depravity, Ferencz walk'd over to the chair in which I was constrain'd to sit, saying, 'My little wife is shaken by this entertainment, Dorottya: see, her face is all o'ercast with sickly pallor.' And he laugh'd. 'What, Elisabeth? Hast lost thy pretty tongue? No epithets, no pious cries? Quite mum? Thine eyes do stream with tears – but whether they be drops of sorrow, or no more than that liquor Nature doth provide to lave thy parching orbs withal, I know not. Let me affirm my fondness for thee, sweetest chuck, and relieve thy lovely eyes of their hindrances.'

So saying, he remov'd the iron rings, and I blink'd, my lids comforting my burning eyeballs like healing poultices.

'Know, then,' Ferencz continu'd, 'that I intend thee nothing hurtful, unless thou dost prove tiresome by stubborn protestations – yet this thou wilt not, I believe. Art silent still? 'Tis well, for thou hast much to learn, and it is meet that thou shouldst meekly listen:

'This wanton, wise, and artful gypsy wight, this Dorottya, hath been my ardent mistress since before thine own fair beauty snar'd my heart.

With her, I have known deep delights surpassing those pale, milky pleasures other folk enjoy. For most men and their dames are plodding, stale, proscrib'd, bound in by limitation, fear, denial, an host of guilty doubts and shames. To but a few is granted spirits broad and questing, undismay'd, which freely vault o'er pretty confines, to range in unexplor'd demesnes; and such an one am I, for those of my blood have ever been impatient with the shackles other men clap round themselves. Thus, from an early age, I sought out bypaths little trod, and cleav'd to those whose passions match'd mine own.

'Dorottya was one such, yet it is too small a thing to call her "one such" – rather, has she been the paramount and chiefest sharer of my joys: pupil and tutor both, purveying and receiving; yet not permitting jealousies to hinder her from being the avenue whereby I met with other congenial spirits.

'Our pleasures were not look'd upon with favour when, from time to time, a whisper would escape from some disgruntled creature we had used; but I would quell such rumours with a show of piety, and all would then again be well.

'But for how long would soothing words and seeming virtue still these grumblings? Not forever, surely. Much need had we to join our forces with those who, sympathetic to our tastes, would yet be sturdy shields, protectors, with blood alliances to noble ministers of mighty sway. 'Twas then we learn'd there liv'd, in a purlieu not far distant from our own, a fair young maid, in whose comely person nubility with nobility were conjoin'd; who counted cardinals and kings among her line; who was a most beloved cousin of that high-placed Gyorgy Thurzo, Prime Minister to His Majesty . . .'

I found my voice at last. 'Oh God! Myself!'

'Thyself,' Ferencz confirm'd.

'But . . .' I stammer'd haltingly: 'didst thou not say, just now, that such highborn allies must needs be "sympathetic to thy tastes"?'

'Ay, little wife. And art thou not of Bathory breed?'

'I am, but what of this?'

'Come, art so innocent? Dost thou not know full well the maim'd repute thy family bears – yet suffers not a jot of open censure, by reason of its powerful affiliates?'

' 'Tis slander!'

'Truly? Is it slander, then, to say thy brother is an unsated ram who spends himself on young and old alike by main force, yet goes unpunish'd? Is't calumny to recall to thee thine aunt, whose lusts consume the choicest youthful blooms her influence and riches can procure, distinguishing not betwixt their genders? Is't falsehood to evoke that uncle who is call'd a warlock, concocter of dread alchemies, whose prayers are offered not to God, but Satan? And, dear Elisabeth, what of thy princely cousin Mad Zsigmond, he of Transylvania? Art thou indeed unknowing of his ways, of how, to entertain him whilst he sups (as others might be cheer'd by songs or stories) he hath serfs dragg'd before his table, that he may watch their coupling, and if he be not pleas'd with their performance, bids his varlets torture them to death, their screams concordant carols to his ears?'

'Nay, these are lies!' I cried.

He did not heed me, but went on. 'And so, on Dorottya's urging, I paid thee court, was welcom'd by thy father, found thee most beauteous, and set about persuading thee to wed me. Young thou wert, and as young mares must needs be broken to the saddle, so must young maids. During this time of tutelage, Dorottya did absent herself from Csejthe. Thine untried ardour soar'd, but still did I refrain from leading thee to arcane joys, for fear of shocking thee and marring all. The mask of sanctimony I put on, and prated like a monk, and anxiously awaited such a time when it would be propitious to bring Dorottya to thee, for different teachings. The king's command well serv'd my purpose; I rode off to rout the Turk; thine unquench'd passions rag'd; and Dorottya, as was my plan, came unto thee to sate them.'

'To . . . sate them?' I said. 'Nay, Dorottya but calm'd me with anointings and sport . . .'

Dorottya, long silent, threw back her head and laugh'd. 'Is't innocence or idiocy?' she said. 'Wert thou indeed purblind, that thou wast unaware how interdicted and unlawful was our congress? Did not these "calmings" and "anointings" and our romps, from which thou didst derive such glee, not once seem contraband or guilty?'

'Nay . . . nay, never!' I rejoin'd.

Ferencz then spake. 'I do believe it, Dorottya. For when, tonight, she lay clasp'd within mine arms, I did attempt to sound her, by talk of "secrets" hidden from me, hints of things unholy in the world, righteous warnings of the faceless sins that "creep unseen into the soul." And not once was she disquieted by guilt or shame, she is so pure. I press'd the point e'en further, bade her read Scripture, spoke of Paul, recited verses that I hop'd would lead her on to fuller guessings.' He look'd down upon me, still manacled, by hand and foot, unto that chair. 'Dost recollect, Elisabeth? Those pagans who, 'tis writ, "worshipp'd and serv'd the creature more than the Creator"? The

Holy Book has ever fill'd thy days, thou saith. Then canst thou not recite the words that follow? "For this cause . . ." '

In memory, the page of Scripture rose before mine eyes: *For this cause God gave them up into vile affections: for even their women did change the natural use into that which is against nature . . .*

'Then I . . .' My voice falter'd and broke.

'Ay, little one,' said Ferencz. 'Thou, either by the fault of too excessive innocence, or the strain of Bathory perverseness in thy veins, hath done things call'd uncleanly and corrupt.'

Dorottya said, 'Thou art now one of us, Elisabeth.'

'Bound to us by bands stouter than the ties of blood,' said Ferencz.

'Ay,' said I in hollow answer, 'and likewise damn'd with ye.'

'If that be so,' said Ferenz, 'then let thine arms embrace damnation like a lover . . .'

'And let us lead thee onward,' added Dorottya, 'to keen delights far stranger and more bold than those thou hast already savour'd . . .'

'Ay, wife,' said Ferencz, 'and be thou Bathory not but in name, but in hot deed, as well!'

'And let us seal this compact with a solemn pledge,' Dorottya said, 'a ceremonial bath to signalize our fealty to sin.'

'We three to bathe?' said Ferencz. ' 'Tis well. And what, of all thy unctions, Dorottya, shall we bathe ourselves withal?'

'One richer far than all the others,' she replied, pointing to the girl who lieth, scourg'd and raw, upon the floor. 'That which floweth in her veins.'

VIII

Grex Sanguinarius

Thou knowest, Lord, that blood bath was the first, but not the last, in which I would immerse myself in all the years that follow'd. As if a gate of Hell had been thrown open, Ferencz and Dorottya, made confident by the bastion of my family name, now steep'd us all in reeking devilish rites, and vilest pleasures; whilst, I, like unto one in whom the soul has died, became a stunn'd, obedient creature, sharing both dark lust and blame.

Whether 'twas truly some streak of grainèd foulness in my stirps that made me such an unobjecting partner in those crimes; or whether disenchantment with my Ferencz and with all humanity had stifled gentler humours; or whether Dorottya's cunning simples had a part in blunting my fair nature (as they had blunted poor Ilona's), I know not. I only know that I became as despicable and perjur'd as Ferencz and Dorottya, for all of us would make a show of most devout obeisance when the village priest would call to say mass: and our confessions were but cynical recitals of small vices and transgressions, nothing more.

As hideous vermin crawl from under lifted stones, now bloated, grinning cohorts stream'd to Csejthe, call'd hither by Dorottya. Thou wert long familiar with them, Lord: the sorcerers Ujvary and Thorko, the first a skilful crafter of new tormentry which far surpass'd in cruel genius those of rack or wheel or any hitherto invented; another witch, call'd Darvula, whose energies and hungers rivall'd those of Dorottya; two serving maids, Otvos and Barsovny, to tend my person, chosen by Ferencz for youth and beauty and total absence of all scruple; and troops of others, nameless to me now.

Pitiful were those who came to Csejthe unwillingly: the blossoming young girls, who, in the mounting hundreds, were requir'd to fan and then appease our raging appetites. Entic'd from the village by pretty Otvos and Barsovny, who told of fair employment and reward at Csejthe; or drugg'd by Dorottya or Darvula; or overwhelm'd and beaten by the hulking Thorko or the slavering Ujvary; these pathetic creatures (all young and fair, for none else did we crave), were herded like swine into our cellars and our dungeons, to await the most deprav'd of our pleasure.

Dorottya told me once she was far older than she seem'd, and that she held the years in check and retain'd the youthful freshness of her skin by bathing in the blood of virgins. She bade me join her, and I did. If such a thing be horrible – the draining of young veins for such a purpose – how much more horrible, and to no purpose whatsoever, was the manner by which these hapless prisoners were put to death: not with the swift, blunt mercy that is dealt even to dumb cattle, but by prolong'd and calculated tortures, which I have not stomach to set down here, so degraded and inhuman were they.

Inhuman, saith I? Nay: the beasts of field and forest, lacking all humanity, e'en the most terrible among these, slay not by long deliberate delaying and for lust. Human, then, indeed, were those fell crimes.

From time to time, my brain – like to a wanderer lost in fog which sometimes lifteth, showing clary sun, only to weave greyly 'round the stumbling wretch again – would comprehend the fullest, deepest horror of our acts; and I would then resolve to end them, by freeing our poor victims, allowing them to spread the tale of our decay throughout the village, till it was arous'd. But never did I this, and now, upon reflection, I do think it was somehow for love of Ferencz that I refrain'; some shred of former feeling clung to me, and I could not bear to think of him haul'd up before tribunals and punish'd.

Then, on one day, fate took that fear from me.

Ferencz was summon'd to the battlefield again to fight the Saracen. As on that night years before, I bade farewell to him whilst cannonades of thunder boom'd through Csejthe and pelting rain curtain'd the countryside.

'Dost recollect,' I ask'd him, 'what words thou spake that other time thou left me for the wars?'

'Nay,' he answer'd, 'what said I then?'

'Thou didst declare: "God's my guardian, thou my guerdon: how else, then, can it be but I will triumph over Death and foe alike?" '

'A pretty speech,' he said, and mounted his palfry.

'Say it now!' I bade him.

'Art silly still?' he scoff'd.

'Say it, Ferencz!'

'Nay, have done. Fare thee well, and —' (irony congeal'd his face) '— prithee, do not pine away in solitude!' He goaded his mount, and rode into the night.

Less than a score of days from then, a courier deliver'd unto me the news: Ferencz was dead, 'honourably slain in batttle, by the heathen Turk who long hath ravag'd and lain waste our land.' The King himself had signed it.

O fortunate husband! Dead with honour; whilst I still languish'd in a filthy sty of sin. 'Twas then I cast from me all caution, and conspir'd to let the world know of the foul blight Castle Csejthe had now become.

One morning, my gore-streak'd companions still abed, so worn were they by ghastly revels in the night, I stole into the dungeons and unlock'd the shackles from the limbs of a single youthful captive, destin'd soon for torture and for death. I bade her flee to the village, and tell all – 'Spare nothing,' I beseech'd her, 'relate all horrors thou hast seen, all gushings of fair maidens' blood, all gloating torments, all!'

The frighten'd maid, at first, thought 'twas some trick, some game design'd to raise her hope, then dash it to the ground and thus torment her further. I begg'd her to believe me, trust in me (why *should* she trust in one who had partaken of such infernal rites?), and perchance for some sincerity that shineth from mine eyes, she believ'd me and did as she was bidden.

She was not miss'd by Dorottya or the others ('twas for this reason I but set free a single prisoner), and word soon spread. Grumblings commenc'd to reach us at the castle; village girls no longer were so easefully accessible to our procurers.

But there it stopp'd: rumblings and rumours; frighten'd glances cast toward Csejthe; a need by us of greater stealth; from the village church, veil'd sermons which, by indirections, weakly touch'd on a certain 'bloody band' abhorr'd by God, yet even these pale warnings couch'd in Latin – '*grex sanguinarius*' – which the villagers could scarce divine. And still our base carousals went uncheck'd!

Slowly, my dull mind fathom'd why: and, in its own way, the cause was far more crushing to my spirit than the grossest horrors we had wrought in Castle Csejthe.

IX
The Curse of Cats

For Ferencz had spoke true.

My name was too refulgent, my family too high-plac'd: who dar'd chastise us? My cousin, Gyorgy, Prime Minister to the King, ignor'd all tales he heard of our debauches, so that his own escutcheon might not be stain'd thereby.

When this execrable truth became clear to me, my heart sank. Was this humanity? Was this nobility? Was this the Christian glory that presum'd to hold itself above the heathen Turk? To suffer innocents be sacrific'd on an altar of corruption, merely that a lofty family be spar'd discomfiture? Oh, this was tenfold more abominable than the crime itself, that high authority should wink at it! Dismay'd, revolted, heartsick, I in that moment of black revelation forswore mankind, abjur'd all ties of family, renounc'd and disavow'd sweet Christ Himself.

Why did I not, disgusted by the perfidious world, plunge with refreshen'd appetite into those hellish orgies? I know not. Some almost dead, not quite extinguish'd lamp of good, perchance, prevented me; and I instead sought out Ilona.

I spoke to her as in far bygone days: 'Sweet nanny . . . dear old lady, dost thou hear? Put by thy dreaming ways, and list. Nay, nanny, do not drowse – thou must needs hear me! I'll give to thee a letter, which I'll straightway indite, and this I charge thee carry to good King Matthias – ay, to His Majesty, Ilona! Dost grasp my words?'

The good old lady nodded; the clouds lifted from her eyes. 'What kind of letter, child?' she ask'd.

'A document describing all heinous, dire iniquities that hath sprouted here like poisonous weeds. An humble, penitent confession of mine own part in them. A strong entreaty that His Majesty send troops to storm this castle and ensnare this whole foul company of demons! Such a letter shalt thou bear, Ilona.'

The old nurse strok'd my hand, as she was wont to do of yore. 'Dear child,' she said, 'my little babe, thou wilt be tried before stern judges, put to torture . . .'

'It is no matter. I yearn to be dismember'd on the rack, or disembowell'd, or burnt alive, to expiate my sins! No penance less will serve, Ilona; the time for pious mutterings of *mea culpa* is long past, it is too late! Thou *must*, dear nanny, do this thing for me!'

'Send *thee*, Elisabeth, to such judgement? . . .'

' 'Twere best, Ilona. In thine own unblemish'd conscience, thou know'st it must be done.'

My old nurse said no more, but obediently awaited my writing of the letter. This I did; and seal'd it with the signets of both Bathory and Nadasdy; and put it in her hand; and watch'd her until she was safe away from Csejthe.

The rest Thou knowest, too, O Lord:

How clement Matthias grew outrag'd, and made Gyorgy Thurzo storm my castle on the very eve of the New Year; how those captives left alive were freed; how all my despicable minions were put in chains and carried off to trial; how all, save me, were put to death.

Ay, all save me: that mercy was as bitter gall to me, who crav'd atonement. I, who wish'd for rack and fire, wast but condemn'd to stay in solitude, wall'd here within my chamber for the remainder of my days – for even when the grisly truth was told, my cousin interceded for me, and my life and comfort spar'd.

In all this tainted record, in all this sorry blot on privilege and authority, is there not one redeeming ray? One good and golden thing to shine in Heaven's book and expiate, in some small part, this race of man?

Verily, there is one. One who, from loyalty and love, could not endure to see me dragg'd before the seat of mortal judgement; one who, lest such a fate befall me, took all blame, all censure, all chastisement, said, ' 'Twas not the Countess brought these witches to the castle; nay, 'twas I, and only I.'

Too late I learn'd of dear Ilona's act: of how she made her way to His Majesty's court, was recogniz'd as my old nurse and so admitted, and how she then (having destroy'd my letter) told the King an host of horrid truths, and one unselfish lie: her false confession.

And, for that glorious sacrifice, which I neither desir'd nor deserv'd, the noble dame was grimly martyr'd: for though Ujvary, Thorko, Darvula, Otvos, and Barsovny were swift despatch'd by the head-man's axe, a most particular doom was meted out to those two thought the most despicable of that band: Dorottya and Ilona. Both luckless women (one a fiend, and one a blessed saint) were condemn'd to have their fingers, one by one, ripp'd off their hands, before they were conducted to the stake and burnt alive.

And soon I, too, will die, for I have left untouch'd for many days the food that has been brought me. Before I die, O Lord, I ask that I be granted but one boon:

I ask that Thou send cats – lean, vicious cats with teeth and claws as sharp as daggers – and set them on all pious souls who, when they knew full well what things were being done at Csejthe, sat idly by and mumbl'd orisons and cross'd themselves, and did no other thing. On my too generous cousin, Thurzo, set these clawing beasts; on that o'ercautious priest down in the village, who water'd down his Christian zeal into an insipid broth; and on all others of their ilk, rain yellow-eyed, mad, scratching, squawling cats! Do this, O Lord, I beg!

And, if Thou dost, why, when I see Thee soon, I'll thank Thee. For what should such an inky soul as mine do in the jasper halls of Heaven? I am so dipp'd in blood of innocents that my intolerable stench would cause the angels to stop up their nostrils at me! And so, instead, I have consign'd myself to Thee, for in Thy realm I am assur'd of welcome. I come, then, like a mistress, to Thy terrible Arms, and offer up mine own immortal soul to Thee – my Sovereign Lord, great Lucifer!

Thine own
ELISABETH

Author's Note

Without exception, every person and place named in this story existed. The main lineaments of the narrative are reconstructed from events that did, in fact, occur. Elisabeth Bathory died, as close as can be determined, on August 21, 1614, in a walled-up apartment of Castle Csejthe, county of Nyitra, northwestern Hungary. After her death, the village priest testified that he had been savagely attacked by a multitude of cats which, after biting and scratching him severely, vanished like mist.

Count Dracula

WOODY ALLEN

Since Bram Stoker's creation of Count Dracula in 1897 he has become probably the most imitated, copied and parodied character in fiction. A seemingly endless line of new books, films, radio and television adaptations, not to mention comic book versions and video games have provided a bonanza for authors, scriptwriters, artists and merchandizers in general all over the world: each and every one of them owing a debt of gratitude to the man who took those legends of Vlad and Elizabeth Bathory and mixed them into the novel which will soon be celebrating the centenary of its first publication. What Dracula begat now fills whole libraries and where short stories are concerned, historian Donald F. Glut in his comprehensive survey, The Dracula Book (1975) devotes over forty pages to the dozens of short pieces of fiction which have resurrected the Count in one shape or another. And that listing is now 20 years out of date! Count Dracula is without any doubt one of the half dozen most famous characters in all of literature.

Authors of every kind have been drawn to the figure of the vampire Count – from a great many leading horror story writers to literary figures including Walter de la Mare, Lawrence Durrell, Kingsley Amis and even such an unlikely figure as the multi-talented film maker and comedian Woody Allen (1935–). Woody, whose understated wit has dominated American humour since the mid-Sixties in print, on recordings and on the stage and screen, is a master of parody and has deservedly won many awards for his work. Here in a story written in 1981 he tackles the Dracula legend, and thanks to his inimitable style it may never be quite the same again . . .

*   *   *

Somewhere in Transylvania, Dracula the monster lies sleeping in his coffin, waiting for night to fall. As exposure to the sun's rays would surely cause him to perish, he stays protected in the satin-lined chamber bearing his family name in silver. Then the moment of darkness comes, and through some miraculous instinct the fiend emerges from the safety of his hiding place and, assuming the hideous forms of the bat or the wolf, he prowls the countryside, drinking the blood of his victims. Finally, before the first rays of his archenemy, the sun, announce a new day, he hurries back to the safety of his hidden coffin and sleeps, as the cycle begins anew.

Now he starts to stir. The fluttering of his eyelids are a response to some age-old, unexplainable instinct that the sun is nearly down and his time is near. Tonight, he is particularly hungry and as he lies there, fully awake now, in red-lined Inverness cape and tails, waiting to feel with uncanny perception the precise moment of darkness before opening the lid and emerging, he decides who this evening's victims will be. The baker and his wife, he thinks to himself. Succulent, available and unsuspecting. The thought of the unwary couple whose trust he has carefully cultivated excites his blood lust to a fever pitch, and he can barely hold back these last seconds before climbing out of the coffin to seek his prey.

Suddenly he knows the sun is down. Like an angel of hell, he rises swiftly, and changing into a bat, flies pell-mell to the cottage of his tantalizing victims.

'Why, Count Dracula, what a nice surprise,' the baker's wife says, opening the door to admit him. (He has once again assumed human form, as he enters their home, charmingly concealing his rapacious goal.)

'What brings you here so early?' the baker asks.

'Our dinner date,' the Count answers. 'I hope I haven't made an error. You did invite me for tonight, didn't you?'

'Yes, tonight, but that's not for seven hours.'

'Pardon me?' Dracula queries, looking around the room puzzled.

'Or did you come by to watch the eclipse with us?'

'Eclipse?'

'Yes. Today's the total eclipse.'

'What?'

'A few moments of darkness from noon until two minutes after. Look out the window.'

'Uh-oh – I'm in big trouble.'

'Eh?'

'And now if you'll excuse me . . .'

'What, Count Dracula?'

'Must be going – aha – oh, god . . .' Frantically he fumbles for the door knob.

'Going? You just came.'

'Yes – but – I think I blew it very badly . . .'

'Count Dracula, you're pale.'

'Am I? I need a little fresh air. It was nice seeing you . . .'

'Come. Sit down. We'll have a drink.'

'Drink?' No, I must run. Er – you're stepping on my cape.'

'Sure. Relax. Some wine.'

'Wine? Oh no, gave it up – liver and all that, you know. And now I really must buzz off. I just remembered, I left the lights on at my castle – bills'll be enormous . . .'

'Please,' the baker says, his arm around the Count in firm friendship. 'You're not intruding. Don't be so polite. So you're early.'

'Really, I'd like to stay but there's a meeting of old Roumanian Counts across town and I'm responsible for the cold cuts.'

'Rush, rush, rush. It's a wonder you don't get a heart attack.'

'Yes, right – and now – '

'I'm making Chicken Pilaf tonight,' the baker's wife chimes in. 'I hope you like it.'

'Wonderful, wonderful,' the Count says, with a smile, as he pushes her aside into some laundry. Then, opening a closet door by mistake, he walks in. 'Christ, where's the goddamn front door?'

'Ach,' laughs the baker's wife, 'such a funny man, the Count.'

'I knew you'd like that,' Dracula says, forcing a chuckle, 'now get out of my way.' At last he opens the front door but time has run out on him.

'Oh, look, mama,' says the baker, 'the eclipse must be over. The sun is coming out again.'

'Right,' says Dracula slamming the front door. 'I've decided to stay. Pull down the window shades quickly – *quickly*! Let's move it!'

'What window shades?' asks the baker.

'There are none, right? Figures. You got a basement in this joint?'

'No,' says the wife affably, 'I'm always telling Jarslov to build one but he never listens. That's some Jarslov, my husband.'

'I'm all choked up. Where's the closet?'

'You did that one already, Count Dracula. Unt mama and I laughed at it.'

'Ach – such a funny man, the Count.'

'Look, I'll be in the closet. Knock at seven-thirty.' And with that, the Count steps inside the closet and slams the door.

'Hee-hee – he is so funny, Jarslov.'

'Oh, Count. Come out of the closet. Stop being a big silly.' From inside the closet comes the muffled voice of Dracula.

'Can't – please – take my word for it. Just let me stay here. I'm fine. Really.'

'Count Dracula, stop the fooling. We're already helpless with laughter.'

'Can I tell you, I love this closet.'

'Yes, but . . .'

'I know, I know . . . it seems strange, and yet here I am, having a ball. I was just saying to Mrs Hess the other day, give me a good closet and I can stand in it for hours. Sweet woman, Mrs Hess. Fat but sweet . . . Now, why don't you run along and check back with me at sunset. Oh, Ramona, la da da de da da de, Ramona . . .'

Now the Mayor and his wife, Katia, arrive. They are passing by and have decided to pay a call on their good friends, the baker and his wife.

'Hello, Jarslov. I hope Katia and I are not intruding?'

'Of course not, Mr Mayor. Come out, Count Dracula! We have company!'

'Is the Count here?' asks the Mayor surprised.

'Yes, and you'll never guess where,' says the baker's wife.

'It's so rare to see him around this early. In fact I can't ever remember seeing him around in the daytime.'

'Well, he's here. Come out, Count Dracula!'

'Where is he?' Katia asks, not knowing whether to laugh or not.

'Come on out now! Let's go!' The baker's wife is getting impatient.

'He's in the closet,' says the baker, apologetically.

'Really?' asks the Mayor.

'Let's go,' says the baker with mock good humour as he knocks on the closet door. 'Enough is enough. The Mayor's here.'

'Come on out, Dracula,' His Honour shouts, 'let's have a drink.'

'No, go ahead. I've got some business in here.'

'In the closet?'

'Yes, don't let me spoil your day. I can hear what you're saying. I'll join in if I have anything to add.'

Everyone looks at one another and shrugs. Wine is poured and they all drink.

'Some eclipse today,' the Mayor says, sipping from his glass.

'Yes,' the baker agrees. 'Incredible.'

'Yeah. Thrilling,' says a voice from the closet.

'What, Dracula?'

'Nothing, nothing. Let it go.'

And so the time passes, until the Mayor can stand it no longer and forcing open the door to the closet, he shouts, 'Come on, Dracula. I always thought you were a mature man. Stop this craziness.'

The daylight streams in, causing the evil monster to shriek and slowly dissolve to a skeleton and then to dust before the eyes of the four people present. Leaning down to the pile of white ash on the closet floor, the baker's wife shouts, 'Does this mean dinner's off tonight?'

West of October

RAY BRADBURY

Just as Dracula *inspired Woody Allen to write his little comedy masterpiece, so it played a significant role in the development of a series of stories about the Family, a clutch of vampires living in middle America created by Ray Bradbury in 1944 and about whom he has written at regular, if not frequent enough intervals, ever since. The first of these tales was 'The Homecoming' which, extraordinary as it may seem, was first submitted to* Weird Tales *and rejected, but instead found a place in one of America's leading slick magazines of the post-war period,* Mademoiselle. *Its publication represented another landmark in the history of vampire fiction, according to William F. Nolan, 'because Bradury succeeded in making a clan of vampires delightful and presented them to a host of feminine readers mainly unfamiliar with vampires as fiction fare.' Just how wrong the decision of the editor of* Weird Tales *had been was underlined in 1947 when 'The Homecoming' was selected for the O. Henry Memorial Award Prize. When Ray wrote a second story about the Family called 'The Traveller' in 1946, however,* Weird Tales *did not make the same mistake twice and published the tale in its March issue. This was followed by 'Uncle Einer' (*Dark Carnival, *1947), 'The April Witch' (*Saturday Evening Post, *1952) and 'West of October' which was originally written in the Sixties as 'A Trip to Cranamockett' but was not published until Ray had substantially revised it in 1988. (One of the gems of my archive of Bradbury material is a copy of the original version of this tale.)*

Ray Bradbury (1920–) is arguably the world's leading writer of fantasy-horror fiction – his novels and short stories have been translated all over the world and a number of them, such as The Martian Chronicles *(1950),* The Illustrated Man *(1951) and* Fahrenheit 451 *(1953) have also been made into films and TV specials. Dracula was, he says, one of the first horror stories he read as a child in Waukegan, a little town in Illinois, and its influence is also to be found in a number of his other works aside from those about the Family. Pre-eminent among these is the novel,* Something Wicked This Way Comes *(1962) which Stephen King has put at the top of his list of 'Ten Favourite Fantasy-Horror Novels', and the short stories 'The Exiles' (1951) and 'A Medicine for Melancholy' (1959). But it is the most recent story of the family of vampires which appears here, and any reader discovering this unique brood for the first time will probably need no further encouragment to find out more about their history from the earlier tales . . .*

*   *   *

The four cousins, Tom, William, Philip, and John, had come to visit the Family at the end of summer. There was no room in the big old house, so they were stashed out on little cots in the barn, which shortly thereafter burned.

Now the Family was no ordinary family. Each member of it was more extraordinary than the last.

To say that most of them slept days and worked at odd jobs nights, would fall short of commencement.

To remark that some of them could read minds, and some fly with lightnings to land with leaves, would be an understatement.

To add that some could not be seen in mirrors while others could be found in multitudinous shapes, sizes, and textures in the same glass, would merely repeat gossip that veered into truth.

There were uncles, aunts, cousins, and grandparents by the toadstool score and the mushroom dozen.

They were just about every colour you could mix in one restless night.

Some were young and others had been around since the Sphinx first sank its stone paws deep in tidal sands.

In all, in numbers, background, inclination, and talent, a most incredible and miraculous mob. And the most incredible of them all was:

Cecy.

Cecy. She was the reason, the real reason, the central reason for any of the Family to come visit, and not only to visit but to circle her and stay. For she was as multitudinous as a pomegranate. Her talent was single but kaleidoscopic. She was all the senses of all the creatures in the world. She was all the motion picture houses and stage play theatres and all the art galleries of time. You could ask almost anything of her and she would gift you with it.

Ask her to yank your soul like an aching tooth and drift it in clouds to cool your spirit, and yanked you were, drawn high to drift in such clouds as sowed rain to grow grass and seed-sprout flowers.

Ask her to seize that same soul and bind it in the flesh of a tree, and you awoke next morning with apples popping out of your branches and birds singing in your green-leafed head.

Ask to live in a frog, and you spent days afloat and nights croaking strange songs.

Ask to be pure rain and you fell on everything. Ask to be the moon and suddenly you looked down and saw your pale illumination bleaching lost towns to the colour of tombstones and tuberoses and spectral ghosts.

Cecy. Who extracted your soul and pulled forth your impacted wisdom, and could transfer it to animal, vegetable, or mineral; name your poison.

No wonder the Family came. No wonder they stayed long past lunch, way beyond dinner, far into midnights the week after next!

And here were the four cousins, come to visit.

And along about sunset of the first day, each of them said, in effect: 'Well?'

They were lined up by Cecy's bed in the great house, where she lay for long hours, both night and noon, because her talents were in such demand by both family and friends.

'Well,' said Cecy, her eyes shut, a smile playing about her lovely mouth. 'What would your pleasure be?'

'I – ' said Tom.

'Maybe – ' said John.

'Take you on a visit to the local insane asylum,' guessed Cecy, 'to peek in people's very strange heads?'

'Yes!'

'Said and done!' said Cecy. 'Go lie on your cots in the barn. 'They ran. They lay. 'That's it. Over, up, and – out!' she cried.

Like corks, their souls popped. Like birds, they flew. Like bright unseen needles they shot into various and assorted ears in the asylum just down the hill and across the valley.

'Ah!' they cried in delight at what they found and saw.

While they were gone, the barn burned down.

In all the shouting and confusion, the running for water, the general ramshackle hysteria, everyone forgot what was in the barn or where the high-flying cousins might be going, or what Cecy, asleep, was up to. So deep in her rushing sleep was this favourite daughter, that she heard not the flames, nor the dread moment when the walls fell in and four human-shaped torches self-destroyed. The cousins themselves did not feel the repercussions of their own bodies being snuffed for some few moments. Then a clap of silent thunder banged across country, shook the skies, knocked the wind-blown essences of lost cousin through mill-fans to lodge in trees, while Cecy, with a gasp, sat upright up in bed.

Running to the window, she looked out and gave one shriek that shot the cousins home. All four, at the moment of concussion, had been in various parts of the county asylum, opening trapdoors in wild people's heads and peeking in at maelstroms of confetti and wondering at the colours of madness, and the dark rainbow hues of nightmare.

All the Family stood by the collapsed barn, stunned. Hearing Cecy's cry, they turned.

'What happened?' cried John from her mouth.

'Yes, what!' said Philip, moving her lips.

'My God,' gasped William, staring from her eyes.

'The barn burned,' said Tom. 'We're *dead!*'

The Family, soot-faced in the smoking yard, turned like a travelling minstrel's funeral and stared up at Cecy in shock.

'Cecy?' asked Mother, wildly. 'Is there someone, I mean, *with* you?'

'Yes, me, Tom!' shouted Tom from her lips.

'And me, John.'

'Philip!'

'William!'

The souls counted off from the young woman's mouth.

The Family waited.

Then, as one, the four young men's voices asked the final, most dreadful question:

'Didn't you save just *one* body?'

The Family sank an inch into the earth, burdened with a reply they could not give.

'But — ' Cecy held on to her own elbows, touched her own chin, her mouth, her brow, inside which four live ghosts knocked elbows for room. 'But – what'll I *do* with them?' Her eyes searched over all those faces below in the yard. 'My boy cousins can't stay here. They simply can't stand around in my *head!*'

What she cried after that, or what the cousins babbled, crammed like pebbles under her tongue, or what the Family said, running like burned chickens in the yard, was lost.

Like Judgment Day thunders, the rest of the barn fell.

With a hollow roar the fire went up the kitchen chimney. An October wind leaned this way and that on the roof, listening to all the Family talk in the dining room below.

'It seems to me,' said Father.

'Not seems, but *is!*' said Cecy, her eyes now blue, now yellow, now hazel, now brown.

'We must farm the young cousins out. Find temporary hospices for them, until such time as we can cull new bodies – '

'The quicker the better,' said a voice from Cecy's mouth now high, now low, now two gradations between.

'Joseph might be loaned out to Bion, Tom given to Leonard, William to Sam, Philip to – '

All the uncles, so named, snapped their hackles and stirred their boots.

Leonard summed up for all. 'Busy. Overworked. Bion with his shop, Sam with his farm.'

'Gah – .' Misery sprang from Cecy's mouth in four-part harmony.

Father sat down in darkness. 'Good grief, there must be *some* one of us with plenty of time to waste, a small room to let in the backside of their subconscious or the topside of their trapdoor Id! Volunteers! *Stand!*'

The Family sucked an icy breath, for suddenly Grandma was on her feet, but pointing her witch-broom cane.

'That man right there's got all the time in the world. I hereby solicit, name, and nominate *him!*'

As if their heads were on a single string, everyone turned to blink at Grandpa.

Grandpa leaped up as if shot. 'No!'

'Hush.' Grandma shut her eyes on the question, folded her arms, purring, over her bosom. 'You got all the time in the world.'

'No, by Joshua and Jesus!'

'This,' Grandma pointed around by intuition, eyes closed, 'is the Family. No one in the world like us. We're particular strange-fine. We sleep days, walk nights, fly the winds and airs, wander storms, read minds, hate wine, like blood, do magic, live forever or a thousand years, whichever comes first. In sum, we're the Family. That being true and particular there's no one to lean on, turn to, when trouble comes – '

'I won't – '

'Hush.' One eye as large as the Star of India opened, burned, dimmed down, shut. 'You spit mornings, whittle afternoons, and catbox the nights. The four nice cousins can't stay in Cecy's upper floor. It's not proper, four wild young men in a slim girl's head.' Grandma's mouth sweetened itself. 'Besides, there's a lot *you* can teach the cousins. You been around long before Napoleon walked in and then ran *out* of Russia, or Ben Franklin got the pox. Good if the boys were tucked in your ear for a spell. What's inside, God knows, but it might, I say might, improve their posture. Would you deny them *that?*'

'Jumping Jerusalem!' Grandpa leaped to his feet. 'I won't have them all wrestling two falls out of three between my left ear and my right! Kick the sides out of my head. Knock my eyes like basketballs around inside my skull! My brain's no boardinghouse. One at a time! Tom can pull my eyelids up in the morning. William can help me shove the food in, noons. John can snooze in my cold pork-marrow half-into dusk. Philip can dance in my dusty attic nights. Time to myself is what I ask. And clean up when they *leave!*'

'Done!' Grandma circled like an orchestra leader, waving at the ghosted air. 'One at a time, did you *hear*, boys?'

'We heard!' cried an anvil chorus from Cecy's mouth.

'Move 'em in!' said Grandpa.

'Gangway!' said four voices.

And since no one had bothered to say which cousin went first, there was a surge of phantoms on the air, a huge tide-drift of storm and unseen wind.

Four different expressions lit Grandpa's face. Four different earthquakes shook his brittle frame. Four different smiles ran scales along his piano teeth. Before Grandpa could protest, at four different gaits and speeds, he was run out of the house, across the lawn, and down the abandoned railroad tracks toward town, yelling against and laughing for the wild hours ahead.

The family stood lined up on the porch, staring after the rushing parade of one.

'Cecy! *Do* something!'

But Cecy, exhausted, was fast asleep in her chair.

That *did* it.

At noon the next day the big, dull blue, iron engine panted into the railroad station to find the Family lined up on the platform, Grandpa leaned and supported in their midst. They not so much walked but carried him to the day coach, which smelled of fresh varnish and hot plush. Along the way, Grandpa, eyes shut, spoke in a variety of voices that everyone pretended not to hear.

They propped him like an ancient doll in his seat, fastened his straw hat on his head like putting a new roof on an old building, and talked into his face.

'Grandpa, sit up. Grandpa, mind your hat. Grandpa, along the way don't drink. Grandpa, you *in* there? Get out of the way, cousins, let the old man speak.'

'I'm here.' Grandpa's mouth and eyes gave some bird-like twitches. 'And suffering for their sins. *Their* whiskey makes *my* misery. Damn!'

'No such thing!' 'Lies!' 'We did nothing!' cried a number of voices from one side, then the other of his mouth. 'No!'

'Hush!' Grandma grabbed the old man's chin and focused his bones with a shake. 'West of October is Cranamockett, not a long trip. We got all kinds of folks there, uncles, aunts, cousins, some with and some without children. Your job is to board the cousins out and – '

'Take a load off my mind,' muttered Grandpa, a tear trickling down from one trembling eyelid.

'But if you can't unload the damn fools,' advised Grandma, 'bring 'em back alive!'

'If I live through it.'

'Goodbye!' said four voices from under his tongue.

'Goodbye!' Everyone waved from the platform. 'So long, Grandpa, Tom, William, Philip, John!'

'*I'm* here now, *too!*' said a young woman's voice.

Grandpa's mouth had popped wide.

'Cecy!' cried everyone. 'Farewell!'

'Good night nurse!' said Grandpa.

The train chanted away into the hills, west of October.

The train rounded a long curve. Grandpa leaned and creaked his body.

'Well,' whispered Tom, 'here we are.'

'Yes.' A long pause. William went on: 'Here we are.'

A long silence. The train whistled.

'I'm tired,' said John.

'*You're* tired!' Grandpa snorted.

'Bit stuffy in here,' said Philip.

'Got to expect that. Grandpa's ten thousand years old, aren't you, Grandpa?'

'Four hundred; shut *up!*' Grandpa gave his own skull a thump with his fingers. A panic of birds knocked about in his head. 'Cease!'

'There,' whispered Cecy, quieting the panic. 'I've slept well and I'll come for *part* of the trip, Grandpa, to teach you how to hold, stay, and keep the resident crows and vultures in your cage.'

'Crows! Vultures!' the cousins protested.

'Silence,' said Cecy, tamping the cousins like tobacco in an ancient uncleaned pipe. Far away, her body lay in her bedroom as always, but her mind wove around them softly; touched, pushed, enchanted, kept. 'Enjoy. Look around.'

The cousins looked.

And indeed, wandering in the upper keeps of Grandfather's head was like surviving in a mellow attic in which memories, transparent wings folded, lay piled all about in ribboned bundles, in files, packets, shrouded figures, strewn shadows. Here and there, a special bright memory, like a single ray of amber light, struck in upon and shaped here a golden hour, there a summer day. There was a smell of worn leather and burnt horsehair and the faintest scent of uric acid from the jaundiced beams that ached about them as they jostled invisible elbows.

'Look,' murmured the cousins. 'I'll be darned. *Sure!*'

For now, quietly indeed, they were peering through the dusty panes of the old man's eyes, viewing the great hellfire train that bore them and the green-turning-to-brown autumn world swinging by, all of it passing as traffic does before an old house with cobwebbed windows. When they worked Grandpa's mouth it was like ringing a dulled clapper in a rusty churchbell. The sounds of the world wandered in through his hairy ears like static on a badly tuned radio.

'Still,' Tom admitted, 'it's better than having no body at all.'

'I'm dizzy,' said John. 'Not used to bifocals. Can you take your glasses off, Grandpa?'

'Nope.'

The train banged across a bridge in thunders.

'Think I'll take a look around,' said Tom.

Grandpa felt his limbs stir.

'Stick right where you are, young man!'

Grandpa shut his eyes tight.

'Put up the shades, Grandpa! Let's see the sights!'

His eyeballs swivelled under the lids.

'Here comes a pretty girl, built one brick atop another! Quick!'

Grandpa tightened his lids.

'Most beautiful girl in the *world!*'

Grandpa couldn't help but open one eye.

'Ah!' said everyone. '*Right*, Grandpa?'

'Nope!'

The young woman curved this way and that, leaning as the train pushed or pulled her; as pretty as something you might win at a carnival by knocking the milk bottles down.

'Bosh!' Grandpa slammed his windows shut.

'Open, Sesame!'

Instantly, within, he felt his eyeballs redirected.

'Let go!' shouted Grandpa. 'Grandma'll *kill* me!'

'She'll never *know!*'

The young woman turned as if called. She lurched back as if she might fall on *all* of them.

'Stop!' cried Grandpa. 'Cecy's with us! She's innocent and – '

'Innocent!' The great attic rocked with laughter.

'Grandfather,' said Cecy, very softly. 'With all the night excursions I have made, all the travelling I have done, I am not – '

'Innocent,' said the four cousins.

'Look here!' protested Grandpa.

'No, *you* look,' whispered Cecy. 'I have sewn my way through bedroom windows on a thousand summer nights. I have lain in cool snowbeds of white pillows and sheets, and I have swum unclothed in rivers on August noons and lain on riverbanks for birds to see – '

'I – ' Grandpa screwed his fists into his ears – 'will not listen!'

'Yes.' Cecy's voice wandered in cool meadows remembering. 'I have been in a girl's warm summer face and looked out at a young man, and I have been in that same young man, the same instant, breathing out fiery breaths, gazing at that forever summer girl. I have lived in mating mice or circling lovebirds or bleeding-heart doves. I have hidden in two butterflies fused on a blossom of clover – '

'Damn!' Grandpa winced.

'I've been in sleighs on December midnights when snow fell and smoke plumed out the horses' pink nostrils and there were fur blankets piled high with six young people hidden warm and delving and wishing and finding and – '

'Stop! I'm sunk!' said Grandpa.

'Bravo!' said the cousins. 'More!'

'– and I have been inside a grand castle of bone and flesh – the most beautiful woman in the world . . . !'

Grandpa was amazed and held still.

For now it was as if snow fell upon and quieted him. He felt a stir of flowers about his brow, and a blowing of July morning wind about his ears, and all through his limbs a burgeoning of warmth, a growth of bosom about his ancient flat chest, a fire struck to bloom in the pit of his stomach. Now, as she talked, his lips softened and coloured and knew poetry and might have let it pour forth in incredible rains, and his worn and iron-rusty fingers tumbled in his lap and changed to cream and milk and melting apple-snow. He looked down at them, stunned, clenched his fists to stop this womanish thing!

'No! Give me back my hands! Wash my mouth out with soap!'

'Enough talk,' said an inner voice, Philip.

'We're wasting time,' said Tom.

'Let's go say hello to that young lady across the aisle,' said John. 'All those in favour?'

'Aye!' said the Salt Lake Tabernacle choir from one single throat. Grandpa was yanked to his feet by unseen wires.

'Any dissenters?'

'Me!' thundered Grandpa.

Grandpa squeezed his eyes, squeezed his head, squeezed his ribs. His entire body was that incredibly strange bed that sank to smother its terrified victims. 'Gotcha!'

The cousins ricocheted about in the dark.

'Help! Cecy! Light! Give us light! Cecy!'

'I'm here!' said Cecy.

The old man felt himself touched, twitched, tickled, now behind the ears, now the spine. Now his knees knocked, now his ankles cracked. Now his lungs filled with feathers, his nose sneezed soot.

'Will, his left leg, move! Tom, the right leg, *hup!* Philip, right arm, John, the left! Fling! Me for his flimsy turkey-bone body! Ready! Set!'

'Heave!'

'Double-time. Run!'

Grandpa ran.

But he didn't run across the aisle, he ran down it, gasping, eyes bright.

'Wait!' cried the Greek chorus. 'The lady's back there! Someone trip him! Who's got his legs? Will? Tom!'

Grandpa flung the vestibule door wide, leaped out on the windy platform and was about to hurl himself out into a meadow of swiftly flashing sunflowers when:

'Freeze! Statues!' said the chorus stuffed in his mouth.

And statue he became on the backside of the swiftly vanishing train.

A moment later, spun about, Grandpa found himself back inside. As the train rocketed around a curve, he sat on the young lady's hands.

'Excuse,' Grandpa leaped up, 'me – '

'Excused.' The lady rearranged her sat-on hands.

'No trouble, please, no, no!' Grandpa collapsed on the seat across from her, eyes clammed shut. 'Damn! hell! Statues, everyone! Bats, back in the belfry! Damn!'

The cousins grinned and melted the wax in his ears.

'Remember,' hissed Grandpa behind his teeth, 'you're young in there, I'm a mummy out here!'

'But – ' sighed the chamber quartet fiddling behind his lids – 'we'll act to *make* you young!'

He felt them light a fuse in his stomach, a bomb in his chest.

'No!'

Grandpa yanked a cord in the dark. A trapdoor popped wide. The cousins fell down into a rich and endless maze of colour and remembrance. Three-dimensional shapes as rich and almost as warm as the girl across the aisle. The cousins fell, shouting.

'Watch it!'

'I'm lost!'

'Tom?'

'I'm somewhere in Wisconsin! How'd I get *here?*'

'*I'm* on a Hudson River boat. William?'

Far off, William called: 'London. My God! Newspapers say the date's August twenty-second, nineteen hundred!'

'Can't be! Cecy?!'

'Not Cecy! Me!' said Grandpa, everywhere at once. 'You're still between my ears, dammit, and using my other times and places as guest towels. Mind your head, the ceilings are low!'

'Ah ha,' said William. 'And is this the Grand Canyon I gaze upon, or a wrinkle in your nut?'

'Grand Canyon,' said Grandpa. 'Nineteen twenty-one.'

'A woman!' cried Tom, 'stands before me!'

And indeed the woman was beautiful in the spring, two hundred years ago. Grandpa recalled no name. She had only been someone passing as he hunted wild strawberries on a summer noon.

Tom reached out toward the beautiful memory.

'Get away!' shouted Grandpa.

And the girl's face, in the light summer air, flew apart. She drifted away, away, vanishing down the road, and at last gone.

'Damn and blast!' cried Tom.

The other cousins were in a rampage, opening doors, running paths, raising windows.

'Look! Oh, my gosh! Look!' they all shouted.

The memories lay side by side, neat as sardines a million deep, a million wide. Put by in seconds, minutes, hours. Here a dark girl brushing her hair. Here the same girl walking, running, or asleep. All her actions kept in honey-combs the colour of her summer cheeks. The bright flash of her smile. You could pick her up, turn her round, send her away, call her back. All you had to say was Italy, 1797, and she danced through a warm pavilion, or swam in moonlit waters.

'Grandfather! Does Grandma know about her?'

'There *must* be other women!'

'Thousands!' cried Grandpa.

Grandpa flung back a lid. 'Here!'

A thousand women wandered through a department store.

'Well done, Grandpa!'

From ear to ear, Grandpa felt the rummaging and racing over mountains, scoured deserts, down alleys, through cities.

Until John seized one lone and lovely lady by the arm.

He caught a woman by the hand.

'Stop!' Grandpa rose up with a roar. The people on the train stared at him.

'Got you!' said John.

The beautiful woman turned.

'Fool!' snarled Grandpa.

The lovely woman's flesh burned away. The upraised chin grew gaunt, the cheeks hollow, the eyes sank in wrinkles.

John drew back. 'Grandmother, it's *you!*'

'Cecy!' Grandpa was trembling violently. 'Stash John in a bird, a stone, a well! Anywhere, but not in my damn fool head! Now!'

'Out you go, John!' said Cecy.

And John vanished.

Into a robin singing on a pole that flashed by the train window.

Grandmother stood withered in darkness. Grandpa's gentle inward gaze touched her again, to reclothe her younger flesh. New colour poured into her eyes, cheeks, and hair. He hid her safely away in a nameless and far-off orchard.

Grandpa opened his eyes.

Sunlight sprang in on the last three cousins.

The young woman still sat across the aisle.

Grandfather shut his eyes again but it was too late. The cousins rose up behind his gaze.

'We're fools!' said Tom. 'Why bother with old times! Now is right *there!* That girl! Yes?'

'Yes!' whispered Cecy. 'Listen! I'll put Grandpa's mind over in *her* body. Then bring her mind over to hide in Grandpa's head! Grandpa's body will sit here straight as a ramrod, and inside it we'll be acrobats, gymnasts! fiends! The conductor will pass, never guessing! Grandpa will sit here. His head full of wild laughter, unclothed mobs while his real mind will be trapped over there in that fine girl's head! What fun in the middle of a train coach on a hot afternoon, with nobody knowing.'

'Yes!' said everyone at once.

'No,' said Grandpa, and pulled forth two white tablets from his pocket and swallowed them.

'Stop him!' shouted William.

'Drat!' said Cecy. 'It was such a fine, lovely, wicked plan.'

'Good night, everybody,' said Grandpa. The medicine was working. 'And you – ' he said, looking with gentle sleepiness at the young lady across the aisle. 'You have just been rescued from a fate, young lady, worse than ten thousands deaths.'

'Beg pardon?' The young lady blinked.

'Innocence, continue in thy innocence,' said Grandpa, and fell asleep.

The train pulled into Cranamockett at six o'clock. Only then was John allowed back from his exile in the head of that robin on a fence miles behind.

There were absolutely no relatives in Cranamockett willing to take in the cousins.

At the end of three days, Grandfather rode the train back to Illinois, the cousins still in him, like peach stones.

And there they stayed, each in a different territory of Grandpa's sun-or-moonlit attic keep.

Tom took residence in a remembrance of 1840 in Vienna with a crazed actress, William lived in Lake County with a flaxen-haired Swede of some indefinite years, while John shuttled from fleshpot to fleshpot, 'Frisco, Berlin, Paris, appearing, on occasion, as a wicked glitter in Grandpa's eyes. Philip, on the other hand, locked himself deep in a potato-bin cellar, where he read all the books Grandpa ever read.

But on some nights Grandpa edges over under the covers toward Grandma.

'You!' she cries. 'At your age! Git!' she screams.

And she beats and beats and beats him until, laughing in five voices, Grandpa gives up, falls back, and pretends to sleep, alert with five kinds of alertness, for another try.

First Anniversary

RICHARD MATHESON

One of the landmark vampire novels of the second half of the twentieth century has proved to be I Am Legend *by Richard Matheson (1926–) which was first published in 1954. This story of a future world where the entire population – with the exception of one man – have become vampires, has had a profound influence on the genre, been filmed several times, and also made its author famous. All this recognition notwithstanding,* I Am Legend *was not Matheson's first excursion into vampire lore: in 1951 he had written two fine short stories, 'Drink My Red Blood' and 'Dress of White Silk' in both of which children were, unusually, the protagonists. The author's own interest in vampirism had, in fact, been sparked during his childhood in New Jersey as a result of reading the classic horror novels and seeing the famous Universal movies at the cinema. What he later brought to fiction was an original way of treating old themes in contemporary settings: a facility which has also shaped his career as a major novelist and now one of the leading Hollywood scriptwriters.*

The first attempt to bring I Am Legend *to the screen was actually initiated in 1957 in England by Hammer Films with Matheson himself writing the screenplay. Sadly, however, even though filming began on* Night Creatures *– as the adaptation was to be called – once a copy of the script was seen by the British Board of Film Censor's office, Hammer were summarily informed the picture faced an outright ban if it was ever released. The company had no alternative but to immediately halt the project.* I Am Legend *has, however, subsequently been filmed twice in more enlightened times – first as* The Last Man on Earth *starring Vincent Prince (1967) and then as* The Omega Man

with Charlton Heston *(1971)* – but Matheson worked on neither
picture and both undoubtedly lack the sense of paranoia of the
original novel. The book was also the inspiration for George A.
Romero's Night of the Living Dead *(1968), a film which, in its turn,
has initiated a whole new genre of movies about the animated undead.
Among Matheson's own work for the movies, he has scripted two
Dracula pictures,* Dracula Walks The Night *(1972) and a faithful
version of* Dracula *(1973) filmed in England and Yugoslavia starring
Jack Palance. One of his later vampire short stories, 'The Funeral'
(1955), about Dracula turning up to the funeral of another vampire,
was adapted in 1973 for Rod Serling's TV series,* Night Gallery *with
Victor Buono as the Count. In 'First Anniversary' (1960), which is
again about the animated undead, Richard Matheson once more
utilizes an ancient concept in a modern setting – and the story is
notable, too, for containing some similar elements to those which
made* Night of the Living Dead *such a ground-breaking movie . . .*

*   *   *

Just before he left the house on Thursday morning, Adeline asked
him, 'Do I still taste sour to you?'
Norman looked at her reproachfully.
'Well, do I?'
He slipped his arms around her waist and nibbled at her throat.
'Tell me now,' said Adeline.
Norman looked submissive.
'Aren't you going to let me live it down?' he asked.
'Well, you *said* it, darling. And on our first anniversary, too!'
He pressed his cheek to hers. 'So I said it,' he murmured. 'Can't I be
allowed a faux pas now and then?'
'You haven't answered me.'
'Do you taste sour? Of course you don't.' He held her close and
breathed the fragrance of her hair. 'Forgiven?'
She kissed the tip of his nose and smiled and, once more, he could
only marvel at the fortune which had bestowed on him such a
magnificent wife. Starting their second year of marriage, they were still
like honeymooners.
Norman raised her face and kissed her.
'Be damned,' he said.
'What's wrong? Am I sour again?'
'No.' He looked confused. 'Now I can't taste you at all.'

*

'Now you can't taste her at all,' said Dr Phillips.

Norman smiled. 'I know it sounds ridiculous,' he said.

'Well, it's unique, I'll give it that,' said Phillips.

'More than you think,' added Norman, his smile grown a trifle laboured.

'How so?'

'I have no trouble tasting anything else.'

Dr Phillips peered at him awhile before he spoke. 'Can you smell her?' he asked then.

'Yes.'

'You're sure.'

'*Yes*. What's that got to do with – ' Norman stopped. 'You mean that the senses of taste and smell go together,' he said.

Phillips nodded. 'If you can smell her, you should be able to taste her.'

'I suppose,' said Norman, 'but I can't.'

Dr Phillips grunted wryly. 'Quite a poser.'

'No ideas?' asked Norman.

'Not offhand,' said Phillips, 'though I suspect it's allergy of some kind.'

Norman looked disturbed.

'I hope I find out soon,' he said.

Adeline looked up from her stirring as he came into the kitchen. 'What did Dr Phillips say?'

'That I'm allergic to you.'

'He didn't say that,' she scolded.

'Sure he did.'

'Be serious now.'

'He said I have to take some allergy tests.'

'He doesn't think it's anything to worry about, does he?' asked Adeline.

'No.'

'Oh, good.' She looked relieved.

'Good, nothing,' he grumbled. 'The taste of you is one of the few pleasures I have in life.'

'You stop that.' She removed his hands and went on stirring. Norman slid his arms around her and rubbed his nose on the back of her neck. 'Wish I could taste you,' he said. 'I like your flavour.'

She reached up and caressed his cheek. 'I love you,' she said.

Norman twitched and made a startled noise.

'What's wrong?' she asked.

He sniffed. 'What's that?' He looked around the kitchen. 'Is the garbage out?' he asked.

She answered quietly. 'Yes, Norman.'

'Well, something sure as hell smells awful in here. Maybe – ' He broke off, seeing the expression on her face. She pressed her lips together and, suddenly, it dawned on him. 'Honey, you don't think I'm saying – '

'Well, *aren't* you?' Her voice was faint and trembling.

'Adeline, come on.'

'First, I taste sour. Now – '

He stopped her with a lingering kiss.

'I love you,' he said, 'understand? I *love* you. Do you think I'd try to hurt you?'

She shivered in his arms. 'You *do* hurt me,' she whispered.

He held her close and stroked her hair. He kissed her gently on the lips, the cheeks, the eyes. He told her again and again how much he loved her.

He tried to ignore the smell.

Instantly, his eyes were open and he was listening. He stared up? He turned his head and reached across the mattress. As he touched her, Adeline stirred a little in her sleep.

Norman twisted over on his side and wriggled close to her. He pressed against the yielding warmth of her body, his hand slipping languidly across her hip. He lay his cheek against her back and started drifting downward into sleep again.

Suddenly, his eyes flared open. Aghast, he put his nostrils to her skin and sniffed. An icy barb of dread hooked at his brain; *my God, what's wrong?* He sniffed again, harder. Adeline mumbled indistinctly and he stopped. He lay against her, motionless, trying not to panic.

If his senses of taste and smell were atrophying, he could understand, accept. They weren't, though. Even as he lay there, he could taste the acrid flavour of the coffee that he'd drunk that night. He could smell the faint odour of mashed-out cigarettes in the ashtray on his bedside table. With the least effort, he could smell the wool of the blanket over them.

Then *why?* She was the most important thing in his life. It was torture to him that, in bits and pieces, she was fading from his senses.

*

It had been a favourite restaurant since their days of courtship. They liked the food, the tranquil atmosphere, the small ensemble which played for dining and for dancing. Searching in his mind, Norman had chosen it as the place where they could best discuss this problem. Already, he was sorry that he had. There was no atmosphere that could relieve the tension he was feeling; and expressing.

'What *else* can it be?' he asked, unhappily. 'It's nothing physical.' He pushed aside his untouched supper. 'It's got to be my mind.'

'But why, Norman?'

'*If I only knew,*' he answered.

She put her hand on his. 'Please don't worry,' she said.

'How can I help it?' he asked. 'It's a nightmare. I've *lost* part of you, Adeline.'

'Darling, don't' she begged, 'I can't bear to see you unhappy.'

'I *am* unhappy,' he said. He rubbed a finger on the tablecloth. 'And I've just about made up my mind to see an analyst.' He looked up. 'It's got to be my mind,' he repeated. 'And – damnit! – I resent it. I want to root it out.'

He forced a smile, seeing the fear in her eyes.

'Oh, the hell with it,' he said. 'I'll go to an analyst; he'll fix me up. Come on let's dance.'

She managed to return his smile.

'Lady, you're just plain gorgeous,' he told her as they came together on the dance floor.

'*Oh, I love you so,*' she whispered.

It was in the middle of their dance that the feel of her began to change. Norman held her tightly, his cheek forced close to hers so that she wouldn't see the sickened expression on his face.

'And now it's gone?' finished Dr Bernstrom.

Norman expelled a burst of smoke and jabbed out his cigarette in the ashtray. 'Correct,' he said, angrily.

'When?'

'This morning,' answered Norman. The skin grew taut across his cheeks. 'No taste. No smell.' He shuddered fitfully. 'And now no sense of touch.'

His voice broke. 'What's wrong?' he pleaded. 'What kind of breakdown *is* this?'

'Not an incomprehensible one,' said Bernstrom.

Norman looked at him anxiously. 'What then?' he asked.

'Remember what I said: it has to do only with my wife. Outside of her – '

'I understand,' said Bernstrom.

'*Then was is it?*'

'You've heard of hysterical blindness.'

'Yes.'

'Hysterical deafness.'

'Yes, but – '

'Is there any reason, then, there couldn't be an hysterical restraint of the other senses as well?'

'All right, but why?'

Dr Bernstrom smiled.

'That, I presume,' he said, 'is why you came to see me.'

Sooner or later, the notion had to come. No amount of love could stay it. It came now as he sat alone in the living room, staring at the blur of letters on a newspaper page.

Look at the facts. Last Wednesday night, he'd kissed her and, frowning, said, 'You taste sour, honey'. She'd tightened, drawn away. At the time, he'd taken her reaction at its obvious value: she felt insulted. Now, he tried to summon up a detailed memory of her behaviour afterward.

Because, on Thursday morning, he'd been unable to taste her at all.

Norman glanced guiltily toward the kitchen where Adeline was cleaning up. Except for the sound of her occasional footsteps, the house was silent.

Look at the facts, his mind persisted. He leaned back in the chair and started to review them.

Next, on Saturday, had come that dankly fetid stench. Granted, she should feel resentment if he'd accused her of being its source. But he hadn't; he was sure of it. He'd looked around the kitchen, asked her if she'd put the garbage out. Yet, instantly, she'd assumed that he was talking about her.

And, that night, when he'd waked up, he couldn't smell her.

Norman closed his eyes. His mind must really be in trouble if he could justify such thoughts. He loved Adeline; needed her. How could he allow himself to believe that *she* was, in any way, responsible for what had happened?

Then, in the restaurant, his mind went on, unbidden, while they were dancing, she'd, suddenly, felt cold to him. She'd, suddenly, felt – he could not evade the word – *pulpy*.

And, then, this morning –

Norman flung aside the paper. *Stop it!* Trembling, he stared across the room with angry, frightened eyes. It's me, he told himself, *me!* He wasn't going to let his mind destroy the most beautiful thing in his life. He wasn't going to let –

It was as if he'd turned to stone, lips parted, eyes widened, blank. Then, slowly – so slowly that he heard the delicate crackling of bones in his neck – he turned to look toward the kitchen. Adeline was moving around.

Only it wasn't footsteps he heard.

He was barely conscious of his body as he stood. Compelled, he drifted from the living room and across the dining alcove, slippers noiseless on the carpeting. He stopped outside the kitchen door, his face a mask of something like revulsion as he listened to the sounds she made in moving.

Silence then. Bracing himself, he pushed open the door. Adeline was standing at the opened refrigerator. She turned and smiled.

'I was just about to bring you – ' She stopped and looked at him uncertainly. 'Norman?' she said.

He couldn't speak. He stood frozen in the doorway, staring at her.

'Norman, what is it?' she asked.

He shivered violently.

Adeline put down the dish of chocolate pudding and hurried toward him. He couldn't help himself; he shrank back with a tremulous cry, his face twisted, stricken.

'*Norman, what's the matter?*'

'I don't know,' he whimpered.

Again, she started to him, halting at his cry of terror. Suddenly, her face grew hard as if with angry understanding.

'What is it now?' she asked. 'I want to know.'

He could only shake his head.

'I want to know, Norman!'

'No.' Faintly, frightenedly.

She pressed trembling lips together. 'I can't take much more of this,' she said. 'I mean it, Norman.'

He jerked aside as she passed him. Twisting around, he watched her going up the stairs, his expression one of horror as he listened to the noises that she made. Jamming palsied hands across his ears, he stood shivering uncontrollably. *It's me!* he told himself again, again; until the words began to lose their meaning – *me, it's me, it's me, it's me!*

Upstairs, the bedroom door slammed shut. Norman lowered his

hands and moved unevenly to the stairs. She had to know that he loved her, that he wanted to believe it was his mind. She had to understand.

Opening the bedroom door, he felt his way through the darkness and sat on the bed. He heard her turn and knew that she was looking at him.

'I'm sorry,' he said, 'I'm . . . sick.'

'No,' she said. Her voice was lifeless.

Norman stared at her. 'What?'

'There's no problem with other people, our friends, tradesmen, . . .' she said. 'They don't see me enough. With you, it's different. We're together too often. The strain of hiding it from you hour after hour, day after day, for a whole year, is too much for me. I've lost the power to control your mind. All I can do is – blank away your senses one by one.'

'You're not – '

' – telling you those things are real? I am. They're real. The taste, the smell, the touch – and what you heard tonight.'

He sat immobile, staring at the dark form of her.

'I should have taken all your senses when it started,' she said. 'It would have been easy then. Now it's too late.'

'What are you talking about?' He could barely speak.

'It isn't fair!' cried her voice. 'I've been a good wife to you! Why should I have to go back? I *won't* go back! I'll find somebody else. I won't make the same mistake next time!'

Norman jerked away from her and stood on wavering legs, his fingers clutching for the lamp.

'*Don't touch it!*' ordered the voice.

The light flared blindingly into his eyes. He heard a thrashing on the bed and whirled. He couldn't even scream. Sound coagulated in his throat as he watched the shapeless mass rear upward, dripping decay.

'All right!' the words exploded in his brain with the illusion of sound. 'All right, then *know* me!'

All his senses flooded back at once. The air was clotted with the smell of her. Norman recoiled, lost balance, fell. He saw the mouldering dead bulk rise from the bed and start for him. Then his mind was swallowed in consuming blackness and it seemed as if he fled along a night-swept hall pursued by a suppliant voice which kept repeating endlessly, 'Please! I don't want to go back! *None of us want to go back!* Love me, let me stay with you! Love me, love me, love me . . .'

So Near The Darkness

THEODORE STURGEON

Another writer who pushed the vampire story a significant step forward in the Fifties and early Sixties was Theodore Sturgeon with his novel, Some of Your Blood *(1961) and a varied group of short stories including 'The Professor's Teddy Bear' (1948) about a child with a blood-thirsty plaything; 'The Music' (1953) a story told from the vampire's viewpoint; and 'So Near The Darkness' (1955). Of the novel, Robert Hadji has written in* The Penguin Encyclopedia of Horror and the Supernatural *(1986):* 'Some of Your Blood *is a significant modern vampire novel, yet remains curiously neglected, perhaps because of its refusal to observe generic conventions . . . and it shatters a major taboo in having its hayseed vampire feed on menstrual blood.' Sturgeon's short stories are equally startling, ironic and horrific in a manner that made his work stand out from that of so many of his contemporaries.*

Theodore Sturgeon (1918–1985) was born Edward Hamilton Waldo but changed this after his mother's remarriage. As a child he dearly wanted to be a gymnast, but a lengthy illness weakened his heart and put an end to any such ambition. After a period as a seaman, he found his metier as a writer and contributed a number of highly regarded if bizarre tales to the fantasy and horror magazines of the time – including 'Bianca's Hands' (1947) about a man with a morbid desire to be strangled which no American magazine would publish, but instead won Sturgeon a £500 first prize in a literary competition run by the British magazine, Argosy! *Just as* Some of Your Blood *offered a new angle on the vampire theme, 'So Near The Darkness' brings together the idea of the vampire as a member of a separate species –*

and not necessarily one of earthly origin – along with the older concept of energy-draining predators or 'psychic sponges', in a way that no previous writer had envisaged. When first published in Fantastic Universe *magazine in November 1955, the editor Leo Margulies hailed it as 'a tale as darkly terrifying and as fraught with November direfulness as midnight's frightful liaison with a demon moon.' The passage of forty years has done nothing to diminish a single word of Sturgeon's unique combination of fantasy and science fiction . . .*

       *   *   *

This is the story of a Chinese silver cigarette case, some Vaseline hair tonic, a gooseneck desk lamp, and two girls – one nearly always beautiful, and one always nearly beautiful. It also may or may not concern a creature called Arrara, so named because of its peculiar snarl.

The girl who was nearly always beautiful had been christened Organtina, but when she heard a snide and subtle remark about it from one of the long-haired gentry in Greenwich Village she determinedly omitted the first two syllables. Tina was attractive in an almost miraculous way, and struck such a perfect balance in the colour of her hair between blonde and brunette that one can only describe it as being the colour of hair which is soft in the shadows, and breathtakingly bright in the sun.

Tina sold seashells in Chelsea, a fact which caused her considerable difficulty in describing her occupation whenever she became emotionally agitated. In her colourful little shop on the fringes of the Village, she displayed seashells and parts of seashells arranged and assembled into dolls, turtles and comedy masks.

She also conducted a flourishing trade in geegaws and a very special assortment of bric-a-brac and izthattas. The izthattas differed from the geegaws and the bric-a-brac in that the latter are unfunctional but pleasing decorative things, whereas the izthatta is a purely functional object. She loved both the izthattas and the geegaws and she made them as fast as she could. And so accomplished was her artistry that they sold like hotcakes. She knew because she had received comparative figures on hotcakes from Eddy Southworth.

The merchandizing of an izthatta is very simple. You make up an object by cementing a razor-shell to a sea-snail, crowning it with a clam and spraying on some Paris Green. Almost certainly the next customer in the place will ask: 'Is that a napkin ring?' or 'Is that a paper weight?' or 'Is that a salad fork holder?' The correct reply should be: 'I really like to deal with customers who show both good taste and insight. But of course it is! And this morning a lady was in –'

Your next cue is to laugh gaily while the customer reaches into her jeans for the exorbitant price of the izthatta, Chelsea being near enough to the Village for jeans on ladies to be *de rigeur*.

Tina's window displays were changed weekly, and brought in a lot of trade. Now it would be a spread of fragile coral-lace and crabclaws, largely labelled: SKELETON ART. (No mussels). And next week the display would be a highly abstract piece of business all made of urchin-quill and mother-of-pearl, captivatingly captioned: UNCON-CHIOUS ART, without, of course, a conch in sight.

In the third week of a warm March, Tina was busily working with tweezers, cement, Swiss pattern files and a set of surgical tools. She worked in a small alcove separated from the rest of the shop by a curved partition, with a splendid assortment of her wares spread out under a gooseneck lamp of high voltage.

The opening in the partition between the workroom and the shop was small – but so was Tina. Her knowledge of a customer's advent was gained in two ways. First, there was the photo-electric beam which crossed the outer doorway, in such a way that its interruption would actuate a mellow chime. Second, there was a hole cut through the partition. The aperture was at her eye-level as she sat at work and it enabled her to see clearly everything that went on in the shop.

Imagine, then, her astonishment when she looked up from her work and saw through the peephole that there was a man in her shop. Eddy Southworth, whose hobby was electronics, had assured her that no one could possibly pass through the outer door without breaking the photo-electric beam. Yet the chime had not rung, and indisputably there was a man in the shop – a slender, graceful man with black hair like a carapace and heavily knitted brows.

Tina rose quickly, straightened her hair and squeezed through the partition. 'Yes?' she inquired, confronting the intruder so abruptly that he recoiled a step.

'Yes indeed,' said the man. He was young, and he had a voice like the middle register of an oboe. He looked up quickly and back to the showcase on which he had been leaning, the darting swiftness of his glance subtracting nothing from its thoroughness. Tina felt like a filedrawer from which inventory cards had been quite deliberately spilled.

'Would – would you like something?' she asked faintly.

She stepped hopefully behind the showcase, but to no avail. He promptly turned his back, to gaze up and across, down and around the shop.

'The old shell game,' he said as if in amazement to himself.

'There was a time,' she said pleasantly, 'when I had only heard that once in connection with this business, which was founded by my grandfather. Is there anything – uh – inanimate here which appeals to you?'

'Oh yes,' he said, turning finally to face her. He had, it appeared, disturbingly ironic eyebrows. 'Where were you on the night of March twenty-fifth, two years ago?'

She stared at him. 'Are you serious?'

'I certainly am,' he said soberly, 'I would really like to know. It's difficult for me to explain, but you must believe that it's important to me.'

'I don't think I can – Wait now.' She tilted back her head and closed her eyes. Two years ago. Of course. She had been in Rochester, and – 'I do remember!' she said. 'It's strange that you should ask me. I was staying with an aunt in Rochester that spring, and I had a violent quarrel which seems very silly now. I was quite the Girl Scout then. I was so angry I got my kit and headed for the hills. I didn't see a soul I knew for almost two weeks.'

'No one?' He stared at her intently. 'Think now. Didn't anybody know where you were?'

'Not a soul,' she said positively. 'And where were *you* that night, if I'm not being too curious? Just where, precisely?'

He smiled a very white smile. His teeth seemed to be pointed. 'I *am* sorry,' he apologized. 'That was very rude of me. Would you like to make some money?'

Tina nodded energetically. 'By selling seashells.'

'I mean real money.'

'How? By selling thousands of seashells?'

He sighed. 'There's one thing I'm sure of,' he said. 'You are being stupid on purpose.'

'I shall take that as a compliment,' she said, and added, 'I wonder how much more I'll have to take.'

He laughed engagingly. 'Your sense of humour seems to stay with you no matter what the provocation. I've noticed your window displays, for example. Laughing in the face of a business recession. You'd probably remain buoyant in the face of any menace.'

'You try me,' she said without inflection. 'I rather think you'd be surprised.'

The eyebrows tensed like the wings of a gliding gull. 'Perhaps I will.'

'What has my sense of humour to do with all this,' she asked, meeting his gaze defiantly.

'More than you might suspect. I have a job to do, and I need a girl like you to assist me.' He straightened, his long face all clear planes and forced patience. 'Cigarette?'

He took a silver cigarette case from his pocket and offered it to her unopened.

She stopped her head in mid-shake and took the case. 'What a lovely thing!' she exclaimed.

'Is it?' said the man.

'Surely there can be no doubt about it. What a beautiful dragon!'

'There are seven dragons,' he pointed out.

'Sev – Oh, I see. Two around the edge here, all curled around each other. Uh-huh – and one peeping around the pagoda.'

'There are a good many pagodas around Peiping, too.'

'Hey!' she laughed. 'That was my line. Now, let's see – that makes four dragons.'

'There are two more on the back,' he murmured.

She turned the case over. 'I don't *like* those. They look positively ferocious.'

'They've been fighting again. But most dragons do look ferocious.'

She looked at him quizzically. His calm, handsome face had grown, if anything, more sardonic. Recognizing that he was willing to let the impossible conversation go on until closing time, she dropped her eyes to the case.

'Where's the seventh dragon?' she asked.

Arrara-arrara said the case. It spoke softly, like a lisping child with moist red lips. Tina gasped, and closed her eyes. The case moved gently but firmly in her grasp, just as if someone were trying to twist it away from her. She trembled and opened her eyes. The young man was trying to pry it from her fingers. She raised it with a shudder of revulsion.

Arrara, said the case indignantly. The man said, 'Shut up, you.'

Tina said, 'I didn't say anything.'

'Not you,' he said to Tina. 'I was just thinking aloud, in reference to something else. Cigarette?'

'Thanks no,' said Tina swiftly, her eyes on the case in horrified disbelief as it went back into the man's pocket. She wet her lips. 'The other dragon's inside, huh?'

'That's right. Now, about this little job. I can make it decidedly worth your while if you'll come in.'

'I don't doubt that,' said Tina, moistening her lips. 'But if I should consider it I'd like to know in advance what it is I may have to say "No" to.'

'Well, it's like this. I have a friend who wants to get married, in a manner of speaking, and you're the ideal – Oh, see here now. Stop shaking your head like that.'

'I can't help it. That "in a manner of speaking" just about does it. Goodbye.'

'Goodbye. My name is Lee Brokaw. I'm a dancer – adagio.'

He looked her up and down and smiled. 'Of course I didn't really mean "goodbye". I wish you would save both of us the trouble involved in my becoming insistent,' he said smoothly. 'How about dinner tonight?'

For reply she marched to the doorway and stood there. The photocell chime crooned from the back of the shop. She threw up a firm thumb. 'Come along, little man. Actually, it's past my customary closing hour.'

As if this were a cue, he nodded with feigned resignation and passed through the door. 'See you tomorrow,' he promised.

Shaking her head, Tina went back into the shop. She was sharpwitted enough to realize that she must depend for the support of her unusual trade on unusual people. Of these she certainly had had more than her share, from the gentleman who would buy no ornament at which his schnauzer would not wag its tail, to the woman who had three rooms of her house redecorated to suit a purple tie-rack she had purchased at a fire sale. But this Lee Brokaw character was strictly eggs in the beer. What *was* it he kept locked up in that cigarette case?

II

Tina had dinner with Eddy Southworth. He was an artist who lived and worked in the Village, but unlike most artists, he put in regular hours. He was locally well-known, and his works were considered delicate, tasteful and distinctly on the light side. He made flapjacks in the window of the Blue Tower Cafeteria, and anyone who watched his ambidextrous hot-cake-tossing knew that here indeed was an artist. Having dinner with him meant sitting across the counter, snatching phrases between servings, and filtering romantic comments through a mouthful of the *spécialité de la maison*, as follows:

'Hya, cinth.'

'Lo, quacious.' This was a routine, an intimacy, and a mental exercise. 'Stack them with cherry syrup.'

'Food of the Gods! How's it with you, Tina?' Before she could reply he was gone to the front of the place, to fill the air with somersaulting pancakes. On his way back with a batter-bucket, she determinedly clipped his elbow.

'Eddy, what kind of a man could walk between a photocell and a light and not ring an alarm?'

'A ghost,' said Eddy solemnly. 'Or a vampire. Did you have one in the shop today?'

She nodded. 'That's nice,' he said, automatically. He went to the mixer at the back of the cafeteria and began to fill his bucket. '*What?*' he bellowed suddenly, and came back. 'What about this guy? Did he wear a black cloak? Did he have a widow's peak, pointed teeth and a demon in his pocket?'

'No – I mean yes. And he has a dragon in his cigarette case.'

Her hotcakes arrived. Eddy sprinted to the front, tossed and stacked eight additional cakes, rocketed to the back and turned off the battercock just as the batter was forming a reverse miniscus. Then he peered over the edge of the bucket, and went back with it at a dead run, the bucket describing one single arc, like a pendulum-bomb, from the mixer to the griddles, without losing a drop. Someone up the line applauded. Eddy squirted a dozen discs of batter onto the griddle and came back to Tina.

'Are you kidding?'

'Ah thirtny am mot,' she said through a hotcake.

'You just mean a wolf. Not a werewolf.'

'Ath a matter of ah,' she said, and swallowed, 'he isn't. I mean, he didn't seem to be. He wants me for something, he says.'

He nodded eagerly. 'But he's not a wolf. You're sure of that?'

'I think,' she twinkled – and it cost her an effort – 'that he wants me for a fate worse than a fate worse than death.'

She changed her mouth from a bow to an O, and stoked. Eddy picked up two turners instead of one, a sign of deep thought.

'What's with this dragon you spoke about?' he asked.

'It's in the most gorgeous silver cigarette case you ever saw.'

'What does it do?'

'It goes *arrara*.'

Eddy jumped back. 'Don't do that,' he gasped. 'For Pete's sake –'

'I'm sorry, Eddy. Terribly sorry. But that's exactly what it does. I – I'd like some coffee.'

'Black with one!' Eddy bellowed. 'Where does this apple tend bar?
Or does he panhandle on the Bowery?'

'He's a dancer,' Tina said. 'When he left he pointed to the Mello
Club and said, "Look at that." After I shut up shop I looked. He's
billed there – "Brokaw and Rapunzel, adagio." '

'I'm out of grease,' said Eddy to the waitress. 'Tina, I don't like the
sound of this guy.'

'Yes, Eddy.'

'See you tomorrow?'

'Yes, Eddy.'

'Stay away from the Mello Club.'

'Yes, Eddy.'

So Tina went to the Mello Club to catch Brokaw's act.

The Mello Club was a cramped and crowded bistro in which the
ceiling, having heard so many cutomers ask 'How low can you get?'
seemed to have accepted the challenge. The lighting was of a dimness
to which the human eye could not become accustomed, because of its
reluctance to recognize such atrocious colour combinations.

The dimness was functional, insofar as the place had a function. It
kept the customers in obscurity, so that each customer thought his
own disgust was unshared, and therefore remained. It kept the
customers' disgust from reaching the master of ceremonies while he
cremated it. It suited the quality of the air, so that taint did not intrude.
In short, a fine, healthy place.

Tina fumbled her way down the steps and into the club, sighted a gleam
of brass from a trombone bell, pointed her elbow at it, closed her eyes and
walked. She was small, but she had the directness of a destroyer escort.
She brought up against a table not ten feet from the dance floor, which
was, of course, two-thirds of the way to the wall. She sat down.

Hardly had she done so when the up-beat cacophony from the
orchestra came to a screaming stop and the master of ceremonies came
out, dragging with him a microphone with a head as polished and
featureless as his own. Into it and the glare of a ceiling spot which
painfully flooded him, he began to recite what had happened to him on
the way to the club that night.

Tina rested her elbows on the table as the most comfortable way to
keep her hands over her ears, and tried to locate Lee Brokaw in the
babbling gloom. Occasionally she lifted her hands enough to find out
if the emcee's droning obscenities were turning into anything like an
announcement.

It was hot. Someone was breathing down her neck. She leaned forward a little and found herself breathing in someone's armpit. She leaned back again. It must have been then that the announcement was made, because suddenly, shockingly, the lights went out.

For a moment someone with the touch of a fly's foot seemed to be brushing a cymbal, and then there was not a sound from the tables. Slowly a blue-green light began to glow, so faintly at first that it could have been there for seconds before she noticed it at all. Gradually she became aware of a figure standing in the middle of the dance floor. The emcee? No, for he had been wearing a dinner jacket. This was something bone-white and slender. The light increased, or her eyes sharpened, and she suddenly saw that it was a girl, nude, splendidly if slightly built, and wearing some sort of a tall hat or – a crown. The light steadied, but did not become bright enough to show anything clearly.

The girl began to dance. There was no sonorous music, only a faint, flute-like plucking which she recognized as a melody played solely in the harmonics of a guitar. The girl moved slowly. She took two small steps forward, and then sank to her knees and touched her forehead to the floor.

The music stopped, but the heartbeat drum quickened as she straightened up again. There was a moment when it missed one beat, and the shock of that was followed by a blaze of yellow light and a painful, discordant blare from every brass in the orchestra.

Tina's aching eyes caught one brief glimpse of the girl's body as the dancer shook her head. Her crown was hair – real spun-gold hair that cascaded down and around her like water. She knelt there, head raised, wide blue eyes staring, arms up and out, cloaked in shimmering blue-green gold. And only then did Tina see Lee Brokaw.

He was standing behind the girl, looking down at her impassively. It was he who held her white arms up, with his long fingers around her slender wrists. Slowly he brought them together and grasped both wrists in one hand. She turned toward him and rose. Her hair was impossible – bewildering. It fell to the floor in a mass that was thick and delicate at once. It was liquid fire; it was smoke. It was like no other hair Tina had ever seen. She remembered the name of the act then – Brokaw and Rapunzel. 'Rapunzel, Rapunzel, let down your golden hair . . .'

The music burst hoarsely into a travesty of the Apache dance. With slow, feline steps they moved about the floor. Brokaw's handsome, almost beautiful face held the girl's eyes. Her features were as motionless as wax.

As they danced, he took one of her arms behind her and apparently began to twist it. Her body stiffened and arched backward; and her head too went back. Brokaw bared his teeth in a frightful smile, bent his head and put his mouth to her throat. They danced that way for four slow measures, and when he lifted his head, the marks of his teeth were easy to see.

Abruptly he pirouetted away from her, and around her. She held her arms over her head, her hands touching his, her eyes glassily staring. The tempo of the music rose. Brokaw spun the girl to him and away, to him and away, as the music sped up to its climax. He stopped her in a final pirouette, both her arms pinioned behind her.

In a crescendo of noise and light, he raised his fist and smashed it into her upturned face. She dropped like a rag doll, and, as the cymbals crashed three times, and with his face as calm as a sunlit cathedral, he stamped on her head, crushing it flat.

In the silence and the blaze of light, Lee Brokaw stood up, smiled, and bowed from the waist. Then a woman screamed, and applause broke out in one great shout which changed to a roar of bruising palms and stamping feet. Brokaw bowed again, scooped up the limp collection of long limbs and golden hair, and tossed it over his shoulder. Sawdust trickled from the flattened head, and the clever hinging of one white elbow could be seen.

'But – she danced by herself!' Tina said aloud.

'In what kind of light?' said a man next to her, pounding the table. 'And him in black!'

The thunder rose, and rose again as the lights dimmed to toxic obscurity. And finally Lee Brokaw came out to take a second bow.

He stepped out to meet the sudden spotlight, and as it fell on him he turned pale and clutched his chest. Something made the ringsiders shrink back from him. Something – the faintest of sounds.

Arrara . . .

'He's sick!' whispered someone.

A woman half-rose and cried, 'His heart!'

'Has he got a heart on the right side?' asked the man next to Tina.

Tina said clearly, 'He has a dragon in his cigarette case.' But of course no one paid her any attention.

Brokaw bowed stiffly and went out. The chrome-plated master of ceremonies returned with his pasty-faced microphone, and Tina rose, dazedly made her way to the exit, handed a palm which materialized before her the cover charge plus ten per cent, and escaped up the stairs.

The outside air tasted so good it made her sneeze. She was still

shuddering inside over Brokaw's finale. She walked briskly homeward, and gradually the shock of that terrifying performance was
replaced by curiosity.

What manner of man *was* Lee Brokaw? With an act like that, why
wasn't he on Fifty-second Street? Or even on Broadway? Why, if he so
casually offered that cigarette case around to chance acquaintances
was he so profoundly affected when it growled *at him*?

How had he been so sure she would see him again? Did he have her
figured so well that he had known she would be at the performance?
Most of all, what on earth could he want with her?

Turning in at her apartment house, she fingered her cheek and jaw.
Maybe he wanted a dancing partner who would spar a little and thus
add a certain colour to the climax. Of course, she had to admit that all
that hair *was* becoming . . .

III

Tina undressed, went into her pyjamas. She felt much better after that.
She loaded her night table with sketching materials, a book on design,
and two volumes of the *Encyclopedia Britannica* which had plates of
shells. Two button sets and an izthatta later, she was happily asleep.

It must have been four hours afterwards that she awoke. She opened
her eyes very quietly, without moving. Something urged her not to
start up, but to relax and look the situation over. The situation was Lee
Brokaw's smooth, imperturbable face, slightly larger than life size. It
floated, apparently, in mid-air between her and the opposite wall. It
wore a gentle smile which ended at the cheekbones. The eyes were as
steady and as deep as ever.

She said, 'Wh-wh —' and the face turned chillingly upside down, got
quite pink, then scarlet — a real blood-scarlet, as if it were looking at
her through red glass — and then slowly disappeared.

Tina blanched and dived under the covers. In a moment one arm
crept out and, feeling along the night table, turned on the lamp. She
worked the blanket over her head and face, found an edge, doubled it
into a sort of peephole, and peered out.

There was nothing to see.

She took a deep breath, held it, flung the covers off, bounded across
the room and switched on the overhead light.

Still nothing. She withdrew into the centre of the room and gazed slowly around. A movement caught the corner of her eye, and she cried out in terror as she turned to face – her own reflection in the bathroom mirror!'

'Great day in the morning! Is that me?' she muttered, staring in shocked belief at the dilated pupils, the chalky countenance.

'Bad dreams,' she told her reflection reassuringly. 'Some way or other, sister, you're not living right.'

She washed her face and went back to bed. She lay a moment in thought, then got up again and located a pair of nub-spiked golf shoes. These she put on the night table. Then she rolled over, tucked herself in, threw back the covers, got up, switched off the bathroom light, the overhead light, and, at last, the night-table lamp.

She was, by this time, much more annoyed than frightened. It had been many a moon since she had let anything throw her into such a dither. She fell asleep angrily, almost by an effort of will, and found herself in a fine technicolour nightmare involving a purring dragon which wanted to stamp on her head.

She came up out of it fighting, only to find Brokaw's glowing face staring at her again. This time she was prepared, and in a single fluid movement she let fly with one of the heavy shoes. The shoe struck the face right between the eyes. There was a loud crash and a torrent of profanity from the street below.

Tina turned on the light, peered around her, and went timorously to the window. She peeped out – no difficult feat since her shoe had passed completely through the pane and apparently collided with the head of the policeman who was standing in cold-eyed fury directly below, kneading his skull and looking up. He fell silent the instant she appeared.

She realized much too late that he did so admiringly. There was plenty of light behind her.

A policeman! She'd soon find out how Brokaw was pulling this little stunt! She'd slap him in jail until he begged for mercy and the devil called him Granddad! She'd –

Her brain raced. She'd do what? Say to the officer: 'There was a face floating in my room and I threw a shoe at it and it disappeared and I want you to throw Lee Brokaw in the clink'?

Oh, no.

She turned to her empty room and screamed, 'I'll teach you to come home at this hour, you heel!'

'Lady,' said the policeman, 'talk to him more quietly or I'll have to take a hand in this.'

'I'm *so* sorry, officer,' she called down, and then even more loudly into the room, 'now see what you've done!'

As she left the window she thought she could hear the policeman saying sadly, 'The poor guy. I wouldn't be in his shoes.'

The following morning she arrived at her shop a few minutes later than usual. Not only had she overslept but she had been compelled to explain to the superintendent of her building that he had cleaned the windows so very clean that she had gone and stuck her silly head through one of the panes. She felt somewhat less than rested, and probably the least popular person in her cosmos was Lee Brokaw.

She opened the door, glanced around at her displays, and went back to the workroom. With grim deliberation she turned on the gooseneck lamp and the photocell, and settled down to work.

Then she saw what was inscribed on the black blotter to her right. It had apparently been written with the silver pencil which was bundled up with all the other colours at the back of the table. It said, simply, 'Here I am.'

It was written in a neat, possibly hurried hand, with fine lines and an even slant. It was almost a feminine handwriting.

'All right,' she muttered. 'Here I am, too.' Tight-lipped, she picked up the blotter.

There was another blotter underneath it – a white blotter. On it, very much less than life-size, was the same face she had seen in her bedroom. It did not turn upside down. It simply faded slowly and disappeared.

Tina sat tensely watching the blank blotter, her hands achingly clasped. She sat like that until the blotter began to blur. Then she closed her eyes.

Aloud she asked herself, 'Can I say it now, Tina? Can I, huh?' She nodded in reply. 'Go ahead,' she said to herself. 'You'll feel better if you do.' A pause. Then: 'All right, I will. I'm really and truly scared, and I should never have listened to Eddy and I should never have gone to s-see that devil last night.'

Tina realized suddenly that this couldn't go on. Either she got away from Lee Brokaw, Chelsea, New York itself – or she stayed. Going away was impossible from a business point of view and unthinkable from an ethical one. Then she must stay. But if she stayed, she couldn't just wait for something even more terrifying to happen. She had to smoke out the trouble. If things got worse, at least she'd know what she was up against. If things got better, well – that was what she wanted.

What to do, then?

Find Lee Brokaw, obviously, and get his story. Force him to talk even if she had to pound it out of him with a conch shell.

The chime sounded. She put her face back together and went into the shop. 'Eddy!' she exclaimed, and hoped he wouldn't notice how close she was to tears.

'Hi, falutin'.'

She forced herself to smile. 'Lo, brow.'

Eddy picked up an abalone shell and began toying with it absently. 'How much were you kidding about that Lee Brokaw character last night?' he asked.

'Not a bit,' she assured him.

'You said he was a vampire.'

'*You* said he was,' she reminded him. 'All I really know is that he walked in here with some proposition that I couldn't let him finish, that he had a cigarette case which growled at me, and that he –'

'Go on.'

'Nup.'

He knew that monosyllable well enough to leave it alone. 'Okay, let's take it as it comes. All you know is that he walked in here – *without* the photocell noticing him. He made you some offer which you insist wasn't what one would assume it to be, though you don't seem to know why.'

'I just *know*,' said Tina defensively. 'Look, Eddy, if you think that Lee Brokaw is assuming the proportions of a deadly rival, you can think again.'

'I'm not worried,' said Eddy in an unconvincing voice.

'Eddy,' she said thoughtfully, 'what is so fascinating about Lee Brokaw just now? I've never seen you fret about anything like this before.'

'I've never run across anything like this before,' Eddy said. 'I'll tell you what I know, Tina. Maybe a couple of things will clear up. Last night about half an hour before closing time, Shaw was in. You know him – manager of that smoke-hole where Brokaw has his act. He was in a fine froth. He wanted to know where Brokaw was. He stood up in a chair and yammered at the customers. Seems he had a second show in a few minutes and Brokaw was among the missing.'

'Any luck?' Tina asked.

Eddy shook his head. 'None of the customers seemed to know anything. I remembered what you said and called him over. He told me that he had hired a ham act and that Brokaw had come up with something that wowed the customers. He was afraid that some competitor had bought him away, I think – though he pretended to be worried about the dear boy personally.

'I asked him what he knew about Brokaw – maybe we could locate the kind of place he might be found in. He didn't know a thing. Brokaw'd been in two days before and described his act and had done a short solo. Shaw never dreamed it was anything good.'

Tina shuddered. 'It was awful.'

'Most of those acts are,' said Eddy. 'Anyway, I told him – what did you say? How do you know it was awful?'

'I saw it, Eddy.'

'You saw – Didn't I tell you to keep away from there?'

'Yes, Eddy. You told me,' she said, and her voice was altogether too gentle. 'You didn't *ask* me, though.'

'I didn't – Oh, I see. Little Miss Muscles can't be given orders, eh? All right, Tina. I'll stay out of your troubles. You can take care of yourself, and so forth. Only, when you're in up to your neck, don't –'

'I know, I know. I'm not to come yelling for you. Don't worry, I won't.'

He went to the door. 'I wasn't going to say that. I was going to say don't forget whom to yell for.'

The chime sounded his departure. Not loudly, but with a faint tinkling sound that slowly died away into silence.

IV

She started after him, then stopped abruptly and dropped her arms. Why did men have to be so pig-headed? Why did every man who got interested in a girl appoint himself as braintrust, bodyguard and duenna? Just to top it, the men who liked her invariably said they liked her because she was independent and self-sufficient. She compressed her lips and half-snorted, half-moaned in aggravation.

The moan was answered from the back of the shop.

Tina froze.

The moan was repeated. It was not so much a moan of pain, though pain was there. It was a moan of desolation – of utter hopelessness and despair.

Eddy was only a half-block away. Perhaps she should – on the other hand, Eddy was an egocentric, puffed up creature with a dictator complex who wanted his women helpless. She'd investigate herself. She squared her shoulders and went into the back room.

There was nothing there but the moan. She looked under the settee and in the closet. Then she heard it again. It was outside, in the alley.

With some difficulty – the door was almost never used – she shot back the bolts and pulled it open. She looked to right and left. The noise was there again, faintly, almost behind her. She looked down a short flight of cellar steps. Near the bottom was Lee Brokaw.

'M-Mr Brokaw?'

He started violently, staggered to his feet and shrank against the wall behind him. He was tattered and dirty, and his fine jaw was covered with harsh stubble. But none of this subtracted one whit from his incredible grace.

'You,' he breathed, and his voice was still the mellow tenor she had noticed before. But now it was faint and frightened.

'What's the matter? Are you hurt?' she asked with alarm. 'Come up out of there!'

'Will you take me inside where no one can see?'

'Come on. No one will see,' she promised.

He tiptoed up, crouching, his eyes on her face. They were full of eagerness and hope, and a terrible fear. *He dances every minute*, she thought.

Every single minute.

He flowed around her and into the open door like a feather borne on an eddy of wind. 'Lock it,' he said, and while she complied he went to the partition and peered out.

'The chime will ring if anyone comes into the shop,' she said.

'Will it?' he asked, and smiled.

Remembering, she said, 'Oh.' She pushed past him and sat at her work table. 'Stretch out on the settee,' she said briskly. 'I can see if anything comes in.' Why she said 'anything' instead of 'anyone', she didn't know. 'Are you in trouble?'

He nodded, sinking gratefully back on the settee.

She stared at him. He looked so young, so tortured. The face was so different from the bland, cruelly smiling one she had seen in her room. But she could not deny it was the same face.

'I saw you last night,' she told him, on sudden impulse.

'I know you did,' he said, putting his hand to his breast pocket. 'I didn't see you, though.'

'Oh – the cigarette case! I remember. You don't mean it growled because *I* was there?'

'It did.' He took the case out and tossed it carelessly into her lap. She recoiled, staring at it. She was afraid to touch it, even to drop it. But she had to know. She gritted her teeth, lifted it, and said, 'I'm going to open it.'

'Go ahead,' he said, as if he had much more important things on his mind.

She looked at him sharply. His eyes were closed, and a furrow of concentration was drawing together the inner ends of his brows. She drew a deep breath and – touched the clasp. The case sprang open.

Of all the things she expected to find in that case – the little crawling horrors, the amulets, the runes on parchment, even perhaps the electronic gear that had so cleverly made the growling sound – what she *least* expected to find in it was what it actually contained. The shock of it was almost more than she could stand.

What she felt was the utmost refinement of the feeling you have when, in a dream, you mount ten steps where only nine exist. True, there was a dragon there. It was etched on the inside of the lid, but it was no more ugly than those on the outside, and it even wore a smile. Otherwise the case held, of all things – cigarettes.

'This,' she said, when she could at last say anything, 'is positively the last straw. Lee Brokaw, who are you, and what makes you think you can frighten me? Why have you done things you must know I would refuse to believe – and bitterly resent.'

He rested on one elbow and looked at her. Again his eyes were unfathomable. 'I am a dancer,' he said. 'If you tell me what you think I have done, maybe I can explain. I want you, very desperately, to do something for me. I want you, because you're exactly suited to the task.' He spread his hands, as if to say, 'Could anything be simpler?' and lay back.

'What is this task?' she demanded.

'You mean – you'll do it?' There was sudden hope in his eyes.

Tina shook her head. 'I certainly said nothing of the sort.'

'I can't tell you about it if there's any possibility of your *not* doing it,' he said.

'Well, then, drop dead or something,' Tina flared. 'I have a job!'

'You'll see me everywhere if you don't,' he said. 'At your home and at work.'

'I've had a couple of samples of that,' she replied acidly. 'I could get used to it.'

'It will get worse,' he said, almost pleadingly, as if he did not want it to happen. 'Other people will have my face when you speak to them.

You will feel my hands on your face and your body. You will hear my voice when you listen to music, and later, you will hear it more and more until the whole world is filled with my voice and my face and my touch. You will go mad.'

'I can keep you out,' she said stoutly. 'You can't walk through walls.'

'Or through light-beams?'

Tina gulped. 'I don't care what you do, or how much of it. You're crazy. I'm warning you now – there's nothing you can do to persuade me to do anything for you.'

Arrara . . .

'Oh, please,' gasped Brokaw. He swung off the settee and came to her, sitting at her feet with his easy, drifting motion. He took her hands in his long, strong, slender ones, and turned his face up to her. It was changed now. His eyes were wide with terror, and the delicate lips worked.

His voice was a whisper, shrill with fright. 'That was the last warning. It will be sometime today, or tonight. Please help me, Tina – please, *please*. Only you can help me . . .' and he buried his face in her lap.

She looked down at his shivering shoulders, and thought of the calm strength he had radiated; thought of his symmetrical, unshakeable expression of objective power. Then her mind returned to the poor broken thing before her.

She stroked his sleek black hair. 'You poor thing,' she said. 'I'll help you. You mustn't cry, Lee, you mustn't. I'll help you . . .'

He sprang to his feet joyously, and grasped her shoulders. 'You mean it, don't you? You really mean it?'

'My speciality,' she said through a tight throat, 'is sick kittens.'

'You're an angel,' he said hoarsely, and kissed her. It was a surprisingly gentle kiss, just between her left temple and her eye.

'Now sit down and pull yourself together, Lee. I've promised. You'd better tell me what this is all about.'

'I killed a man,' said Lee. Keeping his eyes on her face he moved backwards and sank down on the settee. 'I killed him when he was asleep. I hit him with a bronze book-end and then I opened the side of his neck with a little knife. His skin was tough,' he added, 'and the knife wasn't very sharp. It seemed to go on for hours.'

'I see,' said Tina, holding tight to herself. She began to force a smile but decided against it; her cheeks might crack. 'And it left you with a psychic trauma.'

'I suppose so,' he said seriously, ignoring the weak attempt at facetiousness. 'But that wouldn't be anything by itself. I'd be glad if that were all. But, you see, after I did it, I had to get away, and I couldn't. People knew me. I was one of those noticeable individuals, I suppose.'

'You are.'

'Am I? Well, it doesn't matter now. I'm not what I was then. I've changed. I sold my – my soul.'

'What kind of mad talk is that?' said Tina, straightening in alarm.

'Go ahead. Take it for granted that I'm a psychopath. But you're going to help me, and you'll see. Don't you know that there are more forms of life on earth than the ones you read about in the biology books? You deal in shells. You know the shapes and forms they take. You know the differences in the substances shellfish feed on. You know the peculiar variations that occur. Do you know there's a shellfish in the Great Lakes that makes its shell –'

'– out of strontium carbonate instead of calcium carbonate. Of course I know. So far this is my lecture, not yours.'

'Please listen,' he said, 'I don't know how much time I have . . . There are creatures which feed exclusively on cellulose, and creatures which feed on the excreta of the cellulose-eaters.'

'You've got termites there,' said Tina. She was beginning to feel a little better. She knew enough about abnormal psychology to be able to pigeonhole some of this.

He ignored her. 'There are creatures which eat granite, and lichens which live on them. But why go on? The world is full of this symbiosis, even in human beings. There are microbes living in us without which we would die. And I tell you that there are creatures on earth which can't develop a soul any more than a termite can digest cellulose. These creatures feed on the souls which we humans build!'

'That's at least logical,' said Tina. 'Even if it happens to be untrue.'

'We can no more understand them and their motives and methods and hungers than can the hungers, and dark biological urges of a bass be understood by the intestinal microbes of a minnow which it may have swallowed.'

'Very clear reasoning,' said Tina, hoping that her mental reservation did not show. 'How do you know that such a creature wants to eat your soul?'

'I promised it,' said Lee miserably. 'You've heard the tales of selling your soul to the devil. They're poppycock, believe me. What I promised to give up, though, must be called a soul, because there is no other name for it. All those legends are true in essence. Heaven knows how many people lost their essence, their vitality – whatever you want to call it. These soul-eaters are psychic creatures. The psychic pressure of – you may call it the ethics, if you like – of a true promise, is binding. They give you what you want, in exchange for the promise of your soul.'

'That's a little nonsensical,' said Tina flatly. 'If they had access to souls at all, why don't they just gobble them up and have done with it?'

'Do you,' he asked, his voice too patient, 'gobble up a steak in the butcher store? No. You carry it home. You store it for a while. You season it. You cook it – so much on this side, so much on the other. You serve it. Perhaps you add a touch of salt, or sauce, or tabasco. Only then do you eat it.'

'And what, pray tell me, are these psychic sauces?'

'Emotions,' he said. 'Fear. Humour. Terror. Disgust. Pity.'

'I see. And you're convinced that you are now basted for the last time and ready to take out of the oven?'

'If you want to put it that way,' he said, unhappily.

'Don't mind my flippancy,' she said with sudden gentleness.

'I know why you do it,' he answered, understandingly.

'Now,' she said, 'tell me all about this thing, and skip the theory. You killed this fellow. I imagine you had reason for it.'

'I had,' he said briefly, with such terrible emphasis that she all but tangibly felt the wave of hatred. 'After I killed him, there was nothing I could do, no place I could go. I'd be seen leaving the house. I'd be remembered at the depot, at the airport. Sooner or later I'd be found.

'I was pacing back and forth in the library, trying to think of a way out, when I heard somebody cough. I was frightened out of my wits. There was a little man standing in the corner, smiling at me and rubbing his hands together. He looked perfectly ordinary. In fact, you see thousands of faces like that every day, and never remember them. The only thing unusual about him was his hair. He hadn't much, but, in that shadowy corner, it glowed.

'He told me not to be frightened. He said he knew what I had done, and the position I was in. He said he could help me. I believed him. I was desperate, frantic, ready to believe anything. He said that he could tell me just what I could do to get out of my trouble, and be free. He said I need never pay the legal penalty for what I had done.'

Lee paused and moistened his lips. 'I begged him to tell me. He played with me for a while, wanting to know how much I would give him.

Finally I shrieked at him to tell me what he wanted. He told me. He gave me two years. *Two full years.* That looked like forever to me. I agreed. He got my solemn promise, and believe me, I was sincere. Then he taught me how to change.'

Tina waited while Lee sat brooding. She realized that he was finished. 'What sort of change?'

'I – don't want to tell you that. You wouldn't believe it. Nevertheless, I changed, and he kept his promise. I got away free, and came to New York. You know how I make my living. Of course, I don't push my luck. I think I could go to the top. I won't, though, unless I can live out the two years and beyond. I am morally certain if I can keep my – my – what it is he wants, I'll be safe from him and from the law for the rest of my life.'

'Quite a tale,' said Tina. 'Now you'd better tell me how the silver cigarette case enters into it.'

'I got it the night I promised,' said Lee. 'I – I can't seem to dance without it. I've tried, but without it I am no good at all. It seems to be just an ordinary cigarette case, but –'

'But indeed,' shuddered Tina. 'Still – I don't know. Lots of actors carry around a charm or a rabbit's foot. Tell me – what about those fantastic threats you made a moment ago?'

'I'm glad I won't have to do any of those things,' he said. 'You see, when the Eaters feed, they do not take all of a person's essence. The body dies, of course, and what they want is eaten. But there is a good deal left over.'

'Bones and suet, kind of,' she said helpfully.

'Kind of.' He smiled, but she could see it was an outward smile solely. 'That remnant still has a life of its own. Much of it is ugly and evil. I imagine most "haunts" are exactly those left-overs, drifting around the places where they used to live and, depending on their quality, clinging to places where something bad has happened, or to the places where they were happy.'

'Hm. And which would I be, if you haunted me?'

'If you had refused to help me, it would have been bad. Bad.'

'Okay, Lee. Now suppose we go back to my original question. What must I do?'

'It's very simple. Just go with me when the time comes. You may not know what a remarkable person you are. You positively radiate goodness, and courage, and humour. Perhaps I'm hypersensitive, done to a turn –' he smiled – 'but I feel it vividly. I get it from you, and I think I re-radiate it. I think that if you were with me, with your wry wit and your psychic strength, and if I opened myself to you, I would prove distasteful to the Eater, and he would discard me.'

'Burn the roast, hey? Too much salt in the cabbage? Is that all I have to do? Stay with you?'

'That's absolutely all. And in the good clean outdoors, too, right here in the city. At the corner of Bleecker and Commerce. No pentagrams, no witch's brew, no dark caverns. You heard the cigarette case a while ago. I have until ten o'clock.'

'You want me to stay with you until then?' she asked.

'It won't be necessary,' he assured her. 'What time do you close?'

'On Tuesdays, about nine.'

'Good. I'll drop by –'

'No,' said Tina, suddenly thinking of Eddy Southworth and the big, strong, misunderstanding feet he would put into this if he knew about it. Eddy would have to be stalled off. 'I'll meet you at the drug store at the corner.'

'It's a date,' he said.

He got quickly to his feet, looking younger than he should with his stubble and his hollow eyes, and went into the front of the shop. She followed him with deep concern in her eyes.

'Aren't you afraid of whatever it was you were hiding from?' she asked.

He shook his head. 'I'm not afraid of anything any more, thanks to you.' He opened the door, and stepped gallantly aside. Urged by reflex, she preceded him through. The chime hummed. She stood in the doorway as he slipped past her.

'I'm not going anywhere,' she said. She realized only after he was gone that for the second time he had been in and out of the place without activating the chime. On both occasions she had just happened to be standing in the beam when he went out. She shrugged and went inside.

The store seemed unusually deserted, chill and spiritless, as though in departing he had stripped away its individuality.

V

'I think I can,' said Eddy Southworth. He called to the pancake artist on the early shift. 'Joe! Can you hang on a little longer? Tina wants to talk something over.'

'For you, no,' said Joe, flashing a large smile. 'For Tina, yes. Take your time, Eddy.'

Eddy steered her to a booth in the back. 'What is it?' he asked.

She began her reply with an apology. 'Eddy, hon, I'm sorry I barked at you this morning,' she said. 'But if there's anything I can't stand it's some good-hearted bumbling *man* being protective and laying down the law.'

'All right, Tina. I'm sorry, too. But I happen to be fond of you – all of you, including your neck.'

'My neck?'

'The thing you stick out.'

'Oh, that. Well, you'll see that I am doing nothing of the kind. This Lee Brokaw business is coming to a head tonight, and I don't want you messing around with it. Now sit quietly and I'll tell you all about it from the very start. Maybe then you'll see it's all right and let me handle it my way.'

'All right. I'm listening.'

She told him everything, from the face in her bedroom up until Lee's departure that noon. Early in the account Eddy began to sputter. She frowned at him until he stopped. Very soon afterwards his jaw began to swing slackly. She stopped talking and aped him until he closed it. Finally she was through. It had been quite a recital, since her memory was good and her language vivid.

'And just what are you going to do?' Eddy demanded.

'Exactly what he asked me to do,' was her instant reply.

'But Tina!' Eddy protested. 'You're crazy! The man's a confessed murderer!'

'Which would hold up in court only if supported by the evidence,' she told him. 'And if there were any evidence, he'd have been caught. You know what passes for evidence nowadays. A trace of dust, a couple of hairs . . . No, I don't think there was any murder.'

'Then what about this fantastic business of the face in your bedroom, and the cigarette case, and all that?'

'Those faces I saw – well, I told you about his act, Eddy. Why don't you jump to the conclusion that I'm a poor impressionable female when you have the chance? I'm quite convinced that I'm seeing things.'

'I must admit it sounds like it. But why must you concern yourself with this at all? You say that Brokaw doesn't mean anything to you.'

'Every human being should mean something to us, Eddy. Lee's a dancer – better than good. He's great. He's a very sensitive boy. He's gotten a weird fixation, but fortunately there's a very definite time limit on it. If my not being with him means that he goes off his rocker, perhaps permanently, I don't want it on my conscience.'

Eddy looked at her with troubled eyes. 'There is still one thing that troubles me. Why are you telling me all this?'

'Eddy, I've made my own way since I was a kid, and when I marry it's going to be because the man I love and a girl named Tina are travelling together in the same direction at approximately the same speed, and each under his own power. I won't be steered, towed, nor provided with an icebreaker. This business with Brokaw is for the record. It wouldn't do any good to tell you about it afterwards.'

He looked at her in awe. 'Hi, tension,' he grinned. 'That was a speech!'

'I'm just telling you, Eddy – if I see you at the corner of Bleecker and Commerce Streets at ten o'clock, so help me, I'll never see you again as long as I live.'

'You won't,' he promised. 'It's a quarter to nine now. Will you drop back here around eleven?'

'Sure, Eddy.'

'Tina –'

She waited.

'Good luck.'

She smiled, put a kiss on her fingertips and brushed them across his mouth.

When she had gone, Eddy walked to the front. 'Joe,' he called.

'Huh.'

'I'll give you five bucks if you hang on for a couple of hours.'

'Nope.'

'Ten, Joe. This is important.'

'Nope. I'll do it for nuttin'. I know when a guy's got trouble.'

'Gosh, Joe. You're a real pal. If there's ever anything I can –'

'Beat it,' growled Joe. Eddy did, clasping, in his pocket, Tina's keycase, which he had filched from her purse.

VI

Tina and Lee Brokaw walked down Barrow Street. They had spent most of the past hour in a quiet bar and Lee still had not shaved. He was reserved and apparently in excellent control of himself. He spoke in monosyllables. As they turned into Commerce Street, Tina slipped her hand around his arm.

'Do you feel all right?' she asked.

'I feel fine,' he assured her. But he was trembling, ever so slightly. He walked slowly, gazing ahead, his eyes flickering over the four corners of Commerce and Bleeker. There were a few people around, but apparently no one was waiting on the corner.

'Maybe he's late,' murmured Tina.

'He won't be late,' said Lee. He looked at his watch. 'Four more minutes.'

One and a half of the minutes were used up in reaching the corner. Tina felt as if she were carrying a bier.

'Did you hear about the nudist who went to the fancy dress ball with an egg-beater over his shoulder?' she asked.

'No,' said Lee, smiling. 'What was he masquerading as?'

'An outboard motor,' said Tina, and then added wildly, 'that's the whole thing in a shellhole. My brain is certainly working on all fours tonight.'

'Tina, Tina, hold on to yourself. It'll be all right. Just as soon –' He broke off with a sharp intake of breath. Before them stood a slender little man with a partially bald head and a very ordinary expression on his face, who looked from one to the other of them.

'Is this the girl you were talking about?' he asked mildly.

'Here she is,' said Lee, and viciously shoved Tina forward.

'*Lee!*' she cried, utterly shocked.

The bald man put out a hand – to stop her, to catch her, to ward her off, she did not know. She twisted away from him, almost fell, staggered upright. Lee Brokaw was springing away down Commerce Street. She started after him.

Over her shoulder she saw the bald man coming after her, a bewildered and anxious expession on his mild little face. She put on a burst of speed, blessing her good sense in wearing ballet shoes, and for a brief moment gained on Brokaw.

'Lee!' she called.

Suddenly something big and black leaped out of a doorway and shouldered into Lee Brokaw. Caught in midstride, he caromed off into a lamp-post with bone-shaking force. The shadow caught him up, pinioning his arms behind his back and lifting him clear of the ground, bore him grimly along towards Tina.

Tina tried her best to stop, but skidded past. Brokaw, dangling in that relentless grip, lashed his body about, biting and spitting like a cat. Suddenly he began to scream – terrible, high-pitched screams.

The man carrying him said gruffly: 'This is the one you want,' and flung Brokaw down at the panting bald man's feet.

The bald man bent and grasped Lee's shoulder. Lee screamed again as if the hand were made of white-hot metal. He screamed twice more, writhing and twisting on the ground, and then lay still.

The big man said, 'Tina, are you all right?'

'Eddy! Oh, Eddy, Eddy darling!' She flew into his arms like a bird into a large tree. He put his face in her hair. 'I told you so, you idiot,' he said, 'and I promise not to say it again.'

The bald man said hesitantly, 'I have a warrant here for the arrest of a suspect in the case of Homer Sykes.'

'Never heard of him,' said Eddy.

'Take me home, Eddy.'

'I'm very sorry,' said the bald man. 'You'll have to come with me.'

Through the gathering crowd loomed a policeman. The little man rapped out instructions about a radio car and an ambulance. Another policeman rounded the corner. The man gave him orders about staying with Lee Brokaw until the ambulance arrived. Both policemen saluted.

'We can walk,' said the bald man gently. 'It's only just over the block. That man, by the way, is dead.'

Tina and Eddy looked at each other. Eddy shrugged. 'You're the doctor,' he said to the bald man.

They went to the police station. There were a very friendly desk sergeant and three very sour policemen and a triply sour matron. They went to work on Tina with a great deal of efficiency. They took her fingerprints, but not Eddy's. They just asked Eddy questions about himself.

Finally they were told to sit there and wait. They sat. Tina got as close to Eddy as she could without unseating him and asked, 'We murdered someone called Sykes?'

He patted her shoulder. 'No, darling. It'll all come out all right. Shall I tell you a story?'

'Tell me a story.'

'Once there was a big lug who liked a girl who got into some fantastic trouble. So while she went on into her trouble, he swiped her keys and went on a pilgrimage.'

'Tell it straight,' begged Tina.

'Okay. Well, maybe I'm just incapable of jumping to as many conclusions as you. I don't know. Anyway, Brokaw's photocell beam stunt bothered me. I kept thinking about it until I suddenly hit it. I bought a flashlight and went to your shop. I turned on the rig. I found that anyone who wants to look for the cell can see it, and the light-cowl across the doorway too, for that matter.

'Now, if you want to pass a photocell without interrupting the light that goes into it, you shine a light into it, step through the beam, and take away your light. The poor photocell doesn't know the difference. Not a simple rig like what I built, anyway.'

'I'll be darned.'

'Then I don't know what you'll be when I tell you the rest of this. Here.'

Eddy pulled something out of his pocket and dropped it into her palm. It was a ring of transparent plastic, slightly warped and sticky on one face. Around the edges were little curls of what looked like fused movie film.

'This little treasure,' he said, 'was stuck to the bulb of your gooseneck lamp. Unless I'm quite mistaken, it had a disc cut from a colour-photo transparency mounted on it. It was aimed at the black blotter. When you came in, you switched on the light, diddled around a minute and then sat down. The black blotter did not show anything up. The white one acted as a screen on which was projected a nice clear picture of your friend's pretty face – until the heat of the bulb ruined it. I found jimmy-marks on the alley window.'

'But, why on earth should he –'

'Ask questions later. Listen. That projection deal woke me right up. I didn't even have to go to your place. That shoe you threw – did you hit the face that was floating in your room?'

Tina nodded. 'Right between the eyes.'

'Then what happened to the shoe?'

'It went straight out the win – oh!'

'Yes, *oh*. The face wasn't in the room. It was on that tight mesh-lace curtain you have tacked over the lower pane.' He shrugged. 'So, I went looking for some sort of a projector that could do a job like that. I went just down the street to the Mello Club. I got hold of Shaw, the manager. He's a slimy little scut. I told him I had something hot on Lee Brokaw, but I'd have to check his dressing room to be sure.'

'Shaw didn't like the idea much, but he's so crazy to get a line on Brokaw that he'd give away his mother's left leg if he had to. He showed me the place. He crabbed about the lock on the door. Brokaw had had it put on. It was quite a place. You should see those mannequin heads that Lee made. I went through the drawer, and found what I was after. I swiped it. Here.'

Out of the same capacious jacket came a specially built five-cell electric torch. Around the lens was a spring clip. 'Here's a whole set of slides. Coloured ones, and this.' He handed her the glass disc. It was black, except for a spot in the centre, which, when held up to the light, held a miniature transparency of Lee Brokaw's almost beautiful face.

'They clip right on here like this,' and Eddy snapped a black glass over the lens. 'Brokaw just aimed that thing at your window, and then, probably, tossed a pebble or something at the glass. He held it until he saw your light go on. After that he could probably see you.'

She blushed. 'He probably could.'

'Shaw told me something else. He's a low little scuff, as I said before. I just stood there looking thoughtful, and he volunteered the information that he actually had a periscope – can you imagine it? – from his office next door, so that he could keep a dirty eye on whoever was in the dressing room. And he found out something really choice about our friend, Lee Brokaw.'

'What?'

'I think I'll wait and let the sergeant over there tell you. He's bound to come up with it before he lets us out of here.'

'How on earth did you get that gadget out of Shaw's hands?'

'This searchlight thing? Oh, I just said something about the back room. Those joints always have a back room. He was very nice to me after that.'

'Eddy! You might have gotten into some serious trouble!'

He laughed. 'That – from you! Well, after that I hightailed it for Bleecker and Commerce, and hid in a nice dark doorway. I don't know what would have happened if Brokaw had run up the other street. There goes the desk phone. Listen.'

The sergeant picked up the instrument briskly. 'Speaking,' he said. 'Yeah, we've still got 'em. You don't say!' Then followed an infuriating series of grunted affirmatives while he wrote. Then, 'Okay. Soon's I write it up. There may be a couple more questions.' He hung up, and began to write.

'Master mind,' said Tina while they waited, 'can you tell me why Lee did all those things?'

'I can guess,' said Eddy. He leaned back and caught his knee between his palms. 'Lee Brokaw, for all his skill and sensitivity, was the victim of a very real delusion – that soul-eater business. You, my child, were a substitute.'

'Me!'

'Yes, you. He saw in you courage and humour. He probably felt he had the same. Perhaps he did. But he needed some more things that you had. The – what was it? – the seasonings. Fear, terror, disgust, pity. That's what he was conditioning you with.'

'But how could he imagine that the soul-eater would mistake me for him?'

'For the same reason he thought the law would. He played it very cagily. That murder, now, was apparently a perfectly genuine one. He called up the police and tipped them off that the Sykes murderer would be at Bleecker and Commerce Streets at ten o'clock. I think he figured that the soul-eater, on seeing the surrender, would quickly jump at the first seasoned meat he saw that looked like the right one – rather than break his promise of keeping the murderer clear of the law. I imagine Brokaw was a little surprised to find only one person there – the detective.'

'Unless that detective is also a soul-eater,' said Tina brightly. 'But Eddy, I still don't understand how he could dream that the soul-eater could make such a mistake.'

'Sergeant,' called Eddy, 'could we be getting out of here soon? I'm supposed to be working.'

'Oh, I guess so,' said the sergeant cheerfully. 'There don't seem to be much more to figure out now. It all ties up.'

'Mind telling us why we were delayed?'

'I s'pose not, young feller. Seems like about two years back, this feller Sykes got married and killed the same night. They never did find the missus, and there wasn't a fingerprint in the place. It must have happened within an hour after they got to his place, and every fingerprint was wiped clean. Sykes had brought this girl from out of town. No one knew her. It was obvious she done it, but there wasn't but one clue as to who she was or anything about her. Even her license information was false.

'But there was one piece of evidence she didn't know about, or she'd have gotten to that, like as not. It seems Sykes sent a picture of her to his sister, and in the letter he said she had a great ugly mole on her back shaped like an angelfish. Well, now we know. She's been operatin' here for the past year and a half as an actor, ventriloquist, and dancer under the name of Lee Brokaw.'

'Lee Brokaw is a *girl*?'

'Was, ma'am. Dead now. Coroner says she apparently died of fright when she was nabbed. What we held you for, young lady, is because you are the spit an' image of Mrs Sykes, before she cut and dyed her hair according to that picture. If it wasn't for that mole on Brokaw-Sykes' back, you'd have a time proving you didn't do it.'

'He – he needed a shave!' she said desperately.

'Phony stubble, ma'am. Got it right here in the report.'

'Mad, mad, crazy as a loon,' murmured Tina as they went out. 'The poor kid. How on earth did she ever dream up this soul-eaters thing?'

'Paranoid logic, I guess,' said Eddy, who reads books. 'A persecution complex and an absolute genius for rationalizing it.'

They walked in silence for a block. 'I'm glad,' she said, 'that that soul-eater's hypothesis is rationalized. That was a pretty convincing – *awk!*'

'What's the matter?'

'Someone in that doorway,' she shuddered.

It was dark there, but there seemed to be something . . . he pulled out Brokaw's flashlight and switched it on.

It gave a peculiar, dim light. Standing in the doorway was a mildlooking little man, almost bald. He was looking at them and rubbing his hands.

His fringe of hair glowed a ghostly green.

'On your way, I see,' said the little detective happily. 'A most unpleasant experience.' He came closer. Tina shrunk away from him.

'Mind if I ask you,' said Eddy faintly. 'D-do you use Vaseline in your hair?'

The man touched it. 'Why yes. Why?'

'Ha ha, good stuff, hey?' said Eddy, and, scooping up Tina, he all but galloped away.

'It's all right, Tina,' he said as they hurried. 'It's perfectly all right. I still had that black disc on the flashlight. It's an ultra-violet filter. Vaseline fluoresces just fine under ultra-violet.'

What he did not tell her, and what he sincerely hoped she would never find out, was that Vaseline fluoresces blue, not green.

Daybloog

ROGER ZELAZNY

It was perhaps no surprise that the vampire genre should receive a fresh infusion when a trio of writers, Samuel E. Delany, Harlan Ellison and Roger Zelazny emerged in the mid-Sixties as the leading and most representative figures of the American 'New Wave' Science Fiction with its concentration on inner-space stories rather than those dealing with the hard sciences. In the context of this collection, Roger Zelanzy (1937–), the Hugo and Nebula award winning author from Ohio who worked in the US Social Security Administration before becoming a full-time writer, is the most interesting of the three for, as John Clute has written in The Encyclopedia of Science Fiction *(1979), 'A favourite Zelanzy protagonist is the extremely long-lived or immortal (or somehow invulnerable) human who lives a kinetically active but highly cultured life.' This interest has naturally led Roger into the vampire tradition, but like Matheson and Sturgeon he has always sought to update the old concepts. He was particularly active in this respect in the mid-Sixties writing these highly regarded stories about the undead, 'On The Road to Splenoba' (Fantastic Stories of Imagination,* January 1963), *'The Stainless Steel Leech' (Amazing Stories, April 1963) and 'The Graveyard Heart' (Fantastic Stories of Imagination, March 1964), all of which have been included in the collections of his short stories. (Shortly after this, in 1969, Roger wrote the novel for which he is probably best known,* Damnation Alley, *the story of a post-Holocaust motorcyle journey across a savage America, which was filmed in 1971.) Roger has recently returned to the vampire theme in the next story, 'Daybloog', which appeared in the May/June 1985 issue of* Twilight Zone. *It is everything fans have come to expect of Zelazny – a journey into the senses of a very long-lived person that proves to be both intriguing and ultimately surprising. When 'Day-blood' was first published it was prefaced by a warning from TZ's editor: 'Beware that rarest of beings – a vampire's vampire . . .'*

*   *   *

I crouched in the corner of the collapsed shed behind the ruined church. The dampness soaked through the knees of my jeans, but I knew that my wait was just about ended. Picturesquely, a few tendrils of mist rose from the soaked ground, to be stirred feebly by predawn breezes. How Hollywood of the weather . . .

I cast my gaze about the lightening sky, guessing correctly as to the direction of arrival. Within a minute I saw them flapping their way back – a big, dark one and a smaller, pale one. Predictably, they entered the church through the opening where a section of the roof had years before fallen in. I suppressed a yawn as I checked my watch. Fifteen minutes from now they should be settled and dozing as the sun spills morning all over the east. Possibly a little sooner, but give them a bit of leeway. No hurry yet.

I stretched and cracked my knuckles. I'd rather be home in bed. Nights are for sleeping, not for playing nursemaid to a couple of stupid vampires.

Yes, Virginia, there really are vampires. Nothing to get excited about, though. Odds are you'll never meet one. There just aren't that many around. In fact, they're damn near an endangered species – which is entirely understandable, considering the general level of intelligence I've encountered among them.

Take this guy Brodsky as an example. He lives – pardon me, resides – near a town containing several thousand people. He could have visited a different person each night for years without ever repeating himself, leaving his caterers (I understand that's their in-term these days) with little more than a slight sore throat, a touch of temporary anaemia and a couple of soon-to-be-forgotten scratches on the neck.

But no. He took a fancy to a local beauty – one Elaine Wilson, ex-majorette. Kept going back for more. Pretty soon she entered the customary coma and underwent the *nosferatu* transformation. All right, I know I said there aren't that many of them around – and personally I do feel that the world could use a few more vampires. But it's not a population-pressure thing with Brodsky, just stupidity and greed. No real finesse, no planning. While I applaud the creation of another member of the undead, I am sufficiently appalled by the carelessness of his methods to consider serious action. He left a trail that just about anyone could trace here; he also managed to display so many of the traditional signs and to leave such a multitude of clues that even in these modern times a reasonable person could become convinced of what was going on.

Poor old Brodsky – still living in the Middle Ages and behaving just as he did in the days of their population boom. It apparently never occurred to him to consider the mathematics of that sort of thing. He drains a few people he becomes particularly attracted to and they become *nosferatu*. If they feel the same way and behave the same way, they go out and recruit a few more of their caterers. And so on. It's like a chain letter. After a time, everyone would be *nosferatu* and there wouldn't be any caterers left. Then what? Fortunately, nature has ways of dealing with population explosions, even at this level. Still, a sudden rash of recruits in this mass-media age could really mess up the underground ecosystem.

So much for philosophy. Time to get inside and beat the crowd.

I picked up my plastic bag and worked my way out of the shed, cursing softly when I bumped against a post and brought a shower down over me. I made my way through the field then and up to the side door of the old building. It was secured by a rusty padlock which I snapped and threw into the distant cemetery.

Inside, I perched myself on the sagging railing of the choir section and opened my bag. I withdrew my sketchbook and the pencil I'd brought along. Light leaked in through the broken window to the rear. What it fell upon was mostly trash. Not a particularly inspiring scene. Whatever . . . I began sketching it. It's always good to have a hobby that can serve as an excuse for odd actions, as an ice-breaker . . .

Ten minutes, I guessed. At most.

Six minutes later, I heard their voices. They weren't particularly noisy, but I have exceptionally acute hearing. There were three of them, as I'd guessed there would be.

They entered through the side door also, slinking, jumpy – looking all about and seeing nothing. At first they didn't even notice me creating art where childish voices had filled Sunday mornings with off-key praise in years gone by.

There was old Dr Morgan, several wooden stakes protruding from his black bag (I'll bet there was a hammer in there, too – I guess the Hippocratic Oath doesn't extend to the undead – *primum, non nocere*, etc.); and Father O'Brien, clutching his Bible like a shield, crucifix in his other hand; and young Ben Kelman (Elaine's fiancé), with a shovel over his shoulder and a bag from which I suspected the sudden odour of garlic to have its origin.

I cleared my throat and all three of them stopped, turned, bumped into each other.

'Hi, Doc,' I said. 'Hi, Father. Ben . . .'

'Wayne!' Doc said. 'What are you doing here?'

'Sketching,' I said. 'I'm into old buildings these days.'

'The hell you are!' Ben said. 'Excuse me, Father . . . You're just after a story for your damned newspaper!'

I shook my head.

'Really I'm not.'

'Well, Gus'd never let you print anything about this and you know it.'

'Honest,' I said. 'I'm not here for a story. But I know why you're here, and you're right – even if I wrote it up it would never appear. You really believe in vampires?'

Doc fixed me with a steady gaze.

'Not until recently,' he said. 'But son, if you'd seen what we've seen, you'd believe.'

I nodded my head and closed my sketchpad.

'All right,' I replied, 'I'll tell you. I'm here because I'm curious. I wanted to see it for myself, but I don't want to go down there alone. Take me with you.'

They exchanged glances.

'I don't know . . .' Ben said.

'It won't be anything for the squeamish,' Doc told me.

Father O'Brien just nodded.

'I don't know about having anyone else in on this,' Ben added.

'How many more know about it?' I asked.

'It's just us, really,' Ben explained. 'We're the only ones who actually saw him in action.'

'A good newspaperman knows when to keep his mouth shut,' I said, 'but he's also a very curious creature. Let me come along.'

Ben shrugged and Doc nodded. After a moment Father O'Brien nodded too.

I replaced my pad and pencil in the bag and got down from the railing.

I followed them across the church, out into a short hallway and up to an open, sagging door. Doc flicked on a flashlight and played it upon a rickety flight of stairs leading down into darkness. Slowly then, he began to descend. Father O'Brien followed him. The stairs groaned and seemed to move. Ben and I waited till they had reached the bottom. Then Ben stuffed his bag of pungent groceries inside his jacket and withdrew a flashlight from his pocket. He turned it on and stepped down. I was right behind him.

I halted when we reached the foot of the stair. In the beams from their lights I beheld the two caskets set up on sawhorses, also the thing on the wall above the larger one.

'Father, what is that?' I pointed.

Someone obligingly played a beam of light upon it.

'It looks like a sprig of mistletoe tied to the figure of a little stone deer,' he said.

'Probably has something to do with black magic,' I offered.

He crossed himself, went over to it and removed it.

'Probably so,' he said, crushing the mistletoe and throwing it across the room, shattering the figure on the floor and kicking the pieces away.

I smiled, I moved forward then.

'Let's get the things open and have a look,' Doc said.

I lent them a hand.

When the caskets were open I ignored the comments about paleness, preservation, and bloody mouths. Brodsky looked the same as he always did – dark hair, heavy dark eyebrows, sagging jowls, a bit of a paunch. The girl was lovely, though. Taller than I'd thought, however, with a very faint pulsation at the throat and an almost bluish cast to her skin.

Father O'Brien opened his Bible and began reading, holding the flashlight above it with a trembling hand. Doc placed his bag upon the floor and fumbled about inside it.

Ben turned away, tears in his eyes. I reached out then and broke his neck quietly while the others were occupied. I lowered him to the floor and stepped up beside Doc.

'What –?' he began, and that was his last word.

Father O'Brien stopped reading. He stared at me across his Bible.

'You work for *them?*' he said hoarsely, darting a glance at the caskets.

'Hardly,' I said, 'but I need them. They're my life's blood.'

'I don't understand . . .'

'Everything is prey to something else, and we do what we must. That's ecology. Sorry, Father.'

I used Ben's shovel to bury the three of them beneath an earthen section of the floor toward the rear – garlic, stakes, and all. Then I closed the caskets and carried them up the stairs.

I checked around as I hiked across a field and back up the road after the pickup truck. It was still relatively early and there was no one about.

I loaded them both in back and covered them with a tarp. It was a thirty-mile drive to another ruined church I knew of.

Later, when I had installed them safely in their new quarters, I penned a note and placed it in Brodsky's hand:

Dear B,
Let this be a lesson to you. You are going to have to stop acting like Bela Lugosi. You lack his class. You are lucky to be waking up at all this night. In the future be more circumspect in your activities or I may retire you myself. After all, I'm not here to serve you.
Yours truly,
W

PS. The mistletoe and the statue of Cernunnos don't work anymore. Why did you suddenly get superstitious?

I glanced at my watch as I left the place. It was eleven fifteen. I stopped at a 7–11 a little later and used their outside phone.

'Hi, Kiela,' I said when I heard her voice. 'It's me.'

'Werdeth,' she said. 'It's been a while.'

'I know. I've been busy.'

'With what?'

'Do you know where the old Church of the Apostles out off Route 6 is?'

'Of course. It's on my backup list, too.'

'Meet me there at twelve thirty and I'll tell you about it over lunch.'

Vampirella

RON GOULART

Just as the Sixties were about to end, the first new female vampire icon since the French actress Musidora had brought the voluptuous Irma Vep to the cinema screen half a century earlier, made her debut in America as a comic strip heroine. She was Vampirella, an incredibly well-endowed beauty whose long, black hair and revealing one-piece costume was a throw-back to Irma Vep — but cut to the verge of nudity for the era now famous as the 'Swinging Sixties'. Within just a few years she would not only make the transition into a series of novels, but also have her own fan club, inspire a whole range of merchandizing from T-shirts to posters, and inspire a movie. Her appeal was undoubtedly based as much on the sensual and erotic drawings of her by artist Jose Gonzales as to her capabilities as a vampire. Indeed, just how Vampirella managed to stay inside her tiny costume — cut just above the line of her pubic hair and with two tiny strips of fabric across her huge bosom so narrow as to reveal a bat-shaped birthmark on her right breast — considering the hectic adventures into which she was pitched was nothing short of a miracle of design. But her countless fans on both sides of the Atlantic undoubtedly loved it all!

Vampirella had actually been created by the Hollywood film historian, Forrest J. Ackerman (1916–) as an unashamed imitation of another French comic strip heroine, Barbarella, who had been brought to the screen by Jane Fonda in 1968. 'Vampi' — as she was sometimes called — had apparently originated on the planet Drakulon which was inhabited solely by vampires who received their nourishment from rivers of blood. It was the onset of a drought and the unexpected arrival of a NASA space craft that prompted Vampirella's

journey to Earth and her new life on this planet. The first issue of
Vampirella *magazine in September 1969 from Warren Publications
was a smash-hit and in the next few years both the sales of the
magazine and the inventiveness of Vampirella's adventures grew
enormously. In 1970, for instance, she found herself being pursued by
a blind psychic named Conrad Van Helsing, intent on continuing the
vampire hunting tradition of his family; while by 1972 she was in
opposition to a revived and very handsome Count Dracula who,
readers were informed, had himself been an inhabitant of Drakulon
long before taking up residence in Transylvania! The success of the
series was undoubtedly influential in a host of similar comic strips
featuring near-nude heroines such as Devilina, Satana and Lilith,
daughter of Dracula, all of them endowed with enormous breasts and
supernatural powers! The transfer of Vampirella's adventures onto
the printed page did not begin until 1975, however, when the versatile
Californian-born SF and fantasy writer Ron Goulart (1933–) who is
famous for his zany humour and clipped writing style, began a series of
novels with* Bloodstalk (1975) *and followed this with* On Alien Wings
(1975), Deadwalk (1976), Blood Wedding (1976), Deathgame
(1976), Snakegod (1976) *and etc. As a result of the cult status that
Vampirella has come to enjoy, copies of the earliest of these books are
now rare and much sought-after by collectors. In the following
episode, Goulart explains Vampirella's origins and how this 'Huntress
from the Stars' brought yet another new dimension to the vampire
genre . . .*

✳   ✳   ✳

Shortly after the manned space flight to the moon, a second flight
was launched by NASA. Unlike her sister ship, the second craft's
launch was shrouded in secrecy, and today is denied by the authorities.
Officially, the ill-fated excursion never happened.

Some years earlier, an obscure scientist had mathematically determined the existence of a planet half a billion miles from Earth.
Computers verified the findings. In the name of science, the planet
must be reached and explored.

The Starcraft reached its goal. Drakulon was there – a planet of rare
and alien beauty. Where burnished bronze spires rose majestically in
the light of ancient twins moons. Where bizarrely twisted trees
bordered rivers of flowing crimson. Blood rivers that nourished a
gentle race who bent to drink.

Yet the Earthship came at the sundown of a once-lovely dream.
Drakulon was dying – its scarlet waters drying and powdering to dust.
The crew members died on the doomed Drakulon, but their spacecraft
returned to Earth. When it crashed in a remote New England forest, it
was empty save for a single stowaway traveller. A girl who had flown
on alien wings to survive, the last of the Drakulon race. And she would
survive. She had found new rivers of life-giving blood coursing
through the veins of her adopted planet's inhabitants.

Earth people would call her a vampire, sharpen their stakes and
mark her to die. But she would live. She was the huntress from the
stars. She was: VAMPIRELLA.

Blood.

Blood raining down from the scarlet skies, flowing in streams down
rocky hillsides.

Blood to drink, to give life.

Twins suns blazing in the sky. Burning away everything, killing the
planet.

Not this planet, no.

A distant planet, in a distant system. Drakulon.

The double sun. Burning, burning.

The thirst, the hunger, the craving for blood.

Fireworks.

A rocket blazing away from Drakulon.

Alone.

The blood raining down.

No, not here. Here you must kill for blood.

Kill humans, people so much like yourself.

No other way. No other way, except to die.

I don't want to die!

Falling. Falling down through space and time.

Falling to Earth.

I don't want to die!

Falling toward the giant mountains.

The plane is going to crash!

No, that's not . . .

Everything is swirling, mixing, coming together and falling apart.
Memories fall like snowflakes. Hundred of remembrances flickering.

Landing on Earth. That was . . . months ago.

Blood.

If I don't get it, I'll die!

The plane is going to crash! Crash into the jagged mountains.
I won't die!
A man in the snow. Saying something. Don't listen. Don't listen!
He's rising up.
He has no face! Not a man . . . some kind of beast. Huge, with great pawlike hands reaching out.
Don't touch me!
Falling. Falling down through darkness. Home is lost forever.
There is no home. Except here on Earth.
I didn't want to kill him!
No other way. It's that or —
'How are you feeling this afternoon?'
Someone out there. Is that a voice you can trust? Yes, but —
'I think you're looking much better. These past few days I've been very concerned, but I feel confident now.'
Days? Vampirella opened her eyes. A lean-faced blond man with rimless plastic glasses was watching her from the side of the bed. 'I'm afraid,' she said, 'that I don't — '
'We found you wandering in the snow, last week,' said the man. 'I'm Tyler Westron, a doctor.'
She sat up in the four-poster bed, looking around the room. 'Am I . . . is this the old house I saw?'
'Yes, you're a guest at the Westron Sanitarium,' explained the doctor. 'This house was built in the 1980s by a very wealthy, and very antisocial, copper millionaire. He had his reasons for wanting isolation; so do I.'
'A sanitarium? For what sort of patients?'
'Wealthy ones, mostly.' Westron smiled down at her. 'My speciality is orthomolecular psychiatry. Which is why your case is so interesting to me.'
Vampirella placed a hand to her breasts and noticed she'd been undressed and a lacy night-dress had been put on her. 'My case? You mean the effects of the exposure and the crash I — '
'I mean the vampirism.' Westron's smile grew a little strange around the edges. Seating himself on the edge of the bed, he began, 'It's been quite fascinating. So much of what we do here has become routine. A case like — '
She stiffened. 'How do you know about me?'
'You talked considerably in your delirium, Vampirella,' Dr Westron answered with a smile, 'aided at times by certain drugs. At first I thought it was nothing more than babbling, fever dreams. Then, after

a few tests, I became convinced that what you were saying was absolutely true.' He reached out to the carved bedside table to pick up a small beaker. 'Here, drink this.'

'What is it?'

'Medicine. Take it.'

Somewhat reluctantly, the dark-haired girl swallowed the thick, scarlet liquid.

'Very good,' said Westron. 'You are now freed of your greatest worry, Vampirella.'

'What do you mean?'

'Freed, I hasten to add, so long as you remain on friendly terms with me.' He smiled again, watching her. 'What you've just drunk is a blood-substitute serum . . . a little invention of my own. You must drink . . . let's not be too technical . . . let's say a short glass full every twenty-four hours. Do that, and you will have absolutely no craving for human blood.' He leaned closer. 'That will save you a good deal of embarrassment, won't it?'

She was not certain he was telling the truth. 'Why have you – '

'Why have I cooked up the serum? The challenge of the problem, of finding the right molecule, as it were. For another, I find you a very attractive young woman. I want to help you.'

'I see.'

'Yes, I imagine you do,' said Westron. 'The situation, to make everything perfectly clear, is this, Vampirella . . . you are to remain here, and to be, shall we say, obliging to me. Do that and you get your blood-substitute. Otherwise it's out in the snow with you.' He laughed.

'You want me to be your mistress,' said Vampirella. 'What did you do before I arrived?'

'I have been involved with . . . one of my nurses,' said the doctor. 'Lenore, I'm afraid, has grown increasingly tedious. Lord, if you knew how long I've actually had to . . . no matter. All you need concern yourself with is pleasing me. Since you're still recuperating I won't make any demands on you as yet.' Dr Westron put one hand on her shoulder, the other inside Vampirella's nightdress. He fondled her breasts as he kissed her.

She allowed that.

'Oh, and one other thing,' he said, getting off the four-poster. 'There have been some peculiar rumours about the recent crash of that airliner up in the mountains. The condition of one of the passengers was very strange. Seemed the poor devil lost an enormous amount of blood . . . and yet there was no blood at all around the place where he was found. Things like that do happen with a crash, I suppose, and yet . . .' He bowed in her direction. 'Ah, but so long as you're pleasant and well-behaved, Vampirella, no one need know what really happened up there in the mountains.' With a smile he left her.

She couldn't find her way out through the wall. The door of her bedroom was securely locked. Vampirella prowled the midnight room. She knew she was completely recovered from the effects of the plane crash and exposure and from the drugs which Dr Westron had administered to her while she was still only half-conscious. Westron must be aware of her recovery, too, and he'd soon be making further demands on her.

'Better find that formula right now,' Vampirella told herself, 'and then bid the good doctor a fond farewell.'

The leaded windows were barred. No one could get out that way.

No person, at least.

Now that she was completely recuperated, Vampirella could use all her powers and abilities.

She opened one of the barred windows a few inches. Wind and drizzling rain rushed in from the darkness outside.

The dark-haired girl took a step back. She narrowed her eyes and concentrated.

Her voluptuous body seemed to shimmer. Then the girl was gone. In her place a large black bat hovered a few feet above the floor.

The winged creature flapped toward the open window and flew out into the rainy night.

Getting Dead

WILLIAM F. NOLAN

'Getting Dead' is a classic example of the lure of the vampire tradition ultimately proving irresistible to even the longest serving of writers in the horror genre. Although Bill Nolan has been one of the busiest authors around for over forty years – slipping effortlessly from novels to short stories, and from scriptwriting to editing – this is his very first vampire tale: a fact made all the more curious because of his long-time friendship with Ray Bradbury, creator of the Family. 'Getting Dead' is also making its first appearance here in book form after its initial publication in Iniquities magazine in 1991.

William F. Nolan (1929–) is a former commercial artist and racing car driver, who came into fantasy fiction as a fan and then through editing a fanzine in San Diego and finally as the managing editor of Gamma magazine from 1963–4. His name became widely familiar as the co-author with George Clayton Johnson of Logan's Run (1967) which was filmed in 1976 with Michael York and Jenny Agutter, and then became a TV series a year later starring Gregory Harrison and Heather Menzies. This story of a future world where the problem of overpopulation is resolved by the compulsory death of men and women at the age of 21, has subsequently been continued by Bill in parts two and three of Logan: A Trilogy. He also scripted Burnt Offerings and Trilogy of Terror, twice won the Edgar Allan Poe Special Award for his contributions to the mystery genre, and has appeared in over 200 anthologies. 'Getting Dead' adds another to this remarkable achievement as well as providing the vampire genre with one more ingenious not to say humorous new contribution . . .

*   *   *

He'd been trying to commit suicide for the past six thousand years. Off and on. No real pattern to it, just whenever he got really depressed about having to live forever, or when one of his straight friends died (for the most part, he found other vampires a gloomy lot and had always enjoyed outside, non-blood contacts).

But suicide had never worked out for him. His will to survive, to live forever, was incredibly intense and fought against his sporadic attempts at self-extinction. He'd locked himself out of his castle several times and thrown away the key, figuring if he couldn't get inside to his casket before sunrise he'd be cooked to a fine black ash. (He'd seen dozens of movies about vampires and always enjoyed it whenever the sun melted one of them.) Yet each time he locked himself out he found a way to slip back into the damn castle . . . as a bat, or a wisp of smoke, or (twice) as a toad. His infernal shape-change ability invariably defeated these lock-out attempts.

Then, several times down the centuries, he devised ways to drive a stake through his heart . . . but never got it right. Helsinki: stake through his shoulder. London: stake through his upper thigh. Dusseldorf: stake through his left foot (he limped for six months) and so on. Never once in the heart. So he gave that up.

He tried boiled garlic in Yugoslavia. Prepared a tasty stew and had the garlic dumped in by a perverted dwarf pal of his. Devoured the entire bowl, belched, and sat back to die. But all he did was throw up over the dwarf, who found the whole incident most disgusting.

In the Black Forest of Germany he leaped from the roof of a village church onto a cross, ending up with some painful skin blisters where the cross had burned through his cape – but it didn't come *close* to killing him.

He drank a quart of holy water at Lourdes, resulting in a severe case of diarrohea.

And, naturally, he had talked several of his straight friends into attempting to kill him at various times, but either he killed them first or they bungled the job.

So here he was, Count Arnold Whatever (he hadn't been able to remember his last name for the past seven hundred years), walking the night streets of Beverly Hills in the spring of 1991, determined to do away with himself but lacking a conclusive plan of action.

That was when he saw the ad.

It was block-painted on the wooden back of a bus stop bench:

ANYTHING, INC.

Come to us if all else fails.
For the proper fee, we'll do anything.
Open 24 Hours!
We're Never Closed to YOU!

And the address was right there in Beverly Hills. On Rodeo Drive near Wilshire.

Arnold was in a hurry, so he shape-changed and flapped over. He came through the office door as a bat (lots of screaming from the night secretary) and changed back into human form at the desk.

No appointment. He'd just flown in to demand service.

'Who the hell are you?' asked the tall man (he was flushed and balding) behind the desk of ANYTHING, INC.

'I am Count Arnold, and I am here to test the validity of your bus stop advertisement — that for the proper fee you can do anything.'

Mr Anything (for that is how Arnold thought of him) settled back in his chair and lit a large Cuban cigar. 'I got two questions.'

'So ask.'

'What do you want done, and how much can you pay me to do it?'

'I want to stop being a vampire. And I will pay with these.' Arnold produced a bag of emeralds and rubies, spilling the jewels across the desk.

Mr Anything put a glass to his eye and examined each stone. That took ten full minutes. Then he looked up and smiled. 'How old are you?'

'I am just a shade over ten thousand years old,' said Arnold. 'And for the first four thousand years I was content to be a vampire. Then I got bored. Then depressed. I have not been really happy for six thousand years.'

Mr Anything shifted his cigar. 'I don't believe in vampires.'

'I didn't either until I became one.'

'Show me your teeth.'

Arnold did. The two hollow fangs, needle sharp, with which he sucked blood were quite evident when he opened his mouth.

'You live off human blood?'

'That is correct.'

'What's it taste like?'

'Depends. Most of the time it tastes fine. Then again, I've had some that was downright bitter. But I never complain. I take it as it comes.'

Mr Anything got up from the desk, walked to the door and closed it firmly. '*Prove* to me you're a vampire.'

Arnold shrugged. 'The only way to do that would be for me to suck all the blood from your body over a period of weeks – starting tonight.'

'All right,' said Mr Anything with a note of sourness in his voice. 'I'll take your word for it.'

'I have tried literally everything to get rid of me,' Arnold told him. 'But I am very clever. I keep outsmarting myself, and just go on living. On and on and on. Living, living, living.'

'I get your point,' said the tall man.

'So . . . you have the jewels. They are worth a king's ransom. In fact, at one time in Bulgaria, they *were* a king's ransom, but that's neither here nor there. What I wish to know is,' and Arnold leaned close to him, 'how do you intend to dispose of me?'

Mr Anything took a step back. 'Your breath –'

'I know. It's foetid. There's just no way to keep it fresh.' He frowned. 'Well?'

'I could chain you to a post in full daylight and let the sun –'

'No, no, that's absolutely no good,' said Arnold. 'I'd just shape-change into a sewer rat and head for the nearest sewer. Sunlight's not the answer.'

Mr Anything paced the room, puffing out cannon bursts of cigar smoke. 'I'm sure that a stake through the heart would –'

Arnold shook his head. 'I've tried the stake thing over and over and I'm telling you it's a waste of time.'

'C'mon, you gotta be kidding. You mean even with you all snug in the coffin and me leaning over you with a big mallet to pound it into your chest while you sleep?'

'Won't work. Vampires are light sleepers. When we feel the point of a sharpened stake tickle our skin we jump.' Arnold sighed. 'I'd just reach up from the coffin and tear your throat out.'

Mr Anything thought that over. 'Yeah . . . well, that would not be so good.'

He kept pacing. Then he stopped, turned to Arnold, and clapped him on the shoulder. 'I got it.' He grinned. 'Your troubles are over.'

'Really?' Arnold looked sceptical.

'Believe me, you're as good as dead. I mean *dead* dead. My word on it.'

And they shook hands.

A week later, on a clouded night, Arnold woke up. Mr Anything had obviously used some kind of drug on him. So he couldn't shape-change.

His neck was sore.

He reached up to touch it. Something had bitten him. The wound was newly-inflicted; there was blood on his finger-tips.

This was stupid. You don't kill a vampire by having another vampire bite him (or her). That's how it all starts in the first place.

He felt the wound again. Multiple teeth bites – not just the usual twin fang marks.

Something else had bitten him . . . *changed* him.

The clouds parted and the moon was full.

Hair was sprouting out of skin in rough brown clumps. And he felt his jaw lengthen.

Arnold howled.

And he happened to be knowledgeable enough about the real world of Night Creatures to know that a silver bullet was totally ineffectual.

Damn!

Reader, I Buried Him

BASIL COPPER

Of the many non-fiction books written about vampirism in recent years, The Vampire In Legend, Fact and Art *by Basil Copper (1924–) which appeared in 1973 is probably the widest in scope, the most painstaking in research and certainly among the most interesting to read. The author has, in fact, spent many years of his life studying and writing about the vampire tradition in literature and on the screen in his capacity as a journalist, novelist and one of the leading collectors of rare vintage films in the country. Aside from this non-fiction work, Basil has written the sleeve notes for the record album* Dracula *(1974); been highly praised for his novels such as* The Great White Space *(1974) – which earned him the accolade, 'the best writer in the genre since H. P. Lovecraft' – and* The House of the Wolf *(1983); and written two superb vampire short stories, 'Dr Porthos' which I first published in 1968, and 'Reader, I Buried Him!' which is also appearing in print for the first time in this book. The title may well strike a chord with readers familiar with* Jane Eyre *– for it is an ironic distortion of the opening line of the last chapter of Charlotte Brontë's classic – but what is more remarkable is that the genesis of the story itself is* true.

I have therefore decided to let Basil himself preface the fiction which follows with an account of the facts that inspired it. 'In the autumn of 1993 while I was in France there was an extraordinary item on French TV,' he says. 'Dozens of sheep had been found dead by shepherds and farmers in a wild and remote mountainous area of the Var. The sheep had been attacked during the night as they grazed by something which crept beneath them and with a sucker-like mouth had drained all their blood. In front of the TV cameras, a farmer held up one sheep which had survived the attack and there was a large hole in its stomach about the size of a fifty pence coin. The police were baffled – as they say – and medical experts and scientists, after careful examination of the area and the dead animals, were equally mystified. So far as they knew there was no such creature known to science as the one which had killed the sheep. I must confess my hair stood up on end!' The mystery did more than stand Basil Copper's hair on end – it also set his imagination to work and resulted in the following story. And not only does it add yet another new dimension to our theme, but just as that original TV report affected the author, so I must confess that his final line sent a genuine shiver up my spine!

I

Dr Irving is coming tomorrow. That was all Renwick could think of. The epidemic was getting out of hand and he, as the Chief Medical Officer of the Outstation, was baffled. He was grateful for Irving's agreement to come. He was the leading British specialist in blood disorders and the diseases connected therewith. Renwick adjusted the trim of the anglepoise lamp to give a better light on the paper before him and wiped his aching eyes with his handkerchief.

God, I'm tired, he thought. The situation in which he was involved seemed never-ending. He had not bargained for this when he had accepted the position in this remote outpost. With its chill winds and temperatures that froze one to the bone, it put the seal on what his predecessor had called one of the most God-forsaken places on earth.

Now he bent forward again, jotting his observations in the Station Logbook, which he was obliged by law to enter every day. The photocopies were faxed directly to the headquarters of the Central Committee, who could direct his activities within a few minutes if an emergency arose. Renwick remembered the words of Cartwright, the former Director of the station, and his gaunt white face vanishing into the mist as the relief launch took him back to the mainland.

'You'll find things here, man, that are beyond belief.'

He had paused, his grim jaw jutting out beneath the rim of his meerschaum pipe.

'And beyond all medical science,' he had added.

He had spat philosophically overboard into the scummy water. His last words had been, 'Pernicious anaemia, be damned! There's something far deeper and more sinister involved that would baffle the greatest medical scientists, let alone poor humble specialists like ourselves. Good luck to you!'

Renwick had been left with the impression of his glowing eyes and his white, tragic face that had rapidly been enveloped in the thick fog that always descended on the islands. Two months later he was dead; no-one knew the cause. In a letter received a few days before the news came through, he had confided to Renwick, 'I am on the brink of something interesting. If not a breakthrough then at least an inkling of what we might be up against. More later.'

But nothing had ever come and Renwick had been left with a great question mark. His inquiries of the Central Committee had resulted in no further data, and apparently, according to McIver, he had left no notes that made any sense. There was something weird about the whole set-up, Renwick realized. It was as though strange forces were at work to combat the researches of the Outstation.

Professor Quintain had been on to something as well. The island had been uninhabited for years, which was why the Central Committee had chosen it. It was untainted, unlike the mainland, and research could be carried out there, free from the constraints which obtained elsewhere. But the virus may have been airborne, for no sooner had the large number of scientists and ancillary staff been established there, than things resumed their old course.

It had taken some months, it was true. Quintain had been the first person to pinpoint it. He was a gigantic, bearded man, of Scandinavian extraction, and brilliant in his own field, which was that of virology. Almost alone among the personnel on the island, he had discounted the windborne virus theory. He felt the disease was spread by human contact and had directed his researches to that end. This was reinforced by the presence of the strange, sucker-like mark on the abdomen of each of the dead, which no-one could explain. He had come to Renwick some months earlier, when the wind was buffeting at the windows of the Outstation and dark storm clouds were scudding over the sullen sea.

His theory, which was fanciful in the extreme, was that some sort of vampiric influence was at work, attacking the victims and *leaching* their blood away; it was true that the victims became extremely emaciated and their blood count low, but despite the strange abdominal markings, the theory was fantastic in the extreme, Renwick felt. He himself now clung to the notion that some rarer form of pernicious anaemia was at work, of which the abdominal wounds were the culmination, not the commencement. The most awful thing about it all and Renwick, being a scientist, was not an emotional man – was that the symptoms, once appearing, rapidly developed and almost always ended in death of the most excruciating kind.

In the two years since the Outstation had been estbalished, at least twenty of the personnel on site had died and their bodies had been cremated, lest others be contaminated. And of those cases with which Renwick was familiar, a number of medical people who had left the island, had later succumbed to the bizarre disease on the mainland. The most sensational and at the same time most promising develop-ment had been some months ago, shortly after Quintain first came to see him. Since then he had further developed his theories and had noted something that had escaped the observations of the rest of the Outstation's staff.

There were large numbers of wild sheep on the island, which was of vast extent and largely unexplored. It was mountainous, inhospitable terrain and as the scientific establishment had obviously been built at the nearest point to the mainland, few people there had bothered to venture more than a mile or two from its perimeter, particularly as the level ground shortly ran out into steep hillsides covered with shale and boulders. But Quintain was a bold and adventurous man and his explorations often took him several miles inland and he would sometimes stay away one or even two nights, taking a small tent and iron rations with him.

What he had discovered and what his photographs confirmed was that some sort of creature hitherto unknown to science was at work in these barren wastes; findings which were beginning to erode Renwick's own feelings about the disease.

During his wanderings Quintain had discovered the bodies of a number of dead sheep, scattered over an area several miles square, not only on a plateau but on the lower slopes of the foothills where these hardy beasts grazed. Renwick was about to point out that this was entirely normal and that sometimes the beasts lost their footing and could have fallen to their deaths or died from exposure or natural causes, but there was something about Quintain's manner that stopped the words in his throat.

'I have never come across anything like it,' the latter said. 'All these animals, which were otherwise healthy and well-nourished beasts, had been entirely drained of blood, and what's more, on the bellies of each there was a large circular hole – a suction point revealing strange indentations, through which the life had been drained out of them. Some creature had stealthily crept beneath them and quietly and cautiously had leached the vital essence out of them until they were nothing more than lifeless husks! This might explain some of the strange marks on the stomachs of our dead colleagues.'

Despite his phlegmatic nature Renwick could not suppress a slight shudder at these last words, the nature of which had been reinforced by the bleakness of their surroundings, slightly distorted by the thick quartz windows of the laboratory. He had put forward a number of possibilities which Quintain had had no difficulty in dismissing out of hand and truth to tell Renwick himself felt his possible explanations to be thin and unconvincing. Nothing further was said and on parting Quintain had asked him to say nothing to any of the others. Renwick had kept his word and so far as he knew Quintain himself had not confided in anyone else. He had buried those sheep he had found, the ones nearest the Outstation, and his photographs and a number of sketchy notes on the phenomenon he had left with Renwick.

Perhaps he had a premonition – for the last time the two had met, Quintain had expressed doubts about the future and when he had handed his material over to his companion he had urged him to put them in an anonymous brown envelope and keep them under lock and key. This he had done, but afterward he could not forget Quintain's parting words. 'It is my contention that we are up against some superhuman agency that is perhaps taking over mankind for some purpose of which we are unaware.'

Renwick had smiled at this, but shortly after Quintain had disappeared on one of his expeditions. Some days later he was found dead on a remote hillside. Dr Sanders, who carried out purely medical functions at the Outstation, had given the cause of death as heart failure, but Renwick was not satisfied. He had gone to the post-mortem room late at night with a purloined key. He was shocked at what he found. This great man was shrunken, his complexion dead white, his body obviously drained of blood. Renwick was used to death, but he was staggered to the very core of his being when he saw in the centre of the corpse's stomach, a large circular indentation; a suction point which bore the marks of extremely tiny teeth.

He had seen nothing like it before; in the other examples it was as though an abscess had burst. Fortunately he kept this new knowledge to himself, replacing the key in secret. There was nothing of these findings when he read Dr Sanders' report and the next day cremation had taken place in the normal way. From that day forward Renwick was on his guard for he now regarded each of his colleagues as a possible source of evil.

2

Quintain used to say, 'In this life you get only the label on the bottle. Nothing else.' Meaning don't look for anything other than what you expected. He was right, of course. Only in this instance, it looked as though the label on the bottle indicated its contents as poison. But Renwick kept his own counsel and studied each of his more intimate colleagues searchingly, while at the same time trying to avoid any suspicion on their part that he was doing so. He was impatiently awaiting the arrival of Dr Irving, who had been delayed, owing to some administrative difficulties with the Central Committee.

But eventually, some weeks after Quintain's death, the day arrived and Renwick was among the small party on the jetty awaiting the advent of the great man. Renwick's initial impression was disappointing. Despite his great height – Irving was just over six feet four inches tall – he was cadaverous in aspect, with a strong, square chin that gave him a prognathous aspect. His complexion was chalky white, but his eyes were a brilliant green and he was animated enough, inspiring confidence in those around him.

He was a fountain of ideas, spraying out instructions and observations to the laboratory staff, with most of whom he was soon on confidential terms. But something within Renwick held back; beneath his habitual reserve, there was something else; something on which he could not put his finger at the moment. It had crystallized around the figure of Dr Sanders and the fact that he had reported nothing of the bizarre circumstances surrounding the death of Professor Quintain. If Renwick confided in Irving, then that would set the wheels in motion; the last thing he wanted was a confrontation with the latter. That would put him on his guard immediately.

No, all the sensitive antennae with which he was equipped, ruled against this. He must wait, bide his time, and strike when the moment was appropriate. Sanders must make a false move at some point; Renwick could see that Irving's arrival had caught him off balance and made him uneasy. He had only to wait; the time for conveying his suspicions to the newcomer was not yet. In the meantime, as the Chief Medical Officer, he was in Irving's confidence, and the two men had a number of private meetings, in which they exchanged views on the plague for it was nothing less that was blighting the world.

Renwick in turn gained strength from Irving's confidence and authority. He was active from dawn to dusk; striding about the station; calling for private documents and reports; requesting information from the secret archives of the Central Commitee; and actually going out on solitary expeditions among the bleak landscapes of the island, just as Quintain had done. Renwick was a little perturbed at these latter exercises but he kept his thoughts to himself, even accompanying Irving on one occasion, though he marvelled at the older man's energy and stamina.

Irving strode and scrambled across the rocky terrain at such a pace and with apparently undiminished vigour, that Renwick was hard to keep up with him. But later, thinking over Quintain's comments, on many a lonely night watch, he wondered why Irving spent so much time out alone at night, which was completely contrary to the practice of the other members of the research staff. It was true Quintain had done the same thing, but he had a definite purpose in view. Renwick had said nothing to Irving of his suspicions, though naturally the two men had gone deeply into the medical problems involved in the treatment of the disease.

For month after month before Irving's arrival Renwick had spent long nights in the laboratory, examining the writhing organisms revealed by the powerful lenses of his microscopes. Now he had confided his medical theories to the newcomer and had made available to him the detailed notes that occupied the pages of three thick journals. These dealt, of course, with medical problems only, and were entirely different to the secret diaries to which Renwick confided his inmost thoughts and conjectures concerning the plague which had so afflicted his colleagues.

Gradually, his mind had been turned in a certain direction. The Outstation was the principal research unit which contained the finest brains which were currently exploring ways of combating the dreadful disease. If it were a disease. But the Outstation, on an island supposedly free from the plague, was prey to some intelligence that was slowly and invisibly cutting down these fine minds. A human agency somewhere was determined to prevent the secret of the vampiric virus from being discovered. The premise was so simple and so obvious that Renwick had completely overlooked it in his calculations: now it came as a blinding ray of light into his consciousness.

He was torn in two directions. The imperative on the one hand was to confide in someone in higher authority so that proper steps could be taken. On the other, it was impossible, at this stage, for him to decide whom to trust. In the end he compromised, as he had to. There was no other choice. He determined to keep close watch on both Irving and Sanders. If Sanders were involved he might try to make some attempt on Irving's life. But if Irving had his own suspicions and struck first, then Renwick must aid him with everything within his power. It needed a very fine judgement.

His opportunity was to come more quickly than he had anticipated. One evening, as dusk was beginning to fall, Irving went out across the foothills. The big windows of Renwick's laboratory commanded the only entrance to the Outstation and all personnel had to pass in and out beneath these windows. Furthermore, a security light, which was controlled from the laboratory itself, burned there all night, so that anyone coming or going could be easily identified. About ten minutes later, Sanders himself went out, making for the rough ground of the low foothills in the same direction Irving had taken.

Renwick took only three seconds to make up his mind. His anorak was to hand on the peg near his desk; he thrust a sheath-knife into his right hand pocket and he could not have said why he picked up an emergency pack from a rack in the corridor outside the laboratory.

This contained a torch, handtools, a self-powered electric drill, and a short metal spade, its edge honed to maximum sharpness to combat the tough sea-grass which grew so profusely in these parts. He fixed it by the canvas straps to his back and in reply to questions from colleagues he met in the corridor, he merely muttered that he was routinely collecting some core samples from the soil.

No-one queried this and in another two minutes he was outside in the windy dusk, where white spume was being blown from the wave-tops down on the shore. Irving had long since disappeared, but the thin form of Sanders was still visible on the furthermost ridge. Then it too faded from sight. Renwick walked aimlessly at first, but in the general direction which he guessed Irving had taken. He had been with him once to a high, grassy plateau where the sheep grazed. He made his way up a steep ravine in the purple dusk, at a tangent to the route Sanders had taken, his breath hissing in his throat with the exertion on the precipitous slopes.

It was still light when he gained the plateau and there was no sign of either of the two men. But Renwick had a strange feeling this evening and something impelled him to keep on walking in the same direction.

A short while later he could make out the dark silhouettes of a number of sheep, fringed with the last traces of an angry red sunset. There was something else too; something so inexpressibly sinister that he could not believe his eyes. He stopped quickly, and silently lowered the pack to the ground, eased out the spade and extended the metal handle to its full length before locking it in place.

What he saw was some sort of huge white slug slowly making its way across the grass, where it settled like some obscene incubus beneath the belly of the nearest sheep. Renwick's heart was thudding in his throat as he went forward, tightly clutching the metal spade . . .

3

From the secret diary of Dr Donald Renwick.
Section No. 46. Asylum No. 134.

They will not believe me. But now that I have had six months to think things over, I realise that Sanders could not take the risk of killing me. I knew too much, it was true, but what was that weighed against the stake these creatures were playing for? It was better to have me quietly removed to the mainland; then to spread reports and have people in high places – even those on the Central Committee – to sign documents, while doctors, so-called, processed the papers which eventually found me here, helpless and unable to warn anybody of the horrors awaiting mankind.

There had been too many deaths of high-ranking personnel on the island, you see, and they could not afford to eliminate the Chief Medical Officer. Better by far to say that the strain of my duties had unhinged my mind: that would account for the preposterous accusations I was about to make. But I am writing these notes in the hope that somewhere, some day, an incorruptible person in high authority will find them and bring the truth before unimpeachable Centralists while there is still time.

I reiterate again and again the same facts; it is gospel truth what I say, even though it may appear fantastic. Dr Irving has never been seen since that night, of course. Should I, in fact, have brought back witnesses; have taken photographs; have tried in some way to alert the world to these vampiric horrors?

In the long run, I think not. It would have done no good and the menace that threatens mankind must be fought in the same subtle way that these creatures employ. They hold all the aces in the pack while they remain invisible, in the middle of society, yet unsuspected. What I saw that night has been burned inexorably into my brain, and will remain with me until the day I die.

As I stepped forward with the spade I saw with a shudder of indescribable terror that the long, glistening slug-creature that undulated across the rough grass, its sickly white envelope glistening with some noxious fluid, bore the head of Dr Irving whose eyes glared into mine as its sucker mouth with its minute teeth were about to sink themselves into the underbelly of the sheep. The abomination writhed aside, but I was too quick for the loathsome thing. I stepped forward swiftly and with the strength of desperation gripped the spade and sheared the head clean off the foul hybrid which went wriggling blindly across the grass.

I must have had the strength of ten men that night and I do not know how I found the courage to do what I did. They will never find the remains of Irving if they search for a thousand years; there are so many wild and secret places on the island. Did I do right? Who is to say? It was the most difficult decision of my life and as a medical man I should have ordered a full autopsy so that science could gain more knowledge of the darker secrets of the world.

And yet, and yet . . . There was so much horror and disgust; no-one but myself could realize the half of it. For the dismembered portions of this vile creature kept on living and wriggling in torment; there were vent-like mouths all along the slug body on either side.

And the disembodied head opened and closed its eyes, and the mouth was moving as though it were pleading with me. I was sick to my soul, but I did what I had to do. He was still alive, as I say. But . . . Reader, I buried him!

The Bleeder

RICHARD LAYMON

Of the latest generation of major horror story writers – Stephen King, Dean Koontz, Clive Barker, James Herbert et al – the horror story writer's writer is undoubtedly Richard Laymon. King has said of him, 'If you've missed Laymon, you've missed a treat', while Koontz seconds this: 'No one writes like Laymon, and you're going to have a good time with anything he writes.' Among his best-selling novels have been Flesh – *which was voted Best Horror Novel of 1988 and short-listed for the prestigious Bram Stroker Award* – The Stake (1990) – *about a horror novelist who discovers a corpse in a coffin with a stake through the heart – and* Savage (1993) *in which Jack the Ripper returned with an even more monstrous appetite than before. Laymon has also written short stories for prestigious journals such as the* Ellery Queen Mystery Magazine *and* Alfred Hitchcock's Mystery Magazine.*

    Richard Carl Laymon (1947–) was born in Chicago and horror became the dominant influence in his life after the night his parents allowed him to stay up late to watch Boris Karloff in Frankenstein *on television. After gaining a BA in English Literature at Williamette University in Oregon, he worked as a schoolteacher, librarian and report writer for a law firm before sales of his first book,* Flesh, *exceeded 300,000 copies in the US alone and freed him to become a full-time writer. A mild mannered, gentle man, Richard now lives in Los Angeles where he dreams up his uniquely gruesome plots mingling gore and humour which have made him one of the biggest sellers in the horror market. He recently summed up his philosophy as a writer in these words: 'Villains may inspire fear, but horror is made of sterner stuff. Horror requires monsters to be monstrous. It is villainous to put arsenic in someone's soup, but it is monstrous to serve soup in which the floating chunks of meat have toenails.' Laymon's story here, 'The Bleeder' which originally appeared in the Winter 1989 issue of New Blood, is full of just such ingredients and may well be as startling to some modern readers as Stoker's Dracula was to his public a century ago. Don't say you haven't been warned!*

*   *   *

The spot of wetness on the sidewalk at Byron's feet looked purple in the mercury glow of the streetlight. It looked like a drop of blood.

He squatted down and peered at it. Then he pulled a flashlight out of the side pocket of his sport jacket. He thumbed the switch. In the bright, somewhat yellowish shine of its beam, the spot appeared crimson.

Might be paint, he thought.

But who would be wandering around at night dripping red paint?

He reached down and touched it. Bringing his fingertip close to the flashlight glass, he inspected the red smear. He rubbed it with his thumb. The stuff was kind of watery. Not gooey enough for paint. More like blood that had been spilled very recently.

He sniffed it.

He could only smell mustard from the hot dog he'd eaten during the last show, an aroma strong enough to overpower blood's subtle aroma. But it wouldn't have masked the pungent odour of paint.

Byron wiped his finger and thumb on his sock. Still squatting, he let the beam of his flashlight drift over the concrete ahead. He saw a dirty pink disk of flattened bubble gum, a gob of spit, a mashed cigarette butt, and a second drop of blood.

The second drop was three strides away. He stopped above it. Like the first, it was about the size of a nickel. Sweeping his light forward, he found a third.

Maybe someone with a nosebleed, he thought.

Or a switchblade in the guts.

No, a *real* wound and there'd be blood everywhere. Byron remembered the mess in the Elsinore's restroom last month. During intermission, a couple of teenagers had gone at each other with knives. He and Digby, one of the other ushers, had broken it up. Though the kids only had minor wounds, the john had looked like a slaughter-house.

Compared to that, this was nothing. Just a drip once in a while. Even a nosebleed, he thought, would throw out more gore.

On the other hand, the person's clothing, or a handkerchief, might have soaked up most of it – so that only a fraction of the spillage actually hit the sidewalk.

Just a little drip now and then.

Just enough to make Byron very curious.

The trail of blood was going in his direction, anyway, so he kept his flashlight on and kept a lookout.

'Hey, the streetlights aren't bright enough for you?'

He turned around.

Digby Hymus, known to the girls who worked the refreshment stand as the Jolly Green Dork, came striding down the sidewalk. The thirty year-old retired boxer had removed his green usher's jacket. Its sleeves were tied around his neck so he looked as if he were giving a piggy-back ride to someone who'd been mashed by a steam roller. His arms were so thick with muscle that they couldn't swing close to his sides when he walked.

'Hate to tell you this, By, but you look like a god-damn retard with that flashlight on.'

'Appearances are often deceiving,' he said. 'Take a gander.' He aimed his flashlight at the nearest spot of blood.

'Yeah? So what?'

'Blood.'

'Yeah. So what?'

'Don't you find it intriguing?'

'Probably some babe sprung a leak in her – '

'Don't be disgusting.'

'Hey, you're the guy so interested in blood. You've got a real ghoulish streak, you know that?'

'If you can't say something nice, don't say it.'

'Screw you,' he said, and walked across the road to his parked car.

Byron waited until the car sped off, then continued to follow the trail of blood. He stopped at the corner of 11th Street. His apartment was five blocks straight ahead. But the drops of blood went to the right.

He paused for a moment, considering what to do. He knew that he ought to go on home. But if he did that, he would always wonder.

Maybe the bleeder needs help, he told himself. Even a slow leak could be fatal if it went on long enough. Maybe I'm this person's only chance.

Maybe I'll be a hero, my story will be on the news.

Then guys like Digby – girls like Mary and Agnes of the snack counter – wouldn't be so quick to poke fun at him.

His mind made up, he turned the corner and began to follow the blood up 11th Street.

The television. He could see it now. Karen Ling on the five o'clock news. 'Byron Lewis, 28 year-old poet and part-time usher at the Elsinore theatre, last night came to the aid of a mugging victim in an alley off 11th Street. The victim, 22 year-old fashion model Jessica Connors, had been assaulted earlier that evening in front of the theatre where Byron works. Bleeding and disoriented, she had staggered several blocks before falling unconscious where she was later discovered by the young poet. Byron made the grisly discovery after following Jessica's trail of blood. According to paramedics, Jessica was only minutes away from death at the time she was found. Her survival is being attributed to Byron's quick actions in applying first aid and summoning the ambulance. She is currently recovering, and extremely grateful, at Queen of Angels Hospital.'

Byron smiled.

Just a fantasy, he told himself. But what's wrong with that?

The bleeder will probably turn out to be an old wino who cut his lip on a bottle of rotgut.

Or worse.

You'll probably wish you'd gone straight home.

But at least you'll know.

Stopping at Harker Avenue, he found a spot of blood on the curb. No traffic was nearby. But Byron believed in playing by the rules. So he thumbed the button to activate the WALK sign, waited for the signal to change, then started across.

If the bleeder had left any drops in the road, passing cars must have obliterated them.

He found more when he reached the other side.

The bleeder was still heading north on 11th Street.

And Byron realized, with some dismay, that he had crossed an invisible border into Skid Row.

In the area ahead, many of the streetlights were out. They left broad pools of darkness on the sidewalk and road. Every shop in Byron's sight was closed for the night. Metal gates had been stretched across their display windows and doors. He glanced through the checkered grating in front of a clothes store, saw a face at the window, and managed to stifle a gasp of alarm.

Just a mannequin, he told himself, hurrying away.

He made a point to avoid looking into any more windows.

Better just to watch the sidewalk, he thought. Watch the trail of blood.

The next time he looked up, he saw a pair of legs sticking out of a tenement's recessed entryway.

The bleeder!

I did it!

Byron rushed to the fallen man. It was a *man*, unfortunately. A man with holes in the bottom of his shoes, whose grimy ankles were blotched with scabs, whose trousers were stained and crusty with filth, who wore a ragged sweatshirt that had one empty sleeve pinned up.

No left arm.

His right arm was folded under his head like a pillow.

'Excuse me,' Byron said.

The man kept snoring.

Byron nudged him with a foot. A twitch jumped up the body. The snoring stopped with a startled gasp. 'Huh? Whuh?'

'Are you all right?' Byron asked. 'Are you bleeding?'

'*BLEEDING*?' the man squealed and bolted upright. His head swivelled as he looked down at himself. Byron helped by shining the light on him. 'I don't see no blood. Where? Where?'

Byron didn't see any blood on the man, either. But he saw other things that made him turn away and try not to gag.

'Oh God, I'm bleedin'!' the man whined. 'They musta bit me. Oh, they's always bitin' me. Why they wanna bit ol' Dandy! Where'd they get me? They after ol' Dandy's stump again? Jeezum!'

Byron risked a look at Dandy and saw that the old man was struggling with his single arm to pull his sweatshirt off.

'Maybe I've got the wrong person.'

'Oh, they's after me.' The shirt started to rise. Byron glimpsed the grey, blotchy skin of Dandy's belly.

'Gimme yer light, duke! C'mon, gimme!'

'I've gotta go,' Byron blurted.

He staggered away from the frantic derelict – and saw a spot of blood farther up the sidewalk.

Dandy wasn't the bleeder, after all.

'I'm sorry,' Byron called back. 'Go back to sleep.'

He heard a low groan. A voice sunken in fear and disgust said, 'Aw, looky what they's done to me.'

If only I'd left the guy alone, he thought.

Real neat play. I should've gone home.

But he'd come this far. Besides, he couldn't turn back without passing Dandy. He might cross to the other side of the street, but that would be cowardly. And he was no less curious than before.

The drops of blood led him to the end of the block. He waited for the traffic signal to change, then hurried into the street. This time, the trail continued over the pavement. A good sign, he thought. Maybe the bleeder had crossed so recently that no cars had yet come by to wipe out the spots.

I'm gaining on him. Or her.

Oh, he did hope it was a woman.

A slender blonde. Slumped against an alley wall, a hand clamped to her chest just below the swell of her left breast. 'I'm here to help you,' he would say. With a brave, pained smile, she would say, 'It's nothing. Really. Just a flesh wound.' Then she would unbutton her blouse and peel the bloody side away from her skin. She wore a black lace bra. Byron could see right through it.

He imagined himself taking out his clean, folded handkerchief, patting blood away from the cut, and trying not to stare at her breast. His knuckles brushed against it, though, as he dabbed at the wound. 'Excuse me,' he told her. 'That's okay,' she said. 'Come with me,' he suggested. 'I'll take you to my apartment. I have bandages there.' She agreed, but she was too weak to walk without assistance, so she leaned against him. Soon, he had to carry her in his arms. He wasn't huge and powerful like Digby, but the slim girl weighed very little, and –

'Hey, you.'

Startled, Byron looked up from the sidewalk. His heart gave a quick thump.

She was leaning against the post of a streetlamp, not against a wall. She was a brunette, not a blonde. She wasn't holding her chest.

Her hands, instead, were roaming slowly up and down the front of her skirt. The skirt was black leather. It was very short.

Byron walked toward her. He saw no blood on her shiny white blouse. But he saw that most of the buttons were undone. She didn't wear a black lace bra like the bleeder in his fantasy. She didn't wear one at all, and the blouse was open wide enough to show the sides of her breasts.

'Looking for someone, honey?' she asked. Running the tip of her tongue across her lower lip, she squirmed against the light post. As her hands slid upward, the skirt rose with them. It lifted above the tops of her black fishnet stockings. The straps of a garter belt were dark against her pale thighs.

Feeling a little breathless, Byron looked her in the eyes. 'You aren't bleeding, are you?' he asked.

'What do you think?' She eased the skirt higher, but he didn't allow his eyes to wander down.

'I don't think you understand,' he said. 'I'm trying to find someone who's bleeding.'

'Kinky,' she said. 'What's your name, sweet thing?'

'Byron.'

'I'm Ryder. Wanna find out how I got my name?'

'Have you been standing here long?'

'Long enough to get lonely. And hot.' One of her hands glided up. It slipped inside her blouse. Byron saw the shapes of her fingers through the thin fabric as they fondled her breast.

He swallowed. 'What I mean is, did you just get here?'

'Few minutes ago. You like?' She eased the blouse aside, showing him the breast, stroking its erect nipple with the edge of her thumb.

He nodded. 'Very nice. But the thing is . . . did you see anyone go by?'

'Just you, Byron. How about it?' She stared at the front of his slacks. 'You look mighty sweet to me. I bet you taste real fine. I know *I* do. You wanna find out just how fine, too, I'll bet.'

'Well . . . see, I'm looking for someone who's bleeding.'

Her eyes narrowed. 'That'll cost you extra.'

'No, really – '

'Yes, really.' She curled her lower lip in and nipped it. Then she pushed the lip outward, as if offering it to Byron. A trickle of blood rolled down her mouth. When it reached her chin, she caught it on the tip of her index finger. She painted her nipple with it. 'Taste,' she whispered.

Byron shook his head.

Ryder smiled. More blood was dribbling toward her chin. 'Oh? Do you want it someplace else?'

'No. I'm sorry. Hunh-unh.' He backed away from her.

'Hey now, buster . . .'

He whirled around and ran.

Ryder yelled. He understood why she might be upset, but that was no reason to call him such names. They made him blush, even though nobody seemed to be around to hear.

I'm hearing, he thought as he dashed up the sidewalk. And I'm not half those things she's calling at me. She knows it, too. She saw.

Crazy whore.

By the time he reached the other side of the next street, she had stopped shouting. Byron looked back. She was gone.

While he gasped for air, he swept the beam of his flashlight over the sidewalk. He saw no blood spots.

I lost the trail!

His throat tightened.

It's all her fault.

He stomped his foot on the sidewalk.

Calm down, he told himself. It's not over yet. You still had the trail when you ran into her.

The DON'T WALK sign was flashing red, but Byron didn't care. After all, he hadn't even looked at the signal the first time across. Now, it just didn't matter.

Old Dandy'd been bad enough. But Ryder!

Running into people like that made traffic signals seem pretty trivial.

No cars were coming, so he hurried back across the street.

Nothing to it.

He smiled.

When he found a spot of blood on the sidewalk, a thrill rippled through him.

'Ah ha!' he pronounced. 'The games afoot!'

Now I'm talking to myself? Why not? I'm holding up fairly well, all things considered.

Spying a second drop of blood, he understood how he had lost the trail. The bleeder hadn't crossed the road, but had headed to the right along Kelsey Avenue.

Byron quickened his pace.

'Gaining on you,' he said.

As he hurried along, he realized that the spots on the sidewalk were further apart than they used to be. The distance between them had been irregular from the start — but anywhere from three to five feet, usually. Now, it seemed more like eight to ten feet from one drop to the next.

Is the wound coagulating? he wondered. Or is the bleeder running dry?'

What if the blood stops entirely?

If that happens, I'll never find her.

Or find her too late — dead in a heap.

Neither outcome suited Byron.

He broke into a run.

A few strides after passing the entrance of an alley, he lost the trail again and staggered to a halt. Turning around, he returned to the alley. His flashlight reached into it, and a spot of red gleamed on the pavement two yards ahead. Odd, he thought. In his fantasies, he'd imagined finding the bleeder in an alley. What if *all* would happen just the way he'd pictured it?

Too much to hope for, he told himself.

But he felt a tremour of excitement as he entered the alley.

He shined his light from side to side, half expecting to find a beautiful woman slumped against one of the brick walls. He saw a couple of garbage bins, but nothing else.

She might be huddled down, concealed by one of the bins.

Byron stepped past them. Nobody there.

He considered lifting the lids, but decided against it. The things would stink. There might even be rats inside. If the bleeder was in one of them, he didn't want to know.

Better not to find her at all.

This was supposed to be an adventure with a glorious and romantic outcome. It would just be too horrible if it ended with finding a body in the garbage.

He kept going.

Ten strides deeper into the alley, his pale beam fell upon another drop of blood.

'Thank God,' he muttered.

Of course, there were several more bins some distance ahead – dark boxes silhouetted by faint light where the alley ended at the next road.

I'll find her before then, Byron told himself.

Any minute now.

A black cat sauntered across the alley. It glanced at him, eyes glowing like clear golden marbles.

Good thing I'm not superstitious, he thought, the back of his neck tingling.

'If only you could talk,' he said.

The cat wandered over to the right side of the alley. Back hunched, tail twitching, it rubbed its side against a door.

A door!

Byron tipped back his head and inspected the building. He thought that it might be an apartment house. Its brick wall was three stories high, with fire escapes at the windows of the upper floors. All the windows were dark.

He stepped toward the door. The cat leaped and darted past him.

He almost grabbed the knob before noticing that it was wet with blood.

A chill crept through him.

Maybe this isn't such a great idea, he thought.

But he was so *close*.

Still, to enter a building where he didn't belong . . .

This might very well be where the bleeder lived. Why had she entered from the alley, though, instead of using the front? Did she feel that she had to sneak in?

'Strange,' Byron muttered.

Maybe she simply wandered down the alley, lost and dazed, and entered this door in the hope of finding someone who would help her. Even now, she might be staggering down a hallway, too weak to call out.

Byron plucked a neatly folded handkerchief from his pocket, shook it open, and spread it over his left hand. He turned the knob.

With a quiet snick, the latch tongue retracted.

He eased the door open.

The beam of his flashlight probed the darkness of a narrow corridor. On the hardwood floor gleamed a dot of blood.

He stepped inside. The hot air smelled stale and musty. Pulling the door shut, he listened. Except for the pounding of his own heartbeat, he heard nothing.

His own apartment building, even at this hour, was nearly always filled with sounds: people arguing or laughing, doors slamming, voices from radios and televisions.

His building had lighted hallways.

Hallways that always smelled of food, often of liquor. Now and again, they were sweet with the lingering aromas of cheap perfume.

Nobody lives here, he suddenly thought.

He didn't like that. Not at all.

He realized he was holding his breath as he started forward. He walked slowly, setting each heel down and rolling the shoe forward to its toe. Sometimes, a board creaked under him.

He stopped at a corner where this bit of hallway met a long stretch of corridor. Leaning forward, he aimed his beam to the left. He saw no blood on the floor. His light reached only far enough down the narrow passage to reveal one door. That door stood open.

He knew that he should take a peek inside.

He didn't want to.

Byron looked to the right. Not far away, a staircase rose toward the upper stories. Beyond that was a foyer and the front entrance.

He saw no blood on the floor in that direction.

I'll check that way first, he decided. He knew it would make more sense to go left, but heading toward the front seemed safer.

He turned the corner. After a few strides, he twisted around and checked behind him with the light. That long hallway made him very nervous. Especially the open door, though he couldn't see it from here. Instead of turning his back on it, he began sidestepping.

He shined his light up and down the stairway. The balustrade flung crooked, shifting bars of shadow against the wall.

What if the blood goes up there?

He didn't want to think about that.

He checked the floor ahead of him. Still no blood. Coming to the foot of the stairs, he checked the newel cap and ran his light up the banister. No blood. Nor did he find any on the lower stairs. He could only see the tops of five, though. After that, they were above eye level.

I don't want to go up there, he thought.

He wanted to go up there even less than he wanted to search the far end of the hallway.

Sidestepping through the foyer, he made his way to the front door. He tried its handle. The door seemed frozen in place.

He noticed that his light was shining on a panel of mailboxes. His own building had a similar arrangement. But in his building, each box was labelled with a room number and name. No such labels here.

This came as no surprise to Byron. But his dread deepened.

I've come this far, he told himself. I'm not going to back out now.

Trembling, he stepped toward the stairway. He climbed one stair, then another. The muscles in his legs felt like warm jelly. He stopped. He swept his light across the two higher treads that he hadn't been able to see from the bottom. Still, no blood.

She didn't go this way, he told himself.

If she did, she's on her own.

I didn't count on having to search an abandoned apartment house. That'd be stupid. God only knows who might be lurking in the empty rooms.

Byron backed down the stairs and hurried away, eager to reach the passage that would lead to the alley door.

He felt ashamed of himself for giving up.

Nobody will ever know.

But he hesitated when he came to the connecting hallway. He shined his light at the alley door. Twenty feet away. No more than that. He could be outside in seconds.

But what about the bleeder?

You'll never know.

You'll always wonder.

Suppose it *is* a beautiful young woman, wandering around in shock, slowly bleeding to death? Suppose you're her only chance?

I don't care. I'm not going to look upstairs.

But what about that open door?

He could take a look in there, couldn't he?

He swung his light toward it.

And heard the soft murmur of a sigh.

Oh my God!

He gazed at the doorway. The sigh had come from there, he was sure of it.

'Hello?' he called.

Someone moaned.

Byron glanced again at the alley door, shook his head, and hurried down the corridor.

So much for chickening out, he thought, feeling somewhat pleased with himself in spite of his misgivings.

I'll be a hero, after all.

'I'm here,' he said as he neared the open door. 'I'll help you.'

He rushed into the room.

He jumped the beam of his flashlight here and there. Shot its bright tunnel into the corners of the room. Across bare floorboards. Past windows and a radiator.

At his back, the door slammed shut.

He gasped and whirled around.

He stared for a moment, not quite sure what he was seeing.

Then a small whisper slipped from his throat and he stumbled backward, urine running hot down his leg.

The man standing beside the door grinned with wet, red lips. He was hairless. He didn't even have eyebrows. Nor did he appear to have a neck. His head looked as if it had been jammed down between his massive shoulders.

His bloody lips grinned at Byron around a clear plastic tube.

A straw, of sorts. Flecked inside with red.

The tube curled down from his mouth to a body cradled in his thick arms.

The limp body of a young man whose head was tipped back as if he found something fascinating about the far wall. He wore jeans and a plaid shirt. The shirt hung open. From the centre of his chest protruded something that resembled a metal spike – obviously hollow inside – which was joined with the plastic tubing. A single thin streamer of blood stretched from the hole, across his chest, and down the side of his ribcage.

It was the streamer, Byron knew, that had left the trail of drops which led him here.

He pictured the monstrous, bloated man carrying the body block after block down the city streets, drinking its blood as he lumbered along.

Now, the awful man shook the body. His cheeks sank in as he sucked. Some red flew up through the tubing. Byron heard a slurpy hollow sound – the sound that comes from a straw when you reach the bottom of a milk shake.

Then came another soft sigh.

'All gone,' the man muttered.

His lips peeled back, baring red teeth that pinched the tube.

He dropped the body.

The spike popped out of its chest and swayed at the end of the tubing.

'Glad you're here,' he said. 'Got me an awful thirst.'

Wrapping his thick fingers around the spike, he stepped over the body.

Byron spun around, ran, and leaped. He wrapped his arms around his head an instant before hitting the window. It exploded around him and he fell until he crashed against the pavement on the sidewalk. Then he scurried up and ran.

He ran for a long time.

Finally, exhausted, he leaned against a store front. Panting for air, he looked where he had been.

Now *that's* a trail of blood, he thought.

Too weak to go on, he let his knees unlock. He slumped down on the sidewalk and stretched out his legs.

His clothes, he saw, were shredded from the window glass.

So am I, he thought.

But that *thing* didn't get me.

Smiling, he shut his eyes.

When he opened them again, he saw a woman crouching beside him. A young slim blonde. Really cute. She looked a lot like the one he'd hoped to find at the end of the trail. 'You'll be all right,' she said. 'My partner's calling for an ambulance.'

She nodded toward the patrol car idling at the curb.

Dracula: The Real Story

JACK SHARKEY

*This final tale brings the vampire theme back full circle to its origins —
or Bram Stoker's novel to be precise. There are those cynics reared on
the real-life horrors of twentieth-century holocausts, wars and serial
killings who find the old horror classics tame, even amusing by
comparison. Yet there is still something unique about the great
masterworks like* Frankenstein, Dr Jekyll and Mr Hyde *and, of course,*
Dracula, *that enables them to survive the passage of time and
changing tastes to enthrall each new generation. But would they now
benefit from some judicious editing? A few changes here and there to
some of the more implausible names, dates and situations? And even,
possibly, being uprooted from the past and transplanted into modern
times? Jack Sharkey, the author of this final contribution, suggests
they might and without losing any of their impact. Heresy or not,
that is what he set out to do in a series of short stories he wrote for*
Playboy *magazine under the generic title, 'I Want A Ghoul'. Aside
from the aforementioned trio of classics, he also revised Frank R.
Stockton's* The Lady or the Tiger?, The Tell-Tale Heart *by Edgar
Allan Poe,* The Phantom Ship *by Captain Frederick Marryat and the
Sherlock Holmes adventure,* The Hound of the Baskervilles *by Sir
Arthur Conan Doyle, bringing them all 'kicking and screaming into
the modern era' to use his own expression.*

*Sharkey (1931–) a versatile American author, playwright and
editor, has contributed innumerable short stories to crime, fantasy and
horror magazines, and the theme of vampirism has featured in a
number of them. Believing that terror is relative to the times it is
written in and that, 'finding one's midnight bedroom shared with a*

moaning, blood-flecked phantom might be a relief from the nightly phantasmagoria of TV news,' he set out to parody Bram Stoker in just a thousand words. The result is, I think, a wholely successful imitation of Stoker's prose in which Jonathan Harker believes he has at last found a way of escaping from Dracula's Castle. But just as I am sure no reader of this book really wants to escape the delights of the vampire story, so Jack Sharkey flatters to deceive and in so doing ensures that the tradition will continue its allure into the twenty-first century – just as it has done in the two hundred years which have now passed . . .

＊　　　＊　　　＊

Jonathan Harker's Journal –

An untoward event has occurred. The door of my room has been locked, bolted from the outside. When I discovered it this morning, I at first thought there had been some error and waited patiently for the servants to come to my door with the announcement of breakfast. About midday, when no one had yet turned up, I grew worried. Then, I heard footsteps in the stone passageway outside and hurriedly moved to my door to attract the attention of whoever was passing. But something – some instinct, I know not what – restrained my hand just before it would have rapped upon the heavy oaken portal. There was a cadence – how can I describe it? – not *right* about those steps in the passageway. Even as I stood listening to them, to my nostrils came the musky animal odour that one associates normally with the deepest woods where sunlight seldom penetrates. And softly mingled with the strangely shuffling steps came the sound of a low growl – a sound that surely never emanated from the throat of any human. I remained where I was, not so much as daring to lower my hand from where it hovered near the wood of the door, until the sound of the footsteps faded down the passageway. I am terribly, mortally, frightened.

Later –

The sun is setting over the black crags outside my window. Half a dozen times, now, I have gone to the brink of that cold dark abyss that lies just beyond the casement and have had to withhold myself by sheer dint of will from casting myself out into space, toward the tenderer mercies of the rocks below. I do not know precisely what it is that I fear will happen when the last rays of the sun have gone, but fear it I do. I know I cannot bear to face once more the count, should he reappear, as is his wont, shortly after sunset. I am still not over the terrible shock

I received the other morning when he came up behind me as I shaved and I could not detect his approach in the glass of my shaving mirror – nor can I forget the way his eyes lingered, fairly dwelt, upon the slight trickle of blood down my throat, caused by my uncontrollable start at finding him so close, and so inexplicably near at hand. I have a plan. I pray I have the strength to carry it to fulfilment. I will continue later – if I can . . .

Moments later –

I have done what I can. I have placed one of my slippers at the foot of the open casement and by careful aim have managed to drop from that same casement my white silken scarf, so that it caught upon a rough projection of the stone some feet below the window over the sheer drop to the valley below the precipitous castle wall. It is my hope that when the count appears and finds the slipper, he will look from the window and espy the scarf. Then, thinking that I have taken that dread plunge to which I am so fearfully drawn in reality, he will rush from the room and – if luck is with me – not bother to refasten the door behind him! Then, when I am certain he has gone, I shall creep stealthily from this cramped closet in which I am presently secreted and somehow make my way down to the gates of the castle, and thence to freedom. I can hear the count coming, even now. I can hear his hand upon the bolt of the door – there, he has pulled it back! Now, all I can do is remain here, huddled fearfully in the suffocating confines of this closet, and hope with all my heart that my plan works. I dare not so much as even breathe now, as I hear his soft footsteps treading across the ancient stone of the roughhewn floor. He must go to the window. He must! It is my only salvation! If only – oh, if only – this electric portable typewriter on which I am constructing my journal did not rattle so loudly as I write!

Acknowledgements

The Editor is grateful to the following authors, agents and publishers for permission to include the copyright stories in this collection: Carnell Literary Agency for 'I, The Vampire' by Henry Kuttner; Avon Books for 'Nosferatu' by Paul Monette; NBC Publishing Division for 'The Bat' by Bela Lugosi; A. M. Heath Literary Agency for 'Son of Dracula' by Peter Tremayne; John Hamilton for 'The Baghetta' by Val Lewton; Hammer Films for 'Dracula – Prince of Darkness' by Jimmy Sangster; Anthony Blond Ltd for 'Incense for the Damned' by Simon Raven; Metro-Goldwyn-Mayer Inc. for 'Dark Shadows' by Marilyn Ross; New English Library and Hodder/Headline Publishing Group for 'One For The Road' by Stephen King; Little, Brown for 'Interview With The Vampire' by Anne Rice; Transatlantic Review and Allison & Busby for 'Uncle Vlad' by Clive Sinclair; Bantam Books for 'Sanguinarius' by Ray Russell; Virgin Publishing & W. H. Allen for 'Getting Even' by Woody Allen; Harper/Collins for 'West of October' by Ray Bradbury; Abner Stein Literary Agency for 'First Anniversary' by Richard Matheson; King-Size Publications Inc. for 'So Near The Darkness' by Theodore Sturgeon; Montcalm Publishing Corporation for 'Dayblood' by Roger Zelanzy Warner Books Inc. for 'Vampirella' by Ron Goulart; William F. Nolan for his story 'Getting Dead'; Basil Copper for his story 'Reader, I Buried Him!'; International Scripts for 'The Bleeder' by Richard Laymon; Playboy and HMH Publishing for 'Dracula, The Real Story' by Jack Sharkey. While every effort has been made to contact the copyright holders of stories in this book, in the case of any accidental infringement, concerned parties are asked to contact the Editor in care of the publishers.